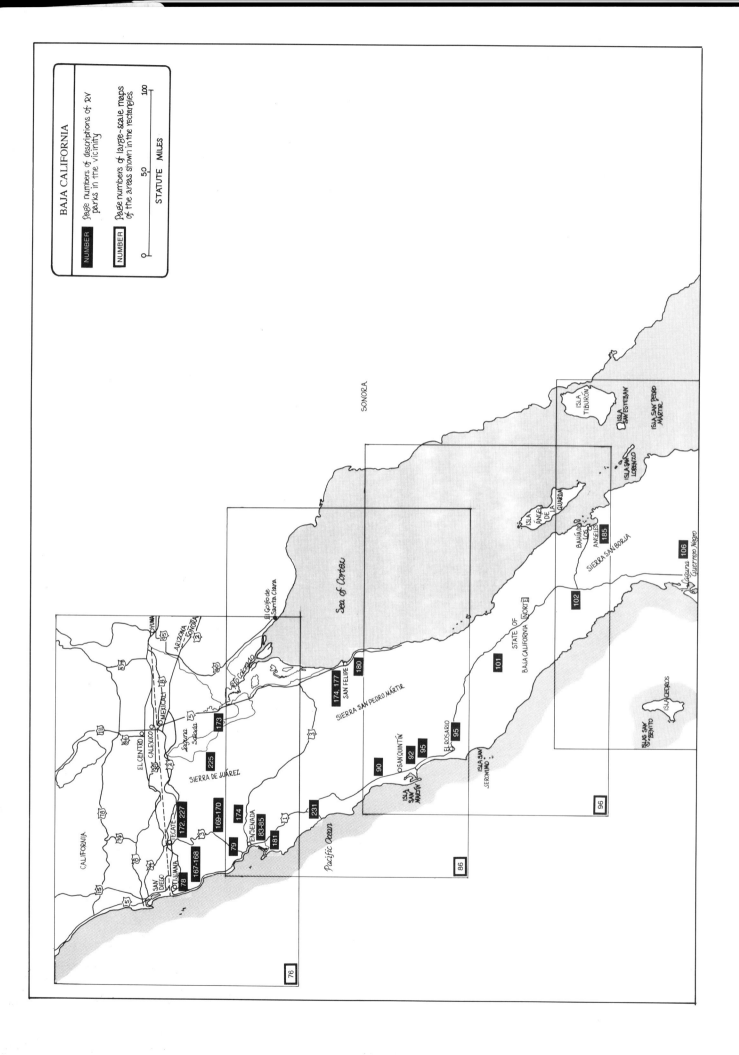

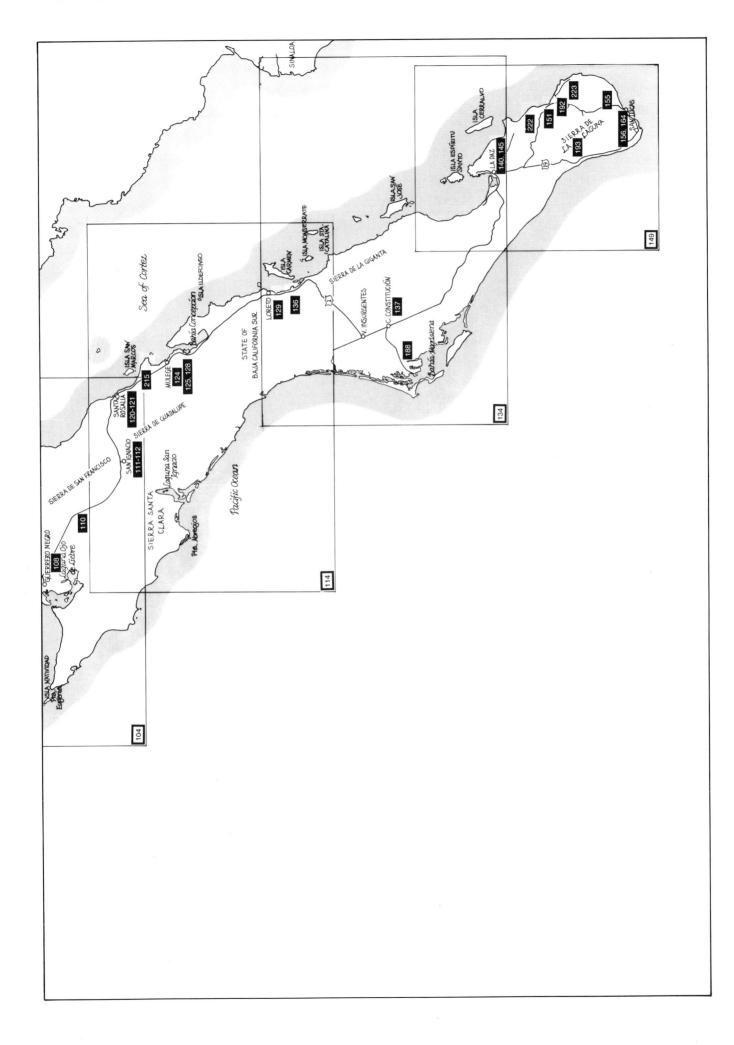

Exploring
BAJA
By RV

*A detailed guide containing everything you need to know
to have an enjoyable, safe, and inexpensive RV vacation
to one of the most interesting places on earth*

by
Walt Peterson
Author of the acclaimed Baja Adventure Book

and
Michael Peterson
His son, a Baja adventurer for seventeen years

WILDERNESS PRESS
Berkeley

FIRST EDITION September 1996

Copyright © 1996 by Walt Peterson and Michael Peterson

Design by Thomas Winnett and Kathy Morey
Cover design by Larry Van Dyke
Front cover photo: copyright © 1996 Erik Cutter
Back cover photos: copyright © 1996 Walt Peterson *(boat, fishermen)*
                copyright © 1996 Sven-Olaf Linblad *(landscape with succulents)*
Maps by Judith Peterson
Photos by authors except as noted

Library of Congress Card Number 96-14683
International Standard Book Number 0-89997-177-6

Manufactured in the United States of America

Published by **Wilderness Press**
            2440 Bancroft Way
            Berkeley, CA 94704
            Phone (800) 443-7227
            FAX (510) 548-1355
            Write, call or fax us for a free catalog

Library of Congress Cataloging-in-Publication Data

Peterson, Walt.
   Exploring Baja by RV / Walt Peterson and Michael Peterson.
      p.   cm.
   Includes bibliographical references (p.   ) and index.
   ISBN 0-89997-177-6
   1. Baja California (Mexico : State)--Guidebooks. 2. Recreational vehicles--Mexico--Baja California (State) --Guidebooks. 3. Camp sites, facilities, etc.--Mexico--Baja California (State)--Guidebooks. 4. Recreation areas--Mexico--Baja California (State)--Guidebooks. I. Peterson, Michael, 1973– . II. Title.
F1246.2.P48   1996
917.2′204835--dc20   96-14683
                                                              CIP

Front cover: **RV camping at Bahía Concepción**

Contents

The Authors

Walt holds bachelor's degrees from the US Coast Guard Academy and Rensselaer Polytechnic Institute, and a master's from the University of Southern California. While a cadet and an officer in the Coast Guard, he sailed across the Atlantic twice on the square-rigged sailing bark *Eagle*, visited many foreign countries, and traveled to the Arctic and Antarctic aboard an icebreaker, becoming a "six circle sailor" (Equator, Tropic of Capricorn, Tropic of Cancer, Arctic Circle, Antarctic Circle, Greenwich Meridian/International Dateline). In addition to shipboard duties, he has served as a civil engineer and in management positions. He is an enthusiastic outdoorsman, has set two world fishing records, and has been a scuba diver and underwater photographer for many years. After retiring from the Coast Guard, he has written three books, *The Baja Adventure Book*, *5,000 Ways to Say No to Your Child*, and *Exploring Baja by RV*.

Judy holds a bachelor's degree from the University of Washington and a master's from New York State University at Albany. She has been a teacher and a vice principal, and has served as principal at three schools. She is now the principal of a new high school in Issaquah, WA, construction of which will be completed in 1997. In recent years, Judy has become a dedicated scuba diver, and she enjoys sewing and her three thoroughly spoiled cats. She served as cartographer and researcher for *The Baja Adventure Book*, as well as *Exploring Baja by RV*.

Michael, now 23 years old, is a graduate of Phillips Exeter Academy, and earned a bachelor's degree with honors in biology from Stanford University in 1995. He played hockey in high school and at Stanford, joined the Stanford University Marching Band as a tuba player. Working as a research assistant in a molecular biology laboratory at Stanford for four years, he is co-author of two papers in the scientific literature. Michael is now a medical student at the University of California San Diego. He made his first visit to Baja California when he was six years old, and this is his first book.

Prior to Michael's arrival, Judy and Walt drove the Pan American Highway through Mexico and Central America to the Panama Canal, returning on a merchant ship with their Volkswagen as deck cargo, and they have driven the Alaska Highway. The family lived aboard a sailboat for two years, exploring southeast Alaska, British Columbia, and the Inside Passage. Wanderlust continues to claim Judy and Walt, and in the last three years they have visited Australia, New Zealand, England, Italy, Egypt, and China, and they have explored the underwater regions of the Red Sea, the Barrier Reef, and Papua New Guinea. Michael joined them for a trip to Cozumel, Mexico, as well as a trip to Japan, Malaysia, and Singapore, with a visit to Borneo to dive Sipadan Island. Among the places they have visited, Baja remains a favorite.

Preface

Walt Peterson's *The Baja Adventure Book*, first published by Wilderness Press in 1987 and now in its second edition, has been widely acclaimed as the most comprehensive, useful, and entertaining book on travel, outdoor adventure, and natural history in Baja California ever published. It has become an indispensable companion to fishermen, divers, boardsailors, surfers, boaters, kayakers, rock climbers, hikers, backpackers, bicyclists, and others intent on the pursuit of adventure in Baja's rugged mountains, remote deserts, sandy shores, and underwater regions.

This new book describes adventures of a more leisurely kind. As will be seen in later chapters, few places on the continent can match Baja California for the variety of interesting and exotic locations available to those traveling in motor homes, trailer rigs, campers, and other vehicles. The weather is usually fine, local staple foods are inexpensive, some RV parks charge as little as $3 a night, and there are innumerable beaches, coves, and clearings that cost nothing. An RV trip to Baja is a very different proposition than one to Yosemite or Yellowstone, and there is much to know. *Exploring Baja by RV* (referred to from this point on simply as *Exploring Baja*) is designed to provide the information you will need to have an enjoyable, safe, and inexpensive vacation to one of the most interesting places on earth.

The book was coauthored by Walt's son Michael, a Baja adventurer for 17 years, who wrote many passages, and served as computer operator, photographer, darkroom worker, cook, dishwasher, driver, and library researcher, at one point taking 7 weeks off during the 1995 Winter term at Stanford to make a 7,000-mile trip throughout Baja with his

While Dad dozes off, Michael burns the midnight oil on the manuscript of Exploring Baja by RV

dad, visiting every location described in the book. Judy Peterson, wife of one author and mother of the other, spent hundreds of hours preparing the maps, helped with research, edited the manuscript, and retouched many of the photographs. Bilingual Abel Hernandez and June Ann Campbell spent a great deal of time and energy assisting in the preparation of Appendix E, and Mimy Eng read the manuscript and provided many valuable suggestions. Tom Winnett and the staff of Wilderness Press stood guard over dangling participles and misplaced modifiers, and used their many skills to turn the 210,502-word manuscript, 26 maps, and hundreds of photographs into the book now in your hands.

Things to Know About the Book

What is a recreational vehicle?

The term "recreational vehicle" ordinarily refers to motor homes, trailer rigs, campers, and van conversions. However, in this book it refers to any vehicle equipped to provide its occupants with at least a minimum ability to prepare meals and spend a few nights away from the comforts of civilization. Many of Baja's attractions and activities are not found at convenient distances apart, where you can expect to leave one RV park in the morning, pursue a full day of exploring, sightseeing, golfing, fishing, diving, or other activities, and arrive at the next RV park as evening falls. In addition, nights spent in solitude on a wild and deserted beach, with only the surf and the howling of coyotes breaking the silence, and with a sky full of more stars than you ever thought possible, are among the supreme Baja experiences, not to be missed.

So, if your vehicle is just a pickup, a station wagon, or even a sedan, don't hesitate to load up your tent, an air mattress, a stove, a cooler, a few cooking and eating utensils, and some food and water, and head south. Occasional "pit stops" for a hot shower, a soft bed, and a few hours of the Simpsons can be made at any of the many hotels and motels noted in the text.

Scope of the book

Exploring Baja is not an "everywhere" book. Some geographic locations in Baja are of limited interest to most readers. In locations having numerous RV parks, such as San Felipe, which has perhaps 50, coverage is limited to those we judged to be of the greatest interest, based on their price, location, facilities, ambiance, and general level of cleanliness and repair. Similar criteria were applied to restaurants. Some RV parks and restaurants in strategic locations are included because they are the only ones available. A number of RV parks are not included because they cater only to permanent residents. Many hotels are listed because they have restaurants, dive shops, reservations desks, lead-free gasoline, or other attractions of interest to RVers.

Tijuana, Tecate, and Mexicali are sizable modern cities having many of the services, facilities, and businesses found in cities of similar size in the US. However, their urban nature and close proximity to the border render them of limited interest in a book on exploring the peninsula by recreational vehicle. In addition, each has a tourist bureau that can provide voluminous amounts of information by mail or telephone, the addresses and phone numbers of which are found in Appendix C. Thus, other than providing border crossing information, and the location of consulates, legal assistance offices, and places where local information can be obtained, *Exploring Baja* does not include these cities.

Many organizations offer "package" trips to Baja from the US and Canada, involving fishing, diving, visiting the whales, exploring, boardsailing, kayaking, bicycling, surfing, golfing, and so forth, and many of these trips can be made by individuals on their own initiative. However, because this is a book about exploring the peninsula by recreational vehicle, the activities described are limited to day-long ventures. Those interested in lengthy side trips away from their RVs, or commercial package trips, should refer to Peterson 1995, Romano-Lax 1993, Wong 1988, Robinson l983, or Curcione 1985, all described in Appendix F. In addition, any travel agent can provide information on commercial trips.

Maps, place names, and travel directions

The maps in the book are based on topographic maps prepared by the Mexican government. They have been corrected and updated with information from many sources. During the seven-week trip mentioned in the Preface, we determined the correct location of many locations throughout Baja using a Global Positioning System (GPS) receiver. This system of 24 satellites permits extremely accurate readings of latitude and longitude, which have been used to make many corrections, producing maps of unprecedented accuracy. Appendix D provides a map key and a table of distances for the Transpeninsular Highway, as well as conversions between metric and standard measurements.

Official place names assigned by the Mexican government have been used throughout the book, although a few have been converted to their English equivalent to promote euphony and brevity. The English translations of Spanish place names having a provocative or descriptive meaning (Isla Piojo is "Louse Island") are provided at the appropriate places in the text. Coined English names assigned by visitors such as "East Cape" and the "Midriff" are placed in quotation marks when first used. To avoid confusion with the popular name of the peninsula, the State of Baja California is referred to as "Baja California Norte" or "Baja Norte," and the southern state as "Baja California Sur" or simply

"Baja Sur." Also, the State of California (ours) will often be referred to as "Alta (Upper) California." The Index lists all place names used in the text.

Travel directions are keyed to the kilometer markers found on virtually all paved highways and on many unpaved roads. No knowledge of the metric system is required—just look at each KM marker as a little lighthouse, providing unmistakable identification as to geographic location. For instance, if you are south of Santa Rosalía and encounter the KM 156 marker, the road you see to the east leads to Punta Chivato. A "+" after a kilometer number means that the site occurs about halfway between that marker and the next **higher** marker. Where markers are not available, distances are cited in miles. The numbers on the KM markers along some stretches of the Transpeninsular are ascending, along others descending, so take care not to become confused.

All distances are in statute miles over land, in nautical miles over water. Elevations are in feet, and temperatures are in degrees Fahrenheit. All maps have true north at the top, and compass bearings are magnetic. The variation in most of Baja is 13° east, so to convert magnetic bearings to true, add 13°, and to convert true bearings to magnetic, subtract 13°.

Icons

In Chapters 4, 5, 6, and 7, the following icons will be found in column margins, beside mention of locations of particular interest to RVers:

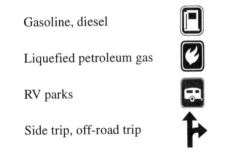

Gasoline, diesel

Liquefied petroleum gas

RV parks

Side trip, off-road trip

Plant and animal species

The names of plant and animal species are in English wherever possible. However, some species have no widely accepted English name, and hence appear in Spanish or in their scientific ("Latin") name. If there is a meaningful Spanish name, many Spanish/English translations will be found in Appendix E. (Like Americans, who apply the names "bass" and "perch" to a variety of fish, the Mexican people have similar words that are of little value in identifying species.) As with place names, coined English names, such as "boojum," are placed in quotation marks when first used.

Businesses and organizations

The addresses of most businesses and organizations mentioned by name in the text are contained in Appendix C. A number in parentheses following a name in the text means

that its location is shown by that number on the accompanying town/city map. To aid you in locating these numbers, they are assigned in an organized manner; beginning at the north edge of each town/city map, (1) will be the first encountered, then, as you move south down the map, (2) will be the next encountered, then (3), and so forth. Many businesses and services not specifically mentioned in the text, such as grocery stores and auto repair shops, are identified on the town/city maps by an alphabetical key, given in Appendix D.

Money and prices

Units of money in the book are dollars, preceded by the "dollar sign," $. The dollar sign is also used in Mexico to denote the nuevo peso, usually as "N$." Visitors should keep this in mind when afield in Baja, for an item costing $5 is almost 8 times as dear as something costing N$5.

Many factors make stating the exact price of everything in the book an exercise in futility. The relationship between the dollar and the nuevo peso changes continuously, and has complex effects on the prices of many things. The proprietors of stores, restaurants, and RV parks follow the laws of supply and demand, and change their prices accordingly, and there are seasonal, holiday, weekend, daily, and even hourly aspects to prices. Hourly? How about happy hour at the Giggling Marlin? In addition, many RV parks, restaurants, and stores offer discounts, based on travel club membership, senior-citizen status, etc. Finally, as in all of Mexico, the prices of many things are subject to bargaining, especially jewelry, arts and crafts, clothing, souvenirs, and boat rentals.

Despite this, we will provide general information on the major, unavoidable cost items that will be encountered on a trip—food, fuel, and insurance—as well as typical prices for such optional things as RV parks, restaurant meals, fishing licenses, boat permits, and rentals of boats, sailboards, and ATVs. Those individual businesses whose prices we found to be exceptionally high or low are identified by adjectives like "expensive," "pricey," "inexpensive," and "modest." Use this information as a general guide, expect change, and with a little care and some shopping around, you will find your Baja RV trip to be very inexpensive.

Hidden agendas?

This book is not a travel agency in disguise; we are trying to "sell" Baja on its merits—dandruff, flat feet, bad breath, static cling, and all—and have avoided putting a false gloss on the place with overstuffed adjectives and lyrical phrasing. There are no deliberate semitruths, omissions, or exaggerations to please Mexican tourism officials or business owners; if we are wrong, we are honestly wrong. Since we spent virtually none of our time hanging around hotel bars, we are not part of the Baja "establishment," and are not selling club memberships or insurance, nor advertising any product or service. When we render opinions, they are based on our own experiences.

It's not our fault

Sincere efforts have been made to insure that *Exploring Baja* is correct and current as of the date of publication. However, to err is human, and Baja California is a land of rapid change. Readers planning activities that are regulated, such as fishing and diving, attending festivals, holidays, and celebrations, or making trips that involve travel to mainland Mexico by ferry, should obtain current information from the many sources identified in the text and Appendix C. Although the authors and the publisher cannot be responsible for the consequences of errors, we will gladly receive corrections, comments, and constructive suggestions; write to us in care of Wilderness Press.

Chapter 1

The Lay of the Land

A land accursed by God?

Following its "discovery" by Europeans in late 1533 or early 1534, the peninsula was visited by a variety of explorers and missionaries, few of whom found much to admire. Jesuit Father Johann Jakob Baegert, who spent 17 years in Baja as a missionary in the mid-1700s, described the peninsula in harsh terms, "Everything concerning [Baja] California is of such little importance that it is hardly worth the trouble to take a pen and write about it. Of poor shrubs, useless thorn bushes and bare rocks, of piles of stone and sand, without water or wood...what shall or what can I report?" He further lamented: "The soil itself consists mostly of sand and fine gravel. For this reason I had the four walls of my cemetery filled in almost to the top with soil, to lessen the work of the grave diggers and to spare the iron tools."

In 1866, explorer J. Ross Browne published a description of the place that showed that its reputation had not improved with time, "All the vegetation visible to the eye seems to conspire against the intrusion of man. Every shrub is armed with thorns; the cactus, in all its varieties, solitary and erect, or in twisted masses, or snake-like undulations, tortures the traveler with piercing needles and remorseless fangs. Burrs with barbed thorns cover the ground; the very grass, wherever it grows, resents the touch with wasp-like stings that fester in the flesh; and poisonous weeds tempt the hungry animals with their verdure, producing craziness and death. Add to this the innumerable varieties of virulent reptiles and insects that infest those desolate regions in summer; the rattlesnakes, vipers, scorpions, tarantulas, centipedes, and sandflies; the rabid polecats that creep around the campfire at night, producing hydrophobia by their bite; the scorching heat of the sun, and the utter absence of water, and you have a combination of horrors that might well justify the belief of the old Spaniards that the country was accursed by God."

Judy Peterson has provided a modern description, "A million acres of kitty litter," which, even if numerically inaccurate, describes the attitude of the unenlightened. Why would anyone of sound mind want to visit such a place? Baegert and Brown had their own agendas (saving souls and commerce, respectively), and shared the common attitude of their times towards "uncivilized" places. However, things are seen through the eyes of the beholder, and from today's perspective their complaints seem laughable. Baja California is now recognized as a unique and largely unspoiled treasure of desert and mountain wilderness. While a good deal of the peninsula remains inaccessible to all but the most hardy adventurers, there are few places on the continent where an ordinary vehicle can carry visitors to more interesting, exotic, and even world-class locations. The possibilities are numerous: drive your rig to the shores of the lagoon that is the winter home of the famous friendly whales; park on a white sand beach at Cabo San Lucas and fish for marlin in the offshore waters, one of the world's great sports fisheries; bring your boat along and troll the rich offshore banks near Bahía Magdalena. There is more: park next to one of the few coral reefs in North America and enjoy some fantastic snorkeling; lash a sailboard to the top of your rig and try out Bahía las Palmas and Santa Rosalillita, only two of many fabled windsurfing spots that are accessible by ordinary vehicle. In addition, your rig can take you to the jumping-off point for trips to places where you might get to ride on the back of a manta ray, encounter such creatures as black jackrabbits, rattle-less rattlesnakes, and bats that catch fish, or to

As depicted by an illustration from an 1869 article by J. Ross Browne in **New Harper's Monthly Magazine,** *early travelers had doubts about Baja California*

STAMPEDED BY A POLECAT.

where a burro will carry you to see some of the most magnificent rock art on the continent.

If your goals are less demanding, there is some fantastic scenery to enjoy, including forests of oak, pine, and fir, deserts filled with exotic plants, the brown islands, white sand beaches, and baby-blue waters of Bahía Concepción, and the plunging gorge of Cañon del Diablo (Devil's Canyon), a short hike from a road accessible by all but the least nimble RVs. There are hundreds of miles of magnificent but deserted beaches, their sands rarely marred even by footprints. If your goal is simply profound silence, there is plenty of that left, for large areas of Baja are still among the most "empty" on the continent.

A land accursed by God? Perhaps it was in the days of Father Jakob and J. Ross, but could it be that God has wrought changes in recent years? Later pages describe these and other marvels, so read on and judge for yourself.

Geological beginnings

The idea that continents and other land features were moveable, not fixed, entities was first suggested in 1596 by

After a day of hand-to-hand combat with the virulent reptiles, rattlesnakes, vipers, scorpions, tarantulas, and rabid polecats that so worried J. Ross Browne (see illustration above), the senior author reaches a place of safety and sustenance, a pool-side bar in San José del Cabo

Dutch cartographer Abraham Ortelius. Father Baegert observed large rocks and marine shells embedded in the soft sandstone near his mission, miles from the Sea of Cortez, and wondered, "...whether subterranean fires, an earthquake, or some other upheaval did not create this land and cause it in time to rise from the sea, after the creation of the rest of the world." Although they presumably knew nothing of plate tectonics, both were close to the truth. About 5 million years ago, the Cortez did not exist, and the land mass of today's peninsula was firmly attached to the mainland. However, a gigantic fault had formed in the earth's crust. Running roughly northwest/southeast, it joined the famous San Andreas Fault, which runs north across Alta California, diving into the ocean near Point Arena, 105 miles north of San Francisco. Driven by tectonic forces still not fully understood, the land mass west of the fault split off from the mainland. Moving at a rate of about 0.25 inch per year, the southern tip of the new peninsula left the mainland at the approximate location of today's Puerto Vallarta, and by about 3 million years ago, Baja was a well-defined peninsula and the Cortez a prominent body of water. Oddly enough, the northern Cortez is thought to be older than the southern. How could this be? The southern part was a long, narrow channel at first, while the northern part was a much larger basin. The land west of the fault is still being carried to the northwest, and in about 40 million years the two Californias will be an island lying off British Columbia. In about 10 million more, they will be subducted into the Aleutian Trench, finally solving the smog problem in Los Angeles.

Today, at 800 miles long (the great circle distance from the point where the border fence ends at the Pacific to the furthest south point just west of Cabo San Lucas), Baja is one of the longest peninsulas in the world, exceeded only by the Malay, Antarctic, and Kamchatka peninsulas. The peninsula is also very narrow, averaging less than 70 miles in width, the narrowest part being the 26 miles from the western shore of the bay near La Paz to the Pacific, and the greatest being 144 miles at the latitude of Guerrero Negro. From the perspective of an astronaut, Baja is thus one of the most striking geological features on earth. Land area is 55,634 square miles, and the shoreline on both coasts totals 1,980 miles, excluding the interiors of enclosed bays.

Baja's mountains are not exceptionally tall, the double peak called Picacho del Diablo (Devil's Peak), Baja's highest, being only 10,154 feet and 10,152 feet. A series of mountain ranges form a largely unbroken barrier up to 2,000 feet in altitude, with about half the length of the peninsula blocked up to 3,000 feet. The western slopes of the Sierra de Juárez and Sierra San Pedro Mártir, extending south about 160 miles from the border, are fairly gentle and descend to coastal plains along the Pacific. Most of the eastern slopes, however, are steep escarpments, plunging down to sweltering lowlands along the Río Colorado and the Cortez. Both escarpments have been eroded into a series of major canyons, a few of which are accessible by RV.

A series of mountain ranges runs south from the Sierra San Pedro Mártir, including the Sierra San Borja, the

Beautiful canyon country in the Sierra de San Francisco

A long series of maps soon appeared, some correct, some not. In 1636, Frans Visscher of Holland produced a reasonably correct version, but later changed his mind, apparently without benefit of any new information, and his prestige caused many other geographers to fall into line. About 1680, young Peter the Great of Russia was given a giant globe of the world, taller than a man. Its details of Europe, Africa, and the east coast of America were remarkably accurate, but California was again shown as an island. Jesuit Father Eusebio Kino published a map showing the correct geography in 1705, but it was generally disregarded. In 1746, Father Fernando Consag, another Jesuit, headed north with a crew of soldiers, Indian neophytes, and Yaqui Indians in four canoes to explore the northern end of the gulf. After a month, they came to the mouth of the Río Colorado, and found the water to be sweet, not salty. The idea that California was an island was deeply entrenched, and efforts were made to refute Consag. However, the facts that Baja California was a peninsula and Alta California was part of the mainland slowly gained acceptance.

Surrounding waters

The waters along Baja's Pacific coast are similar to those of Alta California, being characterized by ocean swells, heavy surge, and upwellings of nutrient-laden deep water. Because of the vast fetch (the distance traveled by waves with no obstruction) of the Pacific, distant weather patterns can produce heavy surf for weeks at a time. The southerly sweep of the California Current keeps water temperatures lower than would otherwise be expected, normally ranging between 50° and 75°, gradually warming as the water moves south.

To many scientists, the Cortez is one of the most interesting bodies of water on earth. Over 600 miles long, having an area of almost 60,000 square miles, spanning 9° of latitude, and with deep basins in its central and southern portions—one more than 14,000 feet in depth—the Cortez is the world's largest deep gulf. Lands on both sides of the geologic fault that formed it are still moving relative to each other, and the sea bed of the Cortez is one of the world's most seismically active areas. A number of settlements on the peninsula have had disastrous earthquakes, including San Ignacio in 1811 and Loreto in 1877, and they continue—in June 1995, La Paz experienced a 6.1 quake, whose epicenter was in the bay in front of the town. In spite of its strength and location, it fortunately did little damage. Although tsunamis ("tidal waves") have not been recorded in historic times, Indians who lived in the area had words in their vocabulary that apparently described them.

The Cortez has been characterized as a "caricature of oceanography" because of its extreme dynamics. Its long, narrow configuration produces one of the largest tidal ranges in the world, up to 31 feet at the north end. Materials eroded

Sierra de San Francisco, the Sierra de Guadalupe, and the Sierra de la Giganta, ending north of La Paz. The central part of the Cape region south of La Paz is occupied by two rugged mountain ranges, the Sierra de la Victoria and the Sierra de la Laguna. Since both ranges are widely referred to by their second name, it will be used throughout the book.

■ Island California

The earliest maps of the North American continent, published by cartographer Gerhardus Mercator in 1531, showed that Baja California was a peninsula. This fact was proven by explorer Francisco de Ulloa in 1539, but was generally disregarded by geographers. However, about 1602, Antonio de la Ascension, a Carmelite priest, prepared a map showing Alta California (now ours) and Baja California (now Mexico's) to be an island. He probably got this idea due to a misunderstanding of reports prepared by explorers Juan de la Fuca and Martin d'Aguilar on their earlier voyages. Ascension's map was sent to Spain, but the Dutch captured the ship and brought the map to Amsterdam, and the erroneous information was widely distributed. Henry Briggs's 1625 map of North America, unambiguously showing both Californias to be an island, was apparently based on this information.

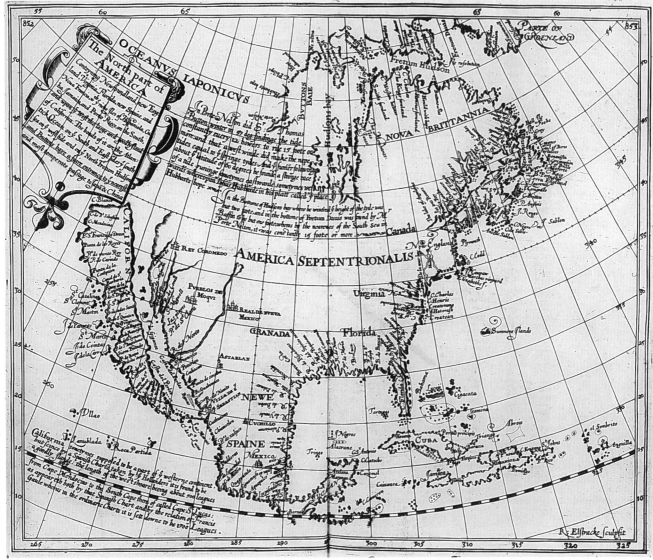

Courtesy of Library of Congress

Henry Briggs's map of North America, 1625

out of today's Grand Canyon and surrounding lands over millions of years have been deposited at the north end of the Cortez by the Río Colorado, and low tides uncover mud flats up to 3 miles wide. Until it was tamed by dams, the tidal bore that ran up the Colorado was so powerful that it once sank a sizable ship. Tidal currents form huge whirlpools and rips in the "Midriff" region of the central Cortez, and velocities of over 6 knots have been recorded. Because there is no long fetch, large swells do not build up as they do in the ocean and there is little horizontal surge. Variations in water temperature also are extreme, inshore surface waters reaching 91° in the south during summer and 47° in the north during winter. Since freshwater transport into the Cortez is less than evaporation, it is more saline than the Pacific.

Rivers, streams, and lakes

Baja lays claim to only two permanent rivers, the Río Colorado and the Río Mulegé, but both claims are tenuous. The Colorado is a "Baja river" only in the sense that it forms

the boundary between the Mexican states of Baja California [Norte] and Sonora. Draining 260,000 square miles of the western US along its 1,450-mile course, the mighty Colorado cut the Grand Canyon out of rock over the millenniums, and deposited vast amounts of silt and mud into the upper Cortez. However, it has now been dammed and utilized for human purposes to the point that it is now a mere trickle of its former self by the time it reaches the Cortez.

The Chamber of Commerce of Mulegé would have you believe that a river courses through the town, but the "Río Mulegé" is actually a brackish arm of the Cortez, although it does receive small amounts of fresh water from springs above a dam. Other than these, Baja has no rivers, and there are only about six small streams that reach salt water on a more or less permanent basis.

There are only two sizable lakes in Baja. Laguna Salada, in the lowlands south of Mexicali, receives widely varying amounts of water from the Río Colorado from year to year: in 1987, the lake was 60 miles long, but in recent years, the drought prevalent in the Southwest has reduced it to perhaps 20. Laguna Hanson, in the Sierra de Juárez, is less than a mile across and is shallow and muddy. There are a number of ponds so small that they are not even graced with names.

The wind and the weather

True to its desert image, Baja California is one of the hottest and driest regions of the North American continent. Between El Rosario and La Paz, rainfall is extremely low, averaging between 2 inches and 4 inches a year, sometimes almost nothing for years at a time. There are four main desert areas: 1) the San Felipe Desert, composed of the area east of the Sierra de Juárez and the Sierra San Pedro Mártir, extending from the US border south to the vicinity of Bahía de los Angeles; 2) the Central Coast Desert, which extends from Bahía de los Angeles along the western shore of the Cortez to the Cape, including most of its islands; 3) the Vizcaíno Desert, starting in the vicinity of El Rosario and extending south to San Ignacio; and 4) the Magdalena Plain Desert, extending from San Ignacio south along the Pacific almost to Todos Santos. However, the northern and southern ends of the peninsula get significant amounts of rain. Winter storms, often generated as far away as the Gulf of Alaska, provide the areas west of the escarpments of the Sierra de Juárez and Sierra San Pedro Mártir with up to 12 inches a year, enough to support sizable forests at high elevations. The rain-in-the-winter rule for the north is not hard and fast: in 1891, an August storm dropped huge amounts near Tecate, depositing 11.5 inches in 80 minutes at Campo, just north of the border and a bit west of Tecate.

In the south end, tropical storms called *chubascos* can bring torrential rains and heavy winds from mid-May to mid-November, peaking in August and September, although abnormal water temperatures can cause exceptions. Most such storms affect only the southern part of the peninsula, but they occasionally move up the Cortez to go ashore at San Felipe or into Sonora. In September 1995, a *chubasco* went ashore at Topolobampo, Sinaloa, on the eastern shore of the Cortez at the same approximate latitude as Santa Rosalía, and wreaked havoc, causing over 100 deaths and the loss of many homes and fishing vessels. Although varying greatly from year to year, the Cape region averages 8 inches to 16 inches of rain a year, and isolated areas in the Sierra de la Laguna can get up to a distinctly nondesert 30 inches. For comparison, Seattle, famous for its rain, gets an average of just over 38 inches.

There are other weather patterns that are of interest to visitors, especially to those planning activities on the water. During fall and winter, a high pressure area often forms over the interior of the southwestern US, creating a strong, persistent wind. Known in Southern California as the "Santa Ana," it can affect Baja from Tijuana to the Cape, especially in coastal areas. The *cordonazo* (lash) is a severe but usually short storm encountered in the Cortez, generally developing in the summer months during periods of southerly winds. Mountains along Baja's eastern coast often cool rapidly at night, causing gravity to funnel strong winds down through

Stunning coastal beauty just south of Ensenada

the arroyos. Bahía de los Angeles is famous for katabatic winds (cold air traveling downward, propelled by the force of gravity) so strong and persistent that they can confine you to Corona and canasta for up to a week. Between November and May, prevailing winds in the Cortez are from the north, generally light and unpredictable. However, they are strong and dependable enough in the East Cape area that thriving boardsailing resorts have been established there. ("East Cape" is an informal term for the area between Punta Pescadero and somewhere short of San José del Cabo.)

The relatively cool waters of the California Current keep air temperatures along Baja's Pacific coastal areas comfortable most of the year, but temperatures soar along the western coast of the Cortez during the summer. The area around Mexicali consistently experiences summer temperatures in the 104° to 108° range, occasionally getting up to 120°, and on a windless summer day, Santa Rosalía can seem as hot as a blast from the town's copper smelters. A breeze called the *coromuel* blows from the south in the La Paz area almost every day from late spring to early fall, starting in the late afternoon and continuing until morning, pulling down temperatures in these otherwise hot months. The Cape region tends to have moderate temperatures all year. As in desert areas elsewhere, day-to-night temperature variations are extreme, and it is not uncommon for RVers to run their heaters early in the morning and their air conditioners in the afternoon.

Despite its normally warm and dry weather, Baja occasionally provides a few surprises. Mountain areas can be very cold in winter: while traveling in the Sierra San Pedro Mártir in 1905, adventurer Arthur North was surprised to find that his canteen had frozen solid. These mountains can accumulate up to 8 feet of snow, and the Ensenada rescue squad has been called out a number of times to retrieve stranded hikers. Snow can occasionally fall at lower elevations; in 1987, 5 feet fell at the 4,200-foot level in the Sierra de Juárez, trapping nine teenagers. After six days of confusion, a convoy of farm tractors, military vehicles, and four-wheel-drives, led by a bulldozer, broke through the snow to find the boys holed up in a cabin, out of food and firewood, three of them sustaining frostbite. Although it is very rare, snow occasionally falls near sea level, and we once drove through a full-fledged snow storm near Camalú (the snow melted immediately upon reaching the ground).

As every experienced desert rat knows, Mother Nature often opts for extremes, and too much water can be more of a problem than too little. In the days before the Transpeninsular Highway was constructed, a rainstorm could strand travelers for days after many arroyos became torrents, but this was usually accepted as a fact of life in the desert and part of the adventure. The budget for the Transpeninsular Highway was so small that construction was limited largely to bulldozing a roadbed and laying a very thin layer of pavement, with no money left over for such amenities as bridges and culverting. Predictably, little more than a light rain was required to sweep away sections of the highway.

In recent years, modern concrete bridges have been constructed over such troublesome locations as the Río Santa María, just south of San Quintín, and the Río del Rosario near El Rosario, providing travelers with a sense of permanence and security. However, in January, 1993 a series of storms over a two-week period dumped record amounts of rain on Southern California and northern Baja, up to 22 inches in some locations, causing havoc on both sides of the border. The Transpeninsular was cut in numerous places, and both bridges noted above were destroyed. Many travelers, estimated at between 500 and 1,000, were stranded, although a few managed to escape by taking the unpaved road from

the vicinity of Laguna Chapala to San Felipe, and others made it across the torrents in the tow of tractors. Some of those south of the damaged highway simply turned around and caught the Santa Rosalía ferry to Guaymas. A number of college students used their initiative and got back to the border on foot and by bus.

Living things

Father Baegert complained "There are...hardly any animals [or] plants...in [Baja] California...." His lack of awareness is understandable, for its native plants and animals often do little to serve the causes of man, providing neither lumber, food, nor fur. To the uninitiated, desert areas have a certain sameness about them—once you have seen one desert you have seen them all, the standard cactuses, perhaps some lizards and coyotes, and possibly a few road-runners thrown in to liven things up, but little else. Even scientists can fail to appreciate desert diversity: a 1942 article in *National Geographic* quoted a well known naturalist as stating "I have made twenty-three trips down that peninsula in the past nineteen years. From a scientific standpoint, I think the peninsula is about cleaned up. Scientists have nearly everything named and classified." He was far off the mark, of course. Recent estimates have been made that 60% of the invertebrate species on the peninsula and in the Cortez remain undescribed. In a modem search of several library data bases at Stanford, Michael found references to 41 "new" species that have been identified since 1989, including a long-nosed snake from Isla Cerralvo, a lamprey-like eel from Bahía la Paz, a tortoise species found near La Paz, and a fly from the East Cape area.

When last tallied, about 3,000 species, subspecies, and varieties of native and introduced (non-native) vascular plants (the "higher" plants, having vessels or ducts carrying sap) have been recorded in Baja. As might be expected, the plants of northern Baja are closely related to those of Southern California. Much of the land below 3,000 feet west of the Juárez and San Pedro Mártir escarpments is covered by chaparral consisting of chamise, manzanita, laurel sumac, sage, and other plants, giving way at lower elevations to a coastal scrub of agave, cliff spurge, buckeye, buckwheat, and bladderpod. Plants in the Cape region are closely related to those of the nearest areas on the mainland, with complex communities of cacti, yuccas, and various shrubs and trees like *palo blanco* and *palo verde* at low elevations. Between these northern and southern areas, many familiar desert plants are found, including ocotillo, ironwood, creosote bush, mesquite, agave, and various cacti, including the infamous jumping cholla.

The aftermath of a torrential downpour on the Río Santa María before the bridge was constructed

Jumping cholla gets its name from the fact that the spines are barbed and the stems break off when touched; they are so easily detached that they almost seem to "jump" onto passersby

■ Coming from the right side of the hill

Similar to the importance of coming from the "right side of the tracks" to humans, growing on the "right side of the hill" is important to Baja's plants. South-facing slopes receive more direct sunlight and tend to be hot and dry. The soils are thinner and have little organic matter, supporting a sparse vegetation that does little to slow down the wind, further increasing the loss of water. In contrast, north-facing slopes are cooler and wetter, and often support a denser, taller, more lush plant community, one more able to hold down wind velocities. The two plant communities are so different that you should have little trouble finding examples of this phenomenon while underway in central Baja.

Most RVers, confined largely to paved roads and possessing a stereotypical vision of what Baja "ought" to look like, would express disbelief about what is to be found in some areas. In spite of Baja's "burning-desert" image, there are relatively well-watered areas that support a distinctly nondesert vegetation, especially the higher reaches of the Sierra de Juárez and the Sierra de San Pedro Mártir, where forests of pine, cedar, fir, aspen, and oak are encountered. The latter area even has a version of a Canadian boreal forest, complete with lodgepole pine and white fir. The considerable rainfall in the Sierra de la Laguna supports woodlands of oak and pinyon pine, sometimes guarded by an almost impenetrable underbrush. In addition, there are tiny Shangri-las, microenvironments of verdant palms, park-like meadows, mangrove lagoons, fresh- and saltwater marshes, streams, and even waterfalls, often in the most unexpected places. Some of these areas can be visited by those traveling in RVs, and descriptions and travel directions will be provided in later chapters.

Encounters with coyotes and roadrunners might not surprise you, but there are also mule deer, mountain lion, bighorn sheep, and a few antelope, as well as many smaller mammal species such as fox, rabbit, bobcat, skunk, badger, raccoon, ring-tailed cat, ground squirrel, chipmunk, gopher, mice, and rat, plus feral (domestic animals gone wild) cat, pig, and goat. Well adapted to Baja's climates, many reptile species inhabit the peninsula, including such familiar and expected animals as various species of rattlesnake and whiptail, king, and gopher snakes, and numerous iguanids, geckos, and lizards. Tree frog, salamander, and pond turtle don't seem to be the sort of animals you would expect to encounter in Baja, but they are present, along with a number of species of toad.

■ The desert bighorn sheep

There was a time when Baja California was popular with big game hunters from the US, and for good reason. In 1914, a license which cost $5 in gold allowed a hunter to take up to 6 desert bighorn. Articles appeared in *Field and Stream* describing hunts where 10 or more bighorn were taken. Gold and mineral strikes occurred in a number of areas, and the bighorn were

A pair of magnificent bighorn sheep

Gary Kramer

sorely pressed by hungry miners. In 1942, Frederick Simpich told of counting 32 pairs of horns in a small mining camp.

Many recent factors have combined to greatly reduce bighorn populations: the locals do a bit of poaching; there is competition with domestic animals for forage and water, especially with goats; diseases have been introduced by feral animals; and human encroachment continues to reduce their range. Never numerous, bighorn survive today in remote mountainous areas, the main populations found on the eastern side of the peninsula, from the border to north of La Paz. Estimates of their populations are often little more than guesses, but in 1992, a helicopter survey of the northern two-thirds of the peninsula produced estimates of between 780 and 1,170 animals.

You are unlikely to encounter a bighorn crossing the road ahead or placidly grazing in a field; if you want to see one, you will have to earn the experience. There is one place where this is possible without a major expenditure of time and sweat—see page 136.

Baja's diverse mix of deserts, bays, mangrove lagoons, forested peaks, and islands, together with its strategic location on many flyways, promotes an equally diverse mixture of bird life. Check lists differ, but some identify over 400 species that live in, breed in, or pass through Baja and over surrounding waters. There are vast numbers of quail and

The Transpeninsular passes through some beautiful desert scenery near Cataviña

dove, and many sea birds, including ospreys, frigates, pelicans, and gulls. The most common raptors include red-tailed hawks, American kestrels, peregrine falcons, and owls, and you may be lucky enough to see a golden eagle or a crested caracara. Turkey vultures seem increasingly common, and you may see frigates, normally sea birds, far inland. A number of special birds will be described in later chapters.

Marine life

The southerly sweep of the California Current insures that snorkelers and fishermen will find it difficult to differentiate the flora and fauna of the Pacific waters off northwestern Baja from those of Southern California, and extensive kelp beds and such fauna as ling cod, abalone, and sea urchins are common. Starting at about San Quintín, however, some of the plants and animals adapted to cool water start to disappear, and forms that are adapted to more tropical conditions become increasingly common. By Punta Abreojos, the underwater environment becomes distinctly tropical, although some cool-water life like abalone can be found all the way to the Cape. Occasionally El Niño, a warm current formed in the Pacific, provides a few surprises: in the Summer of 1993, several Cortez angelfish, normally a tropical species whose presence in Baja waters is confined largely to the Cape, were seen in the San Diego area, mako sharks, skipjack, dolphinfish, and broadbill swordfish were hooked in the Bay Area, and a marlin was caught in Oregon.

The diversity of fish in the Cortez is extreme due to its great variations in water temperature and depth, and great range of bottom topography, from great shallows with flat, silty bottoms to vertical rock walls. Although early explorers thought Baja to be an island, there has been no direct connection between the northern Cortez and the Pacific at any point in the geological history of the peninsula. It might be hard to convince a fisherman or diver of this fact, however, for the northern Cortez is home to a rather odd assortment of fish, with more in common with Southern California than with the rest of the Cortez. Among the "California" fish to be found are white seabass, ocean whitefish, several species of rockfish, sheephead, and California halibut. Although some Baja residents claim there is a tunnel under the peninsula connecting the Cortez and the Pacific, a more likely reason for the presence of these species in the northern Cortez is

A Panamic green moray claims a small area of the Cortez as home territory, not to be invaded even by passing divers

get together in larger groups, and 27 were once seen feeding together in the Cortez. Similar in appearance but smaller and less gregarious than finbacks, Bryde's whales are also seen along the Pacific coast and throughout the Cortez.

Humpbacks, with their long white flippers and musical talents, inhabit the Cortez and waters off the Cape in winter, especially the latter area. Blue whales, at 100 feet and 150 tons the largest animals ever to live on earth, cruise off the Pacific coast, some visiting the Cortez between late winter and late spring. A "school," or better yet a "university," of 12 blues was seen a number of years ago, feeding west of Cedros. Sperm whales are seen occasionally, sometimes traveling in large groups. Fifty-two of them stranded on a beach north of Mulegé in 1979 and died in the hot sun. Other whales that might be encountered include Sei, Minke, Cuvier's beaked, pygmy sperm, northern pilot, orca, and false killer. Orcas often stay near the Islas San Benito, where they are attracted by large numbers of sea lions, a favorite delicacy. In 1978, a pod of an estimated 40 orcas was seen attacking a blue whale off Cabo San Lucas, biting its lips and flukes for over an hour.

The smaller cetaceans in Baja waters include harbor porpoise, Dall's porpoise, common dolphin, Risso's dolphin, Pacific white-sided dolphin, Eastern Pacific spotted dolphin, spinner dolphin, and Pacific bottlenose dolphin. Bottlenose and common dolphins are the most abundant, often racing at the bows of passing boats. We were once rounding the south cape of a small island just south of Isla Tiburón when

that their ancestors arrived during a period when Cortez waters were cooler than today. At the southern end of the Cortez, Indo-Pacific species like Moorish idols and longnose butterfly fish can be seen, and there is even a sizable coral reef.

While a visitor to Baja is unlikely to see a large, wild, four-legged land mammal (the two-legged variety is common), the waters surrounding the peninsula contain an abundance of marine mammals, and over 20 species of cetaceans (whales, porpoises, and dolphins) have been identified. The most numerous large whales in Baja's Pacific waters are the gray whales, described in the next section. A full-time resident population of finback whales lives in the Cortez, often concentrated in the Midriff region, and others can be seen in the Pacific in winter. Finbacks are large, and at up to 80 feet they are second only to blue whales. They sometimes swim in groups of 2 to 10, their spouts shooting up like geysers. On rare occasions they

A troop of passing acrobats puts on a show

we came upon an unbelievable sight to the west—although the Cortez was flat calm, an area of about 10 acres was being churned into whitecaps. Only when great numbers of black and white shapes leaped into the air did we realize that it was a group of a hundred or more common dolphins.

Pinnipeds (seals and sea lions) are common in Baja waters, although few are to be seen in locations accessible to RVers. California sea lions, elephant seals, and harbor seals breed and calve on the larger islands along the Pacific coast. California sea lions often entertain human divers at the islands north of La Paz with barrel rolls and somersaults. Sea lions are not often appreciated by local fishermen, who see them as competition, and they are sometimes killed and used as shark bait. However, scientists have found that 90% of their diet consists of fish with no commercial value. Elephant seals are most common at the San Benitos, although they also haul out on the Islas los Coronados, San Jerónimo, and San Martín as well. Harbor seals often can be seen on San Martín, San Jerónimo, and the Coronados, and occasionally on the Islas de Todos Santos, west of Ensenada. Stellar sea lions and northern fur seals are seen from Cedros north, but only rarely.

The world's most popular whales

Articles frequently appear in the nation's magazines and newspapers proclaiming that yet another species of animal has become extinct or is in danger of becoming so. There is one prominent victory, however, the gray whale, a species which has made a happy comeback from the edge of oblivion.

Early each October, the grays begin a 5,000-mile journey from the food-rich Chukchi and Bering seas to Laguna Guerrero Negro, Laguna Ojo de Liebre, and Laguna San Ignacio. These large lagoons on Baja's western coast, with their warm, shallow and protected waters and lack of natural predators like the orcas, provide ideal places to give birth and to undergo reproductive rituals. Smaller numbers continue on for several hundred miles to vast Bahía Magdalena, or on to the western coast of mainland Mexico, a few even ending up in the Cortez.

The first contingents normally arrive in the lagoons in late November, and the last in February. Among the mature females, about half are pregnant from last year's visit and ready to give birth, the other half, having given birth the previous year and their calves now weaned and independent, are ready to fill their role in the biological imperative and repeat the cycle again. A number of young females are also ready for their first attempt at reproduction. Adult males, and some precocious adolescents, do not share this two-year cycle, and the ratio of willing males and receptive females is thus more than two to one. The result is a melee of comical proportions, with as many as 20 whales participating. In the past, writers often claimed to have seen two or more males "assisting" each other in copulating with a female. Although the image of cooperation during such events has a certain appeal—the whales as "gentle giants"—scientists

A competition developed between mother and child; who was going to be first to be petted and scratched?

now know the truth; the males, intent on fulfilling their biological mission and wishing to garner a reward for 5,000 miles of swimming, will barge right in if necessary, having little respect for the human concept of waiting one's turn, nor concern for the privacy of a loving couple.

One way or another, the job gets done, and about 1,500 grays are born each year. Giving birth to a whale calf is not an easy chore, for they are about 15 feet long and weigh between 1,500 and 2,000 pounds. The mother can provide up to 50 gallons of milk a day, enabling her calf to grow rapidly. Within several months it can reach 20 feet and 4,000 pounds, and be able to undertake the rigors of the sea. The return migration to northern waters begins late in January, a few mothers and calves remaining until May or June.

■ A highly unscientific theory

Why do the grays make such an exhausting migration, the longest of any mammal? The obvious answer, that the warm, safe waters of the lagoons insure a high success rate, gives cause for second question—how could the whales have known about the Baja lagoons in the first place? After all, they are 5,000 miles away from their main food source. Did adventurous whales once undertake voyages of exploration, surveying the shores of the Pacific for the best locations? No one will ever know the answer for sure, but during campfire debates over the years, aided by generous supplies of margaritas, we have cooked up an explanation.

About 400 million years ago, the earth consisted of a single huge continent named Pangaea, circled by an enormous ocean. Tectonic forces gradually caused the land mass to break up and drift apart, forming the seven continents and five oceans we know today. Somewhere during this unfolding of events, the ancestors of the whales visited lagoons very near the cool ocean waters providing their food sources, and found them to be good places to carry out their reproductive duties. Slowly, however, the land surrounding the lagoons drifted away, at a rate that might be fractions of an inch per year. Each year, for millions of years, the distance between the sources of food and the lagoons grew larger, but the whales persisted, until it now requires a 5,000-mile journey.

You may have cause to doubt the scientific validity of this theory, but please consider the following: the Pacific Plate is carrying the lagoons north, and the voyage gets shorter every year. Doesn't this suggest that the whales know something about continental drift?

A deadly new predator finally arrived, one that would almost exterminate the whales. Although an English whaling vessel entered Baja waters in 1795, large-scale whaling in the eastern Pacific did not begin until the mid-1800s. In the Winter of 1857–58, Captain Charles Scammon rediscovered Laguna Ojo de Liebre, first visited by Juan Rodríguez Cabrillo in 1542. The lagoon was full of adult gray whales and their babies, and a terrible slaughter began. The bomb lance, equipped with an explosive charge, was often used to subdue the prey. Calves were often killed first because the whalers knew the cows would not abandon their babies, and as a result became easy targets. Scammon told of a calf that waited for its mother for two weeks after she had been cut up and rendered into oil, and about infuriated adults that gave chase to the whale boats. Tremendous blows from their flukes stove in many boats and killed a number of men, and the species acquired a reputation for ill-tempered, aggressive behavior and were nicknamed "devilfish." From the standpoint of the hunted, their hostility toward the hunters was eminently understandable.

The whale lagoons drew ships from many parts of the globe, including one from Russia and one from Germany, and by 1862, whales had been virtually eliminated from Scammon's. However, Scammon later discovered a similar lagoon to the south, now called Laguna San Ignacio. Between whales taken by ships in the lagoons and those taken along the coast of the Californias, the number of grays declined rapidly. Scammon estimated the population at between 30,000 and 40,000 in 1853; 28 years later it was between 5,000 and 9,000. These estimates were little more than guesses, and scientists now believe the population in 1846, before commercial whaling for grays began, to have been between 12,000 and 15,000. Regardless of which figures are used, many naturalists thought the species was headed for extinction. However, in 1937 the grays were given legal protection. In 1994, the US Fish and Wildlife Service took the gray off its endangered species list, and their numbers are now estimated at 21,000, possibly more than before whaling commenced. This is good news to some, but others fear that killing grays will begin again, despite a number of laws still protecting them. Several Native American groups in Alaska have claimed that treaties enacted long ago allow them to take grays, and they plan to take a small number for "cultural" purposes, possibly encouraging claims by other groups. Several dozen grays that migrate from the Arctic to Korean waters are still on the endangered list, and some scientists are concerned that they may face problems caused by the extremely small gene pool.

With the increase in their numbers has come a better understanding of the animal, and the relationship between whale and human has been transformed to a degree that Captain Scammon might not be able to comprehend. Rather than being the hunter, humans are now cast in the role of active protector. In 1988, a rescue mission was undertaken to save 3 grays that became trapped by ice when they stayed too long in their summer feeding grounds near Alaska. One died, but the other two were eventually freed with the aid of Soviet icebreaking ships and Alaskan volunteers, who carved breathing holes in the ice with chain saws.

The annual migration of the grays has become the object of great interest. Large numbers of people in the US watch from shore or go out on private boats, and hundreds of commercial craft offer daily whale-watching trips out of coastal ports. It is estimated that over a million humans see the gray whales each year, making them the "most-seen" whales in the world.

In recent years there has been a new surge of interest in the grays because some are "friendly." Such whales can be encouraged to come right up to a boat in several Baja locations, the best being Laguna San Ignacio. Since getting there involves only 40 miles of unpaved road from the village of San Ignacio, you can easily have the world-class experience of scratching and petting a 30-ton whale. The details of this marvelous adventure will be found beginning on page 213.

Unfortunately, the travails of the whales at the hand of man may not be over. In 1995, the Mexican government and the Mitsubishi Corporation of Japan announced that they had entered into an agreement to establish a major salt extraction plant at Laguna San Ignacio. This would involve pumping 462 million metric tons of salt water from the lagoon into 70 square miles of evaporation ponds each year. The expected annual yield of 6 million tons of salt would then be transported by a 15-mile conveyor belt to a mile-long pier at the mouth of the lagoon, and which may involve dredging a channel. Environmentalists say that the construction and operation of such a facility would have a disastrous effect on whale breeding. Two departments of the Mexican government are at odds over the project, and many environmental groups have submitted protests. Japan has earned an unenviable reputation in ecological matters, being one of the few nations still hunting whales, taking 300 Minkes each year with the transparent excuse that this slaughter is necessary for "scientific research." Whale meat from many species continues to be a popular menu item in Japan, and in 1994, American scientists were stunned when DNA analysis of whale meat routinely purchased in Japanese markets proved it to be from humpbacks, the taking of which has been banned world-wide for 27 years. In this case, let us hope that the "good guys" win, and that Mitsubishi leaves Laguna San Ignacio to the whales and returns to more acceptable pursuits.

■ Doing what it takes

In the harsh environment of central Baja, it often does not rain for years at a time, and the law of survival of the fittest has resulted in many adaptations. Many desert plants, most notably creosote, are allelopathic, emitting toxic substances that discourage other species from competing for valuable water and space. To discourage animals in search of supper, many plants have spines or thorns, and often taste or smell terrible, cause diarrhea, act as a diuretic, produce an allergic reaction, or leave a rash. A few are outright poisonous, like jimson weed and tree tobacco. Many plants have abandoned water-wasting leaves, and among those that have remained leafed, many have down-pointing, spiked leaves designed to collect dew and cause it to fall to the ground near the roots. Some plants have a waxy or resinous covering, reducing transpiration of water, and others develop huge root systems. Some are able to store great quantities of water: almost 95% of the weight of a well-watered cactus may be water. Some plants, *palo verde* and smoke trees among them, have developed a clever strategy: these species require an ample supply of water, and to insure that seedlings do not take root in unfavorable years, the seeds have a hard coating that must be scarified (scratched) before they can germinate. Since this generally occurs when a flash flood has carried them down a gully, they awaken to a life well endowed with water, at least for a while.

The rare and unusual

By now you are probably thinking: "So what's new? Except for the friendly whales, I have encountered all these animals and plants in the southwestern US, and in mainland Mexico. What's so special about Baja?" The answer is: a great deal—look closer! There are striking plants adapted to extreme dryness that are endemic (found only in one area) to Baja, such as *copalquín*, *cardón*, and "boojum," which are found only in Baja and small areas on the mainland, and *torote*, a "tree" virtually identical in appearance to *copalquín* found only in Baja, mainland Mexico, and small areas in the southwestern US. These and a number of the more interesting and common plants will be described in later chapters at the first point those headed "south" are likely to see good specimens along the road in places where it is safe to park. In many cases, their actual range extends well to the north.

As the peninsula split away from the mainland in the manner described above, the Cortez became wider and longer, and the animals and plants living on the peninsula became isolated—to visit the mainland with breeding in mind, for instance, a bird had to fly over a lot of water or make a long detour. As a result of this isolation, a number of bird species evolved in ways different from their mainland counterparts. There are now four endemic bird species and subspecies to be found in Baja, three of which are so numerous that you should have little problem sighting them. The endemics and a number of other birds will be described in later chapters.

The Cortez even has its own endemic marine mammal, the Gulf of California harbor porpoise. Found only in the northern Cortez, it has the smallest range of any cetacean and is one of the least-known and most endangered marine mammals on earth.

■ Maurice

Whales are not the only friendly animals in Baja's waters. In February 1983, a young sea lion approached the whale-watching vessel *Pacific Star* in Laguna San Ignacio and started playing with the inflatable boats tied off at the stern of the vessel. The crew started to throw small fish to him, and within several days he had become very friendly. One day he climbed aboard the vessel and spent the night, wrapped in a blanket on the deck. On later trips Maurice, as he became known, took to riding in the inflatables on sightseeing trips with the other tourists.

What animal would be so foolish as to try to make a lunch out of the golden-spined cactus?

Islands in the sea

Parked on the shores of the Cortez and enjoying margaritas in the comfort of your Winnie, you may wonder about the brown islands dotting the brilliant blue waters. From a distance, they seem barren and almost lifeless, the homes of nothing more than cacti, lizards, snakes, and sea birds. However, upon close inspection, they will be found to be a treasure of diverse and unusual life forms. Had the navigator on the *Beagle* been a little less skillful, Darwin's *On the Origin of Species* might have made the Cortez islands the subject of the scientific interest and legal protection that the Galapagos now enjoy.

The more curious island animals include a "rattle-less" rattlesnake, and a black jackrabbit. Unlike ordinary rattlesnakes, the small, docile, and very rare snake found on Isla Santa Catalina sheds its terminal scale with each molt, and thus never develops a rattle. First described in 1953, their days are probably numbered, since feral cats on the island prey on them. The black jackrabbit of Isla Espíritu Santo can be spotted from 200 yards away, apparently defying the laws of natural selection. Isla Tortugas has an endemic species of rattlesnake, as well as an endemic mouse, the latter presumably placed there by Mother Nature as food for the former. There is also an endemic bat found on a few Cortez islands that makes its living catching fish.

In addition, the islands have the most spectacular concentrations of nesting seabirds on the west coast of North America—San Pedro Mártir, Raza, and San Lorenzo being among the most important. Raza is the nesting site for an estimated 90% of the world's Heermann's gulls and elegant terns, while San Lorenzo and two nearby islands collectively have the world's largest colony of nesting brown pelicans. Although the yellow-legged gull tends to nest alone or in small groups, the largest number of nests in the world is found on San Lorenzo. Isla San Pedro Mártir, the most remote of the Cortez islands, is surrounded by deep water and subject to heavy currents, and an extensive food chain is supported when tidal mixing causes plankton to thrive. The island is thus home to myriad sea birds, the colonies of blue-footed boobies and brown pelicans being among the world's largest. Since rainfall averages only 3 inches a year, guano collects year after year, giving the island the appearance of an iceberg and altering its climate by reflecting solar radiation.

Many of the islands have land mammals: Tiburón has 13 species, San José 7, Espíritu Santo 6, Carmen 4, and even tiny Mejía, located at the north end of Guardian Angel, has 3. Most are small rodents like mice and rats, but larger mammals such as ring-tailed cat, fox, coyote, brush rabbit, and jackrabbit are found on Espíritu Santo, Tiburón, and San José, and mule deer on Tiburón and San José.

Reptiles and amphibians thrive, with 25 species on Tiburón, 20 on San Marcos, 16 on Carmen, and 15 on Guardian Angel. Even some of the tiniest islets have one: Islotes las Galeras, a group of small islets north of Isla Monserrate, have a species of lizard. An endemic lizard is so prolific on

San Pedro Mártir that the island has one of the highest densities of reptiles found anywhere in the world.

One might expect to encounter only cactus and agave on the islands, but many other species of plants are to be seen: Tiburón has 298 species of vascular plants, Guardian Angel 199, Espíritu Santo 168, and Carmen 163. Isla las Ánimas Sur, little more than a rock sticking out of the sea northeast of Isla San José, has 11. Even Isla San Pedro Mártir, with its fertile but dry and seemingly impenetrable covering of guano, has 27. The more unusual species include a large endemic barrel cactus found on Isla Santa Catalina, which often reaches 10 feet in height and 3 feet in diameter, and the torchwood plant of the same island, which bears two distinct types of flowers.

Rob Watson

Julie Watson inspects a large Catalina barrel cactus

In the past, the islands have been protected from the intrusions of man for very simple reasons: they have few economic attractions, and except on the larger islands, no surface water is available. A number of seabird rookeries have been subjected to heavy pressure by egg collectors, there is a major gypsum mine on San Marcos, salt works have been in operation on Carmen and San José, and some guano collecting still goes on, especially on Isla Patos. Rats were inadvertently introduced to Isla San Pedro Mártir over 100 years ago, severely affecting other species. Despite this, most communities of flora and fauna have remained largely intact, and many scientists consider the Cortez islands, especially those in the Midriff region, to be among the world's last major refuges of relatively undisturbed low-latitude island life.

In recent years, however, a new menace has developed. The islands have become popular stops for yachtsmen and boaters, and for tourists on natural history trips, and increased numbers of outboard motors have made possible more frequent visits by the local people. Even remote Isla San Pedro Mártir sees between 300 and 700 people a month in its offshore waters, about 17% of whom go ashore. Although these visitors intend no harm, it is a fact of desert island life that the mere presence of humans can upset the balance of nature, and laws have been passed controlling many activities. Raza became a seabird sanctuary in 1964, and in 1978 all Cortez islands were granted wildlife-refuge status. Hunting and foraging are prohibited, and a permit is needed to collect or otherwise disturb the flora and fauna.

A capsule human history

Over the millenniums, a low, treeless tundra formation called the Bering Land Bridge has arisen a number of times in the narrow and shallow Bering Strait, joining the Asian and North American continents. Anthropologists believe that nomadic hunters arrived in the New World by simply walking east from the Old. Access by way of this convenient route ended about 13,000 years ago, when the sea level began to rise due to the melting of the last of the great continental ice sheets.

Until recently, anthropologists were certain that the first Americans had spread out over the vast continent by about 12,000 years ago. A stone spear point found in 1933 among mammoth bones near Clovis, New Mexico, has been widely accepted as being 11,500 years old, and other evidence points to this date as well. In recent years, however, doubts have begun to arise, some anthropologists placing the date of occupation much earlier. A hearth site in Brazil has been dated at between 30,000 and 50,000 years old, and recent DNA analysis at other locations points to an arrival almost 30,000 years ago.

At an unknown date, nomadic groups drifting to the south fell into the geographic *cul de sac* of the Baja peninsula. At the time the first European explorers arrived in late 1533 or early 1534, the population of the peninsula is believed to have been between 30,000 and 50,000 people, and "Indian" society had evolved into 4 groups, speaking different languages and having little contact with each other. The Pericú lived from Cabo San Lucas to the latitude of Santiago, the Guaycuras occupied the region from there north to roughly the latitude of Loreto, the Cochimí lived from there north to a latitude just south of Ensenada, and the Yumano from there north. All were nomadic hunter-gatherers, having no agriculture. Because of their wandering lifestyle and lack of pack animals, they had no permanent or even temporary dwellings, and early Europeans were amazed to find that the Indi-

ans would simply lie down for the night wherever they were when the sun went down. The Indian diet, which included snakes, lizards, mice, insects, the remains of beached whales, and even lice pulled from their heads, pulped, dried, or roasted as desired, was horrific to the Europeans. During the brief growing season in the spring, several species of cactus produce bright red, sweet-sour fruits that were highly prized by the Indians. Even while basking in the glow of well-filled bellies, their thoughts still revolved around food, for they would collect their fecal matter, pick out the seeds of the fruit and grind them for later consumption. Jesuit Father Francisco María Píccolo, unaware of this "second harvest," was subjected to teasing by the other priests when he consumed a gift of such flour.

I don't care if the Cochimí liked them. Why don't you be the first to try them?

By modern standards, the Indians led unhappy lives, lacking such necessities as cars, remote TV controls, and disposable diapers, but it seems that by lacking everything, they had everything. Baegert wrote: "The native Californians seem to thrive on anything. For them this is the most delightful place on the face of this earth, either because they know no better or because of the innate love of all people for the place of their birth.... One might consider them among the poorest and most pitiable of God's children, yet I will state without fear of contradiction that, as far as this earthly life is concerned, they are incomparably happier than those who live in Europe. A native Californian sleeps as gently and as well on the hard earth, under the open sky, as any European in his soft feather bed.... In all his life the native Californian never seems to have anything to distress him, to destroy his joy for life, to make death desirable...[and has] no one to plague or persecute him, to throw a lawsuit about his neck, to lay waste to his land, no fire or lightning to burn his farm.... These Californians seem to have nothing, yet at all times they have what they need.... It is no miracle that hardly a one among them has gray hair, and then only very late in life.... They are always in good spirits, they laugh and joke continuously; they are always contented, always joyful, which without a doubt makes for real happiness...."

Rock art treasures

Unknown to the vast majority of Baja RVers, serene, safe, and insulated in their vehicles, the sere hills and remote mountains of Baja California contain unique and frequently spectacular art treasures. At more than a hundred sites scattered from the California border to the Cape, explorers, miners, ranchers, and archeologists have discovered that the ancient Indians had graced their barren peninsula with rock art treasures ranging from simple petroglyphs pecked on exposed rocks to enormous murals painted on the walls of caves. Some of these murals contain figures of men and animals painted life-size or larger, extending 500 feet in length and to a height of 30 feet. Some of the murals are so grand in scale and the individual figures so large and high off the ground that local legends insist that the artists were giants.

Although examples of rock art have been found scattered throughout Baja, the most spectacular lie in the "Great Mural area," the canyons of the interior mountains of the southern end of the Sierra de San Francisco and the northern end of the Sierra de Guadalupe, an area once inhabited by the Cochimí Indians. The Transpeninsular Highway roughly bisects this area near San Ignacio. Although the sites are often called "caves," they are more accurately termed "rock shelters." They are generally formed by the repeated sloughing off of the softer layers of a canyon wall in response to the forces of water and changing temperatures. Many are found hundreds of feet up from the canyon floor.

The murals generally depict humans, deer, mountain sheep, and rabbits, but some also may include mountain lions, birds, fish, sea mammals, raccoons, and rats. No plants are recognizable and, except for arrows and spears, few man-made items are depicted. Human figures tend to be angular and highly stylized, with height accentuated. The sex of the figure is occasionally evident: some paintings show breasts as if they were sprouting from the arm pits, and classic vulva symbols, similar to those found throughout the world, are fairly common. A figure has been found of a male with truly heroic reproductive proportions, and a painted figure at Rancho el Progreso near Bahía San Francisquito appears to be a male endowed with three appendages. A number of animal figures show arrows sticking in them or lying

across their bodies. Relatively few human figures show arrows, but when they do, they can be veritable pincushions, with up to 10 arrows, some as long as 6 feet.

Many figures show the "bicolor" tradition, whereby figures were painted in two colors, sometimes divided vertically, but more often horizontally at waist level. Another important characteristic of the art is "overpainting," where the artist painted new images over those painted at an earlier time, sometimes building up as many as four layers. Known at other sites around the world, the effect can be startling, a cacophony of animal and human figures with no seeming order or logic. The manner in which succeeding images were placed suggests that each succeeding artist was oblivious to the work of his predecessor. The effect is disturbing to some, and one modern critic has deeply criticized the long-dead artists for this "indifference;" he would apparently have had the images lined up like ducks in a shooting gallery. In the minds of others, overpainting adds to the artistic value and power of the murals, and provides valuable clues to their meaning. In addition to representational paintings, those which attempt some realism in portraying animals or humans, the Great Mural area has examples of abstract art. Many of these take the form of "checkerboards," where intersecting lines form a series of squares, each filled with color, while others take various geometric or curvilinear forms.

When were the murals painted? Evidence has been sketchy, but a few clues are available. Some of the wooden artifacts found in Gardner Cave, north of San Ignacio, proved to have radiocarbon dates of between 1352 and 1512. A knife with an iron blade was also found in a crevice in the cave, and instead of a curved cutting edge, it was straight, with

Part of the Grand Mural at Gardner Cave

the back of the knife curved. The shape of the knife and its material suggest that it was made after the arrival of the Spanish. Father Consag wrote in 1751 that Indians in the area possessed metal knives, which they obtained by trading with people from the south. The early Jesuits commented that the murals appeared fresh in appearance and in good condition. Also, some sites contain figures of pack animals and Christian crosses, obviously created after the arrival of Europeans.

These clues do not date the murals with certainty—the artifacts could have been left at the site at any time after these dates, or they could have been made fairly recently out of old wood, and the art depicting pack animals and crosses could have been executed at a later time. However, until firmer evidence is available, it seems safe to assume that the Great Mural artists were at work somewhere between the mid-14th and early 16th centuries.

Why did the Cochimí spend a lot of time and effort on their art when their culture had otherwise produced little more than a bare subsistence living? The murals required a great expenditure of time in obtaining pigments and binders, traveling to the site, preparing ladders, etc. Obviously the art is not casual graffito, leading to the inevitable conclusion that it was produced for reasons considered important.

A desire to dominate appears to be a possibility. As noted earlier, the practice of overpainting was widespread, even though many of the caves had abundant unused wall space. Many of the animals that were painted—deer, mountain sheep, rabbits, etc.—were "power" animals, central to Cochimí existence. A statistical analysis of overpainting has shown that humans were painted over animals at least three times as often as could be expected if the overpainting were done at random. These factors suggest that the paintings were intended as magic, to enhance man's dominance over the animals. However, no "chase" or end-of-hunt "victory" scenes have been found. Today's hunters express this with the traditional snapshot taped to the mirror behind the bar; deer, ducks, or rabbits strung up by the heels, with the grinning victors posed with trusty firearms in hand.

The paintings and practice of overpainting thus seem to represent the general concept of dominance, rather than victory over a specific animal or species of animal, a subtle concept for the supposedly primitive Cochimí. Although the Jesuits accused the Cochimí of a child-like immediacy in gratifying their desires, the existence of paintings of fish, sea mammals, and turtles at sites far in the interior mountains suggest that this was not completely true.

Perhaps shamans living around San Ignacio brought initiates to the high country to impress and dumbfound them with the unexpected majesty of the country and the power and magic of the paintings, or to initiate them into a religion or cultural group through labor, discipline, and risk-taking. There are modern counterparts to this idea: Catholic cathedrals and rituals, the Boy Scouts, the Bar Mitzvah, and even Outward Bound. The human figures portrayed in the murals generally have upraised arms, an almost universal characteristic of religions in general. No one who has visited Gardner Cave can deny the stunning emotional impact of the large and powerful mural that is encountered after climbing up from the canyon floor. In fact, every visit to a mural site is a series of surprises, and you get the feeling that they were staged by someone with a fine sense of theater.

The Europeans arrive

This supposedly idyllic lifestyle began its descent into oblivion when Europeans discovered the peninsula. After conquering much of mainland Mexico, Hernán Cortés sent an expedition from mainland Mexico in late 1533 or early 1534 to explore the coast to the north. The crew of one of the ships mutinied and the captain was murdered. After abandoning a number of sailors who had remained loyal, the mutineers sailed across the gulf and into a large bay, today called Bahía la Paz. This proved to be a fatal mistake, for the Indians killed most of the crew when they became too cozy with the local ladies. However, survivors came back with stories of large numbers of pearls.

The stories of the pearls and the accounts of a survivor fired Cortés's imagination. In 1535, he accompanied an expedition to Bahía la Paz, where he established a small colony, christening it Santa Cruz. It lasted almost two years, until sickness, the harsh climate, and the unfriendly attentions of the natives drove the Spaniards out. Unwilling to give up his dream of more riches, Cortés sent Francisco de Ulloa north with 3 ships in 1539. One was soon abandoned, but Ulloa coasted along the eastern shore of an unknown body of water, and reached the mouth of the Río Colorado, diplomatically naming the gulf the Mar de Cortés. Ulloa then headed south along the western shore, rounded Cabo San Lucas and sailed north, discovering Bahía Magdalena and Isla Cedros. In April 1540, one of the ships was sent south from Cedros, carrying a message to Cortés, and Ulloa and his remaining men sailed north, never to be heard from again.

Between 1542 and 1543, Juan Rodríguez Cabrillo explored the west coast of the peninsula. He died at one of the Channel Islands under mysterious circumstances, but the expedition got as far north as southern Oregon, discovering San Diego Bay and Monterey Bay, but somehow failing to detect the one at San Francisco. Succeeding expeditions, most notably those lead by Sebastián Vizcaíno (1596, 1602–03), Francisco de Ortega (1632, 1633–34, 1636), and Pedro de Porter y Casante (1644, 1648), continued to pursue rumors of treasure, but for various reasons, including the lack of a dependable food supply, conflicting goals, disease, and resistance by the natives, there was little success, and the large sums spent on such expeditions returned little or nothing.

Beginning in 1566, ships known as the Manila Galleons began annual voyages between Acapulco and Manila in the Philippines. East-bound vessels carried gold, silk, and spices, as well as coins, gems, at least one "pearle as big as a dove egge," and such exotic items as artificial noses and alligator teeth capped with gold, the west-bound ships carrying less glamorous trade goods. The voyages took between five and seven months, and by the time the ships from Manila reached the coast of California, their passengers and crews were in great need of drinking water. In addition, the ships were so heavily laden that their slow speed made them easy targets for English and Dutch pirates, especially Sir Francis Drake. Secure harbors on the peninsula were thus needed by the Spanish for safety and resupply, and Bahía San Lucas and Bahía la Paz were chosen. However, the safety offered by these harbors proved less than total, and in 1587, Thomas Cavendish caught the galleon *Santa Ana*, and in 1709, Woodes Rogers captured the *Encarnación*, both at Bahía San Lucas. Despite these and other losses, the galleons plied the Pacific for a total of 250 years. The television movie "Shogun" is based partly on this trade.

■ The Baja name game

Place names are slippery and ephemeral things in Baja, even the name "California." The circumstances—the discovery of the new land, the pearls that had been seen, and the location described—all seemed to have been foretold by a Spanish romance novel published in 1510, *The Exploits of Esplandián*. The book described a fabulous island named "Califa," located "on the right hand of the Indies, very close to the terrestrial paradise," and told of a huge lake of pearls guarded by an Amazon tribe, as well as mountains of silver. The name soon caught on and transmogrified a bit, and the peninsula and the area to the north gained their present name, California.

Later generations of travelers and explorers, however, have assigned other colorful and descriptive names and phrases: "Lower California;" "Baja," referring to the entire peninsula; "The Baja;" "The Land Where Time Stands Still;" "The Land of Shorter Shadows;" "The Land of Clear Light;" "The Land Below;" "The Untamed Arm of God;" "Dragon-shaped Baja;" "a long rock jutting out of the sea;" "[The Land] Hanging Like An Icicle;" "The Sleeping Peninsula;" "The Tail End of An Earthquake;" "an afterthought of the Great Creator;" "a crooked dogleg of spiny land mass;" "the Land That God Forgot;" and "A Dried Stick From the Bough of [Alta] California." In recent years the region has come to be called simply "Baja," although some local politicians want it called "Baja California" and recently enacted an ordinance to that effect.

The body of water between the peninsula and mainland Mexico has metamorphosed from the "Sea of Cortez" to the "Mar Bermejo" (Vermilion Sea), the "California Sea," the "Gulf of California," the "Adriatic of the West," the "California Ocean," "the "Blue Sea," and "The World's Largest Fish Trap," and back to the original "Sea of Cortez."

Locally, things are far more complicated. Some names are used repeatedly: on current maps four locations involve the word "Ánimas," and there are seven "Lobos," nine "Blancas" or "Blancos," and six "Coyotes," as well as three "Punta Bajas." Two Cerro Colorados exist less than 30 miles apart, and in the Cortez there are 2 Isla Partidas, 4 Punta Arenas, and 2 Punta Coloradas. Saints are popular, and over 160 names involve "San," "Santo," or "Santa." Names change frequently. Arroyos are often named for a prominent ranch in the vicinity, which is in turn named for its owner, and when he dies or departs everything changes. There are English versus Spanish problems: English-speaking people do not refer to the big island off Bahía de los Angeles as "Isla Ángel de la Guarda," but rather as "Guardian Angel Island," but they call the even bigger island to the southeast "Tiburón," not "Shark," Island. Foreign names are sometimes applied, and sometimes they stick, like "Laguna Hanson," and sometimes they don't, like "Fornication Hole," a bay in Laguna Ojo de Liebre named by scientists studying whale breeding, or "Lottie Smith's Lagoon," named by the survivors of the 1870 wreck of the great paddle-wheel steamer *Golden City* on Baja's Pacific coast in honor of the first woman rescued.

The Mission Period

A permanent settlement in Baja California proved to be an impossibility until October 1697, when the Jesuits, lead by Father Juan María Salvatierra, founded a mission in Loreto. The early priests and explorers found nothing to admire about the Indians, seeing them as objects of contempt, a destitute people without art or culture living a ragged existence at the barest subsistence level. In 1759, Jesuit historian Miguel Venegas, less charitable than Baegert, and using the European standards of the time, wrote, "The characteristics of the Californians, as well as other Indians, are stupidity and insensibility; want of knowledge and reflection; inconstancy, impetuosity, and blindness of appetite; an excessive sloth and abhorrence of all labor and fatigue; an incessant love of pleasure and amusement of every kind, however trifling and brutal; pusillanimity and relaxity; and in fine, a most wretched want of everything which constitutes the real man and renders him rational, inventive, tractable, and useful to himself and society." Even Baegert made efforts to ferret out words, and thus concepts, that did not exist in the culture of his charges, such as "decency," "kindness," "mercy," "moderation," "pious," "pure," "virgin," and "virtue."

Despite their contempt for the Indians, the Jesuit missionary work went on, and between 1697 and 1767, 20 missions were constructed, although it was necessary to abandon some of them soon after they were built due to a lack of adequate water and other problems. A road, called El Camino Real (The Royal Road), was built to connect the missions. Using Indian labor, sometimes under very harsh conditions, surface rubble was removed down to bedrock or to a level surface, usually to a width of 8 feet or 10 feet. The rubble was then stacked in neat rows along both sides of the road. To keep the grade from getting too great, the road switchbacked up and down mountain passes, then proceeded straight as an arrow across the plains. The Jesuit desire for human perfection extended to road building as well, and in many locations the road went straight through obstacles that could have easily been avoided. The main sections of the road ultimately extended from Loreto through Misións San Javier, La Purísima, Guadalupe, San Ignacio, Santa Gertrudis, and San Borja to Misión Santa María. Less well-developed sections were built to serve the missions south of Loreto, where the pattern of travel was not as well established.

The golden altar at the old mission church at San Ignacio

Some Indians revolted when the Spanish padres attempted to interfere with long-established customs. In 1734, the Pericú attacked and burned the missions at Santiago and San José del Cabo, killing their priests, who had demanded that the Indians give up polygamy. At other missions, the priests allegedly found it necessary to use harsh measures to convince the Indians of the truth and beauty of their religion. During an 1844 visit to Misión San Fernando Velicatá, James Bull, an American who traveled in Baja from late 1843 to early 1844, was told that the Indians were roped like cattle

and brought to the mission, where they were lashed, and then baptized. After this initiation, the Indians were forced to labor from sunrise to dark, sustained by corn-meal gruel. If an Indian fell ill, the priests sometimes allowed a day or two of rest, after which the man either worked or was lashed again. Bull reported that an old Indian showed him where the lash had torn away part of his thigh. Whether this was true or not is unknown, since few outsiders like Bull visited the area, and insiders had good cause to remain silent.

Unfortunately, the Jesuits and earlier explorers brought more than civilization with them, and smallpox, typhoid fever, syphilis, and measles soon took their toll. By 1767, the Indian population of the peninsula had dropped precipitously, to perhaps 7,000. In that year, the Jesuits were expelled by royal decree from Baja California and replaced by the Franciscans. On February 2 the next year, the 16 Jesuit priests boarded a ship, amid weeping parishioners. Rumor persisted that the Jesuits had collected huge amounts of gold and pearls, and to this day fortune hunters still use up vast numbers of metal detector batteries and undermine the foundations of mission churches looking for treasure.

The Franciscans founded another mission, and in 1773, the Dominicans took over. They established nine more in Baja and a number in Alta California. El Camino Real was extended to the north, but the grand road of the Jesuits was reduced to little more than a trail, due in part to the greatly reduced numbers of workers available for road building. However, the land that defeated Cortés finally defeated the missionaries as well. The missions could not sustain themselves economically, and their populations of converts were dying off, so by 1840, all but 2 were abandoned by the padres, and these, Santo Tomás and Todos Santos, closed in 1849 and 1854 respectively.

The Indian tribes continued to decline due to disease and assimilation into the new populations, and today only a few groups now exist in scattered locations in Baja Norte and the Río Colorado delta area. The last full-blooded Cochimí was supposedly an old woman who died in Loreto in the 1920s. However, other human traces of the mission era have not disappeared. As the system collapsed, many of the craftsmen and soldiers who built and guarded the missions took possession of the land, and today the names Castro, Villavicencio, Arce, and Cota are common throughout the peninsula.

El Camino Real continued to be used until the late 1800s, and was not totally abandoned until the system of auto roads began to develop in the 1920s. The Transpeninsular Highway approximates the old route only from the vicinity of Misión San Fernando Velicatá north to the US border. Storms, erosion, and modern road building have destroyed much of the old road, but short portions are still in excellent condition. In some locations, the rock layers exposed by road building were white, and from a plane or a mountain top, the results are spectacular. Some of the missions were built from mud brick and have completely disintegrated, and the anticlerical attitude of the modern

Mexican government was such that no effort was made to preserve even those made of sturdier materials. However, there has been a change in outlook in recent years, and a number of them have received some maintenance and repair, and a few remain in active use. Later chapters will take you to the more accessible and interesting sites and describe a bit of their history.

The Mission Period looms large in Baja history, because, in the opinion of some, the construction and operation of the missions are the only events of any consequence that have ever occurred. In a letter to his brother, Father Baegert complained: "There is no news here—and I speak about all of New Spain and North America. In this country one knows no news but one's own. Among the common people the only discussion is how beans and corn grow or will grow."

Independence, coup, and conflict

The tempo of events picked up after Baegert left the peninsula. On September 16, 1810, now celebrated as Independence Day, a rebellion broke out in Mexico, fueled by economic chaos, inequitable land distribution, and what today would be called human rights violations. Mexico achieved its independence from Spain in 1821, but the peace treaty established a constitutional monarchy, and designated the Catholic Church as the state church, much to the unhappiness of many people. There was great confusion and disorder, and 50 new governments were installed in the first 30 years of independence.

In 1833, General Antonio de Santa Ana seized power, revoked the Constitution, and appointed himself dictator. A series of events brought the defeat of the Texans at the Alamo in 1836, American statehood for much of Texas, and the Mexican-American War in 1846 to 1848. There was fighting in Santo Tomás, Mulegé, La Paz, and San José del Cabo, and Mexico City fell to the Americans in March, 1847. The Treaty of Guadalupe-Hidalgo ended the fighting in 1848, but resulted in the loss of Alta California and parts of Texas and New Mexico. In 1853, Mexico's economy was so weak that it became necessary to sell Arizona and southern New Mexico to the US. An American adventurer named William Walker attempted to occupy Baja in 1853, where he set up a republic, with himself as president, of course. He lasted less than a year before he was "impeached." Walker was acquitted of violating US neutrality laws, but was executed several years later after a similar foray into Nicaragua.

Santa Ana ruled until 1855, when the reins of government were taken over by self-appointed sides based in Mexico City and Veracruz. In 1857, Benito Juárez participated in the writing of a new constitution, and in 1861 was elected president. However, in 1864 France invaded Mexico over nonpayment of debts, resulting in the installation of Ferdinand Maximilian as emperor. In 1867 the French were forced to withdraw, motivated by pressure from the US, and Juárez returned to power, to remain there until his death in 1872.

Economic dreams

Baja California has inspired economic dreams for centuries, but by the mid-1800s, the objects of these dreams began to change from gold and pearls to more practical matters. Reports circulated about a large mountain lake north of Bahía Vizcaíno, and of mountains having perpetual snow, the melt water from which could be used to irrigate crops. In 1888, an Ensenada newspaper reported that a sheaf of wild oats, sent from El Sauzal, measured 4 feet in length and hung heavy with grain, noting that "immense fields of them go to waste for want of stock to eat them." Another report described a twig six inches in length, cut from a tree in Maneadero, on which were eight full-grown plums, the tree supposedly being only one year old. The peninsula seemed to be an ideal location to live and prosper, with an area south of Ensenada providing an "equitable climate and invigorating breezes...mineral wealth..., good soil, abundant fuel, cheap Indian labor, and water abundant in quantity and unsurpassed in quality." There were tales that during a season of drought, cattle and horses from Los Angeles and San Diego were driven to Baja California to save them from perishing. The tall trees in what is now Parque San Pedro Mártir were coveted, and reports said that local streams could be used to float the logs downstream to mills, as done in Wisconsin and Michigan, and that the water could then be used for irrigation. The difference between reality and the picture of the peninsula painted by these stories is a tribute to human optimism and inventiveness, and illustrates the peninsula's remoteness and the difficulties it presents to exploration and exploitation, attributes that persist today.

Hoping to establish an economic base for the peninsula, Mexico granted huge concessions to American and English companies between 1880 and 1889, including huge tracts of land around San Quintín, where wheat farming was planned. Baja had a short-lived gold rush in 1890, which inflamed new interest in the territory. A number of grand schemes were proposed but never carried out, including the digging of a canal across the peninsula.

Revolution, turbulence, and statehood

The Mexican Revolution began in 1910 and continued for a number of years, caused by the familiar problem of socioeconomic inequalities, with the forces of Francisco Madero pitted against those of the dictator-president, Porfirio Diaz, who had governed Mexico in the interests of the privileged few for many years. The legendary soldier-bandit Francisco "Pancho" Villa and the revered Emiliano Zapata gained control of parts of Mexico, and in May of 1910, Diaz resigned and Madero became president. Madero fell prey to the many factions involved in the struggle for power, and was executed in 1913. The Revolution had its effects in Baja California (see page 118).

Germany tried to secure the aid of Mexico in the First World War by means of the famous "Zimmerman Telegram," which offered to "Make war together, make peace together,

Courtesy John Mills

A mule team at Catarina, after unloading a wagon-load of onyx, circa the 1920s. Note the schooner offshore

[to provide] generous financial support, and an understanding on our part that Mexico is to recover the lost territory in Texas, New Mexico, and Arizona." Despite this tempting offer, Mexico wisely remained neutral.

In 1917, a new constitution was enacted, providing for the breakup of large land holdings. However, President Venustiano Carranza did not enforce its provisions, and three years later Álvaro Obregón, a successful general in the Revolution, overthrew Carranza. Plutarco Elías Calles assumed the presidency when the anticlerical Obregón was assassinated by a fanatical Roman Catholic before he could take office for another term. Calles participated in the establishment of the PRI (the Spanish acronym for the National Revolutionary Party), which is still in power.

Baja was divided into two territories in 1887, with La Paz and Ensenada as their capitals. In the 1920s, Prohibition north of the border produced boom conditions to the south, and tax revenues allowed the construction of many roads and schools. The Northern Territory was the more prosperous, and gained full statehood in 1952, becoming known as the Estado de Baja California. Lacking the north's proximity to the US and to rich natural resources, it took the Southern Territory until 1974 to gain statehood, becoming Estado de Baja California Sur.

Continuing socioeconomic and political problems

The fiscal system in Mexico is highly centralized, and almost all taxing and spending are carried out by the federal government. Virtually all decisions of any consequence are made in Mexico City, and the only way to get a road paved or other capital project underway is to go with hat in hand to the federal government. Fiscal centralization thus works against democracy, and gives the PRI immense power, often used for personal and political aggrandizement.

The old problems concerning socioeconomic inequalities have not been resolved, as evidenced by an uprising by Maya Indians in the southern state of Chiapas that began in 1994 and has continued to date. The PRI is the world's longest-lived one-party system, but it has lost some of its previously unshakable power. In the August 1994, elections, judged by many observers to be the most honest in Mexico in this century, the PRI won, of course, but the center-right, business-oriented PAN (the Spanish acronym for the National Action Party) took 27% of the votes, up from only 16% in the 1988 election. State elections in August 1995, featured unfamiliar, American-style political ads sponsored by the newly-emboldened PAN, one television spot showing a young lady sipping a can of soda labeled "PRI." "What's that taste like," a man asks, and her reply is "Corruption."

In 1875, a peso was worth almost exactly a dollar, but since then it has experienced an irregular but precipitous slide to about 3,500 to the dollar. Rather than dealing with the underlying reasons for the decline, President Ernesto Zedillo Ponce de Leon, inaugurated only 3 weeks earlier, devalued the peso on December 20, 1994, and the next day let the peso "float" in the currency markets, bereft of government support. The government then issued "nuevo (new) pesos," simply knocking three decimal places off the old. Within weeks the nuevo peso had lost 40% of its value, resulting in panic on stock markets in Mexico, Argentina, Brazil, Chile, Peru, and the US, the Mexican exchange losing a third of its value. The effects on currency markets were felt as far away as Sweden and Hong Kong. (From this point on, we will refer to nuevo pesos simply as pesos unless otherwise noted.)

President Zedillo also installed a package of wage controls and austerity measures, and Mexican officials have suggested selling off CFE, the state electricity company, and even PEMEX, the state petroleum industry, the crown jewel of Mexico's public sector, as well as port facilities and railroads. However, the Mexican Constitution says that natural resources belong to the people, and that production facilities must remain in the state's hands, portending great political and legal struggles should a major sell-off of state assets get underway.

None of these measures have impressed international investors, who have lost more than $10 billion. By the end of 1995, the peso had declined to the point that it took almost 8 of them to buy a dollar. There have been massive demonstrations against the austerity measures the government deems necessary to stabilize the peso, and the year-end holiday season ending on January 6, 1995, was a disaster for Mexican retailers, with consumers unable or unwilling to part with their money.

Support for President Zedillo and his measures continues to erode, and many doubt his ability to manage the economic and political situation, citing dithering, a lack of will power, a lack of consistent policies, and an inability to inspire confidence. There have been calls to bring his predecessor, Carlos Salinas de Gortari, to trial for "economic mismanagement," an interesting, if unlikely, change in the unstated but cardinal rule that an ex-president is immune from legal liability.

What the future holds

Although there are positive signs, the North American Free Trade Agreement (NAFTA) among Canada, Mexico, and the US, creating the world's largest free-trade zone, has not yet borne much fruit, at least as far as the average Mexican can see. Despite the fact that Mexico is already our third-largest trading partner, behind only Canada and Japan, NAFTA has many opponents on both sides of the border, and the recent economic problems have promoted a chorus of "I told you so's." Investors from Japan and other Asian nations have been flocking to Mexico, driven by NAFTA's content rules, which require that most of any given product must be manufactured in the US, Canada or Mexico if it is to receive tariff-free status. Large Japanese companies such as Sanyo and Sony have been moving production from Asia to Mexico as a way to retain their high market share in the US, although the effects of the political and economic problems may dampen their enthusiasm. Rather than simple *maquiladora* plants, which assemble parts made elsewhere and capitalize on untrained but inexpensive labor, these operations will be complete, vertically integrated production facilities requiring a well-trained work force and educated professionals.

Despite the many problems, there are grand predictions that Tijuana will become a blue-collar suburb of "San Dijuana," a vast and powerful megalopolis including San Diego, Tijuana and their surrounding areas. Some predict that San Dijuana will eventually be joined to the Los Angeles area, and with the addition of Tecate and Mexicali to the east, become one of the most densely populated and richest urban areas of the world. If these predictions are to prove correct, many complex and interacting problems involving economics, water supply, transportation, ecology, law, and sovereignty must be resolved. Because Tijuana residents have voted for PAN candidates, the area has not received much in the way of funding for infrastructure, and with narrow streets, no harbor, the lack of a railroad spur to the docks of Ensenada, a poor water supply, and inadequate sewage treatment, the city needs billions to achieve this promise.

South of the border cities

Most of the peninsula south of the border cities seems to be doing fairly well economically. There has been a good deal of new construction in Ensenada and in La Paz, producing hotels, homes, businesses, and several large marinas, and the Cabo San Lucas area, with many new hotels, condos, restaurants, golf courses, and a fine new marina, is undergoing a boom. San Felipe and Bahía de los Angeles are stalled economically, at least temporarily. Loreto is adrift now that construction of hotel, condo, and marina facilities at Escondido has been halted, and the hotels, condos, and golf course at Nopoló have not attracted the horde of dollar-bearing Americans that had been anticipated. The economy of Santa Rosalía may benefit from new mining activities undertaken by a Canadian company, and by a new gypsum mining operation a few miles to the north. Nothing, of course, ever changes in Mulegé and San Ignacio.

The rusted, rattletrap, oil-burning cars and pickups encountered by those who first drove the Transpeninsular when it opened in 1973 are mostly things of the past, and have been replaced by a fleet of vehicles not much different from those in many American towns. Modern 18-wheelers ply the Transpeninsular night and day, and the old highway buses, rusted, dilapidated, dripping oil, and leaving a wake of blue smoke, have been replaced by sleek, modern, air-conditioned models. There are auto dealerships in a number of towns, there is a jet ski dealer in La Paz, you can make calls on your cellular at the north and south ends of the peninsula, and an increasing number of homes, even the very modest ones, sport the satellite dishes necessary to allow the inhabitants to keep up with the latest on MTV.

The lost world

While the political, social, and economic matters described above continue, there are vast areas of the peninsula that have been bypassed by "progress." Many are virtually uninhabited, and much of the peninsula is thus a rarity in the modern world—an accessible wilderness. Maps can be misleading, for the place names shown are often nothing more than tiny ranches, or even where tiny ranches used to exist. Much of the fascination and the air of mystery of the peninsula lie in the ease with which a traveler can convince himself he is the first person to see a particular canyon or walk a stretch of desert. We once encountered a group of bicyclists camped near Abreojos. Around the campfire that night, it was amusing to hear their descriptions about the remoteness and mystery of the area, all the while sitting so close to the town dump that the flickering flames illuminated the vast assortment of beer bottles and bean cans discarded by the citizenry over the years.

There are people living in this lost world in a manner that is almost beyond the comprehension of those of us used to the comforts and luxuries provided by our crowded technological society. The isolated reaches of the Sierra de San Francisco north of San Ignacio, the Sierra de Guadalupe to the south, and the Sierra de la Giganta, south of Loreto are far from any road, paved or unpaved. Many of the people living on ranches in these areas are descendants of officials, soldiers, and craftsmen who came to Baja California during the Mission Period. The mountains in these regions are not tall by any standard, but they are very rugged. Steep arroyos have been cut by water, and their bottoms are often in the shade early and late in the day. There are no electric lights and no loom from distant cities, resulting in a darkness and a display of stars unknown to city dwellers. Homes are placed well above the bottom of the arroyos and are of simple construction, with woven palm matting for walls and palm thatch for roofs. Architectural adornments are absent, but brilliant bougainvilleas grace many entrances.

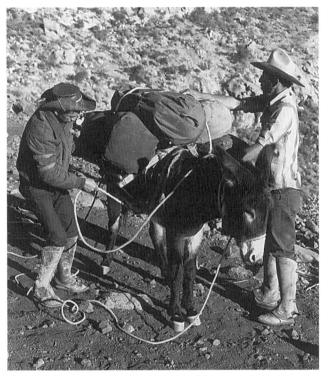

Several mountain men load a patient burro

Outsiders often utilize such adjectives as "quaint" and "primitive" to describe the social and economic conditions of the people living on these ranches. However, in many ways the mountain people have more complicated lives than those making such judgments, as well as having a much larger repertory of skills. A man has to be rancher, farmer, tanner, butcher, civil engineer, leather worker, hunter, carpenter, weather forecaster, and veterinarian, to name only a few skills, and a woman must cook, preserve food, sew, care for children, milk goats, make cheese, and tend to numerous other chores. Many city dwellers in the north make their living by rather simple and repetitive means, such as soldering transistors into circuit boards, waiting on tables, welding mufflers, flipping burgers, driving buses, installing windshields on the GM assembly line, or keyboarding information into a computer. Most have a lot of free time, sometimes utilized in socially undesirable ways. The people of the mountains do not lack meaningful ways to spend their time, and no one suffers from phlebitis or carpal tunnel syndrome.

The soil of most canyon bottoms is too thin to support agriculture, and surface water is limited at best. However, thriving orchards and gardens will be found at many ranches, the product of incredible efforts. Mules and burros are loaded with soil, often found at great distances, who then carry it to a selected location. Flumes are constructed from palm logs, carrying water from a spring or *tinaja* (natural water hole), sometimes more than a half mile away. Despite its shortage, the mountain people understand the power of moving water, and levees of large stones are constructed to divert flash floods. Month after month, year after year, the back-breaking work goes on. With luck, the gardens and orchards will provide a cornucopia of citrus fruits, pomegranates, figs, squash, dates, grapes, beans, and onions for many years, until a *chubasco* overcomes the levees and the water carries everything away, at which time the process begins again.

Cattle and goats are allowed to roam free, but few stray far from surface water, and they are thus easily recaptured. Goat milk is often converted to cheese, which is preserved with salt and carried by burro to villages and towns in the lowlands 50 miles or more away; you will frequently see hand-lettered signs offering *queso de montaña* (mountain cheese) for sale. Occasionally animals are slaughtered for food, and their hides, along with those of a few unlucky deer, are converted into leather by a method thousands of years old, using only local materials such as bark from the *palo verde* tree and lime. The resulting leather is used to make shoes, belts, chaps, and saddles, some of which are sold to provide cash income.

Despite the harsh surroundings, the heavy work, the lack of medical attention, and the vagaries of Mother Nature, the mountain people seem more secure in many ways than city dwellers. Rather than being an impersonal cipher, one face out of a hundred thousand on the freeway each morning, each person is an individual. They are their own masters, few seem to need to vent aggression, and there is no possibility of young people becoming the targets of bullets from passing cars because their shoe laces are the wrong color. Children begin early to learn the practical skills needed for survival in the harsh land. Since they are not segregated by age in a school and they live in extended families including a half dozen or more adults, ranging up to great-grandparents, they have many good role models and are not subject to the damaging peer pressure that occurs in our society. There is no unemployment, no welfare, and no Social Security. Old people work until they are no longer able, but at that point they are not trundled off to rest homes or hospices. Rather, they spend their last years with their families.

I (Walt) once attended a wedding at one of these remote ranches. The room was filled with awkward young girls, self-conscious in lipstick and lace dresses, uncomfortable men in unfamiliar and ill-fitting dark suits, and a few old-timers, hunched over but still attentive. The ceremony was solemn, and except for the incantations of the visiting priest, dead quiet, but when the last word was spoken, the joy seemed to burst like an over-filled dam. A total stranger when

I wandered by on my motorcycle, I was invited to join the party and within a few minutes felt like I had always been there.

The picture just painted is a glimpse of a life-style-in-passing, and the young people are drifting away, attracted by the bright lights and high times of Guerrero Negro and San Ignacio. Finding the unadulterated "real thing" is by now probably impossible. Roads are being cut into the wilderness, portable radios can be heard, and coffee, sugar, candy, and other store-bought items are found everywhere. By definition, no one in an RV can visit a roadless ranch, but you might get an fleeting glimpse of what life was like on one by a trip to the village of San Francisco (page 213), Rancho Santa Martha (page 215), or Comondú (page 219), all now accessible by unpaved road.

● ●

❝ *Changing impressions*

A number of years ago my friend Rob Watson and I dragged a trailer down to the El Rosario area, planning to spend several days wreck diving and fishing Sacramento Reef and Isla San Jerónimo before heading for the Cape. The first night near El Rosario, however, we decided to stay longer, for the diving and fishing were fantastic. The trailer was too big to bring all the way to the beach, so the next morning we stopped at a ranch near the river and asked whether we could park it for about a week. The lady was pleasant and pointed out a good spot.

That night Rob and I began talking, and like many people from north of the border, we found we both had a number of preconceived ideas. The ranch house was not much by our standards, with a concrete floor, concrete block walls, and a corrugated sheet-iron roof, and the car parked in front was dilapidated. Without actually admitting it, both of us felt sorry for the woman and her three children, whom we judged to be living in poverty.

Each afternoon we stopped and gave the family some fish we had caught. The children playing in the back of the house seemed lively and intelligent, and were often seen consuming ice cream bars and drinking Fantas. This was certainly not good for their teeth, but it meant that the family

had some discretionary income. We returned at dusk one day and were invited in for coffee. The family was having supper, and there were plates of fish, corn, and other vegetables, as well as the traditional tortillas, so no one was going hungry, and in fact they were eating better than we were, with our diet largely made up of granola bars, Pringles, and Coke. The kitchen was equipped with a stove, a refrigerator, and a sink, and running water was available. There didn't seem to be an adult male around, but we didn't ask why.

Day by day, our impressions kept changing. Rather than living in dire poverty, the family wasn't doing all that badly. Two of the children attended school regularly, and a mildly retarded daughter was getting professional help. The house was spotlessly clean, and each child had a well-made bed and a number of toys. The garden in back was thriving, providing corn, tomatoes and beans, and several trees were heavy with oranges. The children had been assigned various chores, and they could be seen hoeing the garden, feeding the numerous chickens, and doing dishes, all without complaint. Using her feminine intuition, the lady answered a question even before we asked it—where was the man, if any? Her husband had been herding cattle high in the mountains for several months, and was expected back within a week.

The last morning was spent readying the trailer, and that afternoon we joined the family in a sort of indoor-outdoor picnic, and the last lingering doubts were allayed. Friendly and unpretentious, they seemed to be better off in many ways than a good portion of the population north of the border. The things they didn't have, a giant-screen color television, for instance, were things they were probably better off without. There was no smog, crowded freeways, or hour-and-a-half commutes. Everyone was fairly busy each day, but there was time for play. These people were not poor, at least in any way that really mattered, and in fact led secure, warm, and productive lives.

After hitching up, we walked over to the house to say our good-byes and were invited in. As we drank a last cup of coffee, the lady went over to a dresser and picked up a photograph of a young man. Without intending to be rude, I bluntly asked who and where he was. It was her eldest son, who was in Mexico City attending dental school. ——Walt ❞

● ●

Chapter 2

Planning and Getting Ready

Gangster Willie Sutton was once asked why he robbed banks, and he replied "That's where the money is." If someone asks why should anyone go to Baja, the answer is similar—that's where the adventure is! However, if you are going to take full advantage of what Baja has to offer, you will have to do some planning. Baja adventure takes many different forms, and for some, travel itself is the adventure, but to others, the RV is just the means of travel between adventures. The first step in planning is thus to decide what interests and activities you would like to pursue.

A Baja RV trip offers a wide and diverse range of activities—far more than, say, a trip to Yosemite or Cape Cod. These include: boating; fishing; diving and snorkeling; boardsailing; surfing; kayaking; hiking and exploring; beachcombing; nature watching; rock-art viewing; off-road driving; golfing; tennis; tours, sightseeing, and shopping; and holidays, events and other activities. The following paragraphs will provide you with basic information on each.

Boating

Unless your interests are strictly landlocked, you will probably want to bring a boat to Baja. Although there are many *pangas* for hire throughout Baja Norte and Baja Sur, and a number of cruiser fleets are available in Baja Sur, they are not always to be found when and where you need them, and they can cost a pretty penny. Besides, many fishermen, divers, and explorers find that piloting their own boat is part of the fun. (*Pangas* are open skiffs, made of fiberglass or plywood, about 22 feet in length, powered by an outboard engine of about 40 horsepower. They are used throughout Baja for sport and commercial fishing.)

New roads and improvements to existing roads have opened up great adventures for small-boat sailors, especially the roads to Bahías Tortugas and Asunción. In the past, this stretch of coast was very difficult to get to with anything short of an oceangoing yacht, but now it is possible to haul in cartoppers and inflatables with only modest vehicles, and although there are no paved ramps and over-the-beach launches are necessary, adventurous trailer-boat sailors can make the trip without undue difficulty. The San Evaristo road makes it possible to dive the wall at Isla las Ánimas Sur and the caves of Isla San Diego out of an inflatable or a cartopper,

and the road south from Bahía de los Angeles to Bahía San Francisquito makes it possible to get close to the Midriff region. It is great fun to explore vast Bahía Magdalena, and seaworthy boats can head for Banco Thetis for marlin and wahoo. Trailer boaters often launch at Bahía San Quintín and spend time at Isla San Martín, diving and fishing around Johnston's Seamount and Roca Ben.

The ultimate boat for fishing, diving and short-range exploring Baja's inshore waters may be the largest aluminum boat you can carry on the roof of your vehicle, probably a 15-footer if you have a full-size pickup or van, equipped with a 15 to 25 horsepower engine. Recreation Industries Co. makes loaders that allow carrying a boat on the top of various types of vehicles, including large motor homes, cab-over campers, and pickups towing fifth-wheel trailers. A bow line and extra tie-downs are necessary to resist lateral and vertical loads caused by crosswinds and from wind blast created by 18-wheelers on the narrow Transpeninsular.

The qualities of inflatables make them useful for Baja adventuring: they are light and portable, and their stability, load-carrying ability, and low freeboard make them especially attractive to divers. In heavy weather, an inflatable is far safer than an open aluminum boat. While driving off-road, an inflatable in the back of a pickup will be a lot less hassle than a boat on top. On the negative side, they tend to be wet, take more engine horsepower, use more fuel, have relatively little load volume, are vulnerable to hooks, knives, and fish spines, and attaching downriggers, rod holders, and transducers can be a problem. In addition, they take valuable cargo space: an aluminum boat on the roof takes less usable space than an inflatable in the back.

A wide variety of boats have been successfully trailered to Baja, ranging from miserable 1950s fiberglass runabouts with imitation Cadillac tailfins to the latest in Boston Whalers and Farallons, but no one type or make is clearly best for all situations and interests; the choice depends on how and where you plan to use it, seaworthiness, personal preference, and pocketbook. While the comfort, safety, and range of large trailerable "yachts" are desirable, they are hard to handle on the Transpeninsular and difficult to launch in most locations, and obtaining a supply of gasoline can be a problem in some

Reeve Peterson

Our trusty 15′ Gregor cartopper proved to be an ideal boat for exploring the Cortez

so on, and in summer the migration is reversed. Those who arrive on the scene of this migrating horde, by luck or design, will be treated to some fantastic fishing. There are many other locations that seasonally offer fine fishing for those with access to boats: the San Quintín area, Bahía de los Angeles, the seamounts that dot the Pacific coast, the Bahía Magdalena area, and others. For those who prefer beach-casting, the great sweep of Pacific beaches between El Rosario and Guerrero Negro, and between Bahía Tortugas and Bahía Magdalena, especially the outer beaches of the islands forming the latter bay, can be outstanding, and there are places where dolphinfish, marlin, and yellowfin tuna have been caught from shore.

Because of its importance to many visitors, fishing is described in detail in an appendix all to itself, Appendix A, which includes tips on favorite species, tackle, natural and artificial baits, cruiser and *panga* fleets, the rental costs of such boats, tackle shops, beach-casting, licenses and regulations, seasons and locations, and fishing conservation.

areas. There is no sharp limit, but it is probably unwise to trail boats over 24 feet to Baja.

Fishing

Despite many years of heavy commercial and sports fishing, many locations remain world-class, especially the Cape region. The waters around Cabo San Lucas provide perhaps the finest marlin fishing in the world, and you have an excellent chance of catching one, even if your boat is a small cartopper or an inflatable. The coast from Cabo San Lucas to Bahía de la Ventana remains one of the most productive sports fisheries on the globe, with catches of enough blue marlin, dolphinfish, and sailfish to keep the campfire stories going on for years—in one year, fishermen were complaining that hordes of dolphinfish and sailfish made it difficult to catch blue marlin in the Bahía las Palmas area! Punta Arena de la Ventana and Ensenada Muertos are the finest roosterfish grounds anywhere, and the channel between Ventana and Isla Cerralvo has excellent fishing for striped marlin, wahoo, sailfish, and dolphinfish.

There is fine fishing elsewhere. The warm months bring dolphinfish, the perfect game fish, to the Loreto area, and they are readily accessible, especially to those with boats large enough to get well away from shore. The California yellowtail is one of the most abundant and popular gamefish in Baja's Pacific and Cortez waters. As the northern Cortez cools down in winter, yellows head south, leaving Bahía Gonzaga and showing up at Santa Rosalía, then Mulegé and

Diving and snorkeling

Dave Miller seems pleased with his tuna

Baja California has the most diverse and interesting diving attractions found almost anywhere in the world. On a single trip a diver can hunt for ling cod in a cool-water kelp environment, visit a coral reef, make friends with a huge manta ray, hitch a ride on the fin of a gigantic whale shark, watch sand cascade down steep underwater canyons, and photograph such Indo-Pacific beauties as Moorish idols and longnose butterfly

fish. A visit to a mysterious Pacific seamount, where life competes so vigorously for living space that not a square inch of bare rock can be seen, may be followed days later by a dive on a pristine sand bottom devoid of life—devoid, that is, unless you approach slowly and quietly, to find hundreds of slim garden eels swaying in the underwater breezes, ready to disappear instantly into the sand. Individually, these marvels are found elsewhere, but collectively they make Baja unique.

There are many prominent diving locations: the Islas de Todos Santos, the Punta Banda peninsula, Roca Ben, Johnston's Seamount, Sacramento Reef, Pulmo Reef, Isla las Ánimas Sur, and Marisla Seamount are but a few. Chapters 4 through 7 contain detailed information on these and many other dive sites, as well as the locations and descriptions of dive shops and decompression chambers.

If you are interested in becoming a scuba diver, why not combine an RV trip with a certification course, or, if you are already certified, take an advanced course? The courses offered by the various shops and organizations in Baja range from resort/refresher, through certification and open-water, to such specialties as advanced open water, rescue diver, wreck diver, deep water diver, divemaster, underwater photographer, and underwater naturalist. The weather, scenery, and ambiance at the places where these courses are offered are great, there are a number of good RV parks or boondocking sites close to all of them, and good restaurants and lively night life are to be found near the ones in the larger towns.

Do you suppose that those blips are chests of gold or just some more nails?

Boardsailing

Baja is in the midst of a boardsailing boom, and for good reason, for there is everything anyone could want, ranging from mill ponds to rolling ocean swells, from gentle zephyrs to boom-bending blasts, and vast areas that never see more than a board or two at a time. The orientation of both coasts is roughly northwest/southeast, and since prevailing winds are northwest along the Pacific coast and north in the Cortez, fine, reliable side-shore conditions are frequently encountered.

Along the Pacific coast, KM 38+ (El Portal) on the Free Road is an old favorite with boardsailors, but it is getting too popular with their surfer brethren. Bahías San Quintín, Magdalena, and Almejas provide long rides in good winds, with no ocean swells. Bahía Santa María (the "outer bay" at San Quintín) sometimes has a refracted swell and there are ocean swells at the point, but the winds are good and there are fine sand beaches. Bahía Santa Rosalillita, also a favorite with surfers, often has strong, reliable winds, giving it a reputation as something of a "jock" area. One boardsailor recently spent six weeks there, and was skunked only two days. Waves range from the calm of the bay to perfect sets of big waves off the point, providing a fine place for intermediate sailors making the transition to waves. Bahía Tortugas is not often visited by boardsailors, but it is free of ocean swell and frequently has heavy winds, and you can't get carried too far if you have trouble with waterstarts and tacking. Punta Abreojos is very windy, and the heavy June thermals that are the bane of local fishermen are a joy to boardsailors. El Conejo, too, is a favorite with heavy-weather sailors. There are, of course, many "secret" locations, small bays and coves offering fine sailing, but by and large most other Pacific coast locations are for experts only, due to large swells, tidal currents, and fog.

At the Cape, Playa el Médano at Cabo San Lucas and the small coves to the east attract novice and intermediate boardsailors. Cabo San Lucas is generally out of the area affected by the heavy north winds that funnel down the Cortez in winter, but southern fronts provide fine onshore and cross-onshore conditions in summer. With a large body of warm water and a major land area to the east, a ocean to the south, and mountains and an ocean to the west, East Cape gets brisk, dependable winds between mid-November and mid-March, making it the most popular boardsailing location in Baja, the Cabo Pulmo and Bahía las Palmas areas being favorite places. There are also fine beaches and good boardsailing around Cabo Frailes, Punta Arena Sur, Punta Colorada, and Playa Punta Arena, but the Canal de Cerralvo offshore of the last beach is largely for experts, with heavy currents that change direction and velocity with the tides. During the warm months, a strong afternoon breeze of almost clock-like regularity blows at La Paz, providing fine conditions, especially at Balandra.

Loreto has good winds and general side-shore conditions, February being the big wind month. Placid Bahía Concepción is the ideal spot for beginners, for the wind often funnels down the bay, resulting in side-shore conditions in many locations. The shape and orientation of the sand spit and island at El Requesón allow novices to find good side-shore conditions no matter which way the wind is blowing. Santispac is fun and compact, but the surrounding hills keep the winds down. At the north end of the bay, Punta Arena often has the heaviest winds, since the surrounding land is low. Low Punta Chivato, north of Mulegé, sticks out well into the Cortez, freeing it from the influence

Courtesy Baja Surf Club

A great day of sailing at East Cape

You say that you have always wanted to learn to sailboard but never had the chance? An RV trip to Baja may be the time to remedy the situation. There are a number of thriving boardsailing operations offering package trips that include round-trip transportation, lodging, meals, equipment and instruction. However, they attempt to accommodate walk-ins, and will provide equipment and instruction, subject to first call by their guests. Each is located near a good RV park or boondocking area, and learning to sailboard could thus be an enjoyable part of an RV trip to Baja.

Surfing

With almost 1,100 miles of shoreline along its Pacific coast line and with its varied geography, the peninsula has some outstanding surfing. There are two basic surfing regions. The first, between Tijuana and Ensenada, is essentially an extension of Southern California conditions. The weather, water, beach litter, and most of the people are the same, and San Miguel is as well-known to generations of Southern California surfers as Rincón. There are a number of good RV parks along the Tijuana-Ensenada Toll Road, and a few days spent surfing these locations would be an enjoyable part of any trip. However, for those looking for something a little less tame and familiar, there is a world-class location just off Ensenada. Located at the Islas de Todos Santos, this place ably lives up to its name, "El Martillo" (The Hammer), and is rated by many to be on a par with such locations as Waimea Bay in Hawaii and Mavericks in California. El Martillo often has 10 feet or 12 feet faces when surfers at San Miguel, only 8 miles away, are sitting in their pickups wishing. Those with their own boats can launch at La Jolla Beach Camp, an RV park on the north shore of the

of the higher topography to the west, and providing the best in speed sailing conditions during the prime months of December, January, and February.

Bahía de los Angeles is the eastern end of the famous "Baja Shuttle." In winter, the bay has frequent katabatic (gravity-driven) winds, but no swell builds up since they come from the north and the west. When the winds are up, boardsailors try speed sailing, and when it's calmer they play and explore the many islands. When a Pacific front approaches, they pack up and head west for Santa Rosalillita, only 74 miles away, to take advantage of the wind and the waves. When the front dies, everyone rushes back to Bahía de los Angeles. Since the two types of wind have separate causes, one or the other is often at work, providing almost continual boardsailing action in a variety of conditions. Chapters 4 through 7 contain detailed information on the boardsailing locations mentioned above and many others accessible by RV.

El Martillo's name ("The Hammer") seems well justified; those tiny black dots are surfers

Punta Banda peninsula, or at La Bufadora, on its southwest shore (the ramp here is suitable only for cartoppers and inflatables). La Bufadora Dive offers surfing trips to El Martillo, and a group of divers could also hire a boat in Ensenada for such a trip.

The second region, the coastline from Ensenada to the Cape, has almost every conceivable kind of surfing condition. Prevailing winter northwesterlies produce a succession of highly reliable point breaks on the many capes dangling south from the Pacific coast like icicles. Stretches of beach sweeping between them may work well only a few days or weeks a year, but so many miles are involved, with so many combinations of exposure, bottom terrain, beach curvature and angle to the swell, that there is usually little difficulty in finding something that is working well. With the coming of summer, south winds and waves from tropical storms produce a far greater variety of conditions and enough lefts to keep an army of goofy-foots happy, and opening up locations that work best in south waves like the Cape region.

Any list of the top surfing locations on the coast from Ensenada to the Cape would include Puntas San José, San Telmo ("Cuatro Casas"), San Jacinto ("Freighters"), Baja, Santa Rosalillita, Abreojos, and El Conejo. All are accessible by unpaved class 1 or 2 roads. (Unpaved roads are rated by class; see page 197.) Surfers in search of adventure may wish to consider Isla Natividad. There are those who claim that "Open Doors," at its east end, is the best beach break on the west coast of North America. The island is only 6 miles off the village of Punta Eugenia, which has class 1 road access from the Transpeninsular, and *pangas* are available for hire. However, Natividad is primarily a summer site, dependent on big south waves that often wipe out the landing at Punta Eugenia. If you have a suitable boat, a beach launch could be made in Bahía Tortugas; the run to the island is only 20 miles from the mouth of the bay.

These and many other surfing sites are described in Chapters 4 through 7. There are a number of surf shops in Baja: Tony's in Rosarito, San Miguel in Ensenada, Killer Hooks in San José del Cabo, and Costa Azul, just west of San José.

Kayaking

Rivaled only by boardsailing, kayaking is Baja's most rapidly expanding outdoor activity, and a number of locations are of special interest to those wishing to include hours- or day-long excursions. Bahía de los Angeles has many is-

lands to explore, and the bay's natural beauty and relatively compact area make it a favorite. Bahía Concepción is calm and scenic and is a great place for a novice kayaker to practice paddling, self-righting, and self-rescue procedures. Many kayakers like to launch at Puerto Escondido and explore Isla Danzante. Novice kayakers often launch at Cabo San Lucas and explore "Lover's Beach," Playa el Médano, and the coves to the east. The scenic Punta Banda area just south of Ensenada, with its many coves and beaches, is one of the finest areas in Baja for a day-long kayak trip.

Viajes Mar y Arena in Loreto has kayak rentals and local trips. Baja Outdoor Activities in La Paz offers instruction and rentals by the hour or day. Aqua Adventures offers an unusual activity at Laguna Manuela, kayak wave surfing. Villas de Loreto is home to more than a half dozen kayak companies. Although their primary business is package trips, all will accommodate walk-ins on a space-available basis, renting kayaks and equipment by the hour or day, and providing instruction. Kayaks can be rented at a number of other locations; see the index.

Baja Tropicales/Mulegé Kayaks, located at Santispac in Bahía Concepción, offers a day-long kayaking activity that is of special interest to RVers, a "paddle, snorkel, dive and dine" kayak trip, visiting beautiful coves, hot springs, a shipwreck, etc. The scenery is beautiful, the bay is normally calm, and the locations visited are interesting.

Will Waterman

Kayakers end a long day of exploring

Hiking and exploring

Baja's arid climate renders much of the peninsula of limited interest to most hikers. However, accidents of geology and meteorology have provided places where it is possible to take enjoyable hikes. There are two national parks in Baja, Parque Nacional Sierra San Pedro Mártir, and Parque Nacional Constitución de 1857. The first is Baja's premiere hiking location, and a description of the park and a contour map showing hiking trails are provided later in the book. Parque 1857 has little in the way of trails, but several short hikes are described. A description of the route to the Cañon Tajo overlook is provided, and good hiking is found around the Cañon Guadalupe campground. See the index for these and other hiking locations. In addition, there are hundreds of miles of wild and deserted beaches and innumerable canyons that can be explored.

*A **hiker** explores the mouth of mighty Cañon del Diablo*

Beachcombing

The combination of prevailing northwesterly winds, the southern set of the California Current, and the hook-like configuration of Bahía Sebastián Vizcaíno make the sweep of beach from Guerrero Negro to Punta Eugenia one of the most productive beachcombing areas in the world. Because it is accessible by an unpaved road, Malarrimo is the most frequently visited and well-known location, but there is no reason to believe that the rest of the 60-mile beach is not equally productive. All manner of flotsam has been found, ranging from catsup bottles to a ceramic urn identified by the Smithsonian Institution as having been manufactured between 1690 and 1710 in the Westervald region of Germany. This urn and other evidence suggest that the winds and currents once carried a Manila galleon to "Sand Island," just west of Guerrero Negro, possibly the *San Francisco Xavier*, which disappeared after leaving Manila in 1705.

While none can match the Bahía Vizcaíno beaches for productivity, those in the vicinity of Eréndira are no slouches. Although they require a boat and a good deal of effort to reach, the outer beaches of the islands forming Bahía Magdalena can be very rewarding. In addition, there are hundreds of miles of beaches along the Pacific that are so

rarely visited that treasures brought by the wind and waves can sit months or even years before being discovered. See the index for a number of sites.

Nature watching

Many of the natural wonders described in the previous chapter are accessible by RV. By our way of thinking, the number-one nature-watching attraction in Baja, or the world for that matter, is an encounter with the friendly gray whales of Laguna San Ignacio. This involves only 40 miles of unpaved road from the village of San Ignacio, and all but the least nimble RVs can carry you to the place where you can have the experience of scratching and petting a 30-ton whale. The details of this marvelous adventure will be found beginning on page 213.

Whales can be seen at other locations in Baja, sometimes at close quarters. Although whales can occasionally be seen at a distance from many locations along Baja's Pacific coast, Guerrero Negro is the first place south of the border where visitors may be able to get a close-up view. Whales can also be seen at Parque Natural de la Ballena Gris, 17 miles from KM 208 on the Transpeninsular, southeast of Guerrero Negro. The best place for shore-bound viewers, however, is the narrow channel called Curva del Diablo (Devil's Curve) near Puerto López Mateos.

If you are willing to spend a bit of money, organized day-long trips to see the grays are available. Ensenada Sportfishing Center takes whale-watchers on trips during the winter season. Three-hour whale-watching trips on an outboard-powered barge are offered daily during the winter at Guerrero Negro, departing from the old salt pier. Viajes Mario's in Guerrero Negro offers similar trips. Fishermen at Puerto López Mateos, Puerto San Carlos, and Lagunas Ojos de Liebre and San Ignacio are often willing to take people out to see the whales. Cabo Acuadeportes and Amigos del Mar in Cabo San Lucas also offer whale-watching trips, although the number of whales to be seen is more limited than in the lagoons. In the Cortez, Raul Espinoza takes visitors on trips in the Bahía de los Angeles area, during which visitors might see a variety of whales and lesser cetaceans. Deborah and Alberto Lucero offer similar trips in the Bahía San Francisquito area. Aqua Adventures offers Baja whale-watching ventures aboard kayaks.

You should plan a trip up to Parque San Pedro Mártir. Although at least two or three days is best, a round trip from the Transpeninsular and a bit of local exploring can be made in a day, and will serve to completely undermine your preconceived ideas about Baja's "burning desert" image and prove Father Baegert to be misinformed on yet another point.

As pointed out in the previous chapter, over 400 species of birds live in, breed in, or pass over Baja, and birdwatchers will find much to enjoy. Some of the prominent birding areas, including Guardian Angel Island, Islas San Pedro Mártir, San Esteban, Partida Norte, Raza, San Lorenzo, and Ildefonso, and the south end of Isla San José, require lengthy travel by boat, but others, such as Laguna Hanson,

Bahía San Quintín, Bahía de los Angeles, Laguna Ojo de Liebre, Laguna San Ignacio, and Bahía Magdalena, can be reached by RV.

Presuming you take time to stop for contemplation and examination, just traveling along the highway is a great way to do some nature watching, especially in the spring. Beginning south of El Rosario, the Transpeninsular passes through areas with unusual plant life, such as the bizarre boojum and the ponderous elephant tree. Passages describing the natural history of a number of plants will be found in Chapters 4–7 at the first place you are likely to encounter them. Passages are similarly placed for a number of animal species.

You need not be a certified scuba diver to enjoy some marine nature watching. The use of mask, snorkel, and fins involves no special skills beyond normal swimming if you don't dive below the surface, and there are many warm, safe, non-threatening areas where the water is shallow enough that brilliantly colored fish and hosts of strange creatures can be enjoyed.

Rock art

Some of Baja's rock-art treasures are readily accessible to visitors. The "Playhouse Cave" near Cataviña is an easy 15-minute hike from the Transpeninsular. Cueva Ratón, a site near San Francisco, can be visited by most RVs, requiring only a two-minute hike. Gruta Borjitas, north of Mulegé, is considered a major site, and is only a 15-minute hike from a roadhead, and guided trips can be arranged at the hotels in town. The "Unhappy Coyote" in the Bahía Concepción area is just a 15-minute walk off the pavement. Although none of the sites at La Trinidad are considered important, the first requires only a 20-minute hike. The second, however, involves an unusual mode of transportation, swimming. Each of these sites is described in detail at the appropriate place in later chapters.

Raul Espinoza offers bus trips to see Cochimí art sites in the Bahía de los Angeles area. Cueva Palmarito, north of San Ignacio, can be approached within several miles by vehicle and hence can be visited in the course of a day. Guides can be obtained at nearby Rancho Santa Martha. Guided trips to Palmarito and other sites can be arranged in San Ignacio. Museums in Bahía de los Angeles, La Paz, Todos Santos, and elsewhere have artifacts and photographs; see the index.

Off-road driving

With the exception of the fantastic fishing, nothing in the legend and lore of Baja occupies more time around evening campfires than "Off-Road Baja," the areas of the peninsula not served by paved roads. Beginning in the 1920s, travelers returning from the great desert wastelands to the south began publishing articles and books about their adventures, which were usually centered around unpaved roads so bad that 10 miles a day in a sturdy four-wheel-drive was considered good progress. This reputation has survived, and today "Baja off-road rated" is still the supreme boast of tire and shock-absorber manufacturers, and thousands thrill to the rugged Baja 1000 race.

The paving of the Transpeninsular Highway was completed in 1973, and Off-Road Baja became much smaller. However, a vast network of unpaved roads still covers much of Baja. These roads are generally no place for RVs, but one of the great joys of Baja RVing is a bit of boondocking on a remote beach or in an unspoiled canyon, far enough off the pavement to permit the enjoyment of several circumstances unusual in the modern world—silence and solitude. And besides, who dares to return home and admit to the neighbors that the tires never left the pavement during your trip to fabled Baja? It is, in fact, possible to visit some of Off-Road Baja with all but the most cumbersome RVs, and to drag small travel and boat trailers into a few locations. In addition, ordinary pickups and four-wheel-drives, freed from the encumbrance of trailers, should be able to handle virtually anything Baja has to offer, and RVers often bring along motorcycles, ATVs (all-terrain vehicles), or dune buggies, vehicles eminently suited for off-road forays.

The term "off-road" is often used for trips off the paved roads, but it is misleading, for other than driving on beaches, dry lakes and similar special situations, there is no "off-road" driving in Baja, nor should there be. Driving across untracked desert creates environmental havoc, tearing up slow-growing desert vegetation and leaving scars that endure for generations. Such driving is almost always unnecessary, since unpaved roads will usually be found to take you anywhere worth going. In addition, it can often result in severe tire damage within a few hundred yards, and even the fabled Baja 1000 racers wouldn't go a mile if the race were truly off-road. Thus, although the term "off-road" is widely used, what is meant is off-**pavement** driving.

Chapter 7 provides information on so-called off-road driving, including special preparation and equipment, road classification, and driving tech-

Artist Will Ashford makes a wax rubbing of a petroglyph

Crossing a stream on the way to La Bocana

niques, as well as detailed descriptions of dozens of unpaved roads, ranging from those that can be managed easily by a softly sprung sedan to a few that will challenge even a sturdy four-wheel-drive.

● ●

❝ *A matter of contrast*

An RV would have no chance in the Baja 1000, but watching it makes a fine spectator sport. However, stay out of the way! My dad and I were putting along a trail on our modest Honda Trail 90, making perhaps 3 miles an hour, when we hit a sandy area and fell over on one side, at the feet of several Mexicans. They grinned widely, and we sheepishly began to extricate ourselves from under the motorcycle. However, seconds later several motorcycles roared by, followed by a group of pickups and dune buggies. One driver shouted something, but the only word we could make out was "race." Digging away the sand with our hands, we tried to puzzle out what he had said, when we noticed that the two Mexicans were no longer grinning—they were convulsed with laughter, aimed our way. In a flash it all became apparent: we were on the route of the Baja 1000!

We felt foolish as we dug away the sand, stood up and pulled the bike off to the side of the road. The reason for the laughter was apparent: the contrast was priceless—the racers roaring by without even slowing down, and the two motorized buffoons, first putting along at walking-speed and then being defeated by a few yards of sand. ——Michael ❞

● ●

Golfing

Golf, in "burning desert" Baja? You bet there is! There is a course just north of Rosarito (Real del Mar Golf Club), one just north of Ensenada (Bajamar Oceanfront Golf Re-

sort), one just south of Ensenada (Baja Country Club), at Loreto (Campo de Golf de Loreto), at San José del Cabo (Campo de Golf San José), three on the highway between San José del Cabo and Cabo San Lucas (Palmilla Golf Club, Cabo del Sol Golf Club, and Cabo Real Golf Club), and one in Cabo San Lucas (Cabo San Lucas Country Club). That is not all; Hotel Punta Chivato has an informal eight-hole desert course (no turf), and some of the RV parks have putting greens. Finally, an RV park just north of San Felipe (Pete's El Paraíso Camp) has an impromptu desert course, and the town is planning to build a large course.

The new golf courses in Baja are first-class in every respect, some having been designed by Robert Trent Jones, Jack Nicklaus, and Roy Dye, and most come equipped with chipping and putting greens, driving ranges, pro shops, clubhouses, restaurants, and lounges. The Cape region is perhaps the busiest golf course construction location in world, and there may be 180 holes in use by the year 2000. Many of the physical settings are beautiful, with grand vistas at almost every hole. Some claim that the course at Cabo del Sol at the Cape is one of the most spectacular golf courses in the world, "the Pebble Beach of Baja." Jack Nicklaus designed the Palmilla course, and describes it as the "Palm Springs by the sea." The vegetation surrounding the greens may be somewhat exotic to golfers from the US: *palo verde, palo blanco,* elephant trees, and cactus.

The courses are described in Chapters 4, 5, 6, and 7. All are open seven days a week. The costs and the availability of carts, rental clubs and shoes vary from place to place and time to time, so check when you make your reservation. Dress codes are in effect: no swim wear, cut-offs, halters, or tank tops are permitted, and a few are more restrictive. The green fees shown in the text are those charged in 1996, and are subject to a 10% sales tax. Green fees and tee-time reservations noted apply to those who are not members of the club or property owners. Make a reservation if you can; it's strictly a space-available proposition for walk-ins.

What would Father Baegert say if he were transported back from the place assigned to the souls of dead Jesuits, "Where the heck are they getting all the water?"

Tennis

Like golf, the vision most people have of Baja does not include tennis. However, bring your tennis racket and balls along, for many parks, hotels, resorts, and golf clubs have courts. The Loreto Tennis Center is the largest, with nine lighted courts. There are too many to list individually;

see the index. Sporting-goods stores in the larger towns sell tennis equipment, and it is even possible to get your racquet re-strung (Deportes Blazer in Loreto), and some of the towns, Ensenada for instance, sponsor tennis tournaments.

Tours, sightseeing, and shopping

Later chapters describe walking tours of Ensenada, Santa Rosalía, Mulegé, downtown La Paz, San José del Cabo, and the downtown district in Cabo San Lucas. Because of their lengthy, one-main-drag nature, motorized descriptions of Rosarito, San Quintín, Guerrero Negro, and Ciudad Constitución are provided below.

A number of escorted tours are available, including a cultural/historical tour of Ensenada, a tour of Ensenada's restaurants and night life, a visit to the vast salt ponds at Guerrero Negro, a tour of East Cape to see whale bones and to have lunch at an exotic desert waterfall, a Pacific Cape tour traveling to secluded beaches and a fruit plantation, with lunch in Todos Santos, and a dune-buggy tour of the areas around San Felipe. The larger towns, Ensenada, Loreto, La Paz, San José del Cabo, and Cabo San Lucas, and even Guerrero Negro, have a number of travel agents and "activity centers" that specialize in things visitors from the north like to do, and can arrange a wide variety of tours and sightseeing ventures.

The citizens of Baja take pride in their history and culture, and museums are to be found in the larger towns, such as Loreto, La Paz, and Ensenada, the last of which has five, right down to unexpected places such as Estero Beach, San Vicente, El Rosario, San Ignacio, Mulegé, San José del Cabo, Rosarito, KM 57 on Route 5 south of Mexicali, Bahía de los Angeles, Todos Santos, and Francisco Zarco. The last is largely devoted, believe it or not, to Russian culture in Baja. A number of old mission churches can be visited, some of which are accessible by RV, including San Ignacio, Loreto, Santa Rosalía de Mulegé, and San Javier. The road to the last may tax the ability of the more ungainly RVs, but van tours can be arranged in Loreto. The wineries in Ensenada, Bodegas de Santo Tomás and Cavas Valmar, which advertise themselves as the largest and the smallest wineries in Mexico, respectively, and the Domecq Winery near Francisco Zarco sponsor visits and tastings.

Towns that cater to visitors have a wide variety of shops, selling everything from tacky junk to fine works of art. Avenida López Mateos, Ensenada's primary tourist street, is lined with stores selling clothing, ceramics, guitars, T-shirts, curios, sea shells, leather goods, jewelry, electronics, ironwood carvings, and *serapes* (colorful blanket-like shawls, often used as wall hangings). In 1996, many featured fake Dooney & Bourke handbags at 10% of the state-side price of the real thing. A number carry "Rolex" watches, at significant savings from the genuine. There are several large malls, containing just about the same kind of shops that you would expect to encounter in a mall in *El Norte* (The North, referring to the US). Some Ensenada stores do sell high quality merchandise, including elegant designer jewelry, fine watches, and Lladró porcelain, as well as products bearing

A typical shop along Avenida López Mateos in Ensenada, almost bursting at the seams with **serapes***, jewelry, toys, chess pieces, souvenirs, handbags, and a hundred other things*

the familiar names Gucci, Chanel, Revlon, Levi, and Cartier.

Far to the south, La Paz is the home of Dorian's and La Perla de La Paz, both large, modern department stores, again featuring Gucci, Chanel, Revlon, Levi, and Cartier. Avenida Agosto, between Aréola and 16 de Septiembre in La Paz, has been made into a mall, with boutiques, gift shops, and stores selling imports from Taiwan, England, and California. There is a large number of small shops selling T-shirts, sea shells, carvings, paintings, *serapes*, posters, jewelry, and just about anything else you could desire. Some of the clothing is very stylish, and the art can be first-rate, especially the carvings and paper mâché figurines.

The Los Cabos area seems to have the best shopping on the peninsula. (The term "Los Cabos" refers to San José del Cabo and Cabo San Lucas and the highway corridor between them.) Whether this is true, and if so why, may be the subject of debate, but perhaps the construction of the many new hotels, condominiums, and shopping malls, and the nature of the foreigners on the streets are responsible. It takes a well-stocked wallet to fly to Los Cabos and stay in a hotel, and condos go for handsome prices, so the *gringos* on the streets are likely to be better-heeled than, say, those at Ensenada, Rosarito or San Felipe, and it shows in the quality of the goods for sale. At San José del Cabo, shops offer high-quality silver and gold jewelry, handmade glass decorations, sculpture, artistic T-shirts, blouses, blankets, pottery, knickknacks, belts, and wallets, as well as the fake Dooney & Bourke handbags available in Ensenada. In Cabo San Lucas, the arts and crafts items like pottery, carvings, rugs, figurines, glassware, paper mâché birds, curios, and *serapes* are often of high quality. Women's clothing stores often have very stylish items, as well as the raunchiest T-shirts on the peninsula. Some jewelry stores have large selections of silver and gold items.

Everything has its price, and "list prices" in Baja are usually high. However, like elsewhere in Mexico, prices at stores, other than fancy jewelry stores and large department stores, are usually subject to negotiation, and no one is twisting your arm. Don't expect fire-sale prices, and do expect to pay a hefty 10% sales tax, but with some effort spent shopping and a little bargaining, you should be able to obtain some very handsome things at reasonable prices.

Don't be too quick to brush off the street vendors and bypass the open-air stalls. In Ensenada and Los Cabos, the *serapes*, *huaraches* (leather sandals), jewelry, ironwood carvings, handicrafts, figurines, T-shirts, and knickknacks are sometimes rather nice. In Ensenada, we almost automatically ignored the children that approached us offering hand-made woven necklaces and bracelets, but we finally realized that they were colorful and well-made, and were available for just a few dollars. Some of the silver jewelry offered by peddlers in Ensenada and Los Cabos appears equal in quality to that sold in the shops, and with a bit of hard negotiating, you may be able to come up with some bargains, since the price does not have to include rent or overhead.

What about the other towns? San Felipe is a smaller version of Ensenada, and caters to the same crowd, so expect about the same in the way of arts and crafts. Since their economies are not dependent on tourism, San Quintín, Guerrero Negro, Santa Rosalía, and Ciudad Constitución have little to offer. San Ignacio and Mulegé are so small that there are only a few gift shops and stores carrying souvenirs and knickknacks. Although Loreto sees many visitors, shopping there is surprisingly limited.

The pottery, jewelry, paper mâché figurines, *serapes*, and *huaraches* seen in the shops are almost automatically accepted as being of national vintage, but look closely; some shops also sell purses and handbags made in Guatemala, for instance. Where do you go to get art, crafts, leather work, and other items made in Baja, hopefully from the person or persons who made it? Artesanias Cuauhtemoc in La Paz sells fabrics, place mats, tablecloths, tapestries, bed spreads, and clothing of cotton and wool, made on foot-powered looms in the shop. Children sell hand-made straw baskets alongside the road in El Triunfo. The leather shop in Miraflores makes saddles, chaps, knife sheaths, and other articles for the locals, but also sells belts, wallets, and purses for visitors. Cuca's Blanket Factory in Cabo San Lucas will produce a custom-designed *serape* to your specifications on a foot-powered loom. The Glass Factory in Cabo San Lucas turns discarded beer and tequila bottles into tumblers, pitchers, vases, and other useful objects, as well as knickknacks. Their products are not high art—we purchased a half dozen of their distinctive hand-made, blue-rimmed tumblers, and each is unique, with ripples, bubbles, and sags, and varying in height and diameter, one leaning like the famous Italian tower. However, their charm lies in their nonconformity, and they swiftly sent their machine-made, flaw-free, American-made cousins to an idle existence in the back of our kitchen cabinets.

One other place deserves special mention, Todos Santos. This pleasant little town is the home of a number of painters, potters, woodcarvers, and other artists, some Mexican, some American, and you can buy paintings, carvings, pottery, locally made furniture, Mexican clothing, handi-

crafts, hand-woven upholstery fabrics, and hand-made tiles forming a map of Baja.

A number of shops, department stores, malls, open-air markets and so forth will be described in later chapters. However, don't limit your shopping efforts to just these, for there are far too many to list individually—there are 321 pages in the Yellow Pages in the Baja Sur telephone directory, and 201 in Ensenada's. Each reader has his or her own ideas on quality, price, and desirability, and part of the fun is exploring the towns and cities and ferreting out what you want at the best price.

■ Hey, *gringo*!

The word *gringo* has probably been heard in every movie involving Mexicans and Americans ever made, and most people automatically assume it to be an insult. It does not depend on analogy by comparing a person to an unpleasant part of the anatomy, or to another species like "pig" or "rat," nor is it a recent invention, like "honky." One popular theory is that during the Mexican-American War between 1846 and 1848, Mexicans heard American soldiers singing a marching song with the words "green grow the rushes O," a traditional song in many cultures and languages. The association between the song and the soldiers endured, and the "green-grows" eventually became *gringos*. The first written record of its employment by Mexicans referring to Americans was in 1849. However, its lineage is much older. The Spanish expression *hablar en griego* means "to speak in Greek," that is, to speak in an unintelligible way. In time, *griego* came to mean "foreigner," and the word finally transmogrified to *gringo*. A dictionary published in Spain in 1787 indicated *gringo* meant a foreigner whose accent prevented him from speaking Spanish well

Today, Spanish dictionaries usually indicate that the word simply means "stranger, especially North American," some suggesting that it has derogatory connotations. How should you react if a local calls you a *gringo*? The best way is to evaluate its context and the body-language used: if it is said with a sneer and a swagger, as when Alfonso Bedoya, of "Badges? Badges? I don't have to show you any steenking badges" fame calls Humphrey Bogart a *greeengo* in *The Treasure of the Sierra Madre*, you have been insulted; if it is said in passing, take no offense. The most frequent users of the term are *gringos* themselves.

Holidays, events, and other activities

Holidays are a national passion in Mexico, and Baja is no exception. There are numerous legal holidays, such as Cinco de Mayo and Mexican Independence Day, and a number of traditional civil holidays, like Mother's Day. Many towns have civic holidays; San José del Cabo, for instance,

A troop of "vaqueras" joins the parade celebrating the founding of San José de Cabo

celebrates the town's founding. There are often parades, with marching bands, floats, fireworks, and an elected princess riding in a convertible, and traveling carnivals bring merry-go-rounds, Ferris wheels, games, and sideshows. In addition, religious holidays are celebrated, such as Easter and Christmas, and any city, village, or settlement named for a saint, such as San José del Cabo and San Ignacio, will probably have a fiesta to celebrate the birthday of its patron. The religious holidays tend to be more subdued than their legal and civic counterparts, with processions, candle-lighting, and the breaking of colored egg shells filled with confetti, although Carnival permits Catholics to kick up their heels a bit in anticipation of Lent.

In addition, many places have civic events that cater largely to visitors, such as La Paz Race Week and the Rosarito-Ensenada Bicycle Ride, as well as totally disorganized events like spring break, where *gringo* college students invade Baja with dissipation on their minds. There are numerous other events, including volleyball, soccer tournaments, bi- and triathlons, martial arts demonstrations, regattas, chili cook-offs, music festivals, sportfishing tournaments, bicycle and jet ski races, Lions Club and Rotary conventions, and so forth.

Baja is host to one of the world's premiere off-road races, and it makes a grand spectator sport. Held annually since 1967 (except in 1974), the Baja 1000 has gained international attention, attracting competitors from Argentina, Australia, Belgium, Canada, England, Finland, France, Germany, Guam, Holland, Italy, Japan, New Caledonia, Saudi

Arabia, South Africa, Spain, Sweden, and the countries that made up the Soviet Union, as well as the US and Mexico.

The Baja 1000 is usually held in November, and it follows a different route each year, including Ensenada to La Paz, the longest, which is scheduled every 3 or 4 years, and shorter routes staying within Baja Norte, such as Ensenada to the boondocks and back to Ensenada, and a loop starting and ending in Mexicali. Needless to say, partying goes on into the wee hours before and after the race. SCORE International, the sponsor of the race, has several other events in Baja, including the Tecate SCORE Baja 500, usually held in early June, and the Tecate SCORE Baja 250, normally held in February. Information on routes and schedules is available from SCORE.

In the tourist-oriented towns, you can rent ATVs, Hobie Cats, jet skis, wave runners, and dune buggies, and go for rides on banana and glass-bottomed boats. Hang gliding and parasailing are popular in a few suitable locations like Cantamar Dunes and near El Faro Viejo at the Cape. There are a number of beautiful beaches for picnics and swimming, especially those at La Paz, San José del Cabo and Cabo San Lucas. Information on night life will be found in the following chapter.

When should you go?

What is the best time of year to take a trip to Baja? It depends on the weather and the activities you intend to pursue. Some people choose the fall: the weather has cooled off, but not too much; the water is still warm; many migratory fish species are still around; there is little danger of *chubascos*; and the RV parks and the beaches are uncrowded. Many people, especially snowbirds escaping the freezing blasts of the northern US and Canada, make trips in the winter, motivated not only by what they will encounter, but what they will avoid. Some of the activities described above, including tours, sightseeing, shopping, beachcombing, golfing, and tennis have no particular seasonal aspects, and you should go when the weather suits you. Weather and time of year affect all the others, and should be considered when planning your trip.

Boating and kayaking can be year-around activities on the Cortez, although periods of strong winds in the winter months can be a problem. Activities on the Pacific side are strongly influenced by winter surf and storms. Although the warm months are the most popular for diving and snorkeling, they can be year-around activities. However, if you want to encounter a manta or a whale shark, you have to be there when the critters choose to appear. Encounters with friendly mantas are too rare to allow accurate predictions, but the best months at Marisla Seamount have been August and September, and the recent encounters at Cabo San Lucas were in January and February. Meeting a whale shark is little more than a chance encounter, but the chances are best in the spring.

Off-road exploring is generally a year-around activity, although interior areas can get blazing hot in the summer, and winter rains may be a problem in the north, summer rains in the south. If you plan to visit the mountain areas of Parque Nacional Constitución de 1857 or Parque Nacional Sierra San Pedro Mártir, it is best to go in the spring, when the snow has melted and things are in bloom, or in the fall, when the temperatures have moderated. In winter, there is a possibility of snow at both parks, especially the latter.

Boardsailing, surfing, and nature watching have strong seasonal aspects, which have already been described; there is little use in driving to Laguna San Ignacio to see the whales in July. Although some species are biting almost everywhere year-around, fishing is very dependent on the season; see the calendar in Appendix A. Those activities that involve physical exertion out in the boondocks, far from a cool shower and a source of cold Dos Equis, such as hiking, exploring, and rock-art viewing, are best left for the cooler months.

Most legal, religious, and civic holidays occur at more-or-less fixed dates each year, while events like the Newport-to-Ensenada yacht races, SCORE off-road races, soccer tournaments, bi- and triathlons, chili cook-offs, music festivals, bicycle races, and Lions Club and Rotary conventions are scheduled by their sponsors. Appendix B provides a calendar of major holidays and many events. If you have your heart set on attending any of these, it is essential that you get current information from the appropriate tourism office, for the dates can change inexplicably or don't seem to make "sense"—don't bother to look in the encyclopedia to determine the birth date of a given Catholic saint, for the village by that name does not necessarily schedule festivities on that date.

A pack train winds through the mountains north of San Ignacio en route to Gardner Cave

What will it cost?

The next step in planning your trip is to figure out how much money will be required. Food costs will be much lower than at home if you utilize Mexican-made products bought in Mexico. The cost of a "shopping bag" of several dozen common foods produced in Mexico and sold in the CCC supermarket in La Paz in 1996 averaged 43% of what your would pay in a US supermarket for similar products. By way of contrast, a shopping bag of several dozen common American-made foods from the same CCC cost 141% of what they would in the US.

Your fuel costs will be a bit lower than in the US; in 1996, lead-free gasoline went for the equivalent of $1.08/gallon, diesel for $.83. Insurance costs will be discussed later in this chapter. Also, set aside some money for minor expenses like ice, liquefied petroleum gas (LPG), and toll-road fares.

To food, fuel, insurance, and minor expenses, add the cost of optional items such as RV parks, restaurant meals, boat permits, boat rentals, launch ramp fees, fishing licenses, equipment rentals, and tours. There is no place on the continent that has more fine boondocking sites than Baja, but many RVers choose to spent some of their time in parks. In 1996, costs at the 150 Baja RV parks we analyzed ranged from $3 for a no-frills-or-hookups places, to $43/day at a posh RV resort. However, if you drop out a number of low-cost places offering nothing more than a parking space (why pay for nothing when you can boondock on a beautiful beach for nothing?), and eliminate Baja Seasons and the Oasis Hotel and RV Resort, by far the most expensive parks in Baja, the average park costs $11 a day, and they typically range between $7 and $14.

As you might expect, restaurant meals vary wildly in price, depending on the season, the place you choose, and the food you order. Almost certainly, if you choose restaurants whose clientele is *gringos*, such as resorts, tourist hotels, and fancy restaurants, you are going to pay top dollar, but if you dine where the locals dine, you will dine cheaply. However, if you choose a mix of the less expensive tourist restaurants and the better restaurants catering to the locals, it is possible to come up with some acceptable figures. In early 1996, a full (non-Continental) breakfast cost about $4.25, and normally ranged between $2.60 and $5.90. A lunch was slightly higher. A nice supper in a clean, pleasant, mid-scale restaurant, perhaps with a beer or two to wash things down, averaged $7.50, with a normal range between $3.50 and $11.80. There are restaurants outside the normal range, of course, and it is very possible to get a good $2 breakfast if you look around. A lavish meal at a top-of-the-line restaurant might go for $25 to $30, or more depending on the dessert and the wine you choose.

The cost of boat permits is discussed later in this chapter, and that of boat rentals and fishing licenses in Appendix A. You may wish to rent some toys. Kayaks vary considerably by season and type, $25/day usually being the cheapest, $45 the most expensive; by the hour about $10. Sailboards usually rent for about $15/hour, Hobies $25, ATVs $15, and wave runners $60. Eighteen holes of golf averages $66, but ranges from an incredible $20 to a painful $120 (there are several modest courses that charge nothing). The costs of whale watching, rock art, dune buggying, diving, sightseeing and similar day-long excursions vary greatly according to season, length, and the food, drink, and services provided; use Appendix C to contact the proprietors to get the latest prices and information.

Within the context of these costs, there are two extremes—dirt-cheap trips and expensive trips. A 10-day, dirt-cheap trip from the Tijuana border crossing to Loreto (and back) for 2 people, in an RV worth $20,000 (the value of the vehicle affects insurance costs) getting 10 miles to the gallon, who do not bring a boat nor go fishing, prepare almost all their own meals, mostly from local staples, dine out only a few times at inexpensive restaurants, and boondock most nights and stay at modest RV parks the others, works out to about $500. This assumes that a 10-day, Mexican 5-risk insurance policy is purchased (more on this later), and that the consumption of beer, sodas, and snacks is moderate. A similar 16-day trip to Cabo San Lucas would cost about $800. This works out to about $25/day/person for each trip. Few people will choose such Spartan trips, of course, but the Loreto-for-$500 and Cabo-for-$800 figures serve as bottom lines for initial planning.

At the opposite extreme, things can be at least as expensive as in the US. The fanciest RV park in Baja, the Oasis Hotel and RV Resort, costs a princely $43/day, and if you insist on buying foods imported from the US, especially fancy cuts of meat, making margaritas with Sauza Conmemorativo, eating supper out each night at such places as the Rey de Sol in Ensenada and El Galeón in Cabo San Lucas, and fishing for marlin in large hotel cruisers, the sky is the limit—there is a fishing cruiser at Cabo San Lucas that goes for $925 a day.

Somewhere in between, there is the "happy medium" that most people will opt for, staying at "average" $11-a-night RV parks perhaps 75% of the time, while boondocking the other 25%. Almost all breakfasts, most lunches and perhaps half the suppers will be "at home," beginning the trip with foods and beverages bought in the US, and toward the end utilizing many items bought in Baja. Suppers "out" will be at mid-scale restaurants, with a splurge once or twice. A boat may be brought along for fishing, diving and exploring, and if not, a *panga* may be rented for a day or so of fishing or diving. Such a happy medium, 10-day, 2-person trip to Loreto might cost $900, and a 16-day trip to the Cape

would be about $1,500. This works out to roughly $45/day/person for each trip. If you rent sailboards, kayaks, jet skis or ATVs, play some golf, etc., it will be higher, of course.

How much time should be set aside?

Once you have decided where you wish to visit and the activities you would like to pursue, you can then make an estimate of how much total time should be set aside for your trip. For driving time, look up the mileage between points along the Transpeninsular in Appendix D, and calculate driving time assuming an average of 40 miles per hour, and double it for the round trip. Add the time you plan to use at stops along the way pursuing such activities as fishing, diving, golfing, whale watching, sightseeing, enjoying the towns, and so forth.

Depending on their interests, most people find that trips to Ensenada and San Felipe are worthy of 4 days, the intermediate trips to Santa Rosalía, Mulegé and Loreto not less than 10, and 16 as a bare minimum for a trip to Cabo San Lucas, especially during the winter, when safe driving time is limited by the short hours of daylight. Many people do not set aside enough time, and end up missing some of the high spots like the friendly whales at Laguna San Ignacio, the coral reef at Pulmo, and marlin fishing at the Cape, or end up driving at night and feeling harried. Caravans sponsored by Point South RV Tours and similar organizations require 24 to 26 days for a leisurely round-trip, border-to-the-Cape foray, allowing plenty of time for sightseeing, shopping, and story-telling.

Clothing and appearance

The choice of wardrobe depends on what time of year you go and where you plan to visit. Year around, you should bring clothes appropriate for warm, dry, sunny weather, including short- and long-sleeved shirts and short and long pants, all in light, reflective colors (you will be cooler), a swim suit, a wide-brimmed hat and, of course, socks and the requisite underthings. Due to the brilliant sun, a pair of sunglasses is a good investment. In addition, a windbreaker will be needed to combat wind chill, especially in damp coastal locations along Pacific shores. During winter, many locations can get downright cold, especially in windy locations, and you should have a heavy coat and a sweater or pullover. A trip into the high country of either national park in winter can involve temperatures into the teens, and wind-chill below zero, so be prepared to bundle up. The longer your visit, and the longer you stay in areas lacking laundromats or laundry service, the larger the wardrobe required. The locals are rather conservative in their outlook, and extremes in dress—especially see-through blouses, net shirts, hot pants, g-strings, thong bikinis, and the lack of shoes—will be viewed with a degree of disapproval, almost always unspoken but rating frowns. There are two rules, however, that must be observed everywhere. Beachwear is permissible only at the beach, and those wearing it into, say, downtown La Paz or Ensenada, may encounter outright hostility. In churches, men must remove their hats and women must cover their heads.

"Look like a bum, be treated like a bum" is a world-wide axiom. Dirty, ragged Levis with the butt and the knees gone will fail to impress the locals with your sophistication, as will purple or violet hair, thick lipstick, heavy mascara, obscene T-shirts, heavy chains and handcuffs, and the like. Except for the ear lobes, one piece for each, jewelry involving body-piercing—noses, eyebrows, stomachs, breasts, lips, and elsewhere—should be left home.

The ultimate Baja rig? Note that even the boat trailer has a trailer

The Vagabundos del Mar

The Vagabundos del Mar Boat and Travel Club bills itself as Baja's first and foremost travel club, and that is no idle boast. With over 10,000 members, the club provides opportunities to meet people with common interests in travel and fun in the sun. The club sponsors fiestas, outings, and parties, long-range fishing trips out of San Diego at group rates, guided adventure tours to Baja and other locations, and fishing tournaments for everyone, ranging from beginners up to experienced anglers.

The club offers its membership a wide variety of services and benefits, including Mexican auto, RV, marine, aircraft, and homeowner's insurance; full roadside services; Mexican legal services for travelers; medical air service in the US and Mexico; books on Baja and elsewhere at special rates; discounts at many RV parks, restaurants, and other businesses in Baja, the western US and other locations; and discounts up to 35% on marine accessories. In addition, the club can provide boat permits, tourist cards, and fishing licenses.

Headquartered in Rio Vista, California, the club office is open from 8-5 weekdays to serve the needs of its members. *Chubasco*, the club's monthly newsletter, provides information of interest to Baja RVers. The $35 per year membership is a bargain, and you will more than recoup its cost in savings on your first trip.

Organized caravans

Some choose to join organized caravans, and it is not uncommon to see a million dollar's worth of Southwinds, Winnebagos, and Airstreams pull into a Baja RV park. Point South RV Tours, Inc., and Tracks to Adventure operate Baja caravans, often accompanied by a wagonmaster, a mechanic, and a tailgunner. Best Value Quality RV Tours offers trips

that reach the Cape, as well as shorter "sampler" trips that get as far south as Guerrero Negro. Prices range from $795 for a 13-day trip, to as high as $2,000 for a 20-day trip, with several 26-day trips ranging between $1,395 and $1,795. This rather peculiar rate structure reflects differences in what is provided, such as meals, fiestas, and entertainment. Get brochures from each company and study them carefully. The Vagabundos del Mar and Good Sam also sponsor caravans for their members, and Airstream sponsors trips for Airstream owners.

What can you do if you don't own a rig?

Every RV rental company has its own policy concerning taking rigs into Mexico. El Monte RV Center and Cruise America rent RVs and will allow them to be taken into Baja, while some others will not. The best way to find out is to get on the phone and start making telephone calls. If you are planning to make the trip with an organized caravan, you might ask the company or club for suggestions.

Preparing your vehicle

Because large areas are remote and under-populated, and because there is no infrastructure of dealers, mechanics, and parts stores catering to RVers, a Baja trip requires better preparation than one in the US or Canada. The most common problems are the same ones encountered in driving anywhere: flat tires, engine overheating, failure to start, getting locked out, and running out of gas, and all can be eliminated or at least minimized by careful preparation and outfitting.

In the days before the Transpeninsular Highway was paved, adventurous travelers would bring two or three spare tires, often lashed prominently on top of the vehicle to present a rakish appearance, but today tire problems on the paved road system are normally limited to simple punctures, assuming the vehicle is not overloaded and speed is held down. Since there are many tire repair shops along the paved road system, it is not normally necessary to carry more than one spare. The best flat preventer is good quality tires with lots of tread, so if your tires are treadless wrecks, replace them. If you do have to replace a tire in Baja, dealers are to be found in the larger cities, and used tires can be found for sale in many locations, some in surprisingly good condition. Odd-sized tires, such as those for 16.5-inch rims, and small trailer tires can be difficult or impossible to find.

If you have been having engine overheating problems in the US they won't go away in Baja, so have the vehicle checked over before your trip. The water pump and thermostat should be in good condition, belts and hoses should be near-new, and the belts should be adjusted to the proper tightness. Inspect the cooling fluid, and if it looks scummy have the system flushed. If the front of the radiator is full of bugs, clean them out. If your radiator fan has a clutch, make sure it works: when the engine is hot the fan should revolve.

Failure to start is usually caused by the need for a tune-up, or by a bad battery or alternator. If your vehicle needs a tune-up, get it done before you leave, for most repair shops in Baja lack the computerized equipment required by many vehicles. Rough roads cause sediments to drift down to the bottom of the battery case, resulting in internal shorts as the battery grows older. If there is any doubt about the condition of your battery, have it replaced, and make sure it is held firmly in its mount. Replacement batteries can be purchased in the larger Baja towns, but not necessarily the exact type and size your vehicle requires.

Getting locked out of your vehicle in a remote area can be a real problem, at least if you value your glass. Far more serious is losing your keys altogether. Spares, including those for door, ignition, spare tire, and trailer should be wired to an inconspicuous place under the vehicle, using stainless wire. Magnet boxes can jiggle off on rough roads.

Drivers north of the border give little thought to the possibility that gas stations may not have fuel available. However, in Baja it can happen, especially along the Transpeninsular during long holidays and in winter. Petroleum products in Mexico are sold by PEMEX, an inefficient government monopoly. More information on PEMEX will be found in the following chapter.

There are two things you can do to avoid gasoline problems—plan ahead, and carry extra gas. The basic rule in the notorious "gas gap" between San Quintín and Guerrero Negro is to top off at every opportunity. This is a nuisance, but it at least brings peace of mind. Carrying extra gas is hazardous, but many do it anyway. The traditional five-gallon metal GI can is the safest; plastic jugs can puncture or chafe while being bounced around, and they melt quickly if subjected to fire. The standard flexible GI can spout is too big in diameter to fit the gas tank opening on vehicles using unleaded fuel, so you will need a spout that is smaller in diameter or a long-necked funnel.

Other mechanical matters

In addition to the matters just mentioned, you should take the time and money to insure that your vehicle is in top condition; things are not going to get better just by heading south. Baja is no place for your vehicle if the bands in the automatic transmission are slipping so badly you can't pull up your driveway, if the roaring noises coming from your differential are frightening neighborhood children, if engine oil is gushing out the tailpipe, or if the screeches from your brakes are attracting hopeful tomcats. Fix it **before** you leave.

Tools and equipment

Every vehicle venturing into Baja should carry a lug wrench, jack, flashlight, double-bitted (slotted and Phillips) screwdriver, medium Crescent wrench, regular, needle-nose and ViseGrip pliers, fan belts, tire air gauge, fuel filters, extra fuses, and emergency flares. Consider carrying an emergency fan belt, NAPA part 730-4006: it can be cut to any length and will enable you to help others, as well as yourself. A set of open-end wrenches might prove handy, and it would be well to carry a set of jumper cables. Make sure the lug wrench fits the wheel nuts on the vehicle and the trailer,

and that the jack is suitable for the vehicle in design and capacity, as well as for your trailer. Also, carry a small plastic drop cloth or a dish towel. This should be placed under the scene of all repairs and adjustments: nothing can be more maddening than a search for a small part in the sand. Finally, bring a roll of duct tape, which is useful for fixing cracked water containers, closing-off small slits around windows that let in dust, temporarily repairing rips in awnings, and many other chores.

For reasons that will become apparent in the following chapter, you should prepare for stays at locations with something less than well-planned, full-service, fully operational RV parks. Many parks, especially those in remote areas, do not have full hookups, and problems with water and electrical systems are common everywhere. Bring extra lengths of water and sewer hose, and an electrical extension cord, since water, sewer, and electrical connections in some parks are on the "wrong" side or are otherwise distant. A 20-foot sewer hose is far better than a 10-footer for that reason. Thirty-amp electrical service is not too common, so a 30-20 amp conversion plug is essential. A few parks still use ungrounded electrical outlets, so a "cheater" plug is also needed. An electrical generator will come in handy for those unpredictable nights when the power fails, and for nights spent boondocking. If your rig does not have a generator built in, a portable should be able to provide all the AC and DC power you need. Some parks have washers but not dryers, so if your trip is lengthy, bring a clothes line and some pins. Buy all the holding tank chemicals you will need before you leave, for you will not find them in Baja. Finally, you should carry a shovel; a small GI model found in surplus stores is ideal. Not only might this come in handy if you become stuck, it will be necessary to dig gopher holes for sewage disposal while boondocking.

What happens if you have a mechanical breakdown south of the border, despite your careful preparation? The next chapter describes how to obtain parts and repair services. If you plan some driving on unpaved roads be sure to read Chapter 7, which has additional suggestions on preparation and outfitting.

● ●

❝ *Be prepared*

My dad and I had been doing some diving off Bahía Agua Verde, and just after we got back on the Transpeninsular and headed west, we saw a stake truck ahead of us on the side of the road. Both of its dual tires on the left rear were flat, and the gray-haired Mexican driver was bent over, operating a tiny air pump. The truck was piled high with wooden boxes, it was hot, and he was red-faced and sweating profusely. In good English he said that although he had a spare, the only jack he had was a small scissors type found on autos. He didn't think the jack would hold the load, and didn't want to have to unload the truck to install the spare, so he had come all the way from the Santa Rosalía ferry, pumping up the tires every half hour. And besides, he couldn't find his tire wrench.

He thought he could make it to Villa Insurgentes before they went flat again and asked if we had a better pump. We did, a gasoline-driven air compressor that we used for diving. We set up the compressor, attached an air chuck to its hose, and fired the engine up. In several minutes the outside tire was filled, to the joy and disbelief of the trucker.

The inside tire would not harden up, and it turned out that the valve stem had been ripped off its innertube by driving on the under-inflated tire. The spare had to be installed, but the thought of removing all those boxes was not too appealing. I had an idea: we had a HiLift with us, a brawny heavy-duty jack with a capacity of about 7,000 pounds. I scrambled into the back of the camper and soon found the jack. Several minutes later the wheels were off the ground. We broke out a set of socket wrenches, a ratchet, and an extension and began to remove the wheels and replace the offending one with the spare. As we worked, we watched a series of expressions flash over the man's face, first a smile, then a frown, and then back to a smile.

*Fifteen minutes later the truck was ready to roll. He thanked us, and we said we would follow him to Villa Insurgentes to see that he made it safely. On the outskirts of town he stopped and signaled us to pull over. He thanked us again, but the pensive look on his face told us something was bothering him. We asked what he was thinking, and it all came out. He was grateful that we had stopped to help him—a hundred Mexicans had whizzed by without even slowing down—but did all gringos coming to Baja worry about the place so much that they felt it necessary to be equipped with gasoline-driven air compressors, giant jacks, and dozens of tools? After all, the Transpeninsular might not be exactly a superhighway, but it wasn't **that** bad, was it? We couldn't help laughing, but he took it the right way and grinned back. No, gringos don't think the road is all that bad, and we explained that the compressor was used for diving, and that the big jack was along because we planned to do some driving in the boondocks. With everyone smiling, he went his way and we went ours. ——Michael* **"**

• •

Compasses

Like a picture, a compass bearing is worth a thousand words, or at least 500—the description of the route to the launch ramp at San Carlos on page 188, for instance, is clear, concise, and short because of the use of compass bearings. A purely verbal description would be lengthy and difficult to follow. Many travel directions and observations of interest in the book are phrased in terms of general directions ("north," "southeast," etc.), or in exact magnetic bearings. In addition, it is easy to become confused in unfamiliar towns, especially large ones whose streets are not laid out in the normal north/south manner, such as La Paz.

To increase your enjoyment of the peninsula and the usefulness of this book, we urge you to install an auto compass. Make sure it is of the "compensating" type, allowing

the compass to be adjusted for the deviation caused by the magnetic influence of the vehicle. An Airguide auto compass, stock number 1699, found in many auto supply stores, is a compensating type, costs less than $10, and can be attached with double-faced tape to the windshield, where deviation is normally at a minimum.

All vehicles traveling off the paved road system **must** have a compass, as there is often a confusing maze of roads, and it is very easy to become lost. And remember, this applies not only to four-wheeled vehicles but to ATVs, motorcycles, dune buggies, and bicycles, and to all **rented** vehicles—it is all too easy to tear off into the boondocks on a rented ATV and become lost. Also, anyone hiking or exploring outside of the visual range of their vehicle **must** have a compass. A good choice would be Coghlan's lensatic engineer compass, stock number 8164, available at many outdoor stores and large drug chains for about $10. Needless to say, all boats must have a compass.

■ Getting a slant on things

No way do I need a compass, you are probably thinking—I was a Boy Scout and know how to find north. Moss grows on the north side of trees, and there is a way you can use a watch: you point the hour hand towards the sun and 6 o'clock will point to north. Well, there isn't any moss that grows on Baja trees in that matter, and your watch may be digital. Is there a way? Fortunately, the answer is yes. The "compass cactus," *Ferocactus acanthodes* to scientists, *biznaga* to the locals, is one of a series of species collectively known as "barrel" cacti, due their branchless, chunky shapes. The compass cactus has a tendency to reduce the intensity of the light falling on it by leaning toward the south or southwest. Separating the compass cactus from the other species is a job for a botanist, and don't bother to ask the locals, to whom all barrel cacti are *biznaga*, but if you are lost and encounter a leaning, branchless, chunky cactus with reddish thorns on top, as well as yellow flowers if it's spring, you will at least have a good idea of where south or southwest lies. Oh, yes, you remember from your Boy Scout days that water can be extracted from barrel cacti? Yes, it's true, but Mother Nature will cause you to regret ignoring our advice about not damaging the fragile desert by providing you with a memorable case of diarrhea. You will be able to see compass cactus at KM 144 on the Transpeninsular, south of El Rosario.

Travel trailers

If you plan to tow a travel trailer, make sure both the tow vehicle and the trailer are up to the task. Is the weight of the tow well within the maximum allowed for the tow vehicle? Based on your own experience, does the tow vehicle actually perform as stated in the owner's manual? The most challenging upgrades on the paved road system are 3 miles of 14% going north on the Transpeninsular between KM 56 and KM 51+ just north of El Rosario, and 2.5 miles of 16% going west on the Transpeninsular between KM 13+ to 17+, just north of Santa Rosalía. To place things in perspective, the maximum grade normally encountered in the mountainous areas of the Interstate Highway System in the US is 6%; the relatively few over that are signed. The grades in Baja are by no means world-class, but if you are driving a heavily loaded, under-powered three-speed vehicle and pulling a large trailer on a hot day, they are worthy of respect.

Rough, narrow roads and frequent crosswinds make a load-leveling hitch and a sway-control device advisable on all but the smallest trailers. Is the hitch ball the right size? A ball even a bit too small will cause stressful pounding. Is the shaft of the ball the same size as the hole in the hitch? If the shaft is smaller, put in a bushing, for motion between the hitch and the ball can cause the nut to loosen. Is the nut lock-washered? Are safety chains long enough that sharp turns can be made, but not so long that they drag on the ground? Once the trailer is loaded make sure the hitch weight is within the maximum permitted for the tow vehicle and the hitch. Some manufacturers recommend that tongue weight be between 9% and 11% of the total trailer weight, but not in excess of the limits of the hitch and tow vehicle. Determine tongue weight with a bathroom scale if you are not sure. Never allow the hitch weight to become too light; see the story on page 165.

Most trailer problems in Baja involve tires and springs, caused by the excessive weight and high speed to which they are often subjected, and the rough roads. Trailer tires should be in excellent condition, and a mounted spare should be carried. Will your lug wrench fit the lugs on the trailer? Is the capacity of the jack in the tow vehicle adequate for lifting the trailer? Is the jack of a type suitable for lifting a trailer (bumper jacks don't work well)?

The same advice on batteries given above for vehicles applies to travel trailers as well; get a replacement before you leave if there is any sign of a problem. A battery in a trailer may prove to be a hidden asset: we once encountered the unhappy driver of a trailer rig who had been stranded south of Nuevo Chapala for several hours when he could not get his truck started due to a dead battery. The look on his face was priceless when we pointed out that he already had a spare, the one in his trailer.

Service all trailer wheel bearings and brakes, and make sure the brake controller mechanism in the tow vehicle is operating properly. Trailer wheel bearings are sometimes standard automotive parts, and may be available in Baja auto parts stores, but for peace of mind it would be well to bring an inner and outer bearing and race assembly, a seal, and bearing grease, as well as a grease cap, which is often lost when a bearing fails. If you are a worrier, you might also consider bringing a gas pilot control, a thermocouple, extra fuses, and a brake magnet replacement kit. A battery isolator will minimize the chances of waking up to find that last night's party lasted so long that your starting battery is dead. Remove the hubcaps; they are easily lost and can be hard to replace, and they interfere with a daily check of wheel bearing temperatures.

Because of the warm climate, transmission coolers are a real asset when towing heavy trailers. Since shoulders are rare and the side of the road is often rough, skid wheels are needed on trailers and RVs with long overhangs. Spare keys for a trailer should be wired in a hidden place to avoid "we-came-back-from-fishing-and-you-were-still-gone" problems.

Boat, motorcycle, and utility trailers

For unknown psychological reasons, Baja RV adventurers often take great pride in their boats, motorcycles, and ATVs, but ignore the trailers that carry them. Like those of their larger brethren, most problems with small trailers are caused by excessive speed and loading. When towing a small trailer, you should reduce your speed to about 80% of what would be safe when not so encumbered. The general rule is to avoid loading a trailer more than half of its rated capacity. Also, the trailer must not be loaded too lightly, for it may bounce when bumps are encountered, subjecting it and its cargo to heavy stresses. The wheels on small trailers have to work much harder than those on the tow vehicle; if you are doing 50, the small tires on the trailer are doing the equivalent of about 80. Wheel bearings should be serviced before you leave. You might consider bringing a bearing assembly, grease, and a cap.

Avoid putting containers of fuel and water and heavy coolers in boats carried on trailers; if you must do so, put them directly over the axle. Careful attention should be paid to securing the cargo to the trailer. Horizontal and vertical forces caused by bumps and potholes are considerable, and the resulting strain on tie-downs and their attachment points can be enough to break tie-downs or bend parts.

If you are going to tow a boat trailer, adjust the trailer's bunks and rollers as suggested by the boat or trailer manufacturer, make sure the bow of the boat is snug against the bow stop, and adjust the winch height so that the winch line does not pull the bow down with excessive force. Firm tension must be maintained on tie-downs, so use adequate line and trucker's hitches, or better yet use a nylon strap and a lever device, or a strap winch. There should be a large area of contact between boat and trailer or you will experience cracks and other damage. Do not depend solely on the winch line to hold the front of the boat in place; use extra line. Since tar and gravel will eventually erode that shiny gelcoat, fenders are required.

Towing another vehicle

If you plan to tow another vehicle, the same basic advice discussed above applies. Read the instruction book for the towed vehicle, for many have special requirements. Does the towed vehicle require a dolly? Is it necessary to disconnect the drive shaft or axles? Is towing limited to low speeds? Does the towed vehicle have an ignition steering lock mechanism? If so, avoid putting the ignition key in the "lock" position, since the front wheels can not caster properly. Are a spare tire, jack, and lug wrench available for the towed vehicle? Also, if you plan to visit mainland Mexico towing (or carrying) another vehicle, including a motorcycle, an ATV, or a dune buggy, make sure you are familiar with the regulations discussed on page 52.

Getting motorcycles, ATVs, and dune buggies ready

Service and bring your machine up to top condition before heading south. Tires should have plenty of rubber left, and tube liners should be installed to help reduce the number of flats. Synthetic oil is not available in Baja, so bring what you need. Large quantities of dust will be sucked into the engine intake, so install a washable air filter and clean it frequently.

There are a few motorcycle repair shops in Baja (see the city/town maps), but their parts selections are limited and the brands they handle are often unfamiliar, so you should have a supply of plugs and points, a condenser, chain repair links, and other items that you may need—you know your own machine best. In addition, chain lube, a spare tube (two if the tires are of different sizes), a tire repair kit, an air pump, and a tow rope should be carried. Carry the pump in a plastic bag to keep grit out. Also include a small plastic painter's drop cloth, which can be spread under the bike to avoid the loss of small parts if repairs are necessary. All this will not fit in the bike's standard tool kit, so make a cylindrical container out of plastic drainage pipe and caps, and hold it on the rear rack with a bungee cord. Wire a spare ignition key in a hidden location on the bike.

A helmet, eye protection, gloves, and boots suitable for hiking are essential equipment for every rider, as well as plastic guards to keep thorns and cactus spines away from vulnerable hands. All Baja dogs hate all motorcycles, and since you will be sitting on one, you will be guilty by association. A can of Halt carried on a handlebar clip should save tooth marks on your boots, torn pants, or worse.

The words above on motorcycles apply to ATVs and dune buggies as well. ATVs handle sand better than motorcycles, but are prone to more flats, so make sure your tire repair kit is up to the job. The celebrated instability of three-wheel ATVs is not altered by crossing the border, so bring along a helmet for every rider. The chances of finding parts for ATVs is poor, although you might get lucky in visitor-oriented towns like San Felipe and Cabo San Lucas, where ATVs are often available for rent.

● ●

" *Autopsy on a Honda*

*Baja can be tough on motorcycles if you go off-road, **really** off-road. A number of years ago, we bought a Honda Trail 90 to explore off-road Baja. During the next four years, we made explorations up dry arroyos, forays down almost nonexistent trails to secret coves, ventures into the mountainous regions, and excursions along deserted beaches in search of shipwrecks and treasures. Several canyons were so precipitous that we experimented with a come-along to see if it could drag the bike up over obstacles it could not manage otherwise, and it was once necessary to literally carry it out of a tidal swamp. Finally, with 7,500 miles on the odometer, we did an autopsy and here is what we found:*

Engine shot: valve noise, piston slap, burning oil

Clutch slipping

Saddle reduced to rags

None of rear spokes original equipment, 50/50 in front

Rims on both wheels damaged and out of alignment

Guard under engine twisted and torn

A dozen repair links in the chain (our fourth)

Front shocks leaking oil

Handlebars and both fenders badly bent

Both mirrors torn off

Front and back turn signal bars bent 45°

Tires wrecked (our third pair)

Dozens of patches on tubes

Muffler squashed and split

Half of red paint missing

Battery jiggled to death (our third)

Bikers get help at Alfredo's

Headlight broken

Speedometer cable ripped off

Trailing arms on rear suspension badly
bent

Rear rack welded a half-dozen times

Kickstand vibrated off and nowhere to be
found

Both footrests smashed into uselessness

Pinhole leaks in exhaust manifold

Foot shifter pretzeled too many times to
recall

Gas tank rusted out, the victim of a high
tide one night

*In addition, the pounding had semipermanently
recontoured my dad's posterior into a close match to a Honda
saddle and mine into that of a luggage rack. We thought of
bronzing the corpse and donating it to the Smithsonian, but
there was a sentimental attachment, for despite all the abuse,
we never had to walk back, and it was finally given a decent
burial at the dump. ——Michael* **"**

● ●

Readying your boat

Your boat should be equipped with all safety equipment required by the US Coast Guard, as well as a small
auxiliary outboard motor capable of being started manually
and steered independently. The sun can be fierce and a Bimini
top is a real asset. True to the mariner's ancient maxim, the
best emergency bailing system is "a frightened man with a
bucket," so even if you have an electrical bilge pump, get a
metal bucket and tie it to the boat so it will not be lost if you
swamp. Due to the lack of swell in the Cortez, the disturbances and foam that mark rocks and shoals are often absent, and a depth finder is thus desirable for larger boats. In
the Midriff and the upper Cortez, tides and tidal currents will probably be greater than anything you have
ever experienced outside of Alaska, so bring a set of
tide tables. Tables for the Cortez are available from
the University of Arizona and Cruising Charts. The
*Tide Tables for the West Coast of North and South
America*, published by the National Oceanic and At-
mospheric Administration have tidal stations along
Baja's Pacific Coast, up the peninsula's east coast
and along the mainland.

Parts and service for Evinrude and Johnson outboards are available in Ensenada, San Felipe, Loreto,
La Paz, and Cabo San Lucas, and there is a Mercury
dealer just north of Ensenada and one in La Paz.
Mariner dealers are found in Ensenada and La Paz,
and a Yamaha dealer is located in Ensenada. There
are a few independent repair shops shown on the
town/city maps in later chapters. These businesses
cater to local fishermen, and generally have a limited selection of parts, especially for very small and

very large engines, so if there is a particularly vulnerable
part on your engine, such as the water pump impeller, fuel
pump, or reed valve, consider bringing spares. Parts and service are generally not available for inboard/outboards, although the Mercury outboard dealer in La Paz handles
MerCruiser. Automotive parts may fit, but they can be dangerous in marine service, especially those related to the fuel
system. A shop service manual and a parts list will greatly
simplify handling engine problems. Two-cycle oil is hard to
find in Baja, so bring a supply.

Getting ready for diving

Divers traveling by RV have great mobility and will
encounter a wide variety of conditions, requiring a full range
of equipment. Most people need a quarter-inch wet suit year-
around along the Pacific coast south to Abreojos, and in the
Cortez north of the Midriff region from late fall to late spring.
Lighter suits may be in order elsewhere, depending on your
metabolism and the thickness of your subcutaneous fat. In
protected areas of the Cortez, even shorty suits may not be
necessary during summer. Since you will probably end up
doing a lot of free-diving, a low-volume mask and a shotgun snorkel are assets. A supply of batteries, bulbs, O-rings,
rubbers, wishbones, and wet-suit cement is essential.

Detailed information on dive shops can be found in
Chapters 4 through 6; see the index for their locations. None
of the shops will pump out-of-hydro tanks, and a few ask for
VIP. All require certification from those requesting air, scuba
equipment sales or rentals, and scuba trips, so don't forget
your C card. Many sporting goods stores, hardware shops,
and supermarkets carry masks, snorkels, and fins, generally
of modest quality. If you are an underwater photographer
and your rig floods out or malfunctions, all is not lost—there
is a new shop in Cabo San Lucas that sells and rents underwater camera and video equipment.

John Anglin motivates a reluctant purple-lip

Licensing requirements, species, seasons, and so forth described in Appendix A for fishermen generally apply to spearfishermen as well. Specific bag limits apply to spearfishing, and the taking of corals and gorgonians is prohibited. Spearfishing is limited to free-diving and rubber- or spring-powered guns only. Regulations change frequently, so get a current copy of the regulations and study it thoroughly.

Sailboard preparation and equipment

Baja's remote conditions require additional attention to safety matters. Should the universal break or pull out of the mast foot, a leash between the two will keep them together. A wet suit is a necessity on both coasts because of wind-chill. Make sure your equipment is in top shape and bring essential spare parts and plenty of sail tape. Due to the wide variety of conditions, it will pay to bring both a short and a long board and a full quiver of sails. A kayak paddle can turn your board into a vessel for exploring on no-wind days.

Boardsailors construct elaborate arguments for not wearing life jackets: they are not needed, sailboards can't sink and they always stop when a rider falls off, there is no place to stow a jacket, you can't swim well in a jacket, and the best place to be in the surf is often 5 feet or 10 feet down. These arguments have a certain validity, but all are based on conditions "back home," where there is safety in numbers—if you get in trouble there is always someone around to help. However, few boardsailors have any experience out on the water alone, really alone, as you may be in Baja. Think it out; what will **you** do to stay afloat if you are injured and no one is around? The same thing holds for helmets; you may be the biggest thing around in hot-dogging and wave-sailing circles back home, but what will **you** do if your mast decides to bend itself double over your skull? Think it over, and if you can force yourself, bring a jacket and helmet along; in most locations there isn't going to be anyone around to smirk and make rude noises.

Television

Broadcast television is very limited south of the border cities, although a few RV parks now have satellite systems. If you will miss a daily dose of sex and violence, bring along a television, a VCR, and a supply of prerecorded tapes. If you don't have a generator and plan to do some boondocking, you can still operate them with a 12-volt DC-to-110 volt AC converter, available from Radio Shack. These inexpensive gadgets generate a square wave rather than a sine wave, but this does not seem to cause problems with most equipment.

Citizen band radio

CB radio is monitored by many boaters, RV drivers, and organizations such as the Green Angels, various rescue teams, and CB clubs in Ensenada and La Paz. Local citizens often use CB as a substitute for a telephone system. There is little agreement as to the proper channel for emergency communications. As in the US, channel 9 is the most frequently monitored, but some organizations monitor channel 1, 3, 4, 7, 10, or 16, so if you are listening for others needing help, use your scanner. You are allowed to broadcast only on channels 9, 10, and 11, and only for personal communications and emergency assistance. Amplifiers that increase broadcast power to over five watts are prohibited. Some caravan operators strongly advise participants to get a CB.

Since January 1, 1991, permits for CB radios have been no longer required for US and Canadian citizens. However, the regulations concerning permits seem to change weekly, and if you plan to bring a CB, contact a consulate or tourism office beforehand and get the latest information.

Cellular phones

Baja Cellular has brought cellular service to Baja, at least in the very northern and southern areas. If you plan to make or receive calls near Tijuana, Rosarito, Ensenada, or Mexicali, contact your cellular company before you depart for information concerning automatic roaming, receiving roamer calls placed in the US and in Mexico, rates, airtime free calls, etc. Baja Cellular also operates in the La Paz and Cabo San Lucas areas, and there are plans to include Ciudad Constitución. Roaming status can be established at any Baja Cellular office, a number of which are identified in the text and the index.

Photography, film, and processing

Baja presents challenges to photographers, one of the most important being keeping dust out of the equipment. Never store a camera in a trunk, a camper, a trailer, or in the back of a pickup. These places are usually loaded with dust, especially if you do some off-road driving; let the camera ride up front with you. If your camera is a single-lens reflex, install an inexpensive ultraviolet filter so that you need not clean dust off the lens itself, producing scratches and removing optical coatings. Bring along a supply of large Ziplock bags to store cameras and film, and keep them away from excessive heat; the film in a camera sitting on a dashboard will be cooked to death within hours. (Ziplocks have a number of other uses—more on this later—but are hard to find in Baja, so bring a good supply in a variety of sizes.)

The choice of film is important. The peninsula is a place of high contrasts, and a single photograph may have to encompass a brilliant blue sky and deep shade. The ability of a film to deal with both at the same time is called its "exposure latitude." Some films have a poor exposure latitude, leading to washed-out skies that look almost white, and shadows that look like black blobs, lacking in detail. However, Kodak Gold and Kodak Royal Gold color print films are very "forgiving," with excellent exposure latitudes of -2 to +3 EVs ("stops"). These films, especially the latter, are extremely sharp and render colors faithfully. As its name implies, Royal Gold is the better film, but it costs more. If you have a single-lens reflex, look into installing a polarizing filter, which will help a lot with washed-out skies. There are two types, linear and circular, so look in your camera manual to see which is appropriate. They cost about $45 if purchased from a large New York City dealer by mail, but you will not need the ultraviolet filter recommended earlier.

As with so many other consumable items, you should buy what you will need before you leave home. If you must buy film in Baja, the most readily available sizes are 35mm and 110. Most Baja camera shops carry either Kodak Gold or Royal Gold in these sizes. Film in 126 size is hard to find, and medium-format 120 and 220 films are basically impossible, and should you find either of the last two, it has almost certainly been baking on a hot shelf for several years. The "speed" (ISO number) of 35mm color print films available north of the border runs between 25 and 1,000, good choices in sunny Baja being 200, or 400, combining good depth of field with excellent sharpness, as well as allowing shots in low light conditions. One or more of the "low," "medium," and "high" speeds, 100, 200, and 400, are usually available in Baja shops, but films at the extremes will probably not be found. With 110 film, you will have to be content with ISO 100.

If your camera beaks down or you decide that a scene absolutely must be recorded, many shops sell "disposable" (single-use) cameras, as well as a limited selection of 35mm and 110 cameras, generally of poor quality. If you can't wait until you get home to see your photos, there is hope, for automatic "one-hour" processing machines are becoming available even in towns of moderate size. They can deal with Kodak Gold and Kodak Royal Gold and any other type of film using process C-41 (look on the film canister), but generally only in sizes 35mm and 110.

Color slide films, like Ektachrome and Kodachrome, are very "unforgiving," having a latitude of only -⅓ to +⅓ EV. They are difficult to find, even in towns as large as Cabo San Lucas, and are very expensive, probably two or three times what you would pay at home. They cannot be processed in the C-41 machines, and although some camera shops can arrange to get such films developed, it takes a great deal of time.

Other companies besides Kodak produce film, of course, most notably Fuji and Konica, which have lines of color print and slide films equivalent to Kodak's. Fuji is fairly available in Baja, and Konica is seen occasionally, and their color print films can be processed in the C-41 machines. Check out things like exposure latitude and color rendition before you leave home.

Prescriptions, syringes, eye glasses, hearing aids, and first aid

There are numerous pharmacies in Baja, and the regulations concerning drugs allow the direct sale of some that in the US would require a prescription, often at a lower cost. Despite this, it will pay to bring an ample supply of all over-the-counter and prescription medicines you will need, for inventories are smaller and the language barrier may be a problem. If you use a prescription drug that contains a narcotic or a habit-forming drug, bring a letter from your doctor or a copy of the prescription, and keep the drug in its original container. If you are diabetic or otherwise must travel with syringes, it is wise to have a letter from your doctor stating that they are medically necessary. If you are Canadian, remember that some of the over-the-counter drugs available in Canada require a prescription in the US; discuss the matter with your pharmacist before leaving Canada.

If you wear glasses, bring a spare pair; there are opticians in Baja, but obtaining a new pair will take time. If both of your eyes have the same correction and you have no astigmatism, "store bought" glasses available in the larger towns should prove satisfactory. Cleaning fluid for contact lenses is available in many Baja pharmacies. A malfunctioning hearing aid cannot be repaired or replaced readily in Baja, at least south of the border cities, so bring a spare. Many hearing-aid dispensers in the US sell good used or reconditioned aids for as little as $100, a small cost certainly preferable to several weeks of silence. Above all, take care of your aid and don't do what your senior author did; during a recent scuba diving trip to the Red Sea, I (Walt) was at 65 feet photographing the beautiful reef fish, when I found my $1,900 hearing aid still firmly lodged in its accustomed place.

It is advisable to carry a small, general-purpose first aid kit, with nostrums for two of the most common maladies encountered in Baja, sunburn and diarrhea. If you have doubts as to the adverse effects of sunlight, look at a recent photograph of Brigitte Bardot, the sex- and sun goddess of the 1950s and 60s. Various sunburn lotions can be purchased in Baja in the tourist areas, but not always in the stronger strengths and not in the boondocks, so before you depart, purchase a broad-spectrum waterproof sunscreen with a sun-protection factor of at least 30. We both have light complexions, and it used to seem that we could even get burned in the presence of Governor Brown, but with these modern sunscreens, we can now make lengthy trips to Baja and return home only slightly pink. Lips are susceptible to burning, but effective balms containing sunscreens are available. If small children or persons with sensitive skin are along, try to find one advertised for children, which does not contain PABA (para-aminobenzoic acid) or fragrances. Read the label to determine if the sunscreen is recommended for infants under six months old.

Diarrhea is the most talked-about and feared malady in Mexico, but during our many trips to Baja, we have experienced it only once, its source being the most expensive restaurant in Cabo San Lucas. Although there are other causes, the water usually gets the blame. However, all cities and most larger villages have installed modern systems, and residents of San Diego visiting Mulegé, for instance, sometimes complain that they can't get water that good back home. Some of the remote villages, including Abreojos, La Bocana, and Bahía Asunción, have desalinization plants that turn out better water than anything you have probably ever drunk. In addition, clean, inexpensive bottled water is available in virtually all food stores in Baja. It is thus possible to completely avoid water problems with little expense or trouble by simply using bottled water for drinking and food preparation, and reserving local water for washing and flushing. If you must use local water, treat it with bleach (8 to 16 drops per gallon), or with Microdyn, available in many Baja supermarkets and pharmacies, or boil it for 20 minutes. Microdyn and bleach can also be used for disinfecting fruit and vegetables. Even so, bring some Imodium A-D along in your first aid kit—it is highly effective and is available in tablet form. It can be found in some Baja pharmacies.

The following chapter will provide information on sunburn prevention, as well as tips on avoiding the other causes of diarrhea.

Small batteries

The cameras and hearing aids discussed in the last two sections require batteries, as do strobes, watches, flashlights, calculators, dive lights, Walkmans, and many other gadgets. Once again, the advice is to bring your own and any spares you will need. The only small batteries to be found without a struggle in Baja are 1.5 volt D, C and AA sizes. Anything else, such as 1.5 volt AAA, N-type, any 3, 6, or 9 volt battery, and large 9 volt batteries for your portable depth finder or lantern, will be a problem. Small "button" batteries used in some cameras can be found in the larger towns. Tiny hearing aid batteries are very difficult to find everywhere, and are apt to be the old mercury types, not zinc-air. If your batteries are rechargeable, bring the charger—Baja uses the same 110 volt, 60 cycle electricity found north of the border.

Tourist cards

Citizens of the US must have a tourist permit (everyone calls them tourist "cards," for reasons that have been forgotten) in order to stay more than 72 hours in border areas, or to travel south of Maneadero or San Felipe. Recent magazine articles have advised Baja travelers that tourist cards are not necessary, since the requirement "is never enforced." This is very bad advice: we have been asked for ours on several occasions, and should you be arrested or be involved in a traffic accident, a card is essential to prove your status in the country.

There are two types of cards. A single-entry card is good for one visit of up to 180 days; the exact length will be determined by the Mexican immigration official who validates the card once you are in Mexico. If you get less than the full 180 days, you can ask for a longer period at the time the card is validated, or at any Immigration office in Mexico at a later date. The second type, multiple-entry, allows any number of visits during its 180-day period.

Technically, single-entry cards must be turned in at the border when you depart Mexico, but few people actually do so. The big problem with both types of cards is that there is little or no parking provided at the border crossings for "checking-out," something necessary if you expect to return

to Mexico with a multiple-entry card without a hassle. Also, multiple-entry cards can be a source of complications if you attempt to validate them anywhere except at the border crossings. For these reasons, the multiple-entry card is not recommended.

Single-entry cards can be obtained at the Mexican Consulate General, Mexican Consulates, or Mexican Government Tourism Offices, from some airlines, insurance companies, and travel agencies, and from clubs such as the Vagabundos del Mar, and from any Immigration office in Baja. Obtaining a card and filling it out before crossing the border will save hassle and time, especially on holidays and weekends. In addition to the card, you must have proof of US citizenship, such as a birth certificate, valid US passport, military ID, or military discharge papers (if they show the place of birth). Naturalized US citizens can use a valid US passport, a Certificate of Naturalization, or a Certificate of Citizenship. The card must be used within 90 days of issue, and the document used to prove citizenship must be carried while you are in Mexico. The documents required to prove citizenship must be the originals; copies are no longer accepted. Possession of a card is not enough; you must have it validated at an Immigration office inside Mexico, a topic discussed in the following chapter.

Bringing the kids

Kids like Baja just as much as their parents do, so bring them along. In addition to a tourist card, a person under 18 traveling without *both* parents present should have a notarized letter granting permission to travel in Mexico. The letter must be signed by the parent not present. If the child's parents are separated or divorced, the parent having custody must sign the letter, which is to be accompanied by the separation or divorce papers. If one parent is dead, the living parent should sign the letter, which must be accompanied by the death certificate. If both parents are dead, the child's guardian signs the letter and provides the guardianship papers. These requirements are often ignored by border officials in Baja California.

Disposable diapers, infant formula, and baby food are available in all but the smaller towns, and there are a number of shops whose entire economic existence is tied to selling diapers—look for a sign proclaiming PAÑALS. Snorkeling and fishing equipment will provide endless hours of enjoyment and tales to tell when the child returns to school. If a bicycle is brought along, so should a helmet be, for the rocks in Baja can break heads, just like those north of the border.

Bringing Fido and Fifi

To take a dog or cat into Mexico, you must obtain a certificate that the animal has been treated for rabies and other specified diseases, and an Official Interstate and International Health Certificate for Dogs and Cats (Form 77-043), signed by a licensed veterinarian not more than 72 hours before the animal enters Mexico. In practice, these requirements are often ignored in Baja.

To get back into the US, cats and dogs have to be free of evidence of diseases communicable to man when examined at the port of entry. They must have been vaccinated against rabies at least 30 days prior to entry into the US, except for puppies and kittens less than 3 months of age and for dogs and cats originating or located for 6 months or more in areas designated as being free of rabies. If a certificate is not available or the 30-day period has not elapsed, the animal can still be admitted with some hassle; information can be obtained at the border. US Customs has a booklet available, *Pets, Wildlife*, publication number 509, describing regulations on dogs, cats, birds, monkeys, and other pets and wildlife. We have returned to the US from Baja many times with our dogs and have never been asked for proof of vaccination or even been asked a question concerning them.

Canned dog food is available in many stores in Baja Norte. Cat food is hard to find south of the border cities, but inexpensive canned tuna or mackerel is readily available. In Baja Sur both canned and dried dog and cat foods are usually easy to find in the large towns. Cat litter is hard to obtain everywhere. Although virtually all are involved in large-animal practices, there are many veterinarians and a number of veterinary pharmacies. Many are shown on the city/town maps.

● ●

❝ The piscatorial pointer

Soni, our German Shorthair, lived to hunt. No conceivable activity on earth interested her more, and if I picked up a shotgun, even to clean it, she would instantly begin frisking and pawing at the door. Even her dreams were filled with the chase as she relived the routine learned from a lifetime of hunting: the search, a point, the sound of a shot, and a fallen bird to be retrieved. Lying on her side with eyes closed, all four legs would furiously twitch back and forth for a minute or two, when she would suddenly freeze as if cast in stone. Finally, there would be growls and groans, and more leg twitching, followed by the snapping of teeth. We had always assumed she dreamed about pheasants, but I finally came to realize that her hunting instincts included other quarry as well.

We had parked our trailer on the shores of Bahía San Quintín, but I couldn't interest Michael or my wife Judy in a scuba dive at Roca Ben, a seamount located several miles south of Isla San Martín. Even Soni didn't seem interested, but as I loaded my equipment into the cartop boat, she suddenly came to life at the sight of my speargun, apparently realizing that some kind of a hunt was in the offing. Frisking around and ignoring my loud command "No, Soni!," she jumped into the boat. I pushed her out, but as I pulled away from the beach she started swimming after me and I relented.

The bay was alive with brant, and true to her instincts, Soni froze on a rigid point as we passed a flock of them rafted up in a small cove. Motionless on the front seat, she realized that something was wrong; just as she had been trained, she had found the game and pointed their location out to me,

but the next step was missing—there was no gunshot. A flight of brant came by, and she pointed and froze again, but when the birds passed and there was still no shot, she very slowly and deliberately turned and looked me right in the eye, and it was not difficult to guess what she was thinking—"Shoot, stupid!"

As we turned northwest from Cabo San Quintín, a dozen pelicans glided by in single file and Soni dutifully pointed them, as she did passing gulls and terns. Finally over the seamount, I began to suit up, and noticed that Soni was on point again. Laughing, I yelled at her to knock it off; those were the wrong kinds of birds, dummy! I struggled to get the tight-fitting top to the wet suit over my head, and when I could see daylight again Soni was still on point. I put on a weight belt, backed into the scuba harness, purged the regulator, and put on fins and mask, but when I picked up the speargun, she went wild for a few moments, barking and frisking, and then went back on point over the bow. As I sat on the side of the boat to roll backwards into the water, Soni began barking wildly and seemed about to jump in herself. I couldn't stop laughing, but this was getting tiresome. Although she loved to swim, there was no way she could get back aboard the boat alone, and I might be gone for an hour. I stood up and grabbed her collar, intending to tie her to a thwart, but she jerked out of my hand and began pointing again. Only then did I look over the bow at the source of her interest; this time it wasn't brant, gulls, or terns, but several large sharks, cruising leisurely in circles several feet below the surface. Somewhere between eight and nine feet long, they seemed to be waiting for something, possibly lunch, which was probably going to be me.

To this day I have never figured out whether Soni was trying to warn me or simply home me in for the kill. I lost interest in Roca Ben, and ran the boat over to the island, anchored it, and dove the south shore. Ever the hunter, Soni jumped over the side, swam ashore, and spent the next hour locked on point in front of a flock of seagulls. ——Walt ❞

● ●

Vehicle regulations

Your driver's license is valid for driving your own vehicle or a rental. You must have valid original registrations or notarized bills of sale for all motor vehicles, driven, towed, or carried, and for trailers and boats. If there is a lien on any of these, or if any are borrowed or rented, you must have a notarized letter from the lienholder or owner authorizing you to take it to Mexico, who will probably require that you provide proof of insurance. You cannot lend, rent, or sell your vehicle to a Mexican, and it cannot be abandoned or used for financial gain. If you bring a vehicle to Mexico, it must depart with you when you leave. If it is wrecked or stolen, or if you must leave Mexico temporarily without it, you must contact the nearest office of the *Registro Federal de Vehículos*. These are elusive, tending to open, close, and move without notice; ask the local civil authori-

Beautiful country north of Comondú

ties about their locations. Check with nearby RV parks; some are authorized to take custody of a vehicle if you must leave Baja without it.

Insurance

Mexico does not require vehicle insurance, but it would be most unwise to drive without it. Mexican law treats accidents seriously, and they may be considered as criminal as well as civil matters. If you have an accident, the police will determine whether you are responsible. You will usually be free to leave in a few hours if you are not at fault, or the next day if written statements are necessary. If you are at fault, your vehicle may be impounded, and you will be charged and brought before a judge. You may be held until judgments against you are satisfied, and a Mexican insurance policy is a swift way of proving financial responsibility and reducing red tape. Although some American and Canadian policies partially cover vehicles for physical damage while in Mexico, the Mexican government does not recognize such insurance as valid in Mexico as proof of financial responsibility.

In general, Mexican policies can be written to provide the same five basic coverages available in the US: collision and upset; fire and total theft; property damage liability; bodily injury liability; and medical payments. Unfortunately, uninsured motorist coverage is not available. According to one company, about 92% of Mexican drivers do not carry auto insurance, so if you are in an accident and the other party is at fault, you almost certainly will never collect a dime. Motorcycles can be insured only for public liability and property damage. Theft coverage provides only for total theft, not pilferage of contents (your homeowner's policy may cover this). You will invalidate coverage if you are drunk or under the influence of drugs, if you are unlicensed, or if you permit an unlicensed driver to drive. If you are towing a trailer, it has to be insured along with the tow vehicle. Under such coverage, a boat is insured only while being towed or attached to the insured tow vehicle, not while afloat.

Policies for one day or more are available at many insurance offices in the US near all border crossings, some having drive-up services open seven days a week. Instant Mexico Auto Insurance Services, for instance, located at the last exit before the San Ysidro border crossing, is open 24 hours a day, and will write policies for a stated number of days while you wait. You must present your registration or notarized affidavit from lien holders and your driver's license. They offer discounts for long policies, ranging from 10% for 30 days to about 70% for 360 days, and accept VISA, MasterCard, and American Express cards. In addition, they offer tourist cards, fishing licenses, and boat permits. There are other companies offering such around-the-clock, drive-in services.

As far as we know, the best annual insurance rates are offered by the Vagabundos del Mar. Where is the break-even point, where it pays to buy an annual policy, even though you plan to be in Baja less than a year? The standard wisdom is 30 days, but an analysis of the daily and annual rates from a number of companies and organizations says something different. To some extent, it will be comparing apples and oranges, since the policies and benefits are not exactly the same, but, roughly, if you own a rig valued at $10,000, the break-even point is about 13 days, and it ranges down to about 10 days as the value of the rig increases. Despite the fact that some companies selling daily policies offer discounts ranging from 10% at 30 days up to about 70% at 360 days, the savings of an annual policy grow with the length of the trip. The bottom line: if you will be in Baja for more than several weeks, major savings can be obtained by getting a Vagabundos annual policy, rather than a daily policy.

The Vagabundos also have special low rates for motor home policies covering Canada, the US, and Mexico (no liability coverage in Mexico). However, this policy, combined with the Vagabundo's low-cost Mexican liability-only policy (currently $53/per year), can produce significant year-around savings for motor home owners.

Some American insurance companies provide full coverage while in Mexico. United Services, for instance, extends all coverages, including uninsured motorist, to vehicles within 75 miles of the border. In addition, the company's umbrella policy will extend the liability limits of a Mexican policy, providing that it covers at least $100,000/person and $300,000/accident for bodily injury. If your Mexican policy has lower limits, you will be responsible for the "gap" between the Mexican policy and your umbrella policy. There are problems, however. For instance, the 75-mile limit will let you go as far south as Ensenada, but not to San Felipe, nor even to the junction at Crucero la Trinidad, and your American policy will not be accepted by Mexican authorities as proof of financial responsibility. Other American insurance companies have their own rules, so you should check with your company about coverage. Some American insurance companies can provide Mexican policies for their customers through Mexican affiliates.

There are an almost infinite number of combinations of vehicle value, coverage, deductibles, excess liability, length of trip, towing services, shipping of parts, emergency road service, discounts based on senior-citizen status, club membership, etc., features like legal aid insurance and so forth, and you can also get marine and other forms of insurance. Also, there are other companies selling Mexican insurance, including International Gateway Insurance Brokers and Oscar Padilla Mexican Insurance, and they have different rate structures and features. Further dwelling on insurance is thus not profitable. All of the various companies and organizations writing Mexican policies will provide quotes and information by phone and by mail. You know the value of your rig, the coverage and features you desire, and how long you will be gone, so do some shopping. The addresses and telephone numbers of the Vagabundos and the commercial companies noted above are contained in Appendix C.

Boat permits

The Mexico Department of Fisheries requires that **all** boats carrying fishing equipment have an annual boat permit, and that all persons aboard have fishing licenses, regardless of age and whether fishing or not. These can be obtained from the Department of Fisheries at their offices in San Diego and by mail. Their prices are currently as follows: less than 23 feet, $17.20, and between 23 feet and 29 feet 11 inches, $34.40. The Vagabundos del Mar, some travel clubs and insurance companies, and a few fishing tackle stores in San Diego can also provide them. As required for vehicles and trailers, you must carry your registration papers and a notarized letter from any lienholders giving you permission to bring the boat into Mexico. The details of these requirements have been in a state of flux, so telephone the Department of Fisheries office in San Diego to get current information well before you plan to depart. The department now has an automated telephone message describing requirements, prices, and procedures.

Canadians

The rules described above for American citizens generally apply to Canadians as well. A valid Canadian passport or birth certificate is required to get a Mexican tourist card. A Canadian consulate is located in Tijuana. The Canadian Department of External Affairs publishes a useful booklet, *Bon Voyage, But...*, describing visas, medical matters, import controls, consular matters, foreign laws, money, and many other subjects of interest to Canadians. The services of the Attorney General for the Protection of Tourists are available to Canadians (more on this in the next chapter).

Because of unfamiliarity with the currency and a lack of information as to the current exchange rate, Canadian dollars and travelers checks are not readily accepted in Mexico, and problems are sometimes encountered even in Southern California. Canadians should change their money into American dollars at the US-Canadian border and into pesos at the US-Mexican border. Because of the automatic conversion on billing, or because the locals don't know the difference, Canadian credit cards seem to be as acceptable as American cards.

The Mexican Ferry System

The Mexican Ferry System operates between Santa Rosalía and Guaymas, between La Paz and Topolobampo, and between La Paz and Mazatlán. In the past, the system was ill-managed and inefficient, information was difficult to obtain, and reservations were sometimes not honored. The system is now operated by SEMATUR, a private company, and increases in the quality of service are being achieved, with a corresponding increase in fares. However, prices are still not all that high, and the trip can be an interesting experience. The ferries can take RVs of any size. Accommodations range from inexpensive salon class, where you get a reclining chair, to private suites with bathroom and shower. You will probably be most happy to spend the money to get some privacy and quiet: the salon class is noisy, people are moving around all night, and many end up sprawled out on the deck trying to sleep. The senior author was once confronted by a dozen rough-looking, wide-awake, and very unhappy Mexican men, who accused him of snoring, an untrue rumor of course, but he plans to go cabin-class on future voyages.

Information and reservations can be obtained from the ferry terminals at La Paz and Santa Rosalía, and from a number of travel agencies. The ferries are sometimes booked full during the Christmas and Easter holidays, as well as during July and August, and reservations should be made months in advance.

There are important paperwork matters to understand before you leave home. Unlike Baja, a Temporary Import Permit is required for vehicles entering mainland Mexico, including those entering by ferry. In addition, you must execute a Vehicle Return Promise Form, and post bond with your credit card guaranteeing that you will return the vehicle to the US and not sell it in Mexico. You won't be allowed on the ferry without both. To get them, you must have your tourist cards and the documents used to obtain them (passport, birth certificate, etc.), the original (no copies) **title** and **registration** for each vehicle (or rental agreement/notarized permission), and a valid American or Canadian driver's license (including extensions). To pay the fee for the import permit and the bond, you can use Visa, Diner's Club, or American Express credit card, and the card must be in the name of the person applying for the import permit. (The booklet *Traveling to Mexico by Car*, noted later in this section, also includes MasterCard, but officials in La Paz insist they can accept only the three noted.) If you don't have a

The Guaymas ferry disgorges an RV in Santa Rosalía

credit card, the hassle factor goes way, way up—you must post a cash deposit or obtain a bond from a commercial bonding company—and the cost is higher.

There are a number of other important complications involved. For instance, only one import permit will be issued per person. If you are alone and are towing your motorcycle trailer, you have a problem. The number of permits issued is also limited to the number of licensed drivers. Your import permit may be limited to the time until your driver's license and car registration expire, so look into this well before you leave home; if they expire during your trip, you have a problem. **Finally, at the present time a temporary import permit cannot be obtained in Santa Rosalía.** What to do? You could attempt to get a permit from a Mexican Customs office at the border when you first cross into Baja. The problem with this is that there is extremely limited parking available, especially for big rigs, and the officials may be a bit perplexed, since this is not in the realm of day-to-day business. You could arrange your trip so that you visit La Paz and obtain the permit there before you cross the Cortez on the Santa Rosalía-Guaymas ferry (the process in La Paz is described beginning on page 147). In addition, you could visit mainland Mexico before crossing into Baja. The best option is probably to forget Santa Rosalía and cross from La Paz. This matter illustrates the frustrations and problems often encountered in dealing with the Mexican bureaucracy—Santa Rosalía is sizable town, and the ferry is regularly scheduled, and there is no way to obtain a permit, in a

country that wishes to promote tourism!

It is essential that if you plan to use either the Santa Rosalía or the La Paz ferry that you contact a Mexican consulate or tourist office to get current information **before** departing home. Ask them to mail you a copy of *Traveling to Mexico by Car*, published by the Secretary of Tourism. This booklet also describes the procedure when you leave Mexico—you must "check out" properly. There is also a hot line for current Mexican vehicle import information, 900-454-8277 (note that a charge for this service will be added to your phone bill—this is a 900 call, not 800). Chapter 5 will provide the locations of ticket offices and the ferry terminals in Santa Rosalía and La Paz and identify several travel agencies in the latter city that can make reservations and provide advice.

Souvenirs, trinkets, and knickknacks

Most people like to buy things in Baja that they need or that will remind them of the good time they had. However, you can't haul back just anything. The most common "tourist" items, like T-shirts and other clothing, leather work, ceramics, glass products, *serapes*, *huaraches*, arts and crafts like ironwood carvings, figurines, silver jewelry, and so forth are no problem. If there is a chance that you may want to bring something home outside these general types of items, US Customs has a useful booklet, *Know Before You Go*, publication number 512, that contains detailed information on restricted or prohibited articles. These include some kinds of fruits, vegetables, plants, plant products, soils, meats, meat products, hard corals, feathers, reptiles, snails and other live animals and animal products. Common items offered for sale in Baja that are illegal to import into the US include Cuban cigars, sea-turtle products such as jewelry and cosmetics containing turtle oil, whale bones, teeth, and baleen, wildlife curios such as stuffed iguanas, some species of cacti, and virtually all live birds. All jewelry made from black coral is prohibited, and it is wise to avoid glazed cups, dishes, and other items intended to serve food—many contain unacceptable levels of lead. To avoid wasting your money on things that cannot or should not be brought home, or encountering difficulties at the border, get a copy of this booklet before you leave home.

Canadians traveling through the US must conform to the American restrictions described above, and should get a copy of *Know Before You Go*. In addition, Canada has its own restrictions. A pamphlet, *Don't Bring It Back*, publication 5054E, describing various prohibited, restricted, and conditional items, is available from Agriculture Canada, and you should get a copy before you leave.

Preparing for a minimum impact visit

After perhaps 10,000 years of human habitation, Baja is showing increasing signs of ecological stresses. There is a great deal you can do to eliminate or at least minimize the impact of your visit. As far as you are able, select products that will enable you to bring all debris back when you return home: every can, every bottle, every pull top, every toothpaste tube, emphasizing those products that can be reused or recycled upon returning. If the nature of the product is such that it is unfeasible to bring it back, pick one that can be burned. Avoid all styrofoam (polystyrene) products—although they burn readily, many seem to end up blowing around the countryside, where they last "forever." If they end up in the water, birds and other creatures sometimes attempt to eat them, with deadly results. Avoid bringing plastic bags or plastic film like Saran Wrap or plastic bags: in the water they look like the jellyfish eaten by some species of turtles. Instead, purchase a variety of plastic containers with snap lids for storing excess food in the refrigerator.

Avoid products with unnecessary packaging; if you must buy them, remove the excess before you leave home. Cup O'Noodles is a prime example: not only is the cup holding the product made of styrofoam, but it is also covered in plastic film and surrounded by a cardboard wrapper. All the information on the wrapper concerning contents and preparation is duplicated on the sealed lid of the cup, and the wrapper thus seems to serve no significant purpose. Many other products utilize unneeded packaging: potato chips often come in numerous small bags, all contained in a larger bag; three small cans of tuna are held together by a cardboard box, and so forth.

Purchase soda and beer in aluminum cans and bring them home for recycling. If you purchase them in case lots, leave the cardboard home. Remove the plastic yokes from all six-packs. These devilish devices have a habit of ending up in the environment, where they are a significant cause of death for birds and small sea mammals. If they get in the water they lie flat, and diving birds like pelicans and boobies all too often make bull's eyes into them. A number of companies have switched to yokes made from biodegradable plastic, and although this is a good move, the same rule applies; don't bring them to Baja, for they can still kill while they are degrading. If any manage to accompany you on the trip, burn them when they are no longer needed.

If you have an infant aboard, you have a choice between disposable and cloth diapers. Studies have shown no meaningful difference in their effects on the environment, despite all the hype. The plastic film on some disposables contains starch that supposedly causes it to break down into small pieces, meaning that instead of one large piece that will be around for decades, you will have many small pieces around for decades. However, washing machines are few and far between in many locations in Baja, and few people are ready, able, and willing to wash diapers by hand in an RV, so disposables appear to be the "least worse" choice. Store the used disposables in an air-tight container until their contents can be burned. Many RV and

outdoor equipment stores carry toilet tissue that is specially formulated for rapid disintegration.

Get an engine tune-up and a new air filter, and if your vehicle is due for an oil change, do it before you leave, for if it is done south of the border, the used oil will certainly be dumped behind the shop. Insure that all tires on your rig are inflated properly—not only will they wear out less rapidly, but you will get better gas mileage, up to 5% more than with under-inflated tires. If your tires need replacing, do it before you leave. In Baja the old tires will be dumped somewhere, while in the States there is some chance they will be recycled or at least disposed of in a better way.

Buy outboard oil in recloseable plastic bottles, as opposed to metal cans with pull-tops. This permits you to add the correct amount of oil for the amount of gasoline added, and to burn the container when empty. While out in your boat insist that nothing be thrown over the side; you are the captain and have responsibilities as well as privileges (marriage at sea, the first and last margarita, no watches at night, etc.).

None of these ideas are Baja-specific, and you are probably doing most of them at home anyway. Think ahead, and do the same things on your trip south. The next chapter will describe ways in which you can minimize the impact of your visit once you are south of the border.

What, me worry?

What should you do if your rig does not conform to the prescriptions above: you don't have a transmission cooler nor a load-leveling hitch, your trailer is a bit heavy for the tow vehicle, etc.? The final judgment is yours, of course, but if you make your plans with the limitations of your vehicle and equipment in mind, and go well prepared, you will find adventure on your own terms. Finally, don't be put off by our many stories scattered throughout the book. Most involve misadventures of one sort or another, but they are the results of many years of actively seeking adventure on the peninsula and its surrounding waters. As pointed out several times, all authors stress the extremes; who wants to write a book describing trips to the vast desert wastelands to the

La Paz and its flotilla of yachts

south during which all went well and absolutely nothing out of the ordinary happened?

● ●

❝ *How not to go on an RV trip to Baja*

My mom, my dad, and I crossed the border at Tijuana and decided to spend the night at Estero Beach, an elaborate resort that includes an RV park, located just south of Ensenada. We unhitched our modest 16-foot Wilderness, had supper, and went to bed. As we were dozing off there was the throaty roar of a diesel engine. It seemed odd—a fancy place like Estero Beach would certainly not let 18-wheelers stop for the night.

The next morning I peeked out beneath a curtain and announced that we had neighbors; a gigantic motor home was parked in the site next door. It was a marvel, about the size of a Greyhound bus, and in back was a gleaming gold Cadillac El Dorado, still hitched to the rear. I could see someone looking at me through the rig's dark-tinted windows, and rather than continue to stare, I went about making breakfast.

An hour later, there were stirrings next door, and a very tall and rough-looking young man stepped out of the motor home and walked around the motor home as if he was looking for something. He finally knocked on the door of the motor home, and a man and a woman got out. They looked about furtively, but finally brought out some aluminum chairs, sat down, and had their morning coffee. Dishes done, we went out to stretch our legs, studiously pretending they weren't there. The older man looked our way and said something we could not hear, and as we walked over, the young man took several steps backward. The older man repeated his good-morning salutation, but when we introduced ourselves he looked the other way and did not offer their names in return.

We got back from a foray into Ensenada that evening, and the man and woman were still sitting there, drinking coffee, the young man standing a few yards away. The third evening was a repeat of the second, as were the fourth and fifth. It was certainly an odd situation, and I pointed out a strange bulge under the young man's left armpit.

The morning of the sixth day, we hitched up and were about to head south, when the young man knocked at our door and asked if we would like to join the others for coffee. With a degree of apprehension, we walked over, opened our aluminum chairs, and sat down. No introductions were attempted again, but a pleasant conversation began. It turned out that they were from San Diego and that the man had "always wanted to see Baja ever since he was a boy," but this was their first trip. After the second cup of coffee I asked if I could see their rig. The man suppressed a frown, pointed a finger first at the young man and then at the motor home. It was a marvel; brand-spanking new, it had every convenience known to man: a microwave oven, luxurious leather captain's chairs for the driver and copilot, air conditioning, and a closed-circuit television so the driver could see the rear of the rig. The refrigerator was crowded with fresh lettuce, milk, steaks, and Perrier. A large television and a sat-

ellite dish were available to provide nightly doses of sex and violence, and should the satellite fall out of orbit, there was a VCR and a large supply of tapes. The dashboard looked like the instrument panel of a 747, and the odometer showed just under 3,000 miles.

*Seated outside again, we awkwardly attempted a conversation, and it turned out they were headed back to San Diego that afternoon. What did they think of Baja? It was a bit disappointing, and they couldn't figure out why some people were so crazy about the place. Had they been to Laguna San Ignacio to meet the friendly whales? No, they had not. How about Parque San Pedro Mártir? The Cadillac was capable of making it, and for that matter so could the motor home. No, they had not been there either. Had they done any marlin fishing at the Cape? No. Had they explored the onyx quarry at El Mármol? No. What did they think of Mulegé? Didn't know; they had not been there. Had they driven up to the rural village of San Francisco to the see the rock art at Cueva Ratón? No. Where **had** they been? Estero Beach; during their five days in Baja they had not left the RV park. When they pulled in the other evening they had come straight from the border crossing. Would they ever come back? Probably not. Was the young man their son? They quickly changed the subject.*

With a sense of awe, we pulled out of the park an hour later. A $200,000 rig and a $40,000 dinghy, and they had seen nothing of the legendary desert wastelands to the south. Other than the clerk at the front desk, they had not spoken to a Mexican. Their tinted windows blocked out the bright desert sun, the air conditioner maintained a perfect 72°, the refrigerator, freezer, stove, and microwave made sure that they would consume only the finest of north-of-the-border cuisine, the rig's large diesel fuel tanks made it unnecessary to stop at a PEMEX, and the ample supply of French mineral water was available to eliminate the risk of alimentary canal distress. The young man was obviously a bodyguard; he was not carrying his lunch in that holster under his windbreaker. I thought to myself; were they actually afraid of being stopped on the Tijuana-Ensenada Toll Road by the fabled bandido roadblock?

Mother Nature did not always do her best work in the most accessible places, and the surveyors who laid out the Transpeninsular did not make their alignments just to please RVers. True to the Protestant work ethic, many of the best places require you to go out of your way, perhaps driving some distance on an unpaved road, and possibly even getting a little hot and sweaty from a bit of hiking. A swift air-conditioned dash down the Transpeninsular and an equally rapid retreat will produce little beyond sore bottoms and boredom. To fully appreciate the place, you must plan your trip carefully, set aside plenty of time, and be ready and willing to do some exploring and poking around. Your efforts will be rewarded, and unlike the motor-home crew, you too may discover what draws some people back 10, 20, even 50 times. ——Michael **❞**

● ●

Chapter 3

Underway

As noted in the previous chapter, possession of a tourist card is not enough; you must have it validated at an Immigration office in Mexico. The offices at the ports of entry into Baja described in this book—Tijuana, Otay Mesa, Tecate, and Mexicali—are often busy, and parking can be hard to find, especially at Tijuana and Mexicali. There are also offices in Rosarito and Ensenada, which are conveniently located and have better parking. The office that was at Maneadero is permanently closed. If you decide to stay longer than you anticipated and need to get your card extended, there are a number of Immigration offices in the larger towns to the south and at ferry terminals and international airports. If you are headed for areas south of San Felipe you should have your card validated before you arrive there, for the Immigration office in San Felipe is currently closed.

Getting along with the locals

The long and complex joint history of Mexico and the US has evolved into a schizophrenic blend of friendship and disdain on both sides of the border. It is important that you understand something about such attitudes and how they developed, and how American visitors are seen by the citizens of Mexico. It will be these reciprocal attitudes, plus demeanor, appearance, and actions, that will determine how well you fare during your trip to this foreign land.

We began making trips to Baja California many years ago, and like many Americans, we had seen movies and read stories that caused us to stereotype its inhabitants into five basic categories: poverty-stricken but cheerful peasants wearing colorful native costumes, waving from the roadside at every passing vehicle; cross-eyed *bandidos* with umbrella-sized *sombreros* and a pistol on each hip; begrimed mechanics who could fix anything for $2; border officials, brooding, dark, and contrary, looking for the slightest transgression or smallest error as a lever to promote a bribe; and grinning little 10-year-old thieves, waiting to pick your pocket or to snatch your purse.

During these trips we learned that some Mexicans also have certain stereotypes concerning visitors from the north: rude, aggressive, over-sexed, crime-prone, loud-mouthed materialists; dirty hippies with knapsacks full of magic powders and heads full of the crazies; and pale ephemeral be-ings peering through the tinted windows of speeding motor homes. I (Walt) once got an inkling of how it must feel to be a Mexican in the presence of *gringos*. After several weeks of exploring the hinterlands around El Rosario and attempting to converse with the local fishermen and divers in their own language, Rob Watson and I made a supply run into town. A few minutes after we began shopping in the supermarket, a middle-aged American couple walked in and started shopping. We found their demeanor abrasive and their loud shirts and short pants outlandish. Their English sounded harsh and rough to our Spanish-tuned ears, much like German does to English-speaking people. We recovered from this momentary culture-warp to realize that, other than our deep sunburns and dusty clothes, we were they.

The experiences of Mexican citizens which have lead to these stereotypes of Americans have a rather direct and personal character to them. Millions of Mexicans have visited the US, not generally as pampered tourists, but as unskilled labor, to be cheated, underpaid, and confined to labor camps and *barrios*. These people return to their homes to tell of their experiences to friends and relatives. Additional millions live permanently in the US and send letters home. To all this is added dollops of exported American culture, such as television and movies which emphasize sex, drugs, violence, and materialism, and a bit of historical perspective starting with the loss of Alta California, Texas, and other choice real estate as a result of the Mexican-American War. For these reasons and many more, the Mexican impression of the US and its citizens is thus often something less than totally favorable.

The American stereotype of the Mexican is apt to be based on a much more narrow range of personal experience. By and large, American visitors to Mexico are treated with deference and courtesy, and there is no American counterpart to the expatriate stoop laborer returning home with tales of mistreatment. Many impressions formed by Americans develop during relatively short forays to tourist resorts, where they associate almost totally with other Americans and have few opportunities to meet local people other than bartenders, waiters, and cab drivers. Other stereotypes come from advertising for American-made products, the Frito Bandido and Speedy Gonzales being the first characters to come to mind. In American movies, Mexicans are often portrayed as simple peasants and snaggle-toothed *bandidos*, as in *The Treasure of the Sierra Madre*, or drunken and incompetent soldiers, as in *Villa Rides*. In addition, except when assisted by *gringos* like Steve McQueen in *The Magnificent Seven*, they are virtually always on the losing side. There seems to be only one movie in memory where they are not only portrayed as steadfast and well-lead soldiers, but they get to win for a change, *The Alamo*, overwhelming even John Wayne. Relatively few Americans have ever seen a Mexican movie, the excellent *Like Water For Chocolate* being a recent exception.

The stereotypical Mexicans and the stereotypical Americans are gross exaggerations, of course, and individuals rarely fit completely into such molds. However, this is not the same as saying that there are no recognizable traits of attitude and motivation in each group of people. There are, in fact, a number of celebrated national traits ascribed to the Mexican people, "*mañana*" (tomorrow) being the most celebrated of all. Mexicans seem to have a different conception of time, and visitors from the north are often offended when the locals are an hour or two late for appointments, and every economic woe in Mexico is blamed on this perceived propensity to put things off.

We had a party with the locals; they brought the bugs, and we brought the beer

Other traits have been identified by generations of travel writers. Mexicans sometimes receive visitors to their country with a somewhat excessive and often undeserved friendliness, a trait called the "Malinche Complex." (Malinche is the name the Mexica Indians applied to Hernán Cortés, and the term refers to the courtesy, generosity, and almost brotherly friendliness extended by the doomed Emperor Montezuma II to Cortés and his *conquistadors* after their fateful first encounter at Tenochtitlan in 1519). There are few countries in the world where a visitor receives a more friendly welcome than Mexico, and this fondness for strangers, a sort of reverse xenophobia, often works to the detriment of the locals. As a corollary to this tendency, Mexicans tend to tell you what they think you want to hear, rather than what you ought to hear, in an effort to please. They have a hard time saying "no," even if they know they cannot make the appointment or complete the job. Mexican men, especially officials, have been known to resort to a tactic called the *Ley de Hielo* (Law of Ice); to avoid admitting a mistake, they simply adopt a stern look and refuse to speak.

Many Mexican men are well-equipped with traditional *machismo*. If you are female and not a relative by blood or marriage you may get a lot of attention, and you will be judged largely in the first few seconds. Most Mexican men do not indulge in casual flirting, and if you are female and try it and then suddenly go about other business, they will think you are merely being coy and may persist in an obnoxious way; today we might call it "sexual harassment." We once met a young bicyclist from New Zealand who was having endless problems with the locals. She was of Maori ancestry, with dark hair and a dark complexion, and was very pretty and dressed to attract attention. The local *machos*, thinking her to be of the local vintage, responded with catcalls, winks, and proposals ranging from immediate marriage to shorter situations.

Mexican women are often closely watched and hard to meet, especially in rural areas. We once needed to ask a few questions and to have a scuba tank filled. The dive shop in the small village was closed, but following the directions on a sign in the window, we went to the owner's home. A young and very pretty American woman came to the door and we stepped in. Her husband was away, she said, but started to answer our questions. After a few minutes she became very nervous and obviously wanted us to leave. An older Mexican woman with a stern look on her face stepped in from another room. We quickly got the message and left, but the young woman followed us a few moments later and said, "I am sorry. I'm married to a very Mexican man and we can't be alone even for a few moments," and ran back to the house.

There seems to be a difference of opinion as to the attitude of Baja's residents toward money. In 1869, J. Ross Browne observed that the inhabitants of Baja California "do many things from hatred and malice, but seldom do anything for money." However, in 1906, adventurer Arthur North had the opposite experience when he hired a native to act as a guide. The man objected when he learned that he would be paid off in paper money rather than silver coin, and North found it necessary to blow the head off a passing jackrabbit with his Colt .45 as a way of demonstrating what would happen if the man pressed his claim much further. Many modern travelers note that vestiges of a certain ambivalent attitude about money seem to persist. The American wishing to obtain a guide, a boat, assistance, etc. who makes a blunt, direct offer of money to a Mexican, especially in a rural area, may be greeted by a cold and baffling attitude. In our money-oriented society, we are used to straightforward business transactions. In Baja, the locals will often simply not be "bought," and a straight-from-the-shoulder, *gringo*-style offer of money may be offensive to them. This is not to say that they are uncooperative, or that money is of no value, but only that you must approach them properly.

● ●

❝ *Mind your manners*

One day Rob and I were in our boat searching for a sunken aircraft wreck off El Socorro, with no luck. We pulled up to a sea-urchin diver's boat, said our greetings and the usual preliminaries, and asked the hose tender if he knew where the wreck was. He very politely said the diver did, and that we should wait. The diver soon returned to the boat, but unfortunately we could not understand his directions, and without thinking, we made a straightforward offer of a substantial sum if he would show us the location, far more than he could make diving. Our intentions were the best— we wished to compensate him for his time—but an immediate change in attitude occurred, for the worse. The diver went down again, and in a rather cursory fashion, the hose tender said the diver would show us, but we would have to wait until he came up again. About a half hour later he was back at the boat, and the two men had a hurried conversation. Rather coldly, the diver said that he wanted twice what we had offered and that we would have to wait until the urchins were cleaned. We sensed a deteriorating relationship, but agreed to wait.

An hour later the urchins were cleaned, but rather than hoisting anchor, the diver headed for the bottom again. When he returned, we again pulled alongside and offered twice the diver's price and asked whether he still agreed to help, and received a simple, cold "no." We pulled away, believing that he was simply too lazy to help us, in spite of our handsome offer. In retrospect, we realized that we had insulted him by being too blunt with our offer of money. ——Walt ❞

● ●

To win friends and influence people in Baja, try the following:

1. Dress comfortably but modestly; as noted earlier, see-through blouses, net shirts, hot pants, g-strings, thong bikinis, ragged Levis with the butt and the knees gone, and the lack of shoes, will lead to unfavorable impressions, far more so than back home, and swim wear is appropriate only at the beach.

2. Don't place Mexican women in compromising situations, by Mexican standards, not yours.

3. Engage in the social preliminaries when meeting someone. Say hello, discuss the weather and what you are doing in Baja. When the proper subliminal clues appear, slowly shift the subject matter to whatever you need: information, assistance, a guide, a boat, etc. Avoid seeming *brusco*, abrupt and overly quick, meeting without greeting and leaving without farewell.

4. Avoid blunt, direct offers of money, especially to individuals not normally engaged in providing the services or products you need. Try to minimize the monetary aspect of the transaction, treating it almost as an afterthought. Depending on the nature of the transaction, bargaining may be in order. Start with an offer somewhat too low, but not too low, for you will come across as a cheat, too high and you may be taken for a fool.

5. Relax. Stop looking at your watch every five minutes and making long mental lists of the exact moment everything must happen; you are on vacation and this is Mexico.

6. Numbers—the cost of a trinket or the peso-dollar exchange rate offered at a gas station—are often the source of unhappy misunderstandings. If you can't comprehend a spoken reply involving numbers, ask the person to write them down; Mexico uses the same kind of number system we do, decimal-based, with the familiar Arabic characters.

7. Watch your language. Mexicans are often well aware of the intent of many four-letter English words, if not their exact meaning, and the reverse is true; if a Mexican called you a *cabrón* (bastard, cuckold, pimp) or a *pendejo* (pubic hair, idiot) you would probably understand the general cant of the conversation. Body language also can have a strong influence on how well you get along: a cold smile (mouth only), a raised eyebrow, leaning away from someone you don't like, a shrug of the shoulders; all convey a message.

The hard-working crew of the La Palma tortillera makes sure that the citizens of Ensenada do not go hungry

■ Silence is golden

Everyone knows how we hate to complain, but we promised to tell the truth, remember? During our travels in Baja we have had many interesting and rewarding experiences, but we have observed that there are four problems, four that friends who have traveled extensively in mainland Mexico assure us to be national in scope: concrete, paving, plumbing, and French fries. Mexican workers do not mix good concrete, using too little cement and too much water, often using saltwater instead of fresh. The result is that within months cracks appear, surfaces begin to spall, and the structure is on its way to disintegration. Paved roads generally have little or no subbase, the pavement is often as thin as a half inch, and culverting and slope stabilization have been forgotten. The result is a constant battle with potholes and wash-outs. The plumbing is hopeless: even in the finest hotels, there is frequently no hot water in the rooms, stains appear on the walls and ceilings where leaks develop, and bathroom tiles often show evidence of frequent excavations to get at valves and fittings. Finally, with few exceptions, the peninsula's cooks have never learned to make good French fries. Many years ago, the Mexican brewing industry learned to make some of the world's best beer from German brew masters, but seem to have learned nothing about making French fries during the rein of Emperor Ferdinand Maximilian, or when the French were busy at Santa Rosalía. Soggy, tasteless, and flaccid, they are the greatest exception to the wonderful culinary traditions of Mexico.

In view of these matters, we must reluctantly add an eighth suggestion about getting along with the locals:

8. Don't mention anything about concrete, paving, plumbing, or French fries.

Speaking Spanish

Concern about the language barrier often causes people heading south on their first trip to worry. However, the lack of Spanish should not be a major problem. Many Mexicans have experience dealing with visitors from the north, and speak English or a close approximation of it. English and Spanish share numerous words, and many others have common Latin roots; if a car marked *policía* pulls you over and the officer writes a ticket for excessive *velocidad* and says you will end up in the *hospital* if you don't slow down, there is apt to be little doubt as to the situation. In addition, hybrid "Spanglish" words, created by adding an *-o* or an *-a* on the end of an English word, are often encountered, *launcha* *rampa*, for instance.

Spanish is an interesting, if often puzzling, language. Feminists have made progress in purging English of sexist words, but they face a far more daunting task with Spanish, for every noun is either masculine or feminine, and adjectives also have gender. Sometimes the "reasons" gender is assigned are hard to fathom: *ropas* (clothes), for instance, is feminine, even those worn by men; *manzana* (apple), is feminine, but *manzano* (apple tree) is masculine. Some nouns can be either gender: "the sea" can be either *el mar* (masculine) or *la mar* (feminine), for instance. Occasionally gender makes sense: *cerebro* (brain) is masculine, and *boca* (mouth) is feminine. (Come on now, ladies, don't get sore—we are just kidding.) Most of the time, however, the assignment of gender is downright incomprehensible. Why is the impolite Spanish word for the male reproductive organ feminine, and that for the female masculine? Why? Because that's the way they do it in Spain—*es la costumbre* (it is the custom). Despite these, well, "inconsistencies," Spanish is much simpler than English, with fewer irregular verb conjugations and fewer words that stray far phonetically from their spelling.

Communicating with the locals in their own language is part of the fun, so give it a try! Appendix E provides a highly simplified approach that almost anyone can master. With this appendix, which includes a dictionary of over 1,100 useful words and terms, you should have little trouble in handing almost any situation. If you are at the counter of a pharmacy in a remote village and need something for your cold, you will fare much better if you know the correct word (*catarro*), and you won't get a blank look at an auto parts counter if you ask for *una cinta de ventilador* (a fan belt).

Although it will pay to review Appendix E before your departure, it requires no lengthy study and no memorization; it is to Spanish as connect-the-dots is to painting. You will not be mistaken for a sophisticated resident of Mexico City, but it will allow you to ask directions, interpret road signs, deal with menus, shop for food and supplies, obtain services, and generally understand and be understood. In addition to basic words and terms involving numbers, time, days of the week, colors, food items, directions, tools, geographic and meteorological terms, "opposites" (left, right, hot, cold, up, down, rich, poor, etc.) and so forth, it includes a number of driving, RVing, and health terms, many of which are not often found in Spanish/English dictionaries, at least those small enough to drag along to Baja.

If you can't get across using Appendix E, there is still hope in communicating. If you don't know the word for a physical object, draw a picture; if you need a spare part, bring the broken one. If all else has failed, there is one last chance—act it out. In the El Rosario supermarket, Rob and I wanted to buy some honey, but could not find it. Neither of us could remember the word, and we did not have a dictionary, so Rob tried to act out what we wanted. Fluttering his hands at his shoulders and skipping down the aisles on tiptoes emitting loud buzzes, he stuck his face into a display of plastic flowers. At first there were dumfounded looks, but with a roar of laughter everyone got the idea at the same time, and there was a rush to show us where the *miel* was to be found. An American RV lady once tried to use this method to explain to a La Paz pharmacist that she needed a box of suppositories. There was a considerable confusion at first over exactly what was required, but the correct message was finally understood.

Security concerns

In many trips to Baja, some almost five months long, we have paid *mordida* (a bribe, literally, the "bite") only twice—traffic cops nailed us in Tijuana and in La Paz and promised to pay the fines for us, totaling less than $20 (they kept the money, of course). We were twice cheated by PEMEX attendants, for less than $10 each time. With these small exceptions, experienced over a period of many years of active travel and adventure in Baja, we have never had a problem with the locals, and have in fact been treated with almost uniform courtesy and honesty. We once had to leave a camper in Santa Rosalía for three months while we returned home. Although it was jammed with outboard motors, scuba gear, a diving compressor, cameras, camping equipment, and tools, we returned to find it intact, not so much as a dust mote disturbed. Could you do this in your home town?

Americans often worry about crime while traveling in Baja, the legendary "Mexican road block" being a typical fear. What's the truth? We are not statisticians and make no claim to omniscience, and you are free to believe or disbelieve the following opinions: south of the border cities, there is less major crime in a year than on a hot Saturday night in Los Angeles, you have little to fear from the locals, and are probably far safer in Baja than in your home town.

Does this mean that you can let your guard down and leave your motor home open and your things lying about while you are in town shopping? Should you stop counting your change at PEMEX stations? Can you feel free to get smashed with a half-dozen rough-looking locals in a cantina and invite them back to your trailer for more of the same? Of course not! Unhappy things happen everywhere, and Baja is no exception; they didn't build that new prison just south of Mulegé for nothing. The best policy is to maintain the same level of security you would at home, and don't set yourself up for problems. Later chapters will identify a few businesses and PEMEX stations that have gained consistent reputations for unhappy transactions.

■ They kill everyone they see

The anguished look on the woman's face showed she believed every word she was saying. "Please don't go down there," she pleaded. "They kill everyone they see!" She had learned that we were about to head for Baja on a four-month trailer trip. We listened attentively to a 10-minute tirade about the dangers we faced, but early the next morning we left the San Diego RV park early enough, we hoped, that she would still be asleep in her trailer next door.

Over the years Baja has gained something of a lurid reputation, and although the lady's opinion carried it to new heights, such ideas about the place are all too common. Stories about the legendary roadblock, about hassles with police officers demanding *mordida* for inadvertent infractions of unfamiliar laws, about youthful pickpockets, and about swift and slippery sneak thieves cause many to head south with some apprehension, or even avoid going at all, like the opinionated lady, who admitted that she had never been there.

Where do such tales come from? Over the years writers seeking sensation have published articles emphasizing the negative aspects of their travels in Baja: hurricanes, bad roads, dirty gasoline, and the slightest transgression by the natives. What writer wants to write a story about not encountering a *chubasco*, not finding any bad roads, and not encountering *bandidos*? These stories feed upon themselves, and each successive generation of writers weaves a new fabric of exaggerations. We too are guilty of this, and many of the stories scattered around this book concern such matters, neglecting to mention the many times we have sprawled out on a pristine and deserted beach, with a campfire crackling and snapping in front of us, sipping margaritas and watching the waves and the pelicans, as a golden sunset gives way to a velvety blue night, thoroughly enjoying the end of a day in which absolutely **nothing** went wrong.

Occasionally, real incidents are blamed on the wrong people. We met a man near San Quintín who complained bitterly that "the Mexicans" had stolen his gas can, apparently willing to blame the entire nation. We asked how he knew who did it and he replied, "Who else would do it?" We pointed out that he was parked amidst a dozen or so trailers and motor homes, and asked how a stranger could sneak in during broad daylight without being seen. How did he know that one of the *gringos* didn't do it, perhaps inadvertently? With tight lips, he replied, "They wouldn't do that." A yachtie in a bar at Cabo San Lucas was complaining bitterly that the locals had stolen his dinghy, and we pointed out that fishermen, ranchers, bartenders, and cab drivers have little use for tiny inflatables with two-horsepower engines. Wasn't it more probable that one of his fellow yachties had made off with it? After all, there were 50 or 60 yachts anchored nearby. The answer was the same, "They wouldn't do that." These two men expected to have trouble with the locals, and when they thought it had happened, it colored their judgment.

Newspapers sometimes contribute to this exaggerated outlook. Back a number of years ago, the San Diego papers blared out "American Woman Killed in Baja California!" It made you want to grit your teeth and say, "They have gone and done it again, killing one of our people." Only by careful reading could you discover that her American husband had allegedly done the deed one night in their RV. Americans love to write letters to newspapers and travel publications on how they think they were cheated out of a dollar or two, and they often get published.

Getting into and out of trouble

The things that are illegal in Baja are probably the same sorts of things that are illegal in your home town. The most common causes of jail sentences or deportation are possession of recreational drugs, problems resulting from alcohol consumption, and working without a permit. Public drunkenness is against the law in Mexico. Leave your stash and your nose candy at home—offenders found guilty of possessing more than a token amount of any narcotic substance, including marijuana and cocaine, are subject to a minimum sentence of 10 years—read it again: a minimum sentence of 10 years—and it is not uncommon for persons charged with drug offenses to be detained for up to a year before a verdict is reached. Worldwide, Mexico has the highest number of arrests of Americans abroad—over 1,000 per year—and the highest prison population of Americans outside the US, about 450 at any one time. Jailbirds are not coddled in Mexico—the sign "municipal dump" pointing to the Ensenada prison says it all.

Most legal rights enjoyed in the US are also found in Mexico, and except for voting and such things, foreigners (you) have virtually the same rights as citizens, but there are important procedural differences. If you need help, there is a American Consulate General in Tijuana, and a new American Consular Agency has opened in Cabo San Lucas (the old office in Mulegé has been closed). The State Department maintains a Citizen's Emergency Center in Washington, DC, which can be reached by telephone. Both the state of Baja California [Norte] and the state of Baja California Sur have established offices to provide free legal assistance to visitors, the *Procuraduría de Protección al Turista* (Attorney General for the Protection of Tourists), with offices in Tijuana, Mexicali, Ensenada, Rosarito, Tecate, San Felipe, and La Paz. In the towns and villages, civil authority is exercised by the *delegado*, an elected official who can be found at the *delegación municipal* (the equivalent of city hall) or the *subdelegación* building. In remote areas, a local citizen may be appointed to similar duties.

● ●

❝ *Jumping to conclusions*

Things don't always go smoothly on Baja trips. During one recent foray to Ensenada, Judy and I got diarrhea in a Mexican restaurant, were besieged by aggressive beggars in the parking lot, got back to our four-wheel-drive to find that our camera equipment has been looted, and had to deal

with surly and disinterested police who could hardly speak English. I was angry until our American insurance company reminded me that the theft clause in our home policy insured the equipment for replacement value, not its depreciated value. So, in trade for 3 cameras—battered, salt-encrusted, dust-filled, 10-year-old wrecks—and 5 lenses of corresponding condition, worth $300 total at most, I got $6,000 worth of brand-new equipment. The thieves had done us a great favor!

Oh yes, I forgot to mention where the unhappy tale reiterated in this little story took place: in Sacramento, the capitol of Alta California, on our way home from Ensenada. ❞
——*Walt*

● ●

Mechanical problems

If you encounter a mechanical problem, all is not lost. Often a little ingenuity can overcome seemingly insurmountable problems. On a trip a number of years ago, the main leaf on a spring of our boat trailer broke, and it looked like we were in trouble—how do you fix a spring or get a replacement in the geographic center of the Baja boondocks? Things looked bad, but after a few minutes of deep thought, we came up with an idea: a temporary repair could be made by removing a U-bolt from a bracket holding the boat winch and using it to shackle the axle to the frame. We had to keep our speed down, but the repair held together for the next 800 miles until we reached home.

Sometimes it pays to take the initiative in making repairs, even if you are not a skilled mechanic. After crossing a knee-deep stream a half-dozen times early one morning, Rob and I (Walt) looked back to see huge clouds of black smoke coming from the left side of our trailer: water had entered the bearing assembly. The bearings and races were melted, the seal was shot, the bearing cap was missing, and the electric brake mechanism was an unrecognizable mess of melted insulation and copper. The problem was not in understanding the various mechanisms—anyone with a basic familiarity with electrical and mechanical matters could easily diagnose the problem. The real problem was simply getting parts. Rather than twiddling our thumbs for days while the local mechanic obtained them, we parked the trailer in a safe place off the road, removed the damaged parts, and I headed for San Diego, while Rob stood guard. I arrived back the following evening, and an hour later we were underway again.

Parts stores in Baja tend to be small, often with incomplete inventories, but they can obtain what you need, given enough time, and you might find gas regulators in general and hardware stores, and potable water pumps and other useful gadgets in marine supply stores. A few marine parts stores, several marinas, and the parts departments at some auto dealerships have limited parts for small boat and

Why fix it here? Because the nearest VW dealer is 400 miles away

utility trailers, such as bearings, springs, tires, wheels, and bunker rollers, and their mechanics should be able to get you going again. There is an RV parts and repairs company, Happy Campers, in Ensenada that may be able to help. They do work on appliances, awnings, generators, electrical systems, plumbing, LPG systems, and air conditioning, and they offer mobile service, where they come to you. See the index and Appendix C for these sources of parts. Specialized, nonstandard parts for large trailers, four-wheel-drives, motor homes, and diesel vehicles, and all parts for off-brand vehicles will almost certainly have to be obtained north of the border.

If you have a mechanical problem you cannot personally deal with, cultivate the ability to wait patiently and be prepared for a certain amount of hassle. There are automobile dealerships with modern repair shops in some of the larger towns. Even some of the smallest settlements have a mechanic, but he is sometimes not in business full-time and may not have a sign posted. While these men often show great ingenuity, parts may take a week to get, and they can do little with electronic ignition, smog-control, or fuel-injector problems. They do not have machine-shop equipment needed for turning down brake drums and discs, planing down warped heads, or facing off flywheels. Work on automatic transmissions must be scrupulously clean, a practical impossibility in rural locations. The town/city maps show the location of many mechanics, dealers, and parts stores, and many are mentioned in the text; see the index.

If needed parts are not available locally, there is a quick way to get them: telephone a dealer in the US, order what you want, have it shipped to you by way of DHL Worldwide Express, and pay for the parts, shipping, and customs with a credit card. DHL has offices in Tijuana, Mexicali and La Paz (addresses and telephone numbers in Appendix C), and delivery time is normally only a day or two. DHL can also provide delivery to other locations; for instance, the La Paz office can deliver to San José del Cabo, Cabo San Lucas, Todos Santos, and Ciudad Constitución; the Tijuana office to Tecate, Ensenada, and Maneadero; and the Mexicali office to San Felipe. Local delivery to these towns usually adds a day or two. NorthSouth de Mexico can provide air service direct to you at Los Cabos. They receive shipments at their facility at Los Angeles International Airport from anywhere is the US, and will process and translate all customs documentation and clear the shipment through Mexican Customs. In addition, if you provide them with a description of what you need, they will contact the supplier directly. They accept Visa and MasterCard, and their telephone numbers will be found in Appendix C.

The famous Green Angel patrol operates over most highways in Baja. It consists of a fleet of green pickups, the driver of each being hopefully proficient in English. They can assist with minor repairs, provide small parts, sell gas and oil at cost, and arrange for towing and repairs. Although some routes are patrolled twice a day in mainland Mexico, in Baja it is more often once a day. Tow trucks are based in the border cities, Rosarito, Ensenada, San Quintín, San Felipe, Guerrero Negro, San Ignacio, Santa Rosalía, Loreto, Ciudad Constitución, La Paz, San José del Cabo, and Cabo San Lucas. If you or someone nearby is bilingual, or if you get along well with Appendix E, simply look in the Yellow Pages under *Grúas*, *Servicios* and make your own arrangements by telephone. If not, seek help from the State Secretary of Tourism, a Green Angel, or any civil authority.

Fuel and service

Petroleum products are sold by PEMEX, a government monopoly. In the US, service stations may be available on all four corners of an intersection, each competing vigorously by offering clean rest rooms, computer-assisted tune ups, parts, and repair services, as well as gas and oil. Operating under monopoly conditions, PEMEX does not find it necessary to work so hard. Stations rarely offer more than gas, oil, and a small selection of filters, additives, fan belts, and minor parts. Multi-grade oils and oils of 30 weight and less are hard to find. Encountering an operational rest room is a cause for surprise, and one both clean and operational is reason for an immediate telegram to the Miracles Department at the Vatican. If you are lucky enough to find a suitable rest room, don't press things too far—bring your own toilet paper. PEMEX does not take plastic, so payment must be in cash. Dollars are usually accepted, but expect to get a poor exchange rate. Stations are rarely open all night and they offer no mechanical services; they are gas stations, not service stations—if you need mechanical assistance you go to a mechanic. Attendants pump the gas, but you will probably have to check your own oil and tire pressure, and many stations do not have an air compressor.

Mexican gasoline comes in two grades, Nova and Magnasin. Lead-free Magnasin is dispensed from a green pump, currently costing about $1.10/gallon. Because local demand for expensive Magnasin is low, it is frequently unavailable in the boondocks, but pumps have been installed at the La Pinta hotels at San Quintín, Cataviña, and San Ignacio (the pump at the hotel in Guerrero Negro is currently out of operation). They are available to all travelers, not just hotel guests. Coming from a blue pump, Nova is leaded and, at $1.06 per gallon, is a bit cheaper than Magnasin. However, since it raises havoc with catalytic converters, it is false economy to use Nova. Diesel is available at many PEMEX stations, dispensed out of a red pump, and some drivers claim that it is more readily available in Baja than in some parts of the US. It currently runs about $.86/gallon.

Mexicans chuckled when Chevy tried to market a car called "Nova" ("no-go" in Spanish). Did PEMEX know something when they gave the same name to their leaded gasoline? Is there hidden meaning in the name of Magnasin? Officially 87 octane, it is actually lower, leading to pinging problems in some engines. "Octane boosting" additives are available on both sides of the border. We have never found one that made the slightest improvement, although some people report success with JB Gas Treatment and Moroso.

Chapters 4 through 7 identify all PEMEX stations known to be in operation in Baja south of the border cities, and their locations are also shown on the town/city maps. The text identifies the types of fuel normally available as M (Magnasin), N (Nova), and D (diesel).

Liquified petroleum gas

The LPG sold in Baja is not 100% propane. To enable excess quantities of butane produced by the manufacture of gasoline to be disposed of, butane and other gases are often mixed with propane in Mexico. The amount of butane present varies widely from place to place and time to time. The characteristics of butane are quite different than those of propane, but the mixture seems to have no major adverse effects on refrigerators, stoves, water heaters, or other appliances designed for straight propane. On a very cold night, your RV furnace and water heater might have trouble keeping up with the demands placed on them, but given Baja's climate, this should not be a cause for concern.

In most large towns, cylinders can be filled at LPG yards, the locations of which are identified in Chapters 4 through 7. Although villages often lack an LPG pump, they can sometimes provide gravity fills, but it will not be possible to completely fill the tank. LPG is not available at PEMEX stations.

On the road

Use a checkoff list to insure that your rig is ship-shape before you depart each morning. Drawers and cabinets should locked, equipment properly stowed, and the refrigerator door pinned. Inspect the hitch and check all tires with an air gauge,

or whack them with a hammer, trucker style. Make sure that the tongue jack is fully up and that all trailer lights are working, including stop and directional signals. To avoid loss of a wheel or enlargement of lug holes, especially in aluminum wheels, check all nuts at least once a week. Walk around the rig after doing some driving and check for over-heated bearings: if it's too hot to keep your hand on it, something is amiss. Keep the tie-downs holding trailer-borne equipment like boats and motorcycles tight. If you are towing another vehicle, it will probably be necessary to detach at almost every RV park, since most do not have pull-through sites.

From both the ecological and the social standpoints, the best place to dump sewage is at a dump station. However, if the circumstances are such that you must do it elsewhere, gopher holes should be dug for black water. Since soft ground is easily found, this is ordinarily not a big chore. Before you depart fill it in, tamp it down, and return the area to its prior condition. Gray water can be dumped in a gravel or sand area away from the road and settled areas without lasting harm.

Mexicans have driving habits that are distinctly different from those of Americans and Canadians. They often use the left-turn signal for highly ambiguous purposes, such as signaling a left turn to show that it is safe for you to pass. Intended as a courtesy, this signal can be dangerous. We have seen this signal from a vehicle moving at highway speed and have started to pass, only to have the vehicle swerve into a left turn, its brake lights out of operation. In periods of reduced visibility, truckers often signal a left turn to oncoming traffic to mark the left margin of their rigs, since their clearance lights are sometimes burned out. We once had an oncoming trucker signal a left during a rainstorm, only to have him suddenly swerve left in front of us, leaving us shaken and angry in the ditch. Both the "safe-to-pass" and "left-side" signals should be greeted with great suspicion—don't leave the driving to others.

Some of the locals are poor drivers, with no training and little experience, and although Baja's increasing prosperity is making them less common each year, a small percentage of vehicles are in very poor condition, with bad brakes, worse tires, and headlights missing or out of adjustment. Their low beams are sometimes burned out, and in approach situations they will sometimes turn off their high-beams in an effort to avoid blinding you, a startling courtesy. What appeared to be an approaching motorcycle once blinded me (Walt) with his high beam. When he switched to low beam, he suddenly seemed to swerve across the road. To avoid a head-on crash I swerved right and thumped across the desert for 50 yards. I was cursing all the world's motorcyclists as he sped away, until I saw a pair of tail lights and realized what had happened; it was a pickup with burned-out right low-beam and left high-beam lights.

Driving the Transpeninsular

Paved road systems have existed in the northern part of Baja Norte and the southern part of Baja Sur for many years, but it was not until 1973 that the Transpeninsular Highway was finally completed. The only paved road extending the length of the peninsula, the Transpeninsular was built to modest engineering specifications. It is narrower than its counterparts north of the border, shoulders are often nonexistent, striping and safety signs are normally absent, and culverting and drainage are poor. The subbase is inadequate and the paving thin, and heavy traffic quickly produces a moonscape of potholes. However, in recent years the government has made an effort to upgrade the highway. Concrete bridges have been completed at a number of stream crossings that used to cause trouble after rains, and parts of the highway are even beginning to sport center lines and warning signs.

Do not depend on finding gasoline at every station along the Transpeninsular, especially on long holidays and during winter. The PEMEX stations at El Rosario, Cataviña, Parador Punta Prieta, and Villa Jesús María are remote from shipping terminals, and tank trucks are sometimes delayed by mechanical, weather, or road problems. Some stations depend on locally generated electricity, often produced by tiny gasoline-driven generators, and if these will not run there is usually no way to operate the pumps. A pump failure once put the station at Cataviña out of operation for two months. If one station can't pump gas, those on both sides quickly run out, and problems spread like falling dominoes. The basic rule for drivers in the notorious "gas gap" between San Quintín and Guerrero Negro is to top off at every opportunity.

There are two basic safety rules on the Transpeninsular: never speed and never drive at night. Speeds over 45 are too fast everywhere, and even 30 is sometimes excessive. Some of Baja is just plain boring, the Transpeninsular between Guerrero Negro and San Ignacio perhaps the most so, but resist the temptation to press on the gas. The Transpeninsular is being kept in better condition than in previous years, but potholes can quickly develop, and fate seems to have placed them at points where it is too late to slow down by the time you see them, especially if you are towing a big trailer rig. If you are taking even a few heavy blows from potholes, you are driving too fast and are risking loss of control, blowouts, and broken springs.

The second rule—never drive at night—is often ignored, but those who do so are simply not familiar with the hazards of the Transpeninsular in the dark. Much of Baja is open, unfenced range land, and cattle, horses, burros, and goats often wander onto the highway. Two experiences have made us believers. We were zipping along at 40, a speed that would probably have been safe on a paved rural road at night in the US, when suddenly an apparition appeared in front of us. I (Walt) could not tell what it was, and I had a few tenths of a second to decide what to do. Brakes locked and tires smoking, we skidded to within inches of a very large cow. The critter was black, entirely black except for the whites of her eyes, making her almost invisible in the pitch-black night. A week later, a bit wary but still

unconvinced, we were again driving at night, when we came upon a series of burning flares leading to an 18-wheeler stopped in the middle of the road. The truck had hit—yes!—a black cow, apparently at high speed. The cow would not have even made good hamburger, and the damage to the truck was unbelievable. The heavy front bumper looked like it had been made of aluminum foil, and the grill had been smashed back, crushing the radiator against the engine block, which in turn was driven into the firewall.

RV parks in Baja California

Anticipating a flood of visitors from north of the border upon completion of the Transpeninsular, a series of RV parks was constructed along the way. However, as so often happens in Mexico, the hopes of the well-intentioned government planners were not realized. Many of the parks were in remote locations, far from the power lines and reliable sources of water. Buildings housing bathrooms and laundry facilities were lightly constructed, and the plumbing seemed to have been designed by xenophobes hoping to save Mexico for the Mexicans. Sources of spare parts and supplies were many miles away, and water pumps, water heaters, and diesel generators were frequently out of operation for weeks or even months at a time. In addition, little attention was paid to developing the infrastructure of restaurants, stores, and other attractions necessary to attract visitors. Finally, many people north of the border knew little about the place beyond that it had first-rate fishing and fourth-rate roads. The information available to most was obtained from magazine articles and books telling adventurous tales of broken axles, of hours spent digging out of sandy washes, and of days spent traveling a dozen miles. While this colorful reputation was an attraction to a few, it was a source of apprehension to many.

For these reasons and many others, the expected crowds never materialized. Many of the government parks have been abandoned, a few of which have been taken over by *paracaidistas* (squatters, literally "parachutists"). Some of these parks struggle along, but finding one with electricity, water, or an operational toilet is akin to winning the California lottery, and one with all three a source of unrestrained joy. Those traveling on the Transpeninsular will search in vain for an attractive, fully operational, full-service RV park in the long stretch between San Quintín and Santa Rosalía. North and south of this area, the situation has greatly improved, not due to the efforts of the government, but rather to private enterprise, and you will find a wide variety of facilities, ranging from luxurious resorts to those offering little more than a place to spend the night. Some of them, especially along the Tijuana-Ensenada Toll Road, are every bit as good as the best in the US. If you are tent camping, or are sleeping on the ground while camping in a pickup or van, most will welcome your visit. The few parks that we know of that have a stated policy against tents or on-the-ground camping, all of them large and very expensive, are identified in the text. A number of places are rather vague about this, so don't be too surprised if things change.

The RV parks listed in later chapters have been rated as class A, B, or C, based on the scope of facilities provided, ambiance, cleanliness, state of repair, cost, and recreational activities available in the park or nearby. (The ratings are alphabetized to avoid confusion with the scheme used for classifying roads, which is numerical.) Very simply, a class A park is highly recommended, a class B park is satisfactory, and a class C park leaves much to be desired and is generally included because little else is available in the vicinity or because the cost is are very low.

Except during holidays and vacation periods, reservations are not normally required for most Baja RV parks. However, if you want to be sure space is available, call or write to the parks at the addresses shown in Appendix C. If you belong to Good Sam, the Vagabundos del Mar, or a similar club, if you are a senior citizen or if you plan to stay for more than a week or so, always ask if discounts are available.

RV parking and boondocking

The expressions "RV parking" and "boondocking" are used throughout the book. An RV parking site has few if any facilities, but you will be charged for its use, while a boondocking area has no facilities and will cost nothing, although you may be asked for a small fee by persons who empty trash and keep the place orderly. No other place on the continent has as many good boondocking sites, and later chapters identify them only if they are in strategic locations or are otherwise notable—there are simply too many to describe individually.

Bahía Concepción has a number of small coves with sandy beaches, a few equipped with **palapas**

Mail

Outside the larger towns, the post office is often in a small store, a tiny sign sometimes proclaiming "*Correo*,"

sometimes not. If you can't find it ask; everyone knows. Postage is very inexpensive. Hours of post office operation are erratic, and service ranges from mediocre to terrible. When addressing letters and packages, print clearly and avoid using middle names and initials. Delivery times to the US range as follows: from Ensenada 5 days; La Paz, Bahía de los Angeles, and Loreto 6; El Rosario 8; Bahía Asunción, Cabo San Lucas, and Bahía Tortugas 10; Mulegé and Guerrero Negro 13. Occasionally the delays can be horrendous; a series of letters, clearly and correctly addressed, and carrying the requisite postage, mailed to us from La Paz and Cabo San Lucas in February 1994, did not arrive at our home in Northern California until October. A letter addressed to a friend in Guerrero Negro came back 14 months later, stamped "box closed."

Because of the delays and unreliability of the postal system, the fax machine has become the preferred method of printed communication between the two sides of the border, and you will note that many of the businesses and organizations listed in Appendix C have fax numbers.

Telephone and telegraph

In the past, the telephone system in Baja provided poor service. However, automatic direct-dial equipment is being installed, and additional areas are getting service. The system has been privatized, which should speed further improvements.

Making a direct-dial phone call from the US or Canada to a location in Baja is simple. First, dial 011, telling the system that this is an international call, then the country code, which for Mexico is 52, and then the 2- or 3-digit city code (the equivalent of our area code). If it is a big city (those with two-digit city codes), the local number has six digits, otherwise it has five. Finally, dial the local number. Many Baja telephone numbers are listed in Appendix C in their full 13-digit form. Direct-dial calls from the US to Baja are a bit dear: a direct-dial call from our home in Northern California to Cabo San Lucas runs between $.80 and $1.27 a minute during working hours, depending on which company and billing plan we use, down to $.50 a minute at night and on weekends.

If you wish to make a call to the US or Canada while in Baja, the least expensive way to do it is to purchase a prepaid TELNOR card, available in 25, 35, and 50-peso denominations from many stores in Baja. These are designed to work in pay phones labeled LADATEL. Simply insert the card, dial 95 and the area code and number. When 20 seconds is left on the card's allotted time, a countdown will appear in the readout window.

Many pay phones will accept US credit cards or Mexican coins. However, things usually seem to go awry, and there are often long and unexplained silences, ending when a computer bursts in with rapid-fire instructions in Spanish. The simplest way for those who do not speak Spanish but want to make a credit card call is to use AT&T, Sprint, or MCI. Each company has a toll-free 800 number that can be dialed directly from Mexico: AT&T is 95-800-462-4240; Sprint 95-800-877-8000; MCI 95-800-950-1022. These numbers directly access company facilities in the US, and from that point things are routine; you can then dial the area code and number you are trying to reach and your credit card number, or, if you must, you can place a collect call. Placing calls with the three companies in this manner can be done from private phones at hotels and RV parks, or from many pay phones.

Direct-dialed credit card calls from Mexico to the US and Canada are more expensive that the TELNOR pre-paid calls. A series of Sprint calls to Northern California, normally made at night, from pay phones all over Baja during our 7,000-mile, 7-week trip in early 1995 averaged $1.10 a minute. A similar series of direct-dialed AT&T calls averaged $1.23 a minute, but since the calls over the two systems were from different locations in Baja, the difference is probably not meaningful. Operator-assisted and collect calls are much more expensive, and may involve a substantial surcharge: a number of AT&T operator-assisted calls from San Ignacio to Northern California cost us $1.70 a minute.

Large towns have telephone company offices, where international calls can also be made. There are also private long-distance stations in smaller towns, usually staffed with an operator and often located in a pharmacy or other business; look for the sign LARGA DISTANCIA. Many hotel operators can also place international calls. If you use the services of these private companies or a hotel operator, they will add a surcharge.

Capital Network, based in Austin, TX, provides the blue-colored phones seen throughout Baja, and offers service at some hotels. A call through Capital is extraordinarily dear—a 17-minute collect call from a hotel in Cabo San Lucas to Northern California using Capital Network cost us $77—that's no typographical error—$77: a $5 surcharge, $8 for the first minute and $4 for each succeeding minute. That's over $4.53 a minute! A 9-minute call from Loreto to Long Beach, CA costs over $45! A 17-minute direct-dialed AT&T credit card call from Cabo San Lucas to Northern California cost us a little over $17. A similar call from Cairo, Egypt to Northern California, at 7,450 miles away almost a third of the way around the world, cost us only $32.00. Thus, the service provided by Capital Network is very costly.

There are lessons to be learned: use a TELNOR pre-paid card if you can, make your calls at night, stick to direct-dial, avoiding operator-assisted and collect calls, and before you call, make sure you know what carrier will be used, and

if it is Capital Network ask for another carrier, send a post card, try transcendental communication, or send a carrier pigeon.

Local and long-distance calls within Mexico are relatively inexpensive. All the Baja numbers listed in Appendix C are listed in their full 13-digit, international-call form. To make a call to one of these numbers from within the same city code, just dial the last five digits (six in Tijuana and Mexicali). A call to a number outside the local area code requires the last eight digits.

Although public telephone service is absent in small villages along the Transpeninsular, many have at least one official telephone, often located in the *delegación municipal* building, which might be made available in an emergency. Phone service is slowly being extended to the hinterlands—remote Bahía de los Angeles now has its first satellite telephones.

As noted in the previous chapter, cellular phone service is available in the Tijuana, Rosarito, Ensenada, and Mexicali areas by a company named, appropriately enough, Baja Cellular. The distance outside these cities from which calls can be placed varies, but hot-tubbers at the Guadalupe campground, 40 miles south of Mexicali, claim they have been able to reach their astrologers with few difficulties. In the La Paz and Los Cabos area, the service is also provided by Baja Cellular. You can register at any of their offices when you arrive and be put on roaming status. The altitude of the antennas is high enough at the Cape that the service extends well off-shore, and if you catch a marlin you can immediately call the gang at work to brag. In fact, why not dial them up when you make the hook-up and give them a blow-by-blow account?

Telegrams can be sent to and from over 40 locations in Baja, including all the larger cities and many villages, right down to small places like Bahía Tortugas, Puerto López Mateos, Punta Abreojos, La Purísima, and the Comondús. Western Union can handle telegraphic money orders to all these locations.

Money and credit cards

Although dollars are accepted almost everywhere, the Mexican national currency is pesos, and that is what the locals use and understand. If you use dollars, businessmen outside of the major tourist towns often do not know the current exchange rate, and will protect themselves by requiring an unfavorable exchange rate. If the person is dishonest, the transaction provides an opportunity for flim-flam. Most money problems can be avoided by a simple expedient: convert some of your money to pesos. The decimal system is used and is easy to understand, and since almost all businesses make change in pesos anyway, you would soon be dealing with an impossible mix of pesos and dollars whether you liked it or not. If this makes you uncomfortable, use a calculator to figure the dollar equivalent of each purchase. The conversion can be made at numerous money-changing offices in most tourist towns, at all border crossings, and at banks throughout Baja. You can convert pesos back to dollars when you return. There is competition, so shop around for the best rates. Hotels and airports offer the worst rates.

The peso comes in a variety of denominations, but don't believe that all bills of a given denomination are the same size, or that the larger the bill, the higher the denomination. The 10- and 20-peso notes, for instance, come in 2 sizes, the larger size being also larger than the 50-peso note. One-, 2-, and 5-peso coins have a brass center with a silvery periphery, while the 20-peso coin has a silvery center and a brass periphery. "Old peso" bills and coins are still in circulation, so make sure you get new pesos when someone is making change; there is a 1,000 to 1 difference between the two. One day we rewarded a small volunteer windshield washer at a PEMEX station with a large handful of "old-peso" coins. We thought we were being generous, but got a very sour look. The peso is in great danger of further loss of value, so don't convert large amounts into pesos or plan to hold them for long periods. Get your pesos in small denominations, for many small businesses and gas stations can't make change for large notes.

It is difficult to cash personal checks in Baja, so the remainder of what you expect to spend should be converted to small-denomination traveler's checks from large, well-recognized institutions such as Bank of America or American Express. Many tourist establishments will honor major credit cards, but don't plan to use them in smaller towns, or at businesses catering to the local people. ATM machines are being installed in the larger towns, dispensing pesos.

Launch ramps

A few of the ramps in Baja, the one at Puerto Escondido for instance, are as good as anything north of the border, but most leave something to be desired. The most common problem is that waves have undermined the outer end, providing a big surprise as you back the trailer out. In addition, the northern Cortez is subject to enormous tides, often leaving the toe of the ramp a great distance from the water at low tide. All ramps in East Cape and San Felipe are in exposed locations, making it difficult to launch and retrieve when a sea is running, especially with a trailer with no guideboards. The slope of the ramp can make things difficult: below about a 12% minimum, the boat may not float off the trailer until the back of the tow vehicle is in the salt water. If the ramp is too steep, above about 15%, getting enough traction to pull the boat out is difficult, especially when the bottom of the ramp is covered with slippery vegetation.

For trailer-sailors with relatively small boats, these ramp problems are minor nuisances at the most. Skippers of large boats, especially those with deep-V hulls, have more significant problems, just as they do with ramps in the US. The ramp may not extend far enough to permit such boats to float off the trailer before the paving ends, especially at low tides, putting trailer wheels into the mud and sand. If the end of the ramp is undermined, getting the trailer wheels up

on the concrete again can be a problem. The best advice is to inspect the ramp thoroughly, and plan to launch and to try to retrieve at high tides.

Later chapters describe every paved ramp open to public use known to exist in Baja. Those in excess of 15% are termed "steep," while those of less than 12% are termed "shallow." There are, of course, many rock, hard clay, and sand areas where boats can be launched, too many to list individually. However, some are in important locations that have no other launch facilities, and are therefore identified and described.

Safe boating

Most sailors recognize the inherent dangers of Baja's Pacific coast and keep their guard up, but the tranquil conditions prevalent in the Cortez can lull you into believing that things are always like that. Don't believe it! The Cortez can turn from flat calm to whitecaps in minutes, just like any other large body of water, and high winds are not always accompanied by dark clouds. There are three basic rules for safe boating in Baja: make sure your boat is in top condition and is equipped with all safety equipment; operate it in a prudent and conservative manner consistent with the weather, the boat's capabilities, and the skipper's experience; and always file a written "flight plan" before you depart. This should describe the boat and list everyone aboard, note where you are going, the time (and date if applicable) you expect to return, and the time (and date) the person receiving the plan should "press the panic button" and act to obtain assistance if you fail to return. Leave this with someone you trust, perhaps a fellow RVer who plans to remain in the area, or the manager of the RV park you are staying at.

Boaters in Mexican waters will not find the extensive communications and rapid response they expect from the Coast Guard in American waters. The Mexican Navy provides search and rescue (SAR) services when vessels or aircraft are available, and Captain of the Port offices sometimes have boats or can arrange for local assistance. Under a bilateral agreement between the US and Mexico, the US Coast Guard can provide limited SAR coverage off the west coast of Mexico, directed by the Coast Guard Command Center in Long Beach, CA. Surface units, fixed-wing aircraft and helicopters from San Diego normally can respond to SAR cases as far south as Isla Cedros, and C-130s from Sacramento can operate the length of the peninsula and beyond.

The Coast Guard can be contacted on VHF channel 16, often as far south as Ensenada. Many other organizations guard VHF channel 16, including Mexican government coastal radio stations at Ensenada, La Paz, Guaymas, and Mazatlán; COTP offices; offices and vessels of the Mexican ferry system; commercial shipping; Mexican naval vessels and bases; and a few marinas. Some operators speak English, although not necessarily fluently. As noted earlier, many other organizations and individuals guard various CB channels.

Oh, no. Not the fuel pump again!

Motorcycles, ATVs, and dune buggies

Once riding in Baja, the uniform of the day should be a helmet, eye protection, gloves, and boots suitable for hiking, just like in *El Norte*. Use sunblock and lip balm generously. Keep your speed down and avoid sharp turns and hard braking. In dusty conditions check the oil level, wash the air cleaner, and lube and adjust the chain every day. Engine oil is a major determinant of engine life, and in dusty conditions a change every 200 miles would not be excessive. A breakdown in the desert can be a more serious proposition than one in a truck, so file a "flight plan," and carry adequate food and water. As noted in the previous chapter, all Baja dogs hate all motorcycles. It seems to be the exhaust noise, so stop, turn the engine off, and they normally end the chase. If not, your can of Halt will almost certainly solve the problem.

Safe diving

When diving out of a boat, always leave someone aboard who knows how to operate it, and use a long trailer line. A diver's knife is essential: there has been an explosive growth of fishing in most of Baja's waters, and there is a remote danger of becoming entangled in a length of monofilament line or a gill net. Although shark incidents are remarkably few, there are large numbers present in some locations, and standard avoidance techniques found in any good dive manual should be followed. All in all, the greatest dangers to divers in Baja are self-inflicted: inadequate equipment, poor training, overexertion, foolishness, and running into cows while unwisely driving at night on the Transpeninsular.

The laws of physics and physiology have not been repealed, and divers can get the bends as easily in Baja as anywhere else. There are two privately owned decompres-

sion chambers in Baja Sur, one at La Paz and one in Cabo San Lucas. In Baja Norte, the nearest reliable chamber is at Hyperbaric Technology, Inc. in San Diego. Chambers also exist at El Rosario, Isla Cedros, Isla Natividad, and Bahía Tortugas. These are owned by the local fishing cooperatives, which may not operate year-around, and some compressors use locally generated electricity or small gasoline engines. Some are in a state of disrepair and are not equipped with filters, heating, or intercoms, and qualified operators and adequate medical attention are virtually nonexistent. Except in the most dire of emergencies, you should not depend on these chambers. The chamber at Punta Eugenia, near Bahía Tortugas, appears to be permanently out of operation. A chamber has been installed in San Carlos, but its operational status is unclear.

Safe surfing and boardsailing

A surfing or boardsailing trip to the regions south of Ensenada is a very different proposition than a day-trip to San Miguel. There are no Coast Guard stations your buddies can call when a rip tide carries you out to sea, and medical attention for bumps, bangs, and sea urchin stabs can be a day away. There is an extensive lobster fishery along Baja's Pacific coast, and pots are sometimes anchored in or drift into surfing and boardsailing areas, their buoy lines waiting to ensnare the unwary. Because of wind-chill, a wet suit is a necessity on both coasts. Watch for changes in wind direction, especially if you aren't big on tacking your sailboard, and for increases in velocity. Unless you like being stranded miles from camp, don't stray too far on your sailboard, certainly not in areas with heavy currents, for Baja winds, especially in the Cortez, can drop to nothing in minutes.

Staying well

Apply your sunscreen before exposure. At the latitudes of Baja (the lower the latitude the more intense the sun), a dark-skinned person will begin to burn in 50 to 55 minutes, a fair-skinned person in only 12, more quickly near the water. If you start using a sunscreen, keep using it, for it offers no residual protection and your skin will not have had a chance to acclimate to the sun. No matter how good your sunscreen is, nor how religiously you apply it, wear a hat, a long-sleeved shirt, and long pants. Also, be careful of exposed feet: sunburned feet can be very painful, especially when returned to the confines of shoes. If you do get burned, get out of the sun and apply cool, wet dressings. To avoid infection do not break blisters, but instead let them dry up naturally.

As mentioned in the previous chapter, the water gets most of the blame for diarrhea, but since safe bottled water is widely available, there is no reason to get sick by this means. Don't forget about the purity of ice. If you have a propane refrigerator with a freezer, make your own ice for drinks out of purified water. If you have only a cooler, be very careful with block ice, for it is usually not made from purified water. Keep food in contact with the ice in Ziplocks, and carefully wipe dry cans and bottles that get wet. Cube ice can be obtained in plastic bags in many stores, but look for the word *purificada* (purified) on the bag.

There are other causes of diarrhea, but you can easily make yourself virtually diarrhea-proof: avoid greasy, highly seasoned, and unaccustomed foods; wash, peel, and/or cook all fresh food; and take care in selecting restaurants. Also, according to recent articles in the scientific literature, studies have shown that two of the most common diarrhea-causing bacteria, *Shigella* and *Salmonella*, are vulnerable to alcohol. So if you want to take a tot or two of tequila or several margaritas with your meals, you now have a scientific excuse. If you do get diarrhea and there are no unusual symptoms, take your Imodium A-D according to the instructions on the box, get plenty of rest, and practice diet control. Drink plenty of fruit juices and treated water, and avoid milk and diuretics like coffee and tea.

Should you need medical attention, you will find doctors, clinics, and hospitals in many locations; see the text and the town/city maps. There are also numerous dentists and opticians. Many doctors and dentists speak English, but few opticians and pharmacists do. Not to worry, for Appendix E has the Spanish translation of words for many common problems, illnesses, and medicines, complete with model sentences and their phonetic pronunciation. Should things become serious and the medical facilities in Baja prove to be inadequate, all is not lost—Air-Evac International, Inc. and Critical Air Medicine specialize in transporting critically ill and injured patients to the US by aircraft, and both operate throughout Baja.

Staying clean

Laundromats can be found from the border to San Quintín, and from Santa Rosalía to the Cape. In between you may be able to find a traditional Mexican washerwoman, and some hotels, motels, and RV establishments provide laundry service if you are a guest. If you are boondocking, fresh water will be scarce, but there is plenty of salt water, so use it for bathing. Vel, a solid detergent bar widely available in Baja, washes human bodies satisfactorily in saltwater, but to avoid a sticky film, don't air-dry yourself, use a towel. Joy dishwashing detergent has long been the standard among yachtsmen for washing dishes in saltwater, so try it out.

Caring for your pet

Once in Mexico, some precautions are necessary concerning the health and well-being of your pet. Do not leave it in a confined space in a car, truck, or trailer, never allow it to roam at will, and never keep it leashed outside unattended, for the local coyotes are always on the lookout for such tender morsels such as Chihuahuas and Persians. To avoid territorial fights, don't allow your dog to mingle with the local curs. Provide safe drinking water and prevent your pet from drinking from stagnant pools.

Shopping for food and supplies

Supermarkets are found in the larger cities and towns. The privately owned stores are comparable in most respects to those north of the border, the CCC stores in La Paz being virtually indistinguishable. The government-sponsored CONASUPERs are large supermarkets, which carry a good selection of meat, fish, poultry, produce, dairy products, and other foods, as well as bottled drinks and water, and household items. Many towns have CONASUPOs, smaller versions of the CONASUPERs. Small, locally owned grocery stores with very limited inventories, can often be found in even the smallest villages. Many towns and settlements have a fruit store. They cater to the locals, and the quality is often suspect; apparently the best is exported. However, the prices are low. Some towns have small factories making tortillas and selling them at very low prices. The peninsula's small bakers turn out first-rate products, sometimes using stone ovens fueled with wood. They tend to have fewer products than their counterparts in the US, and those that are available tend to be simpler, with less fillings and sugar glazes—they are food, not breakfast candy. The bakery in Santa Rosalía has maintained an excellent reputation for more than a hundred years. "Store-bought" sliced breads such as Bimbo tend to have the consistency, taste, and appeal of library paste. If you are diabetic, are on a low-cholesterol or low-calorie diet, or otherwise require or prefer special foods, do not depend on finding them in Baja food stores—bring adequate supplies with you.

The meat found in Baja butcher shops is beef, lamb, and the other species found north of the border, but Mexican butchers often cut them in ways not recognizable to visitors. The Spanish word *carnicería* means both "butcher shop" and "massacre," which says a lot about what you will encounter in a search for a few good T-bones; the shop will indeed seem to be the scene of a massacre, or at least a terrible traffic accident. Restaurants claim they fly in "American-cut" steaks to feed the tourists, but the locals eat range cattle that have never seen a feed lot. The product is usually lean, which is better for you than the fat-marbled product you may be used to, and it is inexpensive. However, it is fairly tough, and a jar of Adolph's Meat Tenderizer is a welcome asset.

Seafood products are widely available in supermarkets and stores, sometimes from the fisherman himself. It is not unusual to encounter hawkers making their rounds, selling fresh fish, shrimp, pismo clams, or other species at relatively low prices.

Selecting a place to eat

The culinary arts have been practiced in Baja California for thousands of years, and great progress has been made since the days of the second harvest. Today's Baja explorers are greeted with a wide variety of foods, ranging from simple tortillas and beans up to such delicacies as sautéed frog legs and creamed quail. As expected, most restaurants serve

Booby parents protect their young from the gulls

Mexican cuisine, but many other culinary traditions are to be found, including Italian, French, German, Austrian, Chinese, Basque, Japanese, Moroccan, Argentine, American, International, and Continental. La Paz even has a vegetarian restaurant.

Despite this variety, it seems wise to stick to what intuition says the locals **ought** to cook best: seafood and Mexican dishes. Fish dinners can be superb, with fresh catch and excellent seasoning, often with lots of garlic. Mexican food prepared by Mexicans for Mexicans with ingredients from Mexico can be wonderful; the plastic-wrapped tortillas bought in American supermarkets are pale imitations of their cousins south of the border, and a simple tamale can be a dining experience to remember. The seafood/Mexican rule is not hard-and-fast: your intuition might cause you to have serious doubts about eating at a French restaurant in Baja, but El Rey Sol in Ensenada is absolutely first-class, with first-class prices to match, and if you hunger for the familiar, the burgers at the McDonald's in Ensenada are indistinguishable from the standard issue back home.

As we complained earlier, Mexico has not yet made progress in preparing French fries, and they are often mushy and greasy. However, the vegetables served in the better restaurants catering to tourists can be excellent, the vine-ripened tomatoes having little resemblance to their pale, tasteless, chemically treated counterparts north of the border. Nonsmokers will be unhappy with the air quality in many restaurants, but a few have established a smoker's apartheid.

Don't make snap judgments based on the outside appearance of restaurants, for they are often better inside than their outside appearance might suggest. Also, don't be mislead by a restaurant's name. These ought to provide potential diners with clues as to what might be expected: for instance, you might expect to be offered squid caviar at El Squid Roe in Cabo San Lucas, and you will not be completely disappointed—they at least offer squid fajitas. However, despite some exceptions, the restaurant owners of Baja seem to have a penchant for obscurity: La Cueva de los Tigres in Ensenada also specializes in seafood, but tigers eat meat, and there seems little reason to expect them to carry fish to their lairs. Should one expect Japanese food at the Callejon Tokio in Santa Rosalía? Does the Bismark II Restaurant in La Paz serve frankfurters and sauerkraut? Should you expect sushi at Restaurant Señor Sushi in Cabo San Lucas? Does the Iguana Restaurant in San José del Cabo serve lizard? Are the shrimp actually happy at being served up for supper at El Camarón Feliz in La Paz? Certainly no to the first four, and we suspect the answer is no to the fifth.

If you are in a remote region or a small town and want to eat out, the best, and often the only, choices are the restaurants in the La Pinta Hotels. The menu is standardized and unimaginative, and you will be paying tourist, not local, prices, but the food is usually good. If you are on a limited budget and can't stand your own cooking anymore, eat where the natives eat; try the small, inexpensive cafés, food stands, and taco shops seen in town squares and along the roads, but exercise caution and look for the presence of running water and refrigeration.

What's the best advice on selecting a restaurant? The chapters that follow provide a sampling of what is available in Baja, in a variety of price ranges and specialties. We have tried to be selective, but menus change and cooks get sick, tired, hired, and fired. Do what you would in an unfamiliar town back home: pick something that sounds good, read the menu posted at the front door, and if it agrees with you, walk in. If the place is neat and clean and the prices are right, stay and enjoy your meal; if not, walk out. Most importantly, don't ruin the fun by worrying, for most of the traditional tales of unhappy visitors with "the trots" involve amoebic dysentery acquired in mainland Mexico, not the occasional tummy upset in Baja due to the unfamiliar flora and fauna in the food.

If you sit at your table long after you have finished eating and the waiter has not brought the check, it is not sloth or forgetfulness. Unlike the US, where the waitress at Denny's has been trained to present the check as soon as possible to clear the booth for the next customer and keep the cash flow moving, in Mexico it is considered impolite to present the check until you have asked for it.

Living it up

Many hotels catering to Americans have discos, or live music and entertainment, and a few put on special events, such as the famous "pig-feed" (referring to the entrée, not the patrons) at the Hotel Serenidad in Mulegé, with its good food, live music, and lively crowd. Ensenada, San Quintín, Guerrero Negro, Rosarito, San Felipe, La Paz, San José del Cabo and Cabo San Lucas have discos, hangouts, and close approximations to north-of-the-border nightclubs. Hussong's Cantina in Ensenada is probably the best known bar in

Mexico, with the Giggling Marlin in Cabo San Lucas in hot pursuit. A number of these establishments will be described in later chapters.

Mexico brews excellent beer, including Tecate, Pacifico, Corona, Dos Equis, and Tres Equis. Local stores often carry beer, liquor, soda, and snack foods, but the cheapest place to buy beer is often the brewery's distributors; look for signs saying CERVECERÍA, AGENCIA, or SUBAGENCIA. Excellent grape wines are made in Baja Norte, including the Domecq, Valmar, and Santo Tomás brands.

Mexican tequila is great, at least after you have accepted the fact that it tastes like turpentine, and it seldom causes morning-after regrets. It is the basis, of course, for margaritas, but a few brave souls prefer it straight. It can go down more easily if you take a little salt first and a little lime later. Also, waiters and bartenders sometimes cover the top on the shot glass and give it a sharp whack on a table, causing the tequila to turn foamy white with air bubbles, which seems to smooth it out a bit. If you can't take it straight, try it with a little Viuda de Sanchez (Widow of Sanchez), the rather ominous brand name of a widely available chaser.

Treading lightly

You can do your bit to help keep Baja the marvelous place it is. If you have room to carry it into Baja, you surely have room to carry it out. By crushing or folding empty containers, your trash should require less than its original volume, not more. The perception that Mexicans are often the worst litter-bugs may be correct, but it is certainly no excuse. Do your best to leave nothing but foot- and tire prints and your smile for the locals to remember you by.

If you are overwhelmed by trash and must get rid of it before returning home, locate the dump used by the locals. However, such dumps are almost never bulldozed under, so items that might blow around, like Frito bags, Twinkie wrappers, and plastic milk and soda bottles, should be burned at the evening campfire.

If you build a fire, use the same place picked by your predecessor. If you want a fire on the beach, build it below the high tide mark, so the debris will eventually be carried away and dissipated. For the same reason, build fires at the bottoms of arroyos, not high on their slopes. If you burn trash, poke through the ashes the next morning to recover aluminum foil and other things that did not burn, and dispose of them properly.

Instead of limiting yourself to maintaining the status quo, why not try to make things better? If you finally park your rig at the secret beach that your brother-in-law claimed no one had ever visited before and find it littered, don't just stand around complaining, clean it up! Collect all plastic, paper, cardboard, rubber, cloth, rope, fishing line, nets, and man-made wooden objects and burn them. If you can, haul out unburnable objects to a proper disposal site. Set a goal—how about a "125%" policy; 100% of your trash and 25% more of that left by the inconsiderate oaf ahead of you? If you can't haul such trash, but are in a coastal area and have

a boat, place steel cans in the fire to burn off paper labels and corrosion coatings. Collect these cans and other metallic items from the fire debris, gather all glass containers and other items, and sink them in very deep water. Aluminum cans should be crushed and brought back, not sunk, for currents can carry them long distances underwater. The result of perhaps an hour's work will be an immaculate campsite you can enjoy for the remainder of your stay. If you are on a 10-day trip this will involve less than 0.5% of your time, a small price to pay for the sense of accomplishment it will bring. In addition, those who follow will be more likely to leave the campsite clean for your next visit.

Avoid driving off the paved and unpaved road system, for vegetation crushed under wheels may show no new growth for years, and wheel tracks can remain visible for generations. Ruts provide a channel for erosion, and some visitors returning after a number of years find a small canyon where they expected to find a road to the beach. And besides, millions of agave spines are waiting to fulfill their mission in life—puncturing your tires.

If you come upon a bird nesting area, avoid the temptation to get close for a better view. Most species react to humans as if they were large ground predators, and if disturbed, adults may abandon their eggs and chicks, leaving them vulnerable to hypo- and hyperthermia, falling off ledges, and other accidents. Gulls are major predators of the eggs and chicks of other species, and since they are less afraid of humans than other birds, they can be seen escorting visitors through nesting colonies, darting in to take advantage of every opportunity. Stay at least 100 yards away and use binoculars. You will have an adequate view of the birds going about their natural business of raising their young, rather than of frightened parents poised to take flight.

Never allow your pet to run loose, for its sake as well as for nesting birds, small land mammals, and other creatures. Be extremely careful when in the vicinity of seals and sea lions, for their sake as well as yours. In the wild they can be extremely shy, and if frightened they sometimes stampede for the safety of the sea, crushing pups and seriously injuring adults, some even throwing themselves off cliffs. If they feel cornered, they will defend themselves, moving with unexpected swiftness on land. Elephant seals may appear largely indifferent toward people, but during the breeding

Graffiti come to Baja

season males can be very aggressive. Although there seem to be no reports of attacks on humans, commercial divers give elephant seals healthy respect and a wide berth.

Information on fishing conservation will be found in Appendix A.

Bringing things back

Upon returning from Mexico, each person is currently allowed a maximum of $400 in duty-free personal and household goods, including one liter of alcoholic beverage, 100 cigars, and 200 cigarettes. The prior chapter mentions many items that are prohibited or restricted, so review that section before you cross the border, as well as your copy of *Know Before You Go* and, if you are Canadian, *Don't Bring It Back*.

There are American regulations concerning the importation of fish caught in Mexico. The Lacey Act authorizes border officers to enforce Mexican licensing and possession limits. A declaration must be filled out at the port of entry, and you must have a Mexican fishing license. The Mexican possession limit is the maximum that may be imported. An entry-dated tourist card, receipts, or other satisfactory proof of the time spent in Mexico must be available to import fish in excess of the daily limit.

• •

❝ *Night on the river*

I was far behind schedule and driving at night, a Baja no-no. It had been raining, and in the days before the bridge was built, the usually-dry Río Santa María south of San Quintín was sometimes the scene of floods, causing travelers long delays. It was pitch-black as I approached the crossing, and I could see several people standing under the canopy of a large motor home. Curious, I stopped and asked what was happening. The couple were on their first trip to Baja and were going to wait until dawn to cross. Sensing their concern at being stranded, I told them how experienced old-time Baja travelers handled such situations: remove the fan belt so the fan will not spray water on the engine, cover the distributor and coil with Baggies, and drive slowly at a steady speed. They watched attentively as I prepared my van, but

when I offered to ready their engine and escort them across the river, they demurred, saying that they were sure that I knew what I was doing, and although a number of RVs had started across in the last several hours, they preferred to wait.

As I pulled into the water, I beeped the horn and gave them a smile and jaunty wave. It was raining heavily and I could not see a dozen yards ahead, but the water was only about a foot deep and things were going well. As expected, the water slowly got deeper. About half-way across, my headlights lit up an awful scene; three motor homes and a pair of pickup campers, all stalled in the torrent. The unhappy motorists were milling about, trying to keep their balance as they figured out how to get their engines started. It was too late to show them how old-time Baja hands dealt with such problems, so I kept moving. However, as I continued, the engine began to sputter and my speed began to drop, and the engine finally stalled and refused to come to life.

There was to be little sleep that night. The rain drummed on the roof and the river kept rising, so I clambered around inside the van, moving vulnerable things to higher locations. The bottom of the van was soon awash, and the water was still rising. By midnight it was only a foot below my bunk, and I began to make preparations to bail out before the van was swept away. I opened the sliding door and emptied a five-gallon water jug to use as a life preserver. Six inches, 3 inches, then a half; when the water was even with the top of the bunk I was going to take my chances.

By two in the morning, luck was finally with me, and the water began to recede. By dawn it was less than a foot deep, and I got out and slogged over to a farmer sitting on a tractor on the far bank. The flood had been a financial bonanza; at 50 bucks a whack, I was the fifth to get a tow, and there were still three cars and two pickups upstream at another crossing. As the farmer's chain began to tighten and pull me ahead, I heard an air horn playing The Yellow Rose of Texas, *and my friends from the previous night pulled by, clean and dry, smiling and waving jauntily out the window of their motor home. ——Walt* ❞

• •

Chapter 4

Down the Transpeninsular— Baja California [Norte]

On the US-Mexican border at the San Ysidro crossing

Those crossing at Tecate should turn to page 169, and those at Mexicali to page 170. San Ysidro is open 24 hours a day, and is the busiest border crossing in the world. Those entering Mexico will normally encounter little delay; those returning to the US may wait in line for lengthy periods during business and rush hours, and at the end of holiday periods. Tourist cards can be obtained and validated at the Immigration office (1), located in a building on the right immediately south of the border. In past years, Tijuana had a dubious reputation, and many a young man has crossed the border from *El Norte* to receive his initiation into high times and the facts of life, but in recent years the place seems on its way to respectability. Tijuana is now a major city, and there are many restaurants, theaters, night clubs, and other facilities catering to visitors, and virtually any product or service you can think of is available. Information can be obtained at the tourism office (2) at the border crossing, and the Tijuana Tourism and Conventions Bureau offices down-town (3) and in San Diego. The Consulate General of the US is located in Colonia Hipódromo (5), and there is a Canadian Consulate (4).

If you are heading for Ensenada from the San Ysidro crossing, you should take the Tijuana-Ensenada Toll Road. The traffic pattern immediately south of the border crossing requires quick wits, since you must get in the correct lane on very short notice. Look for signs saying ENSENADA-ROSARITO and then ENSENADA CUOTA. After a dizzying counterclockwise overpass, you should end up going west on Carretera Internacional, paralleling and adjacent to the border fence. After the road climbs a hill and swings south, go right (west) at the first major interchange, and you will soon be on the Toll Road.

If the San Ysidro crossing is too intimidating, or if you wish to avoid the cost of the Toll Road (about $4 for cars, vans, and pickups, roughly twice that for motor homes and trailers), use the Otay Mesa crossing and head for the "Free Road" (Old Highway 1). Be aware, however, that this route involves dealing with some of the worst traffic in Tijuana. A description of this crossing and the Free Road begins on page 166.

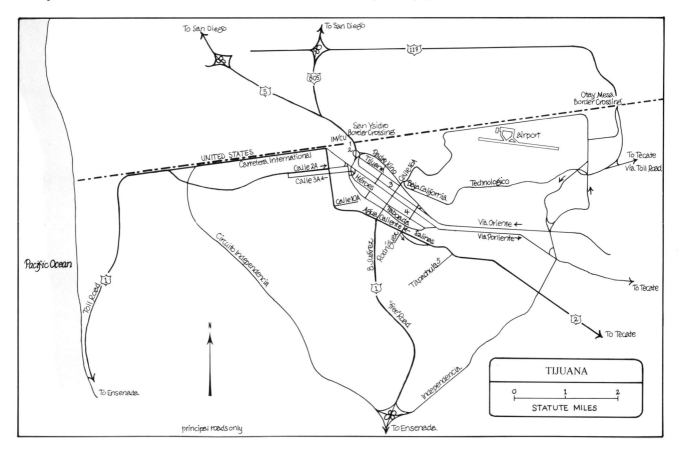

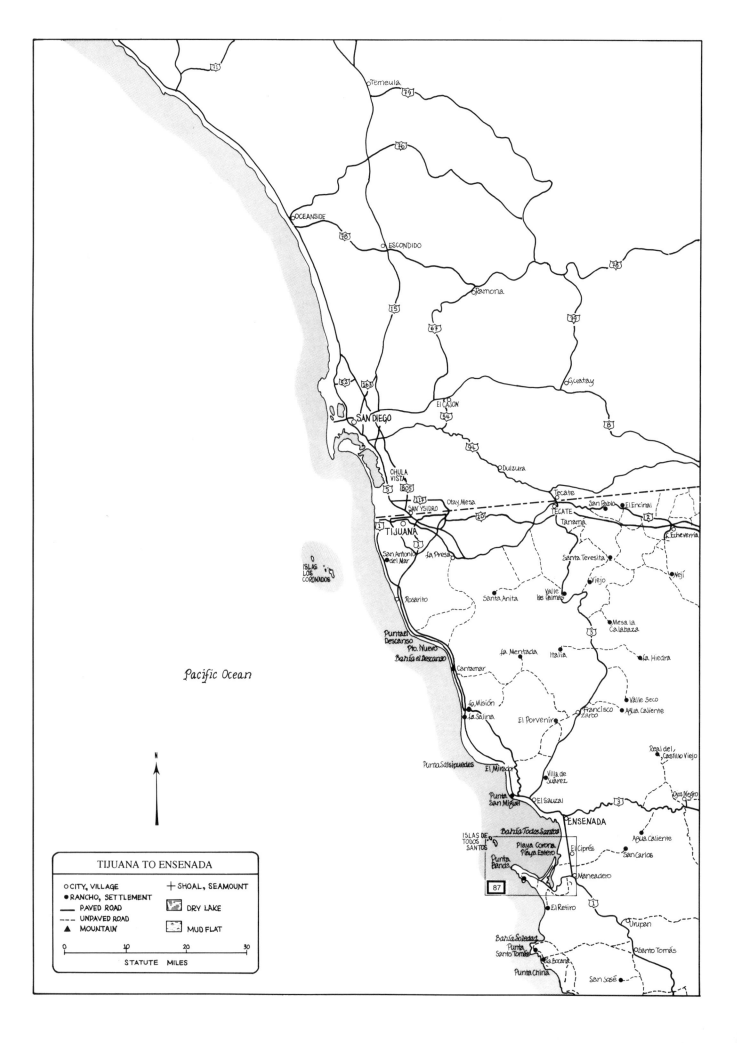

Pacific Ocean

TIJUANA TO ENSENADA

- ○ CITY, VILLAGE
- ● RANCHO, SETTLEMENT
- —— PAVED ROAD
- - - - UNPAVED ROAD
- ▲ MOUNTAIN
- ✛ SHOAL, SEAMOUNT
- DRY LAKE
- MUD FLAT

STATUTE MILES
0   10   20   30

Temecula

Oceanside

Escondido

Ramona

Guatay

El Cajon

San Diego

Dulzura

Chula Vista

Tecate

San Ysidro

Otay Mesa

San Pablo
El Encinal

TIJUANA

Tanamá

Echeverria

San Antonio
del Mar

La Presa

Santa Teresita

Neji

Viejo

Islas
Los
Coronados

Rosarito

Santa Anita

Valle
las Palmas

Mesa la
Calabaza

Punta el
Descanso

Pto. Nuevo

Bahía el Descanso

Cantamar

La Mentada

Italia

La Hiedra

La Misión

Valle Seco

La Salina

El Porvenir

Francisco
Zarco

Agua Caliente

Real del
Castillo Viejo

Punta Salsipuedes

El Mirador

Villa de
Suárez

Ojos Negro

Punta
San Miguel

El Sauzal

ENSENADA

Agua Caliente

Bahía Todos Santos

Islas de
Todos
Santos

Playa Corona
Playa Estero

El Ciprés

San Carlos

Punta
Banda

Maneadero

87

El Retiro

Urupan

Bahía Soledad

Punta
Santo Tomás

Santo Tomás

La Bocana

Punta China

San José

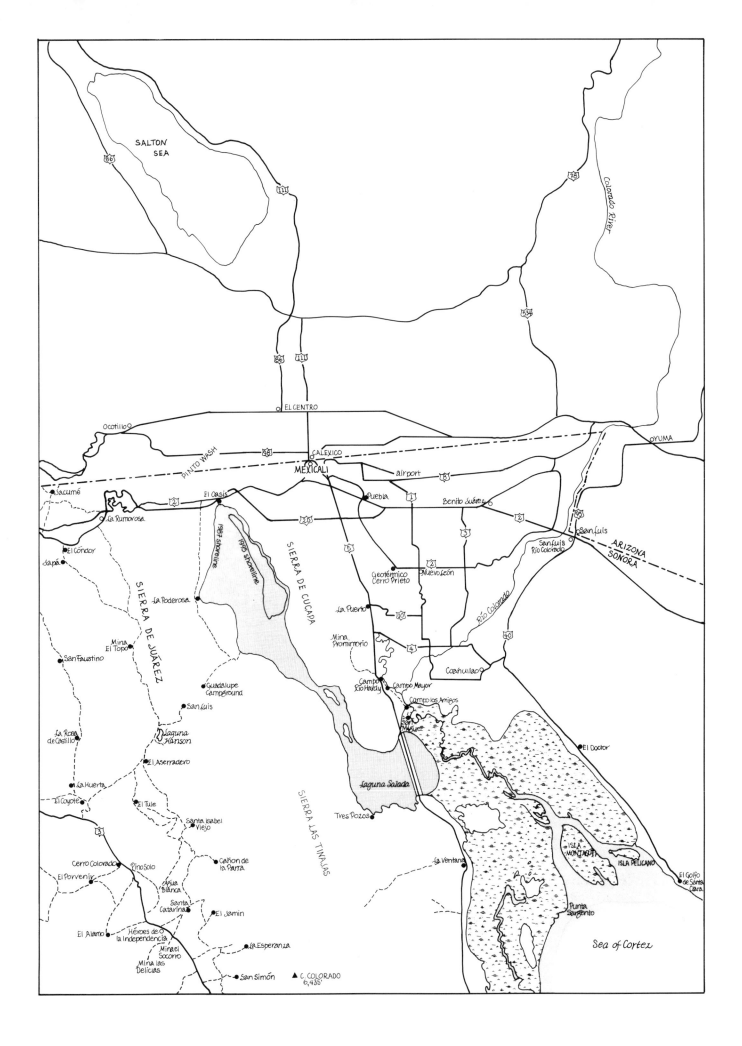

■■■■■■■■■■■■■■■■■■■■■■■■
On the Tijuana-Ensenada Toll Road

KM	Location
9+	Toll booth, information, rest rooms, snacks. There are many solar-powered emergency telephones along the road from this point to Ensenada.

■ Islas los Coronados

The islands to the west at KM 14 are the Islas los Coronados. More people fish and dive these islands than any other location in Baja, and so many *gringo* dive boats, sportfishing vessels, and yachts are present that the place often looks like an American lake. Harbor seals and occasional elephant seals use the islands for haul-outs. Over 160 species of birds have been observed at the islands, and over 30 are thought to have nested on them in past years. Today, only western gulls and brown pelicans nest in significant numbers, the others having been decimated by egg collectors, feral and domestic animals, and pesticides. Unfortunately, a few goats continue to wreak havoc on the southern island. The island was once the home of the Coronado Yacht Club, a casino and hideaway for San Diego sinners in the 1930s, but today the only inhabitants are a few military personnel.

KM	Location
19+	Real del Mar Golf Club; 18 holes, par 72, championship rating 70.5, championship yardage 6460, men 6000, women 5534, club, cart, and shoe rentals. Tee-time reservations can be made no more than seven days in advance. Facilities include a driving range, putting green, chipping green, restaurant, lounge, locker rooms, showers, pro shop, and hotel. As of 1996, there is no sand trap, but one is planned, and a clubhouse will open soon. Green fees are $43 weekdays, $49 weekends and holidays, including cart. A collared shirt is required. Tennis and basketball courts are available.
22	**San Antonio del Mar**. KOA campground, east side of Toll Road; class B but rather expensive, water and electric hookups (some with sewer), dump station, ice, rest rooms, showers, laundry, a small store, views of the Pacific. Many permanents, but space is usually available for short-term visitors. Restaurant la Costa, on the west

side of the Toll Road, is pleasant and nicely decorated, with a menu offering almost every kind of seafood you could desire, even Alaska king crab. Try the clam-chowder-in-a-pastry for lunch. Small grocery store, café serving fish and chips.

KM	Location
25	Oasis Hotel and RV Resort, class A, is easily the most elaborate, and expensive ($43/night for up to 5 people, plus $6 for each extra person) RV park in Baja, with full hookups, rest rooms, showers, beach, beach break, *palapas* (palm-thatched shelters), swimming pools, tennis, volleyball, Jacuzzi, sauna, gym, game room, laundry, mini-market, and small putting green. Tent and on-the-ground camping are not permitted (this does not apply to tent trailers). The menu at the expensive Camello Beach Restaurant is largely seafood, and live music is available in the warm months.
29+	**Rosarito**. A description of this enjoyable, tourist-oriented town will be found beginning on page 166.
35	Toll booth, rest rooms, refreshments, Red Cross clinic. Exit to Free Road 200 yards north of the KM marker. Those on a limited budget headed for Ensenada may wish to escape the cost of the remaining tolls by turning inland on the Free Road, at the price of missing some fine scenery along the coast.
49	**Puerto Nuevo**. Turn to page 168 for a description of the restaurants and attractions in Puerto Nuevo and along the nearby Free Road.
53	**Cantamar**. Turn to page 168.
69	Possible boondocking site (check the signs to see if it is still permitted), sand beach, beach break.
71	Inexpensive RV parking on the beach at end of class 1 road west from the KM marker, just north of the overpass.
72	Baja Seasons. A large, modern, pricey ($35/day for an oceanfront site during the summer, plus $5 extra for each person beyond 2) RV park, class A, with full hookups, rest rooms, showers, restaurant, cantina, store, lounge, clubhouse, laundry, sauna, swimming pool, Jacuzzi, tennis, volleyball, horseback riding, sand beach, beach break with quirky sandbars, fishing, putting green, miniature golf, and satellite TV hookups. Tent and on-the-ground camping are not permitted (this does not apply to tent trailers).
77+	Bajamar Oceanfront Golf Resort; 18 holes, par 71, championship rating 74.9, championship yardage 6968, men 5712, women 4696. Facilities include putting green, chipping green, sand trap, clubhouse, restaurant, lounge, locker rooms, pro shop, hotel, and a new stadium-style, 300-

yard driving range with 40 stalls. Green fees are $45 weekdays and $55 weekends, including cart. Tee-time reservations can be made up to three months in advance, and club rentals and lessons are available. The next 18 holes are due to open in 1996.

84 **El Mirador**. Rest stop, restaurant, bar, crafts shop, picnic tables, children's play area, spectacular views of the coastline. Along the coast to the south, you will note that although most of the coastline is steep, there are many flat areas. These are marine terraces, cut by wave action as the land was repeatedly uplifted by tectonic forces. The islands to the south are the Islas de Todos Santos, off Ensenada. Gray whales occasionally come close enough to be seen with binoculars. You will notice many odd "ups-and-downs" and zigzags in the road as you proceed south. The land under this section of road is unstable, and is very slowly slipping into the sea, requiring almost constant repairs.

99 Toll booth, refreshments, information, rest rooms. San Miguel Village RV Park, class C, just

Victor Cook gave this odd-looking rock a whack, and it split in half to reveal a beautiful fossilized oyster, millions of years old

to the south, has a few sites with water, sewer, and electric hookups, but most are just places to park. Showers and rest rooms are available, usually in poor condition. The small restaurant offers mainly Mexican dishes, plus hamburgers and chicken. This is one of the most popular surfing areas in Baja, often inhabited by dozens and occasionally hundreds of young surfers.

100+ PEMEX (MND), mini-market.

101+ Route 3 north to Tecate.

103 PEMEX (MN). J.A. Servicio; Mercury outboard motor sales, service, and parts.

104 Ramona Beach Trailer Park; class C, water, electric, and sewer hookups. Few people will wish to visit the steep cobble beach. Many permanent sites, but there is occasionally room for travelers.

105 Granada Cove RV Park; class C, water and electric hookups, rest rooms, showers. Although the park is in very poor condition and the beach is steep cobblestone, it is inexpensive and close to town.

106 LPG yard.

107+ Junction. Contrary to what the signs say, avoid taking the left fork; instead, take the right and continue south along the coast until the highway curves left (northeast) in the vicinity of the shipyards, the highway there becoming Avenida Azueta in Ensenada. Many drivers have tried to turn Avenida Azueta into a short version of the Baja 1000, and the city has responded by installing a series of world-class speed bumps, so keep your speed down. Curve right (southeast) at the stoplight onto Blvd. Cardenas, just before the PEMEX (MND). To pick up the Transpeninsular again, continue on Cardenas until you must turn left (northeast) onto Calle Sangines. Continue a half mile to the stoplight, where a right (southeast) turn will put you on the Transpeninsular again.

108 Restaurante Enrique's; International menu, the world's smallest bar.

112 **Ensenada**.

Ensenada

Ensenada almost died at birth. Its founding took place in the 1870s, fueled by the gold rush at Real de Castillo to the east. Hotels, gambling halls, and restaurants were quickly established to meet the demands of the influx of strangers, many of whom were Americans. The cost of living soared, and restaurants demanded and got $2.50 for a breakfast of imported ham and eggs, a princely sum in those days. Most miners went home disappointed, and after the Mexican Revolution began in 1910, the town faded into a small fishing village. However, it started to grow again in the 1930s, due to increasing tourism and the improved port facilities constructed to handle agricultural products from the Mexicali area.

The two-letter symbols on the map stand for the kinds of places shown in the key on p. 255. The numbers on the map show the locations of points of interest mentioned in the text.

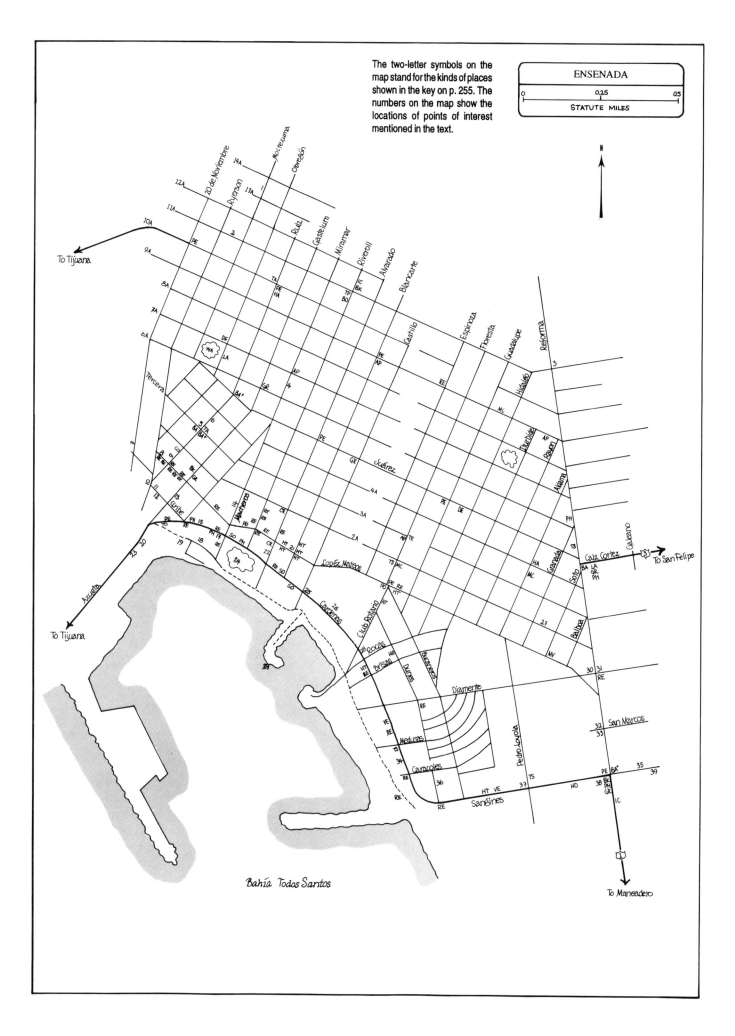

ENSENADA

0   0.25   0.5

STATUTE MILES

Bahía Todos Santos

To Tijuana

To Tijuana

To San Felipe

To Maneadero

Today's Ensenada is a small but bustling city, with an economy largely based on waterfront industries and tourism. It is Baja's largest seaport and a stop for many cruise ships. The city seems to be advancing economically: many new homes have been constructed, and most of the locals drive better rigs than do the authors. Graffiti, cellular phones, junk food, discos, the homeless, and the other trappings of progress are becoming more evident—is Los Angles moving south, or is Ensenada heading north? Despite this, the city retains much of its charm, and the climate is excellent, with mild winters, and summer temperatures held down by sea breezes. Considering the numerous restaurants, shops, and attractions, many travelers like to stop in Ensenada for at least a day or two before heading south. Dollars are readily accepted, so there is no need to exchange them for pesos if this is as far south as you're going.

Ensenada from the top of Chapultapec Hill

A walking tour...

Ensenada is large enough that exploring it completely requires wheels, but fortunately many of the attractions are along Blvd. Cardenas, Avenida López Mateos, and in the western part of town, which can best be explored on foot. The better part of a day should be set aside for this tour.

Park your vehicle near the State Secretary of Tourism Office (28) and begin walking northwest on Cardenas. In the 1930s, the Riviera del Pacifico (26) was a glamorous gambling casino, owned in part by boxer Jack Dempsey, and its clientele included many famous movie stars and prominent civic figures. Today, with its fine Mediterranean architecture and beautifully kept grounds, the Riviera is a cultural and convention center, hosting a variety of events. It also houses an art gallery, a small library, and a museum, Museo de Historia de Ensenada.

The S.S. Catalina (29), in the harbor southwest of the Riviera, was once a ferry carrying passengers from Los Angeles to Santa Catalina Island. It was moved to Ensenada in 1988 to become a floating historical museum and restaurant. It is presently closed, but it may reopen. If you want a better look, you can walk out on the sandy breakwater.

The beautiful Hotel Misión Santa Isabel (25) has a restaurant and a bar, and offers dancing. Just past the hotel, you will begin to encounter curio shops and restaurants on both sides of the road. Plaza Civica (24) has beautiful landscaping, benches, and public rest rooms. It is known locally as the "Three Heads Park," after the large golden-hued busts of three Mexican heroes: Benito Juárez (president 1861-65, 1867-72), Miguel Hildalgo (patriot, hero of the War of Independence), and Venustiano Carranza (hero of the Mexican Revolution, president 1914-20).

Numerous cuisines are represented, including Mexican, Chinese, and French, as well as steaks and seafood. If you have a yen for things Italian, there is a Pizza Hut (17) along the way. Plaza Marina (18), a large shopping center, has recently been completed, but as of early 1996, it had succeeded in attracting only 2 tenants, a toy store and a Denny's Restaurant. The latter is modern and immaculately clean, but distinguished from its northern counterparts only by the Spanish on the menu and several Mexican entrées.

Don't miss the fish market (19), as much a social institution on weekends and holidays as a place to buy and sell fish, with noisy *mariachis* (bands that play traditional Mexican music), street vendors hawking almost everything imaginable, and throngs of people

Service with a smile at the Ensenada fish market

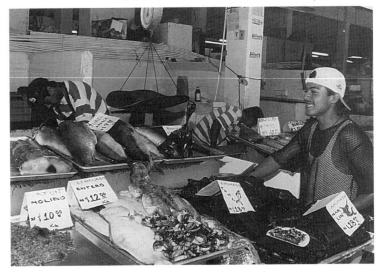

munching on piscatorial treats. There are dozens of species of fish for sale, as well as crabs, clams, oysters, squid, and octopi, and all look fresh, clean, and well cared for. You may have wondered what happens to the marlin once the "victory" photo back at the dock has been taken, and here is your answer—some of them end up for sale at the Ensenada fish market. If you can get a fish vendor aside privately, he may admit that the fish in the taco you just enjoyed was angel shark, a species not ordinarily seen as suitable for human consumption, due to its horrendous appearance, not its taste. Some questions are best left unasked.

Back on Cardenas, walk northwest until you reach Uribe. The Old Jail (13), which houses a museum and the Indian Artists Workshop, can be found just to the northeast on Av. Gastelum. Weavings, pottery, basketry, and other folk arts are on display and for sale. If you are still hungry, you can stop at La Cochinita (10) for some sushi. Next door is the new anthropology and history museum, El Instituto Nacional de Anthropologia y Historia, housed in the oldest building in Ensenada. By continuing on Uribe one more block northwest and turning right (north) on 20 de Noviembre, you will find the new maritime museum, El Museo de la Gente de Mar (7).

Walk north from La Cochinita, and you will immediately encounter Avenida López Mateos, the second half of the walking tour. A visit to Hussong's Cantina (9)—advertised as "The bar that built a city! Until you've been to Hussong's you haven't been to Mexico!"—should be on your itinerary. Hussong's is undoubtedly the best known cantina in Mexico and the subject of countless bumper stickers and T-shirt designs, but at first glance, the reason is not obvious: the attraction can't be the decor—yellowed cartoons and hundreds of business cards tacked to peeling walls looming over battered furniture sitting on the sawdust-covered floor. It can't be the beer or the booze, which are standard issue. Rather, the attraction seems to be the sociology of its American patrons, who come to see and be seen doing things no one would think of doing at home.

López Mateos is Ensenada's primary tourist street, and is chock full of stores selling clothing, T-shirts, native crafts, sea shells, leather goods, jewelry, and curios, and many restaurants. Some shops sell silver jewelry, and it is possible to buy attractive, handmade woven necklaces and bracelets for several dollars. In 1996, many shops featured fake Dooney & Bourke handbags at 10% of the state-side price for the real thing. (That's not a **discount** of 10%, it's 10% of the whole price!) A number of shops carry "Rolex" watches, at significant savings from reality. The exteriors of such creations look reasonably authentic, but it does not require much imagination to realize that inside beats the heart of a gas-station watch. Some shops do sell quality merchandise, including elegant designer jewelry, watches, and Lladró porcelain at Asins (16).

If your timing is right, plan to treat yourself to supper at the El Rey Sol (21), an excellent French restaurant, opened in 1947 by a woman trained at the Cordon Bleu School of Cooking in France. It offers such treats as *Escargot de Bourguignon*, *Duck à l'Orange*, steaks, and seafood, and has all the ambiance you could possibly want, with carpeted floors, carved cane-backed chairs, and Chopin on the piano. While no one comes here to save calories or dollars, the meals are not terribly expensive by standards north of the border: a recent meal for the two of us consisting of French onion soup, boned Cornish game hen in garlic butter sauce, artichoke hearts, carrots, broccoli, boiled quail eggs, Caesar salad, a gigantic margarita, and a glass of wine, cost $54. The real trial comes at the end of the meal, when the waiter puts a plate-full of beautiful flaky French pastries on the table, and asks serenely, "Would you like to have some dessert?," implying that the answer must be yes, for only the unbalanced could refuse. There are high-quality jewelry and art objects to be found next door in the Artes Bitterlin tea salon.

Continue southeast on López Mateos, where a number of hotels will be found, most with a restaurant, a bar, and live entertainment or discos. Turn right (south) on Club Rotario, which will take you back to your starting point.

Even more...

There are many other attractions, too far away to be made a part of a walking tour. The big shopping center (38) at the corner of Sangines (the street name changing to Delante at an unknown point) and Reforma has a bank, a pharmacy, groceries, and a variety of specialty stores. However, it is prudent to leave someone with your vehicle, as there have been recent instances of theft in the parking lot. The La Palma tortilla factory (39) sells fresh tortillas made on the site, and Halitois (35) is a highly recommended seafood restaurant. If your long absence from civilization has produced a hunger that can not be satisfied otherwise, there are a McDonald's (31) and a Winchell's (30). If you would like to shop where the locals shop, try Ruiz north of López Mateos, which has department stores including Sears (5) and Dorian's (6), as well as shops along Avenida Juárez, which runs east/west through the city. A science museum, Museo de Ciencias (1), opened recently, offering marine and oceanographic exhibits. There is an American-style shopping center, Misión Centro Commercial (3).

Bodegas de Santo Tomás Winery (4) is the largest and oldest winery in Mexico, and offers guided tours, with samplings of wines, breads, and cheeses. Cavas Valmar (go north on Riveroll to Calle Ambar (off the accompanying city map; see the address in Appendix C) is advertised as the smallest winery in Mexico, and offers free wine tasting tours by appointment. Viajes Guayacura (22) offers a variety of activities, including a Mexican fiesta and beach party, scuba diving, yacht and sailboat cruises, parasailing, banana boat rides, jet- and water skiing, trips to the Baja Country Club or Bajamar for golfing, a tour of Ensenada restaurants and night life, horseback riding on the beach, fishing excursions, a fiesta at the Riviera Pacifico, a cultural tour of Ensenada, and a motor coach trip to the Domecq winery north of town.

Bajarama Tours (12) offers tours of the countryside and other activities.

Campo Playa RV Park (36), class A, has full hook-ups, rest rooms, hot showers, and a garden setting. It is expensive and traffic noise may be a problem, but its location makes it convenient. In addition, there are many parks along the Toll Road to the north and the Transpeninsular to the south, not far from town. If you choose Campo Playa, pay for your stay with cash; there have been recent reports of fraudulent use of credit cards associated with this park. In addition, do not leave gas cans, aluminum chairs, coolers, and other things out where they may disappear.

Fishing is declining due to heavy commercial netting, but it is often better than in Southern California. There are three primary fisheries: yellowtail and bottom species among the rocks at the end of the Punta Banda peninsula; yellowtail, ling cod, and various bottom fish in the cool water immediately west of the Islas de Todos Santos; and albacore 25 miles or so west of Ensenada. In addition, Ensenada party boats often venture south to other locations along the coast, often in pursuit of prized yellowtail. There are a number of sportfishing boats, and the largest operations are Gordo's Sport Fishing and the Ensenada Sportfishing Center, both of which have offices in the lobby of the new Hotel Santo Tomás (15), providing tickets, tackle sales, rental equipment, bait, and highly optimistic predictions. They also offer whale-

A group of happy fishermen return after a day of trying their luck west of Ensenada

watching trips in the winter months. Nearby Gordo's Smokeshop has facilities for cleaning, smoking, canning, and freezing your catch.

There are currently no good locations in Ensenada to launch trailer boats, for the ramp at Gordo's and one just to the north are virtually inaccessible due to construction and heavy traffic in the area, and parking is almost nonexistent. However, there are ramps along the Punta Banda peninsula to the south, which are described in Chapter 6. If you get

back to Ensenada you may be able to buy live bait from barges anchored in the harbor, although the commercial boats get first call. Frozen bait is usually available at fleet offices.

Diving in the vicinity of Ensenada is poor, and most divers head for Punta Banda or Todos Santos. Almar Dive Shop (14) has a scuba compressor and sells fins, masks, spearguns, regulators, and a wide variety of small, hard-to-find parts such as O-rings, spear points, and rubber mouthpieces, and regulator repairs are available. The shop has no rentals, but makes and repairs wet suits; the turn-around time is two to four days. San Miguel Surf Shop (8) sells boards and equipment, makes repairs, and has rentals. A group of surfers could have great fun by chartering one of the larger sportfishing boats for a day at El Martillo. Also, see page 182.

If this cornucopia of activities is not enough to keep you in a state of exhaustion, there is much more to do: flea markets, swap meets, rodeos, off-road, ATV, motorcycle, bicycle, and sailboat races, beauty contests, dog shows, live theater, musical events ranging from *mariachi* to classical, volleyball tournaments, art exhibits, civic and religious events, environmental classes and workshops, and more. You say you have always wanted to take ballet lessons? There is a full-fledged ballet school in Ensenada, Escuela la Cubana de Ballet (11). Inquire about these and other activities and dates at the State Secretary of Tourism Office. A free English-language newspaper, *Baja Visitor*, covering Ensenada, Tecate, and San Quintín, is available in many public places in Ensenada, and has information on events, attractions, and other topics of interest.

More mundane matters...

If you have vehicle problems, there are many parts stores and mechanics, as well as dealerships for Ford (33), Dodge/Chrysler (32) and Chevrolet (34). A Volkswagen dealer is located on Avenida Gral. Clark Flores (the northwest extension of Calle 10, off the map). There is a Volkswagen parts store on a road leading west from the Transpeninsular just south of town; see page 84. A Nissan dealer can be found on the Transpeninsular at Mile 1.3, just south of the main part of town. Sales, parts, and service for Evinrude outboards and marine supplies, charts, and equipment can be found at Agencia Ajorna (23). Johnson outboard motor sales and service are available at Equipos TerraMar (37), Industria Mexicana de Equipo Marino (27) is a Yamaha dealer, and Promarina (2) handles Mariner. Another Evinrude dealer is located on the Transpeninsular south of the main part of town. A Baja Cellular office is located next to Denny's.

If you can't find the parts or services you need, do what you would do in the US; look in the Yellow Pages. You might also ask questions at the State Secretary of Tourism Office. If you are headed south of Maneadero, remember that you must obtain a tourist card and that it must be validated, tasks which can be accomplished at the Immigration office (20). This office is open during business hours seven days a week, but is sometimes closed when the Immigration officials are dealing with the cruise ships that frequently visit Ensenada.

• •

66 *Let him have it, Lady!*

Judy was apprehensive as we boarded the Ensenada Clipper, *for it was the first time she had ever been fishing. As we headed out of the harbor I tried to answer her many questions: "How will I know when I get a bite? Which way do I turn the handle on this thing? What's this lever for?" A deck hand came around signing up fishermen for the biggest-fish pool, and although I contributed $5, I advised Judy that it was just a waste of money for her to join.*

February is not exactly the peak month in the Ensenada fishing calendar, and after several unproductive stops off the Punta Banda peninsula, the skipper headed for fairly deep water off the kelp beds west of the Islas de Todos Santos. This proved to be a veritable cornucopia, at least by winter standards, and the dozen or so fishermen along the rail began to pick up a mixed bag of perch and rockfish— everyone, that is, except Judy. I tried to coach her: drop a diamond jig to the bottom, reel up a few feet and pump the tip of the rod up and down; try a shrimp-fly rig; confess your sins and pray; but nothing seemed to work. The deck hand began to notice her lack of productivity and came over to provide additional advice. Everyone else was catching fish, sometimes two or three at a time, but Judy's gunny sack remained empty.

After several hours, her lip began to protrude a bit, and it wasn't hard to guess what was going through her mind: "It isn't fair!" Every fisherman has seen it happen; same place, same time, same depth, same bait, but nothing works for someone. The deck hand began to give his undivided attention to the problem and baited up a rock-cod rig with some chunks provided by an unlucky sculpin. Judy lowered it to the bottom and 5 minutes passed, then 10, then 20, but still no luck. Suddenly, she jerked up the tip of her rod and yelled "I think I got something." There was a chorus of cheers, but the tip of her rod gave no sign of a struggle, and the smiles soon disappeared—perhaps she had just snagged a weed. She began reeling in, but suddenly she jerked the rod up, almost bending it double, and screamed, "He's trying to get my fish!" We peered into the clear water and saw what had happened: she had snagged a tiny garibaldi, a small, brilliant-orange, perch-like fish, possibly 4 inches long. Just below it, a huge lingcod was about to make another lunge, and at the last possible instant, Judy gave a mighty heave

and jerked the garibaldi out of its toothy jaws. There was a stampede for the rail, and every eye was intent on the drama below. To a chorus of shouts, "Let him have it, Lady," Judy kept reeling furiously, protesting "No, no, you don't understand! He's trying to get my fish!" About 20 feet from the surface, the ling made another lunge at the garibaldi, which was again jerked away at the last possible fraction of a second. There was another chorus, "No, no, Lady! Let him have it!," and the deck hand, grimacing, gesturing, and stamping his feet, became so exasperated that he burst into a continuous stream of Spanish expletives, which, although mild by most standards, are best left untranslated. As the garibaldi neared the surface, everyone aboard tried one last time; "Let him have it, Lady!" Just as the tiny fish was about to break the surface, Judy stopped reeling, and the ling made a savage rush.

As we headed back to Ensenada there were countless recreations of the incident—"Let him have it, Lady!"—as we drank coffee in the cabin, but the smiles and laughter turned to stunned looks and silence when it came time to award the jackpot; Judy's 18-pound ling was 3 times as large as the second-place fish. All eyes turned to me as she explained why she had not joined the pool, but I had anticipated the confession and was stretched out on a bench, apparently sound asleep. ——Walt 99

• •

At the Intersection of Sangines and Reforma in Ensenada. This is KM 7 for this section of the Transpeninsular, but since many KM markers are missing, miles will be used until Maneadero is reached. Numerous stands along the highway hawk watermelon, cantaloupe, olives, and corn. Set trip odometer.

Mile	Location
0.3	Bowling alley.
0.5	Boat dealer; Evinrude sales, parts, and service.
1.0	PEMEX (MN). Gigante supermarket, Happy Campers Mobile RV Service and Repairs.
1.1	Class 1 road west to La Cueva de los Tigres Restaurant. Located on the beach, the initial impression of the restaurant from the parking lot may cause doubts to arise, but the place is rather pleasant inside, and the magnificent view from its large windows belies its name. The somewhat pricey menu is mostly seafood, but steaks and Mexican are also available. Try the abalone with crab sauce, or the shrimps in garlic butter. There is a Volkswagen parts store on the same road.
1.3	Nissan dealer.
2.8	PEMEX (MN).
3.3	Joker Hotel & RV Park; restaurant, bar, rest rooms, showers, pool, small class B RV park with

shade trees, electrical, water, sewage, and TV hookups, brick barbecues.

3.6 **El Ciprés**. Large ice manufacturing plant across the street from the airport entrance.

4.7 Road west to beach resorts (signed, stop light). Set trip odometer. The area is becoming built-up, with a fishing tackle store, a pharmacy, curios, ice, ice cream, car wash, veterinary office, mechanic, groceries, butcher shops, hardware store, and a number of taco stands. If you want a fancy RV park and plan to do some boating, turn left (160°) at Mile 0.8 for Estero Beach, an elaborate resort with a hotel and an expensive class A RV park. The park has full hookups, rest rooms, and showers, and the facilities of the resort are available, including a restaurant, tennis courts, volleyball, sailboards, water skiing, wave runners, banana boats, Hobies, jet skis, horses, bicycles, kayaks, and a small museum of Mexican culture and folk art. Tent and on-the-ground camping are not permitted (this does not apply to tent trailers). Several good paved launch ramps (14%) lead into Estero Punta Banda, where halibut, croaker, sharks, and other fish can be taken. At high tide in calm weather, boats can run the channel into Bahía Todos Santos, but it would be well to discuss this with local residents first, since channels and conditions change frequently. If you would like a more modest park, continue straight ahead at Mile 0.8 until Mile 1.3. At this point, go straight ahead for El Faro Beach RV Park, class B, with some spaces equipped with water and electricity, a dump station, a fine beach, a small store that carries sodas and snacks, a bar, rest rooms, showers, horseback riding, an area set aside for ATVs, and Leonardo, a very large lion in a very small cage. There are other choices in the area. At Mile 1.3, turn right (340°) for Mona Lisa RV Park and Corona Beach RV Park, both marked by signs. Mona Lisa is rather expensive, class B, and has concrete pads, full hookups, a beach, a small restaurant, and a bar. Corona Beach RV Park, class B and a bit pricey, has a small store selling beer, sodas, and snacks, a recreation room with a pool table and video machines, beach camping, and RV sites equipped with water and electrical hookups. A dump station, showers, and rest rooms are available.

6.8 Road east to Baja Country Club golf course, marked by an elaborate green and white portal. Set trip odometer, arrive at club at Mile 3.1. The course has 18 holes, par 72, championship rating 73.1, championship yardage 6834, men 6500, women 5500. Make tee-time reservations not less than two weeks in advance. Facilities include a driving range, putting green, chipping green, sand trap, clubhouse, restaurant, lounge, locker rooms, and pro shop. Green fees are $34 weekdays and weekends, including cart. Lessons and club rentals are available.

8.0 PEMEX (MN).

8.5 PEMEX (MND).

8.6 **Maneadero**. Stores, groceries, meat and vegetable markets, tire repair, bakery, doctor, dentist, pharmacy, veterinarian, bank, post office, telegraph, auto parts, mechanics, chapter of Alcoholics Anonymous, world record speed bumps. Junction (signed) with paved road west to the Punta Banda peninsula.

Side trip from Maneadero to the Punta Banda Peninsula, with the area's best fishing, diving, and sightseeing. Turn to page 181.

On the Transpeninsular Highway in Maneadero. The Transpeninsular has KM markers from its intersection with the Punta Banda road, which is KM 21. You should have a validated tourist card to proceed south of Maneadero.

KM	Location
22	PEMEX (MND).
41+	**Uruapan**. A park immediately on the left (northeast) has an RV parking site, with spreading oaks, a pavilion, and fireplaces.
45	Spectacular views of the Valle Santo Tomás.
47+	Class 1 road west (signed) to La Bocana and Puerto Santo Tomás.

Off-road trip from KM 47+ to La Bocana and Puerto Santo Tomás, the first relatively unspoiled fishing south of the border. Turn to page 199.

51 **Santo Tomás**. PEMEX (MN), restaurant, groceries, ice, telephone, doctor, tire repair, LPG sales, ruins of outbuildings of Dominican Misión Santo Tomás (1791–1849). Local legend claims that the valley is so fertile that the mission priest absent-mindedly left his cane leaning against the church, and when he found it several days later, it had sprouted leaves and roots, but the authenticity and antiquity of the tale are suspect. Believe it or not, Santo Tomás was once the capital of the northern territory of Baja California. El Palomar Trailer Park, class B, located in a large olive orchard, has full hookups, barbecues, rest rooms, showers, a volleyball court, two tennis courts, a basketball court, two swimming pools (usually empty), a small zoo with a hawk, several monkeys, and a very unhappy bobcat. Use

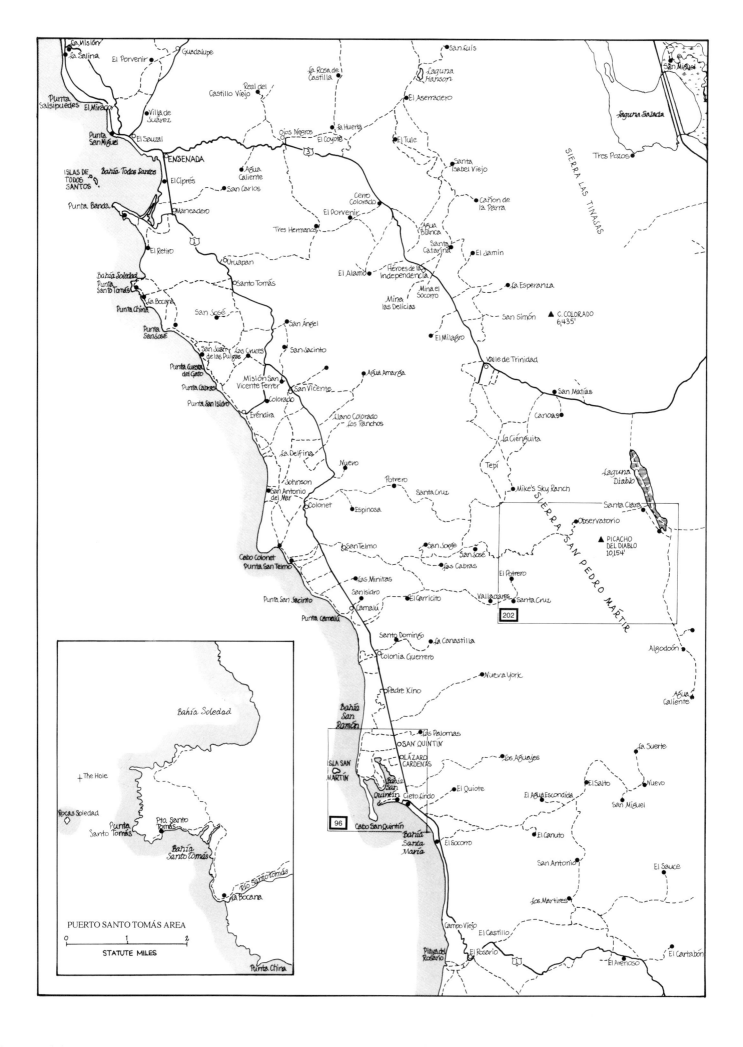

La Misión
La Salina
El Porvenir
Guadalupe
San Luis
San Miguel
Punta
Salsipuedes
El Mirador
La Rosa de
Castilla
Laguna
Hanson
Laguna Salada
Villa de
Suárez
Castillo Viejo
Real del
El Aserradero
Tres Pozos
Punta
San Miguel
El Sauzal
Ojos Negros
La Huerta
El Coyote
3
El Tule
SIERRA LAS TINAJAS
ENSENADA
ISLAS DE
TODOS
SANTOS
Bahía Todos Santos
El Ciprés
Agua
Caliente
San Carlos
Cerro
Colorado
Santa
Isabel Viejo
Cañón de
la Parra
Punta Banda
Maneadero
El Porvenir
Agua
Blanca
El Retiro
Uruapan
Tres Hermanas
Santa
Catarina
El Jamín
Bahía Soledad
Punta
Santo Tomás
La Bocana
Santo Tomás
El Álamo
Héroes de la
Independencia
La Esperanza
Punta China
San José
San Ángel
Mina el
Socorro
C. COLORADO
6,435'
Punta
San José
San Juan
de las Pulgas
Las Cruces
San Jacinto
Mina
las Delicias
San Simón
Punta Cuesta
del Gato
Punta Cabras
Misión San
Vicente Ferrer
San Vicente
Agua Amarga
El Milagro
Valle de Trinidad
Punta San Isidro
Eréndira
Colorado
Llano Colorado
Los Panchos
San Matías
La Delfina
Nuevo
La Ciénguita
Canoas
Johnson
San Antonio
del Mar
Potrero
Santa Cruz
Tepí
Laguna
Diablo
Colonet
Espinosa
Mike's Sky Ranch
Santa Clara
SIERRA SAN PEDRO MÁRTIR
Observatorio
San Telmo
San Jorge
San José
PICACHO
DEL DIABLO
10,154'
Cabo Colonet
Punta San Telmo
Las Cabras
El Potrero
202
Las Minitas
San Isidro
El Carricito
Valladares
Santa Cruz
Algodoón
Punta San Jacinto
Camalú
Punta Camalú
Santo Domingo
La Canastilla
Agua
Caliente
Colonia Guerrero
Nueva York
Bahía Soledad
Padre Kino
Bahía
San
Ramón
Las Palomas
La Suerte
The Hole
ISLA SAN
MARTÍN
SAN QUINTÍN
LÁZARO
CÁRDENAS
Los Aguajes
El Salto
Nuevo
Rocas Soledad
Pta. Santo
Tomás
Bahía
San
Quintín
El Quiote
El Agua Escondida
San Miguel
Punta
Santo Tomás
Cielo Lindo
Bahía
Santo Tomás
96
Cabo San Quintín
El Canuto
Río Santo Tomás
La Bocana
Bahía
Santa
María
El Socorro
San Antonio
El Sauce

PUERTO SANTO TOMÁS AREA
Los Mártires

0   1   2
Campo Viejo
El Castillo
STATUTE MILES
Playa del
Rosario
El Rosario
El Cartabón
Punta China
El Arenoso
1

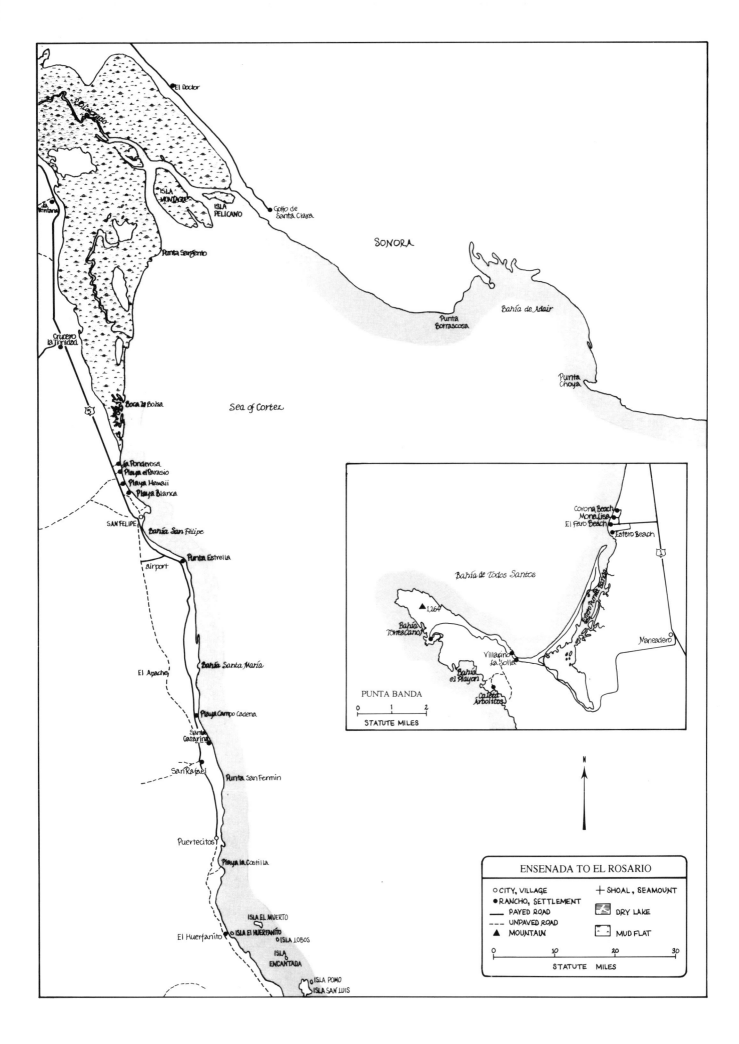

El Doctor

SONORA

ISLA
MONTAGUE
ISLA
PELICANO

Golfo de
Santa Clara

Punta Sargento

La Ventana

Bahía de Adair

Punta
Borrascosa

Crucero
la Trinidad

Punta
Choya

Boca la Bolsa

Sea of Cortez

5

La Ponderosa
Playa el Parasio
Playa Hawaii
Playa Blanca

SAN FELIPE

Bahía San Felipe

Punta Estrella

airport

Corona Beach
Mona Lisa
El Favo Beach

Estero Beach

Bahía de Todos Santos

1264

Bahía
Torres Cano

Villarino
la Jolla

El Apache

Bahía Santa María

Bahía
el Playon

Maneadero

Caleta
Arbolitos

Playa Campo Cadena

Santa
Catarina

PUNTA BANDA

0   1   2

STATUTE MILES

San Rafael

Punta San Fermin

N

Puertecitos

Playa la Costilla

ENSENADA TO EL ROSARIO

ISLA EL MUERTO

El Huerfanito
ISLA EL HUERFANITO
ISLA LOBOS

ISLA
ENCANTADA

ISLA POMO
ISLA SAN LUIS

○ CITY, VILLAGE
● RANCHO, SETTLEMENT
— PAVED ROAD
-- UNPAVED ROAD
▲ MOUNTAIN

+ SHOAL, SEAMOUNT
▦ DRY LAKE
▢ MUD FLAT

0   10   20   30

STATUTE   MILES

care when leaving the park: the access road is steep and it is difficult to see oncoming traffic. The restaurant next to the gas station specializes in seafood and Mexican dishes. Class 2 road south to Punta San José.

Off-road trip from KM 51 to Punta San José, with many secluded coves and beaches, and excellent beach-casting, side trip to points south. Turn to page 201.

■ Quail

With its jaunty topknot, highly organized coveys, and business-like demeanor, the California quail is one of the most engaging birds found in Baja. They are abundant throughout the peninsula at low elevations, often in arroyos and alluvial plains having a mixture of dense cover and open areas. They have an aversion to large open spaces, and will almost always be found within 50 feet of cover. Quail have a well-defined daily routine, which causes them to move among different habitats: at first light they start to feed actively in open areas; by mid-morning they begin to loaf and to drift toward better cover; as dusk approaches they start to feed actively again; and by dark they have selected bushes and trees for roosting until dawn. Although quail obtain moisture from their food, they require a source of surface water and are often found near green areas.

Gary Kramer

A jaunty California quail

Quail are highly social, and if you see one you can be sure a covey is nearby. The species communicates with a vocabulary of 14 different calls, the most frequently used being the assembly call, used to keep the members of the covey together. The colloquial name Mexicans use for quail is *chaquaca*, which is a fine example of onomatopoeia, for the name is an attempt to imitate the sound of the call, "cha-**qua**-cah," in a reedy tone with the first and last syllables of equal pitch, the "qua" higher, and all three equally loud. Once heard and identified, the call is unmistakable and is easy to recognize in the sound tracks of western movies—listen closely the next time you see *True Grit*.

Populations vary dramatically from place to place. Even when ideal conditions are met—low elevation, broken terrain, mixed cover, and open areas, with surface water present—they may be absent, for no apparent reason, though the reverse is rarely true. There are also great variations from year to year, the primary influence being the amount and timing of rainfall. When soil moisture is low, seeds make up most of their diet, which inhibits breeding activity. However, when soil moisture is high, greens make up a large part of their diet, resulting in dramatically different breeding behavior. Like well-fed males of many species, the fathers-to-be become noisy and unusually aggressive, and the hatch is often prolific. A female may abandon her nest after the first hatch, leaving her mate and chicks, take up with a new mate and raise another brood, like some human females. Under extremely favorable conditions three broods in a year are possible, during drought years none. Through this mechanism Mother Nature causes the birds to take full advantage of abundant food to increase their numbers while they can.

Most young birds fall prey to predators, and only about 10% usually survive to adulthood. Since young birds have matured and the less wary ones have fallen to predators, the coveys are markedly "smarter" as winter approaches. An individual quail will often appoint himself as a "watchbird" and remain perched on a bush, ready to warn the covey of approaching danger. Running is their favorite means of escape, and they can easily outdistance a human. They are also experts at concealment and will freeze in hidden positions and allow you to come so close that they are in danger of being trampled. They often get nervous if you stop for several minutes, and will flush with a great whirring of wings, scaring the daylights out of even those prepared for the experience.

KM	Location
78+	Paved road south to Eréndira (signed).

Side trip from KM 78+ to Eréndira, a small village near excellent fishing. Turn to page 182.

88+	Class 2 road southwest (signed) to the ruins of Dominican Misión San Vicente Ferrer, 0.6 mile. Today little more than adobe ruins, the mission was active between 1780 and 1833. There are important copper and iron deposits in the area, and in 1915, a geologist estimated that a hematite deposit several miles from the mission contained 5 million tons of ore.

■ Living close to the edge

As you proceed south, you may notice a odd phenomenon: the vegetation at the edge of the highway is very different from that a few dozen yards away, often consisting of flowering plants instead of cactus and desert shrubs. This is not due to a beautification program undertaken by the highway department, but because opportunistic plants flourish at the side of the pavement, where the microclimate is a bit more favorable due to water running off the impervious pavement. Because the climate becomes more rigorous as you travel south, the effect is more pronounced, and in spring, it is not uncommon to drive past a beautiful garden of yellow, white, purple, and red flowers a foot wide and 100 miles or more in length. One of the most common and beautiful of these opportunists is the brittlebush, a rounded, bush-like shrub up to a yard in diameter, with yellow, daisy-like flowers protruding on long stems from a core of green leaves. This species, common throughout Baja, northwestern mainland Mexico, and the southwestern US, was popular with Indians suffering from toothache, upset stomach, and infections, and it serves as forage for cattle.

90 **San Vicente**. PEMEX (MND), stores, groceries, auto parts, bakery, doctor, dentist, pharmacy, liquor, cafés, post office, motel, fruit stores, butcher's, ice, hardware, welder, tire repair. If your rig finally breaks down completely, there is a used car lot. A small museum of Indian artifacts and local history can be found on the west side of the town square. There is an office of the State Secretary of Tourism (signed) at the north end of town on the east side of the road.

102 The Llano Colorado (Red Plain), named for the red color of the volcanic rock and soil, has some of the largest vineyards and olive orchards in Baja. Although there are wild grape species on the peninsula, most of the vines here descend from those imported in 1732.

126 PEMEX (N), auto parts, grocery stores, restaurant, telephone.

126+ Class 1 road west to San Antonio del Mar.

Off-road trip from KM 126+ to San Antonio del Mar, offering excellent surf casting, a beautiful beach, and RV parking. Turn to page 201.

127 **Colonet**. Groceries, doctor, pharmacy, stores, bakery, butcher shops, cafés, auto

parts, tire repair, mail, long-distance telephone. Shore casting is good for croakers and surfperch, but bottom fishing is often poor. There are good reef breaks on big waves.

140+ Class 1 road east (signed OBSERVATORIO) to Parque Nacional Sierra San Pedro Mártir.

Off-road trip from KM 140+ to Parque Nacional Sierra San Pedro Mártir, Baja's premiere national park, which offers boondocking, striking forest and mountain scenery, and good hiking. Turn to page 201.

142 Class 1 road west to Punta San Telmo.

Off-road trip from KM 142 to Punta San Telmo, site of fine surfing. Turn to page 204.

146 Sodas, snacks, groceries, pharmacy, mail, tire repair, mechanics, long-distance telephone.

150 Class 1 road west (signed) to Punta San Jacinto, 5 miles. This site, named "Freighters" by surfers, even if there is only one shipwreck visible, has excellent right point breaks on large swells. There is plenty of room for boondocking.

157+ **Camalú**. PEMEX (MND), stores, groceries, fruit stores, butcher shops, cafés, auto parts, mechanics, tire repair, long-distance telephone, post office, doctor, dentist, pharmacy. Turn southwest

Heleodoro Ramirez makes some of the best sweet rolls and cookies to be found between Ensenada and La Paz, using a wood-fired stove

at the PEMEX for the beach, which has good right point and reef breaks. Sportfishermen are rare, but a beach launch is possible, *pangas* are for hire, and thresher sharks and a wide variety of pelagic (free roaming, living in the open ocean rather than coastal waters) and bottom fish are taken offshore. Punta Camalú is not too popular with boardsailors, but good conditions occur occasionally, so it's worth a stop to check it out. Diving is poor.

168+　Baja Café; breakfast, hamburgers, Mexican menu, RV boondocking.

169　Class 1 road east (signed) to ruins of Dominican Misión Santo Domingo, 5 miles. Founded in 1775, the original mission church was a cave. The adobe ruins of the mission constructed later have been badly damaged by treasure hunters. The mission closed in 1839, when epidemics decimated the Indian converts.

■ Beep, beep, zoom!

The roadrunners of the Baja deserts have much in common with the bird of movie and television fame: they are cunning, astute, speedy, and given to clowning, like racing RVs and bedeviling Wile E. Coyote. They are common throughout Baja at low elevations, so the chances are good that you will see them along the Transpeninsular. Roadrunners are members of the cuckoo family, and adults are almost two feet long from the end of their long bills to the tip of their lengthy tails. Their coarse feathers are streaked olive-brown and tipped with white, changing to bronze-green at the tail. A small bare patch of skin behind the eyes is blue and red, and their stout legs are bluish.

Since they possess short rounded wings and have feet adapted to running, with two toes on each foot pointed forward and two pointed aft in lieu of the three-one arrangement seen on most other birds, their forte is running, not flying. They can easily reach 15 miles an hour and even reach 20 for short periods if pressed. Their tail has a sort of swivel joint, allowing it to be used as a balance and a rudder by flicking them to one side during sharp turns. They are carnivorous, eating insects, lizards, snakes, scorpions, tarantulas, spiders, centipedes, mice, and birds, including baby and adult quail. They can dispatch a full-grown rattlesnake, darting in to seize it by the head and pummeling it on the ground. They like to sunbathe in

A roadrunner finds lunch

the morning, standing with their back to the sun with feathers erected to expose dark skin.

Roadrunners have more than a dozen sounds, the two most common being a cooing, which appears to be a territorial or mating signal, and a clacking of the beak, whose meaning is not known. They can become quite tame, visiting ranches to beg for food, and will sometimes eat from the hand and will steal food set out for dogs. Great fun can be had by setting out a mirror on the ground—once the "intruder" is spotted by a roadrunner, a great battle between equals may go on for an hour or more. In spring, they build shallow nests about a foot in diameter several feet off the ground in a bush, lining it with leaves, feathers, and grasses. Two to five white eggs, occasionally as many as a dozen, are laid. During the breeding season adult males gain brighter coloration, displaying orange patches and a steel-blue crest. They have few natural enemies, although babies are sometimes eaten by snakes, and adults are occasionally taken by large birds of prey.

Roadrunners are not universally popular, and quail hunters often shoot them on sight, but they have a definite place in the scheme of life in the desert, and add a bit of zest and liveliness—who can resist shouting "Beep, beep, zoom!" as they speed by? However, don't give in to the impulse to race them; we once took off in our pickup in hot pursuit of one. At 35 miles an hour we were occasionally air-borne and gaining rapidly on him, but we lost the race when we skidded into a large cactus and tore off a mirror.

KM	Location
171+	**Colonia Guerrero.** Stores, restaurants, pizza, groceries, fruit stores, butcher shops, bank, post office, auto parts, tire sales and repairs, bakery, tortilla factory, ice, beer, liquor, long-distance telephone, motel, telegraph, doctor, dentist, pharmacy, optician, veterinarian.
172	Office of the State Secretary of Tourism. Look closely; it's in the office of Constructora Ferrex.
172+	LPG yard, PEMEX (MND). Class 1 road west to Mesón de Don Pepe and Posada Don Diego, both of which are class B RV parks, each having some full hookups, rest rooms, showers, and a restaurant. Don Diego has a laundry machine (no dryer, clothes lines provided), and a dump station. The menu at Don Pepe's is the more comprehensive, ranging from a wide variety of seafood such as fish, clams, shrimp, crab, and manta ray, to steaks, rabbit, quail, and Mexican dishes. The beach several miles west has a long beach break and lots of pismo clams.
188	**San Quintín.**

The San Quintín area

Spread along the highway between KM 188 and KM 196, the San Quintín/Lázaro Cardenas area has a wide variety of businesses and services, including doctors, dentists, pharmacies, opticians, veterinarians, health clinics, meat, fish and fruit markets, groceries, tortilla factories, bakeries, ice cream shops, a camera store, liquor, beer, auto parts, mechanics, welders, tire sales and repairs, cafés, motels, sporting goods stores, hardware stores, bank, long-distance telephones, fax service, telegraph, post office, cinema, ice manufacturing plant.

Set trip odometer at KM 188. The Restaurant Misión Santa Isabel at Mile 0.2 is clean and cheerful, and serves mainly Mexican dishes. The Mi Lien Café, Mile 0.9, specializes in Chinese food. The PEMEX station (MND) at Mile 1.1 has established a consistent, long-term reputation for rip-offs, often achieved by the usual methods: by not clearing the readings from the previous transaction, by clearing the new reading quickly and claiming a larger amount, or by short-changing. Occasionally, though, novel ways are employed: young, self-appointed windshield cleaners descend on a vehicle, climb on the hood, and make a mess of dirt and soapsuds that obscures the view of the pump from within. Complaints to the police have brought no action. If you must patronize this station, get out of your vehicle immediately and stand attentively near the pump with eyes open and a calculator in hand.

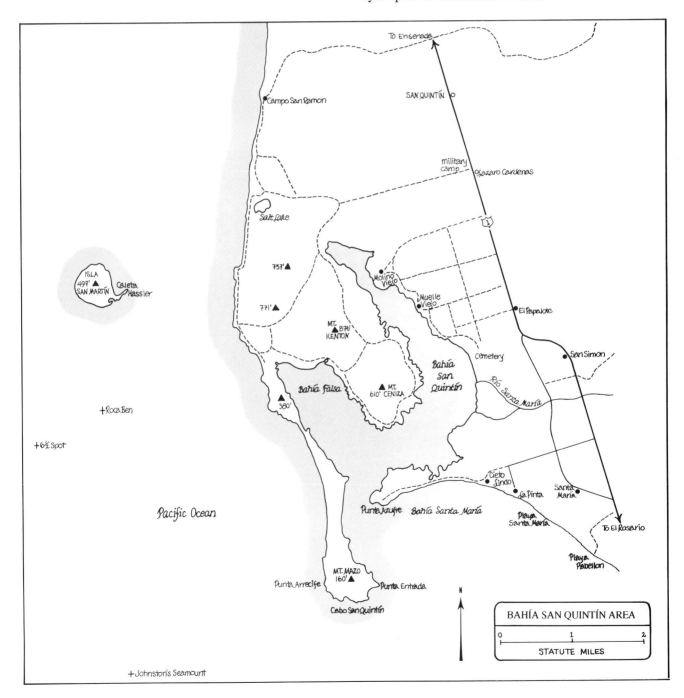

Restaurant Costa Azul, Mile 1.2, has seafood, chicken, hamburgers, and a variety of steaks right up to *filete mignon*, and has a bar, a disco complete with giant speakers and psychedelic lights, and a dance floor. Restaurant el Alazan, at Mile 1.3, serves a number of Mexican dishes, as well as grilled steaks and roasted chicken. The laundromat, Mile 1.6, is the last for many miles to the south. Restaurant la Bota at Mile 1.6 serves steaks, hamburgers, and Mexican food. Restaurant San Quintín, at Mile 1.8, has Mexican, seafood, and steaks, and a bar. The State Secretary of Tourism maintains an office in the restaurant. It would be well to carefully scrutinize transactions at the second PEMEX (MN) at Mile 3.5.

Around 1890, the Lower California Development Company, an English concern, sold tracts of land around San Quintín for wheat farming, dredged the harbor, built a flour mill, started construction of a railroad to Ensenada, and instituted weekly steamer service to San Diego. Trial plantings of wheat in 1889 had produced an abundant harvest, and potential investors were invited to witness its grinding in the mill. However, 1889 proved to be an unusually wet year, and local legend has it that the wheat ground into flour in later demonstrations was imported from more productive locations. The scheme soon failed due to inadequate rainfall, and the defrauded investors lost their money. A large steam engine from the mill can be seen at Molino Viejo (Old Mill, a motel to be described shortly), along with artifacts of a fish cannery. The skeleton of a pier lies several miles to the south of the Old Mill, and the old English graveyard can be seen several more miles to the south.

Today, many thousands of irrigated acres are committed to produce, much of which is shipped north of the border. The area is prospering, and large satellite TV antennas are seen serving even some of the most humble abodes. There are a number of computer and video stores, and a bed-and-breakfast is in business. A regularly scheduled local bus line now serves the area, and a rush hour seems to be developing. However, the weather that sealed the fate of the wheat farming scheme is never far out of mind.

Bahía San Quintín is one of the major geological features of Baja's west coast. Five basalt craters mark its location from many miles away (the sixth crater is Isla San Martín). Shallow mud flats that cover most of the bay are nurseries for hordes of fish, mollusks, and crustaceans, and eel grass attracts large numbers of brant and about 20 species of ducks and other geese each winter. Numerous other species like the place as well, and the bay and surrounding land areas are probably endowed with more bird species than any other location in Baja.

■ The black brant

The bay is the temporary winter home of large numbers of Pacific brant, a small black goose that breeds during the summer in Alaska, northwestern Canada, and Siberia. Many of them winter in saltwater lagoons and bays in Washington, Oregon, Alta California, and Baja California, and along mainland Mexico's west coast. However, increasing hunting pressure and wetlands destruction now cause many of them to avoid lengthy stops in our West Coast states. They are thus common in Baja, often frequenting Bahía San Quintín, Laguna Ojo del Liebre, Laguna San Ignacio, and Bahía Magdalena.

Brant usually begin to arrive at San Quintín in late October, and by mid-November 10,000 to 13,000 birds may be present. Some continue south, while others stop to winter over in the bay, attracted by its 35 square miles of eel grass, their most important source of winter food. The population in the bay remains fairly stable until birds from more southern regions stop in mid-January on their way north. From then until the end of February, the population increases to as many as 35,000. It then declines, and by early May all have left Baja.

The area has both unspoiled fishing and a launch ramp capable of handling sizable boats, and a number of RV parks, restaurants, and other attractions can be found near the head of the bay. To get to the area, turn west on the graded class 1 road at KM 1, opposite a large electrical station. Set trip odometer, arrive at the Old Mill at Mile 3.4.

There have been many changes at the Old Mill in recent years. From an antiquated and sleepy backwater, the Old Mill has developed into a pleasant visitor attraction. Accommodations range from the original brick motel units to new apartment-like units with full kitchens and refrigerators. The class B RV park has full hookups, rest rooms and showers, but is somewhat pricey given the facilities provided. Gaston's Cannery Restaurant serves seafood, including fish, shrimp, crab, oysters, and lobster, as well as steak and Mexican items. If you choose lobster, you can pick your critter from a large aquarium. The ambiance of the restaurant and the adjoining Old Mill Saloon are fine, with a fireplace, *mariachi* music, rustic furniture and, appropriately enough, a "fish cannery" motif, but the prices are a bit high.

Old Mill Bait and Tackle offers boat charters, with 6 cruisers ranging from 20 feet to 25 feet, as well as rods, reels, and other tackle. A fleet of Bertram diesel cruisers was going into service in 1996. Tiburon's Pangas Sportfishing has a 24 feet and several 26 feet cruisers, equipped with bait wells, depth finders, and radios, as well as several *pangas*. Live bait is available upon request. Reservations should be made a week in advance in winter, two weeks in summer. Boats can be stored nearby.

Ernesto's Motel (soon to change its name to Baja Ron's Motel), just to the north of the Old Mill, has a small restaurant and offers fishing trips, but has no RV facilities. Campo Lorenzo, a half mile further north, is completely filled by permanents. Muelle Viejo (Old Pier) Restaurant serves seafood and steaks. RV parking is available, with showers and rest rooms. It can be reached by driving south along the eastern shore of the bay from the Old Mill, or by turning southwest from the Transpeninsular from KM 3+ on the graded class 1 road.

The steep (18%) launch ramp at Molino Viejo has finally been paved, and it's a dandy, 25 feet wide. Channels running south from Molino Viejo and Bahía Falsa join south of Mount Ceniza ("Ceniza" means ashen, in keeping with its volcanic origin) to form a Y, then continue on to Punta Azufre (Sulfur Point). Fishing in the "inner bay" north of Punta Azufre is largely for flatfish, although different species of rock fish are found in deeper areas near the entrance. The flatfish can be big, occasionally in the 20- to 30-pound class, and there are reports of occasional giant sea bass. Fishing off Cabo San Quintín can be excellent for a mixed bag of bottom and pelagic fish. However, three offshore seamounts to the south of San Martín are among the best fishing locations between San Diego and Isla Cedros. It is possible to visit them by trailer boat, and even cartopper in good weather if normal safety precautions are observed. Choose your weather and tides carefully, and while in the inner bay use your depth finder to stay in the channel; for some boaters the run to the seamounts is an easy romp of several hours, while others complain of weed-choked props, heavy tidal rips, and huge waves at the point, and then a long run against heavy wind and waves.

Johnston's Seamount, known to local fishermen as the "240 Spot," is located 6 miles, 240°, from Cabo San Quintín. When you are over the site, Mount Mazo (Mallet Mountain) will bear 052° and the peak on San Martín 340°. The seamount has 2 peaks, one of which rises to within 10 feet of the surface, the other to within 55 feet, both of which are often surrounded by hordes of yellowtail and bottom fish. During the warm months, small numbers of yellowfin tuna and marlin have been known to hang out in the area.

Roca Ben (Ben's Rock), 2.5 miles south of San Martín, is a rocky pinnacle rising to within 12 feet of the surface at low tide. The area is frequented by bonito, ocean whitefish, and a variety of bottom fish, including ling cod to 30 pounds. At low tide, Roca Ben can be found easily, since surf and boils often mark its location. However, at other times it can be elusive and a compass fix may be helpful: when you are over the site, Mount Mazo will bear 110° and the peak on San Martín 346°. Great care must be exercised while fishing in this vicinity. In 1987, the charter fishing vessel *Fish 'N Fool* out of San Diego was overwhelmed by a huge breaker near Roca Ben and sank with the loss of 10 lives. Do not approach the area unless it is flat calm, and stand off at least a half hour to determine if there are any "sneaker" waves coming in.

Because it is about 200 yards in diameter, a shallow area called the "6 1/2 Spot" by fishermen, two miles southwest of Roca Ben, is easy to locate with a depth finder. Bearings to the landmarks just cited are 099° and 010°, least depth 40 feet. Yellowtail are the primary quarry between March and November, when fish migrating along the 100-fathom

curve move in to forage, although some fish hang around all year. Ling, ocean whitefish, and calico bass are also taken in numbers. Between April and November, the prime quarry for those in larger boats is yellowfin tuna, taken 5 to 20 miles offshore.

San Martín is volcanic, its crater rising to 497 feet. A steady procession of gray whales can be seen passing to seaward in winter, often just outside the surf line. In the mid-1800s, ships anchored in the lee of the island to lie in wait for the whales. Sea lions and elephant seals haul out on the eastern shore, and harbor seals can be seen in the small lagoon on the south shore. The areas surrounding the island often produce lots of whitefish, lings, and barracuda, and some yellowtail are present year-around. Sandy bottoms in Caleta Hassler have flatfish and unusually large kelp bass. Although frequently ignored, calico bass fishing can be excellent, and 20 to 30 hookups a day on bonito are possible.

■ Dubious mermaids

Many people believe that the "mermaid" legend, that of a beautiful half-fish, half-woman beckoning seductively to sailors on passing ships, began when sailors saw elephant seals with their heads and shoulders bobbing out of the water. If so, the sailors must have

She may be female, but sailors must have been lonely indeed to mistake an angry face like that on this elephant seal for that of a mermaid

been afflicted with either poor vision or very wishful thinking. Modern observers have more accurate, if less romantic, descriptions, such as "ill-tempered, water-filled Zeppelins," "rotten, peeling, 15-foot sausages," and "giant caterpillars made of Jello."

Northern elephant seals are the second-largest of all seals, exceeded only by their Southern counterparts. Adult males are often 15 feet to 16 feet long and weigh 4,000 to 5,000 pounds, adult females 11 feet and a relatively petite 1,700 pounds. Although they may look ridiculously awkward on land, they are powerful and graceful swimmers, spending almost 90% of their time diving for food, which consists primarily of sharks and squid. Recent research has shown that the elephant seal makes the deepest dives of any air-breathing vertebrate, surpassing even the sperm whale and the leatherback sea turtle. Although dives made by elephant seals are normally around 800 feet, scientists studying them have observed dives deeper than the capacity of their recording instruments, which **end** at 3,300 feet. Although this study was done on females, it is assumed that the larger, more powerful males can dive even deeper.

Except during the breeding season, elephant seals lead solitary lives on the open ocean, but at the beginning of the December-to-March breeding season, males begin to arrive at isolated beaches in the two Californias. Great battles are fought to establish supremacy and territorial rights, the bulls slashing each other's necks with their sharp teeth, occasionally resulting in a copious loss of blood. Nothing can quite match what a male elephant seal does with his nose during threat displays. When inflated, not Carl Malden nor even Gerard Depardieu can compete with these ponderous proboscises. When inflated, the hollow nose acts as a sound resonator, resulting in powerful bellows that carry over long distances. Females begin arriving in late December, to find that they have limited choices in sexual matters: elephant seals are polygamous, and dominant males fight for as many females as they can control. Harems sometimes get so large, up to 60 females, that the lucky males in charge cannot watch everyone, and subordinate males may sneak in to mate with cows in estrus. Competition for harems is intense, and most males can keep one for only three or four years before they are replaced by lusty young competitors.

Cows give birth to single pups that weigh between 50 and 70 pounds. After 3 or 4 weeks of being nursed on rich milk, they may weigh as much as 400 pounds. The greatest danger to pups are the males, which can trample or roll over them. Cows are not friendly toward calves not their own, and will severely discipline any that attempt to nurse, sometimes with fatal bites.

In the past, elephant seals were hunted extensively, not for their scarred and worthless pelts, but for the fine oil that could be rendered from their blubber. Skippers of sealing ships timed their voyages so they arrived at the start of the breeding season, when the seals were hauling themselves out on the breeding beaches and were still fat from months at sea. The supply seemed inexhaustible, but by the late 1830s, the Alta California population had been wiped out. In 1892, a lonely population of 9 was found on Isla Guadalupe, located about 180 miles off Baja's west coast at the latitude of Bahía de los Angeles. The scientists who found this remnant of a supposedly extinct species were delighted, but they unfortunately found it necessary to kill seven for specimens. Luckily, there were others they didn't find, and the seals numbers began increasing slowly after the Mexican government outlawed hunting them in 1922.

Adults are too large and powerful to interest most other species looking for a meal, but killer whales were once seen killing an adult bull, and bite marks from great white sharks have been observed. In recent years, their population has been doubling every 5 years, and the current estimate is about 70,000. They are sometimes encountered at San Martín, as well as Islas San Benito, Los Coronados, and San Jerónimo. Although there has never been a recorded human death resulting from the attack of an elephant seal, and Southern California divers have had uneventful underwater encounters with them, use great care if you do come upon one, for they have no fear of humans despite what the human race did to their ancestors, and can move with surprising speed on land when provoked.

■■■■■■■■■■■■■■■■■■■■■■■■■■■

On the Transpeninsular in San Quintín at KM 196

KM	Location
196/0	Start a new KM numbering sequence.
1	Class 1 road west to the head of the bay, described on page 92.
3+	George's Bait and Tackle sells line, lures, natural baits, and custom rods, and makes rod repairs.
11	Road west to Cielito Lindo RV Park and the La Pinta Hotel. The road is lined on both sides with tamarisks, almost forming a tunnel in some places. Due to its vigorous growth and toleration of saline soils, this non-native tree was introduced to Baja for use as wind-breaks. A mature tree produces over 500,000 seeds a year, and trees damaged by fire can regenerate from

their root systems. These characteristics, plus the fact that each tree transpires hundreds of gallons of water a day, drying out the soils nearby, make tamarisk a vigorous competitor with native vegetation for living space. The last mile to Cielito Lindo is unpaved class 1, but it can get very muddy after rains. The management of inexpensive Cielito Lindo RV Park, marginal class C, does not believe in maintenance, and the showers and toilets at the park are filthy and inoperative, the RV parking sites are littered, and the electrical and water hookups do not work. There is a restaurant nearby. The beach break is good on south swells, and excellent surf fishing for barred surfperch is found south to El Socorro. If you wish to go to the La Pinta, turn left (southwest) at the sign for the hotel about 2.8 miles from the Transpeninsular. The hotel has rooms, restaurant, bar, tennis, horseback riding, a Magnasin pump, and a magnificent beach.

■ The gray thrasher

The endemic gray thrasher is common along Baja Norte's Pacific coast from this latitude south and throughout Baja Sur. They are usually found in desert scrub at low elevations. Look for a slender gray-brown bird with black tear-drop shaped spots on a light-gray or buff breast, and a fairly long, curved, dark-colored bill.

15+ Class 1 road west (signed) to inexpensive El Pabellón Trailer Park, class B, 1.2 miles. (El Pabellón means The Pavilion, although one is not in evidence.) Some sites have water and sewer hookups, and there are rest rooms, showers, and a beautiful sand beach.

23+ Sportfishing and diving boats, guides.

24 **El Socorro.** Beaches, reef breaks. The shoreline south from El Socorro for about 13 miles has good surfing, offering shore and reef breaks. A number of dirt roads approach the water, permitting solitary boondocking.

39 The hills to the east are topped by a weather-resistant Pliocene deposit containing abundant giant barnacles, pismo clams, and sand dollars.

■ Locoweed

The low plants with pinnate leaves (having parts or branches arranged on each side of an axis, like a feather) along the side of the highway in the vicinity of KM 41 are locoweed. The term refers to the fact that the leaves accumulate the element selenium, a poison, and many a horse has allegedly "gone crazy" after eating it. The local Indians reportedly used it for toothaches and sore throats, and, because the dry seed pods rattle when shaken, it was mistakenly thought to be an antidote for rattlesnake bite.

51+ Begin 14% downgrade to El Rosario.

56 **El Rosario.** PEMEX (MN), cafés, stores, restaurants, motels, doctor, bakery, butcher shop, tire sales and repairs, mechanics, auto parts, long-distance telephone. Restaurant Yiyos serves a Mexican menu and is clean and inexpensive. Café Espinosa was the last outpost of civilization in the days before the Transpeninsular was completed, and virtually all travelers stopped to get information, a lobster taco, and one last cold beer before starting out across the wilderness ahead. The supermarket sells groceries, produce (generally of modest quality, but the prices are low), meat, ice, beer, liquor, limited hardware items. A small museum has been established in a white building just northeast of the supermarket; ask for the key at Espinosa's. A fish inspection station is often in operation on the Transpeninsular in the northeastern part of town. Sinai RV Park, class C, at KM 56+, has water, electric, and sewer hookups. Class 2 road to Punta Baja and Agua Blanca.

El Rosario; in the days before the Transpeninsular an important stop before heading south into the wilderness, today just another dusty village

 Off-road trip from El Rosario to Punta Baja and to Agua Blanca, both having excellent bottom fishing. Turn to page 204.

On the Transpeninsular Highway at El Rosario. The PEMEX stations at Cataviña, Parador Punta Prieta, and Villa Jesús María (73, 139, and 198 miles from El Rosario, re-

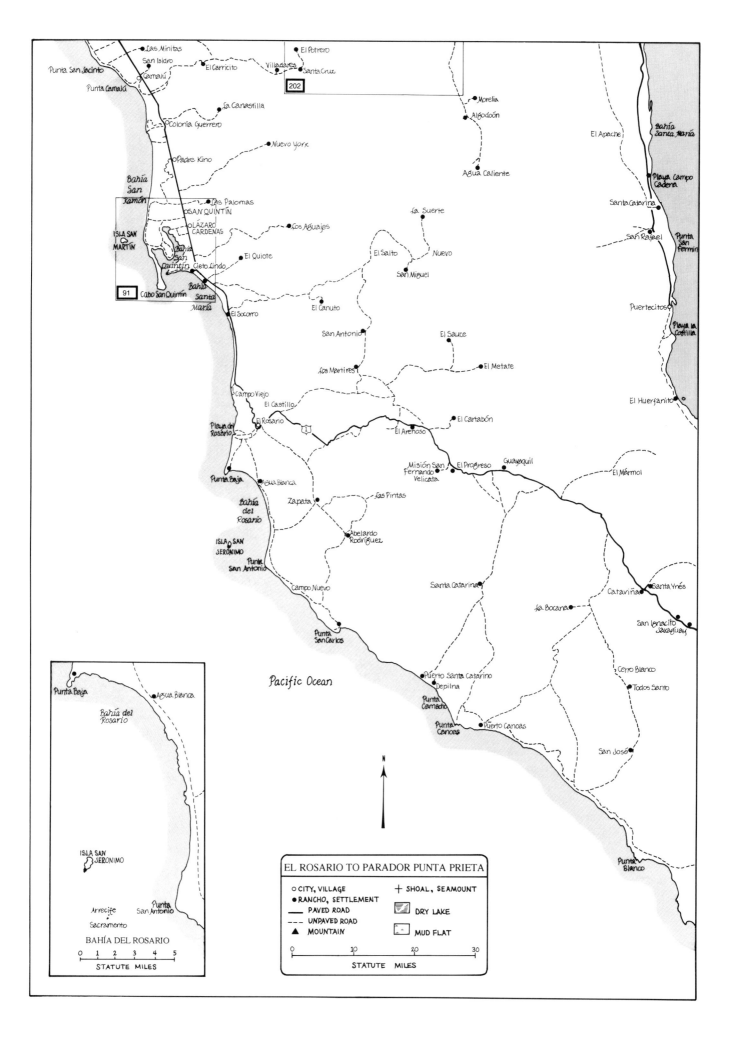

Punta San Jacinto
Punta Camalú
Camalú
San Isidro
Las Minitas
El Carricito
Villadares
Santa Cruz
El Potrero
202
Morelia
Algodón
El Apache
Bahía
Santa María
La Canastilla
Colonia Guerrero
Padre Kino
Nuevo York
Agua Caliente
Playa Campo
Cadena
Santa Catarina
San Rafael
Punta
San Fermín
Bahía
San
Ramón
Las Palomas
SAN QUINTÍN
LÁZARO
CARDENAS
Los Aguajes
La Suerte
ISLA SAN
MARTÍN
Bahía
San
Quintín
Cielo Lindo
El Quiote
El Salto
Nuevo
San Miguel
91
Cabo San Quintín
Bahía
Santa
María
El Socorro
El Canuto
San Antonio
Puertecitos
Playa la
Costilla
San Antonio
Los Mártires
El Sauce
El Metate
El Huerfanito
Campo Viejo
El Castillo
El Rosario
Playa del
Rosario
1
El Arenoso
El Cartabón
Punta Baja
Agua Blanca
Bahía
del
Rosario
Zapata
Las Pintas
Misión San
Fernando
Velicatá
El Progreso
Guayaquil
El Mármol
ISLA SAN
JERÓNIMO
Punta
San Antonio
Abelardo
Rodríguez
Campo Nuevo
Santa Catarina
La Bocana
Cataviña
Santa Ynés
San Ignacito
Jaraguay
Pacific Ocean
Punta
San Carlos
Cerro Blanco
Todos Santo
Puerto Santa Catarino
Depilna
Punta
Camacho
Punta
Canoas
Puerto Canoas
San José
N

Punta Baja
Agua Blanca
Bahía del
Rosario
ISLA SAN
JERÓNIMO
Arrecife
Sacramento
Punta
San Antonio
BAHÍA DEL ROSARIO
0 1 2 3 4 5
STATUTE MILES

EL ROSARIO TO PARADOR PUNTA PRIETA

○ CITY, VILLAGE   + SHOAL, SEAMOUNT
● RANCHO, SETTLEMENT
— PAVED ROAD   ▭ DRY LAKE
-- UNPAVED ROAD
▲ MOUNTAIN   ▭ MUD FLAT

0   10   20   30
STATUTE MILES

Punta
Blanco

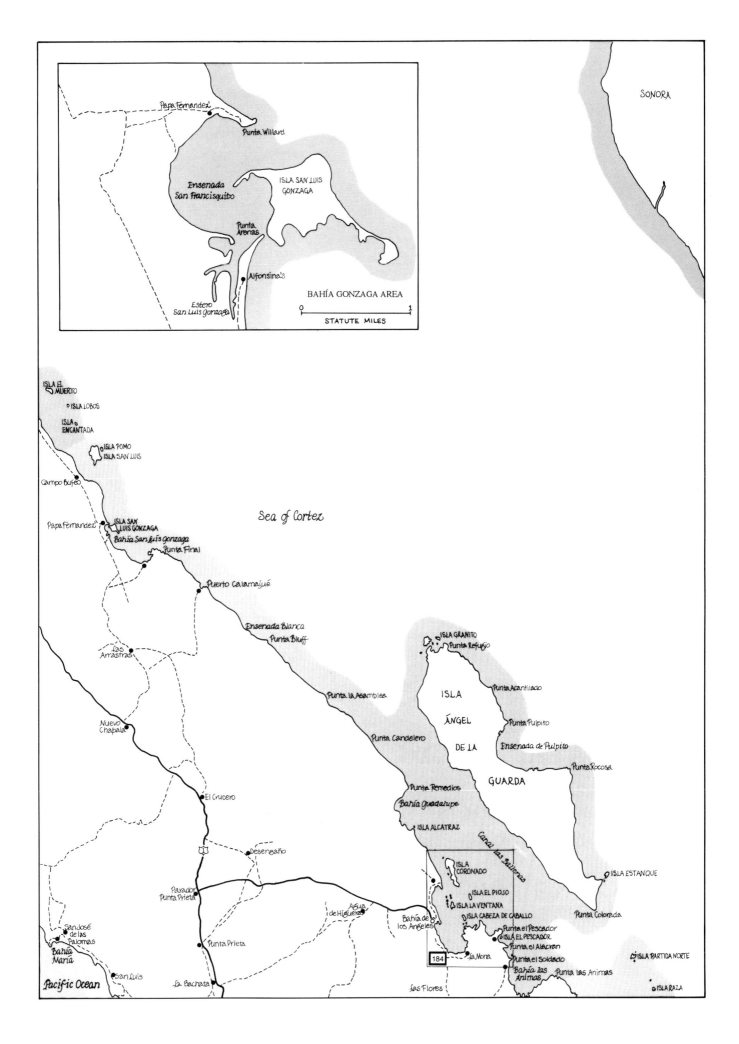

SONORA

Papa Fernandez

Punta Willard

Ensenada
San Francisquito

Punta
Arenas

ISLA SAN LUIS
GONZAGA

Alfonsina's

Estero
San Luis Gonzaga

BAHÍA GONZAGA AREA

0   1

STATUTE MILES

ISLA EL
MUERTO

ISLA LOBOS

ISLA
ENCANTADA

ISLA POMO
ISLA SAN LUIS

Campo Bufeo

Sea of Cortez

Papa Fernandez

ISLA SAN
LUIS GONZAGA

Bahía San Luis Gonzaga

Punta Final

Puerto Calamajué

Ensenada Blanca

Punta Bluff

ISLA GRANITO

Punta Refugio

Las
Arrastras

Punta la Asamblea

ISLA

ÁNGEL

Punta Acantilado

Punta Pulpito

Nuevo
Chapala

Punta Candelero

DE LA

Ensenada de Pulpito

Punta Rocosa

GUARDA

El Crucero

Punta Remedios

Bahía Guadalupe

ISLA ALCATRAZ

Canal las Ballenas

ISLA ESTANQUE

Desengaño

ISLA
CORONADO

Parador
Punta Prieta

Agua
de Higueras

ISLA EL PIOJO

ISLA LA VENTANA

San José
de las
Palomas

Bahía de
los Angeles

ISLA CABEZA DE CABALLO

Punta Colorada

Bahía
María

Punta Prieta

Punta el Pescador

ISLA EL PESCADOR

Punta el Alacran

ISLA PARTIDA NORTE

184

La Mona

Punta el Soldado

Pacific Ocean

San Luis

La Bachata

Bahía las
Animas

Punta las Animas

Las Flores

ISLA RAZA

spectively) sometimes do not have gas, so top off in El Rosario and fill again at every opportunity. The next supermarket is in Guerrero Negro, so get your supplies while you can. Travelers headed "south" early in the day should beware—since the highway runs generally east and southeast for many miles, a blinding sun hovering over the road ahead in the morning increases the hazards of an already difficult stretch of highway. The same applies to those headed "north" at sunset. Until this point, the Transpeninsular has passed through areas that have had substantial populations and paved roads for many years, but the "real" Baja begins here: unfenced ranges, lonely ranches, and mile after mile of almost uninhabited desert.

KM	Location
56	El Rosario.
71	This point marks the beginning of an area where a number of unusual and interesting plants can be seen along the Transpeninsular.

■ A garden of desert plants

The strange plants north of the road at KM 71 are boojums, *Idria columnaris* to scientists. They defy precise description, for the simple reason that analogies fail; there are no other plants quite like them, although "huge, skinny, upside-down carrots" comes fairly close. The Mexicans, though, detect a certain resemblance to candles, hence their Spanish name, *cirio*. Attempting to explain their odd shape, some claim that due to the extremely dry climate, the water in the air due to fogs is greater than that in the ground, so the plant simply puts up its roots into the air, while the branches lie below the soil.

Related to the ocotillo, they are found only from the southern end of the Sierra San Pedro Mártir south to the Tres Vírgenes area, on Guardian Angel Island, and in a small area in the mainland state of Sonora. Boojums reach 60 feet, and are often crowned with a cluster of spindly branches. They grow slowly, and a tall specimen, perhaps 50 feet, may be 360 years old. These no-nonsense plants have few decorative frills, their tapered lower trunks usually sporting no branches larger than pencils, although after rains small green leaves sprout, and yellow flowers may appear at the ends of the upper branches. They bear no edible fruit and make poor firewood.

Despite their Spartan approach to life, boojums quickly become a favorite species with Baja travelers. The reason is hard to pin down, but it seems that their grotesque shapes tickle the imagination; although there are no other plants like them, it is certainly possible to see human characteristics in each of them.

Boojums have the full range of human personalities, ranging from the exuberant to the straight-and-narrow

The plants on the south side of the road at KM 76 that look like giant green porcupines are a species of agave, one of about 20 to be found in Baja. Several species grow slowly for many years, and then suddenly put up a towering stalk covered with flowers, after which they die, a habit leading to the name "century plant." The Indians had a number of uses for the plants. As Father Baegert commented, "The most frequent food use for the Indians is to roast the head of it for twenty-four hours, partly in the fire, partly in the ash and between hot stones. However, many have to wait a long time to eat...,

This beautiful agave manages to prosper on a bleak, inhospitable, wind-swept hillside

for the women have to carry it from a many hour's walk away and do not return until the next evening. It is not a bad meal, and now and then I let the Indians give me a bite...." Baegert also noted that his converts made ropes, nets, and other useful articles out of the fiber, and wished that he could have European flax combers, spinners, and weavers see what they could do with it. Mescal, pulque, and tequila are still made from the fermented juice of some species. Off-road drivers should beware: the pointed spine at the end of each leaf seems to be tailor-made to cause virtually unpatchable sidewall punctures in tires.

The large shrubs growing in the vicinity of KM 90, a yard or two high, with oval, dark green leaves, are lemonadeberry. Their small fruit, about the size of a peanut, tastes good and makes an excellent drink. In her wisdom, Mother Nature designed this system to help disperse seeds, and she added a clever feature— the fruit is also a diuretic, causing you to quickly become thirsty again and prepare more of the drink and thus distribute more seeds, as well as providing them with a plentiful supply of water.

The large, solitary cactus standing north of the road at KM 92 is a *cardón*. Found only in Baja from approximately this latitude to the Cape and in a small area in Sonora, these giants may have 20 or more branches and exceed 50 feet in height. They can be distinguished from the organ pipe cactus described later in that they have a definite main trunk and they usually branch well above the ground. Since they have no leaves, photosynthesis, the process by which plants make carbohydrates, occurs on the green surface of the cactus stem. The stem is fleshy and thick, and can store a large amount of water, and its tough skin keeps the water safely hoarded. The roots spread out near the surface of the soil, enabling the plant to absorb water from a wide area during infrequent rains. As the trunk takes up water after a rain, the accordion-like ribs, 11 to 17 in number, unfold until the cross-section of the trunk is almost circular.

Most *cardóns* are bisexual, their flowers being equipped with both female ovules

A desert giant

and male pollen. However, some are entirely male, producing only flowers with pollen, while others are strictly female, their flowers having only ovules. Since they can self-fertilize, the bisexual plants should seemingly prevail in the long run, but the single-sex plants have an ally, the lesser long-nosed bat. This small animal is fond of the sweet nectar produced by the *cardón*'s perfumed flowers, and while obtaining it, coats its face with pollen. In making its nightly rounds, the bat thus transfers pollen from the male plants to the ovules of females. Apparently recognizing an everybody-wins situation (mutualism to biologists), the *cardón* wisely shapes its flowers to accommodate the cone-shaped head of the bat and opens them during its preferred night hours. The survival of the *cardón* is thus insured by the presence of both the efficient bisexual forms, which require no outside intervention for fertilization, and the sexual forms, which are more adaptable to changing environmental conditions.

The shrubs with dagger-like leaves on the north side of the highway at KM 104+ are *dátillo*, a species of yucca. Up to 15 feet high and having a woody trunk, normally unbranched, and leaves 12 inches to 19 inches long, they are common in Baja Norte. They put out masses of creamy-white blossoms in early spring. Yuccas have an interesting relationship with a tiny, night-flying moth, *Pronuba*—the moth is dependent on the seeds of the plant for food, and the plant is dependent on the moth for pollination, another example of mutualism. *Dátillo* can easily be confused with *dátilillo*, another common yucca, which will be seen along the highway at KM 232+, another 79 miles ahead. Having seen both, you should have little difficulty distinguishing them.

Dátillo

KM	Location
114	Class 1 road southwest (signed) to Misión San Fernando Velicatá, 3 miles.

■ Misión San Fernando Velicatá

This old mission provides clues to the three successive cultures that have occupied the site: Indian, Mission, and Mexican. Prior to the arrival of Spanish missionaries, a band of Indians lived here, drawn by the relative abundance of plant foods and game, and the dependable springs. They pecked, rubbed, and painted many artistic designs on the granite cliffs. While no dating using physical means has been attempted, stylistic comparisons suggest the designs were created between 1000 and 1500 A.D.

In 1768 or 1769 (sources differ), Franciscan Father Junípero Serra founded Misión San Fernando Velicatá on the site. The mission was built primarily for logistic support of the missions in Alta California. Agriculture and domestic animals were introduced, and the mission thrived, the population of converted Indians expanding to about 1,500. To provide irrigation, the cliffs just to the west of the site were quarried to supply stone for an aqueduct, destroying, perhaps purposely, much of the art. In 1773, the Dominicans assumed control of the missions in Baja California, including San Fernando. A disastrous epidemic struck in 1777, and the Indian population was almost wiped out. In 1814 there were only 100 people left, and by 1822, the last padre had departed and the mission closed forever. By 1830 the population had dropped to 19, and 20 years later only 4 were left, all very old. Within a few years the site was silent.

In the last years of the century, the site was reoccupied, and Smithsonian Institution naturalist George Merrill was not too impressed with the level of civilization, "We camped at San Fernando…[now] occupied by Mexicans and their numerous progeny, twice the number of dogs and a million times as many fleas…." Today, a few families live at the site, sustained by ranching and subsistence farming. Their adobe and palm thatch buildings stand close to the crumbling mission, together with the mandatory rusted auto bodies and piles of empty tin cans. A modern graveyard is slowly encroaching into the mission building. Some of the petroglyphs that survived quarrying were obliterated by Mexican road builders in 1973. Vandals have spray-painted names, dates, and crosses in red, blue, and shocking pink.

To see the aqueduct and surviving art, walk to the cliffs a half mile away, bearing 255° from the ruins. Just before arriving at the cliffs look for petroglyphs on the boulders along the trail. Some are visible from the floor of the arroyo, but most will require some scrambling up the rocky cliffs.

The Indians who lived here are now extinct and the missionaries and their charges long dead. In 1988, Father Serra was beatified, the last step before winning sainthood, despite the fate of his flock. Although it is tranquil and time seems to have stopped, a visit to the site makes one wonder if another rolling cultural wave will someday engulf the site. Perhaps you are the beginning; will the site someday sport the Golden Arches? Will it have an economy based on grants, welfare, and tourism, like so much of America? Will it have a methadone clinic?

KM	Location
116+	**Rancho el Progreso**. Food and drink.
126	**Guayaquil**. Tire repair. Groceries in village a half mile north.
144	Tire repair, Lonchería Sonora, a small café. Class 1 road northeast (signed) to El Mármol.

Off-road trip from KM 144 to El Mármol, the site of an abandoned onyx quarry and perhaps the world's most unusual school building, side trip El Volcán, Baja's only geyser. Turn to page 206.

■ The devil's buggy whip

The strange plants with many whip-like branches on both sides of the highway in the vicinity of KM 146 are ocotillos. A common desert plant, they are seen as far south as Bahía Concepción. Often leafless and seemingly dead, these Spartan plants quickly sprout small green leaves after a rain, and unexpectedly beautiful mustard-red flowers appear at the tips of their branches. The world record seems to be held by a specimen with 48 whips, located along the road from the Transpeninsular to El Arco. Ocotillo can be confused with an almost identical plant, *palo adán*, but ocotillo has no trunk, its many whips springing from a cluster on the ground, while *palo adán* has a short, thick trunk.

140	Watch for south-pointing compass cacti in this area.
157	Entering prime desert scenery, with jumbled boulders, stately *cardóns*, and "forests" of boojums.
171+	Arroyo de Cataviñacito.

Arroyo de Cataviñacito

A small stream crosses the highway at KM 171+, watering a number of graceful blue fan palms. With some sandy spots, this area provides a nice stop for lunch and a bit of exploring. If you need a bath, deep emerald-colored pools (in wet years) can be found about a half mile upstream. An interesting and easily accessible display of

Indian rock art can be found in a small grotto near this point. Red, yellow, and black paintings scattered about its walls and ceiling include abstract designs, humans, and a stylized sun. The bicolor tradition is evident on several figures. The grotto is so small that only a few people can crowd in. In fact, it is on such a small scale and the art so simple that one cannot help imagining that it was a playhouse for Cochimí children—hence its unofficial name, the "Playhouse Cave." Look for dark stains on the ceiling from ancient campfires. The exterior of the site has been vandalized with spray paint, but the art was not damaged. The grotto is easy to locate: park on the north side of the highway and sight 359°—the grotto is located among the largest boulders forming the skyline.

The "fat" trees in the vicinity are *copalquín*, or elephant trees, members of the sumac family. Endemic to Baja and widespread, they seem to prosper in poor conditions, sometimes becoming great prostrate giants on desolate lava beds where nothing else grows. They bear two colors of flowers, some white with touches of pink, others pink to light red. Note that the compound leaves are small, that the branchlets are gray, and that balls of parasitic orange dodder grow on many individuals; these observations will be needed to distinguish *copalquín* from an almost identical species that will be described shortly.

A massive, sprawling elephant tree

KM	Location

174+ **Cataviña**. PEMEX (MN; D is improbable), cafés, grocery, tire repair, mechanic. The Hotel la Pinta has a restaurant, bar, pool, and tennis court, and offers horseback riding and local hikes to rock art sites. It also sells Magnasin. Inexpensive Trailer Park Cataviña, class C, has full hookups, rest rooms, and showers, although things almost never work.

■ **Almost twins**

The RV park at Cataviña has been landscaped with desert plants, including *copalquín*, described earlier. However, if you look closely you will note that some of the "fat trees" in the park are not *copalquín*; these have red-brown branchlets, and their compound leaves are much smaller. These are *torote*, also called elephant trees. Despite being almost indistinguishable at first glance and having an overlapping range, they are not closely related to *copalquín*; they belong to the torchwood family. Dodder does not seem to grow on *torote*. These specimens are transplanted, but the two species can be seen growing side by side in the wild in many locations in this region.

176 Paved road northeast (signed) to Rancho Santa Ynés, 0.7 mile. Rooms, bunk beds, showers, hot food, cold beer, and very inexpensive RV parking are available.

186 **Rancho San Ignacito**. Food and drink. In September, 1973, road crews working north and south met here, completing the construction of the Transpeninsular Highway.

205 The Devil used his buggy whip to motivate sinners, using them to stockpile a large supply of boulders, which can be seen to the south. Named Cerro Pedregoso (Rocky Hill), it was much higher in the distant past, but sediments and lava have covered much of it. Having the appearance of an iceberg, it was a handy landmark before the days of the Transpeninsular.

■ **The devil's bowling balls?**

Why are many of the boulders on Cerro Pedregoso and elsewhere in this area rounded, having the appearance of gigantic bowling balls, instead of being ordinary irregular or jagged rocks? Through a process called "spheroidal weathering," sharp edges and corners tend to erode more quickly than flat or gently curved surfaces, leading eventually to a rounded shape, a common phenomenon in arid regions.

229+ Class 2 road northeast (signed) to Puerto Calamajué, Bahía San Luis Gonzaga, Puertecitos, and San Felipe. Turn to page 227 for a description.

230+ **Nuevo Chapala**. Food and drink.

■ **Laguna Chapala**

Laguna Chapala, to the northeast at this point, is

dry for years at a time, and its hard, flat surface, marred only by deep polygonal cracks and a thick layer of dust, was a welcome relief for drivers before the Transpeninsular was opened, permitting high speeds and easy driving, if only for a few miles. One early driver marveled that it was possible to increase the speed of his vehicle from 5 miles an hour to 20, for 2 miles. However, it has no outlet, so when a rain finally came, a lake formed that could be 3 miles in length and 2 feet deep. As the water evaporated, mud of unimaginable depths formed. Nothing, neither man nor beast nor vehicle, could conquer the mud, and travelers had to pick their way around the rocky margin of the lake, at the cost of many shredded tires. One over-confident traveler thought the surface was strong enough and parked for the night, only to find the next morning that his vehicle had broken through the crust and was slowly sinking into the bottomless muck below.

KM	Location

239   Crest of a ridge, magnificent desert views ahead. Some travelers have called this area "lush," but others feel "lush desert" is an oxymoron. Judge for yourself; can a desert be lush?

■ More desert plants

The trees on the southwest side of the road in the vicinity of KM 239 resembling the Joshua tree of the US are *dátilillos*. Growing from this region to the Cape, they are often cut into fence posts, many of which take root and produce a living fence.

Dátillo

They are very common, sometimes forming great open "forests." They can be confused with *dátillo*, noted at KM 104+, but *dátilillos* are generally much taller, and may have branches extending anywhere from the trunk.

The erect shrubs and small trees with blue-green leaves and yellow tubular flowers in disturbed areas

along the road are tree tobacco. A relative of the deadly weed smoked by a quarter of the population in the US, it is poisonous and equally foul-smelling. It repels insects and mammals, but somehow the hummingbirds manage to conquer the stench to obtain its nectar. A native of Chile and Argentina, it has become widespread in Baja, mainland Mexico, and parts of the US.

280   **Parador Punta Prieta**. The PEMEX (M) here is in a key location, but it has the worst record for reliability on the entire Transpeninsular. In March, 1996, the station appeared to be abandoned. The cafeteria is occasionally open, and the junk yard across the highway is a good source of parts. Mechanical repairs and towing service may be available. The inexpensive RV park is not in regular operation and the hookups rarely work. In March, 1996, we were astounded to find that electricity was actually available. Paved road east to Bahía de los Angeles.

■ A heaven full of violins

The organ pipe cactus grows on sandy flats and rocky slopes from this area south to the Cape. It can be distinguished from the *cardón* in that it has only a very short or no main trunk, but has instead a number of upright branches, each having a dozen or more ribs and many small spines. The purple-and-red-tipped white flower blooms from April to July, producing a globular, spiny fruit. Inside, the sweet, slightly acidic pulp is so red that a better term might be "hot-crimson," the color being set off by the numerous small black seeds. Although totally unrelated, the fruit is similar in size, shape, and consistency to the kiwi, with its green flesh and black seeds. The fruit sometimes stains the urine red, causing consternation among the uninitiated. The black seeds were the source of the "second harvest" mentioned in Chapter 1, but you will probably wish to forego this exotic culinary treat.

Father Baegert liked the fruit: "...they bear fruit which one would not be ashamed to be eaten and seen at European and aristocratic dinners." "It tastes sour and is as good as any European fruit known to me." "I make use of [it], add [ing] wine...and sugar and I think I am eating strawberries or even something better." Baegert noted that the fruit served another purpose, as a calendar: "[The Spanish call it] *pitahaya dulce*. But the Indians call them *ambia*, and this serves as their time calendar. For to live in adultery one *ambia* is as much as twelve months, and three *ambia* as much as three years." "They can be eaten from the summer solstice on through two months thereafter. During this time the 'heaven hangs full of violins' and the good Indian thinks paradise has flown to California."

The organ pipe cactus got its name for an obvious reason

A second cactus, *pitaya agria*, produces a similar fruit, which, according to Clavigero (see Appendix F), has a better flavor, although it is not as sweet. *Pitaya agria* is much more common than *pitahaya dulce*, occurring from Ensenada to the Cape. Instead of neat, organized, upright branches of the organ pipe, *pitaya agria* tends to sprawl, its many tangled, spine-covered branches forming almost impenetrable thickets. There is a photograph of a *pitaya agria* fruit in the color section.

You will have to compete with the birds, who also appreciate the fruits of the two cactus, or purchase them in local fruit markets. They do not keep long when fully ripe and should be eaten immediately. If you have a blender along, they make great margaritas.

Side trip from Parador Punta Prieta to Bahía de los Angeles, the quintessential Baja town in the eyes of many. Turn to page 183.

280/0   Start new KM numbering sequence.

13   **Punta Prieta**. Groceries, café, mechanic, tire repair. Fossilized mammal bones 57 million years old have been found near here, including a hyracotherium, a horse the size of a dog.

38+   Class 1 road west (signed) to Santa Rosalillita.

Off-road trip from KM 38+ to Santa Rosalillita, offering excellent fishing, surfing, boardsailing, and boondocking, side trips to surrounding areas. Turn to page 207.

52   **Rosarito**. Groceries, cafés, tire repair.

68   Class 2 road southwest to El Tomatal (The Tomato Field, signed), 2.9 miles, a large boondocking site behind the dunes. If the wind makes camping uncomfortable, a grove of palms about 100 yards inland can serve as a wind-break. Cobble reefs tend to focus the swells, and the waters off the sand-and-pebble beach often have excellent, if incon-

sistent, surfing. The constant side-offshore winds provide good boardsailing. The beaches from here north to Punta Santa Rosalillita and south to Guerrero Negro are among the finest surf fishing locations in Baja. The prime quarry is migratory white seabass, taken with heavy surf rigs during the warm months, although a few are caught as early as January. Look for steep drop-offs with sand and cobble bottoms just offshore, and fling out a squid. Throughout the year you might also find yellowfin croakers in the surf line, and barred surfperch a bit farther out. Halibut, although not often considered a surf fish, are also frequently caught here.

■ The island of trees that drink fog

The large island that can be seen to the west in clear weather is Isla Cedros, about 70 miles away. The word "cedros" means cedar, a seemingly odd name for an island off the coast of Baja. Many thousands of years ago, the island's climate was wetter than today. As it became dryer, its forest of pines died out, except for two stands, which today depend on moisture from fog to survive. Early Spanish explorers thought them to be cedars and hence gave the island its name.

Since the island has abundant food and water, Cedros once had a sizable Indian population, estimated at between 500 and 1,000. In 1539, Francisco de Ulloa "discovered" the island, but the Cochimí inhabitants greeted him with stones and clubs, to which he replied with dogs and crossbow bolts. In 1602, explorer Sebastián Vizcaíno found that local attitudes toward strangers had not changed. However in 1732, Jesuit Father Sigismundo Taraval managed to get in a few words before the clubs and stones started, and the Indians were so impressed with his sweet talk about souls, saviors, and salvation that they agreed to leave the island almost *en masse* and settle around Misión San Ignacio. The few who remained died of smallpox, leaving the island uninhabited for the first time in 2,000 years. Yankees and Russians after seals and sea otters often visited the island in the late 1700s, and in the mid-1800s Chinese and Japanese divers came to take abalone. In the 1960s the island became an important transshipment point for the salt produced at Guerrero Negro, and there is a sizable village. The people living on the island can't share the fog with the trees, and they often rely on water brought from Japan as ballast on ships arriving to pick up cargoes of salt.

KM	Location
84	Note the "living fence" on the east side of the road. Ranchers cut down *dátilillos* to make fence posts, which sometimes spring to life again.

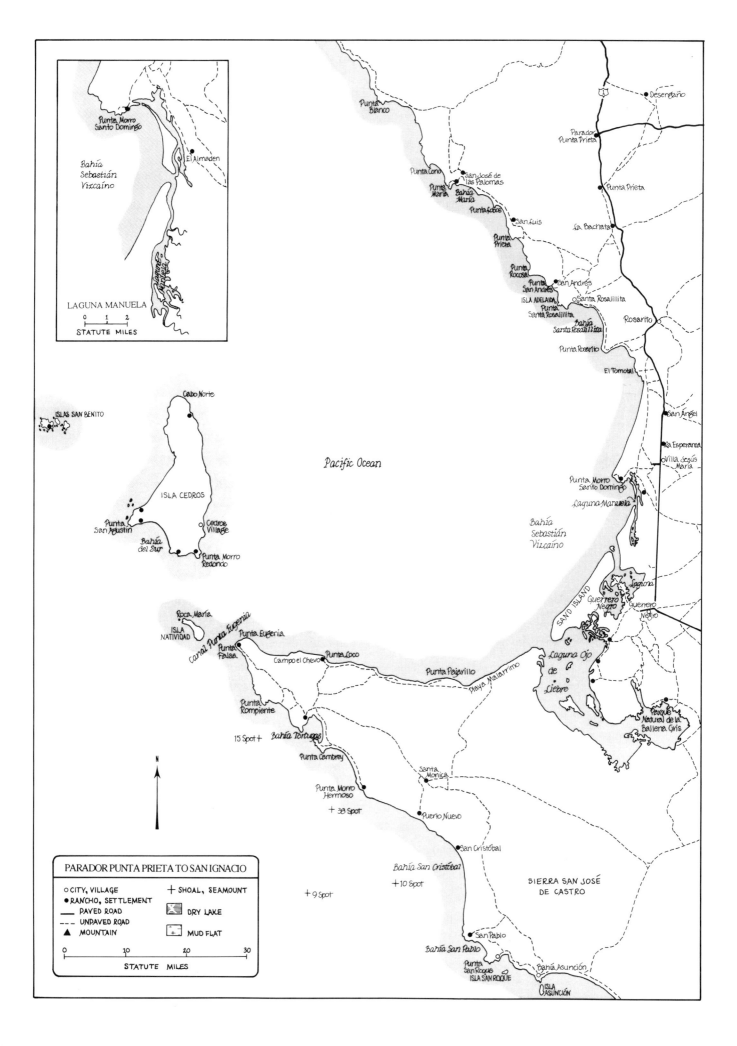

Inset map (top left):

Punta Morro
Santo Domingo

El Almaden

*Bahía
Sebastián
Vizcaíno*

Laguna Manuela

LAGUNA MANUELA

0   1   2
STATUTE MILES

Main map labels:

Desengaño

*Punta
Blanco*

Parador
Punta Prieta

Punta Cono
San José de
las Palomas

Punta
María

*Bahía
María*

Punta Prieta

Punta Acebo

San Luis

La Bachata

Punta
Prieta

Punta
Rocosa

Punta
San Andrés

San Andrés

ISLA ADELAIDA

Santa Rosalillita

Punta
Santa Rosalillita

Rosarito

*Bahía
Santa Rosalillita*

Punta Rosarito

El Tomotal

San Ángel

ISLAS SAN BENITO

Cabo Norte

La Esperanza

Villa Jesús
María

Pacific Ocean

Punta Morro
Santo Domingo

Laguna Manuela

ISLA CEDROS

*Bahía
Sebastián
Vizcaíno*

Punta
San Agustin

Cedros
Village

*Bahía
del Sur*

Punta Morro
Redondo

Laguna

Guerrero
Negro

Guerrero
Negro

SANTO ISLAND

Roca María

ISLA
NATIVIDAD

Canal Punta Eugenia

Punta Eugenia

Punta Coco

Punta
Falsa

Campo el Chevo

Punta Pajarillo

*Laguna Ojo
de
Liebre*

Playa Malarrimo

Punta
Rompiente

Parque
Natural de la
Ballena Gris

15 Spot

Bahía Tortugas

Punta Cambrey

Santa
Monica

N

Punta Morro
Hermoso

38 Spot

Puerto Nuevo

San Cristóbal

9 Spot

Bahía San Cristóbal

10 Spot

SIERRA SAN JOSÉ
DE CASTRO

Legend box:

PARADOR PUNTA PRIETA TO SAN IGNACIO

○ CITY, VILLAGE   ✛ SHOAL, SEAMOUNT
● RANCHO, SETTLEMENT
— PAVED ROAD   ▓ DRY LAKE
--- UNPAVED ROAD
▲ MOUNTAIN   ▨ MUD FLAT

0   10   20   30
STATUTE MILES

San Pablo

Bahía San Pablo

Punta
San Roque
ISLA SAN ROQUE

Bahía Asunción

ISLA
ASUNCIÓN

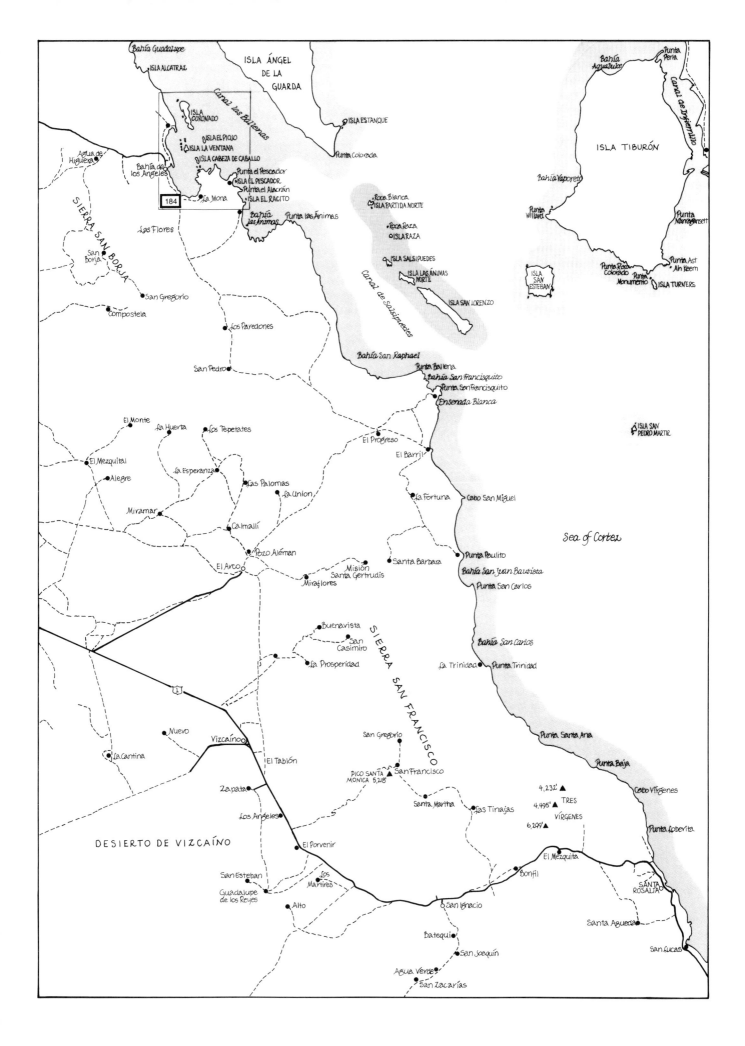

95 **Villa Jesús María**. PEMEX (MND), cafés, groceries, doctor, mechanic, tire repair, long-distance telephone.

96 Class 1 road west (signed) to Laguna Manuela.

Off-road trip from KM 96 to Laguna Manuela, offering boondocking and one of the finest fisheries in Baja. Turn to page 208.

121+ The magnificent dunes a few miles to the west are spread over 16 square miles.

127+ La Espinita Restaurant; seafood, Mexican, free overnight RV parking. The place is clean, and the food and hospitality are getting rave reviews from travelers.

128 Latitude 28° north, separating the states of Baja Norte and Baja Sur. The La Pinta Hotel has a restaurant and a bar, but the Magnasin pump is permanently out of operation. Whale-watching trips can be arranged at the desk. The inexpensive class C RV park has full hookups, showers, and toilets, but things rarely work. This point is also KM 221 for the beginning of a new KM sequence.

■ Oh, oh! Bad news!

We do not wish to be labeled as nit pickers, but there is a matter you should be aware of. The Mexican government has gone to great expense to build an elaborate monument at this point, marking the 28th degree of north latitude, which separates the states of Baja California [Norte] and Baja California Sur. There is only one problem; they built it in the wrong place. We have used our extremely accurate GPS satellite navigation receiver, and found that the monument is 810 feet too far north! The La Pinta Hotel is thus in Baja Norte, not Baja Sur, a matter that may be of interest to the tax officials in both states. A time-zone change occurs here—Baja Sur is one hour ahead of Baja Norte—and employees at the hotel are thus being required get out of bed one hour too early, a matter which should be brought to the attention of their union. A good remedy is not apparent, for the monument seems far too large to move. Instead of calling it the 28th Degree of North Latitude Monument, perhaps they could simply change its name to the 28th Degree 00 Minutes And 08 Seconds of North Latitude Monument.

■ The osprey

The birds nesting in winter on the signposts near the monument are ospreys. Although somewhat smaller than eagles, ospreys are often mistaken for them because of similarities in appearance. They live in temperate and tropic regions of the world near rivers, swamps and other bodies of water, especially in Europe, North America, northern Asia, and Australia.

Also called fish hawks, ospreys seize their favorite prey by plunging feet first into the water, and are well-equipped with sharp talons for that purpose. They are common but dispersed from El Rosario to Cabo San Lucas on the

An osprey shows off its beautiful plumage

Pacific side, and throughout the Cortez side. Because of the large amount of food found in the shallow, highly productive waters surrounding the peninsula, Baja ospreys do not migrate, but those found in other parts of the world go on long annual migrations.

These magnificent birds are highly adaptable, and have taken to nesting on man-made structures throughout the Guerrero Negro area, often favoring high-tension electrical poles. They form monogamous pairs, the male finding food, while the female sits on the nest, often losing considerable weight during nesting. Their nests are an eclectic mixture of twigs, seaweed, fish nets, tapes from cassette cartridges, rope, surprisingly large pieces of driftwood, fish and bird skeletons, and Bimbo bread wrappers. It has been estimated that there are 800 to 900 breeding pairs in Baja. One colony on a small island in Laguna San Ignacio boasts approximately 100 breeding pairs, perhaps the largest colony in the world.

KM	Location
220	Agricultural inspection station for all vehicles.
218	LPG yard.
217	Guerrero Negro Junction. If you are heading north, it is advisable to gas up in town and at Parador Punta Prieta, Cataviña, and El Rosario, as gas supplies are not always reliable. Guerrero Negro is described in the following chapter.

● ●

❝ *The night of the crustaceans*

My dad and I had decided to explore the Bahía San Carlos area, but my mom elected to spend the day reading in our trailer at Punta Baja. As we neared the beach at San Carlos, we saw a frightening scene—two fishermen in a panga *were attempting to come ashore through a thundering 7-foot surf. We soon realized it was all in a day's work for them; circling just outside the breakers, they waited until exactly the right moment on the right wave, and with the outboard engine racing, they skillfully rode the back of a wave onto the beach. We offered them a tow line, and quickly dragged the boat beyond the reach of the waves with our van.*

The sea had been generous, and the catch included perhaps 30 lobsters, several of which must have gone over 10 or 12 pounds. With a dozen or so of the inhabitants of the camp we joined in the celebration, contributing a case of Bud that my dad maintained for such impromptu occasions. As darkness approached, the tired and slightly tipsy fishermen drifted off to their shanties, but as we got up to leave one of them asked if we would drive him to San Quintín. It was a considerable distance, but his truck would not start and we were in no hurry, so we helped him load several crates of lobsters into the truck. Several hours later we were headed back to Punta Baja with a reward—the two giant lobsters, each large enough for a large meal for three people.

Mom was gone when we arrived back at the trailer, but there was a note—she was visiting new friends in a motor home that had arrived while we were gone. The lobsters were still rambunctious, and lacking a suitable box to contain them, I put them on the bathroom floor and closed the door. We were planning an early start the next morning, and suddenly realized that we had forgotten to fill with gasoline, so Dad and I decided to drive to El Rosario. It was after eight when we returned, and as we stopped we noticed that there was no light burning in the trailer. As we got out, there was a piercing shriek, and as we ran towards the trailer, there was another shriek, and my mom flew out the door, clutching at her jeans. Totally confused, we milled about for

No way, Mom. We need a bigger pot

a few seconds, and in a shrill voice she shouted, "There are **things** *in here and they are after me!"*

This tale of terror and tribulation has mellowed in the nine years that have passed. It seemed that when she had returned to the trailer the lights would not work. Waiting patiently, she finally had to answer a call of nature and felt her way to the bathroom. Sitting down in the almost-total darkness, the undertaking was progressing normally, when there was a scraping noise, and something walked across her bare feet. In 10 minutes or so, we managed to calm her down, and the pot was soon boiling, the butter was melted, and one of the culprits was about to get its just deserts, when we discovered that we didn't have a pot big enough to do the job. However, a metal bucket we kept in the boat for bailing solved the problem. ——Michael ❞

● ●

Chapter 5

Down the Transpeninsular—
Baja California Sur

On the Transpeninsular Highway
at Guerrero Negro Junction, KM 217

Use the map on pages 104–105 until San Ignacio.

Guerrero Negro

Guerrero Negro's odd name came from the whaling bark *Black Warrior*. She was wrecked in 1858 at the entrance to the lagoon that now bears her name while being towed out of the lagoon with a full cargo of oil. The name is also odd for a ship: *Black Warrior* is said to have received it because she had once been engaged in trade with Zanzibar.

The town's economy is based on Exportadora de Sal, S.A. (ESSA), which maintains over 300 square miles of diked ponds south of town and around Scammon's Lagoon, producing 6 million tons of salt a year, making it one of the largest such facilities in the world. Shipped in barges to Isla Cedros, the salt is loaded into bulk carrier ships for shipment to mainland Mexico, Japan, Canada, and the US. Whale watching is becoming an important element in the economy, and a number of businesses arranging trips will be identified later in this section.

Except for those stopping for food and fuel, most travelers pass the highway junction without slowing down, for the desolate and windblown look of the place does not suggest that it has anything of interest. In fact, there are things to do and see. The town has many supplies and services, including restaurants, liquor, bank, tire sales and repairs, mechanics, auto parts, hardware, groceries, fruit stores, butcher shops, ice, bakeries, post office, laundry service, tortilla factory, long-distance telephone, telegraph, Pesca office, doctors, dentists, pharmacies, opticians, and a hospital. Guerrero Negro is the first large town south of San Quintín and the last one before Santa Rosalía, and almost all businesses and services are located along Blvd. Zapata. A short motorized tour of the more important attractions follows, starting at the entrance to the town.

Restaurant Puerto Viejo serves seafood, steaks, and Mexican, and has a bar and a disco. The Malarrimo Restaurant has been popular with RVers since the construction of the Transpeninsular was completed, especially with those who like seafood; try the breaded pismos, or the bay scallops sautéed in butter, garlic and wine. The restaurant also has a class C RV park with electric, water, and sewer hookups, showers, and rest rooms. Restaurant Mario's has a seafood and Mexican menu, and a bar, and offers whale-watching trips. Mercado Ballena carries most of the things you would expect in a small supermarket in *El Norte*. Restaurant el Figón de Sal, serving Mexican and seafood, is homey and clean. Laguna RV Park, class C, near the elevated water tank, has water, sewer, and electric hookups, and offers whale-watching trips. Fresk-Pura sells drinking water purified by reverse osmosis.

Fruitería el Triunfo sells a wide variety of fruit and vegetables. The PESCA (Mexico Department of Fisheries) office is located across the street. Can't stand sitting with your spouse in the motor home even one more day? The office of Aerolineas California Pacifico may be able to help. Restaurant Lupita has a Mexican menu and a bar. Supermercado Calimex, smaller than Mercado Ballena, sells basic foods and household items. Farmacia San Martin sells film and can process color prints. Agencia de Viajes Lybsa is a travel agency, and can provide plane reservations, fishing trips, whale watching, Indian art trips, and other activities. Viajes Mario's, across the street, offers the same basic services.

There have been recent reports of rip-offs at the first PEMEX (MND). Restaurant la Palapa, across the street, serves seafood and is clean and neat. The second PEMEX also has MND. BANAMEX can change dollars to pesos and has an ATM machine. Trips to see the salt-making ponds can be arranged at the ESSA offices. If you need to go to the Immigration office, continue going straight ahead at the salt company offices. At the stop sign, encountered after one block, turn left (east), and then right (south) at the second street. The office is on the right in the second block.

A road running northwest from the salt company offices leads past marshes that are home to many gulls, ducks, herons, and other bird species, ending at the old salt pier. A small number of RVers make this their Baja destination and stay for weeks at a time in spite of its lack of facilities, for on occasion, whales come right up to the pier. The area produces enough cabrilla, sargo, and other species to keep fishing interesting. Mullet for bait can be snagged with treble hooks, and small boats can be launched off a sandy area near the pier. Local scallop divers often return to the dock with interesting shells.

■ Life at the extremes

Earlier pages described a number of strange plants adapted to extreme dryness, the boojum being a prime example. However, there are life forms elsewhere on the peninsula and under its surrounding waters which have adapted to even more extreme conditions, one form of which lives in the salt ponds around Guerrero Negro.

A drop of water from the ponds on your tongue will convince you that nothing could possibly survive in such an environment, but you will note that the ponds have different colors, some looking like pink lemonade, others having the light green shade of Gatorade. These colors are caused by algae and other living organisms. The differing degrees of salinity in the ponds favor different organisms, resulting in the various colors. One pond organism, a primitive bacterium of ancient lineage called cyanobacteria, is of particular interest to scientists. Growing in an almost unearthly environment in the highly saline water, and subject to intense sunlight throughout the year, these bacteria thrive. Rather than leading solitary lives like most bacteria, this species is communal, forming layer after layer and slowly build up colonies called "microbial mats." Sediments often cover the mats, but the bacteria start over, only to be covered again. Over the millennia, the alternating layers of bacteria and sediments slowly build up, compress, and fossilize, producing a strange-looking rocky formation called a stromatolite.

Conditions in the ponds are harsh, but scientists have discovered a location even more challenging. The Guaymas Basin, located in the mid-Cortez just south of the latitude of Guerrero Negro, is over a mile deep. The water is very cold, averaging 37°, but a number of hot water vents have been discovered, where the water is 250°, so hot that it would boil if it were at the surface. There is no sunlight, the pressure is about 3,000 pounds per square inch, about that inside a scuba tank, and there are no photosynthetic plants to provide the bottom rung of a food chain. However, recent dives by the research submarine *Alvin* have shown that there is

life down there. Bacteria are at the bottom of the chain, living close to the vents on a strange diet of sulfur and other compounds, existing at a higher temperature that any other organism ever identified. There is a food chain, with tube worms several feet long surrounding the vents and eating the bacteria, and there are crabs that eat the worms. The vents are not permanent; some eventually stop discharging, while new ones form. How the organisms establish themselves at new vents is unknown, since it involves a journey from their accustomed 250° through water just above the freezing point.

Somehow, in the forbidding environments of the ponds and the vents, the DNA, cells, proteins, enzymes, hormones, and other substances necessary for life are constructed. Studies of these organisms may provide clues as to what conditions were like billions of years ago on earth, and suggest that life may exist in other places in the universe other than our own little blue and green watery planet.

KM	Location
208	Class 1 road to south (signed LAGUNA OJO DE LIEBRE) to Parque Natural de la Ballena Gris.
	Off-road trip from KM 208 to Parque Natural de la Ballena Gris, a winter whale-watching site. Turn to page 208.
189+	Road northeast (signed) to El Arco and Bahía San Francisquito.
	Off-road trip from KM 189+ to El Arco and Bahía San Francisquito, with excellent fishing and diving and easy access to the midriff islands. Turn to page 208.

■ For those in need

The residents of Baja California are fortunate to have two powerful home remedies available to treat a particularly annoying condition, impotence. There is a sizable fishery for sea urchins along Baja's Pacific coast, the goal being the creature's roe. Although it tastes approximately like "rotten seagull innards soaked in iodine and then broiled over a fire of old innertubes," the locals put it to good use in times of disappointment, downing quantities of it to cries of *La luz del dia!* This standing joke refers to the hope that the roe will be effective enough to keep one "busy" until the "light of the day." The locals are not stingy, and ship great quantities of it to Japan, where it is used for similar good purposes.

Should urchin roe not prove effective, a small shrub whose usefulness is reflected in its scientific name, *Turnera aphrodisiaca*, is available. If you are in need, scour the hillsides for a small, mint-like shrub having leaves that are smooth and pale green on the upper side, the undersides having a few hairs on the ribs. Popularly called damiana, the aromatic plant often bears yellow flowers. The prescription is simple: just pull off a handful of the tiny leaves and flowers, and boil them in a quart of water for a while and drink when cool. It is found throughout Baja Sur, but those in Baja Norte need not give up hope, for a liquor made from damiana is widely available. Be sparing, for the plant is also reputed to possess laxative and diuretic powers, an unfortunate combination, considering the purpose it is used for.

KM	Location
144	**Vizcaíno**. PEMEX (MND), restaurants, groceries, auto parts, tire repair, stores, ice, liquor, bakery, doctor, pharmacy. The attendants at the PEMEX are magicians, so watch closely. Inexpensive Kaadekamán RV Park, class C and barely so, has water and electric hookups, and an ambiance score of zero. Restaurant la Huerta, across from the PEMEX, has a limited menu, but is clean, pleasant, and inexpensive. Class 1 road to Bahía Tortugas, Asunción, Abreojos, and on to KM 98.

Off-road trip from Vizcaíno to Bahía Tortugas, Asunción, Abreojos, and KM 98 on the Transpeninsular, offering deserted beaches and excellent fishing, side trip to Malarrimo, Baja's best beachcombing site. Turn to page 209.

■ Artistic adventures

Jesuit missionaries spreading their faith in Baja California became aware that rock-art murals existed in the surrounding countryside and asked the Cochimí about them. Most replied that the artists belonged to a race of giants who had migrated from the north. Although the size of the painted figures and their height over the ground must have fostered such a belief, hand prints found at the sites suggest a rather small people. There were scattered descriptions of the art in the writings of the early Jesuits, and in 1883, Herman Ten Kate, a Dutch physician, published an account of his archeological activities in Baja that included a few of the sites. In 1895, Leon Diguet, a French chemist at the mines in Santa Rosalía, published a paper describing many of the sites. However, it took an American writer of mystery stories to bring the art to the attention of the public and generate the great interest that it now enjoys.

Beginning about 1947, Erle Stanley Gardner of *Perry Mason* fame made exploring Baja his vocation/avocation and wrote a series of disjointed and highly subjective books about his adventures. About 1960, he met José Rosa Villavicencio, a descendant of the discoverer of the Santa Rosalía copper deposits. During a visit to the Villavicencio ranch, José told Gardner that he had been born in a mountain village so remote that no "outsider" had ever visited it, and that there was a cave in the vicinity with paintings of giants. Gardner and legendary Baja pilot Frank Muñoz flew over the area and located the village, which proved to be San Francisco, in the high country of the Sierra de San Francisco, about 22 miles north of San Ignacio.

Intrigued, Gardner assembled an expedition in early 1962, equipped with a helicopter. Its arrival caused a sensation in the tiny village, and when José stepped out he became the first person ever to arrive there other than by foot or saddle. After a short visit, they were led to the cave José had described. It depicted deer, rabbits, mountain sheep, men, and a mountain lion, all done in black and red. The next day the helicopter returned to the village and picked up a 17-year-old boy, who had volunteered to show them a larger and better preserved cave some distance away. Terror stricken at first, he soon recovered and guided the pilot to the site, returning to the village an instant hero. Later that day, the pilot made another flight and saw a cave "200 yards long," with an enormous mural of giant men and animals.

Weather problems and plans for explorations in other areas ended the flights in the Sierra de San Francisco. However, Gardner was well aware of the importance of what had been found, and organized another expedition with Dr. Clement Meighan, a prominent anthropologist at UCLA, and Nat Farbman and Bob Wood from *Life* magazine. The Hiller Aircraft Corporation agreed to supply two helicopters, three pilots, and a mechanic, and to pay a part of the cost, and Frank Muñoz was enlisted to provide transportation with his plane. A ground party drove as close as they could and established a base camp, and the helicopters soon arrived. The party quickly began exploring Arroyo San Pablo and photographing the art sites. The "200 yard" cave seen from the air on the first expedition proved to be the crown jewel of Baja rock art, now called Gardner Cave (Cueva Pintada), and a site was found that was unknown even to the villagers.

Under the supervision of Dr. Meighan, a number of artifacts were recovered, including stone scrapers, choppers, metates, awls, scapula saws, arrowheads, fire drills, hearths, an iron knife blade, and possible fragments from a bullroarer (a noise-maker whirled around in a circle on the end of a string).

The village of San Francisco is now accessible by road, and one site, Cueva Ratón (Rat Cave), can thus be visited by those traveling in all but the largest RVs. Arrangements can be made in the village for a three-day burro trip to see Gardner Cave. Appendix F lists a number of books about the art, including Gardner's 1962 book about his trips to the area, *The Hidden Heart of Baja*.

KM	Location
118	Marginal class 2 (trailers and large motor homes inadvisable) road northeast to San Francisco (signed).
	Off-road trip from KM 118 to the Sierra de San Francisco, with some of the most spectacular mountain scenery in Baja accessible by road, and Cueva Ratón, a rock-art site. Turn to page 213.
98	Small café. Class 1 road southwest to Abreojos (described in Chapter 7; see page 209).

• •

❝ *Repast of rattler*

Mexicans sometimes have a distinctly pragmatic attitude towards the local wildlife. We were driving northeast from Punta Abreojos towards the Transpeninsular, when we saw a large rattlesnake slowly crossing the road ahead. We stopped, got out, and began marveling at what a sleek, beautiful, and highly adapted creature it was. I took a twig and threw it towards the snake, and true to its genetic programming, it reared up, faced us, and began making a loud whirring sound with its rattles. It was not eager for combat, and slowly began to head towards a thicket of cactus, when a pickup skidded to a stop in back of our camper. A young Mexican man jumped out and dashed towards us, brandishing a machete. We had some unhappy thoughts for a second or two, but he kept going past us and lopped off the snake's head with a single stroke. We protested that we had been no danger and that killing the snake served no purpose. The Mexican grinned and said that although he was certainly glad to have saved our lives, his real motivation was that it was supper time. A half hour later the snake was skinned out and chunks were browning in the frying pan. It was pretty good, but will never rival Kentucky Fried Chicken. ——Michael ❞

• •

KM	Location
85	Halfway point between the border at Tijuana and Cabo San Lucas.
77+	Restaurant Quichule—Mexican, seafood.

73+ San Ignacio Junction. PEMEX (MND), auto parts, tire repair, welding. San Ignacio RV Park, behind the PEMEX, is a marginal class C. Signs promise full hookups and hot showers, but don't believe a word of it—the place is inexpensive but is not worth a dollar a night.

San Ignacio

The scenery on the Transpeninsular for more than 100 miles has been flat and featureless, the most boring section of the Transpeninsular, and the arrival at San Ignacio, an island of green palms in a sea of brown desert, is one of Baja's most pleasant surprises. Time should be set aside to explore the town, but you should also plan to see what lies outside its boundaries—Laguna San Ignacio, the home of the famous friendly whales, and Cueva Palmarito, a fine rock-art site.

The town is rich in history. A Jesuit mission was founded here in 1728, and a system of stone-lined channels and octagonal cisterns was built to distribute spring water. Many of the converts were Indians who had been persuaded by the good padres to relocate from Isla Cedros. A wide variety of fruits were grown, and some grape vines were planted so long ago that today they have assumed tree-like proportions. Introduced date palms thrived, and as the years passed, they increased their numbers, crowding out the native fan palms and other less-competitive vegetation, to the point that they now dominate everything, although trees hanging with massive numbers of oranges are gaining rapidly.

To protect the agricultural land from floods, Indian converts constructed a gigantic rock diversion wall, which may still be seen today near the town. Constructed of cobbles and mortar, it is 40 feet wide, 10 feet high, and perhaps 3 miles long, making it the largest stone structure on the peninsula.

A more permanent structure than the original adobe church was needed, and construction of a massive stone church with walls of volcanic lava 4 feet thick was begun in the 1760s. The structure was still without a roof when the Jesuits were expelled from Baja California in 1768, but work began again in 1779, and the building was completed in 1786. The church was renovated in 1976, and it is the most impressive Mission Period church in Baja.

■ Dancing the *Fandango*

Everything was not just agriculture and church-building in early San Ignacio. James Bull arrived on a Sunday in 1843, to find a fiesta in progress and the people dancing the *Fandango*. Bull seemed to approve: "The *Fandango* is an exceedingly lascivious dance, or rather a number of dances. Even in the most indelicate dances the women perform their parts without a blush. The music was rather inferior, but what it lacked in harmony was made up by the lungs of the musicians." "The verses are almost always bawdy and when the singer adds something to their lewdness he is greeted by shouts of applausive laughter. The women were not dressed with so much taste as we would find displayed in a ballroom at home, but I think they moved with more ease and grace. It is true their bodies were not confined by stays and tortured into less [than] their natural size, but their limbs were free and moved easily and gracefully in the figures of the dance of their country; and I am not Platonist enough [far removed from sexual interest] to deny that they often appeared bewitching to my sight as they whirled through some of the intricate figures of the *Jota* or passing by me in the less interesting but no less graceful *Jarave*." "It was late when I retired from the scene of amusement, but when I arose in the morning, they were still dancing and did not cease till about 9 o'clock."

Today, the residents of serene San Ignacio largely confine their dancing to La Trampa (The Trap), a large *palapa* dance hall on the road to Laguna San Ignacio. It would be interesting to get Bull's opinion on what he sees on today's Saturday nights; might he become more of a Platonist?

Construction of the massive stone church in San Ignacio was completed in 1786

The village remains amiable, low pressure, and much like it was in the past. Some story telling and loafing go on under the massive Indian laurel trees in the square, and a visit to the church, the new museum, and a walk through the village can occupy several hours. Set trip odometer at the highway. Big rigs should not go into the crowded town square; leave them at the flat area at Mile 0.2 and walk the rest of the way—lighted sidewalks are available for this purpose. RV parking can be found at Mile 0.8; look for the sign on the left. Restaurant las Cazuelas at the Hotel las Pintas at Mile 1.0 is beautiful and serves good meals, if limited in variety. The hotel sells Magnasin.

The road to Palapa Asadero la Presa goes west just before El Padrino (The Godfather) Trailer Park at Mile 1.1. La Presa, an inexpensive class C park, has RV parking and a natural swimming hole. The kids can watch for turtles in the pools, and the nightly frog chorus is the best in Baja. The access road may be a little tight for large rigs. In the past, when it was called La Candelaria, the place was kept immaculately clean, but it is slowly succumbing to litter. Inexpensive El Padrino Trailer Park has a *palapa* restaurant and bar, and RV sites with water and electricity, as well as rest rooms, showers, and a good deal of litter.

Enter the town square at Mile 1.3. With its golden altar, paintings, carved confessional, and stone construction, marred only by fluorescent lighting, vinyl kneeling pads, and loudspeakers, a visit to the mission church will take you back several centuries. The congregation is still active, and visitors are welcome. The birthday of Ignacio Loyola, the town's patron saint, is celebrated on July 31 each year.

A new museum, Museo Local de San Ignacio, has been established. Follow the sign from the southwest corner of the town square. The stone building contains many beautiful photographs of rock art, information on the history of the Indians, reproductions of art sites and artifacts, and an impressive recreation of the art at Gardner Cave. Don't miss it.

An octagonal water reservoir from the days of the Jesuits is still in use, and can be seen by walking 150 yards east from the southeast corner of the town square. It is located just past the post office on the right (south). Restaurant Tota, a modest stone-walled *palapa* just east of the post office, serves budget-priced seafood and Mexican.

A CONASUPO and several other stores in the square sell basic food and household items, and there are a butcher shop, a telegraph office, pay telephones, a bank, and public rest rooms. In 1928, Phillip Townsend Hanna worried that the introduction of electricity and cinema would be the "ruination of one of the most engaging spots conceivable," but these evils have had little influence thus far. However, the new video store in the square may soon cause his fears to be realized. Restaurant Chalita serves inexpensive Mexican food. Guided trips to see the whales and nearby art sites can be arranged at the CONASUPO store. You can also drive to the lagoon and go out with Ecoturismo Kuyima, located just south of La Fridera. Their telephone number is listed in Appendix C.

The new museum at San Ignacio has a re-creation of the rock art site at Gardner Cave

■ The Xanthus hummingbird

The endemic Xanthus, or black-fronted, hummingbird is common from San Ignacio, where it is found at low elevations, south to the Cape Region, where it is found at all elevations. Look for a bird with the trademark hummer size and shape. Males have a black face, a white stripe running aft from the top of each eye, a red bill, green throat, cinnamon belly, and chestnut tail. Females have buff undersides, and the outermost feathers of the tail are rust-colored.

Off-road trip from San Ignacio to Laguna San Ignacio, winter home of the friendly whales. Turn to page 213.

■■■■■■■■■■■■■■■■■■■■■■■■

On the Transpeninsular Highway at San Ignacio Junction, KM 73+

KM	Location
73	Restaurant la Misión—seafood, Mexican, bar next door.
59+	Marginal class 2 (no trailers or large motor homes) road north (signed) to Rancho Santa Martha.

Off-road trip from KM 59+ to the Rancho Santa Martha area, graced by a major rock-art site. Turn to page 215.

53 **Ejido Bonfil**. Cafés, groceries, mechanic, auto parts, tire repair.

■ Belding's yellowthroat

Two subspecies of the endemic Belding's yellowthroat are found on the peninsula, the northern species from San Ignacio to Comondú, the southern from La Paz south, both normally seen in marshy locations. Look for a bird with a yellow belly, chest, and throat, a black mask, and a yellow stripe above the mask, the back, wings, and tail being brown.

41 Tres Vírgenes volcanoes. Jesuit Father Consag's diaries described an eruption that occurred in 1746. In 1792, naturalist José Longinos reported that the area was a source of red, yellow, and black pigments used by Cochimí Indians in their grand rock paintings throughout central Baja. Another eruption was reported in 1811, this one accompanied by an earthquake, which apparently killed some of the inhabitants of San Ignacio. In 1857, large volumes of steam were reported, and recent climbers have reported gas and vapor from fissures near the summit. A geothermal electrical generating plant has been constructed to take advantage of the energy available.

40+ Some of the largest and best-developed specimens of the two species of elephant tree, *copalquín* and *torote*, grow side by side in the lava flows in this area.

17+ First views of the Cortez from the Transpeninsular, begin a 16% downgrade to KM 13+.

11+ LPG yard.

7+ A class 1 road runs north towards an aircraft hangar and then towards the rocky beach, where modest boondocking sites will be found. Avoid parking on the dirt airstrip. Small boats can be launched down a very rough dirt ramp about 100 yards east of the wind sock.

6 Isla Tortugas, 23 miles east, is the tip of a 6,000 feet Holocene volcano, rising from 5,000 feet of water. It is not often visited by sportfishermen, but it sometimes has the best grouper fishing in the Cortez. Described as "barren and useless"

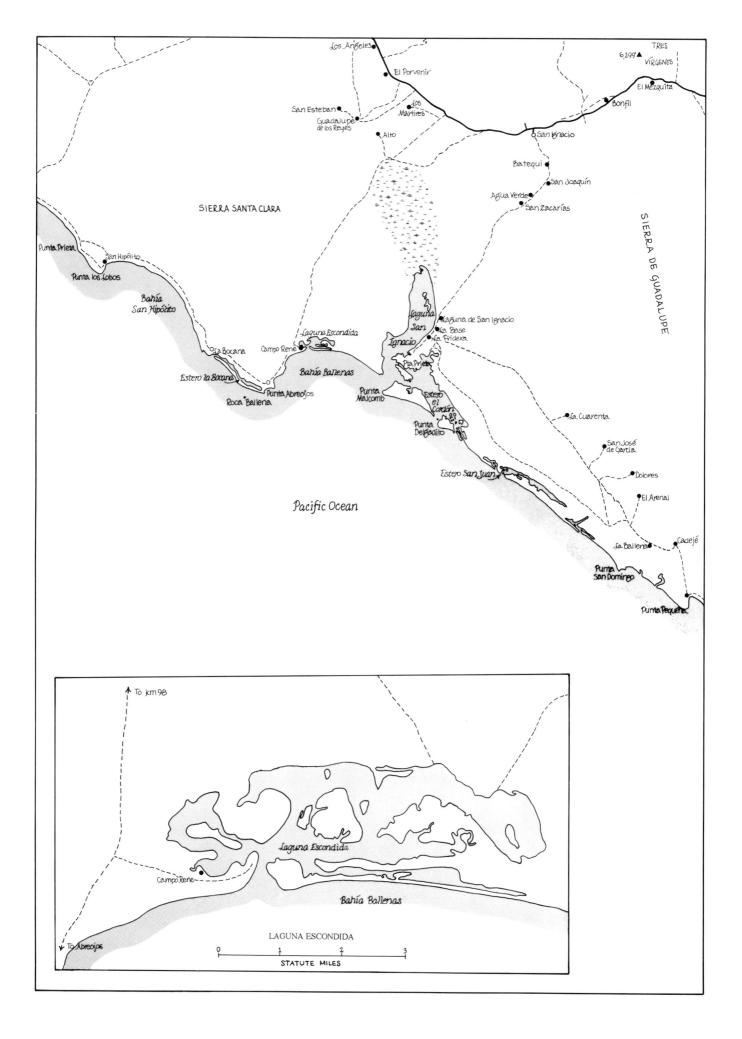

Los Angeles

El Porvenir

TRES
VÍRGENES
6,299'▲

El Mezquita

Bonfil

San Esteban

Los
Martires

Guadalupe
de los Reyes

Alto

San Ignacio

SIERRA SANTA CLARA

Batequi

San Joaquín

Agua Verde

San Zacarías

SIERRA DE GUADALUPE

Punta Prieta

San Hipólito

Punta los Lobos

Bahía
San Hipólito

Laguna Escondida

Laguna
San
Ignacio

Laguna de San Ignacio

La Base

La Fridera

La Bocana

Campo Rene

Bahía Ballenas

Pta Prieta

Estero la Bocana

Roca Ballena

Punta Abreojos

Punta
Malcomb

Estero
el
Cordón

La Cuarenta

Punta
Delgadito

San José
de García

Estero San Juan

Dolores

El Arenal

Pacific Ocean

Cadejé

La Ballena

Punta
San Domingo

Punta Pequeña

To km 98

Laguna Escondida

Campo Rene

Bahía Ballenas

To Abreojos

LAGUNA ESCONDIDA

0   1   2   3

STATUTE MILES

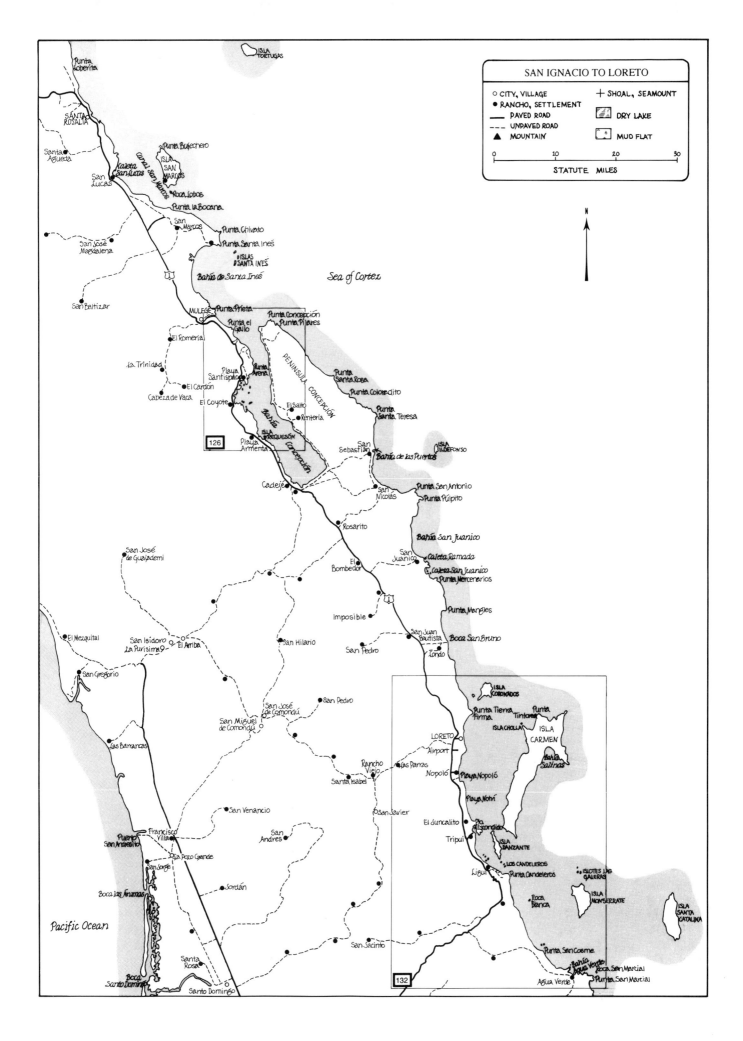

SAN IGNACIO TO LORETO

○ CITY, VILLAGE
● RANCHO, SETTLEMENT
— PAVED ROAD
- - - UNPAVED ROAD
▲ MOUNTAIN
+ SHOAL, SEAMOUNT
DRY LAKE
MUD FLAT

0   10   20   30
STATUTE MILES

N

Sea of Cortez

Pacific Ocean

Punta Roberita
SANTA ROSALIA
Santa Agueda
Isla Tortugas
Punta Bufechero
Caleta San Lucas
San Lucas
Canal San Marcos
ISLA SAN MARCOS
Roca Lobos
Punta la Bocana
San José Magdalena
San Marcos
Punta Chivato
Punta Santa Inés
ISLAS SANTA INÉS
Bahía de Santa Inés
San Baltizar
MULEGE
Punta Prieta
Punta Concepción
Punta Pilares
Punta el Gallo
El Romerial
PENÍNSULA CONCEPCIÓN
Punta Santa Rosa
la Trinidad
Playa Santispac
Punta Arena
Punta Coloradito
El Cardón
Cabeza de Vaca
El Coyote
El Salto
Renteria
Punta Santa Teresa
Bahía Concepción
ISLA PEQUESón
Playa Armenta
San Sebastián
Bahía de las Puertos
ISLA ILDEFONSO
Cadejé
San Nicolás
Punta San Antonio
Punta Púlpito
Rosarito
San José de Guajademi
Bahía San Juanico
El Bombedor
San Juanico
Caleta Ramada
Caleta San Juanico
Punta Mercenarios
El Mezquital
San Isidoro
La Purisima
El Arriba
San Hilario
San Pedro
Punta Mangles
Imposible
San Juan Bautista
Boca San Bruno
San Gregorio
Tondo
San José de Comondú
San Pedro
ISLA CORONADOS
San Miguel de Comondú
Punta Tierra Firma
Tintoreras
Punta
ISLA CHOLLA
ISLA CARMEN
LORETO
las Barrancas
Airport
Bahía Salinas
Rancho Viejo
las Parras
Santa Isabel
Nopoló
Playa Nopoló
San Javier
Playa Notrí
San Venancio
San Andres
El Juncalito
Pto. Escondido
Francisco Villa
Tripuí
Puerto San Andresito
La Pozo Grande
ISLA DANZANTE
San Jorge
LOS CANDELEROS
Ligui
ISLOTES LAS GALERAS
Punta Candeleros
Jordán
Boca las Animas
Roca Blanca
ISLA MONSERRATE
ISLA SANTA CATALINA
Santa Rosa
Punta San Cosme
Boca Santo Domingo
San Sacinto
Bahía Agua Verde
Roca San Marcial
Santo Domingo
Agua Verde
Punta San Marcial

126

132

by passing yachtsmen, the island is in fact unexpectedly rich in flora and fauna, with 79 species of vascular plants, relatively large populations of lizards and rattlesnakes, one species being endemic, and even an endemic mouse. Small fumaroles show the volcano is still active.

■ Tropicbirds

If you are lucky, you may see a red-billed tropicbird winging its way over Cortez waters. With silky white feathers, a red beak, two long, sweeping tail feathers, and a prominent black stripe passing through the eyes, they look like graceful terns. Despite this resemblance, they are more closely related to cormorants, frigates, and the decidedly ungraceful-looking pelicans (all are members of the order *Pelecaniformes*). They are sometimes called bos'n-birds by sailors because the tail feathers bear a fancied resemblance to marlin spikes.

They fly with strong, rapid beats of the wings, giving them the appearance of pigeons from a distance. They do not often settle on the water, but when they do they hold the tail feathers high, as if to keep them dry. They are plunge divers, feeding on fish and squid. Often diving from an altitude of 50 feet or more, they nevertheless do not reach the depths of other plunge divers like the boobies. Although not normally gregarious, they can be seen nesting together on cliffs and in cavities under rocks. Despite being hardly able to walk on land, they are able to scrape and dig spaces for their nests. The courtship display is spectacular, the excited birds plunging and soaring in groups near the nesting sites, their shrill cries cutting the air. Like many seabirds, they lay only one egg. Parents frequently make long foraging trips, leaving the nest unattended, and eggs and chicks are eaten by gulls and other predators, and the mortality rate is thus high.

KM	Location
2	Mouth of Arroyo del Purgatorio, site of a major copper strike in 1868.
0	**Santa Rosalía**.

Baja's copper town

First-time visitors to Santa Rosalía often say something like "Oh, oh. We must have taken a wrong turn somewhere; this can't be Baja." They become more confused in the center of town: rather than adobe or concrete, the buildings are made of wood. Still, the people seem to be no different than elsewhere in Baja, and the streets are named Obregón, Carranza, and Constitución. The products advertised seem to be standard issue—Bimbo, Sauza, and Co-

rona—but some of the buildings on the north mesa look like they belonged on a rubber plantation in the South Pacific. The last straw occurs when visitors try to locate the town's historic stone church, only to find out that it is made of cast-iron. "Darn those Petersons: they sent us to the wrong place."

No, there is no mistake—this is a Mexican town, the most curious place in all Baja. Superficially, the town is gritty and unattractive, an almost comically ugly smelter dominating everything. Even so, the town has a distinct charm and a unique history shared by no other in Baja, and an open-minded visitor will be well rewarded.

In 1868, José Rosa Villavicencio discovered some odd blue-and-green deposits northeast of his ranch, which proved to be a type of high-grade copper ore called *boleos*, due to their ball-like shape. He decided to take immediate advantage of his good luck and sold his mineral rights for 16 (old) pesos, a decision he would come to regret. A copper mine under German management operated until 1885, when a French company, Compagnie du Boleo, was formed. A mining railroad and piers were built, and equipment for a smelter was transported in square-rigged sailing ships from Europe around Cape Horn. The town was laid out on classic company-town lines: straight streets and virtually identical wooden buildings with corrugated iron roofs, their walls painted in horizontal green and white stripes. The distinctive French colonial-style homes on Mesa Norte were inhabited by French mining company officials. Mexican government officials and soldiers dwelt on less-desirable Mesa Sur, and the masses sweltered in the arroyo below.

Soot, gas and ash from the smelter made the town almost uninhabitable. It was noted that the wind regularly blew in opposite directions during different times of the day, and the smelter was operated at the "right" time for a while. However, the scheme didn't work, and there seemed to be only two choices—move the smelter or move the town. Finally though, the engineers worked out a unique solution: a stack was constructed a half mile away and connected to the smelter by a huge horizontal duct. The duct and the stack can be seen best near the Hotel Frances (2) on Mesa Norte.

The mining enterprise was successful from the beginning, and by 1894, production had increased to over 10,000 tons a year. To produce this much copper, the smelter required vast amounts of coke, a fuel produced by heating coal, using twice as much coke by weight as copper produced, and the railroad and the power plant also required coal. Since the coal and transportation industries on the west coast of the US were not well developed, coke was imported from Europe in a large fleet of square-rigged ships. After discharging their cargoes at Santa Rosalía, they often carried lumber and wheat from the US back to Europe. Due to its high value, the copper was shipped out by swift steamer.

By the turn of the century, Santa Rosalía was a major world copper producer, and a parade of square-rigged ships sailed up and down the Cortez. Sailors speaking a dozen tongues walked the streets, seeking the same types of entertainment and social services demanded by sailors every-

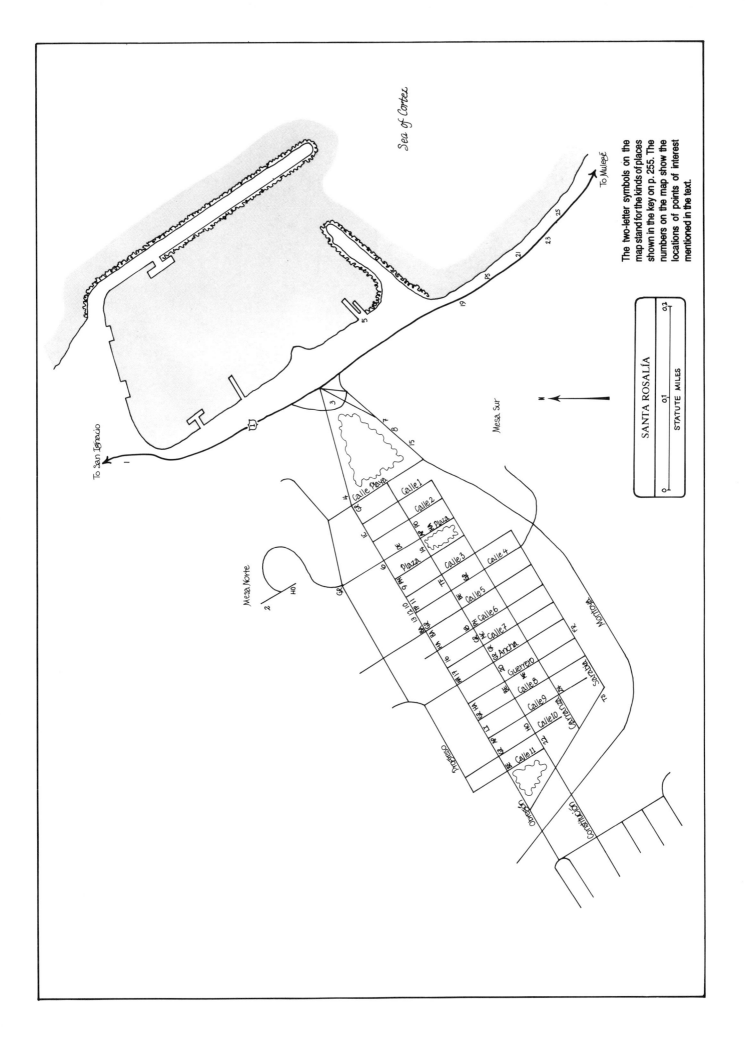

Sea of Cortez

To Mulegé

25

23

21

19

17

SANTA ROSALÍA

N

STATUTE MILES

0   0.1   0.2

To San Ignacio

Mesa Norte

Mesa Sur

Calle Playa

Calle 1

Calle 2

Plaza

Plaza

Calle 3

Calle 4

Calle 5

Calle 6

Calle 7

Ancha

Guerrero

Calle 8

Calle 9

Calle 10

Calle 11

Obregón

Montoya

Carranza

Juárez

Progreso

Constitución

The two-letter symbols on the map stand for the kinds of places shown in the key on p. 255. The numbers on the map show the locations of points of interest mentioned in the text.

The Hotel Frances in Santa Rosalía, built in the days of the French and recently restored, looks like it belongs on a Southeast Asian rubber plantation

The German flag became an increasingly common sight in Santa Rosalía after the opening of the Panama Canal. However, on August 1, 1914, Germany invaded Belgium. Three days later, England declared war on Germany, and a dozen of the big German square-riggers were interned by Mexico and spent the duration of the war swinging at anchor off the town.

The situation in Santa Rosalía seemed ripe for violence; the staff of El Boleo was French, the town was Mexican, and the crews of the interned ships were German. Coke ships from other countries began to fill the void, and sailors from other nations, especially the US, became more frequent on the streets. In spite of the tensions of the war and their vulnerable position, the German sailors encountered few problems and were generally accepted in the cantinas and the brothel. Life on the German ships soon settled down to a deadly routine of blazing heat and dull maintenance work. Weevils procreated happily in the food, the water was poor and rationed, and the sailors were soon reduced to making clothing from flour sacks. Unable to stand the heat and the boredom, some deserted and spread out over Mexico, a few *en route* to the US, some trying to get back to Germany, others settling temporarily or permanently in Mexico, becoming cotton pickers, farmers, prospectors, sailmakers, teachers, circus workers, watchmen, and longshoremen. One even joined the US Army.

where. There was no harbor at the time and no stevedoring services, so the crews had to undertake the hot, stressful, and dirty task of lightering coke ashore, a chore that could take months. The heat was fierce, and other than one brothel and several cantinas and restaurants, there was little to occupy their off hours. Rather than face Santa Rosalía, many sailors tried to desert, and one who succeeded was Frank Fisher, a German sailor on the bark *Reinbek*. After a fist fight with the first mate and a short stay in jail, Fisher started hiking to the northwest until he came to the village of San Ignacio. He soon established himself as its blacksmith, becoming well known to generations of early Baja travelers suffering from broken springs and axles and inoperative engines. His descendants still operate the La Posada Hotel in San Ignacio.

The Mexican Revolution also livened up the existence of the sailors. In the Fall of 1914, Pancho Villa's men occupied Santa Rosalía. One day, however, a vessel began firing at the town, and within a day it was in the hands of Carranza's forces. Their flag was hoisted, new money was issued, Villa's commander was shot, and his men given the chance to change allegiance. At intervals, this scenario reversed itself, the town alternately falling to opposing forces. Some of the German sailors found entertainment value in the change-of-allegiance ceremonies and executions, going ashore to view the festivities.

In 1917, hoping to capitalize on the ill-feelings gen-

Santa Rosalía in the days of the great sailing ships

Courtesy Enrique Patron Lara

erated by General John Pershing's expeditions into Mexico pursuing Villa, Germany tried to enlist Mexico as an ally by offering back the territories in Texas, New Mexico, and Arizona that had been lost to her neighbor. Despite this tempting offer, Mexico wisely remained neutral. On April 6, 1917, the US declared war, blocking the escape of the German sailors to the north. An American consul established offices in Santa Rosalía and developed a blacklist of those supplying the needs of the interned German fleet. The Germans still managed to meet their basic needs through agents and by purchasing food and supplies in Mulegé and Sonora.

Copper production continued after the war. Working for the equivalent of 90 American cents a day, the miners dug 375 miles of tunnels, forming a vast underground network, and more than 18 miles of narrow gauge railroad track were laid. The mines were hot, dirty, and dangerous, where "men's hearts and bodies wilt almost as rapidly as a bride's corsage," as Phillip Townsend Hanna put it. By the 1920s, ore became scarce, but small-scale operators continued work by removing the pillars of ore left to support ceilings in the old shafts, the mining equivalent of a logger cutting off the branch on which he is sitting. Finally, in the 1950s, production ended.

Old-timers remember Boleo with fondness: the work was regular, the mines were relatively safe by the standards of the day, and paychecks were dependable and accompanied by a bottle of wine. Other than the physical aspects of the town, little remains of French culture. *Coq au vin* sometimes appears on menus, but it always turns out to be something totally foreign to the mother country, and the question *Parlez vous francais aquí?* will be greeted with blank looks. In excellent condition due to the dry climate, the old smelter, with its furnaces, extractors, a giant air compressor, huge lathes, metal shears, and other machinery, should be made part of a national park. A restored mining locomotive can be seen in the park at the entrance to the town (3), and another in front of the Hotel Frances. A number of rusted locomotives, cranes, and other machinery can be seen on the highway just north of town (1), next to the old smelter.

A new chapter in the history of Santa Rosalía is un-

folding, however. Several Canadian companies are about to commence a new mining operation. Copper and cobalt will be produced, some of it from ore from the old mines, some obtained from the slag from the old operation: modern methods of extraction are far more efficient than the old, making such a venture economically feasible. In addition, a new gypsum mining operation has begun to the north of town.

A walking tour...

There are many supplies and services in town, including butcher shops, groceries, a tortilla factory, liquor and beer, ice, mechanics, auto parts, hardware, tire sales, pharmacies, doctors, dentists, a health clinic, and banks, as well as numerous pay and credit-card telephones. Due to its narrow and crowded streets, it is inadvisable to drive large motor homes or trailer rigs into the town, and it can best be explored by a walking tour. Parking can be found along the Transpeninsular just north of town. If you must drive into the center of town, be aware that almost all streets are one way, some marked with an arrow proclaiming CIRCULACIÓN, generally posted in the most obscure location available.

We will walk southeast on Avenida Obregón and then northwest on Constitución, with short side trips. Despite its small size, Restaurant Terco's Pollito (4) has a very large menu: salads, shrimp cocktails, clams, octopus, fish, lobster, barbecued chicken, steaks, hamburgers, and Mexican dishes. In 1897, a church (6) constructed from prefabricated cast-iron sections was erected. Designed by Alexandre Gustave Eiffel, of tower fame, it is certainly the most unusual church in Baja. It was designed to be used in France's equatorial possessions, but remained in a warehouse until Compagnie du Boleo purchased it.

During the First World War, there was a legendary brawl at the Hotel Central (9), when the crews of several steamers refused to stand when the band played the Star Spangled Banner. Sailors from two American vessels took exception, and the fight soon spread to the Mexican and German onlookers. The town authorities called in the police and the militia, and the jail was soon filled to overflowing.

The Casa de la Cultura (10) has a display of photos from the days of the square-riggers. Across the street, the tiny Callejon Tokio (Tokyo Alley, 11) serves Mexican and seafood dishes, despite its name. The ISSSTE supermarket (12) carries a variety of food and household products. Smells from the famed El Boleo Bakery (13), established in the days of the French, still make it hard to walk by without stopping. Restaurant el Cachano (16) has a modestly priced Mexican menu. Café Combate (17) sells ground coffee and beans.

An electronics store (22) sells small button batteries for cameras and hearing aids. A shop on Avenida Carranza (24) sells purified water. If the fishing has been bad and you are going to have to endure a lot of teasing back at the trailer, the Pescadería America fish market (20) can help. Lumbago acting up? Plantas Medicanales (18) has herbs that may help:

A locomotive used in the Santa Rosalía copper mines

The interior of the old cast-iron church

azahares, tlanchalagua, te uva (grape tea), *gripyl, cerebyl, axocopaque, boldo,* and *te de la abuela* (grandmother's tea). Need some exercise? Challenge the locals to a game of basketball at the stadium (14). La Hamburgesa Vagabundo (15) is clean and sells good hamburgers and pizza. Both the modest Restaurant el Real (8) and the larger Restaurant las Brisas (7) serve Mexican and seafood.

There is more to see, done best by vehicle. The beautiful Hotel Frances, built in the El Boleo days, with its wide verandahs and polished wooden floors and ceilings, is certainly the most unusual hotel in Baja. It may be one of the few buildings you will ever encounter that have no drywall. The restaurant serves seafood, chicken, beef, and Mexican, and there is a bar. A collection of local minerals can be seen in the lobby.

There are restaurants outside of the main part of town on the Transpeninsular. To the south, Restaurant Selene (21) serves seafood and Mexican. The restaurant is named after the German square-rigger by that name, wrecked in 1890. Rusty plates from her hull can be seen on the rocky beach 100 yards north of the restaurant. Modest Restaurant Regio (23) serves Mexican food. Restaurant el Mirador (25), clean and new, sells steaks, fish, Mexican dishes, hamburgers, sandwiches, sodas, ice cream, banana splits, sundaes, and snacks.

Lavandería las Burbujas will launder your clothes or you can do it yourself in their machines. It can be found north of town. At KM 2, look for two large silver-colored tanks on the hills just to the west of the highway. Immediately south of the tanks, turn northwest, drive 100 yards, and look for the drinking water plant. The laundry is in the same building.

There is only one PEMEX (MND, 19) in town, and in recent years travelers have found it advisable to keep all vehicle and trailer windows and doors locked or attended at all times, to insure that the gas pump reading is zeroed before filling begins, to know approximately how much fuel will be needed to fill the tanks, and the price per liter, and to have a calculator ready to insure that all mathematical calculations of volume and price are on the up-and-up. Also, make sure that your gas comes out of the same pump used by the locals.

Ferries bound for Guaymas leave from the terminal (5). **Remember, temporary import permits are not currently available in Santa Rosalía (see page 55).** There are no RV facilities in town, but parks are located at KM 193+ and 182 to the south. There is a rough, unpaved ramp north of town (already mentioned), and small boats can be launched across the beach at San Lucas Trailer Park at KM 182. However, the nearest paved ramps are at Mulegé.

■■■■■■■■■■■■■■■■■■■■■■■
On the Transpeninsular Highway at Santa Rosalía

KM	Location
0/197	Start new KM numbering sequence.
195+	Hotel el Morro; rooms, restaurant, bar.
193+	Las Palmas RV Park; class B, full hookups, *palapas*, rest rooms, showers, laundry machines, small restaurant, bar. The nightly fee is low if you choose a site without hookups, moderate otherwise.
189+	Place where litterbugs, despoilers of archaeological sites, and those exceeding bag limits may end up.
182+	Restaurant Sara Reyna—inexpensive, good food.
182	**San Lucas.** Class 1 road west to Caleta San Lucas, 0.4 mile.

Caleta San Lucas

Shallow Caleta San Lucas has excellent fishing for snapper, grouper, and halibut. A deep hole at the entrance has immense numbers of bass, and outside lurk leopard grouper, corvina, sierra, barracuda, yellowtail, gulf grouper, skipjack, pargo, roosterfish, amberjack, snapper, dolphinfish, and a dozen or so other species. The best fishing is within a five mile radius from the entrance, and that's a lot of territory! This area is near the juncture of the northern Cortez, with its cool waters, and the more tropical southern Cortez, and migrant species and year-around residents from both are often present. Good fishing is thus possible all year, usually becoming excellent between May and October. A prime fishing area is a half mile east of a solitary hill at the northern end of the rocky arm forming the eastern side of the cove; you can't miss the hill.

San Lucas Cove RV Park, class B, inexpensive, near the north end, is becoming increasingly popular. It has *panga* rentals, rest rooms, showers, *palapas*, and a dump station, but no hookups. The water from their well is of doubtful quality. The best launching location is over the beach (no paved ramp) at the park, since most other beaches in the cove turn into mud flats at low tide. A narrow channel running south from the park winds through the shallows to the entrance.

excellent fishing for yellowtail, barracuda, and grouper, while the south end has some of the best tide pools in the Cortez. Sand and cobble bottoms and rocky reefs are found from San Marcos south three-quarters of mile to Roca Lobos. This diversity of habitat produces fish to match, and it is not uncommon to catch two dozen species in a day. Launch at Mulegé or Caleta San Lucas. A 3-fathom reef, located 1 mile, 060° from Lobos, has produced groupers to 100 pounds.

■ Looking for lunch

Watch the skies in this area for large, black birds soaring in circles over a spot on the ground, rolling slowly from side to side, and you will know several things: they are turkey vultures, and are looking for something dead. Their choice of diet and the rather ugly nakedness of their heads make them few friends among the humans below, but they carry out a valuable service, cleaning up the desert and the highways. They can often be seen roosting in groups on the tops of *cardóns*, waiting until the luck of a cow or a rabbit runs out, or perhaps for cars whose drivers have not insisted that all aboard use their seat belts. They often roost and eat with another carrion-eater, the crested caracara. Look for a large, long-legged dark bird with a white, dark-tipped tail, a reddish face, and a prominent black crest on the top of its head. Both species seem to have become more common in recent years, perhaps because the rather damp, for Baja, weather has caused more abundant plant growth, favoring increasing populations of the animals they eat.

Caleta San Lucas is becoming increasingly popular with RVers.

KM	Location
178	Class 1 road northeast to cobble beaches and modest boondocking sites, 0.7 mile. Once at the beach, a marginal class 1 road leads right (southeast) to additional secluded sites, some shaded by palms.
176	Isla San Marcos, 5 miles to the northeast, was once the bed of an ancient lake. Vast amounts of gypsum precipitated out of the water, and the island is now the site of a large mine. The gypsum is shipped to the US and elsewhere to make drywall and other products. The north point has
156	Class 1 road southwest to Rancho de San Baltizar, signed RUPESTRIAN CAVES SAN BORJITAS, 300 yards north of the KM marker. Gruta San Borjitas, located on the ranch, is among the best known and most studied Cochimí rock-art sites in Baja. Due to the number and quality of its figures and being both well preserved and closely approachable by vehicle, it is the subject of continuing interest. The cave is on private property, and since it is a registered archaeological site, you will need a guide. Trips can be arranged in Mulegé; inquire

156   Graded class 1 road northeast (signed PUNTA CHIVATO) to Puntas Chivato and Santa Inés.

Off-road trip from KM 156 to Puntas Chivato and Santa Inés, their sparkling beaches and good fishing, diving, and boardsailing making them the Baja destination for many Rvers. Turn to page 215.

136+   Auto parts store. Class 2 road west to Rancho la Trinidad, 15.5 miles.

Off-road trip from KM 136+ to Rancho La Trinidad, with Indian art sites in a beautiful canyon. Turn to page 215.

135+   **Mulegé.**

Baja's tropical village

The Tropic of Cancer, the parallel of latitude at 23°27' north of the equator, is the northern boundary of the Tropic Zone. Towns to the south of Mulegé, like San José del Cabo and Cabo San Lucas, are not ordinarily thought of as being tropical, but although it is over 3° of latitude to the north of the tropic, and thus in the Temperate Zone, Mulegé is Baja's "tropical" village. Graced with thousands of graceful palms, thatched roofs, and masses of bougainvillea, it is an unexpected green oasis in a drab brown desert. The name is variously mispronounced as Mule-ah-**gee**, **Mule**-ah-gee, and so forth, but it is Mool-ah-**hay**.

Like so many other towns in Baja, Mulegé was founded by Jesuits, who established a mission here in 1705, at the site of an old Indian settlement. The inhabitants lived quiet lives, enlivened by a 1770 *chubasco* which almost wiped out the settlement. During another storm, this one in 1959, nearby arroyos carried as much as 60 feet of water, and boulders 12 feet in diameter were swept away. American troops occupied it for a day in 1847 in the Battle of Mulegé.

Today, the town manages to maintain a languid, slow-bell approach to life that attracts many repeat visitors; few Americans and Canadians encountered in the streets have been to Mulegé only once. It is the first town south of Ensenada where tourism is a major industry, and there are gift and curio shops, grocery stores, mechanics, tire repair shops, several doctors, a veterinarian, a dive shop, and a number of restaurants, RV parks, and hotels. Despite the fact that it is largely a resort town, most RV parks and local restaurants are rather inexpensive, and even the hotels and their restaurants are moderately priced.

As noted in Chapter 1, the Chamber of Commerce of Mulegé would have you believe that a river courses through the town, but the "Río Mulegé" is actually an estero, a brackish arm of the Cortez, although it does receive small amounts of fresh water from springs above a dam. Level areas nearby

are used to sort and process the date crop. Due to its narrow streets, large motor homes and vehicles towing trailers should avoid using the PEMEX in town, heading instead to the one at KM 130+, just to the south. There is no tourism office, and the American Consular Office that was once here has closed.

A walking tour...

The town is small, the streets are narrow and congested, and there are many that are one-way, so the best way to explore it is to park your rig and go on foot. We will start east from the highway on the "main drag," Martínez, with some side trips. Restaurant la Cabaña (14), a tiny *palapa* at the entrance to town, serves inexpensive Mexican food. The money-changing office (11) will change dollars to pesos, and cash personal and traveler's checks. Turn half-right at the tiny park. The PEMEX (8) carries MN. Mulegé Divers (7) is well-run and relatively inexpensive. It offers scuba and snorkeling excursions, guides, compressed air, equipment sales and rentals, and a scuba resort course (a short course for beginners)." They operate a twin-engine, 20-foot V-hull boat equipped with a Bimini top and a dive ladder, and sell high-quality T-shirts, books, and fishing tackle. Casa Yee (9) is the best stocked grocery store in town, and can provide information on local attractions. Regalos Nancy (5) sells curios, clothing, and gifts.

Take a sharp right around the park and go southwest on Madero. The menu at the Hotel las Casitas (10) is mainly Mexican and seafood. The hotel arranges rock-art tours to Ranchos Baltizar and La Trinidad. The restaurant at the Hotel Hacienda (13) serves only American-style breakfasts—ham and eggs, pancakes, cheese omelets and the like—which are inexpensive and well-prepared, but the orange juice seems to be Tang, which is odd in a town where there are hundreds of orange trees loaded with fruit (this phenomenon is not limited to the Hacienda nor to Mulegé). Its bar is one of the most popular in town. A post office, long-distance telephone, a grocery store, and a tiny ice cream shop will be found at the park at the west end of Madero. Turn north on Zaragoza, and immediately encounter Restaurant el Candil (12). The service is slow, but the food is inexpensive and well-prepared, including steaks, chicken, Mexican, and seafood, and there is usually a guitarist to liven things up. If you want both quantity and quality, try the Mexican combination dinner. There are a number of small gift and curio shops along Zaragoza. Casa Romo (6) sells film and button batteries for cameras and hearing aids. At the corner of Moctezuma, note the modern laundromat (3). Turn left (west) on Moctezuma and encounter Restaurant las Equipales (4), which serves Mexican, steaks, and seafood. The food is among the best in town, but the prices are somewhat more than modest. Take a half-left at the end of Moctezuma, and continue on to the starting point.

Some attractions are best visited by vehicle. The original mission building was destroyed by the *chubasco* of 1770, but it was replaced by one built of stone. Misión Santa Rosalía

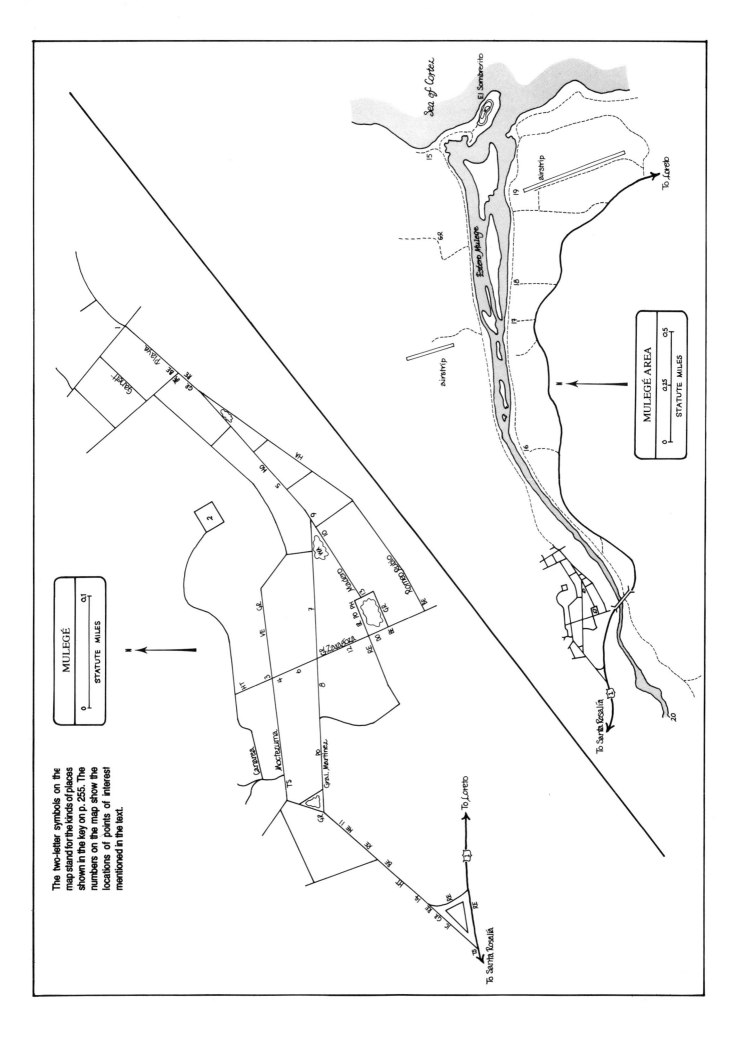

The two-letter symbols on the map stand for the kinds of places shown in the key on p. 255. The numbers on the map show the locations of points of interest mentioned in the text.

MULEGÉ

STATUTE MILES

0   0.1

N

MULEGÉ AREA

STATUTE MILES

0   0.25   0.5

N

Sea of Cortez

El Sombrerito

Estero Mulege

airstrip

airstrip

To Loreto

To Santa Rosalía

Cananea

Moctezuma

Gral. Martinez

Zaragoza

Madero

Romero Rubio

Playa

Gadsel

To Santa Rosalía

To Loreto

de Mulegé (20), was completed in 1766, and although it was abandoned in 1828, it has been remodeled a number of times and is now in active use. To get there, navigate to the south end of Zaragoza. Since the more northern part of Zaragoza is one-way north, it will be necessary to approach by means of Rubio. Once at the south end of Zaragoza, head south, cross under the bridge, swing right (west), and watch for the mission ahead.

The celebrated Mulegé Territorial Prison (2) was in operation from 1907 to 1975 and provided a unique chapter in the annals of penology. At dawn each day, two soldiers would hike up from their barracks, one carrying a conch shell, the other a massive brass key. Upon reaching the prison one would blow a signal while the other opened the massive gate and let the prisoners out! At six in the evening, the gate clanked shut to the sound of the conch, and the prisoners lost their freedom until dawn. Apparently prison officials believed that no one would want to escape from the charm of a town like Mulegé, something certainly believable. A small museum has been established at the prison, which contains historical artifacts from the prison and the town. The days and hours of operation are erratic, so ask in town before you go.

Saul's Tienda (1), on the road to El Sombrerito, is a well-stocked grocery store, and English is spoken. The top of the navigation light at El Sombrerito provides a great view of the area. Despite the exterior appearance of the place, the

Misión Santa Rosalía de Mulegé

tacos and seafood at Café la Almeja (15), a *palapa* on the beach near El Sombrerito, are highly thought of by visitors and locals alike. There are a number of RV parks along the river south of town (some are completely filled by permanents and are thus not described). Orchard RV Park (16), class A, has palm-shaded sites with full hookups, showers, rest rooms, *palapas*, and a dump station. The rough, steep (19%) concrete launch ramp needs high tides, and there is a fish cleaning station nearby. A long-distance phone can be found at the office. Canoe rentals and boat and trailer storage are available. Poncho's RV Park (17) at KM 133, class C, is dirty and ill-kept, and the full hookups are not likely to function. Villa María Isabel RV & Trailer Park (18), class B, has full hookups, *palapas*, showers, rest rooms, and a swimming pool. There is an American-style bakery (sweeter, more fillings than Mexican) here, its location marked by a massive bougainvillea. The steep (17%) ramp has limited parking and maneuvering room, and is best suited for small boats.

The Hotel Serenidad (19) has rooms with showers, cottages, pool, airstrip, tennis, gift shop, bar, and a dining room. It is the scene of famed Mexican fiesta banquets on Wednesdays, complete with *mariachis*, as well as a Saturday night pig feed. The RV park, class B, has full hookups, showers, and use of hotel facilities, but it is not on the river and is surrounded by high walls, and thus lacks some of the ambiance of the parks to the west. The ramp (12%) is often covered with so much sand and mud that it is hard to tell where it is.

All the ramps in Mulegé require high tides. In addition to the ramps already mentioned, boats can be launched near the lighthouse at El Sombrerito on a hard-packed sand and dirt beach. If your boat is sizable and you wish to leave it in the water overnight at the docks there, check with Captain of the Port, who has an office at the lighthouse. Boondocking is permitted on the public beach at El Sombrerito and on the beach south of the "river" entrance.

Yellowtail can be taken by shore-casters off the beaches on both sides of the mouth of the estero, especially from early fall to midwinter, and roosters and a dozen other species are present in the warm month. Fishermen with boats usually concentrate their efforts on yellowtail, amberjack, pargo, and grouper at Punta Hornitos, Punta Concepción,

Punta el Gato, and the eastern coast of Península Concepción. Farther out in the Cortez, yellowfin tuna, dolphinfish, marlin, and sailfish are found in the hot months. Boats and guides can be arranged at Villa María Isabel, at the hotels, and at the landing near El Sombrerito. Live bait may be available from April to June.

Most divers head for Bahía Concepción, Punta Concepción, the eastern coast of Península Concepción, or the Islas Santa Inés. In keeping with its "almost tropical" status, divers in the waters off Mulegé begin to see species such as king angelfish, Cortez rainbow wrasse, giant damselfish, and green moray.

Baja Backroad Adventures provides guided tours from Mulegé by four-wheel-drive, yours or theirs, reaching Misión Guadalupe, San José de Magdalena (the garlic capital of Baja), and Rancho la Trinidad, as well as remote ranches in the back country.

A beautiful cove on the coast south of Mulegé

cleanest. Water temperatures in summer can rise to over 90°. The water stays warm throughout the rest of the year, making it a fine place to swim, water ski, and sail dinghies, Hobies, and sailboards during a winter vacation. Winds often spring up in the afternoon, so divers and fishermen can plan an early day, sailors a late day. There are no public marinas and only one paved launch ramp open to the public, although sizable trailer boats have been launched across the sand beaches at Santispac and Posada Concepción. Serious fishermen tend to avoid the bay, but it can yield pan-sized sierra and cabrilla for the kids, with an occasional surprise like a barracuda, pargo, or snapper to keep things interesting. In September 1914, the German light cruiser *Leipzig*, in need of fuel and attempting to elude warships from Australia and Canada, anchored in the bay.

■ The sand that isn't so

The sand found on Cortez beaches appears to fit the dictionary definition: angular grains formed by the weathering and decomposition of all types of rock, the most abundant constituent being quartz. However, if you look closely with the aid of a magnifying glass, you will find that some Cortez beaches are not sand at all, but rather are tiny particles of mollusk shells. If you have to put a name on it, you could call it "organic sand." Virtually all beaches in Bahía Concepción are of this type, and are the result of the astronomical numbers of shellfish that have lived and died in the bay over the millennia. The beautiful milky, baby-blue color of the bay is caused by colloidal (particles larger than molecules but too small to be observed with a ordinary microscope) lime substances derived from the same shells.

■■■■■■■■■■■■■■■■■■■■■■■■■
On the Transpeninsular Highway at KM 135+

KM	Location
130+	PEMEX (MND), small café, mini-market, long-distance telephone. An excellent boondocking site can be found by following a marginal class 1 road east from a point just south of the PEMEX.
130	Some of the most dramatic scenery in Baja lies along the west shore of Bahía Concepción from this point south, with unexpected panoramas of brilliant blue coves, brown islands, and white sand beaches. The shallow bay is the largest protected body of water in the Cortez, as well as its
118+	Class 1 road east to Playa los Naranjos and Playa Punta Arena. Set trip odometer. At Mile 0.5 encounter intersection; go straight ahead (east) for Naranjos (1.5 more miles), turn right (south) for Arena (1.6 more miles). Both places are low and windswept, with sand-and-pebble beaches. Boats can be launched over the beaches. Inexpensive RV parks at both beaches have no hookups, but rest rooms, showers, and cabin-like *palapas* are

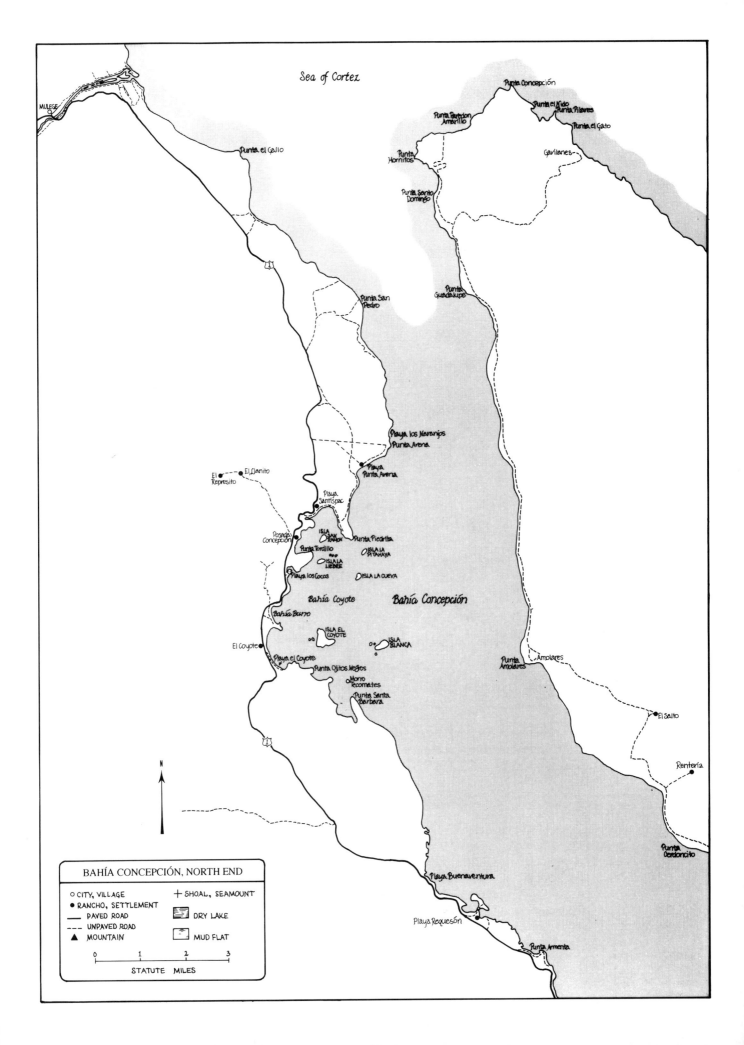

Sea of Cortez

MULEGE

Punta el Gallo

Punta Concepción

Punta el Nido
Punta Pilares

Punta Paredón
Amarillo

Punta el Gato

Punta
Hornitos

Gavilanes

Punta Santo
Domingo

Punta San
Pedro

Punta
Guadalupe

Playa los Naranjos
Punta Arena

El Llanito

El
Represito

Playa
Punta Arena

Playa
Santispac

ISLA
SAN RAMON

Posada
Concepción

Punta Piedrita

Punta Tordillo

ISLA LA
PITAHAYA

ISLA LA
LIEBRE

Playa los Cocos

ISLA LA CUEVA

Bahía Coyote

Bahía Concepción

Bahía Burro

ISLA EL
COYOTE

ISLA
BLANCA

El Coyote

Punta
Amolares

Amolares

Playa el Coyote

Punta Ojitos Negros

Morro
Tecomates

Punta Santa
Barbara

El Salto

Renteria

N

Punta
Cordoncito

Playa Buenaventura

BAHÍA CONCEPCIÓN, NORTH END

○ CITY, VILLAGE
● RANCHO, SETTLEMENT
— PAVED ROAD
-- UNPAVED ROAD
▲ MOUNTAIN

+ SHOAL, SEAMOUNT
DRY LAKE
MUD FLAT

Playa Requesón

Punta Armenta

0   1   2   3

STATUTE MILES

available. There are huge numbers of shellfish offshore, many *chocolate* clams feeling so secure that they do not take the trouble to bury themselves in the sand. Boardsailors like the wide range of conditions, from waves east of the point to calm in the lee. The surrounding land is low, so the winds are often the heaviest in the bay.

● ●

66 *Attacked by flying lizards!*

My brother Reeve and I once had a terrible scare during a night dive near Isla Blanca, in Bahía Concepción. The moonless night was black, only the distant stars in the cold winter sky providing any light. Reeve was still down and the exhaust on the hooka compressor was barking loudly, when without warning, a large dark shape swished by. I ducked down and waited for several seconds, but when I stuck my head up, something again almost parted my hair. Reeve finally returned to the surface, to find me maintaining a judiciously low profile below the gunnel. Just as the words "What's got you?" left his lips, something swished past his head and he too took refuge in the bilge. "What in the hell was that, Walt?" "Darned if I know; the only thing I know is that it's big and it's black and it keeps coming back. Whatever it was, it was half as wide as the boat is long. Maybe it's gone." I had spoken too soon, for just as we stood up, two huge black shapes came right at us and we headed for the bilge again. In a whisper, I said "I'll try to get it in the beam of the dive light," and no sooner had the light gone on than it illuminated a large dark shape for an instant. "Jeez, it looks like a damn pterodactyl. I thought those flying lizards died out with the dinosaurs." After a few minutes Reeve peeked over the side and turned on the light again, and this time it centered directly on a large and evil-looking creature plunging straight at us, almost resulting in the need for an after-dive Lysol rinse of two wet suits. We shut off the hooka, and after 10 minutes with no further "attacks," we pulled the anchor and headed for shore at full speed.

Sitting in the trailer a half hour later, we finally got our wits together and realized what had happened; the creatures were frigate birds. They were apparently buzzing us to protest the loud exhaust noise of the compressor and simply wanted to roost in peace, or perhaps to let us know we were too close to their island.

Called tijeras *(scissors, because of their deep, forked tail) by the locals, frigates are so highly evolved for a life in the air that their wings can span 10 feet and their bones weigh less than their feathers. They have strong, hooked bills, black feathers, and extremely long, deeply forked tails. These features, when combined with their great wingspan and angular form, stir faint apprehensions, perhaps due to some primordial genetic memory of pterodactyls swooping down to carry off the children of our ancestors millions of generations ago. Their diet includes fish, squid, jellyfish, crustaceans, young turtles, and small birds. They often use their ability to outfly other sea birds to steal food, doggedly harassing them until they disgorge their catch. In spite of lives spent over and near the sea, Mother Nature has not seen fit to waterproof their feathers, and they will not land on the water voluntarily, and if accidentally knocked down, they cannot rise. There is a report of a frigate being knocked into the water by a wave. Seeing its struggles, other frigates flew to its aid, picked it up and flew it to a safe altitude and dropped it. They are sometimes willing to make a compromise of sorts—on hot days they swoop down and make belly-slides across the surface of the water to cool off, taking off after a dozen yards or so.*

Even when fishing for themselves, they often enlist help from other species—see page 237. They are common residents of Baja, wandering as far north as San Felipe, and are occasionally seen in the interior. If you see a large black creature soaring in the sky that looks like a hungry pterodactyl, don't worry—it's just a frigate. Probably. ——Walt 99

● ●

KM	Location
114+	**Playa Santispac** (signed). Beach, pit toilets, showers, *palapas*, inexpensive RV parking.

Playa Santispac on a winter day

Ana's Restaurant, serving Mexican and seafood, is popular, and has a bar, a bakery and a grocery store. Truckers sometimes sell block ice and vegetables, fishermen hawk shrimp and scallops, and the "tamale lady" comes around each morning. The beach is jammed on holidays, with dozens of jet-skiers and water-skiers tearing around offshore. Hills break up the breezes, but many boardsailors and Hobie sailors visit the place anyway. Excellent snorkeling can be found among the islands. The old wooden shrimper *San Gabriel*, home to hordes of small fish, lies in 3 fathoms 250 feet northeast of Isla la Pitahaya. (There are differences in the names applied to the islands in the bay by different charts.) Baja Tropicales/Mulegé Kayaks, located on the beach in front of Ana's, offers guided day-long "paddle, snorkel, dive, and dine" kayak trips in the bay, visiting beautiful coves, hot springs, the shipwreck, etc. Reservations and information can be obtained at Santispac, at the Hotels las Casitas and Serenidad in Mulegé, and at the San Diego office listed in Appendix C.

112 **Posada Concepción**. The RV Park here, class B, has full hookups, showers, rest rooms, a game room, and tennis. Most sites are occupied by permanents, but you may get lucky.

111 **Playa los Cocos** (signed). Inexpensive RV parking on one of the best beaches in the bay, but no facilities are available except for pit toilets, a dump station and a few *palapas*. The area is popular with boardsailors, although the surrounding hills tend to keep things gusty and unpredictable.

109 **Bahía Burro**. Inexpensive RV parking, beautiful beach.

108 **El Coyote**. Restaurant Estrella del Mar, a tiny *palapa* restaurant, serves breakfast, Mexican, sodas, and snacks.

107+ Inexpensive El Coyote RV Park, class C, has no hookups, but provides drinking water, solar-heated showers, and pit toilets. A road south along the shore leads to a nicer RV parking area, with *palapas* and trees to provide shade. Fishing is often good along the rocky beaches and cliffs from here south to El Requesón, primarily for cabrilla, pargo, and snapper, plus an occasional barracuda. Isla Blanca has the best diving in the area, with lots of marine life and caves on the southwest side.

106 Rock-art site.

■ The Unhappy Coyote

One of the more engaging examples of Indian rock art in Baja, this painting is of a lop-eared coyote, its mouth open and tail sticking straight astern, its back humped up and its left front paw swollen. At first glance this simple portrait, mottled and indistinct due to aging, hardly seems to rate a second glance, but it seems to grow on most people, at least those with some imagination. The Cochimí artist not only created a coyote, but even managed to convey something of its physical and mental state—it is obviously hassled and dejected, perhaps due to a thorn in its paw. In addition to the coyote, there are over a dozen other painted figures including seven fish, a man, and something that looks like a very pregnant pussycat.

The Unhappy Coyote can be visited by stopping at KM 106. At the marker sight 101° and note the three small rock shelters. Do this quickly and watch for traffic—the shoulder is narrow. Drive 0.25 mile north and park on the east side of the road. The shelters can then be reached by hiking about 400 yards south along the old unpaved highway.

KM	Location
94+	**Playa Buenaventura**. Motel, inexpensive RV parking, showers, rest rooms, *palapas*, beach. The concrete launch ramp (12%) is usable by big deep-Vs only at high tide. Pricey George's Olé Restaurant serves breakfast, burgers, sandwiches, and Mexican, and has a bar.
92+	**Playa Requesón** (signed). Beach, very inexpensive RV parking, pit toilets, *palapas*. The configuration of this area allows novice boardsailors to find side-shore conditions no matter which way the wind is blowing. The name means "Cottage Cheese Beach," applied for unknown reasons.
91+	Class 1 road east to Playa la Perla (signed), 0.4 mile; RV parking, sand beach.
90+	Class 1 road east to Punta Armenta (signed). The road reaches the beach in 0.5 mile and then turns south. Sandy cove, RV boondocking, pit toilets, *palapas*. Fishing camps along the beach to the south sometimes have scallops for sale.

■ A desert nursery

The plants that look like they are standing on stilts at the edge of the bay in this vicinity are mangroves. Forming dense thickets in saline locations avoided by other vegetation, they serve important ecological functions. Their roots offer shelter to hordes of fry and other small creatures, and tend to trap particles, causing the mud flats to extend and thus providing homes for countless worms and mollusks. Their branches and leaves attract many species of birds, whose droppings enrich the environment below. Nevertheless, this, mangrove lagoons are in retreat world-wide and many are filled in to create land. Several mangrove species are found south along peninsula shores from Bahía las Ánimas near Bahía de los Angeles, and in many lagoons on the Pacific side, as well as on some Cortez islands from Isla Coronado south. The greatest mangrove lagoon in the Cortez is at Bahía Amortajada, at the south end of Isla San José.

The graceful trees with green trunks to the west at KM 81 are *palo verde*; those with white trunks are *palo blanco*; those having slender, leathery leaves with rolled margins, 2 inches to 5 inches long, are *palo San Juan*; and the straggling, almost shapeless, trees with sharp thorns that resemble cat's claws are *palo fierro*. Despite sharing the common name *palo* and having overlapping ranges, they are not closely related. *Palo fierro*, also called ironwood because of its dense wood, was widely used for carvings and tool handles, while *palo verde* bark was once popular for tanning leather, so much so that both species became rare in parts of their ranges. The distinctive "bearded" cactus is *garambullo*, found widely in lower elevations throughout much of the peninsula.

The *palo verdes* vary considerably from tree to tree in their genetic makeup, a characteristic that aided an Arizona sheriff in solving a 1992 murder. A number of *palo verde* seeds were found in the suspect's truck, and through DNA analysis, it was possible to identify the specific tree they came from, which proved to be at the scene of the murder.

KM	Location
76+	Class 2 road east to Peninsula Concepción and San Sebastián.
	Off-road trip from KM 76+ to San Sebastián, offering unspoiled surroundings and good fishing and diving. Turn to page 216.
68	The first of the wild and beautiful Sierra de la Giganta can be seen to the south.
60	Class 1 road southwest (signed) to San Isidoro and La Purísima. These towns are of little of interest to most RVers. If you wish to visit the Comondús, use the road from Villa Insurgentes (see page 219).
23	Restaurant el Troyero—Mexican, beer, soda.
0	**Loreto**.

Loreto

Loreto's neighbors to the north, Santa Rosalía and Mulegé, are in a sense opposites, one once a bustling indus-

trial town, the other a sleepy, stereotypical tropical village. Loreto seems to fit somewhere between the two; it caters to visitors from the north, but at the same time it is a busy center for ranching, construction, and commerce.

Loreto was the first permanent Spanish settlement in the Californias, being founded by Jesuit Father Juan María Salvatierra in 1697. The mission building was completed in 1752, using bricks made in Italy and brought to Loreto as ballast in sailing ships. The town thrived at first, serving as a political capital, a military center, and a base for Jesuit operations. A shipyard and a school to teach Indians to handle sailing vessels were established. However, fate was not to be kind. A *chubasco* wrecked the town in 1829, and in 1830 it lost its political status when La Paz was made the capital. In 1877, the town was badly damaged by an earthquake, perhaps generated by the movement on the same geologic fault that created the Cortez. Coupled with an inadequate economic base, these disasters caused Loreto to decline into a backwater for more than three-quarters of a century.

Today, Loreto is fairly prosperous again, due in part to the construction of a hotel complex to the south at Nopoló. The international airport brings in tourists, intent on tennis and lounging in the pool at local hotels, and shuttle busses cruise the streets. Father Salvatierra would probably not approve, but part of the street named in his honor has been turned into a shopping mall.

Loreto is blessed with some good street signs, an almost unique asset among Baja towns; not every street, mind you, but enough that you can get around reasonably well. Loreto's size and spread-out nature do not lend themselves well to a motorized or a walking tour, so the town will be described by category. There are three RV parks now in operation, Villas de Loreto (31), class A, being the nicest of the lot. This is the old Flying Sportsmen's Lodge, one of the original fly-in fishing resorts in Baja, then operating its own DC-3. Refurbished and under new management, it has full hookups, rest rooms, showers, a laundry, a pool, and a beach. Auto, bicycle, and sailboard rentals are available, as well as fishing and diving trips. Loreto Shores Villas & RV Park (32), class B, has a beach, pull-through spaces, full hookups, laundry service, rest rooms, showers, and *palapas* along the beach. The park is nice enough, but does not seem to be prospering. El Moro RV Park (8), class C, has no beach, but is within walking distance of the central part of town, with full hookups, rest rooms, and showers. It does not always operate year-around.

Although the restaurant scene can't compare to Los Cabos, there is a variety of good places in every price range. The El Nido (25), part of a chain by that name, serves steaks grilled over mesquite, and seafood, as well as breakfast and lunch. Rochin's Palapa (27) serves Mexican and seafood. Tiffany's Pisa Parlor (18) is clean and neat, and serves pizza. Restaurant Playa Blanca (16) has Mexican and seafood, lobster being a specialty, all at moderate prices, and has a bar. Restaurant la Palapa (17) has Mexican and seafood, and a bar. The inexpensive chile rellenos and the Mexican combi-

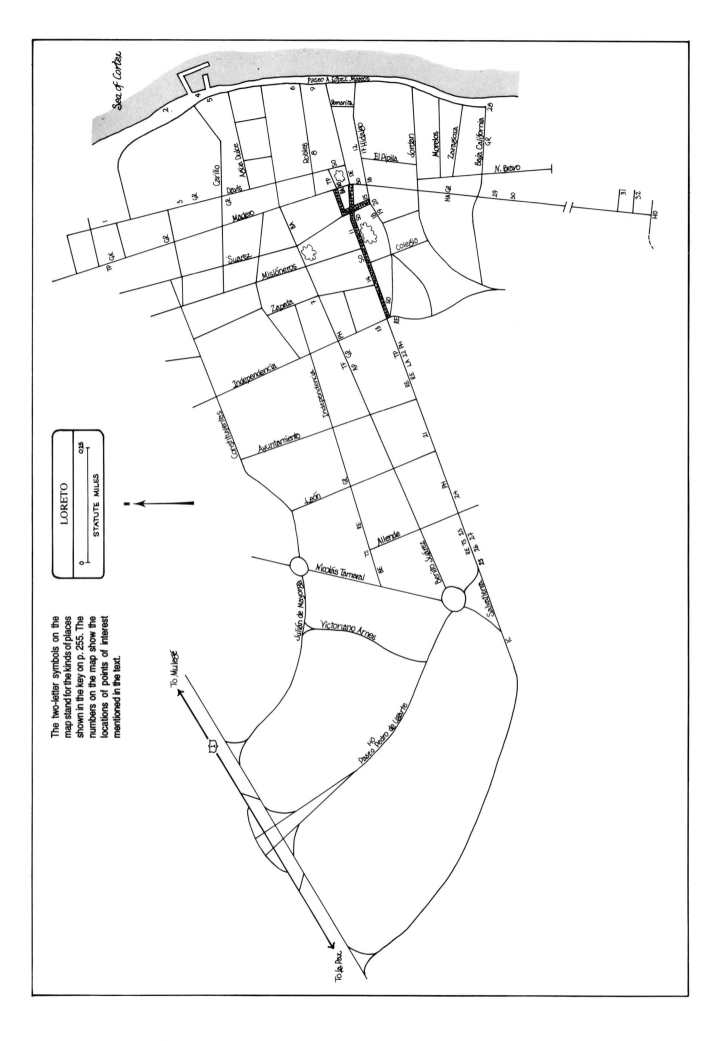

LORETO

STATUTE MILES

0   0.25

The two-letter symbols on the map stand for the kinds of places shown in the key on p. 255. The numbers on the map show the locations of points of interest mentioned in the text.

Sea of Cortez

Paseo A. López Mateos

Yomanita

Carillo

Agua Dulce

Robles

El Hidalgo

El Pipila

Jordan

Morelos

Zaragoza

Baja California

N. Bravo

Davis

Madero

Suarez

Misioneros

Zapata

Independencia

Independencia

Colegio

Ayuntamiento

León

Allende

Benito Juárez

Salvatierra

Constituyentes

Nicolás Tamaral

Julián de Mayorga

Victoriano Armes

Paseo Pedro de Ugarte

To Muleg

To La Paz

nation plate are favorites. Loreto Grill (2), a *palapa*, has seafood, steaks, Mexican food, a small playground for the kids, and giant margaritas for their parents. Restaurant de la Plaza (10) serves breakfast all day, and seafood and Mexican for lunch and supper. Café Olé, just to the south, serves inexpensive breakfasts and lunches. La Fogata (22, The Bonfire), a tiny café, has the reputation of serving the best hamburgers in Loreto. There is an ice cream shop (14), serving generous scoops at reasonable prices. Taking an unusual course in the history of advertising, Anthony's Casa de la Pizza (30) offers the "world's worst pizza," apparently suffering from undue modesty or trying to attract the curious. Should the worst occur after a slice of the worst, there is a funeral parlor in the plaza.

The clock tower at the old mission church in Loreto

There are a number of hotels in town, each with a restaurant, a bar, an excursions reservations desk, and other facilities that may be of interest. The Hotel Plaza Loreto (19) has a restaurant serving steaks and Mexican, and a bar. Hotel la Pinta (1) has a restaurant with a limited selection of Mexican and seafood dishes, and a bar. The restaurant at the Hotel Misión (6) serves seafood, and will cook whatever you drag in, and they have a beer garden. The *palapa*-roofed Oasis Hotel (28) has a restaurant, bar, tennis courts, pool, gift shop, and a sportfishing fleet, and offers whale-watching trips.

Finding what you need should be no problem. The new but smaller (21) and the old but larger (13) El Pescador supermarkets have almost everything you could wish for in the way of food and household items. There are two PEMEX stations (24, MND) and (7, MN). Commercial Marina de Loreto (23) has Evinrude sales, parts, and service. Pescadería Davis (3) is a retail fish market. The plaza near Anthony's also has a bank, long-distance telephone, and a gift shop. The 7-11 Liquor (26) sells spirits, beer, and racy T-shirts. LPG tanks can be filled at an informal operation west of the Transpeninsular. Drive to a point 0.1 mile south of the KM 2 marker, and look for an unmarked marginal class 1 road leading south; it is hard to identify. Set trip odometer. The road immediately swings southwest. At Mile 0.2, the road approaches a power line. Just to the west, look for the sign GAS painted on a concrete power-line pole.

Swing left (south) at the sign to arrive at the yard at Mile 0.3.

There are things to see and do. Misión Nuestra Señora de Loreto (11), constructed between 1704 and 1752, is still in use, repairs and renovations being funded in part by 500,000 (old) pesos won by its priest in the national lottery a number of years ago. An inscription carved over the main door reads CABEZA Y MADRE DE LA MISIÓNES DE BAJA Y ALTA CALIFORNIA (Head and Mother of the Missions of Baja and Upper California.) There is an interesting museum next door, containing exhibits depicting the days of the Jesuits and the founding of the mission, exhibits on whales and whaling, antique sugar presses, swords, firearms, and many other subjects. There is a small entrance fee. The pleasant Malecón (9) has brick paving and benches, half of them facing east for the sunrise, half to the west for the sunset. You could also challenge the locals to a game of basketball at the stadium (29).

Many people like to visit the Islas Coronados, a small volcanic island and a rocky islet about five miles north of Loreto. A cove with a white sand beach will be found, an ideal place for picnics, and the warm and clear water invites snorkelers. Those without a boat can arrange for a *panga* or a cruiser at Alfredo's Sport Fishing (5), Arturo's Sport Fishing Fleet (12), or any of the hotels. Agencia de Viajes Pedrin (20) offers such excursions, as well as fishing trips, public fax, reservations for the Guaymas ferry, car rentals, and visitor information.

Years of over-fishing by shrimpers, squid vessels, tuna seiners, and trawlers have damaged the local fisheries, and the fish available to sportfishermen are declining year-by-year. Town officials have proposed an 80-mile underwater ecological reserve, but this will take years to achieve, if ever. Good fishing is still possible, especially for those with a boat big enough to get well out into the Cortez. The action is quite seasonal, with the warm months being best. In July, the area east of Isla Carmen outside the 100-fathom line, reached about 2 miles east of both Punta Lobos and Punta Baja, provides good dolphinfish action. The waters between Islas Coronados and Carmen sometimes have good runs of yellowtail. Other favorite offshore fishing spots include the areas south and east of Coronados, and the deep water between Loreto and Carmen, which produce yellowfin tuna and sailfish. The shallows around Coronados are the home of snapper, pargo, and cabrilla. The beaches north of Loreto occasionally have roosterfish in the spring, and have yellowtail from October to April.

The grooved concrete public ramp (4, 12%) leads into the small man-made harbor. The parking near the ramp is somewhat limited for larger rigs. There is currently no fee for its use. Small boats can also be launched over the sand beach at the north end of town, and just south of Loremar, where there is plenty of parking. Large trailer boats should be launched at Puerto Escondido, about 15 miles south. If you need a fishing license, there is a Pesca office on the outskirts of town; from Loreto Junction, drive south on the

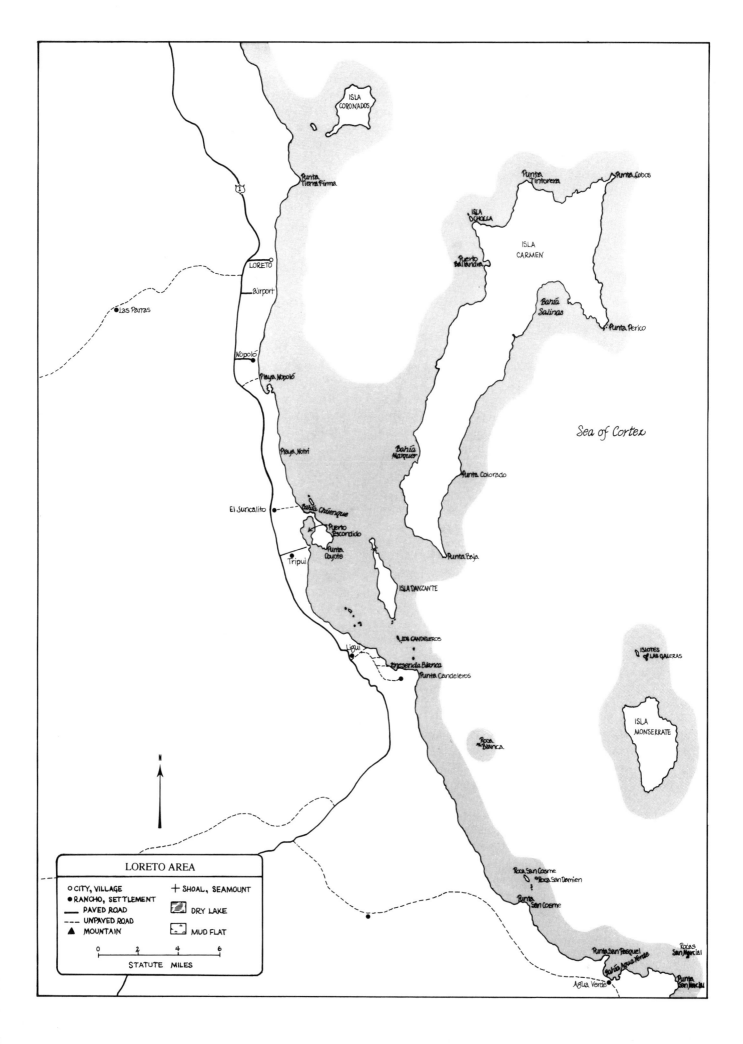

ISLA
CORONADOS

Punta
Tierra Firma

LORETO

Airport

Las Parras

Nopoló

Playa Nopoló

Playa Notri

El Juncalito

Bahía Chuenque

Puerto
Escondido

Punta
Coyote

Tripui

Ligui

Ensenada Blanca

Punta Candeleros

LOS CANDELEROS

Bahía
Marquer

Punta Colorado

Punta Baja

ISLA DANZANTE

Roca
Blanca

Punta
Tintorera

Punta Lobos

ISLA
D'CHOLLA

Puerto
Ballandra

ISLA
CARMEN

Bahía
Salinas

Punta Perico

Sea of Cortex

ISLOTES
of LAS GALERAS

ISLA
MONSERRATE

Roca San Cosme
Roca San Damien

Punta
San Cosme

Punta San Pasquel

Bahía Agua Verde

Roca
San Marcial

Punta
San Marcial

Agua Verde

N

LORETO AREA

○ CITY, VILLAGE	+ SHOAL, SEAMOUNT
● RANCHO, SETTLEMENT	
— PAVED ROAD	▨ DRY LAKE
--- UNPAVED ROAD	
▲ MOUNTAIN	⬚ MUD FLAT

0   2   4   6

STATUTE MILES

Transpeninsular 0.2 mile and watch for several white buildings.

Deportes Blazer (15) has compressed air, limited sales and complete rentals of diving equipment, and has a supply of hard-to-find gadgets like wishbones, sling rings, speargun points, and snorkel tabs. It also sells fishing tackle and sporting goods, repairs rods, sells tennis racquets and balls, and restrings racquets. In addition, there is a dive shop at the Loreto Inn Hotel at Nopoló.

Most divers head for Isla Carmen or Isla Danzante, although those with adequate boats often choose Isla Monserrate or Isla Santa Catalina. Divers will find *chocolates* to be abundant on shallow sandy bottoms off the western shores of Carmen. The best diving is off the north end and along its east coast. Also, a reef about 1,500 yards south of the south cape comes to within 12 feet of the surface and offers outstanding snorkeling. The water is alive with fry and tiny mysids, and large barracuda, leopard groupers, pargo, and snappers are common, along with king angels and several species of grunts. Underwater photographers should stay alert for nudibranchs: the gold-and-blue beauty in the color section was encountered off the western shore. The waters around the island are among the best in the Cortez for encountering blue and finback whales, and those to the south have blue, fin, Minke, and Bryde's whales.

During periods of north weather, Carmen's chain of mountains, some over 1,500 feet, extending over its entire 20-mile length, plus their northeast/southwest orientation, tend to funnel heavy winds through the channel between Loreto and the island.

Villas de Loreto is home to a number of kayak companies. On a space-available basis, all will rent equipment to experienced paddlers, and provide instruction to those who are not. Baja Backroads Adventures has guided trips from Loreto by four-wheel-drive, yours or theirs, to San Javier to visit the mission, on to López Mateos for a bit of whale watching, and a visit to the lush and exotic Comondús.

■■■■■■■■■■■■■■■■■■■■■■■■
On the Transpeninsular Highway at Loreto, KM 0

KM	Location
0/120	Start new KM numbering sequence.
118	Class 2 road west (signed) to San Javier.

↱ Off-road trip from KM 118 to San Javier, a mountain village with a fine mission church. Turn to page 217.

KM	Location
117	Paved road east (signed) to Loreto International Airport.
111	**Nopoló.**

Nopoló

A paved road runs east (signed) to the FONATUR visitor complex and the Loreto Inn Hotel (formerly the Stouffer Presidente). The hotel offers rooms and suites, restaurants, bars, pools, shops, laundry service, local tours, and travel and car-rental agencies. Campo de Golf de Loreto has 18 holes, par 72, championship yardage 6964, men 6334, women 5451. Facilities include a driving range, putting green, chipping green, sand trap, clubhouse, locker rooms, and pro shop. Green fees are $20 for 18, $12 for 9, with a discount for multiple-day use. This course may be the least crowded golf course in North America, and tee-time reservations can be made anytime. The Loreto Tennis Center has lighted courts, which can be used by walk-ins for a $3 fee, and a clubhouse and a bar. Aqua Sport de Loreto at the hotel offers sportfishing, whale watching, boat trips, island tours, kayaking, compressed air, and diving equipment rentals. Resort and full certification courses (NAUI) are available. There are plans to offer sailboards and jet skis in the near future. February is the big wind month. C & C Ground Services & Tours, located in a mini-market at the corner of Misíon San Ignacio and de Sisteaga, offers picnic trips to beaches on Islas Carmen and Coronado, as well as whale watching, fishing trips, and excursions to San Javier. At their "clam bakes" goat cheese, roast baby goat, barbecued chickens, and drinks are served.

Despite its many assets, the Nopoló complex does not appear to be prospering, and it is not uncommon during winter to encounter less than a dozen people who appear to be customers. The reasons include the lack of beaches, the fisheries, and transportation problems. Small jetties extending from shore have been constructed to trap shifting sands, but the beach scene leaves a bit to be desired. In addition, the area lacks the world-class, year-around marlin fishery at the Cape. Also, local businessmen complain that cutbacks in flights into Loreto are strangling business. Finally, the cost of a ticket from Los Angeles can actually be lower to Los Cabos than Loreto. However, these problems are your gain, for where else can you play 18 holes on a beautiful, uncrowded, first-class golf course for $20, or play tennis for a $3 fee?

KM	Location
107+	They don't rival the one at the Golden Gate, but the only two suspension bridges in Baja can be seen here (they carry golfers across tidal inlets).
103	**Playa Notrí** (signed). Boondocking beach, no facilities.
97+	Class 1 road east (signed) to El Juncalito.

El Juncalito

This palm-lined little cove is a favorite boondocking site with many travelers, offering camping, *palapas*, trash cans, and a nice beach. Parking on the beach south of the

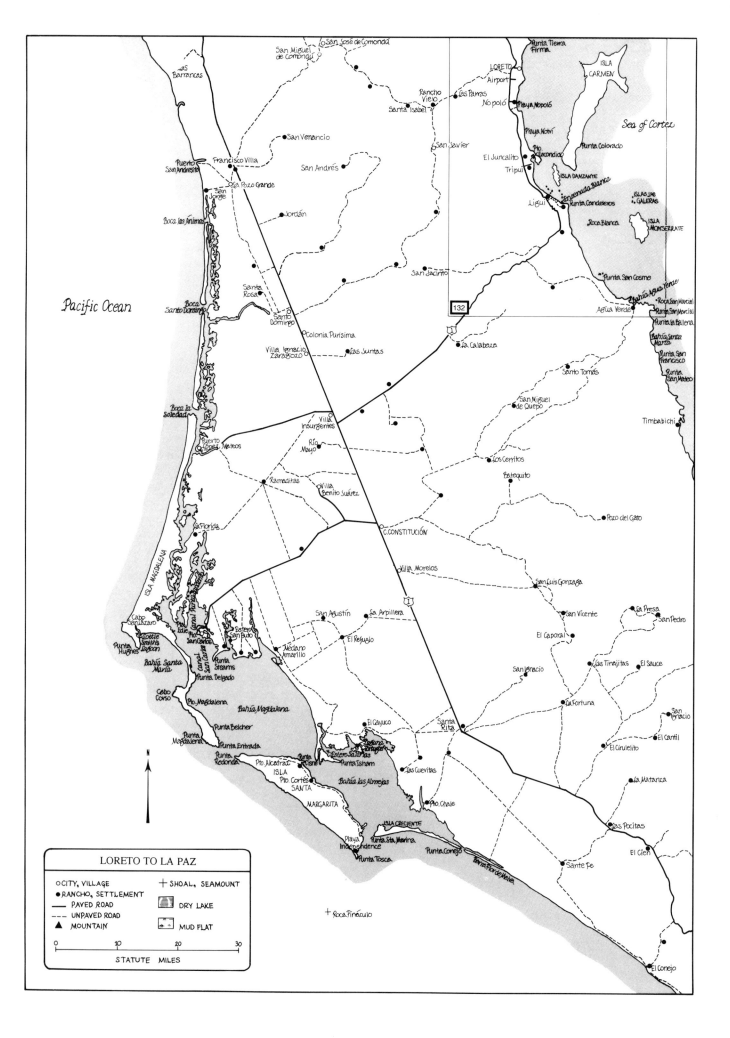

Pacific Ocean

Sea of Cortez

Las Barrancas

San Miguel de Comondú
San José de Comondú

Punta Tierra Firma

LORETO
Airport

ISLA CARMEN

Rancho Viejo
Las Parras
Santa Isabel

Nopoló
Playa Nopoló

San Venancio

Playa Notri

Puerto San Andresito
Francisco Villa

San Javier
El Juncalito
Tripuí
Pto. Escondido

Punta Colorado

San Andrés

La Pozo Grande
San Jorge

ISLA DANZANTE

Jordán

Liguí
Ensenada Blanca
Punta Candeleros
ISLAS LAS GALERAS

Boca las Ánimas

Roca Blanca
ISLA MONSERRATE

Boca Santo Domingo
Santa Rosa

Punta San Cosme

132

Santo Domingo

Bahía Agua Verde
Roca San Marcial
Punta San Marcial

San Jacinto

Agua Verde

Colonia Purísima

Punta la Ballena
Bahía Santa Marta

Villa Ignacio Zaragozo
Las Juntas

La Calabaza

Santo Tomás

Punta San Francisco
Punta San Mateo

San Miguel de Quepo

Timbabichi

Villa Insurgentes

Río Mayo

Los Cerritos

Puerto López Mateos

Batequito

Ramaditas

Villa Benito Suárez

Pozo del Gato

La Florida

C. CONSTITUCIÓN

ISLA MAGDALENA

Villa Morelos

San Luis Gonzaga

La Presa
San Pedro

Cabo San Lázaro

1

San Agustín
La Arpillera

San Vicente

Punta Hughes
Smiths Lagoon
Pto. Eclie
Canal María María Magdalena
San Carlos

El Caporal

Punta Stearns

Estero San Buto
Médano Amarillo
El Refugio

Las Tinajitas
El Sauce

Bahía Santa María

Canal San Carlos

San Ignacio

Punta Delgado

Cabo Corso

Pto. Magdalena

San Ignacio

La Fortuna

Bahía Magdalena

El Cirulelito
El Cantil

Punta Belcher

El Cayuco

Santa Rita

Punta Magdalena
Punta Entrada

Esteros Salitpas
Laguna Brujas
Punta Isham

La Matanza

Punta Redonda
Pto. Alcatraz
Punta Elsner
Pto. Cortés
ISLA SANTA

Las Cuevitas

Bahía las Almejas

Pto. Chale

MARGARITA

ISLA CRECIENTE

Las Pocitas

Playa Independence
Punta Sta. Marina
Punta Conejo
Tierra Flor de Malva

El Cien

Punta Tosca

Sante Fe

LORETO TO LA PAZ

- ○ CITY, VILLAGE
- ● RANCHO, SETTLEMENT
- ── PAVED ROAD
- --- UNPAVED ROAD
- ▲ MOUNTAIN

- ╋ SHOAL, SEAMOUNT
- ▨ DRY LAKE
- ▦ MUD FLAT

N

╋ Roca Pináculo

0   10   20   30
STATUTE MILES

El Conejo

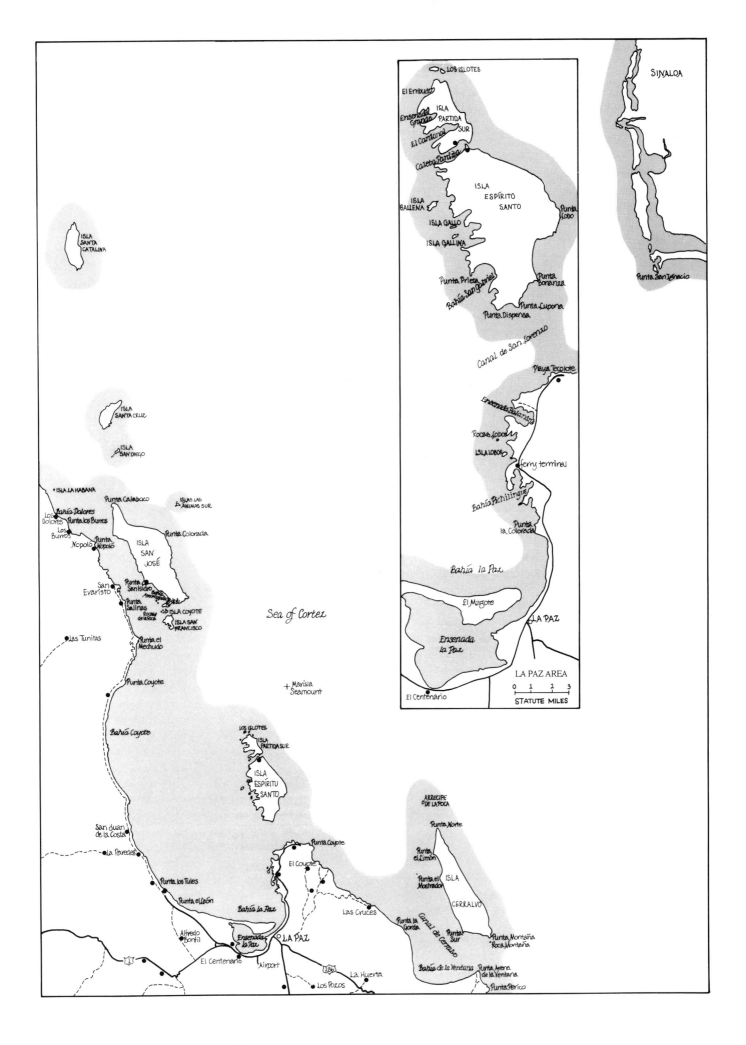

SINALOA

Punta San Ignacio

ISLA
SANTA
CATALINA

LOS ISLOTES
El Embudo
Ensenada
Grande
ISLA
PARTIDA
SUR
El Cardonal
Caleta Partida
ISLA
ESPÍRITU
SANTO
Punta
Lobo
ISLA
BALLENA
ISLA GALLO
ISLA GALLINA
Punta Prieta
Bahía San Gabriel
Punta
Bonanza
Punta Lupona
Punta Dispensa

Canal de San Lorenzo

Playa Tecolote
Ensenada Balandra
Rocas Lobos
ISLA LOBOS
ferry terminal
Bahía Pichilingue
Punta
la Colorada
Bahía la Paz

ISLA
SANTA CRUZ

ISLA
SAN DIEGO

El Magote

ISLA LA HABANA
Punta Calaboxo
ISLAS LAS
ÁNIMAS SUR
Bahía Dolores
LOS
DOLORES
Punta los Burros
Los
Burros
Punta Colorada
Nopolo
Punta
Nopolo
ISLA
SAN
JOSÉ
San
Evaristo
Punta
San Isidro
Punta
Salinas
Rocas
de la Foca
ISLA COYOTE
ISLA SAN
FRANCISCO

LA PAZ
Ensenada
la Paz
El Centenario

LA PAZ AREA

0   1   2   3
STATUTE MILES

Sea of Cortez

Las Tunitas
Punta el
Mechudo

Punta Coyote

Bahía Coyote

+ Marisla
Seamount

LOS ISLOTES
ISLA PARTIDA SUR
ISLA
ESPÍRITU
SANTO

San Juan
de la Costa
La Paredes
Punta los Tules
Punta el León
Bahía la Paz
Alfredo
Bonfil
Ensenada
la Paz
LA PAZ
El Centenario
Airport
La Huerta
Los Pozos

Punta Coyote
El Coyote
Las Cruces

ARRECIFE
DE LA FOCA
Punta Norte
Punta
el Limón
ISLA
Punta el
Mostrador
CERRALVO
Punta la
Gorda
Canal de Cerralvo
Punta
Sur
Punta Montaña
Roca Montaña
Bahía de la Ventana
Punta Arena
de la Ventana
Punta Perico

grave of Bad José is restricted. Launching cartoppers and inflatables over the sandy beach is easy. There is fine beach-casting along the south shore of Bahía Chuenque for yellowtail from November to April, and for jack crevalle and roosters in the spring. Divers will find purple-lip rock scallops among large rocks below the cliffs outside the cove to the south, also the habitat of many sizable snapper, grouper, pargo, and cabrilla. Divers will find the wreck of a DC-3 off Isla Chuenque, the only island in the bay. Maneuver until the central peak of the island bears 342° and the water is about 22 feet deep.

KM	Location
94+	Paved road east (signed) to Puerto Escondido.

TRIPUI, Puerto Escondid, and Isla Danzante

TRIPUI Resort RV Park, class A, a half mile east of the highway, has full hookups, rest rooms, showers, laundromat, restaurant, bar, grocery store, gift shop, pool, tennis courts, and vehicle storage. Two-thirds of the RV spaces are now occupied by permanents, leaving perhaps 30 for transients.

Tidal current flows through the channel at Puerto Escondido (local officials would like to call it Puerto Loreto) at up to four knots. A steep (17%) concrete launch ramp, considered by many the best in Baja, is available inside the harbor entrance, suitable for even large trailer boats. There is plenty of parking. Obtain a ramp permit at the Marina de Puerto Loreto office, a stone building with a metal roof, 100 yards south of the ramp. Construction has been underway for a number of years on a major development of the area, which may some day provide a yacht club, markets, sports club, beach, condominiums, residential subdivisions, and other facilities. In 1996, construction was at a standstill, but rumors persist that things will begin again. RVs may no longer boondock in the area.

Divers will see garden eels and might be able to ride whale sharks, which occasionally visit the area. Several massive black coral trees can be seen in deep water off Punta Coyote, the easternmost extension of the peninsula forming the bay. Divers report that dense schools of yellowtail inhabit this area year-around at depths of 100 feet to 120 feet, a fact apparently not known to many visiting fishermen.

The island about three miles to the southeast is Isla Danzante. There is a good deal of commercial netting in the area, but fine fishing is still available, the most productive locations including the reefs and small islands from Danzante south to Punta Candeleros, and the water outside the 100-fathom line, 5 miles east of Danzante. Diving is best on Danzante's east side and on the reef at the south cape, where garden eels have been seen in the sand at 65 feet, and black coral in deeper water. The south cape is also excellent for

fishing, with barracuda, yellowtail, leopard grouper, and snappers. Fishing and diving are good near a rock visible from the surface 4 miles, 072° from the south cape of Danzante. A large bank offering excellent bottom fishing and diving is located 3 miles, 086° from the south cape of Danzante. With a least depth of 36 feet, it can sometimes be seen from the surface.

Those with adequate boats should visit the reefs and islands south of Danzante. A group of small rocky pinnacles called Los Candeleros is found 2 miles southeast of its southern tip. These are fine deep-dive sites, with plenty of large fish and shellfish. Low-lying Monserrate is 12 miles from Los Candeleros. Its surface looks largely barren, but the surrounding waters teem with fish and lobsters. Islotes las Galeras, a small group of islets 2 miles north of the island, are seldom visited but have excellent fishing and diving on a jumbled bottom, with numerous rocky ledges.

Eleven miles east of Monserrate is Isla Santa Catalina, one of the most famous islands in the Cortez. Home of the "rattle-less" rattlesnake, the island is visited frequently by natural-history tours. Unlike ordinary rattlesnakes, this small, docile, and very rare snake sheds its terminal scale with each molt and thus never develops a rattle. First described in 1953, the species' days are probably numbered, since feral cats prey on them. Another curiosity is an unusually large species of barrel cactus, which often reaches 10 feet in height and 3 feet in diameter. Equally strange is the torchwood plant, which bears two distinct types of flowers. Diving is excellent all around the island, with numerous rock walls, caves, and crevices.

■■■■■■■■■■■■■■■■■■■■■■■■■
On the Transpeninsular Highway at KM 94+

At KM 94+, opposite the road to Escondido, a class 1 road heads southwest 0.7 mile to the mouth of Cañon Tabor, a fine hiking location. At one point, there is a huge boulder wedged in the narrow canyon, making it necessary to scoot under it and then climb a notched log. There are palms and surface water in some places, and you may encounter bighorns. The chances are not very good, but it's worth a try.

Although mostly just steep cobble, the beaches from KM 94+ south to Ensenada Blanca are favorite boondocking areas, and many fishermen prefer them to any other in the Loreto area. There are a number of short, almost unnoticeable class 2 and 3 roads that lead to the beach, permitting some degree of privacy and ready access to Danzante and the other islands. Diving around the small islets just offshore is excellent.

KM	Location
84	**Ligui**. A class 2 road (signed) heads east to a boondocking beach. A half mile from the high-

way, a class 2 road heads right (110°) to Ensenada Blanca. Several spur roads along the way lead to seaside campsites, one with a fine sand beach. Seven percent upgrades and many switchbacks to KM 77.

83

■ A useful relationship

The cliffs along the upgrade from Ligui heading towards Villa Insurgentes often look like someone attempted to improve on Mother Nature with spray cans. However, the large green and orange areas are caused by two species of lichen. Each appears to be a single organism, but they are in fact combinations of a fungus and an alga, living symbolically, each contributing to the welfare of the other. The algae can photosynthesize food from air and water, and the fungus absorbs and retains the needed water. These "pioneer" plants can stand extremes in temperature, and can exist on bare rocks, which, because they produce weak acids, they can erode. The particles freed by this erosion eventually collect with organic debris to form soil, which the less adventurous vascular plants require.

63+   Class 2 road southeast (signed) to Bahía Agua Verde.

Off-road trip from KM 63+ to Bahía Agua Verde, offering uncrowded boondocking and excellent fishing. Turn to page 217.

17   PEMEX (MND), ice, sodas and groceries.

0   **Villa Insurgentes**. PEMEX (two, one MND, the other MN), bank, stores, groceries, bakery, meat and fish markets, restaurants, beer, tortilla factory, ice, auto parts, tire sales and repair, health clinic, pharmacy, veterinarian, telephone, telegraph, and mail.

Side trip from Villa Insurgentes to Puerto López Mateos, one of the best places in Baja to view the whales. Turn to page 187.

Off-road trip from Villa Insurgentes to San Miguel de Comondú and San José de Comondú, two of the most exotic and engaging villages in Baja California. Turn to page 219.

0/236   Start new KM numbering sequence.
221+   LPG yard.
214   PEMEX (MND), auto' parts and service.
213   Chevrolet parts, service, and repairs. Manfred's RV Trailer Park; class B; full hookups, rest rooms, showers, Austrian restaurant.
212+   **Ciudad Constitución**.

Baja's Indiana

Dozens of wells tapping huge underground aquifers have converted the surrounding areas into Baja's equivalent of Indiana, and the town appears to the thriving. There are two automobile dealerships, Chevrolet (1) and Nissan (2). The Chevrolet dealer also has Johnson outboard parts and service. In addition, there are hospitals and doctors, dentists, pharmacies, opticians, veterinarians, PEMEX (two, MND at both), mechanics, auto parts, telegraph, long-distance telephone, new tire dealers and tire repairs, post office (5), department stores, restaurants, butcher shops, beer, hardware, travel agents, banks, hotels, laundromat (4), sporting goods, an ice manufacturing plant, a yoga parlor and a psychiatrist. Foto Studio Karla (9) sells film and has one-hour print processing. Supermarkets Almart (11) and the new El Crucero (13) are close approximations to American-style stores, and there is a homeopathic pharmacy (10). The Secretary of Tourism of Baja California Sur has an office at the AeroCalifornia agency (6).

The restaurants in Ciudad Constitución cater to the locals, but they are quite inexpensive and there are a number of choices. The *palapa*-roofed Restaurant Estrella del Mar (3) is clean and neat and has an extensive seafood menu, plus chicken and a few beef items. The *camarónes* (shrimp) *rancheros* are excellent. However, for a restaurant catering to the locals, prices are a bit high. Super Pollo next door specializes in barbecued chicken. If you crave the Italian, try Pizza el Rey (12). Calafia Restaurant (8) is simple and inexpensive, serving a Mexican menu. There is a small ice cream shop (7).

Campestre la Pila Trailer Park, class B, at the south end of town has a dump station, water and electric hookups, a pool, tent sites, toilets, and showers. Drive south from the downtown area and watch for the large electrical substation on the east side of the road. Turn west and watch for signs in about a half mile.

Side trip from Ciudad Constitución to Bahía Magdalena, offering excellent bay and blue-water fishing. Turn to page 188.

■■■■■■■■■■■■■■■■■■■■■■■■■■■■■■

On the Transpeninsular Highway at the south end of Ciudad Constitución

Except in its final miles, the 131-mile highway between Ciudad Constitución and La Paz is the second-most boring drive in Baja, and the only boondocking sites are little more than side roads away from traffic noise.

KM	Location
198	**Villa Morelos**. Tire repair, groceries, Restaurant Cocina Popular—Mexican.
157	**Santa Rita**. Tire repair, limited auto parts, Res-

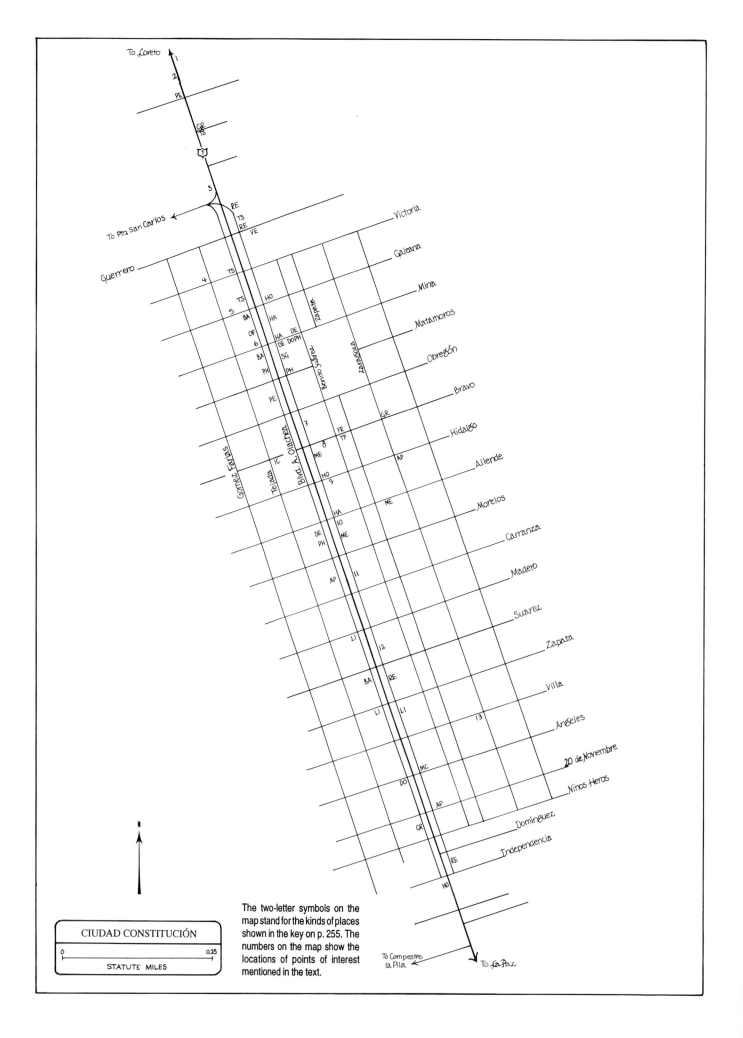

To Loreto

1

2

PE

GP
TS

1

3

RE
TS
RE
VE

To Pta San Carlos

Victoria

Galeana

Guerrero

Mina

TS

4

Matamoros

TS
BA
OP
6
BA
PH

HO
HA
HA DE
DE DOPH
SG
PH

Zapata

Obregón

5

Zaragoza

Benito Juárez

Bravo

GR

PE

Hidalgo

7

FR
TF

8

AP

Allende

Gomez Farias

TC

ME

Tejada

Blvd. A. Olachea

HO
9

Morelos

ME

HA
10
ME

Carranza

DE
PH

AP
11

Madero

Suarez

LI

Zapata

12

BA
RE

Villa

LI
LI

Angeles

13

20 de Noviembre

MC

Niños Heros

DO
AP

Dominguez

GR

Independencia

RE

HO

N

To Compestre
la Pila

To La Paz

CIUDAD CONSTITUCIÓN

0   0.25

STATUTE MILES

The two-letter symbols on the
map stand for the kinds of places
shown in the key on p. 255. The
numbers on the map show the
locations of points of interest
mentioned in the text.

taurant los Pinos—Mexican. Class 2 road southwest (signed) to Puerto Chale.

 Off-road trip from KM 157 to Puerto Chale, where fishermen and divers can gain easy access to Bahía las Almejas, Isla Crecente, Canal Rehusa, and the southern end of Isla Santa Margarita. Turn to page 220.

140	Two-tenths of a mile southeast of the KM marker, a class 2 road leads south a quarter mile to several flat desert boondocking areas. They are out of view from the road, but truck noise may be a problem. You take what you get in this area.
130	One hundred yards southeast of the KM marker, another class 2 road leads south to several other boondocking areas. The plants with lash-like branches seen in this area are *palo adán*, not ocotillo.
127+	Groceries, Restaurant Rancho Rosita—Mexican.
114	Restaurant Rosy—Mexican.
112	**Las Pocitas**. Tire repair, mechanic.
110+	Restaurant Penjamo—Mexican.
110	Restaurant Miriam—Mexican.
100	**El Cién**. Tiny cafés, stores, tire repair, PEMEX (MND).
96	Restaurant Tere's—Mexican.
80	Class 2 road southwest to El Conejo.

Off-road trip from KM 80 to El Conejo, with good boondocking, surfing, and boardsailing. Turn to page 220.

■ The fairy duster

A short hike down the wash on the right (southwest) side of the road at KM 76 will introduce you to another favorite desert plant, the fairy duster tree. A shaggy, well-branched shrub about a yard tall, it has the happy tendency to bloom all year, producing beautiful red flowers, usually erect and shaped like the old-fashioned dusters that were used in homes before vacuum cleaners were invented.

55+	Class 1 road southwest to boondocking areas. This road, which leads to the Punta Bentonita area, is graded but washboarded. Set trip odometer. Go right (200°) at the side road at Mile 0.8. Don't expect too much here; it's just a few flat places with no scenery to speak of, but at least road noise should not be a problem and you won't be impeding traffic on the main dirt road. The side road continues on a short distance and loops back to the main dirt road, and large rigs may have difficulty turning around.
34	Magnificent views of La Paz and Isla Espíritu Santo.

Walt and his brother Reeve managed to bring something back for supper

| 21+ | Agricultural inspection station. |
| 17 | Paved road northwest, signed SAN JUAN DE LA COSTA. |

Off-road trip from KM 17 to Punta el Mechudo, offering excellent fishing and the most colorful display of sedimentary showmanship in Baja, continuing on to Evaristo, with excellent fishing and diving offshore. Turn to page 221.

15+	City View RV Park; class C, full hookups, rest rooms, showers, trailer storage. Given its distance from town and lack of a good beach (the beaches from here into the city tend to be muddy), the place is pricey, but off-season rates are offered.
14+	Oasis los Apripez Trailer Park; class C, full hookups, showers, rest rooms, laundry, restaurant, bar, poorly maintained pool.
14	Cafés, auto parts, mechanics.
11+	PEMEX (MND).
9	Paved road south (signed) to La Paz International Airport.
6	Junction. Turn south for the Cape region, bypassing downtown La Paz.
5+	The offices of the State Secretary of Tourism and the Attorney General for the Protection of Tourists are located on the south side of the road. They share a suboffice downtown in the waterfront area. The Real Hacienda just to the north has the full range of entrées (and prices) you would expect in an elegant restaurant: lobster, fish, shrimp, spaghetti, fettucini, steaks, chicken, and Mexican, as well as seafood cocktails, burgers, sandwiches, salads, soups, and a variety of desserts. However, the "parrot chicken" dish needs some explanation. The shallow (10%) launch ramp at the marina here appears well-constructed and has plenty of parking, but its operational status is unclear. Restaurant Campestre, across the street and a bit east of the Tourist office building, has salad, barbecued ribs, steaks, and Mexican.
4+	Casa Blanca RV Park; class B, full hookups, shade trees, laundry, pool, tennis, showers, rest rooms, small store, long-distance phone.
4	El Cardón Trailer Park; class B, full hookups, showers, rest rooms, dump station, laundry, pool, *palapas*, shade trees. La Paz RV Park; class B, has full hookups, pool, laundry, rest rooms, showers. Priced a bit high, it can be found by driving 200 yards northeast of El Cardón, turning north, and following the signs.
0	**La Paz.**

La Paz

While Santa Rosalía was established as a copper town, and Mulegé and Loreto were founded by the Jesuits for religious reasons, La Paz started out as an outpost for men with a more adventurous quest in mind, the pursuit of treasure. In late 1533 or early 1534, Hernán Cortés, conqueror of Mexico, sent two ships to explore the west coast of Mexico, looking for a shorter way from "New Spain" to the sources of the spices so highly prized in Europe and, of course, for gold and pearls. The crew of one ship mutinied and sailed into a large bay, where most of them were killed by the local Indians. However, the few survivors told of pearls, and in 1535, Cortés himself founded a colony, which failed in less than 2 years. In 1596, Sebastián Vizcaíno attempted to found a colony in the area, which he named La Paz (The Peace), since the Indians were now found to be friendly. However, the stockade soon burned down and the place was abandoned.

In 1683, another colonizing expedition tried again, this one led by Jesuit Father Eusebio Kino and accompanied by Admiral Otondo y Antillión and a group of marines. The Indians had changed their minds again, shooting arrows and carrying on, so the admiral invited a group of them to a feast, which ended when he fired a cannonball into their midst.

By 1720, the cannonball had been forgotten, and a Jesuit mission was established by Fathers Jaime Bravo and Juan de Ugarte. However, there were further uprisings, which ended only after epidemics had killed most of the Indians. With few souls left to save, the mission was abandoned in 1749, and it was not until 1811 that a permanent settlement was established. In 1829, Loreto, the territorial capital, was severely damaged by a *chubasco*, and the growing village of La Paz was named the capital the following year. It was captured by American forces in 1847 during the war with Mexico and held until passage of the Treaty of Guadalupe-Hidalgo ended the fighting in 1848. Adventurer William Walker tried to take over the city in 1853, but failed. By the 1950s, La Paz had become famed for its fine fishing and a vacation destination for Americans and mainland Mexicans. Baja California Sur gained Mexican statehood in 1974, and La Paz was named its capital.

La Paz from the east

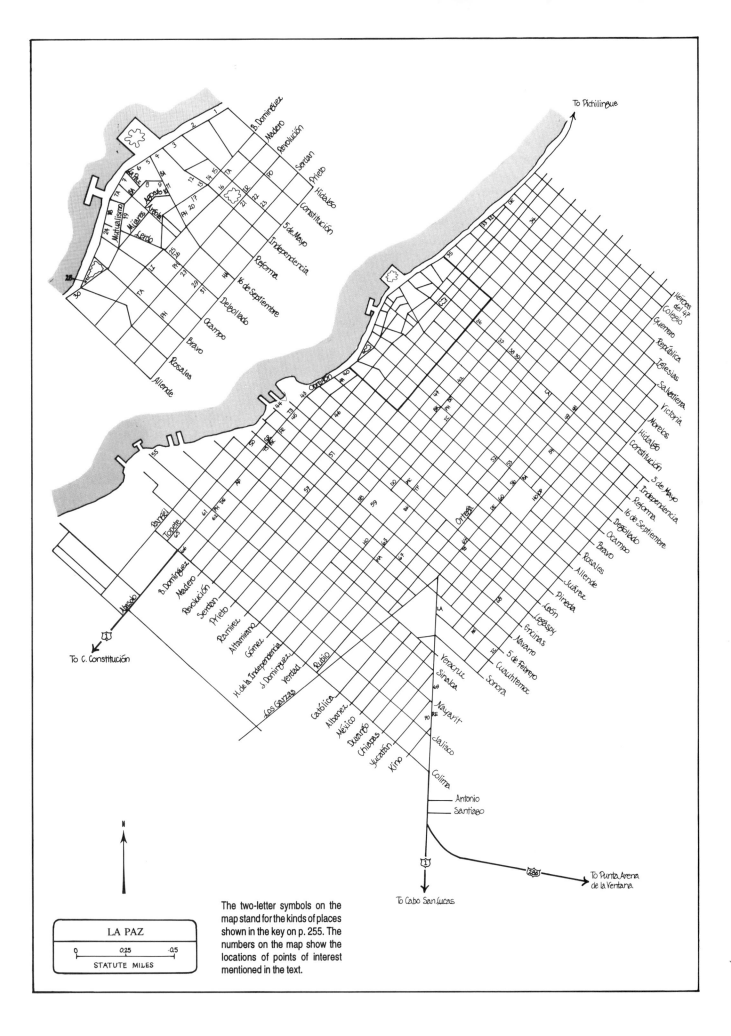

The two-letter symbols on the
map stand for the kinds of places
shown in the key on p. 255. The
numbers on the map show the
locations of points of interest
mentioned in the text.

LA PAZ

0   0.25   0.5

STATUTE MILES

N

To Pichilingue

To C. Constitución

To Cabo San Lucas

To Punta Arena
de la Ventana

Compared to the rest of the peninsula, today's La Paz seems to be a place of extremes, with the prettiest women in the shortest skirts, the ugliest dogs, the most flowers, a riot of color at every part of the spectrum, the least visible one-way signs, and the most *dulcerías* (candy stores) and shoe stores per capita on the peninsula. The place is growing up, cellular phone service is available and you can get a computerized horoscope. As a town modernizes, things become more specialized, and La Paz is no exception: there are a number of health food stores, and even a vegetarian restaurant; Veterinario Madero (46) specializes in the medical difficulties of dogs and cats; and you can get your misplaced teeth moved to more suitable locations by an orthodontist. The T-shirts are becoming racier ("Will Work For Sex"), graffito artists are at work ("Fuck the police"), and local businessmen have found it necessary to use a fleet of armored cars to transfer their assets. The growing number of ice cream shops and *dulcerías* is surely considered a blessing by the town's many dentists. The public market (27) is a riot of activity, with vendors hawking candy, plastic toys, and magazines to people waiting for busses. La Paz is advancing economically, and the tree-shaded streets are being paved, new homes are being built, and the cars plying the streets are of more desirable makes and models than in many an American town.

Despite these changes, La Paz does not seem to be in danger of losing its Mexican identity by assuming a homogenized culture like Cabo San Lucas; it is distinctly Mexican and is fortunately staying that way. Many private businesses observe *siesta* (a period of time traditionally set aside for an afternoon nap) between 1 P.M. and 3 P.M. The weather is fine from November to May, with warm days and balmy nights, and a breeze called the *coromuel* keeps the place cool in the summer. The name supposedly came from the pirate Cromwell, when the locals observed that he sailed out with the strong breeze that sprung up from the south in the afternoon and arrived back with the northwesterlies the next day.

● ●

❝ *Finding Foo*

My mom, dad and I spent 5 months in the Winter of 1986 living in our trailer and exploring Baja. As May arrived, we chartered a sailboat to explore Isla Espíritu Santo and the islands to the north with my uncle and his family. Since my cousin was allergic to cats, we placed ours in the care of a La Paz veterinarian. When we returned two weeks later, we checked into a hotel, and my mom went to the vet's office to pick up the cat. She was abruptly told that although Foo had escaped on the second day, he had been captured a short time later. However, the cat in the cage was not Foo— it was a male blue-point Siamese, but not ours.

Crying, Mom called us at the hotel and we quickly mounted a search of the neighborhood. We attracted a lot of

attention; gringos don't often wander the streets of La Paz poking under wood piles and emitting strange animal cries. A doctor in a white coat rushed out of his office and accosted my dad, apparently thinking he was an escapee from the local asylum, and he had to hightail it around the corner. As night fell we returned to the hotel, worried and extremely unhappy; Foo had been with us for many years and we were very fond of him. We continued the search early the next day, and although everyone we encountered tried to be helpful, we could find no trace of the cat, so on the third day we contacted the La Paz television station, had them broadcast a detailed description of the cat, and offered a $250 reward for his return.

Every man, woman, and child in La Paz, it seemed, suddenly became a cat hunter. A mob of little boys descended on the hotel with cats of every shape and hue in tow: skinny black cats, odd-eyed white cats, pregnant tiger-striped cats, even a Burmese. Twice the bell clerk called our room in the middle of the night to say that the police had captured Foo, but when we rushed to the lobby the cat in the officer's arms was the wrong one. Some of the people could not understand our attachment to the cat. A woman came to the hotel with a basket of kittens and offered 1 of them for $250—we could take our pick. When we said we wanted our own cat back she made a better offer; if we bought one kitten for $250 she would throw in the other seven free. The doctor saw the ad and called the hotel to apologize. A cab driver arrived with four battle-scarred veterans imprisoned in a cardboard box, but just as he was about to show them to us, they burst through the top and escaped. Another woman called to say she had found Foo, and that our "kitty was very, very sad and we should immediately come to her house to get him." When we arrived, the reason the young alley cat was very sad was apparent: he had the worst case of mange we had ever seen. Somehow La Paz does not seem the sort of place one would encounter a lot of Siamese cats, but little boys kidnapped a least six of them from the city streets and dragged them, spitting and hissing, to the hotel. A man offered the free services of his male cat if we wanted a new kitten and said that his neighbor had a willing female, and another offered a $250 dog.

Continuing our search, we handed out hundreds of fliers and put more ads on television, and in the newspaper, and on the radio as well, and no cat in La Paz could safely leave the house for a prowl—a number made two and even three trips to the hotel. Sadly, after 10 days of full-time effort, it became obvious that Foo was gone for good. The wonderful people of La Paz tried hard to find Foo, but we finally had to leave and never saw him again. ——Michael ❞

● ●

A walking tour of the "downtown" area, roughly bounded by Allende, Hildalgo, Prieto, and the Malecón, is a good way to become familiar with the city. (The inset map on the accompanying city map describes this area.) There is no specific route, so go where your interests carry you. There are many souvenir and crafts shops, too many to mention all individually, selling T-shirts, sea shells, carvings, paintings, *serapes*, posters, jewelry, music cassettes of all the latest tunes from Mexico City, *sombreros* large enough to make the most discriminating *bandido* proud, and just about anything else you could desire. Some of the clothing is very stylish, and the art can be first-rate, especially the carvings and paper mâché figurines. The beautiful Malecón has sand beaches, *palapas*, and palm-shaded benches, and vendors hawk snacks and cold beverages from carts.

The Los Arcos Hotel (30) is a nice resort hotel in a central location, and has a coffee shop, travel agency, pool, sauna, bar, and gift shop. The Restaurant Bermejo at the hotel is nice, but a bit pricey. Viajes Palmira across the street arranges fishing, diving, and snorkeling trips, and ferry reservations, and has bike and scooter rentals. El Camarón Feliz (28), a *palapa* just northwest of the hotel, has seafood, steaks, Mexican on the menu, and a bar. Viajes Lybsa (24) can make ferry reservations, and has land tours, sportfishing and snorkeling and scuba tours. La Fuente (18), a small ice cream store, sells 20 different flavors. Carlos 'n Charlie's (5), part of a chain, serves seafood, steaks, and Mexican, amid a funky decor designed to please visitors from the north. BBQ ribs are not ordinarily considered part of the Mexican culinary tradition, but they do a pretty good job on them. A travel agency, the State Secretary of Tourism, and the Attorney General for the Protection of Tourists have offices across the street. Although the pizzas produced by La Fabula (3, also at 22 and 60) bear little resemblance to those of Palermo, they are good in their own right. Restaurant Kiwi (2) was decorated by a talented artist, with a beautiful design worked in the floor with colored tile, and imaginative wall hangings. There is an extensive menu, and an outdoor dining area looking out over the beach and harbor. Restaurant Adriana (1), a large *palapa* on the beach, serves excellent fish dinners, nicely seasoned with garlic, at reasonable prices.

The La Perla Hotel (7) has a reservation desk and a flashy nightclub with plenty of neon and more than sufficient volume. La Terraza Restaurant, in the hotel, has a large menu of fairly inexpensive Mexican, seafood, steak, and Italian dishes. Their glass of fresh-squeezed orange juice is the tallest and best in La Paz. It is open-air, and birds fly in to beg for treats. A constant parade of people passes by: ranchers, farmers, mechanics, tourists who flew in this morning and will fly out tomorrow, "Baja Johnnie"-type Americans wearing raunchy T-shirts and a week's worth of whiskers, and yachties from all over the world.

Deportivo La Paz (6) has sales (no rentals) of diving equipment such as suits, gloves, masks, spear guns, regulators, goody bags, and small, hard-to-find parts like mask straps, spear points, tank valves, rubber slings, and wishbones, as well as fishing tackle and T-shirts. Baja Diving &

Service, 2 doors northeast, is the largest dive operation in Baja California, with 16 full-time employees, including 5 divemasters, and 10 boats ranging from *pangas* to a 45-foot cruiser. PADI and NAUI certification and resort courses are offered, along with trips to all the local dive sites. In addition, they have one of only two privately owned decompression chambers in Baja, located at their facility at Pichilingue. They plan to open a new shop in the new Marina Palmira at KM 3, northeast of town, with complete sales and rentals, and compressed air. Baja Outdoor Activities, 60 yards northeast of Baja Diving & Service, offers local kayaking and snorkeling excursions, as well as trips to Espíritu Santo. Instruction and hourly or daily equipment rentals are available. Walk-ins are welcome.

Mr. Yeti (4) sells ice cream, yogurt, fruit juices, and fruit. Dany's Soda Fountain (15) has hamburgers, sandwiches, and Mexican, as well as ice cream and juices. The movie theater (14) shows such hits as *Tiempos Violentos*, *Street Fighter*, and *La Loteria del Amor*. Las Varitas (12) is a lively nightclub, with live music. Restaurant el Quinto Sol (13) is La Paz's vegetarian restaurant, and you can buy yogurt, raw oatmeal, prunes, "energizing smoothie," cheese pie, and "vegetarian fried steak," whatever that might be. They also sell such nostrums as *tlanachalaqgua, tizana abango, reumatyl*, and *bermzfugo*.

If there was too much tequila last night and things got out of hand, La Novia Elegante (17) sells bridal outfits. A tiny mall (20) has shops that sell shoes, clothing, T-shirts, jewelry, and gifts, as well as watches of dubious pedigree, and there is a video game parlor. Deportes Calafia (11), Deportes America (8), and Deportes Ortiz (26) are close approximations to north-of-the-border sporting-goods stores.

Dorian's Department Store (10), with its marble floors, escalators, and such brands as Gucci, Chanel, Revlon, Levi, and Cartier, may cause you to feel that you have been transported to *El Otro Lado* (The Other Side). Dorian's has one-hour color print processing. La Perla de La Paz (19), another major department store, has tile floors, but is otherwise very much the same. Avenida Agosto, between Aréola and 16 de Septiembre, has been made into a mall, with boutiques, gift shops, and stores selling imports from Taiwan, England, and California. The large MAS store (25) is the rough equivalent of a Target store. Foto Flash (29) promises to return your color prints in 45 minutes, beating the local competition by a full 15. Naturaleza Viva next door sells medicinal herbs and natural remedies.

Nuestra Señora de La Paz (21), on the south side of Plaza Constitución, is a large cathedral. It replaced the original mission church, its cornerstone being laid in 1861, but it has none of the charm of the churches at San Javier or Mulegé. Biblioteca de História de las Californias (16) is a library devoted to books on the history of Alta and Baja California, and it has a pictorial rendition of the early history of Baja California.

The rest of the city is too large to explore on foot. The accompanying map shows the location of many restaurants, stores, and other attractions that may be of interest. There are a number of travel agencies in town that can arrange fishing, diving, and whale-watching trips, horseback riding, ATVs, water-skiing and so forth. In addition, the hotels catering to visitors from the north have reservations desks. Information on other restaurants, hotels, stores, night spots and such can be obtained from the State Secretary of Tourism offices.

The CCCs (57) and (66) are well-stocked supermarkets, every bit as good as the best in the US, and have color print film processing and ATM machines. Stop at Baja Cellular (52) to establish roaming service if you have not already done so at an office in Baja Norte. If you have forgotten a birthday, there is a florist (47). Ace Hardware (39) contains just about what you have come to expect at home. Artesanias Cuauhtemoc (61) sells fabrics, place mats, tablecloths, tapestries, bed spreads, and clothing of cotton and wool. Everything is made on foot-powered looms, the only electricity being utilized by the lights.

There are a number of good Chinese restaurants in town, each with the requisite lanterns, golden Buddhas, and tanks of fish, but not an epicanthic fold to be seen. Restaurant Dragon (9), second floor, is clean, neat, and moderately priced, with the full range of Chinese food, such as shark fin soup, chicken in oyster sauce, egg rolls, chop suey, chow mein, and won ton soup, and the usual Mexican and seafood items, plus some hybrids such as *chorizo chino* (Chinese/Mexican sausage). Restaurant Nuevo Peking (33) is very pleasant, and has an extensive Chinese menu and a bar. Restaurant Jardín Yee, at KM 3 to the west of town, is clean, neat, and relatively inexpensive.

Restaurant el Taste (41) has seafood, Mexican, steaks, and live music and dancing. Sunset Mike's (40) offers Mexican, burgers, and beers, and live music some nights. The Immigration office is two doors to the southwest. Rin Rin Pizza (32) does a good job with the primary entrée. There are only 22 flavors at 33 Flavors Ice Cream (35). The *palapa*-roofed Restaurant Estrella del Mar (43) specializes in seafood. Just to the northwest, the Plaza Coral has a number of shops and cafés, and an interesting view of the yacht anchorage. The large menu at Restaurant Bismark II (42) includes lobster, abalone, carne asada, and deep fried red snapper, but our favorite is *cochinita pibil*, a roast pork dish. Super Pollo (38), one of three in town, fills the role of Kentucky Fried Chicken. Restaurant Samalu (65) is a large *palapa* with an equally large menu of seafood, steaks, and Mexican. Rosticería California (31) specializes in poultry. Modest Restaurant la Mar y Peña (54) has the most extensive seafood menu in La Paz, and meals are quite inexpensive—the locals know it, and you will have to dine early to avoid a wait. Café Combate (51) sells roasted beans and ground coffee. Baja Sur Internacional (34) has scuba air, dive equipment rentals, service, local trips, and guides.

Everything made at Artesianas Cuauhtemoc is produced on foot-powered looms, the only electricity being utilized by the lights

In addition to the RV parks on the southwestern outskirts of town, Aquamarina RV Park (55), class A, has sites with full hookups, shaded by trees, bougainvillea, and other flowering plants, rest rooms, showers, laundry machines, a pool, boat and trailer storage, and a concrete launch ramp (14%). Club Campestre de La Paz, a residential development, has plans for a golf course, but so far little has happened.

The area of the city called Cuatro Molinos (59, Four Mills, referring to the four windmills that can be seen) includes an art gallery, an art school, and the Teatro de la Ciudad, which offers a variety of musical, theatrical, and dance performances. The Museo de Anthropologia (37) has photographs and exhibits on Indian life and rock art, the history of Baja California Sur, folk art, minerals, and fossil shells. There is no telling what you might find at Centro de Arte Regional (68): potters making their wares on foot-powered wheels; people sitting around roasting meat, drinking beer, and loafing; possibly a truck loaded with hand-made wooden furniture, offered at very low prices; women selling beautiful bedspreads; or perhaps nothing at all. Father Baegert would probably not approve of the design of the religious sanctuary Santuario de Guadalupe (56), but it is certainly eye-catching.

Help is not far away should you encounter mechanical difficulties, for there are a number of dealers with repair facilities: Dodge (58), Dodge/Chrysler (49), Nissan (63), Volkswagen at KM 3, west of town, and Ford/Lincoln also at KM 3. The large Chevrolet dealership (53) handles parts and service for Chevys, as well as other GM makes, Johnson outboard parts and service, some trailer items (hitches, bearings), and marine accessories like pumps and anchors. Baja California Motors (67) handles parts for Nissan, Dodge, Ford, and Toyota, as well as Chevrolet and other GMC makes. There are numerous other parts stores, mechanics, radiator and brake shops, and tire sales and repairs. Agencia Arjona (45) is an Evinrude dealer, and sells tools, hardware, camping equipment, and Coleman stoves. Mercury outboard parts and repairs are available (62), and there is a Mariner outboard dealer (69). There are a number of PEMEX stations: (50, MND), (23, MN), (64, MN), (48, MND), (70, MND).

de la Independencia, just mentioned, and Avenida Héroes del 47. To top things off, there are three "date" streets, 16 de Septiembre, 5 de Febrero, and 5 de Mayo.

Marina de La Paz (44) offers the full range of facilities and services you would expect at a marina in the US. The concrete launch ramp (14%) leads to protected waters, although maneuvering room and parking are limited. The marine store carries a variety of maintenance materials, parts, and accessories with familiar brand names, and an inventory of boat trailer parts and equipment, including hitches, rollers, springs, and bearing assemblies. There are also a laundromat, showers, rest rooms, and a long-distance telephone. The Dock Restaurant at the marina serves meals attuned to American tastes: chicken, hot dogs, zucchini sticks, pizza, nachos, beer, milk shakes, banana splits, and ice cream. El Molino Steak House next door specializes in, well, steaks. Other marinas just northeast of town are described beginning on page 190.

The waters north and east of La Paz have long been among the most prominent fishing locations on the continent, and a number of world records for sailfish, roosterfish, and amberjack have been set there. The best fishing is in deep water off the east sides of Islas Espíritu Santo and Partida Sur, primarily for wahoo, yellowfin tuna, and dolphinfish from June to November, and sailfish from July to October. Yellowtail migrate from the upper Cortez and are found in large numbers in winter and early spring off rocky points, reefs, and headlands throughout the region.

The Dorado Velez Fleet operates a fleet of cruisers, and fishes Espíritu Santo, Isla Cerralvo, and the La Paz area. Information and reservations can be obtained at the fishing desk at the Los Arcos Hotel or any travel agency. Bob Butler's Fisherman's Fleet offers complete trips to Ensenada los Muertos, fishing the productive waters around Cerralvo out of *pangas*. Reservations can be made at the Los Arcos or by telephone. Information on other fleets and boats is available from any hotel or travel office in La Paz.

There are three prominent diving attractions in the La Paz area: the wreck of the Salvatierra, Los Islotes, and Marisla Seamount.

Salvatierra...

An ex-US Navy Second World War LST, this vessel sank in Canal San Lorenzo in 1976, and is now one of the premiere dive sites in the La Paz area. Colorful photographic subjects abound, including yellowtail surgeonfish, grunts, goatfish, angelfish, morays, rays, and several species of large parrot fish. Her propellers and rudders are easily accessible, and large schools of fish hide under the stern, often so dense you literally have to brush them aside to swim through. The ship was carrying a cargo of trucks and trailers, and a few still can be seen scattered over the sandy bottom.

■ Sources of confusion

The Baja Name Game in the first chapter described the confusing state of names applied to places on the peninsula, but even street names can be a problem. There are, for instance, two "Avenida Independencias," in La Paz, meeting at right angles. Yes, it is possible to stand on the corner of Independencia and Independencia! One runs northwest/southeast, the second northeast/southwest. The name of the second is actually "Héroes de la Independencia," but the letters of the first three words on the street signs are small. There are also two "Avenida Héroes": Avenida Héroes

The wreck is relatively easy to find. There are two aid-to-navigation structures in Canal San Lorenzo: the southernmost, Scout Shoal Light, is a concrete tower; the northernmost, San Lorenzo Shoal Light, a metal pipe structure. The wreck is located about one mile east of the latter structure. When you are over the wreck Scout Shoal Light should bear 206°, San Lorenzo Shoal Light 267°. She lies in 57 feet of water, her highest part rising to within 23 feet of the surface. Tidal currents in excess of three knots are possible in the channel, requiring divers to plan their activities using the tide tables.

Los Islotes...

Los Islotes are islets located just north of Isla Partida Sur. The greatest attraction is a colony of friendly sea lions, who put on a wonderful show of underwater acrobatics, often doing barrel rolls around divers and indulging in a one-sided game of "chicken," rushing in and veering off at the last second. The best diving is among the boulders on the north and east sides. The site tends to be deep, although there is limited snorkeling close in. Many species of fish can be seen, most notably mantas, sharks, king angelfish, and yellowtail surgeonfish, as well as many octopus.

Michael joins the sea lion ballet at Los Islotes

Marisla Seamount...

Friendly manta rays and not-so-friendly hammerhead sharks have made Marisla Seamount (often called "El Bajo") the most famous dive site in the Cortez. The seamount is located 8.2 miles, 032° from Los Islotes. When you are over the site the largest of the Islotes will bear 212°, the highest point of Isla San Francisco 287°, and the left tangent of Espíritu Santo 166°. Local commercial fishermen often anchor a buoy on the seamount, and in calm weather fish the area in *pangas*. There are 3 distinct underwater peaks arrayed along a 300-yard line running 120/300°, the northernmost rising to within 83 feet of the surface, the central peak to within 52 feet, and the southern to within 69 feet. The

central peak, with its shallow depths and relatively flat top, is the primary dive site and anchoring location, although the hammerheads seem to prefer the north peak. Don't get your hopes too high: the friendly mantas are rare. The best months for them are August and September.

There are other species present at the seamount. John Riffe tells of a group of divers who came up from their first dive raving about the huge fish. One man, though, complained that he had seen nothing. After his second dive he still had seen nothing, so John followed him down on the third dive. The scene was priceless; the diver was found annoying a tiny moray in a pile of boulders, all the time being observed by a gigantic jewfish not three feet away. Garden eels can be observed in sandy areas around the peaks, and marlin, tuna, and jacks have been seen in the area.

● ●

❝ *A creature to be feared*

Man relies heavily on physical appearances when making judgments about the character and intent of other creatures, as Quasimodo, the Elephant Man, and the mantas have found to their sorrow. Found from Santa Barbara to Peru, Pacific mantas are common in the Cortez up to the Midriff. Ugly by some standards, they have whip-like tails, twin horns projecting forward, and flapping wings rather than respectable fins like other fish, and they can be huge, running up to 25 feet across and to 3,500 pounds in Baja waters. Remoras have been seen attached inside their mouths, a location presumably favored only by the most self-confident.

Baja's mantas got a bad press right from the beginning, when Father Antonio Ascension observed in 1602, "One fish which is like nothing else grows there; it appears to be a mossy blanket extending to several unequal points.... Its motion is scarcely perceptible, but when its prey is near it moves with great speed and enfolds and squeezes it. It is a very rare man who can save his life even though he is armed to strike out and defend himself."

In 1863, Baja explorer J. Ross Browne summarized the current understanding of these creatures, "The manta ray is an immense brute of great strength, cunning, and ferocity, and is more the terror of the pearl divers than any other creature of the sea. The habit of the animal is to hover at the surface over the pearl divers, obstructing the rays of the sun, and moving as the diver moves, and, when he is obliged to come up for breath, hugging him in his immense flaps until he is suffocated, when the brute, with his formidable teeth and jaws, devours him with gluttonous voracity. Many fishermen and pearl divers have been killed by them."

The formidable teeth and jaws reported by Browne have proved to be imaginary, for they are plankton eaters, and the only teeth they have is a tiny set on the lower jaw. Although they are harmless, a certain distrust lingers on: in the 1966 movie, Batman kept a spray can of "manta ray repellent" handy.

Events at Marisla Seamount have suggested that the mantas are something entirely different than their appearance and reputation would suggest. In September 1980, a boat carrying a television crew was anchored on the seamount, filming an "American Sportsman" show about schooling hammerhead sharks. Aboard were Stan Waterman, Howard Hall, Ted Rulison, Marty Snyderman, and novelist Peter Benchley, of Jaws *fame. Soon a 16-foot manta came by, swimming slowly, something obviously wrong: ropes were fouled around its left wing and ala, a hornlike appendage used to sweep food into its mouth. Closer inspection showed it also had a number of fish hooks embedded in its wings, and a rope had cut deeply near an eye. Sensing that the divers wanted to help, the manta let them come close, cut off the rope, and remove the hooks. It began swimming more vigorously and allowed one of the divers to climb on its back, taking him for a swooping, soaring ride. Returning the first diver, the fish gave the others a chance, and if a diver dropped off, it would circle back and pick him up. It hung around the entire time the crew was on the seamount, offering rides to whoever wanted them.*

I recently encountered a friendly manta while scuba diving in the Red Sea, and it will be an experience long remembered. When I was about 50 feet deep, the large creature materialized out of the blue, turned directly towards me, veered off at the last moment, did several barrel (belly out) rolls around me, and then several outside (belly in) rolls. He then moved in closer and let me hitch a ride for several minutes, and finally disappeared into the blue. I was stunned at first by what had happened, but when I collected my wits, I realized what the manta was doing; he was showing off! The puny creature with the tank on his back, kicking laboriously along at a quarter of a knot, was put in his place!

Mantas are common in Baja waters, but friendly encounters are rare. Should you see a passing manta, it serves no purpose to begin a pursuit, for with several flaps of its "wings," it can be out of sight in seconds. Rather, simply wait, hope it turns your way and shows some interest, and if so, count your blessings. ——Walt **99**

• •

A diver is taken for a fantastic ride

Ferries to Topolobampo and Mazatlán operate from the terminal at KM 17, northeast of town. If you plan to take the ferry, the first step is to make reservations, assuming that you have foolishly put the matter off this long, not only to make sure you get on, but to avoid waiting in line at the ticket office. In La Paz, reservations can be made at a number of travel agencies, including Viajes Lybsa and Viajes Palmira. Also, make sure you have your tourist cards and the documents used to obtain them (passport, birth certificate, etc.), the **original** title and registration for each vehicle

(or rental agreement/notarized permission), a valid American or Canadian driver's license (including extensions), and a credit card: Diner's Club, American Express, or Visa. (The booklet *Traveling to Mexico by Car* also includes MasterCard, but La Paz officials insist they can accept only the three noted). The original and four copies each of your tourist cards, the documents used to obtain them, title, and registration (or permission) are required, and copy machines are available in La Paz; ask around to find out which ones are currently in working order.

The day before departure, drive to the ferry terminal at Pichilingue with your rig (officials granting import permits must see it), enter main gate, make an immediate right (north), and drive to a small green-and-white duplex office building at the north end of the ferry complex, marked "Banjercito." Go to the office on the left marked "Vehicle Control Office" and present the originals and the copies you made. There is a fee for the import permit of about $11, and you must execute a Vehicle Return Promise Form. Using your credit card, you will be required to post a bond, guaranteeing that you will remove the vehicle from Mexico when your trip is over. When these are completed, they will put a decal on your windshield and give you the import permit.

Early on the day of departure, say 7 or 8 in the morning, drive your rig with all your paperwork (its length must be measured to determine the fare) to the SEMATUR ticket office (36). An employee will hopefully direct those with reservations to go directly to a ticket window. You will get a ticket for your rig and for each person.

Several hours before the departure of the ferry, drive to the ferry terminal and return to the same building where you got your import permit, only this time go to the SEMATUR office on the right, where they will stamp your tickets and return them to you. Locate the trucks and autos waiting to board the ferry, get in line, and follow the instructions of the men supervising the loading. Once aboard, you must then leave your rig and will not be allowed to return to it while the ferry is underway, so feed and water Fifi and Fido. Each ferry has a passenger's desk, where room keys and information on the location of food service, the time of arrival, debarking procedures, and so forth can be obtained.

Side trip from La Paz to Playa Tecolote, with fine sand beaches and boardsailing. Turn to page 190.

■■■■■■■■■■■■■■■■■■■■■■■■■■■■■■■

On the Transpeninsular Highway at La Paz

KM	Location
0/216	Start new KM numbering sequence.
213	Route BCS 286 to Ensenada los Muertos and Playa Punta Arena.

Side trip from KM 213 to Ensenada los Muertos, with world-class fishing, and Playa Punta Arena, with excellent boardsailing. Turn to page 191.

KM	Location
203	LPG yard.
190	**San Pedro**. Groceries, beer, pottery, long-distance telephone, Restaurant el Paraíso, which has a Mexican menu.
185	Mexico Route 19 south to Todos Santos and Cabo San Lucas. Turn to page 192.

■ The rugged Sierra de la Laguna

The intersection of Route 19 and the Transpeninsular Highway marks the approximate northern limit of the granite mountains of the Sierra de la Laguna. The range is a wilderness much different from anywhere in the US, much of it highly isolated and inaccessible even by foot due to difficult terrain and dense vegetation. The axis of the range is roughly north/south, its Pacific slope being much steeper than the Cortez side. Both sides are cut by a series of parallel canyons having an east/west orientation. The range is not high, 6,855-foot Cerro las Casitas being the tallest mountain, but the terrain is so rugged that only a few flat areas of any size exist, the largest and best-known being La Laguna, a meadow about a mile long and a half mile wide, located at 5,600 feet about 3 miles west of Cerro las Casitas. Temperatures below freezing are possible, fog and heavy dew are fairly common, and the sound of thunder is frequent. Rainfall is much heavier than in any other part of Baja, up to 30 inches in some microclimates, most of it occurring between July and

November. Small streams and springs can normally be found in the upper regions of virtually all the larger canyons.

Baja was once cooler and wetter than today. As the climate became hot and dry, the flora and fauna of surrounding lowlands changed dramatically, but in small "island" environments, especially around La Laguna meadow, a wonderful mix of the rare, the ordinary and the seemingly out-of-place remains. An all-inclusive list would be impossibly long, but there are pinyon pine, mosses, prickly-pear cactus, jewel lichen, algae, oak, madrone, fern, marigold, monkey flower, evening primrose, willow, rose, geranium, palmita, strawberry, sorrel, wild grape, watercress, deer, mountain lion, coyote, pocket gopher, water beetle, mosquito, band-winged grasshopper, walking stick, waterstrider, dragonfly, caddisfly, Pacific tree frog, and the exotic-looking sotol, with its yucca-like leaves perched on top of a tall, thin trunk. The mix of birds is equally strange and diverse, and a hiker might be able to identify 50 in a single day, including the endemic Xanthus hummingbird and the uniquely plumaged endemic subspecies San Lucas robin.

Sober-faced naturalists can undoubtedly provide very objective explanations for all this diversity, noting the meadow's altitude, generous rainfall at high elevations, the aridity of the surrounding regions, the influences of the nearby Pacific and Cortez, and the meadow's position just north of the Tropic of Cancer, missing being "tropical" by less than four miles. Still, it seems certain that there is at least a bit of magic involved. So unusual is La Laguna that it has been proposed as a national park. RVers with suitable vehicles can cross the mountain range on the Naranjas Road and learn something of its natural history; see page 224.

KM	Location
169	Rolling hills to KM 103, with moderate grades and numerous blind curves. Watch the hillsides in this area for small trees, perhaps 15 feet high, with large and very beautiful, trumpet-shaped, yellow flowers. These are *palo de arco*, found widely in Mexico and commonly used as ornamentals.
164	**El Triunfo**.

El Triunfo

The area 30 miles south of La Paz was long known to have mineral riches, and in 1748, a silver mining camp and settlement called Santa Ana was established, the first secular, non-Indian settlement in the Californias. However, it was not until foreigners invested large amounts of money that mining grew into a large-scale enterprise.

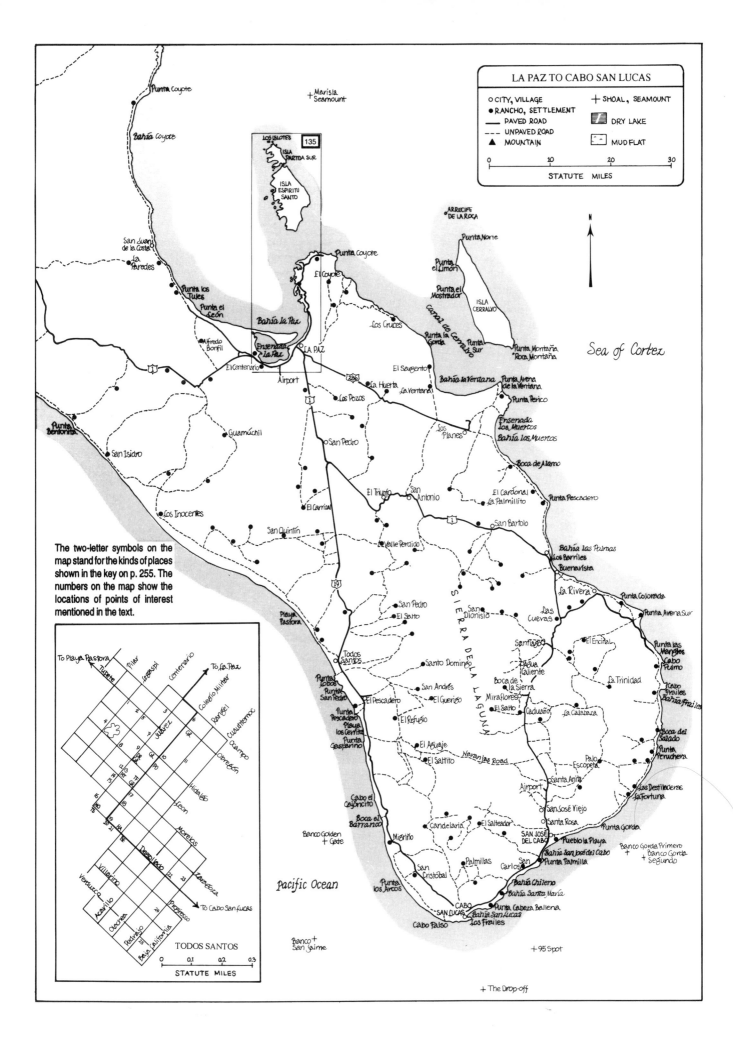

LA PAZ TO CABO SAN LUCAS

○ CITY, VILLAGE   + SHOAL, SEAMOUNT
● RANCHO, SETTLEMENT
— PAVED ROAD   ▨ DRY LAKE
-- UNPAVED ROAD
▲ MOUNTAIN   ⬚ MUD FLAT

0   10   20   30
STATUTE MILES

The two-letter symbols on the map stand for the kinds of places shown in the key on p. 255. The numbers on the map show the locations of points of interest mentioned in the text.

Punta Coyote

Marisla Seamount

Bahía Coyote

LOS ISLOTES
ISLA PARTIDA SUR
135
ISLA ESPIRITU SANTO

ARRECIFE DE LA ROCA

N

San Juan de la Costa
La Paredes
Punta los Tules
Punta el León
Alfredo Bonfil
Ensenada la Paz
El Centenario
Airport

Punta Coyote
El Coyote
Bahía la Paz
LA PAZ
Los Cruces

Punta Norte
Punta el Limón
Punta el Mostrador
ISLA CERRALVO
Canal de Cerralvo

Sea of Cortez

El Sargento
286
La Huerta
La Ventana
Los Pozos

Punta la Gorda
Punta Sur
Punta Montaña
Roca Montaña
Bahía la Ventana
Punta Arena de la Ventana
Punta Perico

Punta Bentonita

San Isidro
Guamúchil
San Pedro
Los Planes

Ensenada los Muertos
Bahía los Muertos
Boca de Álamo

El Triunfo
San Antonio
El Carrizal
El Cardonal
La Palmillito
Punta Pescadero

Los Inocentes
San Quintín
Valle Perdido
1
San Bartolo

Bahía las Palmas
Los Barriles
Buenavista

Playa Pastora

19
San Pedro
El Salto
San Dionisio
Las Cuevas

La Rivera
Punta Colorada
Punta Arena Sur

SIERRA DE LA LAGUNA

Santiago
Agua Caliente
El Encinal
Punta las Mangles
Cabo Pulmo

Todos Santos
Santo Domingo
San Andrés
El Guerigo
Boca de la Sierra
Miraflores
El Salto
Caduano
La Calabaza
La Trinidad
Cabo Frailes
Bahía Frailes

Punta Lobos
Punta San Pedro
El Pescadero

Punta Pescadero
Playa los Cerritos
Punta Gasparino

El Refugio
El Asuaje
El Saltito

Navanjas Road

Boca del Salado
Punta Peruchera
Palo Escopeta
Santa Anita
Airport

Las Destiladeras
La Fortuna

Cabo el Cajoncito
Boca el Barranco

Candelaria
Migriño
El Salteador
San José Viejo
Santa Rosa
Punta Gorda

Banco Golden + Gate

San Cristóbal
Palmillas
San Carlos
SAN JOSÉ DEL CABO
Pueblo la Playa
Bahía San José del Cabo
Punta Palmilla

Banco Gorda Primero + Banco Gorda + Segundo

Pacific Ocean

Punta los Arcos
CABO SAN LUCAS
Cabo Falso
Bahía Chileno
Bahía Santa María
Punta Cabeza Ballena
Bahía San Lucas
Los Frailes

Banco + San Jaime

+ 95 Spot

+ The Drop-off

TODOS SANTOS

To Playa Pastora
To La Paz
Tutate
Pilar
Legaspi
Centenario
Colegio Militar
Rangel
Juárez
Cuauhtémoc
Ocampo
Obregón
Hidalgo
León
Morelos
Degollado
Carrasca
Villarino
Verduzco
Acevlo
Ocotero
Pedrajo
Baja California
To Cabo San Lucas

0   0.1   0.2   0.3
STATUTE MILES

In 1862, the Triunfo Gold and Silver Company began operations, and the town soon had a population of 10,000, the largest mining town in Baja California; the population of La Paz at the time was less than 1,000. Due to a lack of hoisting machinery, the miners tried to avoid constructing shafts, and often dug laterally into the hillsides. Swinging picks, they broke the ore loose, loaded it into knapsacks, and carried it out through galleries so low that they were sometimes forced to crawl. When it was necessary to dig a vertical shaft, ladders were constructed of notched logs. At the entrance, the ore was loaded on mules to be carried to a large stamp mill, where it was crushed, mixed with salt, roasted, and washed. The silver was then removed from the ore by mixing it with mercury and heating the amalgam. Ground water was a problem, and a number of the most productive mines had recurrent flooding problems. The famous hurricane that wrecked La Paz in 1918 flooded many of them.

The primary output of the mines was silver, but gold, antimony, lead, and copper were also obtained. Hopes were high, for one of the mines reported silver ore that assayed at $400 to the ton, and it was possible for miners to earn as much as $16 a day. Veins of metallic ores were traced all the way to the Cortez and to the vicinity of La Paz.

However, expenses were high, one authority complaining that "This rebellious ore had to be calcined, chloridized and lixiviated or cyanided." By the turn of the century, the quality of the silver ore began to decline, and the other metals could not sustain the enterprise. By 1905, only a small force of miners was still employed. The Boleo Company of Santa Rosalía took over after the 1918 flood, but gave up in 1926.

Today, the town gives the impression of being in a state of suspended animation, perhaps recovering from the intense activity of past years. Some mining still goes on, but the town has continued to decline, and now it is little more than a collection of dilapidated old adobe buildings. Only the huge chimney, constructed of brick in 1905 and still in good repair, helps it cling to the name "The Triumph." If El Triunfo were located in the US it would certainly be a national park. The smelter and mill are well worth a visit, and there are dozens of mines within a radius of three or four miles. The strange brick-walled cemetery, about 200 yards east (075°) of the circular stack, contains 13 concrete crypts, unlabeled as to contents, origin, cause, or date of expiration. Many show signs that they have been opened, for there were persistent tales about treasures left behind by Americans fleeing political disturbances or the law.

Artesanias el Triunfo, across from the church, sells locally made hats, place mats, and baskets woven out of straw, and there are several tiny grocery stores and a long distance telephone.

KM	Location
156	San Antonio. In 1756, San Antonio was briefly

the capital of Baja California, and was a great rival to El Triunfo during the mining years. However, San Antonio failed to keep up economically. Today the tables have turned and it is the more clean, pleasant, and prosperous, with a PEMEX (MN), library, grocery and gift stores, doctor, post office, telegraph, liquor, beer, and cold sodas. The architecture of its church, built in 1825 and remodeled a number of years ago, is one of the more unusual in Baja, a massive concrete amalgam of the features of a railroad locomotive and a river steamer.

■ More interesting plants

At KM 153, watch the surrounding trees for the vines they support. If it's anywhere between April and October and the flowers on the vine are crimson, reminiscent of bougainvillea, the plant is the common San Miguel vine. The other vine is yuca (only one c), which produces large, bright-yellow flowers most of the year. The large trees at KM 145, having tiny leaves arranged on each side of a common axis, similar to a feather, are acacias. Since there are perhaps 50 species found on the peninsula, only a botanist could determine which this is. The umbrella-like shape of the tree provides shade, and thus keeps the ground damper, allowing smaller plants to prosper. The many-branched cacti to the left (north) of the highway at KM 138 are candelabra cactus, a Baja endemic, named for obvious reasons. They are common in Baja Norte along the Pacific side, and in Baja Sur along the Cortez side, presumably to take full advantage of winter rains in the north and summer rains in the south.

The strikingly beautiful tree with creamy-yellow bark and bright-green deciduous leaves clinging to the rocks on the north side of the highway at KM 131 is a *zalate*, or wild fig. Found from San Ignacio south, *zalates* often choose exposed locations where no other large trees are able to survive, sometimes clinging to sheer cliff faces, their root systems taking advantage of every available crack. This specimen is not particularly large or dramatic, but it offers one of the few chances you may have to see a mature specimen directly beside the Transpeninsular. If you wish to examine the tree, a flat spot can be found on the south side of the road, but be careful. A large stand of zalates can be seen at Pueblo la Playa, a small settlement on the beach just east of San José del Cabo.

KM	Location
128+	San Bartolo. Cafés, groceries, fruit, sodas, beer, long-distance telephone, famous springs of exceptional purity.
110+	Road east to the shores of Bahía las Palmas.

To see a really big zalate, drive south from Pulmo on the road to San José del Cabo

Bahía las Palmas

Stretching from Punta Pescadero south to Punta Arena Sur, Bahía las Palmas is world-famous for its gamefish. For over 10 miles, the 100-fathom line averages less than a mile offshore, the closest lengthy approach anywhere in the Cape region, which may account for the fine fishing and many successful resorts. Blue and black marlin and sailfish are taken from May to October, sometimes by astonished fishermen in cartoppers. Roosters are caught year-around, but fishing for them is best from May to October. Yellowtail are best from January to April, and striped marlin, dolphinfish, tuna, wahoo, and lesser fish inhabit the area all year, although the warm months are the most productive and December through March can be slow. Four miles south of Punta Pescadero is the famous "Tuna Canyon," where Ray Cannon found depths of 50 fathoms 100 yards from shore and a year-around population of yellowfin tuna. Diving is pleasant, with large sandy areas broken by reefs, and spearfishing for pelagic gamefish should be great.

The bay is the most popular boardsailing location in Baja, with many clean, sandy beaches, pleasant weather, good campsites, and winds often in the 18 to 25 knot range between mid-November and mid-March. Winds during this period are normally from the north, producing side-onshore conditions from Punta Pescadero to the Buena Vista area. The beach from Buena Vista to Punta Colorada has sandy areas and the launch easy, but the shoreline has curved eastward to the point that novice boardsailors may begin to encounter problems with onshore winds. A number of boardsailing operations are located along the shores of the bay.

Although a number of concrete launch ramps have been built through the years, all have been destroyed by waves or deeply buried by sand. All beach launches open into unpro-

tected waters and can be carried out only in calm conditions.

Side trip to Bahía las Palmas, with excellent fishing and boardsailing. Turn to page 192.

109 PEMEX (MND), groceries. Mr. Bill's Boardsailing Adventures is found by driving east on the graded class 1 dirt road across from the PEMEX. RVers can stay one night, but no hookups are available. Several hotels that have restaurants and bars are within easy walking distance. Sailboard rentals and instruction are offered, and transportation is available to other sailing sites and for downwinders. In addition, there is a dive shop that offers rental equipment, clinics, and local trips, and Hobies, Zodiacs, mountain bikes, and sea kayaks are for rent.

108
105 PEMEX (MND), cafés, groceries.
Hotel Spa Buenavista (signed), which has a restaurant, and cruiser and *panga* fleets, live and frozen bait, tackle rental, and snorkeling gear. Boat and trailer storage can be arranged. Vista Sea Sport, near the hotel, offers dive trips ranging from Cerralvo to the Bancos Gorda, and the owners are very knowledgeable about the best dive sites. They have a compressor, a *panga*, and a 22-foot cruiser, full rentals and limited sales, and offer PADI instruction from resort/refresher courses to full certification. To locate them, turn east at KM 105 on the class 1 road, pass the hotel, turn right (south) at the bottom of the hill, and look for a white house with green trim sporting the diver's flag.

103+ Class 1 road east to La Capilla Trailer Park and Ranchero Leonero. Set trip odometer. At Mile 0.6, go straight ahead (005°, signed) for inexpensive La Capilla, class B, at Mile 1.1, which has full hookups, showers, and rest rooms. The beautiful sand beach is only 100 yards north, and small boats are easily launched. To go to Rancho Leonero, turn right (120°) at Mile 0.6, follow the signs and arrive at the ranch at Mile 4.3. Although the sandy class 1 road has some bumpy areas and several 20% grades, it is passable by almost any RV. The ranch has fishing cruisers and *pangas*, live bait, and rental tackle. East Cape Divers at the ranch has two compressors, limited rentals, and sales of small items. Diving is excellent right in front of the resort, and a boat dive to Pulmo Reef is offered.

93   **Las Cuevas.** Grocery store, paved road northeast (signed) to La Rivera and Arricefe Pulmo.

Off-road trip from KM 93 to La Rivera, Arricefe Pulmo, which is one of Baja's premiere diving locations, Bahía los Frailes, and on to San José del Cabo. Turn to page 223.

90   The candelabra cactus and *pitaya agria* described in earlier pages form large, almost impenetrable thickets in this area.

84+   Groceries. Paved road west to Santiago (signed), which has a PEMEX (MND), groceries, stores, clinic, doctor, pharmacy, long-distance telephone, mail, telegraph, cold beer and sodas, ice. Restaurant Palomar can be found by following the signs from the southwest corner of the town square for about 75 yards. This pleasant, shaded outdoor restaurant serves seafood and Mexican. Zoologico Santiago can be found by continuing south past Palomar until reaching the church, where you must turn right or left. Turn right (west), drive 0.3 mile, and turn left (south) at the stop sign. The zoo is on the right in about 400 yards. The zoo is a great surprise for a tiny Baja town, with spider monkeys, a lion, a tiger, a black bear, several guinea pigs, turtles, snakes, a caiman, caracaras, foxes, coyotes, a half dozen deer, bobcats, an ocelot, a peacock, parakeets, a hawk, a badger, three parrots, and other animals.

81+   Tropic of Cancer; those heading south are officially in the tropics.

71   PEMEX (MND). Road west (signed) to Miraflores, which has groceries, stores, doctor, dentist, cold beer, tortilla factory, long-distance telephone. While driving into town, watch on the left (south) side of the access road for the Leather Shop (signed). This shop cures leather and makes saddles, chaps, knife sheaths, and other articles for the locals, but also offers belts and purses to visitors.

55   Naranjas Road (signed).

Off-road trip from KM 55 on the Transpeninsular to KM 71+ on Route 19 via the Naranjas Road, the only road through the Sierra de la Laguna. Turn to page 224.

KM	Location
46+	**Santa Anita.** Grocery stores.
43	Los Cabos International Airport.

■ Trying to explain the unexplainable

Somewhere in this area—the exact location is not known—most people begin an almost magical transformation. It is easier to explain what it is not, rather than what it is. It can't be ordinary excitement, for it is unaccompanied by a quickening pulse and rising blood pressure. It can't be anticipation, because even those who have been to the Cape dozens of times still feel the magic. Many people, newcomers and veterans alike, find themselves grinning, but none find anything particularly humorous.

There is probably no explanation, but the transformation seems to be a change in mood, a step beyond *déjà vu*; you think that not only that you have been here before, but that you **belong** here. There are other Baja places that stir the imagination: El Rosario, when the "real" Baja is first encountered; San Ignacio, a small palm-covered island of green in a sea of brown desert; and the unexpected panoramas of brilliant blue coves, brown islands, and white sand beaches of Bahía Concepción. Still, the Cape is a place apart from the rest of the peninsula.

39+   **San José Viejo.** Groceries, tire repair, fish market, bakery, auto parts, long-distance telephone.

36+   **Santa Rosa.** PEMEX (MND), Volkswagen dealer, car rental, tire repair, fruit stores, butcher shops, café, grocery stores, pharmacies, liquor, new shopping center.

33   Ice manufacturing plant, hardware.

32+   **San José del Cabo.**

San José del Cabo

Beginning in 1566, the galleons coming from Manila, the "black ships" of *Shogun* fame, stopped at San José del Cabo to obtain water and fresh provisions *en route* to Acapulco. A Jesuit mission was founded in 1730, but epidemics quickly killed most of the Indians. In 1822, English sea lord Thomas Cochrane attacked the town, and in 1847, the American frigate *Portsmouth* landed a company of marines to occupy the town during the Mexican-American War. Mexican patriots besieged them for several months, almost wiping them out before reinforcements arrived. Today's Avenida Antonio Mijares is named for a Mexican lieutenant killed in an attack. The mission church was destroyed in the battle, and the present one (8) was built in the 1940s.

Today, San José del Cabo is one of the most beautiful towns in Baja. The pace is slower and more mature than at Cabo San Lucas, and the town does not attract as many collegians on spring break. The raunchiness of the T-shirts for sale is several orders of magnitude less than Cabo, and there are fewer people hawking time-share condos and trinkets along the streets. The town caters to hotel inhabitants rather than RVers, but there are many restaurants, beaches, and other

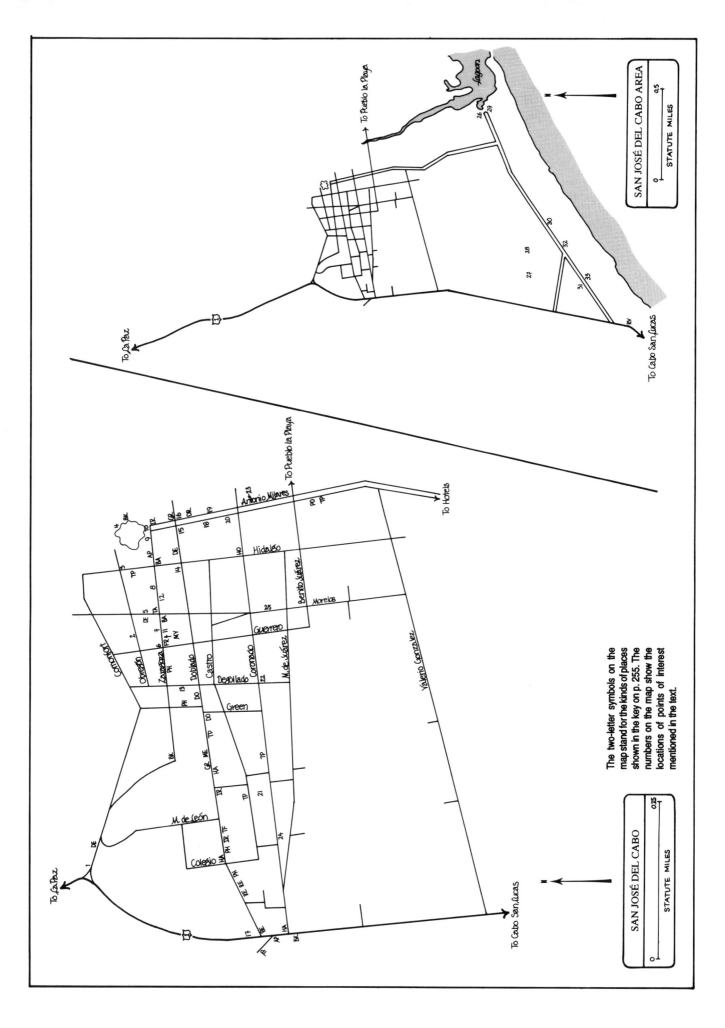

SAN JOSÉ DEL CABO AREA

STATUTE MILES

Lagoon

To Pueblo la Playa

To La Paz

To Cabo San Lucas

SAN JOSÉ DEL CABO

STATUTE MILES

To Pueblo la Playa

Antonio Mijares

Hidalgo

Benito Juárez

Morelas

Guerrero

Castro

Degollado

Coronado

M. de Juárez

Valerio González

To Hotels

Comonfort

Obregón

Zaragoza

Doblado

Green

M. de León

Colegio

To La Paz

To Cabo San Lucas

The two-letter symbols on the map stand for the kinds of places shown in the key on p. 255. The numbers on the map show the locations of points of interest mentioned in the text.

attractions that bring such vagabonds into the area. The central part of town is often congested, and a walking tour is the best way to visit.

There is a municipal tourist information office (10). Restaurant Damiana (4) is very nice, with a menu of seafood and Mexican. They swear that they do not add the herb to their products, a reassuring fact. Modest el Café Fiesta (9) is clean and pleasant, and has a menu of Mexican, burgers, submarines, sandwiches, and salads. The *palapa*-roofed Iguana Restaurant and Bar (18) is fun and informal, with live music and dancing evenings. The specialty of the house is seafood, but the New York steak is excellent, and the French fries are as good as you will find on the peninsula. Restaurant Tropicana at the Tropicana Inn (19) is attractive and clean, serving a large menu of Mexican, American, and seafood. Restaurant Jazmin (5) serves breakfast, lunch, and supper, the supper menu including seafood, chicken, Mexican, BBQ baby back ribs, and steaks. Le Bistrot (25) offers French and European cuisine in a charming atmosphere. Restaurant Abajo del Palmar (2) is a pleasant open-air patio with lots of flowers, serving seafood and Mexican. Ristorante Pietro (7) serves International and Italian cuisine for lunch and dinner. Pizza Fiesta (22) is the local pizza hangout, and has free delivery.

You should be able to find almost anything you need. Almacenes Grupo Castro (17) is a large store, selling groceries, meats, cold cuts, wine, liquor, fruit, and vegetables. Aramburo's Supermarket (6) has meats, groceries, household items, and good produce. Pescadería San Marcos (24) sells fresh fish and fish bait. The Mercado Municipal (21) has many stands selling fresh produce, meat, and fish, and has large baskets of hot peppers, and there are small food stands and a juice bar. The PEMEX (1) sells MND.

Jewelry Amethyst (15) has a good selection of silver and gold jewelry, as well as sculpture. Baja Mar Hand Painted Clothes (20) sells blouses and artistic T-shirts. Curios el Bronco (23) offers pottery, blankets, and knickknacks. Poncho's Leather Shop (16) sells belts, wallets, some made from

The cotton candy man makes his rounds during Carnival at San José del Cabo

rattlesnake, and Dooney & Bourke handbags of dubious pedigree. Fantasia de Cristal (11) sells handmade glass decorations. Fotopronto (12) sells film and claims to be able to process color print film in 30 minutes, the fastest on the peninsula if true. There is a shop (3) whose stock in trade consists of showers and long-distance telephone calls, presumably not at the same time. Killer Hooks Surf Shop (14) sells and rents surfing equipment. Plaza los Cabos (31) has mini-markets, travel agents, handicraft and T-shirt shops, restaurants, airline offices, and long-distance telephone. The Regional Museum (26) is just being established, and so far contains just a dozen or so paintings. However, there are plans to include exhibits on fossils, whales, antiques, and the Pericú Indians, as well as gift and snack shops.

There are a number of hotels in the area that have restaurants, reservations desks, sportfishing fleets, and other things of interest to RVers, including: the Aquamarina (32), Fiesta Inn (33), Howard Johnson Plaza Suites (27), Posada Real Best Western (30), El Presidente Intercontinental (29), Posada Terranova (13), and the Tropicana Inn. If you wish to take a break from RVing, the last is the best bargain in the Cape region in terms of quality, amenities, appearance, comfort, plumbing, and price.

The Costa Azul, one of the most magnificent beaches on the peninsula, sweeps past the town, providing, during low surf conditions, fine swimming and loafing. Care must be exercised, for the bottom offshore gets very deep very rapidly, and a booming surf is sometimes present. Despite the waves, surfers usually head west of town, for the water immediately off the beach is so deep that although large in terms of height, the waves go from crest to crash too quickly to provide good rides. A large lagoon is found just east of town, where more than 180 species of birds have been spotted. The El Presidente Intercontinental has canoes and paddle boats available for birding ventures on the lagoon.

There are no launch ramps nor a harbor in the area, and the sportfishing industry is not as well developed as in Cabo San Lucas. Most hotels have a reservations desk, where *pangas* and cruisers can be hired for fishing and diving trips. Victor's Aquatics, with offices at the Fiesta Inn, the El Presidente Intercontinental, and the Posada Real, can book fishing, scuba diving, and snorkeling trips in *pangas* and cruisers. Reservations are advisable. In addition, *pangas* can be booked at Pueblo la Playa, a settlement on the beach just east of the main part of town. The most popular locations for fishing and diving are at the Bancos Gorda, which will be described later in this chapter.

Campo de Golf San José (28) has 9 holes, par 35, championship yardage 3141, men 2909, women 2444. Tee-time reservations can be made at any time, but allow two weeks for large groups. Facilities include a putting green, chipping green, sand trap, clubhouse, snack bar, locker rooms, showers, and a limited pro shop. Green fees are $15 for 9 holes, including cart. Lessons, club rentals, tennis courts, and a swimming pool are available.

Hikers enjoy a pool at the mouth of Cañon del Diablo

A cooperative manta takes Marilyn Danielson and a pair of remoras for a fantasic ride

A tiny red abalone, about ¾″ across, struts its stuff

Some young ladies enjoy spearfishing

A blue-striped nudibranch, **Tambaja eliora,** *off the western shore of Isla Carmen*

Playa Los Cocos, Bahía Concepción

A crimson **Pitaya agria** *fruit*

Campers at Bahía Concepción

A Spanish shawl nudibranch, Flabellina iodena

Surfing at Morro Domingo

Body surfers near San Miguel

A magnificent bighorn ram

■ The biggest fish in the sea

Man has encountered whale sharks ever since he developed vessels capable of plying ocean waters, but the species was not scientifically described until 1828. Their habit of basking at the surface made them increasingly vulnerable to collisions as ships became larger and faster. Unlike whales, which occasionally survive such encounters, whale sharks inevitably lose, and one giant was even cut completely in half by a steamer. They have cartilaginous skeletons, skin four inches thick, and dorsal fins which can approach six feet in height. The most distinctively marked of all large fishes, their gray-brown sides and backs are covered with a pattern of intersecting transverse and longitudinal stripes. Since they have no known enemies except man and mako sharks, the reasons the biggest fish in the sea needs camouflage are unknown.

Their extreme size and the aggressive habits of their smaller cousins seem to inspire violence. About 1925, Zane Grey was fishing off the Cape, when his party encountered a pair of 40-footers. Grey felt a "boyish desire" to catch one of the monsters, and they somehow managed to set a heavy gaff into its tail. A terrific struggle went on for many hours, with the fish sounding repeatedly to as deep as 1,500 feet. The second shark never abandoned the other, and it was not until the harpoon rope wrapped around the propeller and threatened to bend the shaft that the "boys" cut the line.

The whale sharks have proved to be something other than what their size and family history might suggest. In 1975, a 26-footer was accidentally trapped in a lagoon on Canton Island in the Pacific, and became known as Mimi to local residents. Concerned over her ability to find adequate food, they started to feed her frozen shrimp, pouring buckets-full directly into her gaping mouth. She seemed to love it, and would rub against their skiff and push her mouth against it as if begging for more.

Since they prefer deep water and surface only occasionally to bask and feed, such contact with humans is rare. The emotional impact of the appearance of such a gigantic monster on an unprepared diver can only be imagined: an Australian diver became so frightened when one came by that he grabbed his buddy and held him out like a shield. However, a small number of Baja divers have been able to approach them, sometimes spending considerable periods of time swimming alongside, and a lucky few have had the extraordinary experience of riding on their huge dorsal fins like jockeys. While the experience is undoubtedly the source of a considerable amount of swagger and *braggadocio* upon the return home, the only danger encountered by divers has occurred when they have attempted to hang onto the tail and have been violently swished back and forth in a 15-foot arc, tearing off fins, masks, and scubas.

Should you wish to enjoy an encounter with a whale shark, they are known to frequent the Bancos Gorda. Dive trips to the banks can be arranged at the reservations desk at any of the hotels in San José, at Victor's Aquatics, at Pueblo la Playa, or at a number of places in Cabo San Lucas.

■■■■■■■■■■■■■■■■■■■■■■■■
On the Transpeninsular Highway at KM 32+

KM	Location
32	Restaurant la Parrillada; flame-broiled chicken is a specialty.
31	Los Cabos Autocompactos; Nissan dealer, parts, service, and repairs.
30	Brisa del Mar RV Resort; class A, full hookups at many sites, motel, rest rooms, showers, pool, recreation room, restaurant, bar, laundry, bicycle and water sports equipment rentals, volleyball, horseshoes, fishing trip arrangements, and a beautiful beach. The place is a bit pricey if the site you choose has full hookups and a beach view.
29	"Zippers"; short, fast inside break. Costa Azul Surf Shop sells clothing, as well as selling and renting surfing equipment and snorkeling gear.
28	"The Rock" is the middle break, and "Old Man" is the long outside break. Zippers Restaurant serves burgers, sandwiches, and seafood in an open *palapa* on the beach. RV parking, groceries, liquor, beer.
26+	**Punta Palmilla**. The luxurious Hotel Palmilla has several restaurants and a reservations desk, offering fishing, snorkeling, and sailing excursions. Dive Palmilla, located at the hotel, has full equipment rentals, PADI certification up to divemaster and instructor, compressed air, and trips to Pulmo, the Bancos Gorda, and other local attractions. *Pangas* and fishing cruisers can be rented at the beach. Pepe's Restaurant specializes in lobster and shrimp, and has live music in the evenings. If you have been lucky at fishing, they will cook your catch. The Palmilla Golf Club, north of the highway, has 18 holes, par 72, championship rating 74.3, championship yardage 6939, men 6572, women 4868. Tee-time reservations are accepted not more than 48 hours in advance. Facilities include a driving range, a restaurant, and a pro shop. A new clubhouse is scheduled to open Fall 1996. Club and shoe rent-

Divers check out a "small" whale shark

als and lessons are available. Green fees are $105, and include cart, range balls, and bottled water. Summer rates are applicable from June 1 to the second week of October. When completed, the course will have 27 holes, with 3 sets of 9.

26 LPG yard.

25 Restaurant Da Giorgio; up-scale Italian, with antipasto, salads, various pastas, fish and beef dishes, and "glorious gooey pizza." The Scampi Da Giorgio is exceptional. Very pleasant and spotlessly clean, but a bit pricey.

24 Westin Regina Hotel.

20+ Hotel Meliá Cabo Real.

20 Casa del Mar Hotel. The nearby Cabo Real Golf Club has 18 holes, par 72, championship rating 73.8, championship yardage 7001, men 6437, women 5068. Lessons and club and cart rentals are available. Tee-time reservations can be made any time. Facilities include a driving range, putting green, chipping green, sand trap, and a pro shop, and a restaurant is under construction. Green fees from November 1 to May 31 are $99 for 18, $65 for 9, and $65 and $45 for the rest of the year.

17+ Centro Nacional de Artes Popular combines a restaurant with a number of small shops selling Mexican art, some of it quite good.

15+ Hotel Cabo San Lucas.

15 **Bahía Chileno**. The beach here is public, with fenced daily parking and a rest room. The bay has rocky reefs alternating with sandy areas and shoals of colorful tropical fish. A night dive here is a special treat. Cabo Acuadeportes, at the western end of the bay near the parking lot, has compressed air, and wet suit and dive equipment rentals and repairs. A full array of scuba courses is available, the largest in any location in Baja:

resort/refresher, open water check-out, full certification, advanced open water, rescue diver, wreck diver, deep water, underwater photographer, and underwater naturalist. Scuba and snorkeling trips with bilingual guides are available for trips to the Sand Falls (described shortly), the Bancos Gorda, Pulmo and other prime locations, and night dives in Bahía Chileno. In addition, wave runners, canoes, catamarans, kayaks, and sailboards are for rent, and whale-watching trips are available January through March.

13 **Bahía Santa María**. Public beach with fine diving on coral heads, loaded with brilliant tropical fish. Drive 0.3 mile south on the class 1 road, park at the gate, and walk 5 minutes to the beach.

12 Twin Dolphin Hotel. Class 2 road 0.4 mile to Playa las Viudas (Widow's Beach); look for a sign immediately southwest of entrance to the hotel. The beach alternates between sandy and rocky areas, and is open from 7 A.M. to 7 P.M.

11 Meliá Cabo Real Hotel. Cabo del Sol Golf Club, adjacent to the hotel, has 18 holes, par 72, championship yardage 6403, men 5949, women 5534. Tee-time reservations can be made not more than seven days in advance. Facilities include a driving range, putting green, chipping green, sand trap, restaurant, and a pro shop. A clubhouse will open in Fall 1996, with 2 more 18-hole courses planned. Lessons and club rentals are available. Green fees are $96 between June 1 and October 15, $120 otherwise, including cart, range balls, and bottled water. The course is touted as having "the three best finishing holes in the world."

7 Villa Serena RV Park; class B, full hookups, restaurant, rest rooms, showers, tennis, pool, Jacuzzi, gym, ocean view, trail to rocky beach. Calinda Beach Hotel San Lucas.

5+ El Arco Trailer Park; class B, full hookups, showers, rest rooms, ice. Restaurant el Arco is a large *palapa*, serving breakfast, lunch, and dinner, with a menu largely of seafood and Mexican. Bar, palm-shaded patio with pool and a view of the ocean.

4 Cabo Cielo RV Park; class B, full hookups, rest rooms, showers, mini-market, some sites shaded by palms.

3 Vagabundos del Mar RV Park; class A, full hookups, pool, showers, rest rooms, laundry machines, bar, café, long-distance telephone. This is the nicest RV facility in the Cabo San Lucas area.

2+ Ice manufacturing plant. Cabo San Lucas Country Club, north of the highway, has 18 holes, par 72, championship yardage 7136, men 6840, women 5100. Lessons and club and cart rentals are available. Tee-time reservations can be made anytime. Facilities include a driving range, putting green, chipping green, sand trap, clubhouse, and a pro shop. Green fees are $66 for 18. The par 5, 600-yard 7th hole is claimed to be the longest in Mexico.

0 **Cabo San Lucas**. This is it, the end of the Transpeninsular!

■ Getting your bearings

Congratulations, you have finally made it to the Cape! You may be interested in knowing where you are relative to the rest of the world. At the summer solstice, about June 21, the sun reaches its northern most latitude during its annual cycle, and is directly over the Tropic of Cancer. Since Cabo San Lucas lies 33 miles south of this latitude, you can send postcards to your friends and truthfully say you are enjoying your tropical vacation. Your friends live in Honolulu? Well, they are 2,648 miles west and a mere 87 miles more tropical. Although the two places are very close in latitude, Hawaii is one of the wettest places on earth, and parts of Baja are among the driest. To the east (or west if you prefer), Havana, Cuba; Calcutta, India; Guangzhou (Canton), China; and the island of Taiwan lie on or close to Cabo's latitude of 22° 53' north. To the north on meridian 109° 53' west lies the Four Corners region, where the states of Arizona, New Mexico, Utah, and Colorado meet. If your marlin cruiser runs out of fuel and north winds start to blow, don't worry, for there are 3 places you can obtain dry footing: the Islas Revillagigedo at 240 miles south, Clipperton Island at 745, and Easter Island at 2,735. If you miss all 3, don't give up hope, for you will reach the Antarctic ice pack at 5,565 miles. If you drilled a hole through the center of the earth, would you hear Chinese people talking? No, but you might get an ear full of water from the Indian Ocean. If you could hold your breath and squeeze through the 7,910-mile hole, the nearest point of land to where you emerged, Mauritius Island, is a 757-mile swim to the west. Should a Mac Attack occur, the nearest source of relief is only 743 miles, course 316° magnetic if you fly, 988 miles if you have to drive.

Cabo San Lucas

Time is not being kind to those who love Cabo for what it was in the "old days." In recent years, this quaint fishing village has almost exploded into a retreat for large numbers of people from north of the border. There has been much new construction, including a number of hotels and many condominiums in town and along the highway from San José del Cabo. The character of the town has also changed. To some extent, there are not two ethnic traditions, Mexican and American, coexisting in the same place. Most of the local people and many of the resident Americans now live in a "homogenized" culture, where there is little distinction in dress, where shops may observe only one hour of *siesta*, if any, where words, phrases, and colloquialisms from the two languages are freely interchanged, where the two most popular lunch items are tacos and burgers, where you can buy food in almost any culinary tradition, including a "Swiss enchilada," whatever that may be, where T-shirts showing two dogs copulating below the legend "Bury The Bone" attract titters from Mexican and American women alike. Is this the "melting pot," so dear to liberal professors of sociology?

One thing is certain: you will like the place and feel at ease, more so, perhaps, than in any other place on the peninsula. If you can free yourself of visions of things past, you will realize that while still maintaining some of its old virtues, like its world-class marlin fishery, the "new" Cabo has a great deal to offer. Cabo, pronounced "**kay**-boe" by those wishing to express their sophistication and obvious familiarity with the place, is now the liveliest and most thoroughly amiable town in Baja. No other place, not even Rosarito or San Felipe, is more committed to pleasing visitors, and during the day an almost continuous parade of magnificent motor homes, campers, and trailer rigs clogs the narrow streets. However, Cabo is a cut, really several cuts, above the other two towns, with better construction, more to see and do, and a higher class of handicrafts, native art, scenery, and restaurants. Unlike San Felipe, Cabo is expanding rapidly, and it might take a week, or better two, to explore the shops, bistros, and restaurants, and to participate in the many outdoor activities available. Also, unlike San Felipe and Rosarito, there is excellent diving and world-class fishing just offshore. With its new construction, many restaurants, bars, handicraft and art shops, and fleet of yachts of worldwide origin, Cabo is unique on the peninsula, with La Paz a close second.

A tour of the downtown district is best made on foot. Besides the traffic, there is one hazard to watch out for: people trying to sell you a time-share condo. This is a high-pressure enterprise, and dozens of men stand outside tiny offices, performing the same function as the doorman at a house of ill-repute: get the customers inside. You may be negotiating for the rental of an ATV, or even buying an ice cream cone, and suddenly find yourself contemplating a catalog of condos. Total nonrecognition, a useful modification of the *Ley de Hielo* (Law of Ice) mentioned earlier, is the best tactic, and few salesmen will persist in an obnoxious way.

There are three sizable malls, where you can spend hours poking around. Unlike the neon and plastic glitz and the sameness of malls in *El Otro Lado*, those in Cabo offer a greater range of character, from upper-income slick to the modest and unpretentious. Plaza las Glorias (75) is a new hotel and shopping complex, and is home to a number of businesses. The Tours & Activities Shop in the mall books snorkeling, scuba diving, kayaking, sunset cruises,

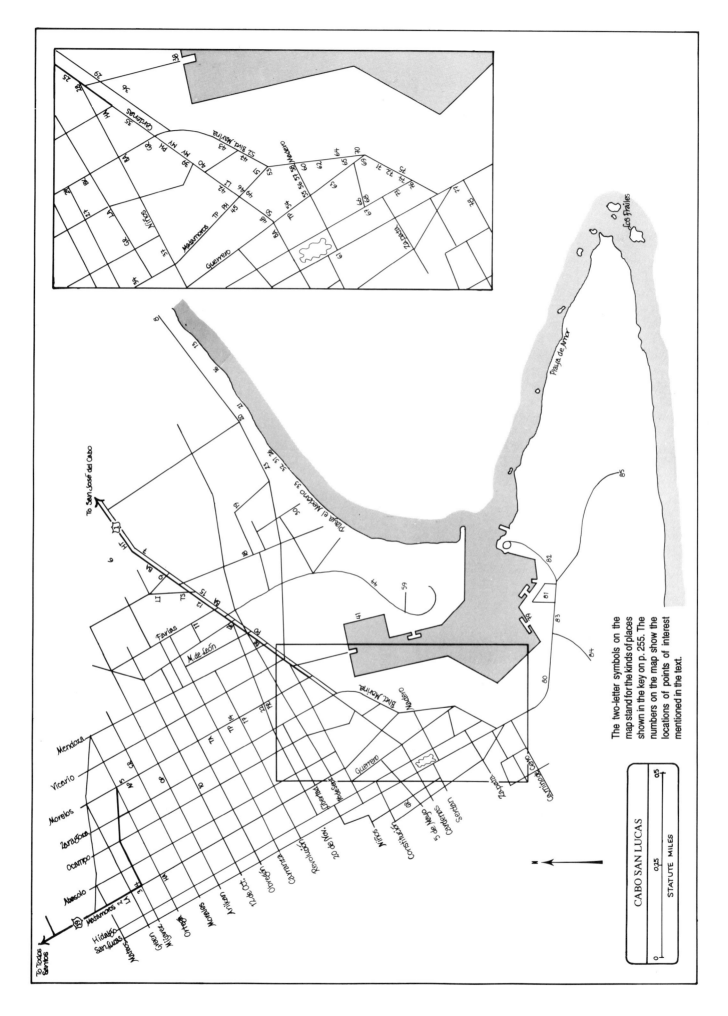

The two-letter symbols on the map stand for the kinds of places shown in the key on p. 255. The numbers on the map show the locations of points of interest mentioned in the text.

CABO SAN LUCAS

STATUTE MILES

0   0.25   0.5

parasailing, helicopter tours, boat rides, water-skiing, and Hobie Cat rentals. Land's End Divers has scuba tours to Pulmo and the Bancos Gorda, equipment rentals, snorkeling tour PADI certification, including open-water, advanced, rescue diver, divemaster, and first-aid/CPR. Dolphin's Head has underwater camera and video sales and rentals, as well as PADI underwater camera and video specialty courses. Baja Outback Tours specializes in four-wheel-drive safaris, including a full day touring East Cape to see whale bones and have lunch at an exotic desert waterfall, and a full day Pacific Cape tour including secluded beaches, a working fruit plantation, and lunch in Todos Santos, plus several half-day tours.

Dos Mares Glass Bottom Boats operates from the Glorias dock, as does *Pez Gato* (*Cat Fish*, since it is a catamaran), which offers a snorkeling tour of Bahía Santa María, and whale-watching trips in season. Margaritaville, a new part of the complex now under construction, will have a number of restaurants, one of which is now operational— Restaurant China Splash serves the usual Chinese items as fast food, or at least semifast: many items are prepared in a deep-fryer rather than a wok. Tables are covered with no-nonsense butcher paper, and the decor is strictly New World, but the food is tasty and relatively inexpensive. Kentucky Fried Chicken is new, immaculately clean, offers the standard products, and has a fleet fleet of new Suzuki motorcycles to speed telephone orders to their destinations. Baja Cantina advertises CABO'S BEST HAPPY HOUR, 3 P.M. TO 6 P.M. It may be the best, but it isn't even close in duration. Sporting events blast from six large television sets, and if you have been away from home for a while and want to get current on football, baseball, tennis, soccer, hockey, and boxing, all at the same time, this is the place. Dollar Moto Rent rents ATVs and offers tours to El Faro Viejo (The Old Lighthouse).

Among its many businesses, Plaza Nautica (70) has a Domino's Pizza, whose products are indistinguishable from those of higher latitudes, and a Subway. Cabo Sports Center and Golf Pro Shop sells limited golf, surfing, and snorkeling gear. Caliente is a sports betting establishment offering alcoholic beverages, not only to quench thirst, but presumably to increase the size of the wagers. There are a Bing's ice cream shop and a 31 Flavors, which could occupy the kids while their parents were losing the family fortune at Caliente. Motos Karlsa rents ATVs. Cabo Foto has film and one-hour color print processing. Mexico Lindo sells jewelry guaranteed to be either 92.5% silver or 14- or 18-karat gold.

Plaza Bonita Mall (36) houses numerous boutiques, T-shirt stores, and knickknack shops, and you will not go hungry or thirsty. Restaurant Chicken Shack supplies chicken in many manifestations, and Salsita's Restaurant serves Mexican, and has an espresso bar. La Trattoria is an upscale and pricey Italian restaurant, with the usual entrées. Francisco's Café del Mundo sells gourmet coffee, cappuccino, and espresso, cold drinks, fruit, and pastries. Restaurant la Terraza offers sushi and teriyaki. There is a book store carrying the *San Francisco Chronicle*, *Wall Street Journal* and *USA Today*, usually only a day or two old, together with books on Baja and trashy soft-cover novels in English.

In addition to these three, there are several very small malls. Plaza de los Mariachis (53) has curio stores, open-air stalls selling jewelry and knickknacks, and several restaurants. Mer Méditerranéo specializes in rather expensive French dishes, including *Coq au vin*, *L'osso bucco*, and *La bouillabaisse de Marseilles*. The owners are French, and the high quality of the entrées proves it. The fresh dolphinfish is delicious. Amigos, Tacos and Beer serves chicken tacos and beer for lunch, and pork ribs and beer for supper. A tiny restaurant offers *crêpe suzettes*. Another little mall (35) has stores that sell ice cream, souvenirs, and T-shirts, one shirt advising "Cabo San Lucas, Save The Rain Forest."

There are almost 50 restaurants in the downtown district in addition to those in the malls, ranging from humble to elite, offering almost every food preference possible, including seafood, steaks, pizza, L.A.-deli, Japanese, Chinese, German, Italian, American, French, Spanish, and even Mexican. El Galeón (83) is an expensive restaurant, serving steaks and seafood, often to the accompaniment of live music, and it has a bar and a view of the harbor. The marine artifacts on which the theme of the restaurant is based are supposedly from an ancient galleon, but many are from the *Oliver J. Olson*, an American schooner that was driven ashore in the vicinity of Cabo Falso in 1911. She was carrying lumber, and served as a free lumber yard for the locals, each year revealing more of her cargo as the sands shifted.

Restaurant Langosta Loco (28) serves omelets with

The Plaza las Glorias and other commercial buildings now dominate the marina district in Cabo San Lucas

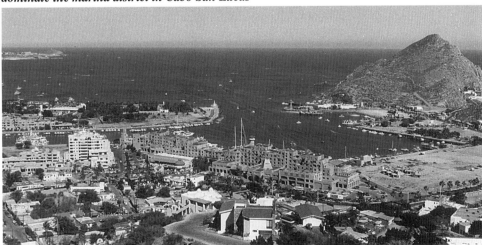

cheese, lobster, or shrimp, an "almost famous" giant burrito, and for those who have trouble making up their mind, lobster in combination with ribs, steaks, scallops, fish, squid, crab, or chicken. Prices are a bit high. Happy hour is 8 A.M. to 6 P.M., 7 days a week. Restaurant Señor Sushi (65), advertising EVERYTHING BUT SUSHI, offers seafood, steaks, and Mexican, but not Japanese. El Coral Restaurant (74) has steaks, seafood, and Mexican. The place is a bit pricey, but they provide all the tequila you can drink after dinner, apparently to relieve the pain when the bill arrives. They claim the longest happy hour in town, 8 A.M. to 6 P.M., apparently unaware that they are tied with the Langosta Loco.

Fisherman's Pescadores (66) serves first-class American breakfasts at modest prices. Mama's Royal Café, next door, has rules: no Jimmy Buffet music, marriages performed by waiters may not be legal in the US, and the waiter is always right. They serve burgers, fish, and Mexican, as well as breakfast—you can choose among 29 kinds of omelets. However, given the competition nearby, some of the menu items are a bit over-priced. Cabo Gourmet (46) sells delicatessen foods, as well as sandwiches and breakfast, and provides box lunches for picnics and fishing expeditions. Latitude 22 (25) advises that it has "served some of the lousiest food in the world, 70,000 meals in 1993, at ridiculously low prices." We planned to give it a try, but there was a sign CLOSED TUESDAYS FOR MENTAL HEALTH, presumably that of the proprietor. The Creamery (71) is an American-style donut shop. Open-air Ali's Burgers (24) is popular with tourists and locals alike, and serves burgers, shakes, and Mexican.

The La Placita Bar and Grill (69) is a pleasant sidewalk café, serving breakfast items such as omelets, French toast, Mexican-style eggs, and the Swiss enchiladas mentioned earlier, plus lunch and an International dinner menu. The Mexican eggs and the mushroom omelet are excellent. Broken Surfboard (67) is popular for breakfast, and they proclaim on a sign at the entrance WE HAVE SERVED A GOOD $2 BREAKFAST SINCE 1973, AS WELL AS SPEAKING PERFECT BROKEN ENGLISH. True on both counts.

Restaurant Romeo and Julieta (78), is expensive-Italian, with antipastos, salads, and almost every Italian entrée you can name, Italian wines, and bread and pizza cooked in a brick oven. Both the aprons worn by the waiters and the tablecloths and napkins bear the national colors of Italy (come to think of it, they are the same as Mexico's). The lasagna would rate rave reviews in Rome, and the only inconsistent note is the music of the *mariachis*. In the unlikely circumstance you are unable to find a place to eat in the downtown district that suits your taste, do not fret, for a Pizza Hut (52) is under construction.

There are four establishments that defy simple explanation and have no common denominator except that they are designed to appeal to the college crowd and to passing yachtsmen looking for the exotic after the perilous weeklong voyage from San Diego. The Giggling Marlin (51) is in competition with Hussong's in Ensenada as to which will be the most famous bar in Baja, and serves burgers, beer, mixed drinks, and a heavy dose of ersatz funk: cartoon characters in the walls are labeled GARTH BROOK TROUT, MACKEREL JORDAN, and FLEETWOOD MACKEREL, and a sign requests IF OUR FOOD DRINKS AND SERVICE ARE NOT UP TO YOUR STANDARDS, PLEASE LOWER YOUR STANDARDS. It sounds sophomoric, but it comes across rather well, especially to the mobs of American college students who patronize the place during spring break (SPAWN BREAK claims a sign over the bar). El Squid Roe, just to the north of the tiny mall mentioned earlier (35), is skillfully decorated to look like a dump, but it turns out to be a rather good restaurant, serving a wide variety of seafood, including squid seviche, BBQ "bones" (ribs), and Mexican dishes. It is also popular with American college students on spring break. Carlos 'n Charlie's (43) has a large menu, with lots of beef and beer, and a gift store selling "fresh" T-shirts, although it is unclear whether this refers to their age or design. Cabo Wabo (54) is another spring break hangout, but a substantial number of students in Cabo must be on 12-month breaks, for they are encountered throughout the year, lured by loud music, dancing, and suicidal, all-you-can-drink specials. In addition, a sign advises WE MIGHT SERVE FOOD.

Baja Travel (64) offers a variety of activities, ranging from fly fishing to outback tours. Open-air stalls (40) along Cardenas sell T-shirts, *serapes*, silver jewelry, colorful belts, figurines, and souvenirs. Cotton Club (39) sells "hip" women's clothing aimed at the young. Zen Mar (42) offers handicrafts, carvings, rugs, artistic masks, T-shirts, and Cuban cigars. Gaby's, next door, sells only *huaraches*, in perhaps 50 different styles. Cuca's Blanket Factory (45) has many different *serape* designs, but if you can't find what you like, they will produce one to your specifications on a foot-powered loom. Plaza del Sol (73) is a jewelry store with a large selection of high-quality silver and gold items.

Open-air stalls (47 and 49) sell T-shirts, *serapes*, jewelry, ironwood carvings, handicrafts, and figurines. The proprietors are not sticklers for the finer points of human sensitivity: a stuffed raccoon, a figure of Buddha, and a crucifix lie heaped one atop the other. The wax renditions of apples, oranges, and bananas look better than the real things. Plaza Indios (50) sells glassware, *serapes*, pottery, paper mâché birds, and handicrafts, some very well done. Mamma Elis's Curio Shop (61) has a large selection of art, handicrafts, and the like. Curios Jacial (68) has many unusual art figurines and curios. Pancho's, next door, claims to serve 80 kinds of tequila and home-brewed mescal, plus Mexican dishes for lunch and supper, as well as breakfast items. Taxco, a half-dozen doors to the southeast, sells high-quality silver jewelry. The open air market (81) may be the best place, in terms of price, to hire a fishing boat or to buy ironwood carvings, *huaraches*, T-shirts, and knickknacks. The silver jewelry seems to be as good in quality as that in the shops, and with some bargaining, you can get a better price.

There are a number of restaurants outside the downtown district. Restaurant Tipico Mexicano (22) serves, well, typical Mexican food. Mariscos Mocambo (14), offering seafood, beer, and sodas, is inexpensive and popular with the locals. Super Pollo (5) is part of a chain selling Sinaloa-style char-broiled chicken. Hamburgesas Andrés (10) offers burgers, corn dogs, nachos, and fries.

The beach to the east of the harbor entrance, called Playa el Médano (Sand Dune Beach), is the best swimming beach in the Cape region. The beach to the west of town is not suitable for swimming for the same reasons at San José del Cabo: very deep water near to the beach, and an often booming surf. Médano is an ever-changing kaleidoscope of color: the great spinnakers of departing yachts, the hand-made baskets being hawked by the locals, the mini-bikinis of the young women, the sails of the boardsailors, the colorful gores of the parasails, together with the light tan of the sand beach, the gray of Los Frailes, the famous rocks that seem to end the peninsula, and the baby-blue of the ocean.

■ Oh, oh! More bad news!

We do not wish to dwell on the negative, but there is another matter that the public must be aware of. Local tourism officials would have you believe that Los Frailes are the southernmost extent of the peninsula. Physically, they fit a romantic vision—they look like the end of a peninsula "ought" to look, and artists have produced immense numbers of T-shirts and paintings portraying the craggy rocks as such. However, we have long doubted whether this was true, and on a March 1995, trip, we finally had a chance to test it. We used our GPS satellite navigation receiver to determine the exact latitude of the rocks. We then drove our four-wheel-drive west, and hiked down to the beach, taking readings of latitude.

We discovered two things. First, the cartographers that produced the US nautical charts of the area inaccurately calculated the position of the rocks themselves; they are 500 yards, 020° true from where they are shown. Second, the rocks are not the southernmost part of the peninsula. The beach at Faro Viejo is 877 yards further south! Sorry, but the truth must be faced.

The Activity Center (32) at Médano offers a cornucopia of things to do and toys to play with: wave runners, snorkeling tours, scuba diving, a glass-bottom boat, sunset tours, whale watching, boardsailing, helicopter tours, water-skiing, banana boat rides, kayaks, ATV rentals, semisubmersible tours, hot-air balloon rides, fishing, scooter rentals, golf, trap shooting, outback tours, horseback riding, mountain bike tours, and parasailing, the last of which they claim is an "airgasmic experience." There is a rather peculiar rate structure for parasailing: naked girls get a 10% discount, while naked boys get charged $5 extra, which is distinctly sexist. Tío Watersports (26) has wave runners, parasailing, kayaks, catamarans, sailboards, snorkeling, scuba diving and instruction, ATV tours, mountain bikes, whale watching, and fishing. Pisces Water Sport Center (21) offers water skiing, jet skis, Hobies, sailboards, parasailing, pedal boats, scooters, kayaks, and snorkeling trips.

There are a number of fast-food and refreshment stands at Médano, as well as some excellent restaurants. Peacock's (18) is expensive, with a small menu of such gourmet dishes as linguini with grilled chicken breast smothered in sun-dried tomatoes and sunflower seeds in basil pesto. Cabo Tavern (19) serves Mexican and German food and beer, and has pool (the kind with cues and balls) and darts. They also offer sports TV by satellite, so you need not miss any Raiders games. Restaurant el Delfín (The Dolphin, 33), a large *palapa*, serves seafood and Mexican, and has a dance floor and exceptionally loud music, apparently intended to permit the hard-of-hearing throughout the Cape region to participate. Las Palmas Lobster House (31) has a menu of seafood and steaks, but the specialty is, of course, lobster. Edith's (30) offers jazz, blues, and salsa, charcoal-broiled steaks, finger food, coffee, a bar with exotic drinks, and a fine view of the bay. Bazar Gattamelata (44) sells high-quality Mexican art, furniture, gifts, and antiques.

The Plastic Surgery Institute, based at the Hotel Hacienda Beach Resort (59) at Médano, performs state-of-the art plastic surgery, and Mom and Dad could undergo abdominoplasty, rhinoplasty, breast enlargement/reduction, liposuction, body sculpturing, permanent eye-, lip-, and brow-liner, baldness surgery, and penile enlargements, as appropriate. The phone number of the institute says it all: 800-FUN-CABO. When both have recuperated, some bungee jumping (16) might be in order.

The waters around Cabo San Lucas provide some of the finest fishing in the world. During our most recent trip, every fishing cruiser returning to the harbor was flying a billfish flag, indicating a catch, most with two or more, and one with seven. On a typical day in April or May, it is not uncommon to see five or six finning striped marlin within a circle 100 yards across, and fishermen often report active competition among the fish over which would be first to take the bait. There is year-around fishing for stripers and sailfish, the warm months being best. Four of the best marlin areas are Banco San Jaime, 18 miles, 252° from Cabo Falso; Banco Golden Gate, 19 miles, 293° from Falso; Banco Gorda Primero, 8.5 miles, 095° from the San José del Cabo lighthouse; and Banco Gorda Segundo, 11 miles, 095° from the San José del Cabo lighthouse. Run 23 miles, 056° from Cabo San Lucas for Gorda Primero. The "95 Spot" and "The Dropoff," 9 miles, 106° and 12 miles, 160°, respectively, from Los Frailes are also good, but harder to find. Many marlin are also caught between Frailes and Falso, where the 100-fathom line comes within a mile of shore.

■ A recipe for marlin

You don't have to be an experienced fisherman to catch a marlin, and you don't need a yacht equipped with outriggers, a fighting chair, and a spotting tower. A modest trailer boat, an inflatable, or a cartopper will do. In addition to rod and reel and other tackle recommended in Appendix A, you will need a large empty cooler and a bucket. Get up early and launch your boat in the inner harbor at Cabo San Lucas. Fill the cooler with sea water and buy live mackerel offered from *pangas* in the harbor; four or five per person should last for an entire day. The bait will stay frisky if you drain half the water every half hour and refill. Run between three and six miles south of Cabo Falso and shut off the engine. Rig a hook and leader, but do not use a weight. Hook a mackerel through the nose, damaging it as little as possible, and simply let it swim about 60 or 80 yards away from the boat before setting the drag, and wait.

It might take five minutes, five hours, or five days, but your chances of getting a hookup using this "recipe" are excellent, the most likely fish being a striper of between 125 and 150 pounds. When it happens, your modest boat has a number of distinct advantages over larger craft: your engine can be tilted up, the shallow hull offers few opportunities for snags, and if the fish runs under the hull you can put the tip of your rod underwater if necessary to keep the line from touching the hull. A fish may drag you for miles, but it will be a fight to remember. Release the fish unharmed if you can, but if this is not possible, don't believe the rumor that stripers are poor eating. Like all marlin, they are excellent, especially if they are bled by cutting the gills and quickly cooled.

There are, of course, numerous other species in Cape waters. Dolphinfish are often taken incidentally by those pursuing marlin. Fishing very deep at night, fishermen have taken swordfish. Bancos Gorda Primera and San Jaime produce many fine wahoo, and when water temperatures are normal (non-El Niño years) they may come close to shore between Bahía Chileno and Bahía Santa María, and between Frailes and Falso. The area south of "Red Hill," just west of Punta Palmilla, is also excellent for wahoo, often in water less than 200 feet deep. Trollers sometimes work roosters right in front of the Hotel Solmar (85), but be careful of the waves, for more than one boat has been tossed here. Excellent fishing for wahoo and dolphinfish can be found in 125 feet to 300 feet of water along the beach from Falso to Frailes. The beach immediately west of Frailes can be a hot spot for shore-casters, and yellowtail, roosters, and even dolphinfish are possible.

Don't worry too much about locating a fishing boat; it is probably the least difficult thing you will do in Cabo San

Lucas. A large and ever-growing fleet is available, and in 1996, they numbered at least 18. Some of the hotels manage their own fleets, including the Hotel Hacienda Beach Resort Fishing Fleet, with 7 boats, and the Hotel Solmar Sportfishing Fleet (82), with 19 at last count, ranging from 26 feet to 60 feet. In addition, there are a number of independent fleets. Ursula's Sport Fishing Charters (76) operates several *pangas* and a cruiser. Los Cabos Fishing Center (56) has *pangas*, cruisers, and a 24-foot Mako center console, and provides all tackle, licenses, and drinks. They also have a tackle store where rods, reels, lures, and line are available. Pisces Fleet (58) offers several options on boats, 4-passenger 28-foot Uniflites, or 6-passenger 31-foot Bertrams. Juantia's Fleet (62) operates 9 cruisers from 28 feet to 33 feet. Others have desks at the Giggling Marlin (ABY Charters) and Hotel Plaza las Glorias (Los Dorados Fleet), and several operate out of offices at the fishing docks, including Baja Mar Fleet and Rafael's Sport Fishing Fleet. Freelance boat operators will also be found at the docks. Some promote high expectations, one claiming "Jacques Cousteau asks our guys where the fish are."

John Anglin's striper was over half the length and three-quarters the weight of our cartopper

Minerva's Baja Tackle (57) stocks a complete line of rods, reels, line, leader, artificial baits, and other needs, plus lunches, snacks, licenses, and boat permits, and has charter boats available. If you are fishing for the record books, Minerva's is an IGFA weigh station. Current information on fishing conditions can be obtained by telephone. Minerva 3, a Bertram 31, released 13 marlin in 3 days in early March 1995. The Tackle Box (55) offers complete tackle sales, plus guided surf fishing trips with Jeff Klassen, six-time IGFA world-record holder. These two shops are the best of their kind in Baja.

The steep (16%) launch ramp (38) has no major tide problems, but maneuvering room is becoming more limited with each passing year. It costs $5 in, $5 out. To park your boat trailer, drive north on the access road from the ramp to Blvd. Cardenas, turn right, drive one block and turn right, and make an immediate right to a dirt lot. There is a public ramp (79, 14%), but parking and maneuvering room are limited. There is currently no fee, but you must get a launch ramp permit, and regulations are in a state of flux, so go to the Captain of the Port office (34) to get information. The inner harbor is often crowded, especially from December to May, and the docks are almost always jammed. Live bait is usually available from *pangas* in the dock area.

One of the most interesting scuba dives in Baja can be made in the outer harbor. The narrow strip of land leading out to Los Frailes is overtopped by waves during storms, carrying sand into the bay. Several tributaries of an enormous underwater canyon begin between the mouth of the inner harbor and Frailes. Starting with a rather modest slope, the canyon begins to descend at an average of about 75% within 200 feet. It then levels off to a slope of 10%, which it maintains until the water is 6,000 feet deep. Granite walls tower over the bottom of the canyon, and at a depth of 5,400 feet, the walls are over 3,000 feet high. Long rivers of excess sand from the beach flow down the tributaries of the canyon, forming sandfalls when they reach cliffs.

The sandfalls should be visited only by certified divers with deep water experience. The best place to start a dive is halfway between the mouth of the inner harbor and Frailes, where an islet with a flat top will be seen 60 yards from shore. Follow the slope down and start watching for falls at 100 feet. Most sandfalls are intermittent, but the chances of seeing at least one cascading over the cliffs are good. Rocky areas are covered with lush growths of corals and gorgonians, and there are many species of fish to be seen, but touch nothing, for the bay is an underwater ecological reserve.

Banco Gorda Primero is another excellent dive site, although it is too deep for all but the most experienced divers, since its shallowest areas are about 110 feet. Nautical charts show one area at eight fathoms, but experienced local divers insist it does not exist. The primary diving attractions at Gorda are the large numbers of heavy-duty gamefish, plus the chance to see black coral. In addition, Gorda is frequented by whale sharks. Some gray whales continue past the Cape during their annual migration, and divers have occasionally

been able to swim with them. Marisla Seamount near La Paz is not the only place graced by friendly mantas: in early 1995, divers just outside the harbor entrance encountered friendlies for a period of almost three weeks.

There are other, less demanding dives in the area. An interesting wreck can be found in 50 feet of water on a sand bottom just southwest of the most southerly rock at Frailes. It is badly disintegrated, but is home to a number of unusual fish, including an occasional longnose butterfly fish. Be careful diving here, for sightseeing and fishing boats studiously ignore diver's flags. The wreck is often festooned with fishing lures, some quite expensive, small treasures for the taking. Big jewfish occasionally visit the wreck in the summer months, and sea lions living nearby often accompany divers.

There are dive shops in addition to those already mentioned. Amigos del Mar, next to the Solmar Sportfishing Fleet offices, has complete scuba sales, rentals, and repairs, snorkeling equipment, compressed air, certification and resort/refresher courses, local snorkel tours, and scuba tours of Pulmo and Gorda accompanied by bilingual guides. The shop operates 2 large trimaran dive boats, a pontoon boat, and a 25-footer with twin engines. They also offer a sunset cruise and whale-watching trips. Cabo Diving Services (72) offers complete rental equipment, compressed air, boat and shore dives, and tours, including a "100% adrenaline" trip to the Bancos Gorda.

Cabo Acuadeportes, at the Hotel Hacienda Beach Resort, has the same basic equipment, instruction, rentals, and services as their facility at Chileno described earlier, and also has a shop in the Plaza las Glorias. Pacific Coast Adventures, in the Plaza las Glorias, offers dive trips to the Bancos Gorda, Pulmo, and local sites, equipment rentals, a resort course, full PADI certification, and advanced courses such as divemaster. Dive Adventures, in the Plaza Bonita Mall facing the marina, has tri-lingual (Spanish, Italian, and English) guides, scuba and snorkel tours, rental equipment, compressed air, night dives, full PADI certification, and a resort course. A decompression chamber is located in the Plaza las Glorias.

There are less strenuous things to do. Pacifico Tours offers snorkeling/luncheon trips and sunset/dinner cruises on the *Sunrider*, a 60-foot motor yacht. Departures are from the Plaza las Glorias pier. Trips on the *Nautilus VII*, a "semisubmarine" with viewing both down and sideways, also departs from the pier. Reservations for both can be made at the Tours & Activities Shop. Wisely putting the huge supply of soda, beer, and tequila bottles generated in town to good use, the Glass Factory (6) produces a variety of tumblers, pitchers and art objects. Their distinctive blue-rimmed glassware is seen in many restaurants throughout the area, and in some stores in the US. Visitors are welcome.

Many people enjoy a visit to El Faro Viejo (The Old Lighthouse). This trip is best made with an ATV or a dune buggy, but nimble RVs can make it to within a half mile. Begin at the intersection of Avenida Cardenas (main drag) and Avenida Morelos. Set trip odometer and drive northwest on Morelos. At Mile 0.7, the road swings left (260°), and at Mile 1.2 you will encounter the intersection with Route 19 to Todos Santos, marked by a large Coca-Cola sign. Turn left (120°) at this intersection, and at Mile 1.4 turn right (265°). Pass an athletic field on the right, go right (265°) at the Y at Mile 1.6. At Mile 2.1, go right (250°), and at Mile 2.3, go left (230°), towards a housing development of white homes. Parallel the north side of the chain-link fence, and at Mile 2.4, make a left (190°) and then an immediate right and drive parallel to the south side of the fence. At Mile 3.5, the road and the fence turn left (195°), and the road can be seen winding into the dunes ahead, with the new lighthouse on the horizon. At Mile 4.2 pass the entrance road to the new light and encounter a parking site in 100 more yards. The old light is down the hill, about a half mile south. If you are driving an ATV or a dune buggy continue; if not park and hike to the light. With its sandy dunes and updrafts, the area is popular with hang gliders and parasailers. It is illegal to drive any vehicle on the beach.

In addition to the RV parks on the Transpeninsular already mentioned, there are a few in town. Club Cabo RV Park (8), class B, has some sites with full hookups, showers, rest rooms, barbecues, and long-distance telephone. Considering the little it has to offer and its small area, this park is somewhat overpriced. El Faro Viejo Trailer Park (4), class B, has palm-shaded sites, full hookups, showers, rest rooms, and a good restaurant serving steaks and seafood. The menu is a bit expensive, but the portions are very large, and two people might be content with sharing a single order. There are numerous hotels having bars, restaurants, reservations desks, fishing fleets, and other fa-

Parasailors prepare for a voyage at the dune area near El Faro Viejo

cilities that may be of interest, including the Finisterra (80), Mar de Cortez (48), Solmar, Hacienda, and Plaza las Glorias, as well as Club Cascades de Baja (20), Marina Fiesta Resort (41), Meliá San Lucas (23), Terra Sol Beach Resort (84), and Villa de Palmar (13).

Obtaining food and supplies will not be a problem. Almacenes Grupo Castro (17) sells groceries, meats, cold cuts, wine, liquor, fruit, and vegetables. Sanliz Supermarket (60) sells imported foods from the US, as well as local meats and vegetables. Panadería San Angel, across the street from Ali's Burgers, sells bakery goods, pastries, cold drinks, and dairy products. There are, of course, many small grocery stores and beer distributors in Cabo. Pollos y Carnes Lizarraga, just north of Ali's, is a butcher shop. Fresh fish is available at El Pescadería el Dorado (37). Fotolab Carrizosa (63) sells film and offers one-hour color print processing. Wetsun (11) sells water purified by reverse-osmosis in large quantities, and can fill RVs.

There are two PEMEX stations (1 and 9, both MND). Proveedora Agricola Automotriz California, S.A. de C.V. (7) is a Chevy dealer, and offers parts, service, and repairs. Refaccionaria López Cinco (2) sells auto parts, and has a machine shop. Celis Automotriz, a few doors southwest of Wetsun, has parts and service for Volkswagen. Taller Miramontes (27) has parts and service for Evinrude outboards. The ship's chandlery store at Cabo Isle Marina (29) is the most complete in Baja California, and has a small selection of parts that may be of interest to RVers, including boat-trailer rollers and shafts, hitch balls, and U-bolts.

Baja Cellular has an office in town (15). There is a Mail Boxes Etc. office on the ground floor of the Marina Fiesta Resort, offering mail and parcel service, office and packaging supplies, stamps, copies, fax, and long-distance telephone. There are several laundromats, including Lavandería Evelyn (3). There are many doctors and dentists. An American Consular Agency (77) has been established in Cabo San Lucas; its mailing address and telephone number are found in Appendix C. There is also a Mexican immigration office (12).

Cabo San Lucas to Todos Santos and KM 185 on the Transpeninsular via Route 19, with many fine beaches and numerous boondocking sites and RV parks *en route*. Turn to page 194.

● ●

66 *The trailer two-step*

Years ago, several friends and I spent an afternoon carefully loading my pickup and trailer, anxious to begin our first trailer trip to Baja. The coolers, outboard engine, fuel containers, scuba tanks, and other heavy gear ended up in the pickup shell, and the trailer carried little more than food and clothing. The next morning, we headed for the border for several weeks of fishing and diving in the Cortez. Although the pickup was heavily loaded, the trailer was a very light 13-foot Cardinal, and the rig handled well.

Our carefully planned loading scheme began to disintegrate the first night in Baja, when someone wanted a tackle box, which was buried in the gear in the back of the pickup. To avoid having to tunnel for it again, the box was put in the trailer. The next day we did some snorkeling, and a speargun ended up in the trailer, for the same reason. Day by day, more and more weight ended up the trailer, including scuba tanks, weight belts, and several coolers, most of it stowed below a table in the rear. The weather was warm, and we ate and slept outside, so the crowded condition of the trailer was no bother. By the time we headed north from Cabo San Lucas, the back of the pickup was almost empty, allowing several weary travelers to stretch out for naps. The tongue weight of the trailer was almost zero, but someone pointed out that this made it easier to hitch up each morning. Great idea, guy!

*The next evening we were winding down the long grade south of Loreto, when the pickup shuddered violently and almost went out of control on a hairpin turn. I glanced out the rear-view mirror and was surprised to see a red and white 13-foot trailer about to pass us. For an instant I thought, "That's a hell of a bad place to pass, Buddy," when I realized that it was **our** red and white 13-foot trailer about to pass us. Going almost sideways, it swerved back out of sight behind the pickup and appeared in the other mirror. I instinctively began to slam on the brakes, but I realized that this would jackknife the rig. Several seconds later the trailer again swerved to the left as we came to another hairpin turn. It looked like we were destined to end up in the bottom of the yawning canyon ahead, but somehow I managed to stay on the road. With my foot off the accelerator, our speed slowly dropped, and the trailer decided to end the worst of its swerving, but even at 25 miles an hour it still kept lifting alternate tires off the pavement.*

Finally at the bottom of the grade, we stopped and had several very foamy Fantas as we straightened out the chaos in the trailer. The scuba tanks had apparently bounced back and forth like ping-pong balls, but fortunately there was no damage beyond several major dents in a cooler and a few gouges in the woodwork.

The moral of this story? Read your instruction book carefully and keep the tongue weight very close to that recommended; you are not doing your tow vehicle a favor by reducing the weight on the hitch. Stow heavy objects in the tow vehicle and lash or brace them so they cannot move around. ——Walt 99

● ●

beer distributors, liquor stores, real-estate offices, tire stores, and tortilla factories. Numerous stands sell pistachio, pecan and pine nuts, cashews, corn, and dried fruits. There are many small factories turning out pottery, ceramics, and cast concrete *objects de arte*, so many, in fact, that it is hard to believe that a person could extract a living from such a crowded enterprise. If you have been yearning to buy something to beautify the front lawn and cause envy among the neighbors, perhaps a birdbath, a statue of a peon riding a burro, or possibly painted plaster figures of Beavis and Butt-head, here is your chance.

We will now pick up the KM marking system, but remember that these designations refer to the Free Road, not the adjacent Toll Road.

KM	Location
28	Interchange, at which you can choose to take the Free Road or the Toll Road. We will continue along the Free Road; readers interested in the Toll Road should turn to page 78.
34	Popotla Trailer Park. This class C park is the long-term home to many permanents, but space is sometimes available for transient RVers. It has concrete pads and full hookups, but the beach is little more than cobbles and empty beer cans, there is no place to launch a boat, and the ambiance leaves something to be desired. There is a restaurant on the grounds.
35	Calafia Restaurant—Mexican, seafood, steaks, bar, disco. Surfers will encounter good waves from here south.
36	Costa Baja Restaurant—Mexican, seafood, bar.
36+	Surfing site, parking on the west side of the road.
42	Raul's Restaurant—Mexican, seafood, ocean view, circular building, circular bar.
43	Bahía Cantiles Restaurant—Mexican, seafood, bar, occasional live music.
44	**Puerto Nuevo**. The local Chamber of Commerce bills this enclave as the seafood capital of Baja, with a higher percentage of restaurants serving fish, lobsters, and clams than anywhere else on the peninsula. There are a dozen or more, some

with steaks, chicken, and other menu items, and competition among them keeps culinary standards rather high. The specialty of most is lobster, available in a variety of sizes, from dainty to diet-demolishing. The restaurants nearest the water, especially the third floor of Ortega's (there are more than one Ortega's—this refers to the one at the western foot of the entrance road), command a panoramic view of the coast. Musicians roam the streets, and a number of stalls sell Mexican blankets, jewelry, leather goods, music tapes (probably pirated), T-shirts, trinkets, and *sombreros*, the last so great in diameter that they could serve as *palapas* should the weather turn bad. An amiable place, Puerto Nuevo is worthy of a stop of several hours. The Hotel New Port Baja, just to the south, has an excellent restaurant and live music.

Can this be Baja; a Moorish castle, rhythm, soul, and Kelly and the Killers?

KM	Location
46+	**Cantamar**. PEMEX (M only), stores, doctor, fruit, bakery, beer distributors, dentists, auto parts, tire repair, pharmacy, and restaurants. There is an interchange here to allow you to get on the Toll Road.
48	The rolling "Cantamar Dunes," here are favorites with off-road drivers, parasailers, and the pilots of hang gliders. Too Much Fun Promotions sponsors an annual motocross event here.
49+	Beach access just north of the bridge, RV parking.
51	Cafe Americana—Italian-American, lobster, steaks, bar, outdoor patio, live music.
52+	Halfway House Restaurant—Mexican, bar.
54+	RV parking, surfing.
59	Ejidal Trailer Park; RV parking, sand beach.

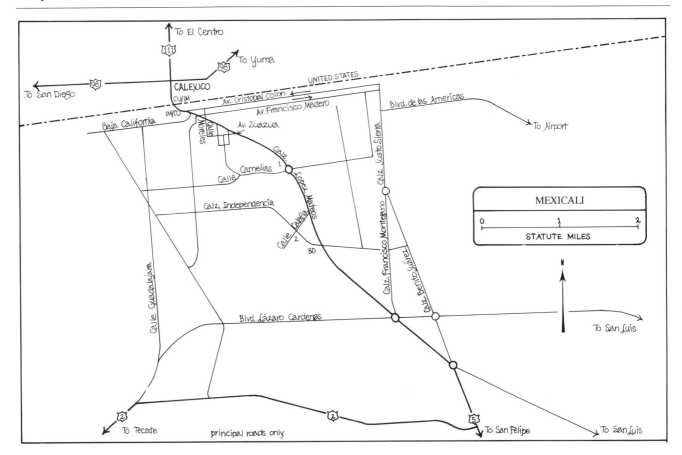

24 **El Oasis**. PEMEX (MND), refreshment stand, road south to Laguna Salada (Salt Lagoon). The exit for east-bound travelers is difficult due to construction of the Tijuana-Mexicali Toll Road.

Laguna Salada

Laguna Salada, Baja's largest lake, can be seen to the south. Once an arm of the Cortez, the lake's level and its salinity have varied greatly over the years. There is a report that it dried up completely in 1924, leaving millions of fish to rot in the hot sun. In 1987, the lake was at a high level due to heavy flows from the Río Colorado. A road south from El Oasis led to a camp on the lake's shores, where fishermen could rent boats to pursue bass, crappie, carp, and huge catfish. Since then, years of drought in the southwestern US have greatly reduced the size of the lake. In 1987, the shoreline was a half mile from El Oasis, but by 1996, the water had receded so far it could not be seen.

Until dams were built on the Colorado, the lake would flood when the river was high, which sometimes happened at the same time the Cortez was having spring tides. This has made the lake the scene of a persistent legend. Having picked up a cargo of valuable black pearls in the lower Cortez, a 16th or 17th Century Spanish explorer entered the Laguna during a flood tide while looking for the "Straits of Anian," a passage around the Californias, which many at the time thought to be an island. As luck would have it, the flood tide receded while the ship was still in the lake, and the crew died or wandered off. The stranded ship, with treasures intact, slowly disappeared beneath the drifting sands when the lake dried up. Thousands, perhaps tens of thousands, of man-made hours and countless metal-detector batteries have been expended to date without a blip, and not a single pearl has shown up to boost morale. But who knows?

Sometimes even inches count on the grade up to
La Rumorosa

KM	Location
26	Rest stop, complete with a large swimming pool, two smaller pools for the kids, refreshments, a restaurant, rest rooms, and a aviary with doves, quail, pigeons, pheasants, and other birds.
28	Class 2 road south to the Palm Canyon area (signed CANON GUADALUPE).

Off-road trip from KM 28 to Canon Guadalupe, which offers RV parking, hiking, hot-tubbing, and loafing in a beautiful setting. Turn to page 224.

| 44 | There are 15 miles of twisting upgrade averaging 5% between here and KM 68. With its craggy cliffs, massive piles of boulders, and grand vistas of the lowlands to the east, many people regard this as one of the most scenic locations in Baja, but your brakes or engine might not be too enthusiastic, depending on whether you are going east or west. |
| 71 | **La Rumorosa.** PEMEX (MND), food stores, bakeries, mail, restaurants, cafes, mechanics, welder, auto parts, tire repair, Red Cross, mini-mart. |

■ Pigmy forests

As you might expect, the sharp gain in altitude has produced changes in the plant communities encountered. This area is home to pigmy forests of juniper and pinyon pine. A variety of conditions—the amount of water available, the lack or excess of minerals or nutrients, the depth of the soil—cause the trees to become stunted, achieving a height only a fraction of those in more favorable locations. It is easy to tell the two species apart: the green "leaves" of the juniper are more like a reptile's scales than proper leaves, while pinyons have regular needles. If you are out of gin, perhaps you could convert a bottle of vodka by pressing some of the fluid out of the juniper's hard, bitter berries. If this is successful, the pinyon nuts that were a staple food for the Indians go very well with a gin and tonic. Both trees are widespread in Baja in their normal form.

| 83 | El Condór. PEMEX (MND). Class 2 road south to Parque Nacional Constitución de 1857. |

Off-road trip from El Condor to Parque Nacional Constitución de 1857, one of Baja's two national parks, and on to KM 55+ on Route 3. Turn to page 225.

| 98 | **Ejido Luis Echeverria Alvarez.** Class 2 road south to Ojos Negros. |

Off-road trip from KM 98 to Ojos Negros, which passes a fine RV park, then crosses rolling chaparral country dotted with pine-rimmed meadows and groves of oaks. Turn to page 227.

104	Club Campestre Eréndira RV Park—class B, shade trees, brick barbecues, playground equipment, rest rooms, potable water, several small lakes for fishing and swimming, but no hookups.
109	PEMEX (MND), tiny cafes, groceries, tire repair, rodeo arena.
112	Rancho Ojai—class B, full hookups, restrooms, showers, shade trees, club house, barbecue area, volleyball, horseshoes, hiking trails, playground, working ranch.
122	**San Pablo.** PEMEX (MND).
132	**Tecate.**

■■■■■■■■■■■■■■■■■■■■■

Intersection of Routes 2 and 5 south of Mexicali to Crucero la Trinidad

87 miles; use the maps on pages 76–77 and 86–87. The road passes through irrigated farm land, with many scattered roadside businesses until approximately KM 48.

KM	LOCATION
0	Start KM numbering sequence.
23	The white plumes seen to the east are from a geothermal electrical generating plant.

■ Doves

Doves are abundant and widespread in Baja, and two species predominate, mourning doves and whitewings. Both breed in Baja from March to September in areas where suitable food, water, and cover exist. They pair up early and have a long nesting season, raising several broods of two young each year. Mourning doves are found throughout the peninsula in virtually all habitats from sea level to 8,000 feet, but they are most abundant in agricultural areas. Large numbers spend the entire winter in the Delta area, north of where the Río Colorado empties into the Cortez. In contrast, white-wings are more of a desert and subtropical species, and they are most abundant in agricultural fields adjacent to desert scrub, and in Baja Sur. Most leave their breeding areas in northern Baja, southeastern California, and southern Arizona in September for points south, and winter in the southern part of the peninsula and on Mexico's mainland.

While both species will share the same feeding, roosting, and watering areas, they tend to congregate in groups of their own kind, especially in roost areas, and you may see mourning doves in one grove of trees, and white-wings in the next. Once airborne it is easy to identify each species even from a distance. Mourning doves, the more familiar of the two to Americans, are smaller and swifter, and given to erratic turning and twisting flight. White-wings are slower, steadier, and fairly predictable flyers, and are somewhat larger. White-wings travel in definite flocks, while mourning doves often fly as singles or doubles, only occasionally in large flocks. The timing of feeding flights from roost areas also differs—mourning doves are usually first off the roost in the morning and the last back to the trees before nightfall.

KM	Location
32	PEMEX (MND), small auto parts store.
33+	PEMEX (MN).
52	A number of very modest RV parks are found along the Río Hardy for the next few miles. The road passes fine marshes, with immense populations of birds, and it is not uncommon to see 30 egrets solemnly surveying a single pond 20 yards across.
57	Groceries, cold sodas, tiny museum devoted to the Cucapa Indians.
60	Class 1 road east (signed) to inexpensive Campo Mosqueda, 1 mile. Some sites have electricity, but there are no other hookups. There are many shade trees, a restaurant, rest rooms, showers, and a small fresh-water lake where catfish and bass can be caught for a fee.
65+	The road starts across the bed of Laguna Salada on a causeway. Due to the continuing drought, the lake was not visible from the causeway in 1995, and only a few puddles and vast areas of dried mud were testimony to its existence.
87+	South end of Laguna Salada. The low, dark mountains to the west are the Sierra de Cucapa.
105	**La Ventana.** PEMEX (MN), cold drinks, small store, beer distributor.
134	Cerro Chinero (Chinese Hill).

■ Several desert phenomena

The surrounding desert exhibits two common desert phenomena, desert paving and desert varnish. For paving, the wind blows the dust and smaller particles away, and alternating wetting and drying causes the remaining pebbles and cobbles to slowly concentrate into a hard mosaic. In some areas, the rocks are covered with a thin, shiny varnish coating that may range from red to black. Rain water dissolves minerals from the desert surface, and as it evaporates, it deposits on the pavement a thin coating of the minerals it carried. Both processes take hundreds of years to become apparent.

It would seem that hiking in the region would be fascinating, but the heat is overwhelming. The name of the volcanic hill to the east commemorates a disaster in the summer of 1902, when a group of 42 Chinese laborers arrived in San Felipe and set out on foot for Mexicali through this area, 130 miles and 120 degrees of blazing heat away. Thirty-five of them died *en route*.

140   **Crucero la Trinidad.** The new restaurant here is pleasant, but has a limited menu. Those traveling to Ensenada should continue reading; those headed for San Felipe should turn to page 174.

■ Creosote

The rangy, multi-stemmed bushes, their leaves almost a shade of olive, along the highway in this area are creosote, one of the most common desert plants in Baja. Because of their rather pedestrian appearance, they usually gain little attention, but they are unusual and interesting plants. This resinous evergreen species puts out large and shallow root systems, "hogging" the water and making it difficult for other plants to gain a foothold. In addition, it maintains its privacy by emitting a toxic substance, a phenomenon known as allelopathy. It develops new stems from the root crown, and as time passes the oldest parts in the center die, and the bush thus grows outward in the form of a ragged circle. Scientists believe that the largest creosote circles are the oldest living things on the planet, ranging up to 12,000 years old. This claim seems tenuous, because although the plant may have had its origins 12,000 years ago, no leaf, stem, root, or cell is anywhere near that old.

Creosote is abundant at low elevations along Baja's eastern shore and in the El Rosario area. The species can reach a height of over 10 feet and it is well adapted to desert living, emitting a sticky, varnish-like coating on its leaves that helps it reduce water loss. Its yellow flowers are found year-around, but are especially common from mid-winter to late spring. A small, almost spherical, fruit is produced, covered by a white fuzz. Some believe the species has medicinal properties, a tea made from its leaves supposedly being good for colds, bronchitis, coughing, and rheumatic pain, and even cancer and tumors. It is imported in small quantities from Mexico to the US, where it is sold in health food stores in powdered form.

■■■■■■■■■■■■■■■■■■■■■■■■
Crucero la Trinidad west to Ensenada on Route 5

122 miles; use the map on pages 86–87.

KM	Location
197	**Crucero la Trinidad**. Begin new numbering sequence.
173	Picacho del Diablo, Baja's highest mountain, dominates the skyline at 196°. In winter, the crest is often covered with snow. Look carefully along the ridge (204°) and you will see a white dot. This is the astronomical observatory in Parque Nacional San Pedro Mártir, described on page 202.
142	**San Matías**. Tiny store.
121	**Valle de Trinidad**. PEMEX (ND, located on the south side of town), mechanic, auto parts, tire repair, stores, groceries, meat, restaurants, doctor, dentist, post office, bakery, ice.
92	**Héroes de la Independencia**. PEMEX (MD, note the antique glass-barrel pump), cafés, auto parts, tire repair, groceries, fruit market, stores, doctor, pharmacy.
86	Class 1 road southwest (signed) to El Alamo.

Off-road trip from KM 86 to El Alamo, the site of an old gold-rush settlement. Turn to page 227.

| 55+ | Class 2 road north to Parque 1857, signed LAGUNA HANSON. This road is described beginning on page 225. |
| 39+ | Paved road (signed) north to Ojos Negros, 1.3 miles, which has groceries, restaurants, post office, limited auto parts, tire repair, doctor, and pharmacy. The Los Casian Trailer Camp, marginal class C, will be found 0.7 mile east on the class 1 road running east from the end of the pavement. It has shaded campsites (no hookups, but potable water is available), a large swimming pool, brick barbecues, rest rooms, showers, and a small pond. The place is dirty, littered and ill-maintained, but seems to be slowly improving with time. To drive north on the Alvarez-Ojos Negros road or to Parque 1857, set trip odometer at the end of the pavement, and drive east. There is a small gas station along the road—follow the signs. At Mile 4.0 note the road ahead winding into the hills and steer for it, arriving at El Coyote junction at Mile 7.7, described on page 227. |

■ **A plant to avoid**

The green plants about a foot tall with large, white, trumpet-shaped flowers (generally open only at night) in the vicinity of KM 29 are jimson weed, a poisonous narcotic plant which has caused many a Hollywood cowboy's cayuse and cattle to go crazy or die. A member of the nightshade family, its relatives include such useful plants as the potato and the tomato, but there are less desirable cousins, including tobacco, a plant that kills more people than any other on the planet. A number of years ago, a group of people in the US became violently ill after eating tomatoes. This made no sense, until epidemiologists found that a local farmer had been grafting tomatoes to jimson weed root systems, producing a more prolific, if poisonous, product.

| 26 | Class 2 road to Rancho Agua Caliente, signed. |

Off-road trip from KM 26 to Rancho Caliente, an RV park having hot springs, a pool, and other attractions. Turn to page 227.

13	Great 13 Recreation Park—playground equipment, restaurant, pool, showers, rest rooms, *palapas*, RV parking spaces, some with water hookups.
11	Large LPG yard.
0	**Ensenada.** Those continuing south on the Transpeninsular should turn left (south) on Avenida Reforma; turn to page 84.

■■■■■■■■■■■■■■■■■■■■■■■
Crucero la Trinidad to San Felipe on Route 5

30 miles; use the map on pages 86–87.

KM	Location
141+	PEMEX (MND). Except for the pumps, no valve, pipe, tank, nail, board, or brick in this station seems to have started its career as part of a gas station. There ought to be a place in Guinness for it. Note the antique glass-barrel gas pump.
178	Class 1 road east to Pete's El Paraíso Camp, 1 mile, offering a beach, a restaurant and bar, rest rooms, a laundry, and showers. This is one of the more well-established RV parks north of San Felipe, but it tends to be inhabited by people with partying, fireworks, ATVs, and dune buggies on their minds, and the din can be terrific. An impromptu 9-hole, par 35 golf course is available.

❝ ❞ *Coyote cuisine?*

My fifth-grade science teacher said that Mother Nature had devised fruits, berries, and melons as ways to get animals to disperse plant seeds. To do this, food had to be sweet and good-tasting or the animals would not eat them, right? If you believe this, a taste-test of the coyote melon, Cucurbita palmata to scientists, will prove to be a memorable dining experience. They look like small watermelons with green-to-yellowish stripes, and are found on trailing vines, mostly in the washes and lower slopes of the hills east of the Sierra Juárez and in desert areas around San Felipe. Their dark green, white-veined leaves have five lobes, the middle one usually being a little longer than the others, and their orange flowers also have five lobes.

The first time we found some, my dad said they ought to taste good, and "nothing ventured, nothing learned," so we both took a big bite. Dad was right on—we did a lot of learning in the first few seconds: the foulest taste I have ever experienced caused my mouth to pucker up, and my eyes began to tear. I spit everything out, but the awful taste would not stop and I began to retch. I ran to the trailer for a drink of water, but that didn't work, so I tried Coke, vinegar, milk, and mouthwash, but nothing helped, not even a good brushing with Crest. The bad taste seemed to be more than a taste; I could "feel" the taste throughout my body. My tongue tasted

awful, so I scraped it against my teeth, and then washed out my mouth with water and ate some sugar. My dad tried the same things, but by dusk he was talking about gargling with gasoline.

Michael samples a coyote melon

What in the world was Mother Nature up to; what possible benefit could such a foul taste provide to the vine? We wondered why it was named "coyote melon," for no coyote except the most intellectually challenged could eat it, at least not more than once. Was the name a trick by the locals to get the coyotes to try it? Two days later we still had the bad taste in our mouths, and even to this day we can remember it when we talk about our first and last meal of coyote melon. ——Michael **❞**

● ●

San Felipe

Santa Rosalía was founded by the French, who were interested in copper, and San Felipe was also founded by foreigners, but this time it was Germans interested in fish. In the early part of this century, Chinese living in Guaymas, a port opposite Santa Rosalía on the eastern shore of the Cortez, discovered that the dried swim bladders of the large bass-like *totuava* had a ready market in China, where they were used in soups. However, the fishermen in their dugout canoes were too successful, and the catch soon declined. A group of German seamen, possibly from the great sailing ships that were interned in Santa Rosalía during the First World War, did some scouting and located virgin fishing grounds in the northern Cortez. Below a rocky headland, they founded a settlement.

The fishermen had apparently learned nothing about conservation from the lessons taught off Guaymas, and their dugouts came back heavily loaded with *totuava*. As had been customary, the swim bladders were removed and the rest of the fish discarded, thus wasting up to perhaps 200 pounds of excellent food from each. The profits were sizable at first, and the settlement grew rapidly. Rumors spread, and several American truckers from Calexico made the hazardous trip across the salt flats and sand dunes, to arrive safely in San Felipe. Buying fresh *totuava* carcasses at the rate of one American cent for 20 pounds, they loaded their trucks and headed north, with the fish unrefrigerated, to the markets of Southern California. Aided by this new financial incentive, the fishery thrived, and in the 1927-28 season, over 1.8 million pounds of fish were landed. Roads from the US were soon paved, and large numbers of sportfishermen began to arrive. It couldn't last, and by the late 1960s, the *totuava* were almost gone.

Today, San Felipe is almost completely dependent on tourism, a place where people from Arizona and Alta California can have an inexpensive beach vacation without a long drive. No one knows with certainty, but the RV parks in the vicinity must total at least 45 or 50, making it the RV capital of Baja. With its numerous restaurants and curio shops, and miles of beautiful sand beaches, the town is lively and pleasant, with a fascinating mix of sights and sounds: vendors walking through the RV parks, hawking everything from ironwood carvings to fresh shrimp; gentle old Mom and Pop, spending the day sitting under the awning of the Winnie talking about their previous trip and planning the next; boardsailors flitting around the bay like a covey of bright marine butterflies; a fat woman with enormous breasts bouncing around an improvised slalom on a three-wheel ATV, unaware that the combined effects of gravity, inertia, and centrifugal force are making her the center of attention.

The peak season at San Felipe is from November to April, when the temperatures are moderate, and the area can

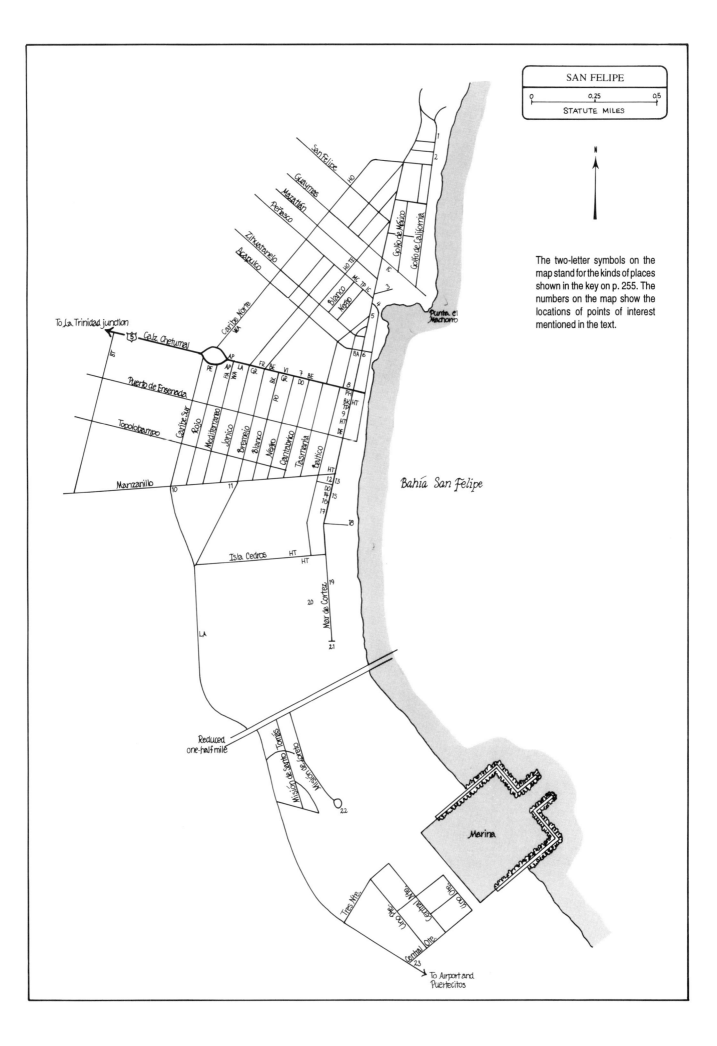

SAN FELIPE

0   0.25   0.5

STATUTE MILES

N

The two-letter symbols on the map stand for the kinds of places shown in the key on p. 255. The numbers on the map show the locations of points of interest mentioned in the text.

San Felipe

Guaymas

Mazatlán

Peñasco

Zihuatanejo

Acapulco

Golfo de México

Golfo de California

Caribe Norte

Punta el Machorro

To La Trinidad junction

Calz. Chetumal

Puerto de Ensenada

Topolobampo

Caribe Sur

Rojo

Mediterráneo

Jónico

Bermejo

Blanco

Negro

Cantábrico

Tasmania

Báltico

Manzanillo

Blanco

Negro

Bahía San Felipe

Isla Cedros

Mar de Cortez

Reduced one-half mile

Misión de Santo Tomás

Misión de Loreto

Marina

Tres Nte.

Central Nte.

Uno Pte.

Central Ote.

To Airport and Puertecitos

get very hot in the other months. During a visit in late August 1994, our thermometer indicated it was 110, which seemed to be an understatement. The air conditioner in our pickup kept things bearable, until the left window popped out of its guides when the door was slammed too hard, letting in the searing blasts. When this was repaired, the air conditioner quickly chose to go belly up, subjecting us to all that San Felipe had to offer. Finally home in cool Northern California, we agreed; better to have the brakes go out than the air conditioner, at least in San Felipe in the summer.

We promised to tell the truth, and no town can be put in a single pigeonhole. In addition to being the RV capital of Baja, San Felipe is the noisiest place on the peninsula. ATVs are great fun, and they are for rent at a dozen or more places. As a consequence, the town is full of men, women, and children buzzing about, creating a loud droning that suggests the town is under attack by killer bees. In addition, fireworks are for sale, and it sometimes sounds like the town is also under naval bombardment. This is great fun for the participants, but the noise can become irksome to others. If you enjoy such things, fine, but otherwise turn off your hearing aid, stuff cotton in your ears, or grin and bear it. These phenomena reach their zenith during holiday and vacation periods and become more bearable at other times, and the din usually tapers off as darkness arrives each evening.

Locating a suitable RV park among the multitude is worth a bit of research, for each tends to cater to a specific clientele. The parks close to the center of town tend to be older and somewhat utilitarian. Expensive Playa de Laura RV Park (15), class B, has full hookups, a beach, rest rooms, showers, and *palapas*. Campo San Felipe Trailer Park (13), class B, has full hookups, a beach, showers, ice, and *palapas*. A bit expensive, Victor's El Cortez RV Park (19), class B, offers full hookups, a beach, rest rooms, showers, *palapas*, and the use of the El Cortez Motel facilities next door. Club de Pesca RV & Trailer Park (21), class B, offers expensive RV sites with electrical and water hookups, a dump station, rest rooms, showers, a recreation room, a store, and a beach. Also somewhat expensive, La Jolla RV Park (11), class B, has full hookups, showers, rest rooms, a pool, a laundry, *palapas*, and, they claim with pride, the only Jacuzzi in San Felipe. These five parks cater mostly to permanents, but some spaces are usually available for transients.

Further afield, very expensive Mar del Sol RV Park, class A, has full hookups, showers, rest rooms, laundry, pool, and *palapas*, with tennis courts available at the hotel just to the north. Very expensive San Felipe Marina Resort and RV Park (23), class A, is the newest and best RV park in San Felipe, offering full hookups, a clubhouse, pool, bar, showers, rest rooms, and satellite TV at the pads, and you can use the facilities of the hotel next door. Tenting and on-the-ground camping are not permitted. The management hopes to eventually make this a membership-only facility.

Ruben's Trailer Park (2) is perhaps the most popular RV park in San Felipe, offering full hookups, showers, two-story *palapas*, restaurant, bar, ice, and a beautiful beach. It rates a marginal class C, not for its assets, but for its ambiance. The park caters largely to exuberant young visitors from the north, who are out to have a ball, and they have a taste for incredibly loud and uninterrupted rap music, something the management seems to encourage. Together with the ubiquitous ATVs and fireworks, the din is awful. However, if you are an exuberant young visitor from the north out to have a ball and have a taste for incredibly loud and uninterrupted rap music, this is the place. Playa Bonita (1), class B, has full hookups, showers, rest rooms, sun shelters, *palapas*, and a beach. Marco's RV Park, class B, across the street from Playa Bonita, has full hookups and sun shelters, but, of course, no beach.

■ The plight of the little cow

About 35 years ago, scientists first identified a "new" species of porpoise, naming it *Phocoena sinus*, the "porpoise of the gulf." It turned out later that the Mexican fishermen of the northern Cortez knew it well, calling it the *vaquita* (little cow), for unknown reasons. It was familiar for a very ominous reason: fishermen frequently found dead *vaquitas* in shrimp trawls and gill nets set for sharks, drowned when they became entangled and were unable to get to the surface for air. Scientists estimate that only a few hundred *vaquitas* may remain, and that between 25 and 35 are killed each year, over 10% of their total number. Unlike fish, where a female may lay thousands or even millions of eggs each year, a female *vaquita* may produce only 10 or 12 young in a lifetime, and the rate they are being killed at means eventual extinction.

The *vaquitas* seem to be the victims of the law of unintended consequences, for they have no commercial value and no one kills them purposefully, and the decline of the species is tied to other events. In the 1920s, the *totuava* fishery developed. Using handlines, spears, nets, and dynamite, local fishermen caught the fish in vast numbers, and unfortunate *vaquitas* were often the other victims. The *totuava* fishery has been closed for many years, but a sizable illegal fishery still goes on, and they can be purchased in San Felipe. While this was happening, the Río Colorado was dammed, reducing its flow of fresh water and nutrients into the Cortez to a trickle. This reduced the biological productivity of the northern Cortez, and creatures high on the food chain, including both the *totuava* and the *vaquita*, found less to eat.

With luck, you may encounter one of these creatures, one of the rarest marine mammals on earth. *Vaquitas* are seen most often in the vicinity of San Felipe. Very shy and not given to riding bow waves like their more gregarious dolphin cousins, they are very small, adults being about 5 feet long. Their bodies are blue-gray to olive- and tawny-brown, and they have black eye and ear patches. Their dorsal fins, pectoral flippers, and caudal flukes (tail fins) are proportionately very large compared to other porpoises and dolphins. They are usually seen alone or in groups of 2 to 4, occasionally as large as 10. They often make three to five rapid surfacings to breath, barely breaking the surface, and then dive for a minute or so. Gulls and storm petrels frequently dive in their wakes.

Scientists hope the species can be saved by tighter enforcing existing laws better, closing certain areas to fishing, designating portions of the northern Cortez as a Mexican marine park, and making gill nets "acoustically visible," enabling the *vaquitas* to avoid them. Despite these efforts, the species seems doomed to extinction before we really get to know it.

"Restaurant Row" is a section of Avenida Mar de Cortez with numerous restaurants offering fish, shrimp, clams, lobster, steaks, chicken, and almost anything else you could possibly want to eat, even frog's legs and quail. You might wish to try the *machaca de mantarraya* at the Corona Restaurant (8), also serving other seafood and Mexican. What? Don't ask. Cachanilla's Restaurant (9) has an international menu. Puerto Padre (14) offers an American, Mexican, and seafood menu. George's Restaurant (16) attracts many visitors, offering Mexican, seafood, and steaks, as well as a bar. El Nido Restaurant (17), part of a chain found elsewhere in Baja, serves steaks and seafood, and has a bar, together with an attractive rustic decor.

There are many other choices, of course. Most of the

hotels and some of the RV parks have restaurants, and there are many inexpensive cafes spread throughout the town. Along the Malecón, the street next to the beach paralleling Avenida Mar de Cortez, there are a number of restaurants and open-air cafes. The modest Cafe Rosita (5), immodestly claiming to be the "Legend of the World," serves seafood and steaks. Despite the raunchy innuendo, the Bearded Clam (4), a circular *palapa* with a bar and an outdoor patio, is a pleasant place to have lunch, with a large menu offering many choices. Culinary civilization has not yet arrived in San Felipe: during our last visit, we were unable to find a McDonald's, a Burger King, a Kentucky Fried Chicken, a Winchell's, or even a Taco Bell. A number of discos will be found—look for the signs. Rockodile (6) is one of the newest and largest, offering a bar and lots of music, in terms of quantity if not quality.

There is much to see and do. Long stretches of beautiful sand beaches invite swimming and loafing, Hobies, sailboards, and jet skis are for rent, and banana boat rides are available. You can rent a bicycle-built-for-two, but it will be one arranged side-by-side so you can make sure your partner does his or her share of the work. You can drive up to the top of the headland at Punta el Machorro to get a good look at the town and the surrounding desert. When the wind is from the east, the gulls and pelicans like to soar past the headland, and since their forward passage is just a bit faster than the wind, they are hardly moving and you can reach out and almost touch them. If you want to try your hand at piloting an ATV, the dune area (20) is great fun.

In addition to being its RV and ATV capital, San Felipe may also be Baja's T-shirt capital, with a bewildering array,

San Felipe and its magnificent beaches from a nearby hill

ranging from the modest to, well, let's just call it the less-than-modest. The Rockodile has the largest selection. Silver jewelry, hammocks, leather goods, and various arts and crafts are sold by individuals who set up shop along Mar de Cortez and the Malecón by simply appropriating a section of the sidewalk. Some of the arts and crafts are quite good.

Through the years, many world fishing records have been set at San Felipe, but as of 1996, only two still stood, white seabass records set in 1953 and 1980. The fishery continues to decline, and only small corbina, cabrilla, and sierra are found in most coolers. Even corvina, mainstay of San Felipe fishing until the late 1970s, can be scarce. Roca Consag, seen on the horizon to the east, 17 miles, 062° from the lighthouse on Punta el Machorro, used to be one of the fabled Baja hot spots. Today, the fishing there is only fair, with a mixed bag of cabrilla, triggerfish, and sierra. There are numerous *pangas* for rent, and limited tackle is available at hardware stores and sportfishing offices.

There are two usable concrete launch ramps in San Felipe. The ramp at the El Cortez Motel, next door to Victor's El Cortez RV Park, is fairly shallow (11%) and rough, but wide and generally in good condition. The ramp at Club de Pesca (13%) is missing a chunk of concrete at its foot, reducing the usable width to about 8 feet. You may or may not be charged a fee, usually depending on whether you are staying at the park—ask at the office. As might be expected, parking your tow vehicle and boat trailer can be a problem during holidays. Because of the enormous tides, the shoreline can extend a half mile at low tide, and these ramps are thus usable at high tide only. Since they lead to unprotected water, afternoon wind and waves can cause difficulty, and guide boards are an asset Drifting sand may cover them, and be on the lookout for the usual drop-off at their lower ends. The ramp at Ruben's has been undermined and broken up, but they have special vehicles for across-the-beach launches. Due to the low slope of the beach, your trailer wiring harness will be submerged in salt water. Winds tend to blow in the afternoon, so head out early. A hardware store (3) has service and some parts for Evinrude and Johnson outboards.

Enchanted Island Excursions (18) offers dune buggy tours, including one to the "Valley of Giants," where a 20-ton *cardón* was selected for transport to the 1992 World's Fair in Seville, Spain, one to the beaches north of town, and one to Valle Chico to see ancient fossil sites and Indian art, with lunch in a canyon at the base of Picacho Diablo. If you already have an off-road vehicle, you can join the tour for a modest fee. They also offer trips on a 37-foot motor sailer from Puertecitos to the Islas Encantadas and Gonzaga, and will arrange custom trips. Gourmet tours, with food prepared by a chef trained in Europe, are also available, as are kayaking and Hobie forays and ultralight aircraft trips over the town.

Charters Mar de Cortez (10) offers sailing trips on a 41-foot trimaran; dune buggy excursions; fishing trips; kayak, sailboard, and Hobie rentals; and horseback riding; and operates San Felipe's only dive shop. PADI certification instruction up to Divemaster is available, as well as air fills, scuba and snorkeling equipment rentals, Zodiac ventures to islands and coves, and scuba trips to Puertecitos and Gonzaga.

The office of the State Secretary of Tourism (12) has many brochures, fliers, and maps to give away. The office of the Attorney General for the Protection of Tourists is located in the same building. At present there is no Immigration office in San Felipe, and those headed south will not find it possible to obtain tourist cards or to have them validated. The two PEMEX stations (both MN) have been known to run out of gas during holidays, resulting in lines at every station all the way to Ensenada. Diesel is available at the commercial marina south of town, but you must bring a large funnel, since the nozzle is too large to fit an automotive tank. There are a number of places to buy food, including a small supermarket (7) carrying most of the items you would find in a similar establishment in *El Norte*. An ice cream truck makes it rounds of the town, its chimes reminding older readers of the Good Humor trucks of their childhood. There are public rest rooms and showers at each end of the Malecón, both charging a small fee.

■ The brown pelican

They are not slim and shaped for high speed, they do not possess mighty talons nor brilliant plumage, their cries do not thrill like the call of the wild, and they serve no purpose of man by providing eggs, flesh, or feathers. Still, they are not noisy and quarrelsome like the gulls, distant and aloof like the ospreys, nor sinister-looking like the frigates, and the thick-bodied,

San Felipe pelicans are a gregarious lot

long-necked, ungainly-looking brown pelican is almost everyone's favorite Baja bird.

They are abundant on both coasts and breed around Bahía Magdalena and along the coasts and islands of the Cortez. They are among the largest bird species, some reaching 30 pounds, and are gregarious, flocking together in colonies to rear their young. They are often seen accompanying one another on fishing trips. They are silent, emitting no sound except for an occasional grunt. Their bills are far longer than their heads, with enormous pouches of skin fastened to the lower mandibles. These hold more than their stomachs, about three gallons when full, and are used as nets as they scoop up fish through their wide-open bills. The fish are held in the pouch until the excess water is squeezed out through the corners of the bill. The female pelican lays one to four bluish-white eggs, and the young emerge in about a month. They live at first on regurgitated food obtained by thrusting their bill down the parent's gullet.

Pelicans are awkward on land, but are among the best of aviators, flying with their heads held back on their shoulders, their bills resting on their necks, propelling themselves with slow, powerful beats of their wings. They often fly in single file with military precision, plunging into the water when prey is seen. They are also skilled mariners, their large webbed feet serving as powerful paddles, and numerous air sacs that make their bodies as buoyant as cork.

During the 1960s and 70s, their numbers declined drastically, largely because of the use of DDT along the Pacific coast of mainland Mexico and in the vast area of the US drained by the Rio Colorado. The pesticide moved up the food chain, and the fish eaten by the birds contained so much DDT that their calcium metabolism was affected, resulting in thin egg shells that often broke, killing the chicks. In addition, they are very sensitive to human intrusions while nesting, and scientists have found that even one visit can have severe and long-lasting repercussions. However, since the use of DDT has been banned in the US, and many Cortez islands have been given park status, their populations seem to be recovering. A closely related bird, the American white pelican, is a winter visitor along both coasts in small numbers.

■■■■■■■■■■■■■■■■
San Felipe to Puertecitos

53 miles; use the map on pages 86–87. The pavement south of KM 62 is rough and potholed. Start south at the intersection of Calzada Chetumal and Avenida Caribe Sur. Set odometer. At Mile 6.1, take the left (090°) turn at the

junction (the road otherwise goes straight ahead to the airport). Commence KM markers.

KM	Location

7   Pricey El Faro Beach Trailer Park, class A, has full hookups, rest rooms, showers, pool, bar, and tennis. A "hole" a mile east of the point in 80 feet of water is the first outpost of good fishing south of San Felipe, mostly for a mixed bag of cabrilla, corbina, sierra, grouper, and an occasional white seabass. Just after slack tide, when the currents are moving but nor roaring along, the fishing in shallow water 200 yards offshore can be excellent. There are numerous private homes and inexpensive RV camps along the beach for many miles to the south, and it appears that someday they will stretch wall-to-wall all the way to Puertecitos.

76   **Puertecitos**. This small village has a PEMEX (N, not always open during business hours), a few RV parking sites, some with *palapas* and occasional electricity, a cantina, several stores with limited produce, ice maybe, the world's smallest public library, and many retired Americans living in ramshackle homes. Diving is poor, but fishing is a noticeable improvement over San Felipe. A steep (16%) and rough launch ramp leading into semiprotected waters can be found at the south point of the peninsula forming the harbor. Although the ramp extends into fairly deep water, the tidal range here is still extreme, so use your tables. There are several natural hot tubs in the rocky beach near the point, each having a different temperature. To try them out, locate the launch ramp, turn around, and drive about 100 yards north, The tubs are on the Cortez side of the peninsula, marked by a scalloped stone fence and a rough concrete path.

■ Besieged

We parked our camper on a beach south of Puertecitos and were having outstanding luck casting feathered jigs from several rocky promontories. Large white seabass would seize them and rip off many yards of monofilament before we could turn them. We landed some and released all but one, which was destined to become supper. Only one thing dampened our enjoyment, the wind. Although the skies were blue, a very strong wind blew from the northwest without cessation, day and night. It ripped at our clothes, it blew dust into everything, it tried to tear the doors off our camper. Day after day of ceaseless wind! We decided to curse the wind, praying that it would stop. Finally one afternoon, we decided that the good fishing could hold us here no longer, but just as we finished packing our gear, our prayers were dramatically answered; the wind suddenly fell to a flat calm. Happy days! At least for a few minutes. We were not even done celebrating when a new plague descended upon us—millions upon millions of *jejénes*, thirsting for human blood. The Mexican equivalent of the North Woods "no-seeum," these small black flies are "pool feeders." Using scissor-like mouth parts they slash your skin and greedily lap up the oozing blood. Freed from the wind, they came out of thousands of nooks and crannies, covering every square inch of exposed flesh. They flew up our noses, and several examined the interior of our ears. They found this location tasty, causing tiny trickles of blood to run out. We began to wonder whether we would be sucked dry, leaving two mummies to be prodded and photographed by future passersby. Praying for the wind to come back, we quickly finished loading the camper, hoping to escape to the comforts of civilization as soon as humanly possible.

Although they relish people slathered in DEET and are so small they can pass through window screening, you should have no fear of an encounter with the *jejénes*. Found in salt marshes, mangroves, and decaying seaweed, they tend to be very localized, and the best defense is thus avoidance; moving your rig as little as a few hundred yards can put you out of range.

Off-road trip from Puertecitos to KM 229+ on the Transpeninsular, one of the most interesting areas in Baja Norte. Turn to page 227.

Maneadero to the Punta Banda Peninsula and La Bufadora

13 miles; use the inset map on page 87. The Punta Banda peninsula is one of the most popular fishing, diving, and sightseeing locations in Baja Norte. The KM markers are absent in many places, so miles will be used. Set trip odometer, turn west from Maneadero on the paved road (signed). The side of the road is building up, and many small businesses sell firewood, baked goods, hamburgers, tire repair,

art objects, welding services, and fishing trips, and there are a pharmacy, several cafés, and a laundromat. Several children's parks with swimming pools are also found along the road. The name of the peninsula, "Banded Point," refers to the many wave-cut terraces that can be seen as you drive west.

Mile	Location
7.6	La Jolla Beach Camp, inexpensive, class B, has RV sites with water hookups, showers, rest rooms, tennis, horseshoes, ice, a mechanic, a pebble beach, and a restaurant. The steep (17%) one-lane concrete launch ramp requires calm water and high tide. The ramp is getting quite rough, and the bottom is often covered with sand and pebbles. Afternoon winds from the northwest can make retrieving difficult. Villarino Camp, class B, next door, has some full hookup sites, showers, toilets, a small store, a post office, a café, block ice, and a pebble beach. Rental boats and bait can be obtained along the beach to the west. A geological fault, Falla Agua Blanca, dives into the sea here, and divers will find gas discharges and hot-water springs along a cleft parallel to shore in 30 feet of water. People have been able to dig private hot tubs in the beach at low tide, served by the water from the fault.
8.0	Class 2-3 road south (signed COLONEL ESTEBAN CANTÚ) to Caleta Árbolitos, Kennedy's Cove, and Bahía el Playon.

Exploring the eastern shore of Isla de Todos Santos Sureste

Off-road trip from Mile 8.0 to Caleta Árbolitos, Kennedy's Cove, and Bahía el Playon, among the most scenic areas in Baja, turn to page 230.

8.7   Class 2 road north, 17% upgrade coming out, leading 200 yards to a small boondocking site. A steep (22%) concrete launch ramp leads into Bahía Todos Santos. It is badly broken up, exposed, and usually covered with pebbles, but cartop and inflatable boats can be launched in calm weather. Masses of fossilized clams can be seen frozen in the cliffs and scattered among the cobblestones. Thriving 70 million years ago, the species was peculiar, for a clam anyway; its two shells were not mirror images. There are several RV parking sites along the road to Punta Banda from this point west, and although very inexpensive, they have no facilities, not even water, and are on steep terrain.

11.0   The two islands to the northwest are the Islas de Todos Santos, the closer one high and rugged, the other flat and featureless. Party boats from Ensenada often fish the islands. Many birds nest on the islands, and a species of cinnamon-colored rabbit can be spotted from 200 yards away, apparently defying the laws of natural selection. Local legend tells that Robert Louis Stevenson used the islands as a model when he wrote *Treasure Island*. Many other islands have also been nominated, but since Stevenson once lived near Ensenada, the legend may be true. The north island is the location of two famed surfing sites, El Martillo and "Killers," the second being the "greatest wave magnet on the west coast" according to some.

■ Caught in the act

Abalone are relatives of the snails, and are widely spread along Baja's Pacific coast. The most common species in Baja waters is the black abalone, which is taken by commercial divers and canned. The larger and more tasty red abalone, reaching 10 or more inches in diameter in its major habitat in Northern California, is found in limited numbers along Baja's northern Pacific coast. The abalone in the color section is a tiny red about 0.75 inch long, caught in the act of displaying its many filigrees and appendages. Note the tiny barnacle.

13.0   **La Bufadora.**

La Bufadora

Located on the shore of Bahía Papalote, La

Bufadora has restaurants, small visitor businesses, inexpensive RV parking, and restrooms. It's the location of a sea spout that sometimes jets a plume of water 100 feet high. The road to the spout is crowded with taco and souvenir stands. Several of the most interesting sea caves in Baja can be reached by the trail running northwest from Mile 11.5. This trail continues to Cabo Banda, where there are great views of the many islets and pinnacles at the end of the peninsula. The California Current produces upwellings of cold water off Bahía Papalote and Cabo Banda, and fishermen will encounter numerous species of bottom fish. Beachcasters willing to do some hiking will find dozens of small coves and beaches along the trail past the sea caves to the point. Stands near the sea spout often sell natural baits. La Bufadora Dive Shop has complete rentals, a new compressor, and three *pangas,* and offers guided dive and surfing trips to the Islas de Todos Santos, as well as kayak rentals. Diving is excellent, and hot springs will be found at the bottom of the small bay. The rocky, rough, and very steep (32%) launch ramp ends on a pebble beach, making it unsuitable for launching trailer boats, although it is handy for cartoppers and inflatables. A fee is payable at the dive shop. Be careful of sneaker waves and surge from refracted swell when launching.

■■■■■■■■■■■■■■■■■■■■■■■■■
KM 78+ on the Transpeninsular to Eréndira

10.7 miles; use the map on pages 86–87. Turn south at KM 78+, set trip odometer. There is a PEMEX (MND), several small stores, groceries, long-distance phone, a motel, tire repair, and a café in Eréndira, beginning at Mile 10.7. The road swings northwest at Mile 11.6 reaching Castro's Fishing Place at Mile 12.7, which has fishing boats, as well as cabins with bunk beds, stoves, and refrigerators for rent. Boats up to 24 feet have been launched here using the steep (22%), grooved concrete ramp. The ramp ends too soon, placing trailer tires in mud and cobble. If your vehicle is not up to the chore, Castro's has *El Chile Verde*, a truck

Yeah, yeah, Dad. I'll remember the next time; never shift gears when you are in soft sand, especially at stream crossings

equipped for launching. Fishing can be excellent for a mixed bag on local reefs and offshore to 10 miles. Shore-casters will find opaleye, cabezon, sheephead, and calico bass close to the landing. Low-cost RV parking can be found on a bluff a half mile west of Castro's.

● ●

❝ *Trying to remain shiftless*

Driving on sand can be a problem: as you move ahead, small "hills" form ahead of the wheels, and your vehicle is thus always going "uphill." In addition, when sand has been disturbed, perhaps by previous vehicles or by flowing water in a stream, it acts almost like a liquid, flowing more readily and letting your vehicle bog down. In such situations, the rule is to drive in low gear, in compound low if you have four-wheel-drive, and never stop. Never attempt to shift gears, for the rolling resistance is so great that your vehicle will come to an almost instantaneous stop when you push in the clutch, and you may be unable to get moving again. And don't think for a minute that four-wheel-drives are invulnerable to these factors.

I learned this the hard way. We decided to cross the stream at Eréndira to explore the coast to the south, and I was driving in second gear in four-wheel-drive. The truck began to slow down because of the high rolling resistance over the sandy bottom, so I naturally began to shift to low. In an instant, two things happened simultaneously: my dad was just beginning to say the word "no," and the truck stopped with a lurch. There we were, down to the axles in the middle of the stream in our four-wheel-drive, with the locals whizzing by in their ordinary Toyota sedans, all with gleeful expressions and shouts of derision. Fortunately, a man with a tractor was working nearby, and we were up and running in less than five minutes.

At the time, my dad thought the scene was hilarious, and I heard about it at regular intervals, but all that changed three weeks later. He was taking photos of the paragliders near Faro Viejo at Cabo San Lucas, when he had to negotiate

a steep slope of soft sand. The truck began to slow down, and guess what? He attempted to shift to low gear, and the truck came to an instant halt! I never got a full account of what transpired from this point on, but I know it involved a lot of digging with a GI shovel, six or eight people pushing on the truck, and cutting some thick branches off a torote tree that got in the way, using the tiny saw of a gadget he carried on his belt. I noticed that from that point on, he never mentioned how funny it had been when everyone had whizzed past me.
——*Michael* ❞

● ●

↱ Off-road trip from Eréndira to Baja Malibu Sur RV Park. Turn to page 232.

■ ■ ■ ■ ■ ■ ■ ■ ■ ■ ■ ■ ■ ■ ■

Parador Punta Prieta to Bahía de los Angeles

40 miles; use the map on pages 96–97.

KM	Location
21	Elephant tree forest
41	The wispy, almost formless trees on both sides of the road are smoke trees. They are intricately branched, and grow up to 24 or 30 feet high. Widespread over the peninsula, they are always found in arroyos, where their water requirements can be met. As noted earlier, their seeds must be scarified by flash floods in order to germinate.
44	Class 3 road south (signed) to Misión San Borja.

↱ Off-road trip from KM 44 to Misión San Borja, site of the first well-preserved mission building south of the border. Turn to page 231.

49	Boojum forest.
52+	Beautiful vistas of the Cortez.
65	**Bahía de los Angeles.**

Bahía de los Angeles

If it was necessary to pick a single location to represent the entire peninsula, there would be little doubt what it would be; Bahía de los Angeles, the quintessential Baja in the eyes of many. Beginning in the 1940s, aviators and four-wheelers returned home to tell of a tiny outpost of civilization that could be found at the foot of a mountain, where friendly fishermen lived in palm-thatched adobe homes, everything and everyone dominated by the desert wilderness on one side, and the incredibly beautiful blue

Yes, you are right, Michael. Never shift gears when you are in soft sand

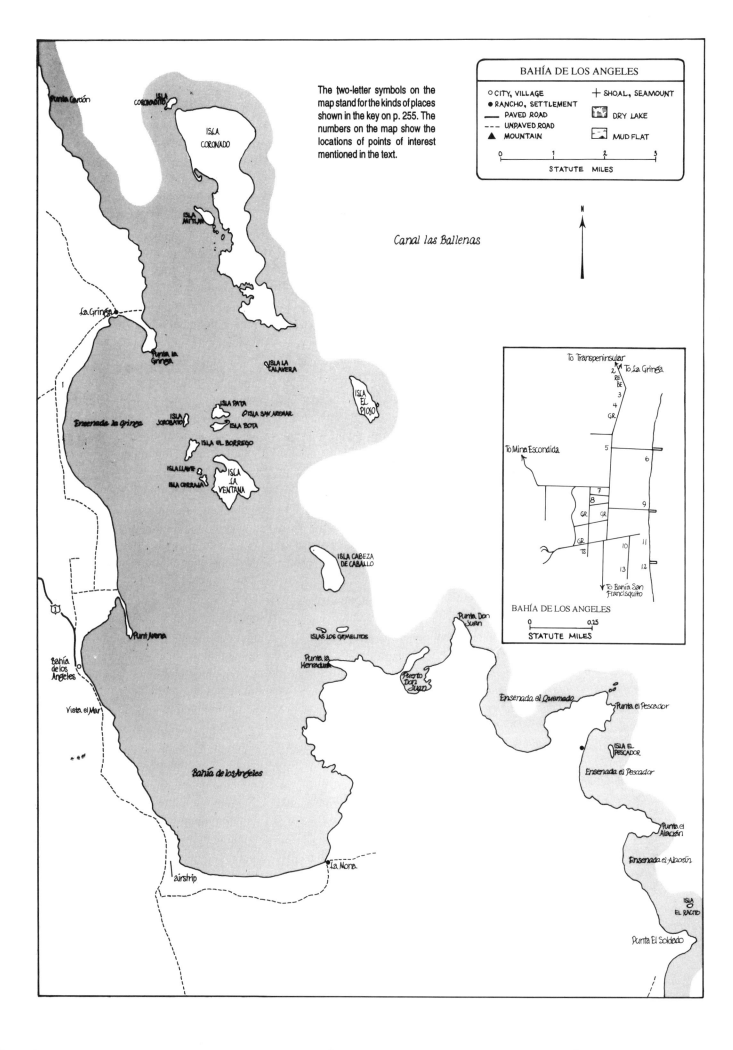

The two-letter symbols on the map stand for the kinds of places shown in the key on p. 255. The numbers on the map show the locations of points of interest mentioned in the text.

BAHÍA DE LOS ANGELES

○ CITY, VILLAGE
● RANCHO, SETTLEMENT
— PAVED ROAD
--- UNPAVED ROAD
▲ MOUNTAIN
+ SHOAL, SEAMOUNT
DRY LAKE
MUD FLAT

0   1   2   3
STATUTE MILES

N

Canal las Ballenas

Punta Cardón
ISLA CORONADITO
ISLA CORONADO
ISLA MITLAN
La Gringa
Punta la Gringa
ISLA LA CALAVERA
ISLA EL PIOJO
Ensenada la Gringa
ISLA PATA
ISLA JOROBADO
ISLA SAN ANDMAR
ISLA BOTA
ISLA EL BORREGO
ISLA LLAVE
ISLA CERRAJA
ISLA LA VENTANA
ISLA CABEZA DE CABALLO
Punta Arena
Bahía de los Angeles
Vista el Mar
ISLAS LOS GEMELITOS
Punta la Herradura
Punta Don Juan
Puerto Don Juan
Ensenada el Quemado
Punta el Pescador
ISLA EL PESCADOR
Ensenada el Pescador
Bahía de los Angeles
Punta el Alacrán
Ensenada el Alacrán
La Mona
Airstrip
ISLA EL RACITO
Punta El Soldado

BAHÍA DE LOS ANGELES (inset)

To Transpeninsular
To La Gringa
2 — RE BE
3
4 — GR
To Mina Escondida
5
6
7
8
GR — GR
9
GR — TS
10
11
13   12
To Bahía San Francisquito

BAHÍA DE LOS ANGELES

0   0.25
STATUTE MILES

bay and brown islands on the other. In recent years, the town has not prospered, and is badly in need of a fix-up, paint-up, and trash removal program. Still, the natural beauty of the area has endured, and once out on the bay fishing, diving, exploring, or whale- and bird-watching, you will find that the visit is a high point in your RV trip.

The RV park situation in town is not inspiring: they are often badly littered, and maintenance ranges from fair to bad, depending on the unpredictable whims of the management. Although you may see water, electrical, and sewage hookups, the chances that they are operational are poor.  Moderately priced Villa Vitta's RV park (5), class C, has a dump station and electric hookups. Inexpensive Guillermo's RV Park (9), class C has full hookups, and the place is often badly littered. Rest rooms and showers are located in a small building just to the south of the associated restaurant. Inexpensive Casa Diaz (10), class C, has full hookups, showers, and rest rooms.

Fortunately, there are other choices a short distance out of town. Inexpensive Campo la Ventana (1), class B, has a beautiful location, breezes keep the temperature down, *palapas* provide shade, and there is fresh water, showers, rest rooms, and a dump station. Kayakers and boardsailors may safely park their vehicles here for a small fee while out on the bay, and boat storage is available. Ventana can be reached by turning north at KM 61 (signed) and driving 1.7 miles on a class 1 road. Gecko Campground, class C, 4 miles south of town on the class 1 road to Las Flores (described on page 232), has inexpensive RV parking, showers, and rest rooms. Boondocking and inexpensive RV parking sites can be found along the northern sweep of the beach from town to Punta la Gringa.

The Villa Vitta Motel across the street from the RV park has a bar, a pool, and a restaurant. The clean and pleasant restaurant serves American-style breakfasts, burgers, tacos, and quesadillas for lunch, and fish, scallops, and shrimp for supper, all priced a bit high. They sell a very limited selection of fishing and diving equipment. Guillermo's Restaurant at the RV park serves American-style breakfasts, seafood, and Mexican. Although the place is clean, the ambiance is only a step or two above a factory cafeteria. There is a small grocery store and a curio shop in the same building. Casa Diaz Restaurant serves seafood, chicken, burgers, steaks, and Mexican. Restaurant las Hamacas (4) serves breakfast, seafood, and Mexican, and is clean and well-run. There is a small motel adjacent to the restaurant.

Cube and block ice can be purchased (6), and there is a PEMEX (11, MND). LPG can be purchased at an unmarked store (2). There is a telephone office (3) and a health clinic (8). A garage (13) makes mechanical and welding repairs and often has diesel fuel available. There are a number of other mechanics, but they may not have signs out—ask around. Postal matters are handled informally; outgoing mail is left at the PEMEX and it collects until someone goes to

Ensenada. There are no auto parts or hardware stores, laundromats, or commercial transportation. Some of the businesses in town keep *siesta* hours from one to three in the afternoon.

A fine museum has been constructed with contributions of money, materials, artifacts, and volunteer labor, and land donated by the local *ejido*. The Museo de Naturaleza y Cultura (7) is open afternoons and has many interesting displays, including geological samples, shells, fossil ammonites, Cochimí art and artifacts, depictions of life on rural ranches, and a replica of a mine shaft complete with railroad, ore cart, and hanging buckets. The skeleton of a young gray whale hangs from the ceiling. Ore samples from local mines are given away, and books and T-shirts are sold to support the museum. A slide show on local fish, birds, turtles, and history is presented twice a month. Don't miss this unusual and interesting museum!

Raul Espinoza, a local resident, is a government-licensed guide and takes groups on fishing, sightseeing, whale-watching, and overnight camping trips throughout the area. From March through early June he takes birding groups to Isla Raza to see the nesting sea birds. Located about 30 miles east of Bahía de los Angeles, Raza is the annual scene of a spectacular pageant of conflict, disaster, death, and renewal when large numbers of elegant and royal terns compete for nesting space on the small island with Heermann's gulls. Don't plan a freelance trip; a permit is required to land, and there may be wardens on the island. In addition, Espinoza has a small bus for trips to see the local Cochimí art, the cactus forests, Misión San Borja, and local gold mines. He speaks excellent English and has a thorough knowledge of the local flora and fauna. He can be found at Campo la Ventana.

There is a shallow (10%) concrete launch ramp at Villa Vitta, the only one in Bahía de los Angeles that is usable at low tide. The steep (17%) ramp at Guillermo's is very rough and requires mid- to high tides for larger boats. The steep (19%) Casa Diaz ramp (12) is rough, but a small breakwater offers some protection. Gecko Campground has a shallow

Guide/naturalist Raul Espinoza explains a bit about gray whale anatomy, using the skeleton washed up on a Bahía de los Angeles island. The skeleton eventually was put on display in the new museum

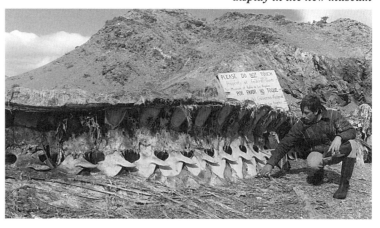

(7%) launch ramp, but it leads to a pebble area and is usable by larger boats only at high tide.

The best fishing is during the hot months, and in midwinter things slow down considerably. The bay is known primarily for yellowtail, which are present from late April or early May through October, and dolphinfish and sierra are available from May through July, white seabass a bit earlier. There are many other species, and the fishery resembles Southern California, with ocean whitefish, various varieties of rockfish, and even sheephead around, the leopard grouper found elsewhere in the Cortez being less common. The result is perhaps the most mixed of "mixed bags" available in Baja, and it is not uncommon to encounter 20 and even 30 species during a week-long fishing vacation. *Pangas* and guides can be arranged at Guillermo's and Casa Diaz, as well as through Raul Espinoza. Live bait is not available for sale, but can be taken with Lucky Joes or snagged with treble hooks near Punta Arena or several miles to the south of the point.

The bay provides good jigging and trolling, especially around the islands. The most productive locations include the east coast of Isla Coronado and the reefs off its north and southeast points, and east of Isla Cabeza de Caballo. The deep water of Canal las Ballenas yields rockfish, various basses, and ocean whitefish, but because of its swift currents, fishing ventures must be planned around the tide tables. Shorecasting with cut bait produces sand bass, triggerfish, guitarfish, and rays. In spring, the shoreline from Punta Arena north to La Gringa is a good place for yellowfin croaker, and halibut to 15 pounds are taken in the inner harbor. Beachcasting equipment is an asset, for it may be the only technique possible during windy periods. Incidentally, when asking a local fishing guide to take you to Coronado, San Aremar, or El Borrego, you may get a blank look: departing from their official names, local usage has identified these islands as Smith, Rasita, and Flecha, respectively.

Whale- and bird watchers can remain engrossed for days or weeks. More than a dozen species of whales and dolphins have been seen in the Canal, including blue, finback, gray, Bryde's, Minke, humpback, pilot, sperm, pygmy sperm, killer, and false killer whales, as well as bottlenose

A patient booby poses for a portrait

and common dolphins. Bryde's whales are the most common, more so than finback whales, for which they are often mistaken. Bryde's whales are seen most frequently in winter, especially January, when they feed on large squid. Finback whales cruise the Bahía de los Angeles area and the Midriff region year-around, peaking in the Canal in spring and summer. Sperm whales are less common, and are seen most frequently in February. Grays are encountered only rarely. Dolphins put on a great show for almost any passing boat, and sometimes break into organized groups in Puerto Don Juan, apparently herding forage fish.

At least 50 species of birds are seen around the bay and its islands, including yellow-legged gulls, a Cortez "almost endemic," and such expected species as pelicans and pink-footed and sooty shearwaters, and various terns, petrels, cormorants, boobies, and other sea and wading birds. There are nesting ospreys on Isla la Ventana, Coronado, and El Pescador, a pelican colony on Isla el Piojo (Louse Island), and a frigate resting site on the southeast point of Coronado.

■ Blue-footed boobies

Blue-footed boobies are among the most numerous sea birds in the Cortez. Their comical and not-too-bright appearance and demeanor are responsible for the Spanish name *bobo,* meaning clown or dunce. They are, however, skilled flyers and plunge divers, and groups of them sometimes make synchronized dives when they see food below the surface. Unlike most diving birds, they seize prey from below and swallow before reaching the surface. Boobies examine trolled lures intently and sometimes make the wrong decision, to the consternation of fishermen and the booby.

In pairing off for mating purposes, boobies go through an elaborate court ship ritual. After a period of waddling, goose-stepping, and showing off its bright blue feet, a bird of either sex may "skypoint," stretching its neck, bill, and tail feathers vertically and canting its wings. Skypointing is accompanied by honks if the bird is a female and whistles if a male. Ceremonies after mating are limited to "foot-showing," when the male lands near the nesting site. Two or three eggs are laid on bare ground. Plunge diving is difficult to learn, and young birds receive food from their parents long after they have learned to fly at seven or eight months. The easiest way to tell male from female is to look at their eyes: a female's black pupil appears to be larger than a male's. Actually they are the same size, but females have a ring of black pigment around the iris.

A closely related species, the brown booby, is frequently seen in the Cortez. A third species, the masked booby, is also seen occasionally in Baja, but the general rule is that if a booby does not have blue feet, it's a brown booby.

Although the area has been popular with divers for many years, there is no dive shop. However, Raul Espinoza can supply compressed air. The channel between Coronado and Isla Mitlan offers good snorkeling. The east coast of Coronado has fine diving, especially about one-third of the way south from the north cape, where rocks and boulders form caves and small crevices. An excellent reef continues from the southeastern tip of the island. Many octopuses live in holes in rocky and gravel areas throughout the bay. Although beach diving is generally poor, the reefs north of La Gringa have brilliantly colored sea fans and encrusting sponges, the latter in a dozen hues.

The 50-foot wooden fishing vessel *Marcelo* ran onto the reef between Ventana and Cabeza de Caballo in 1983, and her wreck now makes a fine dive site. Lying approximately 400 yards southeast of the prominent "window" landmark on Ventana, the reef is about 100 yards long. A half-dozen shallow rock pinnacles are barely covered at moderate tides, so take care approaching the site. The bulk of the wreck is about 20 feet from the southeastern pinnacle in 10 feet to 50 feet of water. Deeper sections of the reef have the most colorful sea life in the bay, and a proposal has been made to make it a national marine park. About 1981, a fishing boat burned and sank off the east side of Isla el Racito, a low, rocky islet 700 yards north of Punta el Soldado, and the wreck presents one of the finest displays of plant and animal life in the Cortez. It lies in 10 feet to 16 feet of water about 100 feet off the east side, midway between the north and south points.

■ Seeing small

Nature watchers usually concentrate on things with the grandest scale—the largest fish, the highest mountain, the tallest tree—but sometimes the smallest things are the most beautiful. Witness the nudibranchs: few people know what they are, and fewer still have actually seen one in the wild. Mollusks, they are closely related to the sea slugs and sea hares, and more distantly to the snails and other shelled creatures. A few species have the ability to swim, a skill shared with few other mollusks except the squid and octopus. They are hermaphroditic, meaning that each is both a male and a female, although some species tend to become females as they get older. This characteristic greatly reduces the search for a mate, since anyone who comes along is available for reproductive services.

The nudibranchs are so colorful and flamboyant that they have been called the butterflies of the sea. However, their beauty is not meant to please the eye, but rather to warn predators that they possess a foul taste. To date, no one seems to have accepted this culinary challenge. The purple-and-gold species in the color section was photographed at Isla el Piojo, probably the best location in the Cortez for

nudibranch-watching. The photograph of the blue-and-gold beauty was taken on the west side of Isla Carmen, off Loreto. Nudibranchs are widespread, so "see small" while snorkeling or scuba diving, and you may encounter an inch or so of luminescent beauty possessed by few other creatures.

Boardsailors can have a ball in Bahía de los Angeles. Many just like to explore the islands, while others enjoy getting someone to drive them to La Gringa and making downwind runs to play in the islands, returning directly to town. Still others like to take advantage of every opportunity; when the famous winds are blowing they try speed sailing, when it's calmer they play around the islands, and if it stops they head for Santa Rosalillita. Most avoid the southern part of the bay, since winds are cut off by the surrounding topography and tend to be gusty and erratic.

The big island off Bahía de los Angeles to the northeast is Guardian Angel, 46 miles long. Once a part of the peninsula and now moved 30 miles south by tectonic forces, the island is the result of sea-floor spreading about a million years ago, its rocks being of Miocene volcanic and Pliocene sedimentary origin. The rocks are colorful, some areas graced with broad layers of gray, white, pink, green, and red. In spite of being mountainous and second in land area in the Cortez only to Isla Tiburón, Guardian Angel has no permanent surface water, although a few sparse palms show there is underground water.

Off-road trip from Bahía de los Angeles to Las Flores and on to Bahía San Francisquito. This trip will take you to a gold mine active in the late 1800s and excellent fishing. See page 232.

■■■■■■■■■■■■■■■■■■■■■■■■■■■■■
Villa Insurgentes to Puerto López Mateos

22 miles; use the map on pages 134–135. The town of Puerto López Mateos can be reached by driving northwest through town and taking a left (262°, signed) 1.4 miles north of the Transpeninsular. The paved road reaches the town at KM 35.

López Mateos has groceries, butcher shop, tortilla factory, restaurants, beer, liquor, ice, long-distance telephone, health clinic, pharmacy, and a Pesca office. Gasoline is available from drums at a place 100 yards northeast of the church. RV parking is available at a large flat area just north of the fish-packing plant in the north part of town. There are rest rooms and taco stands nearby, and small boats can be launched over the beach into protected water. There are limited boondocking sites and over-the-beach launching at Playa el Faro (Lighthouse Beach), just south of the packing plant. A marginal class 1 road leads northwest from KM 33+ to Playa Santa

Elenita and several other boondocking beaches.

López Mateos would normally be of little interest, except for one thing—the whales. During the winter months, especially February, the whales cruise by in the narrow waterway that passes the town, within easy viewing distance, and *pangas* can be hired to get even closer. The best viewing location is at Curva del Diablo (The Devil's Bend), a sharp bend in the waterway where the tides from the north and south tend to meet, located 17 miles south of town. A number of organizations provide whale- and bird-watching tours; look for the signs. Several small shops sell T-shirts and carvings with whale motifs.

■■■■■■■■■■■■■■■■■■■■■■■■■■■■■
Ciudad Constitución to Bahía Magdalena

36 miles; use the map on pages 134–135. Commencing at Boca las Ánimas, a series of narrow barrier islands stretches south for over 130 miles. Two of them, Islas Magdalena and Santa Margarita, form Bahía Magdalena and its southern extensions, Bahía las Almejas. Although this vast area has a great potential for fishing, diving, and other activities, it is not often visited by outsiders. Commercial fishermen tell of 60-pound snook netted in the hundreds of miles of mangrove-lined waterways and small bays, but ordinary techniques common to Baja fishing simply do not work. Storms often cut new channels and silt up old ones, changes not reflected on the marine charts. However, unfamiliarity and mystery are the stuff of adventure, and there is a great deal to see and do.

The bay is best reached by driving west from Ciudad Constitución from the signed intersection at the north end of town. Trailer Park la Curva, class C, at KM 56, advertises sewer, water, and electric hookups, rest rooms, and showers, but appears to be closed, although RV parking and a mud beach are available. San Carlos, at KM 58, is a deepwater port. The small town has a PEMEX (ND), PESCA office, ice manufacturing plant, beer, liquor, mechanics, laundry service, tire repair, doctor, dentist, pharmacy, health clinic, grocery stores, butcher shop, post office, telegraph, and long-distance telephone. The new Museo de la Ballena (Whale Museum) has artifacts and machinery from the old whaling station at Punta Belcher. A decompression chamber has been installed in the Productos Pesquera de Bahía Magdalena plant, but its operational status is unclear.

Restaurant el Galeón is clean and nicely decorated, and offers seafood and Mexican. Hotel Alcatraz has a restaurant, bar, laundry service, telephone, sportfishing, and boat trips, and will cash traveler's checks. Viajes Mar y Arena, with an office in town, offers whale- and bird-watching, marine ecology tours, fishing, hiking, kayaking, snorkeling, and beachcombing. Reservations and information can be obtained at their office.

The town lacks RV facilities, but many flat parking spaces can be found. The old Flying Sportsman's Lodge once operated a fishing camp south of town. It is now out of operation, but RV parking is available. It is found by driving 0.2 mile, 060° from the PEMEX, then 120° for another 1.5 miles. Boats as long as 28 feet have been launched from the rough, shallow (7%) concrete ramp, but tides of at least 3.5 feet are required, and sandy beach launches can be made.

■ The creeping devil

The prostrate, many-stemmed cactus seen in this area is creeping devil. It is endemic to Baja, no other region having volunteered to take the evil-looking menace. The name comes not only from its appearance, but also from its habit of sending branches forward, while the older ones behind die, allowing the species to creep across the desert in a most-unplant-like way, and to increase in numbers. This method of asexual reproduction is often encountered in desert regions, since sexual reproduction involves the production of flowers, pollen, and seeds, and the seeds require water to germinate. No further description is needed—you will know exactly what it is when you see it.

Bay and blue water fishing

Bahías Magdalena and Almejas are shallow, half their area averaging 60 feet or less, and large areas are exposed at low tide. However, the bay east of the shoreline between Punta Entrada and Puerto Magdalena is fairly deep, some locations being over 140 feet, especially north and east of Punta Belcher. In these areas you can catch cabrilla, grouper, yellowtail, and black sea bass. Favorite spots outside the entrance include the area between Punta Magdalena and Cabo Corso, and off Punta Hughes. Surf fishing can be excellent on the beaches north of Cabo Corso. It's too rough to land, pull up on the protected beach several miles north of Puerto Magdalena on the "inside" and hike over the dunes.

Larger boats have access to world-class big-game fishing offshore. The 100-fathom line is 9 miles off Punta Entrada, but sailfish and dolphinfish are caught within 5 miles, marlin preferring it a bit deeper. Banco Thetis is known for marlin, yellowfin, wahoo, and giant sea bass, and is 18 miles, 290° from Cabo San Lázaro, least reported depth 6 fathoms. Thetis has been fished by trailer boats using the launch ramp at Puerto San Carlos. When water temperatures and wind are favorable, boats often get into boils of wahoo so bold that they will attack baitfish seeking refuge in the shadow of the boat. Another fine location is "6 Spot," 16 miles, 266° from Punta Hughes. A seaworthy boat could make productive daily runs to these locations for as long as fuel permitted, anchoring in the lee of Punta Hughes at night. Live bait is no problem, for mackerel can be caught by the ton near Punta Entrada. For those with adequate range, a little-fished 22-fathom spot called Roca Pináculo, 8 miles, 192° from Punta Tosca, offers the same species as Thetis. In addition, "3 Spot," 22 miles, 133° from Tosca, offers good fishing.

The best fishing tends to be in summer and fall, depending on water temperatures and currents. Frequent northwest winds and fog may cause problems. It is common to be able to fish only one or two days a week, and wipeouts of two weeks are possible. April, May, and June are usually the windiest months, September, October, and November the calmest. Alternating shore and sea breezes often push fog back and forth, creating clear and foggy periods, sometimes only hours apart. If it's a total wipeout, cheer up—Puerto Escondido is only 109 road miles away and La Paz 166, and the Cortez will probably be calm.

Fishing the extensive mangrove areas requires special techniques, information on which will be found in Appendix A.

● ●

❝ *Golden visions*

An amusing instance of ignorance and credulity was related about one of the whaling captains who visited Bahía Magdalena about the time of the gold fever in California. He was out one day exploring the interior of Isla Margarita in search of water. Coming upon some outcroppings, he supposed them to be gold and in great excitement he carried down a lot of it to his crew. "Boys," he said," we have been whaling long enough. Here is gold for all of us, and for the owners too. For my part, I am done with blubber hunting. What do you say? Shall we ship a cargo of ore and go home rich, or spend the rest of our lives catching whales and trying out the oil?" The crew to a man were clamorous for the gold. Overboard went the oil, and all hands went to work loading the vessel with the golden treasures of the island. About the time the ship was laden down to the water's edge a practical miner from La Paz, hearing of the excitement, came over, and dashed the hopes of the deluded fortune hunters by pronouncing the gold utterly worthless iron pyrites. An assay was made which confirmed his judgment, and the unlucky party had to go to work again catching whales, wiser if not happier men. ——From an 1868 article by J. Ross Browne ❞

● ●

Other activities at Bahía Magdalena...

The vast expanse of the bay and its breezes make it an excellent location for boardsailing. The downwind ride from López Mateos to Puerto Chale is one of the longest protected runs in Baja, 70 miles. Vast quantities of clams lie scattered all over the bottom of the bay. Gray whales can be seen in winter months, and whale watchers in a boat anchored inside Punta Entrada are apt to see a magnificent ballet of breaching and spy-hopping. An enormous variety of birds inhabits the area, either permanently or seasonally, and a complete check list might go to

100 species, second only to the Bahía San Quintín area in numbers. The many miles of Pacific beach north of Punta Lázaro contain a jackpot of flotsam, but a boat and a motorcycle or ATV are required to inspect them completely.

The sidewheel steamer *Golden City*, one of the largest and finest wooden oceangoing ships every constructed, went aground on Isla Magdalena in a fog in 1870, and the actions of her captain, crew, and passengers provide the great comic opera of Baja shipwrecks. As the lifeboats went over the side, a passenger became involved in a shouting match with Captain Comstock and several officers over whether he or the treasure of gold bars should go ashore first. The choice was easy, and they triced him up by tying his hands behind him and connecting the rope to a spar above, leaving him lurching about the heaving deck, standing on tiptoes. Blustering, cursing, waving a saber in one hand and a revolver in the other, the captain began bullying everyone in sight. Once ashore, a number of steerage passengers got into a fight over a cask of liquor that had washed up, which the captain ended by striking one of them in the face with his saber. A cow that swam to the beach was promptly slaughtered and boiled in a huge pot of sea water. At first light the next day it was found that the steamer had broken in half aft of her paddleboxes, discharging a flotsam of 43,000 chests of tea, hundreds of bales of silk, and more liquor. The steerage passengers began drinking and quarreling, and Captain Comstock found it necessary to strike Mr. James Murphy over the head with a pistol and kick him in the face. Drunken passengers continued to stagger around the beach, Mr. Murphy later having a "fit."

Some time later the steamer *Colorado* appeared off the beach. Since the surf was too rough to permit safe embarkation, Captain Comstock asked that the ship anchor in Bahía Santa Maria. He then assembled the passengers and ordered them to "go down the beach," waving his saber toward the south, swearing and threatening to shoot. With no guidance as to the route to be taken, and without adequate water or food, groups of people started out, a number of old or invalid passengers being carried on litters. One elderly gentlemen was carried seated upright in a chair. Everyone

The Golden City in 1867, three years before her loss on Isla Magdalena

Courtesy National Maritime Museum

finally arrived, safe and reasonably sober. A small lagoon at the north end of the bay was named "Lottie Smith's Lagoon," after the first woman rescued from the ship. The *Colorado* made steam for San Francisco, leaving Captain Comstock, a small crew, and a number of volunteer passengers, duly fortified with a large supply of wine, to guard the treasure and baggage. Two days later, the unfortunate Mr. Murphy was seen jumping over the rail of the *Colorado*. The

The beautiful new Marina Palmira complex

ship was stopped, but no sign of him could be found. Captain Comstock and the others were picked up several weeks later by the steamer *Fideliter*, treasure intact and bottles presumably empty.

The scene of the wreck is littered with massive wooden beams, silverware, bronze spikes, broken pottery, buttons from sailor's uniforms, and other artifacts. It can be visited by those with a boat and a motorcycle or ATV. The most certain way is to drive to Puerto López Mateos, launch the boat, put the vehicle aboard, and land on the north end of the island at Boca la Soledad. Head south on the outer beach until you arrive at the lighthouse at Lázaro, turn around, set your trip odometer and drive back exactly 11 miles. The remains of the wreck will be found behind the first line of dunes. The locals seem to know something of the *Ciudad de Oro*, and if you don't have a boat or vehicle, you might be able to hire a *panga* and a guide, and land on the inside shore of the island, about 4 miles south of La Florida. Locating the wreck in this manner is obviously a chancy proposition, however.

■■■■■■■■■■■■■■
La Paz to Playa Tecolote

15.5 miles; use the insert map on page 135. This trip leads past fine hotels, one of the finest marinas in Baja, the ferry terminal, and a series of beautiful coves, and arrives at one of the nicest beaches in Baja. Begin by driving northeast on Obregón. The fancy restaurant at the Hotel el Morro at KM 2.5 has a menu of steaks, seafood, and pastas, and the shrimp omelet is excellent. The Araiza Inn Palmira, just north of the El Morro, has a restaurant with a coffee-shop atmosphere featuring breakfast, seafood, steaks, and Mexican, a piano bar and a disco, and occasionally offers plays and musical comedies.

The Dinghy Dock Restaurant at Marina Palmira, just north of the Araiza, is a covered patio with a nautical theme and a menu of steaks, seafood, and Mexican, and a buffet. The marina is one of the finest in Baja, and is filled with yachts from all over the world. Marina Palmira offers slips,

storage, gasoline, diesel, repair, and painting, and the marine store has items that may be of interest to passing RVers, such as small trailer tires and hitches, wheel bearing assemblies, water pumps, ice, beer, fishing tackle, and a variety of hardware and electrical items. The steep (17%) concrete launch ramp leads to protected water, there is plenty of parking, and your rig will be watched by guards while you are away. The pleasant La Panga Restaurant has a buffet on Saturdays and Sundays. The Hotel Marina has rooms, a pool, Jacuzzi, and tennis, and books sports fishing, scuba diving, and snorkeling trips.

The Hotel la Concha (formerly the El Presidente) at KM 5 has a restaurant, several bars, a gift shop, and a reservation desk. The sports center offers parasailing, water- and jet skiing, windsurfing, sailing, kayaking, bicycling, scuba diving, and snorkeling, and walk-ins are welcome. The lavish New Year's Night buffet is an experience to remember. There are several coves between the La Concha and the Pichilingue ferry terminal with beautiful sand beaches and small *palapas* offering sodas and snacks. Parque Acuatico el Caimaucito, just to the north of the hotel, has a beach, *palapas*, a restaurant, and a bar, and water sports equipment is for rent.

The ferry terminal is passed at KM 17. The launch ramps north of the ferry terminal can be found by turning left (west) at the *palapa* restaurants at KM 18. The rough concrete ramps (10%) are semiprotected from waves, but there is no security for your rig when you are gone. However, there is adequate parking, and they are the closest ramps to the great fishing and diving to the north and east. At KM 23, a Y is encountered; the left (250°) curves around the north shore of Ensenada Balandra (Sloop Cove), where a beautiful sand beach, *palapas*, and toilets will be found. Watch for herons, egrets, and other marsh birds in the coves in this area.

The right (055°) fork continues for several more kilometers to Playa Tecolote (Owl Beach). The imaginative architecture of Restaurant Palapa Azul is based on a fishing boat. The menu of seafood and Mexican dishes at Restaurant Tecolote seems a bit formal and somewhat expensive for such a setting—no burgers or hot dogs—but the clam chowder is as good as it gets. There is RV parking, a number of *palapas*, some equipped with barbecues, jet ski rentals, public rest rooms, and one of the finest sand beaches in Baja. A small dive shop is under construction. *Jejénes* are sometimes present. Small boats can be launched over the beach, but the place is exposed and waves can make it difficult. Boardsailors will find exposed onshore conditions.

If you can't make a living as a fisherman, just pull the boat up on the beach and go into the restaurant business

■ ■

KM 213 on the Transpeninsular to Ensenada los Muertos and Playa Punta Arena

37.3 miles; use the map on page 149. The waters around Punta Arena de la Ventana (Sand Point of the Window) and Ensenada los Muertos (Deadmen's Cove) are the finest roosterfish grounds in the world, and the channel out to Isla Cerralvo has excellent striped marlin, wahoo, sailfish, and dolphinfish, and merely fine amberjack and grouper. Although there are fish to be caught all year, May through October are the best months, action peaking during the last two weeks of July and the first two in August.

Turn east from the Transpeninsular at KM 213 on to Route 286, signed SJ DE LOS PLANES, 286, about 2.5 miles south of the waterfront in La Paz. There are beautiful views of Isla Cerralvo, Canal de Cerralvo and Bahía de la Ventana at KM 25. At KM 37, a graded, class 1 road leads north to El Sargento (signed).

Off-road trip from KM 37 to El Sargento, with fine beaches, excellent fishing, and boardsailing. See page 232.

At KM 44, enter the town of Los Planes, which has groceries, tire repair, long-distance telephone, doctor, dentist, pharmacy, butcher shop, tortilla factory, and a restaurant. Magnasin is sold from drums at a lot just west of the Supermercado del Pueblo. At KM 46+ the road swings north. At KM 48, pass a small grocery store selling gaso-line from drums, and soon encounter an intersection; take the fork signed ENS DE MUETROS. The pavement ends, the road becoming graded, class 1. Set trip odometer. The road soon curves northeast. At Mile 3.3, note the road north to Playa Punta Arenas (signed), but continue straight ahead. At Mile 5, arrive at Muertos. Diving is only fair, but a huge anchor, metal rails, and ore carts will be found scattered over the bottom, mementos of a silver mining operation in the 1920s. There are numerous boondocking sites along the beach, but no facilities are available. The beach is soft sand with steep cobbles above it, but local fishermen have cleared paths, and it should be possible to launch small trailer boats using sand mats cut from plywood. Cabrilla and pargo are taken in the immediate vicinity, "big fellows" in deeper water. Bob Butler Baja Fishing, based in La Paz, offers *panga* fishing trips out of the bay. Boardsailing conditions are good, with calm water and offshore breezes along most of the shoreline, and waves outside.

For those with adequate boats, outstanding fishing can be found east of Cerralvo at "88-Fathom Bank," 15.5 miles, 040° from the navigation light at Punta Arena. When you are over the bank, the north end of Cerralvo will bear 298°, the south end 246°. This bank gets little traffic from La Paz or hotel boats from East Cape, and the chances are good that you will be alone. The fish are prolific and unsophisticated; there is a record of a triple hookup on a blue marlin, a striped marlin, and a sailfish! If that isn't enough, there are dolphinfish in the 40-pound class, and wahoo to 60.

Cerralvo, 6 miles north of Punta Arena, is the southernmost island in the Cortez. For a number of reasons, both oceanographic and icthyological, many of the fish that migrate in and out of the Cortez pass on either side of the island, often very close to shore. The close-packed schools produce some of the hottest fishing action imaginable, peaking in mid-May and again in October. The fish must be fin-to-fin around Roca Montana, a pinnacle coming within several yards of the surface about 1,200 yards south of Punta Montana. (The rock got its name when the steamer *Montana* struck it in 1874. "Unfortunately" for divers, it did not sink.) Wahoo are often thick offshore. The bottom is crowded with invertebrates, including crown of thorns, sponges, hydroids, gorgonians, cowries, conches, spindle cones, nudibranchs, lobsters, arrow crabs, urchins, sea stars, brittle stars, and several species of coral. There are vast beds of garden eels in sandy areas, and black coral can be seen in deep water. A reef about 1.5 miles north of Punta Montana on the east side of the island also has excellent diving.

To get to Playa Punta Arena, drive to Mile 3.3. Set trip odometer. The road (signed) is class 1, but receives no maintenance. There is a confusing matrix of side roads, so steer for the white lighthouse that can be seen to the north. (At Mile 2.1, there is a road right (east) to Hotel las Arenas, which is closed.) At Mile 3.1, cross evaporation ponds producing salt, and arrive at the beach at Mile 3.4. Punta Arena de la Ventana, on which the lighthouse sits, is low and flat, with a fine sand beach over which small boats can be launched. Boardsailors will find exposed onshore and cross-onshore conditions and good winds. The waters close to the point are shallow out to 1,000 yards or so, with rocky fingers crossing sandy areas, but snorkeling is not too exciting. Boondocking sites can be found just west of the navigation tower. A wrecked ship lies at the water's edge to the west.

■■■■■■■■■■■■■■■■■■■■■■■
KM 110+ on the Transpeninsular to Bahía las Palmas

1 mile; use the map on page 149. A number of RV parks and excellent fishing and boardsailing can be reached by driving east from this point. Set trip odometer.

Mile	Location
0.0	Leave highway at KM 110+, drive east.
0.3	Turn left (000°).
0.4	Encounter a short dirt road leading east to the Hotels Palmas de Cortez and Playa del Sol; follow the signs. Palmas de Cortez has a restaurant, a fleet of sportfishing boats, and a boat launching service, all open to walk-ins. The Playa del Sol has a fleet of cruisers and *pangas*, live bait, rental tackle, and snorkeling gear, and is also open to walk-ins. Vela Highwind Center, located at the Playa del Sol, has boardsailing equipment, instruction, clinics, and high-wind seminars. All facilities are available to walk-ins on a space-available basis. Vela is open from Thanksgiving to early March. Tío Pablo's Restaurant, across from the hotel entrance road, is pleasant, clean, and neat, with humorous art on the walls and fish, Mexican, and steaks on the menu, with a Sunday brunch. There are a few small grocery stores, a post office, and a hardware store in this vicinity.
0.5	Martin Verdugo Trailer Park, class B, has some sites with full hookups, showers, rest rooms, a laundry facility, a restaurant, and a motel, as well as boat charters and a swimming pool. The launch ramp (14%) leads to a sand beach, with very limited maneuvering room, but the park provides a launching service. Juanito's Garden RV Park, across the street, class B, has full hookups, a number of large *palapas*, rest rooms, showers, a laundromat, and bonded boat and trailer storage. The walk to the beach is short, and the park has been surfaced with beach sand, keeping the dust down.
0.9	Playa de Oro RV Resort, class B, is normally

filled by permanents, but a few spaces may be available for transients. It offers rest rooms, showers, laundry, and large shade trees.

1.0	Pavement ends. Class 1 road north to El Cardónal.

Off-road trip from the Las Palmas Resort area to El Cardónal. Turn to page 222.

■■■■■■■■■■■■■■■■■■■■■■■■■
Cabo San Lucas to Todos Santos and Route 1 via Route 19

77 miles; use the map on page 149. Although Route 19 crosses many arroyos, most grades are gentle, and only a few are very long. There are many spur roads to fine beaches and good camping. Birders should keep a sharp eye out, for there are a number of unusual and interesting species.

KM	Location
124	Begin at the intersection of Avenida Cardenas (main drag) and Avenida Morelos. Set trip odometer and drive northwest on Morelos. At Mile 0.7 the road swings left (260°), and at Mile 1.2 you will be at KM 122 on Route 19, the location marked by a large Coca-Cola sign.
102	Marginal class 1 road to Playa las Margaritas. Turn southwest (240°), arrive at the beach in 1.5 miles. Don't attempt to climb the last dune—it is too soft for most vehicles, and driving on the beach is prohibited. There is a large boondocking area behind the dune, and miles of pristine sand beach.
97	**Migriño**. Class 1 road (signed) to a beautiful public beach. Set trip odometer. Turn off the highway and make an immediate right (320°) turn. At Mile 0.1, turn left (255°), arrive at the beach at Mile 0.6. Short beach break, good right point break on the right waves.
90+	Class 1 road southwest (200°) to Boca el Barranco, a sandy boondocking beach. Be sure to camp on high ground, for the water offshore is deep, and the sand beach is exceptionally steep. Waves thus break within yards of the beach, occasionally driving water inland, and many an unsuspecting camper has been flooded out. For these reasons, the surfing is poor, since waves close out in seconds, and swimming is dangerous. The heavy and persistent winds make it a fine heavy-weather boardsailing site.
77	**Plutarco Elías Calles**. Settlement, mechanic, Palapa Marzita with a Mexican menu.

Still up and running, but this surfer at Cerritos has about two more seconds until fate overtakes him

71+   Western end of the Naranjas Road, signed SP. DE LA SOLEDAD.

64   Class 1 road southwest (255°) 1.6 miles to Playa los Cerritos. Public beach, point and beach breaks. As you approach the beach you will encounter a Y; go left (145°) for the abandoned RV park, go right (205°) for a beach. Although the RV park here has no facilities or services, some independent-minded people choose to stop anyway. A small fee is charged, the money going to the town of El Pescadero. Boondocking is available at the sandy beach west of the park.

62   **El Pescadero.** Cafés, groceries, fruit store, tortilla factory, long-distance telephone. The main part of town lies east of the road. The reef and beach breaks in this vicinity consistently produce fine surfing, with steep faces and short, fast rides. Boardsailors also love the place.

Evidence that the wind at Boca el Barranco (blowing from the right) is strong enough for good boardsailing!

59   Class 1 road southwest to San Perdito RV Park (signed). The park is class B, with full hookups, rest rooms, small *palapas*, showers, pool, bar, restaurant serving a limited menu of seafood and Mexican, laundry service, sand beach, good beach break on northwest swells. Playa las Palmas, a fine boondocking beach, can be found by turning southwest at KM 59. Set trip odometer, and turn right (310°) at Mile 0.1 on the class 1 road. At Mile 0.4 take the left (255°), at Mile 1.2 the left (225°), and arrive at the beach at Mile 1.6 (the last 200 yards get a bit bumpy). There are numerous campsites in the palm groves just inland from the beach. The sandy half-mile beach is bounded at each end by rocky headlands.

51+   Todos Santos.

Todos Santos

A pleasant agricultural town, once the site of a Jesuit mission, Todos Santos is now the home of a number of painters, potters, woodcarvers, and other artists, plus a growing community of American expatriate retirees, artists, surfers, and loafers. With its old brick buildings, tranquillity, and leisurely ways, the town is in dramatic contrast to "go-go" Cabo San Lucas. One claim to fame for the place is that it is located directly on the Tropic of Cancer. There are a number of *brujas* (witches), *curanderos* (witch doctors), *sobradoras* (touchers), magnetic therapists, and herbalists whose professional activities in town depend on the Tropic's mystical properties. We are happy to announce that all is well; according to our GPS receiver, the town is only 303 feet too far south, using Room 3 at the Hotel California as a reference.

Restaurant Santa Monica (20) has a menu of seafood, steak, and Mexican, served in a large, open garden setting. Some diners claim that the Santa Monica has the best oysters in North America. Restaurant las Fuentes (19) serves breakfast and Mexican; Casa las Margaritas (24) Mexican and seafood, with a Sunday champagne brunch; Restaurant Carmen's (23) pizza, spaghetti, hamburgers, and "killer salads;" Restaurant Tejitas, at the historic Hotel California (12), is usually open only for breakfast and lunch; Pilar's (18) has a Mexican menu and long-distance telephone; Restaurant Rickles (17) has oysters, shrimp, octopus, clams, and other seafood dishes. Modest Restaurant Costa (6) has a seafood menu; Las Casitas (11) is a bed-and-breakfast hotel; Cafe Todos Santos (5) serves Mexican dishes. Expensive Cafe Santa Fe (8) serves Italian, including antipasto, salad of baby octopus, ravioli, linguini, and fettucini, and is considered by many to be one of the best restaurants in Baja Sur. It is not a Mexican interpretation of an Italian restaurant; with its marble-topped tables and such ingredients as rosemary, olive oil, capers, artichokes, anchovy, mozzarella, ricotta, and cognac, it is emphatically Italian.

Almacenes Grupo Castro (22) has groceries, meats, cold cuts, wine, liquor, fruit, vegetables, and household items, and there is a laundromat (25) and a cinema (4). Perico Azul (2) is an American-run vegetable and fruit market, clean and well taken care of. Tienda ISSSE (15) sells basic food and household items. Cristalina (13) sells ice and purified water. There is a bank (3), and the PEMEX (21) sells MND. A new mini-mall and motel (10) are under construction.

The American-operated book store (7) carries a wide variety of books about Baja and magazines in English, as well as beautiful hand-made tiles forming a map of Baja. Casa Franco (9) offers pottery and handicrafts. Hermanas (14) sells gifts and local art. The Old Casa Cultura (1) has red-dyed skulls of Pericú Indians, pottery, baskets, and other local crafts, historical displays, photos of the old sugar days, and a small collection of rocks and minerals. The remains of an old sugar cane processing mill (16) can be seen. El Molino RV Park, just west of the PEMEX, is filled with permanents. A number of the artists mentioned earlier work out of their homes, and some small shops sell locally made furniture, Mexican clothing, local handicrafts, hand-woven upholstery fabrics, and hand-made pottery. These come and go, and some are open only erratically, so locating them requires some driving around and asking questions.

Fishing trips can be arranged at the Hotel California. The quarry are marlin, wahoo, yellowtail, and dolphinfish, but a trip is not for the faint-hearted, for there is no harbor and boats must negotiate the surf. There is good surf-casting at all local beaches.

There is good boondocking and surfing near town at Playa Pastora. Set trip odometer, drive northwest on Topete on to a graded, class 1 road. Turn left (235°) at Mile 0.2, bear right (250°) at the Y at Mile 0.5, turn left (260°) at the intersection at Mile 0.6, pass two stores at Mile 0.8, and at Mile 0.9 bear right (320°). The road continues northwest, paralleling the beach, about a half mile inland. Pass through a large grove of palms at Mile 4.2. Continue straight ahead until Mile 4.3, where you will turn left (205°), towards the beach. Arrive at Mile 4.5. The beautiful sand beach provides endless boondocking opportunities, and the area is famous among surfers for its point and beach breaks, with surf up to 10 feet or 12 feet on northwest swells.

■■■■■■■■■■■■■■■■■■■■
On Route 19 at Todos Santos

KM	Location
29	Liquor store, Restaurant la Garita (the Sentry Box), with a Mexican menu.
8	Cafeteria, swimming pool, *palapas*.

0	Junction with the Transpeninsular Highway at KM 185.

●●●●●●●●●●●●●●●●●●●●●●●●●●

66 *A token of appreciation?*

The blue-footed boobies seem to have a sense of clan loyalty and are capable of collective action when one of their numbers is threatened. Rob and I had been trolling along a Cortez shore, hoping to catch a yellowtail for supper, but our surface lures had produced nothing. Rummaging through my tackle box, I found a beat-up "Pink Lady," a small plastic paravane that permits trolling at greater depths than lead sinkers allow. I tied the gadget to the end of my line, added a leader, and selected a small chrome spoon for the business end of the rig. The rod bent almost double as we watched the bright-pink gadget disappear into the deep blue water.

As we trolled past a small island a half hour later, there was a commotion ashore, and as if on cue, several dozen boobies took to the sky at the same time. Boobies are plunge-divers, and are somehow able to see food at depths not possible to the human eye, and several began following us, staring intently at a spot about 100 feet aft of the boat. Suddenly, one of the birds dove straight down, hit the water with a splash and disappeared. Seconds later there was a heavy tug on the line and the booby soon popped to the surface with the chrome spoon dangling from its beak. I began reeling in, and Rob stood by with a fish net, but as I pulled, the knot at the front of the paravane let go, and the bird took to the air. The paravane skipped across the surface several times and then dove, jerking the bird to a halt and leaving it thrashing frantically on the surface.

We knew the bird would eventually starve to death unless the lure was removed from its beak, so we slowed the boat down and attempted to catch the line with a gaff. Each time the bird eluded us, taking off and flying a few yards, until coming up short and crash-landing on the water. It quickly became obvious that new tactics were necessary, so we stopped the boat and I went over the side with mask, fins, and snorkel. By that time other boobies had begun to circle over their unlucky friend, and as I got close, they had landed and assembled in an irregular line in front of me. In any other circumstance, boobies may look unconcerned and even a bit comical, but in the water, eye-to-eye, they appeared distinctly hostile. Rather than swimming through them and probably getting a pummeling from their beaks, I made a large circle, trying to approach from the rear. The assembled birds didn't figure out what I was doing at first, but they soon faced me again, and the situation was at an impasse. As I lay on the surface I came up with a plan; I would dive under the birds and grab the Pink Lady, swim underwater as far as I could, come up, and drag the bird to the boat. I hyped up, dove down, leveled out, and grabbed the Pink Lady, and as I broke the surface it seemed that I had outfoxed the birds, which had taken off. The hooked bird, however, had its own ideas, and attempted to swim away, and I knew that I would have to subdue it to avoid breaking its neck. Hand over hand, I pulled on the line, and when the bird was with arm's reach, it began to defend itself, pecking at my hands. As I grabbed it by the feet it aimed at my eyes, but the mask warded off the blows.

Alongside the boat, the bird finally found a weak spot, giving my left ear a painful pinch. Rob caught the bird with the net, I climbed aboard, and with a pair of nippers, we cut the hook away from its beak. As Rob threw the bird up into the air, he said something along the lines of "Awwww, isn't that great! Wow, that must be some kind of grateful bird!" Holding a towel against my bloody ear, I was about to agree, when the bird defecated as it winged away, a statement, perhaps, of what it really thought about the matter, rather than a token of appreciation. ——Walt 99

● ●

Chapter 7

Off-road Baja

Nobody said that some off-road boondocking was going to be like the Marriott

There is a vast network of unpaved roads in Baja, totaling many thousands of miles, some of them providing access to Baja's greatest attractions. Despite the peninsula's celebrated reputation for fourth-rate roads, it is possible to visit some of Off-Road Baja with all but the most cumbersome RVs, and even to drag small tent or travel trailers or small trailer boats into a few locations. In addition, ordinary pickups and four-wheel-drives, freed from the encumbrance of trailers, should be able to handle virtually anything Baja has to offer, and RVers often bring along motorcycles, ATVs, or dune buggies, vehicles eminently suited for off-road forays.

Equipment and preparation

Extra equipment, beyond that described in Chapter 2 needed for all vehicles entering Baja, necessary for off-road forays need not be elaborate or expensive. There are few if any road signs, and there is often a confusing maze of roads, making it is easy to get lost, so an auto compass would be a handy addition. An inexpensive tow line at least 25 feet long with large hooks at each end may prove useful and should cost less than $15 (a shorter line may get the rescuer into the same fix as the "rescuee"). There is a chance of having more than one flat on an off-road trip, and there are no tire repair shops out in the bush, so a push-through patch kit, available in many auto parts stores, may come in handy. Most punctures will be in the tread, and such a kit, together with an air pump, safety glasses, and some water (to locate the leak by means of the bubbles produced), will enable you to repair almost all leaks without even removing the wheel from the vehicle. In addition, you should have adequate water and food along, and every person should have a pair of shoes or boots suitable for long-distance walking—bathroom thongs are the wrong footwear for off-road driving. It goes without saying that the vehicle should be in top mechanical condition, with plenty of rubber left on the tire treads.

The extra equipment described is the minimum needed for short trips over relatively easy unpaved roads. If your trip will be more challenging and you have the mechanical skills to use them, a more elaborate set of tools is in order. Bring three Crescent wrenches, small, medium, and large; Channelock pliers; three ViseGrip pliers, small, medium, and large; a set of socket wrenches, ratchets, adapters, and extension drives; a set of hex wrenches; a ball-peen hammer; a hacksaw with spare blades; a set of various screwdrivers; and a magnetic parts retriever with a ductile aluminum shaft, Sears part number 40766 (this gadget can get into places where ordinary retrievers fear to tread). Beyond this, the sky is the limit—somewhat paranoid off-road travelers bring an elaborate array of tools that would be the envy of the neighborhood garage—impact wrenches, distributor wrenches, multi-meters, taps and dies, gear pullers, and such. However, the chances are excellent that few of these will ever be used—we used to carry a huge assortment, but as the years passed, we learned what is actually used as opposed to what could conceivably be used, and our tool box has gotten lighter every year.

All loose equipment should be wedged or tied in place to avoid chafing and banging. Think small: we put a lead fishing weight and a tube of fishing-reel lubricant together in a tackle box, resulting in a thin gray covering of oil over everything in the box, and a quart of olive oil once got together with 10 pounds of flour, producing a mess of instant pasta. We once opened the back of our pickup to find it filled with a billowy white mass—something had evidently pressed on the top of a can of shaving cream. Use cube ice to fill coolers rather than a block, for the latter can act like a battering ram, reducing the contents to an unrecognizable pulp. The large swinging rear door found on some campers can be forced open by shifting cargo when climbing hills, so lash it closed. Take off all hub caps, since they serve no useful purpose and are easy to lose and hard to replace. Put your cameras, Walkmans, tapes, and CDs in Ziplock bags to avoid a coating of dust that will otherwise be carried into their inner workings and hidden mechanisms. If you plan to drag a trailer, it will be necessary to protect it from flying gravel propelled backwards by the rear wheels of the tow vehicle. This is best accomplished by mud flaps, but some people also attach pieces of plywood in strategic places on the front of the trailer.

Always file a written "flight plan" before you depart. This should describe the vehicle and list everyone aboard, note where you are going, the time (and date if applicable) you expect to return, and the time (and date) the person receiving the plan should "press the panic button" and act to obtain assistance if you fail to return. Leave this with someone you trust, perhaps a fellow RVer who plans to remain in the area, or the manager of the park. If possible, get someone in another vehicle to join the trip, for this solves many problems encountered while traveling on unpaved roads. However, keep an interval of 100 yards or so between vehicles, or the air cleaner in the second vehicle will soon be overwhelmed.

■ The ultimate Baja off-road RV

People go to Baja in all kinds of RVs, ranging from very humble vehicles up to magnificent motor coaches, but Jack and Kay True have assembled the ultimate Baja RV; surely, no more capable vehicle has ever cruised its back roads. Based on a 1964 military Jeep pickup, the rig has an engine that runs on either gasoline or LPG, with plenty of tankage for both. Rock, mud, and sand are no challenge, since the rig has four-wheel-drive, a 9,000-pound electric winch, and a HiLift jack. If a tire needs to be pumped up, the aid of an air compressor can be enlisted. To insure that the desert heat does not cause mechanical problems, it has an auxiliary radiator and a transmission cooler, both equipped with electric fans. To insure that the supply of electricity does not run low, there are three batteries and a solar charging panel. They are never cut off from civilization, for the rig has CB radio, ship-to-shore radio, a cellular telephone, color television, and a stereo system. Creature comforts have not been forgotten, and it has a custom-built camper shell with sleeping quarters, air conditioning, a refrigerator with a freezer, a 150-pound ice chest, a built-in shower, and a Porta Potty. It seems that their rig has everything short of a levitation system to carry it across the potholes on the Transpeninsular.

Road classification

A complex numerical scheme for classifying roads is of little value. An otherwise excellent book on Baja off-road driving published a number of years ago rated unpaved Baja roads on an elaborate 10-point scale, which proved to be meaningless once afield. With our ordinary, heavily loaded, underpowered, two-wheel-drive, three-speed camper van, we negotiated a "class VIII" (four-wheel-drive essential) road without spinning a wheel, but barely survived a class II (family auto possible) section of road.

A good deal of the judgment about roads and roadability is subjective. Years ago, we were creeping along a road in Parque Nacional Constitución de 1857, which we thought to be exceptionally bad. Our camper was slamming and banging along, with lots of wheel-spinning and startling noises. Doubts began to lurk about whether we would arrive at our destination in one piece, when there was a toot from behind; a man in a Chevy station wagon wanted to pass. We once met two senior citizens who had just returned from Parque Natural de la Ballena Gris in a large motor home. The woman was incensed about the condition of the road, 17 miles of graded but sandy washboard, vowing that "We almost didn't make it! We are heading home and shall never return to Baja," forgetting that they did make it, and had seen gray whales and their babies while sitting in their captain's chairs, an experience available in few places in the world.

A lot of the judgment also depends on just how badly you want to get to that secret cove or remote arroyo. Some people get fairly large trailers into some pretty hairy places; a number of years ago, a party dragged a large fifth-wheeler into San Sebastián over almost 15 miles of rather poor, unimproved road. They arrived minus some of the plumbing underneath the trailer, but they had a ball for a month or so once there. A local somehow man-

Jack and Kay True's Ultimate Baja Off-road RV

Jack True

A common problem when trailering off-road

aged to drag a 22-footer into Evaristo, over 46 miles of gravel road containing stretches of loose rock, sharp switchbacks, and grades up to 27%.

Because there are too many variables and too many unknowns to permit a precise classification, unpaved roads in this chapter are described by a simple numerical scale: class 1, 2, and 3. The class assigned is not based on comfort, for some otherwise excellent roads may have stretches of washboard, for instance, but rather the simple ability of the vehicle to get safely down the road. Class 1 unpaved roads are suitable for all but the most ungainly vehicles. There may be occasional soft spots and grades up to 6%, occasionally twice that if the slope is smooth and has good traction. Travel and boat/motorcycle trailers can ordinarily be towed if care is exercised and speed held down. Turning around on class 1 roads is often a problem, since they are almost always one-lane and brush closely borders them. Class 2 roads are suitable for light-to-moderately loaded pickup campers, van conversions, and short, high-clearance motor homes. Such roads may have moderate ruts, sections of sand and loose rock, stream crossings, and grades up to 15%, although short, relatively smooth grades up to 25% providing adequate traction may be encountered. A trailer, even the smallest, is not a good idea unless you are willing to face the consequences, including scratches on its sides due to brush along the way. Class 3 roads are suitable only for rugged, high-clearance vehicles, such as four-wheel-drives and lightly loaded pickups, or small off-road vehicles such as motorcycles, dune buggies, or ATVs. All distances shown are one-way from the point of departure to the final destination stated in the title, and do not include any side trips. Because they offer no significant impediment to RVs, stretches of class 1 roads not over 5 miles long leading to RV parks, restaurants, scenic or historical attractions and the like are contained in Chapters 4 through 6; all other unpaved roads are found in this chapter.

The best advice for drivers of large rigs is to remain on the pavement and do your exploring with your tow vehicle, ATV, dune buggy, or motorcycle. You are the best judge

of the suitability of your rig for travel over unpaved roads, so read this chapter carefully. All drivers should keep in mind that virtually all of Baja's "off-road" roads are civil engineering disasters-in-the-making, with poor or nonexistent culverting, and steep, unstable grades, and a single rainstorm can render one impassable. Do not hesitate to turn back if circumstances dictate. If things go wrong, please do not write unhappy letters to us complaining "You said the road to...was class 2, but we couldn't make it in our pickup 'cause the rain washed out a gully and...."

On the road

Once underway on an unpaved road, keep your speed down; almost all damage on unpaved roads results from excessive speed. A careful driver may get up to 25 miles an hour on the best stretches, and slow down to a crawl on the worst, but over the long run will average about 12 miles an hour. Always wear a seat belt, and keep at tight: hitting the ceiling during a bad bump can do serious damage to your head. In brushy areas, mirrors should be folded back and arms kept inside. If you come to a bad spot, stop, walk the section first. If it begins to rain, turn around and head for the pavement. Although it seems too self-evident to mention, it is unwise to boondock in the bottom of an arroyo: more than one RV has been washed away in a sea of churning water, mud, and boulders.

As you explore Baja's many unpaved roads, watch for changes in the plant communities. Paving a road greatly alters the nearby plant communities. Some plants are opportunistic, colonizing an area only when bulldozers have eliminated the competition. In "civilized" areas, some of the plants you may see are not natives, and were introduced by accident or design, such as tamarisk, which makes a good windbreak; Australian saltbush, which was intended as animal fodder and proceeded to "escape" and become a common plant along the Transpeninsular and in saline areas; or bougainvillea, which is prized for its beauty. Out in the boondocks, look for places where domestic animals have not been present; goats and cows don't or can't eat everything, and what you see in grazed areas is what they left, resulting in distorted plant communities.

Consult your compass regularly. If you come to a fork and don't know which way to go, the best bet usually is to take the one that appears to be the most-traveled. If doubts arise, don't hesitate to ask for directions. Ranchers and farmers usually know a great deal about the local area, and have a name for every canyon, mesa, water hole, and dry lake, and even places where two trails cross, and if you can get close to your destination, they are an invaluable source of information. However, be careful if you are asking directions to a destination more distant, for they often know little or nothing about places even a dozen miles away. Mexicans seem to have no need for maps, and consequently few seem to have any skill at interpreting them, so hunkering over the hood with your battered copy of this book with a local is not likely to produce anything but uncomprehending looks. Based on many attempts, asking Mexican women for travel directions almost always produces either misleading results or nothing at all. The reason seems simple—Mexican women are tied to their homes and families, and simply don't get around as much as the men.

● ●

66 *The worm turns*

We were camped on the beach at Bahía de los Angeles, when two young men drove up and parked nearby. As evening fell, we made a campfire and invited them over for a few beers and some conversation. Their pickup was beauty, a gleaming four-wheel-drive with a chrome roll-bar with "racing" lights on the top, a stereo, air conditioning, and velour upholstery, as well as an electric winch mounted on the front bumper. It was obviously brand-new, and the sales information was still posted proudly in a side window. They were not reluctant to answer a number of admiring questions, but we detected a notable lack of interest in our battered 1975 Chevy van. We swapped stories for an hour or so, but the conversation quickly and inevitably returned to the new pickup—nothing we could say about our 80,000 adventurous miles the length and breadth of Baja in the van elicited the slightest interest. The fire finally died out, and the pair returned to their pickup and broke out sleeping bags and air mattresses. They talked for several minutes, and I distinctly heard the work "junk" muttered three or four times.

Our new neighbors began stirring just after dawn the next morning, and after making breakfast, they came over and said that they were going to try out their new pickup by doing some doughnuts on the beach exposed by a low tide. "I would be careful if I were you; a few inches below the sand, that beach is nothing but mud, very deep and very gooey," cautioned my dad, but they laughed and drove off towards the shore. Things went well at first, but we began to notice that they were going slower and slower, and that the roostertails of mud thrown up by the rear tires were getting higher and higher. Suddenly, they seemed to break through a relatively hard layer of mud, and the pickup came to an abrupt halt. The driver was not going to give up easily, and tried rocking the vehicle, first forward, then backwards, with no apparent effect. One of the men got out, sank up to his ankles in the mud, and struggled to the front of the pickup. He pushed as the driver stepped on the gas, but he succeeded only in covering himself from head to foot in muck. The scene could have been something out of an old Laurel and Hardy movie.

We shouted an offer to help, which was wordlessly refused. The tide was slowly creeping up the beach, and would soon reach the pickup. Finally good sense took precedence over pride, and they asked if we would give them a hand. We detached our trailer and my dad backed the van onto the beach as far as he dared. Our tow line was too short to bridge the gap between the vehicles, and since the front of the pickup faced the water and the bottom of the chassis was sitting on mud, their winch could not be put to use. A man in the gathering crowd of locals gave a shout and ran off, to return several minutes later with a line. The two lines together proved to be a yard short, and several of the locals began to speculate as to how many feet of salt water would cover the pickup at high tide. In a flash of inspiration, I remembered that we had a set of snow chains aboard that would bridge the gap. With 8 or 10 people pushing on the van, the makeshift tow line tightened, and the van leaped up and down as the wheels gained and lost traction. Slowly it got a foothold, and the pickup began to creep backwards out of the bottomless depths of mud. Within a few minutes it was on hard ground, safely out of the reach of the tide.

*Once they were free, the two men thanked us quietly, steadfastly avoiding eye contact. Looking like soldiers from a World War I trench battle, they stripped down to their shorts and T-shirts, climbed into their previously pristine and now experienced Baja vehicle, and drove off without saying another word. There was a lesson to be learned: four-wheel-drives are great, but the people driving them often come to believe they are invincible, which they are not—although they don't get stuck very often, when they do, they **really** get stuck.* 99
——*Michael*

● ●

■ ■ ■ ■ ■ ■ ■ ■ ■ ■ ■ ■ ■ ■ ■ ■ ■ ■ ■
KM 47+ on the Transpeninsular near Santo Tomás to La Bocana and Puerto Santo Tomás

Graded class 1, 19.8 miles; use the map on pages 86–87. This trip will take you to the first relatively unspoiled fishing south of the border, as well as excellent diving. Turn west at KM 47+, set trip odometer. The road reaches La Bocana (The Mouth, apparently referring to the river, not the local *delegado*) at Mile 17.1, which has RV parking and a beach.

The road then swings north after climbing a short, steep (17%) concrete road. For future reference, note the road headed up the hill at Mile 19.3. Arrive at Puerto Santo Tomás at Mile 19.8. Punta Santo Tomás diverts the California Current and creates a circular countercurrent, pulling up cool bottom water containing nutrients and producing a rich underwater environment and limited visibility in the bay. In spite of local commercial fishing activity, Bahía Santo Tomás has the first relatively unspoiled fishing areas encountered south of the border, and the vast underwater plain offshore can provide a fine mixed bag of ling cod, calico bass, ocean whitefish, yellowtail, barracuda, bonito, and several species of rock fish and flatfish.

Pangas can be rented at Puerto Santo Tomás, and a steep (21%) concrete launch ramp runs into a small cove, requiring high tides and calm conditions. Parking is usually no problem. Excellent fishing is found in "The Hole," located due west of an abandoned concrete building foundation on a finger-like point a mile north of Punta Santo Tomás, where so-

Divers working Baja's Pacific coast for sea urchins and abalone

nar shows a steep-sided depression at 150 feet. Fishing varies quite a bit from week to week and year to year, but visitors who frequent the area often use superlatives like "outstanding" and "wow" during the good seasons.

Rocas Soledad, 1.25 miles west of the point, has sheer walls, caves, crevices, pinnacles, abundant wildlife, and excellent visibility. The deep blue of surrounding depths, red urchins, yellow and red encrusting sponges, and the largest specimens of Pacific green anemone on the Pacific coast, with discs that can expand to 14 inches, provide a field day for underwater photographers. Because of their coating of orange-hued encrusting sponge, it is easy to spot large rock scallops, and abalone hide in deep crevices. Schools of ocean whitefish and sheephead often approach within photographic range. Depths of over 100 feet prevail close to the rocks, but a shelf extending 40-150 yards to the south makes it possible to anchor in 40 to 70 feet.

Almost total solitude can be found on Bahía Soledad's (Lonely Bay) south shore, accessible by a class 3 road going north from Mile 19.3. The road gets no maintenance, and has loose rock, ruts, and slopes to 21%. A prominent sea cave on the western end of this shore shows evidence of a large hidden chamber: heavy surf results in booming repercussions as air and water are expelled, producing a violent horizontal geyser hitting the opposite wall. The bay is exposed and shallow, with depths of 20 feet to 60 feet. Thick kelp beds harbor opaleye, kelp bass, and dense schools of fry, and the beaches along the eastern margin of the bay offer outstanding corbina fishing almost year-around.

• •

❝ *Divers of the deep*

Baja California is home to a large number of professional divers, most engaged in the abalone and sea urchin fisheries along the Pacific coast. The most common boats

are pangas, *equipped with shallow water dive rigs, which consist of a cast-off refrigeration compressor driven by a gas engine, a volume tank made from a stainless steel beer keg, about 200 feet of hose, and a battered scuba second-stage regulator.*

The crew is normally three men: a diver, a hose tender, and an oarsman. The diver, equipped with extra weight, goes down with a mesh bag tied to a line from the boat, and walks or crawls along the bottom. The boat is not normally anchored, and the oarsman follows the diver's progress. When the boat crew feels a tug on the line, they pull up the basket full of abalone or urchins, dump it, and return it to the bottom. Urchins are opened with a tool that looks like a giant pair of pliers, except that they have spade-like blades on the end and open when the handles are squeezed together. Using a tablespoon, the gonads, the valuable "meat" of the urchins, are flicked into a bucket. The remains are dumped over the side, causing a commotion of small fish. The species of abalone taken include blue, black, green, and red.

Most abalone is canned, and the urchin meat is processed and flown fresh to Japan, where it is prized for its aphrodisiac properties. In 1995, urchin meat averaged almost $54/pound on the Tokyo wholesale market, and on the retail market 2 to 3 times that. Unfortunately, Mexico is competing with California, Oregon, Washington, British Columbia, Chile, North Korea, Iceland, Russia, Hong Kong, Norway, China, Australia, New Zealand, the Philippines, and Japan, so the three men receive relatively little for a hard day's work, most of the money ending up in the hands of processors and wholesalers. In addition, Mexico is over-harvesting the fishery, and the catch shipped to Japan has declined precipitously.

During a recent trip to Japan, we bought some uni,

as it is called there, as well as a sauce recommended by the shop proprietor. Back in our hotel, neither my mom nor I were brave enough to try the awful-looking substance, and my dad found it to be foul, slimy, and squishy, tasting approximately like rotten seagull innards soaked in iodine and then broiled over a fire of old innertubes.

There are fewer professional divers in the Cortez, since abalone and edible sea urchins are absent. A number of years ago, large numbers of almejas voladores *(flying clams, actually a species of scallop) were found in Bahía de los Angeles and a fishery was established, drawing divers from all over Baja. The beds were quickly wiped out, to the point that it seemed that they got the last male and the last female. A similar approach has been taken towards the clams and scallops of Bahía Concepción, with similar results. Despite a terrible smell and a less-than-appetizing appearance, to put it mildly, the lowly sea cucumber can bring as much as $20,000 a ton in Japan, and divers are now working the Cortez, diligently trying to meet the demand. We saw dried sea cucumber for sale in Malaysia, but even my dad, who will try almost anything once, was not brave enough to sample it. ——Michael* **99**

• •

■ ■ ■ ■ ■ ■ ■ ■ ■ ■ ■ ■ ■ ■ ■ ■ ■ ■ ■ ■
KM 51 on the Transpeninsular near Santo Tomás to Punta San José

Class 2, 25.4 miles, side trip to points south; use the map on pages 86–87. This trip will take you to an area having many small coves and beautiful beaches, almost always deserted. The waves and sloping volcanic shelf rock often make it a hard place to launch a boat, but you might try some beach-casting. The area is popular with surfers.

Two-tenths of a mile southeast of the PEMEX (MN), turn south, and 200 yards later turn right (200°) onto the graded road seen winding up the hills to the west. At KM 23, a road (signed) heads south to Punta Cabras (Goats Point), which should be noted for future use. Turn northwest at the junction at KM 30, arrive at the lighthouse at Punta San José at KM 41. Ammonites can be seen frozen in the sedimentary cliffs throughout the area. An interesting scavenger and fossil beach is found below the first arroyo north of the lighthouse, but access is a problem, since it may not be possible to follow the beach north around the point. Bring a knotted rope to allow you to get in and out.

To visit Punta Cabras and Punta San Isidro, go back to the junction at KM 23, set your trip odometer, and take the class 2 road south. (The old coast road south from the junction at KM 30 reaches Rancho San Juan de las Pulgas (Saint John of the Fleas Ranch) in 3 miles, where a difficult stream crossing may cause problems for those not in four-wheel-drives.) At Mile 7.7, arrive at Punta Cuesta del Gato (Cat Grade Point). The coast to the north and south is broken by a series of volcanic points, where spectacular blowholes expel great jets of water, and many small coves and beaches provide fine beach-casting. A sandy cove at Mile 8.3 has easy access. Punta Cabras is reached at Mile 10.8, and Punta San Isidro at Mile 14.8. At Mile 16.6 arrive at Castro's Fishing Place, described on page 182.

■ ■
KM 126+ on the Transpeninsular near Colonet to San Antonio del Mar

Class 1, 7 miles; use the map on pages 86–87. Turn west, set trip odometer. At Mile 4.5 a road is encountered running north; continue straight ahead, reaching Tony's Camp at Mile 7. There is RV parking, and the beach is beautiful, offering beachcombing, hiking, and excellent surf fishing, although the ambiance at Tony's Camp leaves a lot to be desired.

■ ■
KM 140+ on the Transpeninsular south of Colonet to Parque Nacional Sierra San Pedro Mártir

Class 1, 59.6 miles; use the map on pages 86–87, and the accompanying contour map. Padre Baegert complained, "There is no semblance of a forest in [Baja] California, there is also no trace of a meadow or of a green turf," but as you drive upward to the park you will pass through a fascinating biological transition that will prove him wrong on all counts. Leaving the familiar chaparral of the lower regions, you will first enter a pinyon-juniper zone, with pines, junipers, and oaks, then a zone where the dominant trees are Coulter, Jeffrey, lodgepole, and sugar pine, incense cedar, white fir, and quaking aspen. The rare San Pedro Mártir cypress, endemic to this area, is found in a few isolated locations, the largest known individual having a circumference of 15 feet. Hard freezes are common in winter, and snow sometimes blankets higher elevations. Can this be Baja?

The road is normally well-maintained and can handle virtually all RVs. However, there are fairly steep and lengthy grades, and visits with large motor homes and large trailers are probably not a good idea—you know your own vehicle best. Set trip odometer and turn east. At Mile 5.7 pass through the village of San Telmo, and at Mile 11.4 through a settlement where groceries and sodas can be purchased. A right turn at Mile 30.1 (signed) will take you to historic Rancho San José. Founded in 1907 by the Meling family, this 10,000-acre cattle ranch has guest facilities and offers horseback riding, swimming, bird watching, hiking, and trout fishing, plus mule trips to the high country.

Your arrival at the park entrance at Mile 47.4 may be something of an occasion; during our last trip we seemed to be the only visitors in the entire 170,000-acre park. Firearms and motorcycles are prohibited, and fires must be confined to the concrete fireplaces available in some locations.

Since much of the park is above 6,000 feet, temperatures average 15° cooler than surrounding lowlands. Best of all, you are almost certain to have the silence needed to enjoy this majesty, with no RV generators or rock music to be heard.

Reset trip odometer at the park entrance. At Mile 9.2 the road passes Vallecitos meadow, a pleasant place to spend a day or two. Note the road headed southeast at Mile 9.9 for later reference. At Mile 12.2, a gate may prevent further travel by vehicle. Park and hike up the road, where a number of dome-topped buildings will be encountered, which house astronomical telescopes, the largest an 84-inch reflector. No scheduled public tours are offered, but supervisory personnel may be willing to show you around. Views of the lowlands and the Cortez to the east are wonderful.

The observatory was not located in the park by accident, stargazing conditions are usually superb, and city dwellers are in for some surprises. The night sky in most cities, with its load of pollutants, is gray or a musty blue at best, and the horizons often bright with the loom of man-made light. Although children from time immemorial have believed that there are "millions" of stars to be seen, the number is actually about 300 in the average city. In this park, however, things are very different. The sky is almost black and free from loom, and displays an almost uniform shade from di-

rectly overhead to the horizon. The number of stars to be seen increases 10-fold, to about 3,000. Unknown to most urban dwellers, the Big Dipper's seemingly empty bowl actually brims with a half dozen stars, and the Milky Way will be seen in unexpected glory. At night, starlight can be so bright that it produces shadows, and you can sometimes see a line of light creeping along tree trunks during moonrise. Other than the road, a cow or two, possible jetliner lights in the sky, and, of course, you and your vehicle, this is what Mother Nature intended.

A pair of ordinary binoculars will let you see Saturn's rings. If you are in the park for a few nights, you can see the evolution of one of the strangest sights in the nighttime sky, visible even to the naked eye. First, locate the Big Dipper. Draw an imaginary line from the star forming the "bottom" of the dipper on the handle side and the star at the "top" of the dipper on the side away from the handle, and note the apparent distance between these stars. Proceed along this line (away from the handle) a little over five times that distance—use two fingers as a gage. This will put you in the Constellation Perseus. Look for the second brightest star in this neighborhood, which is Algol, almost directly on the line. Algol is a twin variable star, consisting of two bodies which whirl closely together in a frantic dance, a fantastic

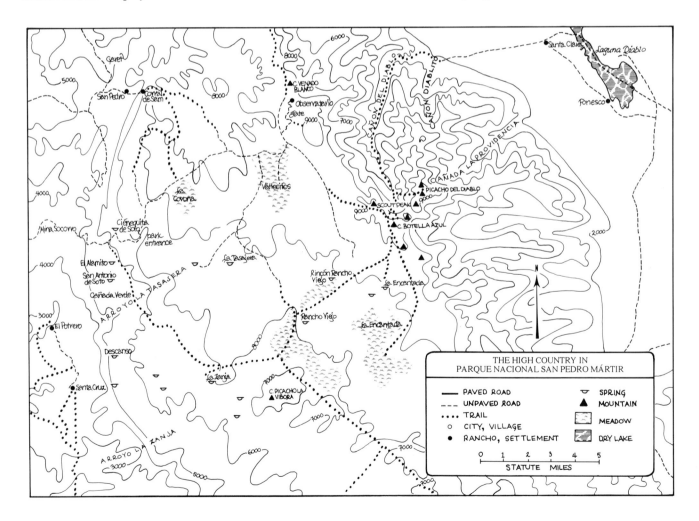

analogy to the square-dancer's "swing your partner." Every 2 days, 20 hours, and 49 minutes, Algol looses much of its light when the two bodies go into eclipse, a sight unknown to those who live their lives submerged in a perpetually hazy sea of smog and looming lights.

Three year-around streams in the park, San Rafael, La Zanja (The Ditch), and San Antonio, have a surprise—trout. The climate would seem too hot and the flows of water too low to support them, but there are indeed trout, a few running to 14 inches. A heat-tolerant species closely related to rainbow, they were identified by naturalist E.W. Nelson in 1905. Originally found only in Arroyo San Antonio, they were transported by mule-back into the other streams in the 1930s. In 1937, some were taken to a hatchery in Redlands, California in an attempt to determine if they could be established in the US, where their ability to withstand heat would be a valuable asset. However, the hatchery and all its fish were wiped out in a flood the next year. Another attempt at an Oregon hatchery failed when a frog climbed into a pipe and caused the pond to drain.

Picacho Diablo is the highest mountain in Baja California. A massive, nearly bare, double peak of pale granodiorite, it rises to 10,154 feet and 10,152 feet from the escarpment that borders the San Pedro Mártir plateau just outside the eastern edge of the park. From October to May the peak is often covered with snow, and because it can be seen from over 75 miles away, it presents a strange spectacle to travelers driving south from torrid Mexicali. The peak was first climbed in 1911, and many hundreds have succeeded since then.

The park offers fine hiking. The trails shown on the accompanying contour map have never been surveyed, and their locations are approximations only. Most are pleasant and undemanding, passing through open, park-like country with little or no brush-busting and no major changes in elevation. Since there are no trail signs, it is easy to become confused, and you must carry a compass and a map. Picacho Diablo can be seen from many high points, forming a useful landmark. Do not expect to be rescued by rangers or passersby, and if you become lost, head directly for the Observatory Road; going in any other direction may result in difficulties. The best time for a hike is spring, when the weather is still cool, nature is in bloom, there is plenty of water, and the fire danger is low.

The most rewarding hike in the park provides smashing views of Picacho Diablo and Cañon del Diablo. Hikers should be in reasonably good condition and have at least a half day available. A class 2 road leads southeast (125°) from Mile 9.9. Set trip odometer. Look for a concrete block shed at Mile 0.4. About 80 yards past the shed you will encounter a Y; take the left (080°) fork. At Mile 2.1, pass between two pines close to the road, the left one having a large scar due to missing bark. In about 200 more yards, pass a large aspen on the left, very close to the road. At Mile 2.25 arrive at the parking place. There is little else to distinguish this spot, so

Ted Robertson and Wayne Campbell explore Parque Nacional Sierra San Pedro Mártir on a brisk spring morning

make sure you have followed the preceding directions exactly; if the road starts to climb and rough stuff is encountered, you have gone too far. Park and start hiking southeast up the arroyo, following its meanders. Most of the route is well ducked (ducks are small piles of stone placed to mark the trail). Set watch. At Minute 30, the route leaves the arroyo and turns northeast at a large cairn to avoid dense brush. At Minute 45, you will be back in the arroyo, near a large grove of aspen. A trail leads from this point a half mile north to the rim of the escarpment, where there is a great view of Cañon del Diablo.

Those with the time and energy may wish to continue on to "Scout Peak." Set watch. From the aspen grove, skirt its south margin, hiking east to a low saddle. Sight 022° and note the striking orange-colored knob rising about 400 feet above the surrounding terrain. Cross the saddle, drop into the arroyo, and continue east on its south side, which is again well ducked. At Minute 75, arrive at a point just south of Scout Peak. The climb to the top of the 9,352-foot peak will be rewarded with splendid scenery.

Another excellent hike will be found by driving towards the observatory. Just short of the gate at Mile 12.2, in the vicinity of a horseshoe bend in the road, a trail will be found heading east. Park and set watch. The trail follows a moderate upgrade until Minute 30. In the midst of a sizable aspen grove, look for a trail heading north to steeper terrain. Follow this trail, and after some rock scrambling, you should be on top of a small knob. The yawning canyon below is spectacular.

The trail descriptions and accompanying map should be adequate for the three hikes just described, and the map useful for casual day-hikes elsewhere in the central part of the park. Those considering lengthy, multi-day backpacking expeditions, climbing Picacho Diablo, or visiting the trout streams should refer to Peterson 1995 and Robinson 1983.

■■■■■■■■■■■■■■■■■■■■■■■■■■■■■■■
KM 142 on the Transpeninsular north of Camalú to Punta San Telmo

Class 2, 6.7 miles; use the map on pages 86–87. The turn is hard to find because of missing KM markers, but it is located 0.75 mile south of the Parque road. Set trip odometer. Turn north at Mile 4.8, and arrive at the point at Mile 6.7. Known to surfers as "Cuatro Casas," this place has fine right point and reef breaks. Low cliffs at the point are no problem, and the beaches are pebble and sand with some shelf rock.

■■■■■■■■■■■■■■■
El Rosario to Punta Baja

Class 2, 10.3 miles, side trip to Agua Blanca, class 2, 7 miles; use the map on pages 96–97. Bottom fishing in Bahía del Rosario can be excellent. Cartoppers and inflatables can be launched off the beach, and *pangas* are for hire, but there is no adequate place to launch trailer boats.

Starting in "downtown" El Rosario, where the Transpeninsular takes a 90° bend, set trip odometer and turn southwest. Take the left (164°) fork just before Mile 0.1, and cross the river at Mile 0.9. This crossing is flat and sandy, and is usually no problem, but look before you leap. Take the right (230°) fork at Mile 1.0, and at Mile 1.5 look on the right for the ruins of Dominican Misión el Rosario (in operation 1774-1832, but these buildings date from 1802). At Mile 2.5 come to a fork and continue straight ahead (245°). Turn left (160°) at the fork at Mile 2.9, signed PUNTA BAJA, and arrive at the settlement at Mile 10.3.

The coast between the mouth of the river and the point has been the scene of a number of shipwrecks, the largest being the wooden steamer *Union*, which hit a reef in calm weather early in the morning of July 5, 1851. The crew and passengers got ashore safely, together with $270,000 in gold coin. When the passengers returned to San Diego the story came out: the crew had celebrated the Fourth of July so enthusiastically that the helmsman was unable to steer. Gold and silver coins still wash up occasionally, probably from baggage left aboard.

Alcohol figured prominently in another wreck, but this time it was the rescuers, not the crew, who had the hangovers; in 1978, the vessel *Noroeste* went ashore with a cargo of 1,000 cases of Tecate beer, leading to a legendary week-long toot in the tiny settlement.

A side trip to the small fishing camp of Agua Blanca (White Water) can be reached by taking the left (228°) fork at Mile 2.5, following the class 2 road for about 7 miles. Although it is more exposed than Punta Baja, the flat sand beach is an excellent place to launch a cartopper or an inflatable, and *pangas* may be available for hire. Pick your weather carefully, for boats have overturned in the surf. Surrounding beaches provide outstanding beach-casting for spotfin and yellowfin croaker, to the point that you may not be able to eat them all.

The island to the south is San Jerónimo, which has a fish camp on its south end. Three miles south of the island is Arrecife Sacramento (Sacramento Reef), which has been described as a "seething cauldron of Hell." Since its shallow reaches are exposed to ocean swells, the reef is nothing but white water in anything short of a flat calm. Many vessels have been wrecked while blindly coasting north or south along the 20-fathom curve, most notably the big American sidewheel steamer *Sacramento*. Carrying a treasure of gold and silver coins and bullion, she was steaming up the coast in December, 1872, when her deck officer smelled kelp. It was too late to do anything, and the ship crashed on the reef. The passengers and crew made it safely to Jerónimo and were rescued. The gold? Newspapers of the day claimed every penny of the treasure was recovered, variously reported as between $335,000 and $2 million, but shipping and insurance companies had a strong self-interest in issuing such proclamations. Today authorities differ, but local sea-urchin divers may reluctantly show Polaroid photos of small bars, which they claim to be gold taken from the wreck of the *muy rico yate* (very rich yacht) *Goodwill*, lost in 1969. However, the location they describe is that of the *Sacramento*, and they seem to know nothing about how the reef got its name.

A dive on the reef will be an experience to remember. Although a place of danger and death to ships and sailors, it pulsates with underwater life, and biologists have termed the reef a "biological miracle." The most outstanding feature is the dense growth of surf grass, with blades up to 12 feet long, forming homes for great numbers of horn sharks. Gray sponges reach huge proportions, and the growths of bryozoans are the most prolific on the Pacific coast. Big black sea bass and large lobsters are common, especially on the eastern margins of the reef.

● ●

❝ Stubborn

The Baja RVer's motto should be "remain relentlessly flexible," for it does not pay to be too single-minded, as the following short history will demonstrate.

Many years ago, my dad and I had planned to do some fishing and diving at a secret beach south of the tiny fishing camp of Agua Blanca. Our van was heavily loaded with a boat, several outboard motors, fishing gear, and a diving compressor, and we were towing a 15-foot travel trailer. We had explored the area on a motorcycle several years earlier, and although the road looked bad, there seemed to be a chance that a trailer could be dragged to the beach.

As night fell we turned west from El Rosario, and met our first challenge at the river crossing. The water was only ankle-deep and the sand seemed hard, so my dad shifted down to first gear and pressed the accelerator. The van began to bog down almost immediately, and I looked out the window and yelled that the sand was almost up to the rims. We knew that we had to keep moving, but our speed kept falling: 5 miles an hour, 4, 3, 2, 1 and then almost nothing. The spinning wheels would occasionally dig through the sand to bedrock and the rear end of the van would leap up and down, then they would lose traction again and the engine would race wildly. Finally, after several minutes of almost imperceptible progress, we gained dry ground on the opposite side.

We had successfully met the first challenge of our adventure, but this minor triumph was to be our only good luck for the next three days. Fifty yards from the crossing we encountered a shallow ditch running across the road. A sign had been posted, proclaiming DESVIACIÓN *(detour), but it neglected to inform travelers just where traffic was being detoured to. The left side of the road was an embankment and the right was blocked by a fence, so we couldn't get around the area, and that left only two options, give up or go straight ahead. No way were we going to give up; we were here for adventure! As we decided what to do, a pickup drove past us and crossed the ditch; an earlier traveler had laid the rusted tailgate off an old truck across the ditch, and trundled a large rock into the ditch the appropriate distance away. Slowly pulling ahead, all went well at first, the right wheels over the tailgate, the left over the rock, and finally the van was across. However, there was a lurch and a crash as the rock rolled under the weight of the left trailer wheel. Cursing, we dug out a ramp in the side of the ditch, which the trailer wheel managed to negotiate after a good deal of engine racing and the pungent smell of burning clutch. Some of the plumbing under the trailer had been rearranged, but nothing was serious.*

After several miles, we turned onto a road consisting of little more than wheel ruts. Things seemed to be going well, until we came to a series of rocky areas. We had enough clearance, but to avoid bottoming out, it was necessary to drive very slowly, at nothing more than a crawl. With a four- or five-speed or an automatic transmission this is no problem, but with a three-speed stick shift, the minimum velocity is too fast, and it becomes necessary to slip the clutch. The van was again filled with the smell of clutch, but we gave no thought of turning back. A mile later the road began to climb, and the clinometer read 6%, 8%, and then 10%. With a four-

or five-speed, such grades are not difficult; in low gear, the engine can maintain high RPMs and transmit plenty of power to the rear wheels, but with a three-speed, the only way to keep up engine speed is to slip the clutch. We stopped to roll down the windows to let the smoke out, but we agreed; we are going to make it to the beach, no matter what! As the clinometer approached 12%, I noticed that my dad was having less trouble in maintaining engine RPMs, despite the increasing grade. The reason quickly became apparent as we slowed to a standstill and the engine kept running; the clutch was slipping.

As any child knows, a temper tantrum often gets quick results, but our diatribes against the makers of Chevy clutches had no effect. It already had 60,000 hard miles on it, so it wasn't too surprising that it wasn't up to the task we were imposing on it. There was nothing we could do to make the rig move uphill, and we could not go sideways, so this left only one direction—we had to use gravity to back out of our predicament. It was pitch-black, and after an hour of yelling instructions back and forth and several close calls with steep slopes, we got to a place where the road was level and just barely wider than the combined width of the van and trailer. We detached the trailer and inched the van past it. Supper was somber that night.

There was still a small amount of clutch left, so at four the next morning we unloaded the boat and all unnecessary weight from the van, and my dad headed north for San Diego, while I stood guard at the trailer.

When he returned, he told me what had happened. He managed to get across the ditch, but he knew that the van would never be able to make the river crossing if it started to bog down. The clutch didn't begin to slip until the van was up to 30, and he made the crossing; apparently the high speed did not allow the tires enough time to bog down. He got up all the speed he could before the 14% upgrade on the Transpeninsular north of El Rosario, but about a halfway up, the engine began to race and he slowly came to a halt, just as the slope was leveling out; so close but yet so far! He spent the next half hour dejectedly trying to figure out how to make the last 100 yards. A 18-wheeler passed with its horn blaring, and he had almost decided to return to El Rosario, when he made one last try; with the clutch slipping badly, he inched ahead, and a few minutes later he finally gained the top of the mesa and made San Diego by nightfall.

He was at the Chevy dealership first thing the next morning, but it proved to be closed since it was Sunday. The following morning a diagnosis was available: the clutch plate was fried to a crisp, the pressure plate warped, and the throwout bearing was a goner. The service manager looked dumfounded and exclaimed "Shooweee Bob! What in the hell caused all this? That clutch is the worst-looking mess I ever saw. There must'a been a quart of sand in the clutch housing." My dad's reply was simple: "Stubbornness, just plain stubbornness."

He arrived back at the trailer late the third night, and over a supper of cold Kentucky Fried Chicken imported from

San Diego, I described what had happened while he was away. I had hiked the road towards the secret beach, and a quarter mile past the fatal slope had found that rains had cut a deep ravine across the road. All our efforts and problems had not been in vain! At least we had an answer to our question; no, it was not possible to drag a trailer to the secret beach. This experience, together with many others over the years, have been reflected in the class ratings assigned to unpaved roads throughout the book—we learned the hard way just what the limits were. ——Michael **"**

● ●

■ ■
KM 144 on the Transpeninsular east of El Rosario to El Mármol

Class 1, 9 miles, side trip to El Volcán, class 2, 4 miles; use the map on pages 96–97. You should plan to spend a few hours exploring El Mármol (The Marble), the fascinating site of an abandoned onyx quarry. Discovered about 1883, the deposit is about 3,000 feet by 1,200 feet in area and averages about 40 feet thick. About 1900, an American company, the Southwest Onyx and Marble Company, still in business in San Diego, began quarrying the stone. Wells were dug, homes, a store, and a jail were built, and the new settlement soon had a population of several hundred people. A schoolhouse was eventually constructed of unpolished blocks of onyx 30 inches thick, the only one in the world.

A gin-pole was erected to move the heavy blocks. A large timber perhaps 40 feet long was held in a vertical position by guy wires anchored into the ground, and another pole was hinged to its base and held up by a guy from the top. The miners used air drills to split the stone into large rectangular blocks, which were then lifted by the gin-pole onto mule-drawn wagons for the 53-mile trip to Puerto Santa Catarina. Deep ruts that formed after rains made travel slow and difficult, so the workers would fill them in with onyx chips, creating another El Camino Real of sorts. At Catarina, the blocks

A study in contrasts; while sitting in the window of the old onyx school house, Michael studies mathematics with a Math-And-Speak machine

were barged out from a dock to waiting ships, which carried them north to the US. High technology came to the operation when the wagons were replaced by trucks with solid rubber tires.

Beautifully veined and subtly colored by impurities into shades of brown, tan, red, and yellow, El Mármol onyx was also prized for its lack of cleavage planes, insuring that the stone would not split as it was cut and polished. In its time, El Mármol provided a major portion of the world's supply of this valuable stone. Craftsmen fashioned it into products ranging from facades for churches, banks, and fine homes to knickknacks and souvenirs. A 3-by-3-by-7 foot block was quarried to make a $10,000 bathtub for actress Theda Bara.

The mine was officially called the New Pedrara Mine, but the settlement soon became known as Brown's Camp, after the mine's American superintendent (whose son later became superintendent). It served as a rest and supply stop for generations of Baja travelers, including adventurers Phillip Townsend Hanna and Howard Hale, and writer Erle Stanley Gardner. The exciting tales told by these men were told and retold by the citizens for generations, but there were incidents at the quarry that gave them a lore of their own. Old men still tell of the time a rare hail storm struck; everyone stood enthralled as hundreds of onyx slabs created a magic carillon of music. Once, the miners were driving wedges into a slab six feet thick, and when it cracked they discovered a small crystal-lined chamber. Carefully enlarging its entrance, they peered in to see a tiny frog living inside. Completely transparent, every bone and blood vessel in its body could be seen. It had apparently been able to live on a tiny trickle of water and the few insects that blundered by, but it finally grew to a size too large to escape, and its palace became a prison. Out of pity, the miners gave it freedom, but the hot sun killed it quickly and the corpse soon turned to dust.

The coming of plastics and modern process building materials doomed the mine, and by 1958 the settlement was deserted. The homes have disappeared, their scarce lumber having been appropriated for more important uses. In spite of its heavily buttressed walls, even the famous schoolhouse is slowly crumbling. However, the place has not been completely forgotten. Occasionally, an open semitrailer will pull in and a crew of laborers will noisily load it with onyx slabs cut years ago. By sundown it will be headed north for an importer in North Hollywood, and the silence returns. In 1983, someone began making repairs to the schoolhouse, for reasons unknown, and the work has continued sporadically to date. A visit to the graveyard shows that someone still remembers; some of the tombstones have been decorated with plastic flowers.

Visitors should not miss a visit to nearby Arroyo el Volcán (Volcano Gully), for here can be seen the process by which Mother Nature creates onyx. The stone is a sedimentary carbonate, a family that includes marble and travertine. Special conditions must be met if onyx is to form. A slowly moving flow of water must pass over beds of calcium carbonate. To dissolve this mineral, the water must be cold, contain dissolved carbon dioxide, and be pressurized. To provide the colors desired in onyx, the water must pick up iron and manganese, which partially replace some of the calcium. It must then vent towards the surface, where the reduction in pressure causes the water to lose some of its carbon dioxide, thus reducing its ability to carry its dissolved mineral load. The water must then reach the surface in an arid area, where runoff will not contaminate the deposit with sand and debris. If these conditions are met, fine onyx will be deposited in layers, sometimes at a rate as slow as 500 to 1,000 years per inch.

The results of this process can be seen in Arroyo el Volcán. A half dozen crystal-clear bubbling springs are depositing a blanket of new onyx over a quarter acre or so. The water tastes acidic and faintly sweet. Immediately to the south a rounded, cone-shaped dome of onyx about 30 feet high graphically shows how a spring laid down successive layers: the small spring at its top deposited minute layers of onyx around the vent, causing the dome to rise to its present height. Freshly formed onyx is often covered by sediments, remaining hidden for millennia, but a thick layer that has been exposed by erosion lies just to the south of the dome.

If you are lucky, really lucky, you may witness the only geyser known in Baja. About once a month, a 60-foot plume of gas and water spouts into the air for a few minutes. The residents of Brown's Camp used it as a calendar; its trembling and noise meant that another month had passed.

To reach El Mármol, set trip odometer and turn northeast at KM 144 onto the class 1 graded road. Just past the corral and windmill at Mile 0.9, take the right (045°) fork, and arrive at the site at Mile 9.0. For the side trip to the El Volcán onyx dome area, sight 040° from the schoolhouse and note the class 2 road in the distance. Set trip odometer. At Mile 4.0 the road crosses the arroyo; the spot will be obvious. Park and hike up the arroyo for

Victor Cook examines the onyx dome at El Volcán

about 15 minutes.

■■■■■■■■■■■■■■■■■■■■■■■■■

KM 38+ on the Transpeninsular north of Rosarito to Santa Rosalillita

Side trips to surrounding areas, class 1 (one 17% upgrade coming out), 9.6 miles; use the map on pages 104–105. This area is the best boondocking location in the vicinity, and has excellent fishing, surfing, and boardsailing.

Turn west at KM 38+, set trip odometer. Note the side road at Mile 8.1 (but don't turn), and arrive at the beach at Mile 9.6. The road is capable of handling fairly large RVs, and there is plenty of parking along the beach and in the dunes north of the point. There is a small grocery store in the village, and limited supplies of gasoline and water may be available.

Boardsailors like the bay for its strong and reliable afternoon winds, large area, and range of wave sizes, from calm inside to sizable at the point. Many boardsailors rate "Sandy Point" as the best wave-sailing beach in Baja, and surfers say the right point break here is the longest in Baja, some riding it for a mile.

A road running to the northwest has improved access to the many wide, uncrowded, and litter-free white-sand beaches along the coast to the northwest. Other than an occasional ranch and several small fish camps, the area is uninhabited. To get to the road, return to Mile 8.1, set trip odometer, and turn northwest (320°) on the class 2 graded road, signed SAN JOSÉ DE LAS PALOMAS. At Mile 4.0, turn left (180°), pass Rancho San Andrés, and arrive at an intersection at Mile 5.5. Continue straight ahead (230°) between the cliffs (if the weather is wet, take the right fork, 280°). The road will cross mud flats, swing north and arrive at the cove in another 1.5 miles. This area, called "Alejandro's," has an excellent sand beach. To continue on to Punta Prieta (Dark Point), return to Mile 4.0 and continue west (280°) until Mile 15.5, where a sharp left turn (160°) onto a class 2 road will take you to the beach in a little over 2 miles.

The curve of Bahía Santa Rosalillita from the settlement to Punta Rosarito offers those with surf-fishing equipment some of the finest white seabass fishing in Baja, 25-pounders not being uncommon. A class 3 road runs south along the bay, leading to many small sand beaches interspersed with rocky points. The summer months are best, especially when the surf is light, the tide is coming in, and the water is clean. Look for a place where a sandy beach and a rocky point meet, with a steep drop-off marked by the dark color of the water. Whole squid is the bait of choice. Those with vehicles unsuitable for class 3 roads can get close to equally good fishing action at El Tomatal just to the south; turn to page 103.

■■■■■■■■■■■■■■■■■■■
KM 96 on the Transpeninsular
near Villa Jesús María
to Laguna Manuela

Class 1, 7 miles; use the map on pages 104–105. The Laguna Manuela area is little known to many *gringo* visitors in spite of the facts that it has one of the finest fisheries in Baja and is close to the Transpeninsular. Set trip odometer. Follow the paved road west to Mile 0.9, turn southwest, and arrive at the beach at Mile 7.0. The graded sand-and-gravel road is often washboarded.

The lagoon was named for the whaling brig *Manuela*, wrecked on the outer coast of the lagoon in 1871. This desolate spot was once served by regular steamship service to San Diego. In the heyday of the gold mines in the Camallí and Alemán areas in the 1800s, the steamer deposited supplies on the beach, which were then hauled to the mines on mule-back, the steamer heading north with the gold.

There is plenty of space to park RVs along the beach, but the shoreline is low, and a high tide can produce surprises. There is no ramp, and trailer boaters will be disappointed unless they are equipped for launching over a low-slope, soft-sand beach. Those with cartoppers and inflatable boats should not have great difficulty. Boats can enter and leave the lagoon through the north entrance, but the south entrance is often unsafe due to heavy surf. The large-scale inset map on page 104 shows the general topography of the lagoon, but the mud flat and shallow areas change frequently.

The lagoon extends south about 9 miles, and is very shallow and often choked with eel grass, its bottom being mixed mud and sand. Surge created by tides and winds may leave a boat anchored in 3 or 4 feet of water high and dry 30 minutes later. These conditions make the lagoon a "biological factory," and the place seems fin-to-fin with yellowfin croaker, corvina, corbina, halibut, and various basses, especially in its southern reaches. For those with a boat, the southern end of the lagoon is one of the finest fisheries in Baja.

In suitable weather, the ocean coves just north of Punta Morro Santo Domingo offer outstanding fishing for corbina, yellowfin croaker, and halibut, especially in the summer, and white seabass, giant sea bass, yellowtail, ocean whitefish, and grouper are also taken. Always be on guard for sneaker waves and heavy tidal currents in this vicinity.

Aqua Adventures offers an unusual activity at Manuela, kayak wave surfing. Taking advantage of the big swells that wrap around the point, their instructors will get you surfing in a fraction of the time that it takes to learn surfboarding. Also, there is great whale-watching just off the point during the winter. Aqua Adventures maintain a camp at the lagoon and will accommodate walk-ins, including both instruction and equipment rental.

■■■■■■■■■■■■■■■■■■■
KM 208 on the Transpeninsular
near Guerrero Negro
to Parque Natural de la Ballena Gris

Class 1, 17 miles; use the map on pages 104–105. This whale-watching site on Scammon's is both a disappointment and a joy. The whales are normally rather far from shore, and binoculars are necessary to see any detail, but on a broader scale, how many places in the world can you drive to in an RV and see three or four whales breaching or spy-hopping simultaneously?

The road crosses a number of salt flats and is badly washboarded. You will be charged a small fee for entrance and overnight parking, and there is a small restaurant. Local entrepreneurs offer whale-watching trips from the park and from the fish camp a mile east. The park is an underwater ecological reserve, and private boats of any kind are not allowed on the lagoon during the whale season. A deposit of fossilized shark teeth can be found mixed in the surface gravel northwest of the park.

Most visitors are so entranced by the whales that they do not recognize that the lagoon, with its shallow waters, extensive mud flats and marshes, and rich production of fish, mollusks, worms, and other creatures, is prime avian territory, with almost 50 species present at one time of the year or another.

■■■■■■■■■■■■■■■■■■■
KM 189+ on the Transpeninsular
east of Guerrero Negro
to El Arco and Bahía San Francisquito

Class 2 to El Arco, 25.4 miles; marginal class 2 to the bay, 48.8 additional miles; use the map on pages 104–105. There is little of interest in El Arco, although those wishing to go on to the Bahía San Francisquito area sometimes choose this route. The road was paved a number of years ago as far as El Arco. However, the construction was poor and maintenance nonexistent, and it is now a moonscape of potholes, local drivers now preferring the class 2 wheel tracks that have developed next to it. The road beyond El Arco, once infamous for a slope so steep (27%) and rugged that it was named La Cuesta de la Ley (The Slope That Rules), is marginal class 2 (no trailers or large motor homes).

Despite this, the road will take you to unspoiled fishing and diving, and provides access to the Midriff islands. Set trip odometer. At Mile 25.4 arrive at El Arco. In 1882, extensive gold deposits that eventually produced over $3 million were discovered at nearby Camallí. Gold was discovered later at El Arco, and in the 1920s about a thousand miners were at work. Today, copper and gold mining continues sporadically at low levels. Hopes are high for newly discovered deposits, but little seems to change from year to year.

"Quo Vadis" is Latin for "Where are you going?" The answer seems simple—to the bottom, unless the fisherman who owns this popular boat cleans it out frequently

To continue on, locate the *Delegación Municipal* building, identified by its twin radio towers, at Mile 25.8. Pass this on your left, continue straight ahead (335°) and immediately drop into an arroyo, staying right (020°) at the intersection at Mile 25.9. Arrive at Pozo Alemán at Mile 27.9, a collection of ramshackle buildings. At the cemetery, take the left (045°) fork. Continue straight ahead (045°) at the fork at Mile 35.8, pass through a great *dátilillo* forest beginning at Mile 50.8, and arrive at the beginning of La Cuesta de la Ley at Mile 54.7. "The Slope That Rules" has been tamed by bulldozers, but even in years past it was overrated; with its 1 mile of grades, the steepest only 27%, it was no challenge to the "Terrible Three" south of Puertecitos. At Mile 62.5 arrive at Rancho el Progreso, turn left (330°) and join the Bahía de los Angeles-Bahía San Francisquito road at Mile 63.2, going east. Stay left (070°) at the fork at Mile 72.6 and arrive at the inner harbor of Bahía San Francisquito at Mile 74.2.

There is relatively little pressure from sport or commercial fishermen, and sea bass and groupers get very, very large. There is an excellent seasonal fishery for yellowtail, which pass the area heading south in early November, returning north in late May and early June. One of the most productive fishing areas is Bahía San Rafael, beginning five miles to the northwest of Punta San Francisquito. Whales often are seen in Canal de Salsipuedes. Diving is good off Punta San Francisquito, but is better around Isla San Lorenzo.

Deborah and Alberto Lucero, local residents, offer fishing, diving, camping, and natural-history trips throughout the area and to the islands in the Midriff from November through April. In addition, they sell hand-painted clothing, desert art, and gourmet Baja cuisine, and he is a welder. Nova is usually available and possibly Magnasin. They have a home on the inner bay. Reservations and information can be obtained by writing to them, but due to the remoteness of the area and the idiosyncrasies of the mail system, on both sides of the border, they suggest writing simultaneously to both addresses shown in Appendix C. Allow a month for a reply.

Vizcaíno to KM 98 on the Transpeninsular

Class 1, 290 miles, side trip to Malarrimo, class 2, 52 additional (round trip) miles; use the map on pages 104–105. One of longest and most interesting "off-road" trips in Baja crosses the Desierto de Vizcaíno to Bahía Tortugas, heads south through Bahía Asunción to Punta Abreojos, and returns to the Transpeninsular in the vicinity of San Ignacio. The attraction is not the scenery, for most of the trip is across flat coastal plains, but rather the remoteness and grand scale of the desert. Once you near the ocean, the reward is more than 60 miles of the most deserted and pristine beaches in North America, plus fine diving and fishing. Large areas inside this great loop are covered with a rare type of sand dune. Called "transverse dunes," they form when winds blow steadily in one direction, causing the surface to look like huge plowed furrows in a farmer's field. Similar dunes have also been observed in northern Australia.

■ Pronghorn

If you see a "deer" speeding across the Vizcaíno, but upon reflection realize that a few things were just a bit peculiar—the coat of the animal wasn't quite the right color, it was a bit too angular, and the "horns" would never make it into the record books—you have been lucky enough to see one of Baja's rarest creatures, a pronghorn. Although frequently called "antelopes," they are not closely related to any Old World species of the same name. One of the fastest animals on the planet, they have exceptionally large hearts and lungs, and can maintain a speed of 40 to 50 mph for extended periods. Their top speed of 60 is second only to the cheetah's 70. They are also very powerful animals, capable of making horizontal jumps of up to 27 feet. In addition, they have the keenest vision of any large mammal on the continent, said to be comparable to 8-power binoculars.

It would seem that with these qualifications—extreme speed, endurance, great power, and exceptional eyesight—the species would be well-qualified for survival, and at one time they numbered in the many millions in western North America. However, pronghorn venison was a mainstay of the pioneer diet in the early 1800s, and was hunted commercially, and within 75 years, the pronghorns had been reduced to small remnant herds. Laws and conservation measures in the US have caused the species to rebound, and today it is second only to deer as the most abundant big game animal.

In Mexico, the species has not been so lucky. It has been estimated that there are only 600 left in the entire country, and their numbers continue to decline. The pronghorns in Baja are a subspecies, the peninsular pronghorn, and while it is little more than a guess, it is thought that perhaps 90 still survive in the Vizcaíno. There has not been an open season since 1921, and the Mexican Fish and Game people have posted many signs saying "Don't shoot the *berrendos*." Such measures are not likely to be taken too seriously by hungry locals living in a sparsely populated desert region wanting a change in a monotonous diet of tortillas and beans, and the future of the Baja pronghorn is in great jeopardy. We have never seen one, and have met only one person who has.

The central Vizcaíno Desert is among the most inaccessible wildernesses left on the peninsula, but change is coming; the roads have been graded, and water and power lines have been extended to the coast. It is now feasible to make the trip in an RV, even towing a trailer boat equipped for over-the-beach launches.

The road to Tortugas is often washboarded, so plan on at least a six-hour journey, one-way. Gas and supplies may or may not be available in Tortugas, Asunción, and the other villages along the way, so make sure you fill at every opportunity. Set trip odometer, turn southwest. For the first several miles there are roadside grocery, beer, and liquor stores. The pavement, much of it in poor repair, ends at Mile 18.3 and becomes a class 1, graded, two-lane gravel road, damaged in sections by erosion, and badly washboarded. Cross the first of three salt ponds on an earthen causeway at Mile 36.1. At Mile 46.2 encounter a class 1 road south (195°, signed), ending on the coast road east of Asunción. If time is short and you are interested mainly in the beach areas southeast of Asuncion, turn south here; otherwise go straight ahead (275°, signed). The road north to legendary Playa Malarrimo will be found at Mile 73.2.

If you have a suitable vehicle, you should plan a side trip to Malarrimo. Long the most famous beachcombing area in Baja, this beach has yielded US Navy mops and firefighting foam containers, human bodies, palm and redwood logs, hatch covers, enormous numbers of light bulbs and Twinkie wrappers, airplane wings, shipwrecks, both in their entirety and in thousands of parts, prized Japanese glass fishing floats, whale carcasses and bones, a 12-foot torpedo emitting buzzing noises, and a soggy package containing a CD by Hootie & the Blowfish. A statistical analysis of the huge crop of cans and bottles would reveal that humans drink a great deal of alcohol, cover their food with layers of catsup, and are deeply concerned about underarm odor. While you are searching, try to figure out why empty catsup bottles are almost always capped, while alcohol bottles are generally open. The beach is slowly advancing, so it might pay to explore areas as far as 500 yards inland. Spend the night—there is usually lots of firewood.

The class 2 road north from Mile 73.2 to Malarrimo is hard to spot; if you miss it, keep going until you see the sign for Rancho San José de Castro, and go back (east) 200 yards. The 26-mile (one way) road has an 18% grade in one stretch. Because of deep sand, those in two-wheel-drive vehicles should stop a half mile short of the beach and walk in; if you can see the water you are already too close.

Continuing on the Bahía Tortugas road from Mile 73.2; at Mile 75.9 note the intersection with the old road to Asunción (120°). Continue straight ahead (235°) for Bahía Tortugas (Turtle Bay) at Mile 107.3. The ramshackle town has groceries, bakery, restaurants, liquor, ice, purified water, laundromat, clinic, doctors, pharmacy, sporting goods, *pangas* for hire, Pesca office, mechanics, auto parts, tire repair, telegraph, mechanics, several motels, tortilla factory, a bank, and a PEMEX (MND). Aerolineas California has an office in town and you can fly to Isla Cedros, Ensenada, and other places on their routes. Inexpensive Restaurante Morocco has a wide variety of breakfast items, seafood, including abalone five different ways, steaks, roast beef, burgers, Mexican, and "tender tits Baja." We were unable to learn the exact nature of the last item.

There are no organized RV parks, but many sandy locations are available around the bay. Boats can be launched over a sand beach west of the pier in town, at a number of locations along the eastern margin of the bay, or over a hard sand-and-gravel beach near the fishing camp at its southwest end. Fishing in the bay is difficult in some areas due to dense beds of sea weeds, but outstanding fishing for sand bass, kelp bass, and ocean whitefish is found outside between Cabo Tórtolo (Cape Turtledove) and Punta Cambrey. The main channel out of the bay, about a mile wide and marked by lighthouses on its north and south margins, offers excellent fishing for bonito, yellowtail, barracuda, and dolphinfish in season, out to about 4 miles. There is good offshore fishing at the "15 Spot," 6 miles, 248° from Punta la Cantina, the point forming the north entrance of the bay; at "38 Spot," 12 miles, 150°; at "9 Spot," 22 miles, 176°; and at "10 Spot," 25 miles, 138°. Handliners working from *pangas* account for part of the commercial catch in the area, and they need bait, so gillnets are maintained along the south shore of the bay. This bait is sometimes sold from a boat anchored off the village and might be available—ask around.

Gray whales come close to shore, occasionally entering kelp beds. We were once fishing near Punta Cambrey, when a gray plowed through the kelp like a gigantic bulldozer not 5 yards away, apparently oblivious to our presence. The bay served as an important base for whaling ships in the mid-1800s. Divers almost acquired a magnificent wreck when the Japanese armored cruiser *Asama* hit a rock at the mouth of the bay while on a First World War patrol, ripping a 15-foot gash in her hull. "Unfortunately," she was refloated three months later and made it back to Japan.

● ●

66 Fiddlin' around

My dad and I were pulling out of Bahía Tortugas in our pickup early one evening, when we came on an unbelievable scene; a full-fledged Mexican band, standing by the side of the road with their thumbs out! The four men were equipped with a bull fiddle, a saxophone, a guitar, and an accordion, along with amps, speakers, and some duffel. My dad slowed down to get a better look, but as we passed them he speeded up and said, "No way; they will never fit in the back." I yelled, "Come on Dad, let's give it a try," and he stopped and backed up, saying "Yeah. What the heck."

The players reeked of strong drink and seemed badly hung over; it hurt me even to look at them. One spoke good English, and it seemed that their gig at the Kaluha Cantina had been a tremendous success. The previous evening the entire adult population of Bahía Tortugas had jammed in and kept plying the players with tequila in an effort to persuade them to stay forever, and if not that, for at least one more day. It worked, and by early the next afternoon the band had simply fallen asleep, still being urged on by the few in the audience still able to function. As dusk approached, one player had awakened and realized that they were due in Vizcaíno at 8, over 100 miles to the east, for another night of music. They had missed their bus, and no one in town was willing, or able for that matter, to drive them.

Loading the back of the pickup was a re-creation of the famous show in the Barnum and Bailey Circus, where two-dozen clowns get out one-by-one from a tiny car, only in reverse. It was pitch-black by the time we got going, and it seemed that every cubic inch was filled by instruments and musicians, who promptly went to sleep and began snoring. The fumes were so thick that I had to open a window. An hour later, we were still far short of Vizcaíno, but the road had been graded recently, and it looked like we would make it on time. One by one, the musicians came to life, and my dad said "¡Música!" in a loud voice. Somehow the rubber-armed accordion player found enough elbow room and began pumping away. Inspired, the others squirmed around to find their instruments. All were soon in hand, except for the bull fiddle, which was at the bottom of the heap and could not be retrieved, and the group began playing.

What a scene! Tearing along in the pitch darkness at 50 on a gravel road with a huge plume of dust behind us, the headlights piercing the black night, jackrabbits fleeing for their lives, cold air blasting through the open windows, the heater on full-tilt, and the band in back playing all the latest hits from Mexico City!

With 10 minutes to spare, we were approaching the Transpeninsular Highway, when one of the players yelled "¡Aquí, aquí!" and pointed to a large stake truck parked on the side of the road. The gear was quickly loaded into the truck and the musicians climbed into the back, all except the

accordion player, who had to be hoisted up, and they drove away shouting "¡Gracias!" The back of the pickup smelled like tequila for a week. ——Michael 99

● ●

Isla Natividad lies five miles west. Although it is within easy range of boats launched from Bahía Tortugas, few sport divers or fishermen head for the island. Surfers claim that "Open Doors," on the island's east end, is the best beach break in North America.

A class 2 road winds south from Tortugas along the eastern shore of the bay, where sandy shores provide numerous places to spend a few days and to launch boats. At Mile 11.0, the road ends at Bahía Cambrey, a favorite place with many visitors. The sandy bottom of the bay is home to astronomical numbers of pismo clams. Stretching east and then arcing south for 5 miles or more, the beds are so dense that the mere act of anchoring a boat can uproot a dinner-load. A foray with fins and mask should prove fruitful. Vehicles can get near the beach, and small boats can be launched, but a rocky berm makes it difficult to launch trailer boats.

Asuncion can be reached in two ways from Tortugas: the new route via Mile 46.2, or the old route via Mile 75.9. The distance from Tortugas to Asuncion is 90 miles if the old route is taken, or 68.8 miles by the new route. Both routes are graded, two-lane, class 1, although there are a number of gully crossings lacking culverts, rendering them vulnerable to rain damage, and in a number of locations the roads are reduced to one lane. There are virtually no ranches along either route once past the Santa Monica-Rancho San José de Castro area. Asunción has a health clinic, pharmacy, mail, telegraph, long-distance telephone, hardware, auto parts, mechanics, Pesca office, beer, groceries, and a desalinization plant. There is no PEMEX, but several locals sell Magnasin from drums. Diesel might be available at the cannery in an emergency.

Rob Watson would rather drown than let go of that pismo

After climbing down low cliffs west of town, surfers will find good reef breaks at the point. Boats can be launched over the beach in town and at a steep unpaved area a quarter mile inside the point. Good fishing for yellowtail and bottom fish is found northwest of Isla San Roque. Large numbers of kelp bass and sand bass frequent the area, and the lobsters get so big you can eat their legs like king crab. Fishing is often excellent on reefs around the island and directly offshore, at "24 Spot," 6 miles, 245° from the south tip of Isla Asunción, and at "6 Spot," 3 miles, 120° from the same place. I (Walt) once fired up my hooka and made a dive off the island. When I reached the bottom, stood up, and looked around, I was stunned to see a dozen, 20, no 40, lobsters within the range of visibility. Had they chosen to act collectively the outcome would have been quite different.

The coast between Bahía Cambrey and Bahía San Pablo is penetrated by only a few class 2 and 3 roads, but many reach the beaches southeast from Punta San Roque. This stretch is a surf fisherman's paradise, perhaps the least stressed and most productive beach fishery in Baja. The beaches between San Roque and Asunción have superb beach-casting for corbina, and the rays of the setting sun passing through the waves often reveal hordes of fish searching for food, a stirring sight to anyone, fisherman or not.

Continuing on; set trip odometer and drive east from Asunción along miles of beautiful sand beach. At Mile 4.6, encounter the intersection with the "new" road northeast to Mile 46.2 on the Vizcaíno-Tortugas Road. At Mile 19.6 take the left (125°, signed) fork. (The right fork, 155°, signed, leads to the tiny settlements of Punta Prieta (Dark Point) and San Hipólito. At Mile 23.6, take the left (085°) at the Y (the right, 110°, returns to the small towns just mentioned, plus some beach boondocking sites). Bahía San Hipólito has a good reef break. The rocky beaches around Mile 43.5 are a favorite with shore-casters, small bits of clam often producing large numbers of yellowfin croakers and sand bass.

The small town of La Bocana (The Mouth, apparently referring to the mouth of the nearby Estero la Bocana) at Mile 49.0, has grocery stores, auto parts, tire repair, small cafés, health clinic, pharmacies, telegraph, mail, and a desalinization plant. There is no PEMEX, but Magnasin and Nova are sold from drums, and diesel may be available at the packing plant. Boats can be launched over the low sand beach south of the packing plant. Large numbers of cabrilla, croaker, corvina, corbina, shark, and halibut are taken inside the lagoon, and although there is an active commercial *panga* fleet, dolphinfish, yellowtail, and black- and white seabass are still numerous offshore. Many areas in the estero are lined with mangroves; see page 238 for some fishing hints.

The road from La Bocana to Abreojos passes close to Estero la Bocana, offering numerous chances to launch small boats. Abreojos, at Mile 60.0, has very limited groceries, beer, Pesca office, telephone, telegraph, ice, auto parts, mechanics, tire repair, health clinic, restaurant, and a desalinization plant. No PEMEX again, but locals sell Magnasin out of drums, and diesel may available at the cooperative. A number of vessels have been lost due to confusion around the many offshore reefs and pinnacles—they didn't name it "Open-Your-Eyes" for nothing. The point has a fantastic right break in the proper swells, some surfing fans claiming that it is the best right point break in Baja. Abreojos is well-known and much discussed among several generations of boardsailors, who capitalize on passing fronts, especially from March to May or June. At the point, conditions are often side-offshore, providing exciting down-the-

The **panga** *fleet at Abreojos*

line wave-sailing. Fishing is excellent, and shore-casters take corvina, corbina, and croakers. The beach sand is hard and the slope shallow, and it should be possible to launch small trailer boats across the beach in town. Wright Shoal, a mile southeast of Punta Abreojos, and Roca Ballena (Whale Rock), 4 miles west, produce white seabass and yellowtail, and a dozen grouper and black sea bass approaching 50 pounds would not be too much to hope for during a single trip, at least one reasonably endowed with luck.

Leaving Abreojos, set trip odometer. At Mile 7.2, a class 1 (dry weather) road signed CAMPO RENE leads to the right (110°) 3.4 miles along a sandy peninsula forming the western margin of shallow Laguna la Escondida (Hidden Lagoon). Campo Rene will be encountered about halfway to the entrance. RVers are welcome, and cartoppers, inflatables, and small trailer boats can be launched in the lagoon across a hard-packed sand-and-sea-shell ramp at higher tides.

The lagoon offers excellent fishing for spotted bass, grouper, corvina, halibut, sierra, barracuda, and maybe, just maybe, snook. Much of the inside of the lagoon is lined with mangrove, so turn to page 238 for some fishing hints. Various basses, croakers, and groupers are taken in the channel leading to the ocean, and the deep area just inside the entrance can be fantastic, as close to fool-proof fishing as can be found in Baja. The lagoon is very shallow and turns into mud flats in periods of very low tides, so check your tide table before coming and avoid low periods. The large-scale inset map on page 114 shows the general topography of the lagoon, but mud flats and shallow areas change frequently. White water is often present on a sandy reef directly south of the channel entrance, and boaters should use great caution, even in periods of relative calm. Boaters have made it safely around this area by heading south out of the channel for a half mile until they clear the beach breakers , then turning east and running a mile or so until the white water area

They said it couldn't be done—the Vizcaíno-Tortugas-Asuncion-Abreojos-KM 98 trip by motor home—but it was

is bypassed. Better yet, watch for local *panga* fishermen heading out and follow them.

The two-lane, graded, class 1 road northeast from Abreojos to the Transpeninsular is sometimes badly washboarded. At Mile 54.3, the Transpeninsular is reached at KM 98.

KM 118 on the Transpeninsular southeast of Vizcaíno to the Sierra de San Francisco

Marginal class 2 (no trailers or large motor homes), 22.5 miles; use the map on pages 104–105. This trip will take you to some of the most spectacular mountain scenery

in Baja accessible by road, with the added attraction of its finest rock-art site close to a reasonably good road. No grades are over 14%, but there are sharp switchbacks and few places in which to turn around. At least six hours should be allowed for the trip.

Set trip odometer. After crossing flat desert for 6 miles, the road switches back a number of times to the top of a narrow ridge, climbing toward massive Pico Santa Monica, at 5,218 feet the highest point in the Sierra de San Francisco. There are deep canyons on each side, and although the road closely approaches their edges, it pays to stop occasionally and look over the edge—the scenery is dazzling.

After passing several small ranches, the road swings around the upper reaches of Cañon San Pablo at Mile 20.0. One of the most magnificent canyons in Baja, it is on a par with, but very different from, Cañon Tajo far to the north. This narrow, 1,000-foot-deep, palm-lined gorge is the location of Gardner Cave, the crown jewel of Baja rock art, as well as several other fine sites. With its treasures of man-made and natural art, the entire area should be made into a national park. At Mile 21.0 arrive at the site of Cueva Ratón (Rat Cave). While not of the caliber of the sites farther downstream, it has a 30 feet-wide mural showing figures of humans, deer, lions, mountain sheep, and other animals, with examples of the bicolor and overpainting traditions. All visitors to the site must register and have a guide, which can be obtained at the village of San Francisco at Mile 22.5. The local policeman keeps a sharp eye. Arrangements can be made in the village for three-day burro trips to see Gardner Cave.

Since you were probably intent on the scenery ahead on the way up, the trip back to the Transpeninsular will be an all-but-new treat: canyon walls resembling a vast book with pages 50 feet thick, and vistas of the head of Laguna San Ignacio and the Sierra Santa Clara, over 40 miles away.

San Ignacio to Laguna San Ignacio

Class 1, 40 miles; use the map on pages 114–115. Laguna San Ignacio is one of the world's major gray whale breeding grounds, and a visit there should be on the itinerary of every winter RV trip. The trip takes three hours (one way), and be warned, sections of the road have world-class washboard.

Starting in town on the south side of the square, set trip odometer and drive east, turn right (170°) at Mile 0.3, and left (090°) at the large satellite dish at Mile 0.5. The road quickly climbs a hill, swings right, and heads south. A number of ranches will be passed in the first 15 miles, and you will encounter the fish camps of Laguna de San Ignacio, La Base, and La Fridera at Miles 36.0, 37.0, and 40.0, respectively. The last name means "trypot," referring to the device used by shore-based whalers located here in the Winter of 1860-61 to reduce their quarry to oil. The scenery is not inspiring, mostly desert scrub, mangroves, and extensive mud flats, and there are no whales to be seen at first, but your disappointment will not last long. Six miles southwest of La Fridera is Punta Prieta, a low-lying point with a rocky margin jutting into the lagoon. The waters surrounding this point and south to the entrance of the lagoon are the winter home of the gray whales.

Except for the lack of music, the dictionary definition of ballet—a classical dance form characterized by grace and precision of movement and elaborate formal technique—certainly fits the show off the point. Grays look awkward, but they are in fact extremely graceful and have a repertory of movements that would test the skills of the best of ballerinas. Instead of pirouette, adagio, or jeté, the most frequent move among the whales is the "spy-hop," in which one pushes its fluke (tail fin) against the bottom, or if in deep water, vigorously beats it, allowing the whale to rise vertically about one-third of the way out of the water. Another move is the "breach," in which one leaps completely out of the water, often repeated two or three times in a row, landing with great splashes. They often "corkscrew," rolling over again and again as they move through the water. The unromantic offer sober explanations for such behavior: spy-hopping whales want a better view, and breaching whales are trying to dislodge parasites, but those who have seen it come to believe it is indeed a ballet, or at least a demonstration of their immense power, perhaps a whale sport—or that they do it just for fun.

Fishermen at La Fridera and the other fish camps can be hired to take you out in their *pangas* to get a front-row view. A few whales may come closer and spy-hop to get a better look at the curious creatures looking at them. Most whales seem unconcerned by the presence of boats, allowing you to get close to see mothers nursing their babies, mating activity, and the repertory of whale ballet.

An event that first occurred in 1976 elevates a visit to the lagoon from merely interesting to extraordinary. A young female whale surfaced next to the fishing vessel *Royal Polaris* while it was in Laguna San Ignacio on a whale-watching trip. She was so curious about inflatable boats that she would lift them with bursts of exhaled bubbles and balance them on her head or back, always being careful to do this only when passengers were not aboard. Such "friendly" behavior had never been seen before, the whales having maintained a safe distance from their old persecutors. However, there may be an explanation: many people believe that the whale was Gigi, captured in 1971 and studied at Sea World in San Diego until she was released a year later. Apparently not holding a grudge over her year of incarceration, she stayed for a lengthy visit. Other friendly cows began making such visits, accompanied by their calves, which in turn have grown up and now allow their youngsters the same experience. Originally observed only in Laguna San Ignacio,

these encounters have occurred recently in Bahía Magdalena, near Vancouver Island in Canada, and in the Bering Sea. Also, the fun is not limited to grays: recent incidents with southern right whales off Australia and Argentina suggest that they too are willing to forget the past and want to become friends.

The motivations of animals can never be known with certainty, and some people insist that grays are not friendly but merely curious. However, based on our experiences during a visit to the lagoon, we have decided they are indeed friendly. Together with several young men we met, we hired a fisherman to take us to Punta Prieta. There were dozens of whales nearby, and as we stopped the boat, a cow and a calf immediately changed course and headed directly towards us. We were soon the recipients of nuzzles and nudges from a 30-ton mother and her 2-ton calf, both intent on being scratched and petted. A person gains a sense of perspective during such an event; the relationship between the weight of a whale and of a human is about the same as that between a human and a rat.

A friendly whale at Laguna San Ignacio pays a call

After we had spent 45 minutes with them, we moved to another area, only to quickly gain the attentions of another pair, and later in the day, a third. Each of the three mothers repeatedly swam under her baby and pushed it to the surface, as if urging it to get a better look at the strange creatures peering down at them. The mothers and the babies seemed playful, and as the babies grew more familiar with us they became bolder, one even becoming something of a brat. Michael, then 13 years old, had the wonderful experience of snorkeling for a short time with a mother and baby.

Already guilty of attributing human motivations to animals by stating that the grays are friendly, we will carry it a step further by claiming that they also have a sense of humor. During Gigi's encounter with the *Royal Polaris*, she came up very close to one side of the vessel, and when everyone rushed over to see her, she submerged and caused another rush when she came up on the other side. She did this more than a dozen times, and observers came to understand that she was teasing them. During our visit to Laguna San Ignacio, the whale mothers occasionally swished their great flukes under our boat, bouncing it on huge boils of water. One rolled on her side and repeatedly vented spray and smelly breath directly at us as we took photographs. This occurred too often to be mere chance, and each time she would roll over a bit to see that the blast had reached its target. Another mother even played a joke on Steve Prasser. He was sitting with his rear hanging over the side of the boat, when she let out a great blast of bubbles and spray directly beneath him. If this is not humor, what is it?

■■■■■■■■■■■■■■■■■■■■■■
KM 59+ on the Transpeninsular east of San Ignacio to the Rancho Santa Martha area

Marginal class 2 (no trailers or large motor homes), 28.3 miles; use the map on pages 104–105. Although the road is rough, this trip passes through fine scenery, and at its end, Cueva Palmarito, a rock-art site, is only a two-hour hike away.

Set odometer. Swing left (330°) off the graded road at Mile 1.0, set trip odometer, and arrive at Rancho el Carricito at Mile 11.3. The road makes an abrupt right (100°) turn at the ranch and then swings north again. The scenery grows more beautiful as you gain altitude, with twisted volcanic shapes and fantastic horizons. Arrive at the ranch at Mile 28.3. Guides can be obtained for a hike to see the rock art at nearby Cueva Palmarito. The hike is a small price to pay: a great mural is worked across the back wall of a rock shelter, 150 feet long and 40 feet high, with figures of red deer, a black mountain lion, and other animals. Over a dozen human figures are shown, many in headdress, some in the bicolor tradition, others in vertical stripes. The ranch can provide horses or burros for those unable or unwilling to hike.

■■■■■■■■■■■■■■■■■■■■■
KM 156 on the Transpeninsular north of Mulegé to the Puntas Chivato/Santa Inés area

Class 1, 14 miles; use the map on pages 114–115. For many miles to the north, most RV facilities have been places to stay overnight *en route* to other places, but the Punta Chivato/Santa Inés area is a place to stay and play. With its sparkling beaches and good fishing, diving, and boardsailing, it is the Baja destination for many RVers. Hotel Punta Chivato, located west of the point, has a restaurant with a grand view to the south, bar, pool, gift shop, and beach, plus fishing boats and guides. A small grocery store can be found nearby, and golfers have not been forgotten: there is a 9-hole, par 27, desert course (no turf) just northwest of the hotel.

The RV park can be found by continuing on the road past the hotel through an area of nice homes; follow the signs. The inexpensive park, class B (but A for ambiance), has *palapas*, potable water, showers, and toilets, but there are no hookups. There is currently no dump station at the park, but one can be found just south of the trailer and boat storage area, west of the hotel. Boats can be launched over the sandy beach, and some protection from waves is provided by small, rocky fingers at some east-facing sites.

Shore fishing can be good, especially for yellowtail near the aid-to-navigation light tower on Punta Santa Inés. Ladyfish action can be found in the hot months by casting small chrome spoons, feather jigs, or soft plastic lures from the shore with light spinning gear at dawn or dusk. Roosterfish are sometimes taken along the beach in front of the hotel. The Islas Santa Inés, to the south, especially the southernmost island, are good for yellowtail, snapper, pargo, and amberjack. Tuna, billfish, and dolphinfish are offshore in the warm months, and close-in there are reefs everywhere with lesser species. Seven miles, 040° from Punta Santa Inés, the water begins to get very deep, in excess of 400 fathoms, and yellowfin tuna are often present in the summer months. There is a shallow (9%) concrete launch ramp just west of the hotel, with plenty of parking and maneuvering room.

A good diving reef extends east from Punta Santa Inés. Mexican divers have found gold coins, the diameter of a silver dollar but twice as thick, in a small bay northwest of Punta Chivato with the intriguing name of Caleta Muertos (Dead Cove). The Mexican fishing vessel *Britania*, lost in 1980, lies 150 feet east and 300 feet to 400 feet south of the northern tip of the southern island at the Islas Santa Inés in 5 feet to 15 feet of water. The historic schooner *Abel Miranda* lies somewhere in the vicinity. Built in 1859, she was the oldest vessel in the Mexican merchant-marine register and the last merchant sail in the Cortez when she was lost in 1957.

Boardsailors will find excellent winds in the December through February season. The bay off the hotel offers speed sailing in flat conditions, with winds accelerated by the venturi effect of the hills to the north, and reaches are measured in miles. Beginners will not be left out; although the winds are usually brisk by mid-morning, they tend to be light earlier, and the south beach is sandy and the bottom shallow. Punta Chivato's north shore provides advanced sailors with a sandy launch, waves, and strong side-onshore winds.

■■■■■■■■■■■■■■■■■■■■■■
KM 136+ on the Transpeninsular at Mulegé to Rancho la Trinidad

Class 2, 15.5 miles; use the map on pages 114–115. The road is mostly excellent graded class 1, but several arroyo crossings near the ranch involve 21% grades and loose rock, rendering the trip a marginal class 2 (no trailers, no long over-hangs). Turn west from the Transpeninsular opposite the auto parts shop, set trip odometer. At Mile 1.2 swing left (southwest). There is a Y at Mile 2.9; take the right (260°). Go straight ahead (240°) at the intersection at Mile 3.0, cross a cattle guard at Mile 5.3, and immediately swing right (180°). At Mile 7.8 there is a sign, SAN

ESTANISLAO, and a Y; take the right (290°) branch. At Mile 8.6, you have a choice: straight ahead, left, or right; take the right (230°). As you approach the ranch, the scenery ahead becomes beautiful, with massive, deeply eroded bluffs, the skyline accented by *palo blanco* trees clinging to their summits. Pass a sign, LAS TINAJITAS, at Mile 12.4, and at Mile 13.2 look for a sign, LA TRINIDAD, and the first Y; take the left (160°). At Mile 14.1, pass through a barbed wire fence, make an immediate right (190°), and arrive at the ranch at Mile 15.5. Since this is private property and an archaeological site, you will need a guide, who can be obtained at the ranch for a small fee. The canyon is the upper reaches of Arroyo Mulegé, which supplies water to the "river," although it disappears underground for a good deal of the way.

A hike of about 20 minutes is required to the first site, over relatively flat country, except when clambering over a stone dam, a feat which requires a certain degree of agility. The art figures include a white, upside-down deer, an "x-ray" fish shot with an arrow, a standing man done in white, and other figures. If the dozen or so white hand prints were those of adults, the Cochimí were a rather small people.

The second site requires a swim through a high-walled canyon. Yes, that's what we said—a swim. You must be in reasonably good condition and dressed for the occasion. If you want to bring a camera, it should be a submersible model

Negotiating the dam on the way to the rock art site at La Trinidad

or you should have some means of floating it safely, such as an inflatable beach mat or an innertube with cloth or plywood covering the center. You must have at least six hours available for the round trip from the ranch to the second site.

The La Trinidad sites have been known for many years, and were number 13 on the list in Leon Diguet's paper. The two art sites are not spectacular (a third site lies further upstream), but the drive and the hike are well worthwhile, and the swim to the second site will certainly be a Baja experience to remember. If you would like to make the trip with a knowledgeable guide, or if your vehicle is not up to the task, contact Backroad Adventures.

■■■■■■■■■■■■■■■■■■■■■■

KM 76+ on the Transpeninsular south of Mulegé to San Sebastián

Class 2, 14.6 miles; use the map on pages 114–115. San Sebastián offers unspoiled surroundings and good fishing and diving. As noted earlier, a number of years ago, a party made up their collective mind to bring a big fifth-wheeler into San Sebastián. It took days of digging down humps in the road, clearing brush, cutting tree limbs, and the holding tank and much of the plumbing under the rig was wiped out. However, they made it, and spent a happy month at the beautiful little bay recalling the experience. Since then, the place has become home to almost a dozen "permanent" trailers. Still, there are a number of 26% slopes with loose rock, and while we rate the road as class 2, it is marginal and we cannot recommend the road to those with large trailers or motor homes, unless you are willing to undertake an adventure (read a degree of substantial risk).

At KM 76+ turn east, set trip odometer and pass an abandoned RV park at Mile 0.5. There are numerous boondocking sites to the east of the camp. Enormous numbers of *chocolates* live in the sandy shallows along this stretch of beach. Divers will find them in as little as three feet of water. Don't bother looking for a vent hole—the really big vents are giant egg cockles—but rather for a small, suspicious-looking indentation in the sand; just plow your thumb through the loose sand. The *cardóns* in the area are favorite resting places for vultures, frigates and occasional caracaras.

At Mile 5.5, take the left (020°) fork and at Mile 5.6 take the right (045°) fork (the left fork, 330°, leads to a class 2 road, providing access to good boondocking sites along the eastern shores of the bay). You will soon pass through a beautiful "forest" of *cardóns*. Arrive at San Sebastián at Mile 14.6.

Isolated and still relatively unknown, San Sebastián has no facilities for visitors, no stores, and no launch ramp, just a few ranch buildings, pigs, goats, and chickens, a steep pebble beach, and shaded RV parking, although you might be able to hire a *panga*. A hundred yards to the west of the cove are palm-shaded boondocking sites. The cove in front of the settlement, called Bahía de los Puercos (Bay of the Pigs), is a Baja rarity, a snorkeling site with excellent beach access, protected waters, and unspoiled conditions, with huge morays, groupers, parrot fish, and possibly a dozen other species. Roosterfish show up in April or May and stay for several months, and in the hot months large numbers of dolphinfish are present. Yellowtail from the north migrate past the area in November and return in June, and grouper, bonito and barracuda stay all year, although the best months are the hot ones.

■ Bats that catch fish

You may be returning in the evening from a fishing expedition around Isla Ildefonso off San Sebastián, or perhaps from the islands southeast of Bahía de los Angeles, and see one of the strangest sights you have ever seen, a tiny animal that looks like a mouse with wings, flying along in the darkness with its feet in the water. No, it's no apparition, but rather *Pizonyx vivesi*, the Cortez fishing bat. Endemic to a few islands in the central Cortez, the animal has supremely designed feet and claws that make it possible for it to make a living catching fish. Having a hydrofoil design that would be the envy of a marine architect, it reduces drag from the water to a minimum. A foil shape on its legs suppresses spray, which further reduces drag and presumably avoids alarming the prey. The reaction time from when the feet collide with a fish till the claws seize it must be measured in milliseconds. The bat flies with its body an inch or so above the water until a small fish with exceptionally bad luck is caught and supper is finally at hand. We wonder what might occur should a fishing bat encounter a skinny-dipper on some dark night, especially should he be doing the backstroke.

■■■■■■■■■■■■■■■■■■■■■
KM 118 on the Transpeninsular
near Loreto to San Javier

Class 2, 22.1 miles; use the map on pages 114–115. This trip passes through beautiful mountain scenery and visits the village of San Javier, home of a fine Jesuit mission. The road is improved, being almost completely graded and having many stream crossings paved with concrete, attempts are made at maintenance, and the locals routinely drive it in sedans. However, the road is subject to weather problems and has grades to 19%, and if there is doubt that your RV can handle it, any of the hotels in Loreto can arrange a van trip.

Set trip odometer. Starting at Mile 1.4, commence moderate up- and down-grades, soon followed by a steady climb. Water may appear in canyon bottoms starting about Mile 8.7, and it might be possible to find a swimming hole. As the road switches back and forth the scenery becomes more spectacular, with *zalates* clinging to almost vertical canyon walls and palms lining the bottom of the canyon.

At Mile 11.9 encounter Rancho las Parras (Grapevine Ranch), with a stone chapel, a small dam, and citrus and olive trees. At Mile 13.0, the road reaches the summit at 1,700 feet, offering fine views of the canyon below and of the Cortez. Occasional small streams and ponds may be found from here to San Javier. Pass Rancho Viejo (Old Ranch) at Mile 16.6. At Mile 18.0 pass a class 3 road right to Comondú (signed). This road cannot be recommended to those wishing to visit these villages in RVs; a far better way to Comondú is to approach from the west—see page 219.

Arrive at San Javier at Mile 22.1. In 1699, Jesuit Father Francisco Píccolo founded a mission at Rancho Viejo. However, in 1707 the site of the present village was developed as a garden and visiting station by Father Juan de Ugarte, and in 1720 the mission was moved there. In 1744, construction of the stone church began, taking 14 years to complete. The golden altar and its paintings were carried by burro and ship from Mexico City. The church has 3 bells, two dated 1761, one 1803. The church is still in use, and parishioners often enjoy the perfume of the nearby orange trees during mass. On December 2 and 3 of each year, the tiny village is filled with people from the surrounding ranches, there to celebrate Saint Javier's birthday. A tiny *palapa* café sells Mexican food and cold sodas, there is a small grocery store, and you can buy oranges from the children.

■■■■■■■■■■■■■■■■■■■■■
KM 63+ on the Transpeninsular
south of Loreto to Bahía Agua Verde

Class 2, 26.1 miles; use the map on page 132. This road is important in that it opens the Bahía Agua Verde (Green Water Bay) area to fishermen and divers having cartoppers and inflatables, who would otherwise have to run over 20 miles from the beaches near Danzante. Set trip odometer. For the first dozen miles, the road is graded, culverted, and equipped with concrete paving at most of the stream crossings, and there are no major grades. However, the road then begins a series of hairpin turns, with fairly steep (16%) grades. Several of the hairpin turns are blind: a driver going down and a driver coming up cannot see each other until only a dozen yards apart, and there are few places to pass and virtually nowhere to turn around. The situation of two large trailer rigs meeting under such circumstances would provide great material for a Laurel and Hardy skit. The road reaches beach level at Mile 14.4, opposite two small islands on the shores of the Cortez, and continues southeast along the shore. The beaches are mostly steep cobble, although short stretches of sand can be found near Agua Verde. The road closely parallels the water, but side roads leading to the beaches are limited, making it important to find a place to park before nightfall.

The scenery alone is worth the trip. The Sierra de la Giganta assume wildly improbable shapes—lopsided domes, fantastic plunging cliffs, strange valleys, and great battle-

The old stone church at San Javier

ments from ancient days, all worked in red and purple rock, disproving Father Baegert's claim that there is no scenery to please the eye in Baja California.

At Mile 23.1, the road climbs a hill, providing a sweeping view of the coastline to the northeast and southwest, allowing some scouting for places to camp. The village is reached at Mile 26.1. Some time ago, the wells turned saline and the place seemed doomed, but water is now piped in from the back country. There are two small grocery stores, a mix of cows, pigs, goats, chickens, dogs, and children wanders around, and there is a blaze of bougainvillea and hollyhock. The largest black-coral forest in the Cortez can be found in 80 feet to 150 feet off the rocky pinnacle of Roca Solitario, a pinnacle rising 115 feet out of the Cortez at the mouth of Bahía Aqua Verde. Large catches of yellowtail, dolphinfish, and roosters are common in season, and excellent diving is available.

● ●

❝ *Getting an eyeful*

Trolling was slow along the remote coast south of Bahía Agua Verde one June morning. I was doing some tax-deductible research for this book about the fabled spring migration of yellowtail. However, the water was cold, the run was late, and I was bored, so I tried an experiment: deep sea fishing, really **deep**, *deep sea fishing. Using my largest reel, I bent on five pounds of lead from my skin-diving weight belt, hooked on a large bait and began lowering the rig into the depths. The 50-pound mono rushed through the guides,*

and after several minutes I began to see metal at the bottom of the spool. I didn't know how deep I was, 1,000 feet perhaps, but I knew that if I were to catch something, it would be far different than anything to be encountered in the sunny upper levels: a sea serpent 100 feet long, a bizarre creature capable of swallowing fish larger than itself, or even me—who could tell?

I dozed off for an hour or so, but there wasn't a sign of a nibble, so I began to crank in. After a few minutes I guessed that the bait was at 500 feet, and continued to crank. It was hard work, and I finally began to realize that it was **too** *hard. At about 200 feet, I could feel something struggling, and at 30 I could see a large shape fighting the line. Suddenly there was an eruption at the surface, and I found myself staring eye-to-eye with a large squid. The look on its "face" was nothing short of malevolent—short of the neighbor's dachshund who had been "Maced" by the mailman, I have never seen an animal so angry. In no more than a second or two, the animal had seen enough to diagnose its problem and figure out a course of action—with a flip of its many arms, it turned and squirted me right in the eyes with a powerful jet of water as big around as my finger. I staggered backwards and almost fell over the opposite side of the boat, and by the time I collected myself and could see again, my line was slack.*

I have always marveled at this experience; how could a "lower" animal, forcibly cranked from its habitat in the inky darkness at 1,000 feet, manage to see anything in the brilliant sun at the surface? After an ascent involving a reduction in pressure of 500 pounds per square inch, why didn't its swim bladder blow up like that of a fish, leaving it helpless on the surface? How could it have known what the tall creature standing over it was, and know that its most vulnerable spots were the two blue globes near the top?

Later I came up with a few answers. Squid have excellent accommodation for changes in light intensity, being able to alter pupil size and the amount of pigment in the retina quite rapidly. They do not "blow up" like a fish because they do not possess a swim bladder; most squid regulate their buoyancy by using ammonium, a chemical they can quickly manufacture or eliminate, depending on the circumstances. For invertebrates, squid have relatively large brains, with big optic lobes, as well as excellent eyes. Although not exactly intelligent by mammalian standards, they are very "competent" animals, in the sense of being well equipped for survival. The squid had apparently recognized my eyes as such and "shot" me, just as he would have done to any enemy. Perhaps squid, with their pea-sized brains, have other abilities we do not understand nor appreciate. ——Walt ❞

● ●

■■■■■■■■■■■■■■■■■■■■■■■■

Villa Insurgentes to San Miguel de Comondú and San José de Comondú

Class 2, 60 miles; use the map on pages 134–135. This trip will take you to two of the most exotic and engaging villages in Baja California. Begin by turning north through Villa Insurgentes. At KM 16, the road will pass through Villa Zaragoza, which has tire repair, groceries, ice, auto parts, liquor, beer, a fish market, and a PEMEX (MND). The arrow-straight road then passes through orchards and fields of corn and wheat. At KM 64, turn half-right (north, signed COMONDÚ) onto the graded class 2, two-lane road. Comondú is no place for a trailer, so if you are towing one, leave it here, hopefully manned by a volunteer to maintain security. A new KM sequence beginning at this point. There will be 3 stream crossings (wet weather) and several 19% grades, but the new road is smooth and the traction good. At KM 33 arrive in San Miguel de Comondú.

The palms are so lush and dense at Comondú that it is hard to believe there is a village down there

The twin villages, known collectively as Comondú, occupy the bottom of a fertile, well-watered canyon. Suddenly you enter a cool sea of green so dense with oranges, sugar cane, figs, corn, grapes, palms, bougainvillea, and a dozen flowering plants that there doesn't seem room for the people. Most of the buildings are traditional adobe, and except for the electric lines, the vehicles, and a satellite TV dish, it could be a scene from the previous century. San Miguel is the older village, established in 1714 by Father Ugarte to supply food for Misión San Javier. Look for antique sugar-cane presses, operated by burros walking in circles. San Miguel has a store that sells groceries, and you can buy gas at a house on the southeast side of road— look for the piles of drums.

To visit San José, keep driving straight ahead. A small plaza will be encountered upon entering the village. The stone building is a missionary house from Misión Comondú, the bell in front dating from 1708 (the church was torn down).

It appears that despite the new graded road, the tranquillity and beauty of the villages, and the wealth of food made possible by Mother Nature, Comondú is dying. Its population is half that of 10 years ago, the handful of businesses has declined to two or three, and most of the faces seen are wrinkled and the hair gray. One wonders—is the decline related to the construction of the new road, or did the road keep it from dying altogether?

■ Stinkers

In the mid-1800s, a group of Americans and Englishmen lived in Comondú, possibly deserters from the whaling ships working Bahía Magdalena. These men earned their living by a somewhat aromatic means. When done flensing (cutting up) the whales, the crews of the ships in the bay would cast away the carcasses. From the "stinkers" that drifted ashore, the men from Comondú would then try out an additional three or four barrels of oil from the fat surrounding the lungs, heart, and intestines. The barrels would then be sold to the whaling ships, whose captains did not seem to mind the source of the oil, nor the odor of the men that offered it.

The church at Comondú

■■■■■■■■■■■■■■■■■■■■■■■■
KM 157 on the Transpeninsular
near Santa Rita to Puerto Chalé

Class 2, 15 miles; use the map on pages 134–135. This road provides fishermen, divers and explorers access to Bahía las Almejas, Isla Crecente, Canal Rehusa, and Isla Santa Margarita. The south end of Margarita was the scene of the greatest maritime disaster in Baja history. Early on a February morning in 1853, the 211-foot sidewheel steamer *Independence* rammed a submerged pinnacle north of Punta Tosca with 400 passengers and crew jammed aboard. The situation was deadly, for heavy surf was breaking at the foot of dark perpendicular cliffs, and no one would survive if the ship broke up in this location. The captain backed the ship off the pinnacle, turned northwest, and slowly ran her along the coast. Steam pressure was falling rapidly, so after about a mile, the ship was turned toward a small beach and purposely run aground. Flames roaring out of the furnaces soon touched wood and spread rapidly. Terrified people began to jump overboard and struggle in the sea, clinging to flotsam. A woman attempting to climb overboard snagged her full skirts on a davit and was left swinging until she was consumed by the flames and dropped into the sea. Rather than let their children burn, parents threw them overboard to an almost certain but less painful death by drowning. Swimmers were sucked under when the ship rose and settled in the waves, and others clinging to chicken coops were swept out to sea. On the beach, men were seen looting corpses and quarreling over the spoils. About 150 people died and were buried in shallow graves high up on the beach and in the canyon beyond. The survivors were soon rescued by whaling ships at anchor inside the bay.

Over 130 years of surf and storm have not succeeded in erasing all traces of the *Independence*, and a visit to the beach will teach you all you want to know about ghosts. The two 10-inch diameter iron shafts that carried her paddle-wheels lie among the rocks on the beach, and several anchors, a capstan, booms, and twisted iron parts can also be seen. Above the beach, numerous shards of pottery and thousands of rusted iron objects lie about, mingled with hundreds of human bones.

"Playa Independence" can be reached in several ways. Launch your boat or hire a *panga* at Puerto Chale, and head for the south end on the island. In Canal Rehusa, a sand spit forms a shallow, sandy lagoon 3 miles north of the lighthouse. An arroyo heading southwest from the south end of this lagoon climbs to a pass and then drops down to the beach, a hike of about 3 miles, one-way. Allow 6 hours for a round trip, including several hours at the site. In calm weather a boat can be landed on the beach: proceed northwest along the outer coast from Punta Tosca for 2.5 miles and look for a sandy beach fronting an arroyo, the first substantial sand beach northwest of the point. A broad stripe of green rock runs diagonally up the hill forming the northwest shoulder of the arroyo.

■■■■■■■■■■■■■■■■■■■■■■■■
KM 80 on the Transpeninsular
south of El Cien
to El Conejo

Class 2, 9.8 miles; use the map on pages 134–135. Long a favorite with surfers, El Conejo (The Rabbit) has easy access and excellent lefts and rights on a small rocky point, working well in almost any swell, although best when they are from the northwest. The place is windswept, with frequent cross-onshore winds, making it popular with heavy-weather boardsailors, especially during frontal conditions. It can be a blow-out all day in summer. Be careful of a strong current paralleling the shore and of frequent sneaker waves. Driftwood sometimes can be found for campfires, and there is good surf fishing. Lobsters and oysters may be purchased from the locals, but the diving potential is almost zero. Secluded beaches and sandy campsites can be found for many miles to the southeast.

The **Independence** *aflame off Isla Santa Margarita*

Courtesy National Maritime Museum

■ Orchilla

The plant resembling Spanish moss seen hanging on shrubs and trees in the Bahía Magdalena-Conejo area is orchilla. A lichen, it colonizes some species of plants, but is resisted by others. Lichens have an odd life style: they consist of two plants, an alga living inside the cells of a fungus. The relationship is beneficial to both, the algae gaining a home and a supply of water, while the fungus gains food from the algae, which can photosynthesize sugars.

Around 1870, it appeared that collecting orchilla was to become the basis of a major industry, since it was used for the manufacture of organic dyes in red, magenta, and violet. A warehouse and a pier were constructed in Bahía Magdalena by an American company, and men began to gather the plant. However, the hopeful entrepreneurs had forgotten that the development of the aniline dye industry had begun in England in the middle of the century, and the further development of these synthetic dyes quickly brought an end to the orchilla industry.

■■■■■■■■■■■■■■■■■■■■■■

KM 17 on the Transpeninsular near La Paz to Punta el Mechudo and Evaristo

Class 2 for 31.2 miles, then class 3 for 14.4 miles; use the map on pages 134–135. As noted earlier, the highway south from Ciudad Constitución is the second most boring section of the Transpeninsular. However, the most boring, between Guerrero Negro and San Ignacio, had a gem waiting near the end (San Ignacio), and this section is no different.

The trip is best made early in the morning in clear weather. Turn north at KM 17 (signed), set trip odometer. The washboard gets bad past the end of the pavement at Mile 14.1. The road follows the shoreline, and there are a number of places to park for the night. Most beaches are pebble and cobble, but sand will be found at Miles 20.0 and 22.8. At Mile 23.8 take the right (010°) fork (the left fork leads to San Juan de la Costa, a phosphate mining town with a public restaurant).

Mother Nature soon begins the most colorful display of sedimentary showmanship in Baja. Some layers of sandstone are graced with easily described colors, such as black, purple, gray, and pink, and there are three shades each of green and beige. Others require physical analogy: persimmon, cinnamon, coffee, guacamole, salmon, and Grape Popsicle. Up close, each color is muted, just touches of pastel in otherwise ordinary rock, but the "big picture," from a distance, is stunning. Erosion has carved strange shapes; there is a turtle with a green shell spotted with brown, and a salmon castle with green battlements.

At Mile 29.0, the road squeezes between the blue Cortez and a cliff of brick-red, green, and tan rock, the most colorful half-mile drive in Baja. Past the cliff, add olive drab, burnt umber, and salmon-tan to the list of colors.

The inshore waters near Punta el Mechudo offer fine fishing, one of the least known and least stressed fisheries in the Cortez, and marlin, sailfish, and dolphinfish have been caught offshore in the warm months. With easy access and numerous places to park a rig, the area would be a good place to spend a few days.

There is another splendid geological display just north of Mile 31.2: the road winds up a huge wedge of rock, and near its top is a castle seemingly molded out of sand, perched on a green cliff plunging into the blue sea. When just past the sand castle, stop and peek over the edge for another visual treat. The road quickly changes to class 3 and soon winds inland to avoid Punta el Mechudo, with loose rock, sharp switchbacks, and grades to 27%. At Mile 33.5, the road gets its turn; ordinary gray to this point, it becomes green, not just faintly green but **green**. The road returns to the coastal plain and to ordinary desert colors at Mile 37.4, and arrives at Evaristo at Mile 45.6.

■ Just deserts

After the "discovery" of the peninsula by Europeans, adventurers carried pearls back to Spain, and La Paz eventually became a center for diving activity, Indians performing the dangerous task, of course. Pearls slowly became harder to find, and in 1874, compressed-air diving equipment was introduced. By the early 1900s, pearls had become so rare that an oyster-cultivation farm was built, whose rock basins and buildings can still be seen on Isla Espíritu Santo, north of La Paz. The scheme failed, and the industry went into a steep decline, ending in 1940, when a blight killed off most of the surviving oysters.

The pearling industry died, but not without leaving a legacy, a literary legacy. There was supposedly a custom among the Indian pearl divers fostered, undoubtedly, by the Jesuit missionaries—to obtain a blessing and a promise of safety, each diver contributed the finest pearl found each day to the church. However, one day, a diver working the oyster beds along the curving coast north of La Paz found a valuable black pearl early in the day. Deciding to keep it for himself, he continued to dive the same area, hoping to find another pearl worthy of the daily blessing. When he failed to return to the surface, his companions began a search for him, and in the process of their diving, they discovered a horrifying sight: a ghostly human corpse, his foot trapped in a huge clam, and his long black hair undulating in the current. The pearl, found clutched in his hand, was dutifully turned in to the Church, but the divers never went back to the area they came to call Cabeza Mechudo, (Long-Haired Head), known today as Punta el Mechudo.

There is some doubt as to the historical authenticity of this tale, for *Tridacna*, the alleged but unproved "killer clam" exists only in the Indo-Pacific region. However, during John Steinbeck's trip with Ed Ricketts to the Cortez described in *The Log From the Sea of Cortez*, he supposedly heard this tale, and he used it as the framework for his novel *The Pearl*.

The main attraction of Evaristo is not Evaristo itself, but the islands offshore. Fishermen and divers equipped with adequate boats, especially underwater photographers, should visit Isla las Ánimas Sur, 9 miles east of Punta Calabozo on the north end of Isla San José. Seen from the west, the island resembles a whale chasing a fish, the aid-to-navigation tower on the island being the whale's spout and a small islet being the fish. Ánimas Sur is one of the premiere deep dives in the Cortez, the sheer sides of the island plunging almost vertically to about 300 feet. So steep is the underwater terrain that it is very difficult to anchor safely, although in calm weather small boats may be able to anchor in 80 feet off the south side. The water is deep blue, providing a clue to its depth, and visibility often exceeds 100 feet. Upwellings of cold, nutrient-rich water promote spectacular growths of gorgonians on the steep walls. Because of the large variety of micro- and macro-habitats available, few locations in the Cortez have such a range in the size of fish present, from clouds of tiny fry through colorful reef fish to heavy-duty gamefish, including grouper, marlin, dolphinfish, and shark. Watch for rare longnose butterfly fish. There are a number of caves, including one on the east side at 60 feet, which you can enter and chimney up through passages. Although this is scuba country, free-divers might get a shot at large groupers and jacks around the pinnacles on the east side.

The southwest reef at Isla San Diego, 10 miles north of Isla San José, is another outstanding dive site, with intricate lava formations honeycombed by grottos. An especially fine grotto system can be found in 30 feet to 40 feet of water near 2 pinnacles awash at the end of the reef. Huge groupers and large populations of lobsters are often seen here, along with orange corals and red, gold, and white sea fans.

Isla San José is about 18 miles long. With a sizable area and some surface water, the island supports a wide variety of wildlife, including such large mammals as deer, ringtailed cats, and coyotes. Scorpions up to 6 inches long wait to terrorize visitors, and bird watchers will be kept busy. The island was home of Pericú Indians until the mid-1700s. There is good diving off the north tip of the island, where diveable depths extend more than a mile from shore, and at Punta Colorada. A sea cave so large it can be entered with a boat will be found near this point. There is relatively little commercial fishing along the east side, so sportfishing is good.

At the south end of San José, the entrance to a large mangrove lagoon will be found along the shore of the beach forming the margin of Bahía Amortajada. It is the largest mangrove area in the Cortez, and a boat trip inside is worthwhile. There are many small channels off the main waterway, and once in the mangroves, it's a whole new Baja experience. Large numbers of birds inhabit the thickets, including the big and obvious ones like herons, egrets, and ibises, and others so small and reclusive you may not be aware of their presence unless you stop the engine and sit quietly for a while. The waters are filled with large numbers of fish, and oysters can be seen clinging to mangrove roots. The visibility is often good, and a snorkeling venture is an experience to remember. Bottoms range from clean sand to the blackest of gooey mud. For the stout-hearted, a night dive ought to be fantastic.

The waters around Isla Cayo have good diving, much of it within free-diving range, and sections of it are loaded with shellfish. Garden eels can be seen in sandy areas. Just south of San José is tiny Isla Coyote, site of a prosperous-looking fishing settlement, with neat homes and a well-cared-for look. Diving is especially colorful among the rock islets to the west, and at the solitary rock to the north, all having huge orange and red sea fans and many reef fish.

Isla San Francisco, just south of Coyote, was worked for pearls from the late 1500s to the early 1900s, and between 1881 and 1886, a German operated a one-man gold mine on the island. The end of the spit provides good diving, with fine visibility in periods of north weather. Watch for garden eels and jawfish on the sandy bottoms. The deep water to the east has good fishing for dolphinfish and yellowfin tuna in season.

■ The yellow-legged gull

The yellow-legged gull breeds entirely within the Cortez and its range is almost, but not quite, limited to those waters: some get as far north in summer as the Salton Sea, and several have been recorded in the Bahía Magdalena area, so it might be termed a Cortez "almost-endemic." It looks like an ordinary western gull, with a snowy-white head, chest, and belly, yellow eyes and bill, and dark slate-colored back and wings. However, it has, obviously, bright yellow legs, not flesh-colored like the western gull. They eat everything from krill to smaller seabirds, and are not adverse to scavenging carcasses and the offal dumped by fishing vessels. Yellow-legged gulls are so bold there is a record of one drinking excess milk off the belly of a lactating female sea lion.

Las Palmas resort area to El Cardónal

Class 1, 12 miles; use the map on page 149. The class 1 road continues north past Hotel Punta Pescadero (no facilities for RVs) to El Cardónal Resort at Mile 12, which has RV parking, a sandy beach, a water purification system, and a store selling limited basic groceries, sodas, and snacks. This inexpensive class B resort offers diving, snorkeling, sailing, kayaking, windsurfing, fishing, hiking, horseback riding, mountain biking, and visits to nearby rock art sites. Diving off the settlement is excellent, with many small tropical fish and all three of the moray species found in Baja waters: Panamic green, zebra, and spotted.

■■■■■■■■■■■■■■■■■■■
KM 93 on the Transpeninsular at Las Cuevas to La Rivera, Pulmo, and Bahía los Frailes and on to San José del Cabo on the East Cape Coast Road

17 miles paved, then 37.8 miles of class 1 and 2; use the map on page 149. This road passes Pulmo Reef, one of Baja's great natural wonders, and Cabo Frailes, with its unusual beach-casting, and then passes dozens of miles of the finest and most pristine beaches imaginable. Most of the road described remains unpaved. However, it is expected that the road as far as Pulmo will be paved in the near future.

Turn northeast at Las Cuevas, and pass through Santa Cruz at KM 3.5, which has a restaurant and groceries. At KM 10+, at an intersection continue straight ahead (northeast) for La Rivera, which has groceries, tire repair, tortilla factory, restaurants, long-distance telephone, cold sodas and beer, ice, doctor, and pharmacy. To find the PEMEX (MND), continue straight ahead (northeast) until you are forced to turn right or left. Turn right (east) on the class 1 road, and find the station in 0.6 mile.

To go to Correcaminos RV Park, turn left (west) at the intersection just noted. The class 1 graded dirt road leads to the park entrance in 3.0 miles. Located in an old mango orchard (the crop is ripe for picking in summer), the inexpensive class B park has full hookups, showers, and rest rooms. The sand beach 0.2 mile to the north is prime boardsailing country, with good winds and frequent cross-onshore conditions. Small boats can be launched across the beach.

To head for Pulmo, turn southeast at the intersection at KM 10+. At KM 19, a class 1 road left (northeast, one 14% grade with loose rock) leads 2.3 miles to Hotel Punta Colorada. The hotel has fishing cruisers, *pangas*, rental tackle, and bait, which are available to walk-ins. Boardsailors will find lots of wind and cross-onshore conditions in this vicinity, and if you are looking for logo waves (waves as high as the logo on a sail), this may be the place. A number of sandy shallow bars about 100 yards out have the reputation of being the best place in Baja for wave-jumping. The hotel will allow RVers to park overnight at the beach just to the southeast of the hotel.

At KM 22, a class 2 road left (north, signed) leads to Punta Arena Sur. Set trip odometer. At Mile 0.7 turn right (100°), at Mile 2.8 go half-left (050°) between several ranch buildings, and at Mile 7 arrive at the beach. This area is the scene of fine beach-casting for roosters. Inshore are jack crevalle, sierra, and ladyfish, and out several miles dolphinfish, skipjack, yellowfin tuna, sailfish, and black, blue and striped marlin in season. The water east of the lighthouse is a top location for high-wind and wave boardsailing. The lee of the point is great for speed sailing, with lots of sand beach and cross-offshore conditions. There are many boondocking locations, but be careful of the soft sand.

Back on the main road, the pavement ends at KM 27+, and the graded, washboarded, class 1 road begins. Set trip odometer. Arrive at Pulmo at Mile 6.2. The name is derived from *pulmón*, the Spanish word for lung, apparently adopted during the days of the pearl divers.

The tiny animals that build coral reefs are among the world's most industrious creatures, being responsible for building Australia's Great Barrier Reef and other immense public works about the world. These animals, jelly-like carnivorous polyps encased in a "skeleton" of calcium carbonate, are delicate and require a strict set of environmental conditions, one of which is being far from the fresh-water discharges of rivers. In addition, the polyps need water temperatures above 72°. In spite of these requirements, their colonies are found over 80 million square miles of the earth's surface, an area 22 times that of the US, generally between 32° north and 27° south latitude.

Corals are not spread evenly between these two latitudes, and a glance at a map showing their distribution reveals a striking oddity; coral reefs are rare or absent along the western coasts of the continents. This is not due to a cultural bias on the part of the polyps, but to the fact that the waters off western coasts tend to be cooler than those off eastern coasts. Because of the earth's rotation and related wind patterns, ocean currents are forced into a clockwise pattern in the northern hemisphere and a counterclockwise one in the southern. On the eastern shores of the continents, warm water is carried towards the poles, extending the area suitable for corals. On western shores cool water is carried toward the equator, restricting coral growth. Corals have managed to establish reefs in only four locations along the west coast of North America—one in Panama, one in Costa Rica, one in mainland Mexico, and Pulmo. (There are, however, coral heads in many Cortez locations, as well as a very small patch in Bahía San Gabriel at Isla Espíritu Santo.)

The corals of Pulmo, shielded from the cold Pacific and finding other conditions to their liking, have constructed a sizable reef. Starting near shore just south of Cabo Pulmo and running in a northeasterly direction, 3 broad rows of coral heads of 2 dominant species continue for 1.5 miles, ending in depths of 70 feet. The row pattern is caused by the geology of the area—the corals are cemented to elongated ridges of basaltic rock protruding from the sandy bottom. The astronomical number of nooks, crannies, and cavelets formed by the reef are home to huge numbers of creatures. In his book *The Log From the Sea of Cortez*, John Steinbeck recounted a visit to Pulmo during a 1940 boat trip to collect biological specimens with Edward Ricketts: "The complexity of the life-pattern on Pulmo Reef was even greater than at Cape San Lucas. Clinging to the coral, growing on it, burrowing into it, was a teeming fauna. Every piece of the soft material broken off skittered and pulsed with life—little crabs and worms and snails. One small piece of coral might conceal 30 or 40 species, and the colors on the reef were electric."

Pulmo is one of the most famed diving locations in the Cortez, second only to Marisla Seamount. The water is warm and the visibility is often 30 feet to 50 feet, occasionally 75. Since the innermost coral heads can be found in only a few feet of water immediately off the beach, neither scuba nor a boat is essential. As you enter the water, be ready for a surprise; at some times of the year small *sardinas* are so numerous that they may envelop you in a silver cloud, bringing on vertigo. Once, in deeper water, I (Walt) was approached by a school of goatfish, which turned and began making endless circles, placing me at the center of a living carousel, its leader apparently having come to the conclusion that he was at the end of the procession rather than at its beginning. Certainly, do not miss a night dive. The small white islet at the south end of the bay is also a fine dive site, with sea fans, cup corals, pargo, and numerous other species.

Another outstanding dive site lies just offshore, Bajo el Pulmo. With a least depth of 32 feet, it is located approximately 2,500 yards, 050° from Cabo Pulmo. A little searching may be necessary, but it should be possible to see it as you approach. With coral heads, deep caves, many species of sea fans, colonies of yellow colonial tulip corals, dog and yellow snappers, grunts, coral and giant hawkfish, bicolor and bumphead parrot fish, sea bass, broomtail grouper, turtles, and an occasional jewfish, the place is spectacular.

Pulmo is an underwater ecological reserve, and fishing, spearfishing, foraging, and shell collecting are not permitted. Small boats can be launched across the beach or the launch ramp noted later, and *pangas* are for hire. Avoid anchoring on the reef, for it can cause severe damage to the coral. There is often a good afternoon breeze, and the bay is popular with boardsailors. In winter, the prevailing north winds often exceed 20 knots, providing excellent cross-onshore conditions. Sailfish are numerous in the deep water offshore, sometimes producing two or three per boat per day.

There is a concrete launch ramp (14%), but it has limited maneuvering room and ends abruptly in rather shallow water, making it a high-tide proposition for larger boats. To find the ramp, drive from Tito's Restaurant 0.75 mile northeast, parallel to the shore, to a stone building near a rocky headland. Check at the restaurant about fees and rules. Pepe's Dive Center has rental equipment, guided tours, night dives, snorkeling, three boats, compressed air, full PADI certification, and a resort course for beginners. Pepe will provide visitors with an orientation on the location and the ecology of the reefs and measures necessary for their protection. He is knowledgeable and speaks excellent English. Cabo Pulmo Divers, located on a beach on the south side of the community, offers NAUI and PADI instruction, rentals, air, guides, boat dives, and snorkeling.

Modest Tito's Restaurant has no official menu, but usually has fish, scallops, tacos, and beer available. Nancy's Restaurant serves meals, cocktails, and snacks, under a *palapa* roof. Cabo Pulmo Beach Resort offers rental homes, *casitas*, and bungalows, all with LPG refrigerators and stoves, some with kitchenettes, with a two-night minimum.

The class 1 road continues, arriving at Bahía los Frailes at Mile 10.9. A deep submarine canyon winds into the bay, having depths of over 400 feet within 400 yards of shore, and shore-casters have caught yellowfin tuna and marlin. The closest approach of the canyon to the shore is at that point on the beach where the right tangent of Cabo Frailes bears 055°. Spearfishermen with sufficient courage will encounter large gamefish by lying in wait in the deep water along the south margin of the point. Divers have seen sandfalls in the canyon. There are numerous boondocking locations along the shore. The new Hotel Bahía los Frailes has diving and snorkeling rental equipment and a *panga* fleet. The class 2 road south of Frailes continues until Mile 38.7, when it approaches the outskirts of San José del Cabo.

■■■■■■■■■■■■■■■■■■■■■■
KM 55 on the Transpeninsular north of San José del Cabo to KM 71+ on Route 19 via the Naranjas Road

Class 3, 30.8 miles; use the map on page 149. Explorers can visit the Sierra de la Laguna on this road, which crosses the range to the vicinity of Punta Gasparino on the Pacific side.

Set trip odometer, turn southwest. The road meanders through brush-covered hills and scenic canyons, with dark emerald ponds shimmering in light-colored rock. There are very few signs of civilization, just a few cows, small flocks of goats, and an occasional ranch. Soon after you start, *zalate* and oak trees will be seen, somehow out of place amid the palms. If you see what looks suspiciously like an ordinary American robin except that it has a light creamy, buff-colored breast rather than brick-red, and has a longer-than-normal bill, it is an endemic San Lucas robin, a colorfully feathered subspecies common in the Sierra de la Laguna. Some experts believe it to be a separate species.

The Pacific can be seen from the crest of the range at Mile 13, the elevation being about 3,400 feet. The road east of the crest is graded, but to the west it is poor, with switchbacks and slopes to 30%. Turn right (004°) at a small cluster of buildings marked "El Aguaje" (The Water Hole) at Mile 23.1. The road quickly swings west, and a power line will be seen paralleling it almost all the way to Route 19. Take the left (252°) fork at Mile 24.7, and at Mile 30.8 arrive at Route 19.

■■■■■■■■■■■■■■■■■■■■■■■■■■■■■■
KM 28 on Route 2 to Cañon Guadalupe

Class 2, 34.6 miles; use the map on pages 76–77. A series of wildly beautiful canyons are eroded into the Juárez

Rob Williams

Two hikers inspect a waterfall near Cañon Guadalupe

escarpment in this area. The road west of Laguna Salada passes through typical desert scrub, but in the canyons California fan palms, blue fan palms, smoke trees, cottonwoods, and elephant trees can be found. The largest canyons, Tajo (Gorge), El Carrizo (The Reed), Guadalupe, La Mora (The Blackberry), and El Palomar (The Pigeon House), have surface water, often inhabited by such unlikely Baja creatures as tree frogs, water striders, and giant water bugs. Large emerald pools make fine swimming holes.

Indians used the canyons as routes between the desert and the pine forests above. Virtually all portable artifacts were carried off long ago, but petroglyphs, pictographs, chipping waste, *metates* (grindstones), and pottery shards are common in the palm groves and around watered sites. Guadalupe has three major blessings: a road into the mouth of the canyon, a campground, and hot tubs full of highly mineralized water at exactly the right temperature for removing desert dust and loosening tight muscles.

The road heads south at KM 28, signed CAÑON DE GUADALUPE. Set trip odometer. At Mile 14.7 encounter Rancho la Poderosa, at Mile 20.7 shacks and a water tank. At Mile 21.4, El Trono Blanco (The White Throne), the greatest rock wall in Baja and a prime climbing site, is in plain

ew up the canyon to the west. It looks deceptively close ҂cause of its massive size; it is actually over 8 miles away. ᴗontinue southeast to Mile 26.8 and swing southwest between irrigated fields. Note the pointed peak dominating the skyline ahead, Picacho Rasco, 4,500 feet, and the sharp spire, which is the Virgin of Guadalupe, named for a fancied likeness to the Madonna.

 Arrive at the campground in Cañon Guadalupe at Mile 34.6. There are a number of RV sites, with tubs fed by hot springs. *Palapas* cover some of the sites, and a large pool holds 1,500 gallons under two enormous boulders, forming a cave of sorts. Some sites also have barbecue pits and tables. A year-around cool-water stream cascades through hundreds of palms and disappears in the alluvial fan below. Views from the ridge above are well worth the climb to elevation 1,800 feet; the view of the mouth of the canyon is breathtaking. The Pool of the Virgin can be found 2 miles upstream. Bounded on three sides by white granite cliffs, surrounded by cottonwoods, willows, ferns, and mosses, and fed by a slender waterfall, it seems out of place.

The best time to visit Cañon Guadalupe is from early November to the end of May. Holding tanks should be dumped prior to arrival at the campground. The hot mineral water is safe to drink, but has a mild sulfur odor, so it may be best to bring your own water for cooking and drinking. There is no electricity or telephones, but a small store sells canned food, snacks, soda, beer, motor oil, and firewood. A restaurant serves Mexican dishes on weekends. Off-road tours to a number of Indian sites are available. Stop at the store for site assignment. The minimum stay is two nights. Prices are a bit high, but the scenery makes it worthwhile. Reservations are required, which can be made by calling Rob's Baja Tours. It is best to call again just before departure to learn about road conditions.

■ ■ ■ ■ ■ ■ ■ ■
El Cóndor to
Parque Nacional Constitución de 1857
and KM 55+ on Route 3

Class 2, 38.9 miles to Laguna Hanson, class 2, 19.3 miles from the lake to Route 3; use the map on pages 76–77. Much of the park is above 4,000 feet, and the chaparral of lower regions gives way to the cool pine forests and dry meadows of the Sierra de Juárez. An ever-changing maze of roads from El Cóndor to the park makes a compass essential.

The road from El Cóndor heads south next to the PEMEX station (MND). Set trip odometer, and take the left (145°) fork at Mile 11.4. The surrounding areas are among the most heavily mineralized in Baja, with many gold, tungsten, manganese, and cobalt mines.

At the crossroads at Mile 17.0, note the sign EVITE INCENDIOS and continue straight ahead (141°). Take the left (128°) fork at Mile 17.5, and at Mile 18.0 continue southeast (125°). An eagle's-eye view of magnificent Cañon Tajo

A hiker gets some chinmeying practice at a site near Cañon Tajo

can be found by hiking from the La Milla campground to a ridge overlooking the canyon. At Mile 20.0 turn east onto a class 2 road signed RANCHO SAN IGNACIO-LA MILLA. Set your trip odometer and turn left (320°) at Mile 1.1. The road will meander north and then east toward the Juárez escarpment. Swing right (090°) at the forks at Miles 1.7 and 1.8, left (090°) at Mile 1.9, and arrive at the campground at Mile 2.8. The campground is a good boondocking site, especially for those seeking solitude. There is no trail to the ridge, but the country is fairly open and hiking is easy. Simply head east from the campground for about an hour, avoiding dropping too deeply into the northwest fork of the canyon, which approaches the campground. The view is well worth the hike.

Back on the Parque 1857 Road at Mile 20; there are great views of "Picacho Row," a line of miniature granite spires rising up to 500 feet above the tableland, with many chimneys and domes. Continue straight ahead (150°) at the intersection at Mile 24.0. Rough stuff is encountered between Miles 25.5 and 28 as the road climbs a ridge. Take the left (114°) fork at the intersection at Mile 30.6. At Mile 35.5 encounter an abandoned forest-fire camp. Laguna Hanson, at Mile 38.9, is less than a mile across, but is home to many water birds. Boondocking sites are available around the shores of the lake, a few with tables. Potable water can be obtained from a tiny seep at the forestry camp a half mile southwest.

Despite its beauty and accessibility, you will rarely see more than a half-dozen people in the park most of the year, but during Easter vacation it can become a scene from Hell: hundreds of people roasting chunks of meat over fires,

the noise from ATVs and trail bikes splitting the blue air. Every square inch seems covered with ruts or broken beer bottles. People sit in aluminum chairs drinking beer and telling stories, occasionally leaping up to take a turn at the wheel. No one attempts to remove a dead dog lying in the middle of the race course, squashed under a dune buggy. A week later the people are gone, the litter has been picked up, and all is quiet again.

Because of its altitude the park is cooler than surrounding areas, and there is little underbrush, making hiking enjoyable. There are no marked trails, and no maps are available from rangers. The 6-mile hike around the lake through the pines and meadows is pleasant. You can see much of the surrounding country from the rocky formations rising to 200 feet, 500 yards northwest of the buildings at Mile 39.4. Picacho del Diablo, 78 miles away, bears 140°. East is the Juárez escarpment, dropping precipitously to the desert floor. The escarpment can be approached on either of two roads south of the lake. Rolling waves of rock are passed before the sudden drop. Views from the top of the sharp-pointed peaks six miles east of the lake are smashing. The highest peak in the Juárez is Cerro Colorado, at 6,435 feet somehow out of place in much lower tablelands 42 miles southeast.

The route to KM 55+ on Route 3 begins at the buildings at the southwest end of the lake. Set trip odometer. At Mile 0.4 pass the forestry camp and small pond, at Mile 1.1 a tree farm, at Mile 2.5 a ranch, and at Mile 3.9 arrive at El Aserradero (The Sawmill). The road from this point on is normally in good condition, with many long downhill stretches. At Mile 6.6, pass more ranches and a pond. A fine shaded boondocking site will be found at Mile 14.8. Encounter a fork at Mile 16.5. Although this fork is important,

Laguna Hanson, as seen from rocky formations to the west of the lake

it is unmarked and looks like just another place where drivers have made parallel roads to avoid bad spots, and if you don't look sharply, it is easy to miss. Take the left branch, which immediately turns southeast to reach a fork at Mile 17.3. Take the right (180°) turn here, and arrive on Route 3 at KM 55+.

■■■■■■■■■■■■
KM 98 on Route 2
to Ojos Negros and Route 3

Class 2, 61.1 miles; use the map on pages 76–77. This pleasant trip crosses fine rolling chaparral country dotted with pine-rimmed meadows and groves of oaks. The road is generally in good condition, with no bad grades, not much change in altitude, and only two sizable stream crossings, both of which are sandy and flat. Although there are many minor forks and intersections, the correct road is usually obvious and there is little danger of becoming lost.

The road starts south 0.1 mile east of the KM 98 marker. Set trip odometer. The road passes a bakery, a tortilla factory, laundromat and a number of grocery stores, but the pavement (rough and potholed) ends at Mile 4.5. At Mile 5.6 go straight ahead (130°). (The right—190°—fork is a class 1 road leading 1 mile to Hacienda Santa Veronica. This beautiful class A park has spreading oaks, open meadows, full hookups, a swimming pool, tennis courts, mountain bike and motorcycle courses, horseback riding, dining room, bar, rest rooms, and showers.) At Mile 8.8 continue straight ahead (183°) at the fork. Rancho Nejí is reached at Mile 11.3. Continue straight ahead (125°) at Mile 12.4, and at Mile 18.8 turn right (140°), passing through El Compadre (The Friend), a small settlement graced by enormous oaks. The road then crosses several streams, passes through large meadows and by several ranches at San Faustino at Mile 29.0, and then runs through a series of majestic oak groves, offering fine boondocking sites. After you pass more oak groves, La Rosa de Castilla, a tiny ranching community, is reached at Mile 42.6.

The tailings of Mina el Fenómeno can be seen on the ridge to the west. As its name implies, the mine was a phenomenon of its time, producing over 2% of the world's supply of tungsten during its short working life. By 1943, the 100,000-ton ore body was exhausted, and today the mine is a totally deserted but fascinating place. The west flank of the ridge has cool, mysterious mine shafts. Look for thousands of cast-iron balls used in the mill to crush the ore.

La Huerta (The Orchard), a small settlement, is reached at Mile 50.8, and at Mile 52.1, El Coyote, an important junction, unmarked except for a barbed-wire fence with metal posts, a rarity in Baja. To continue on to the village of Ojos Negros, drive straight ahead (255°), arriving at Mile 61.1. If you intend to head for Parque Nacional Constitución de 1857 turn left (110°) at Mile 61.1, and you will encounter the KM 55+-Parque 1857 road in 3 miles.

■■■■■■■■■■■■■■■■■■■■■
KM 86 on Route 3 to El Alamo

Class 1, 11 miles; use the map on pages 76–77. The nearby Santa Clara gold placers were discovered in 1888, and El Alamo soon had more than 5,000 inhabitants, a newspaper, a pool hall, and a cantina. Unwashed miners had another source of entertainment: the first captured louse to scurry out of a circle won a poke of gold dust for its handler. Gold seemed unlimited, and a one-ounce nugget was found in the gizzard of a chicken. Famous mystic Eilley Orrum, the Washoe Seeress, soon appeared. In earlier years, aided by a crystal ball, she had provided Nevada miners with advice on where to stake their claims, and which way and how deep to dig. Her advice had made her and a number of miners wealthy. At one point she owned a mansion in Virginia City, but when she arrived in El Alamo she was an elderly widow, down on her luck. Pitching her tent and polishing her ball, she went into business again. Her first "seeing" demonstrated that she knew the commercial value of positive thinking: the ball showed El Alamo's gold fields to be extensive, spreading all the way to San Diego, and the specifics could be known for a price. Finding gold in Nevada was one thing, in El Alamo another. Even Eilley's talents could not sustain the boom, and today El Alamo is almost a ghost town. A few miners still are at work, and gold can be purchased at market prices.

■■■■■■■■■■■■■
KM 26 on Route 3
to Rancho Agua Caliente

Class 2, 5.1 miles; use the map on pages 76–77. With its restaurant and bar (open warm months only), pools, rest rooms, showers, hot springs, shade trees, and RV parking spaces, this recreation area is popular with the locals. However, the maintenance and cleanliness of the place have varied over the years from satisfactory to awful. Unfortunately, you must pay your toll at the gate, which is out of sight of the facilities, and you either pay or don't get in. Once you are in, it seems that there is no refund if you don't like what you see and turn around. During our last visit, the old gentleman at the gate refused to let us in when he discovered that we were working on this book. Short stretches of 23% upgrades going in and out.

■■■■■■■■■■■■■■■■■
Puertecitos to KM 229+
on the Transpeninsular

Class 2, 80.9 miles; use the map on pages 96-97. Many people drive far too fast along this stretch of road; a man recently bragged to us that his wife had made the 48-mile run between Puertecitos and Alfonsina's in an hour in her "hot-rod sand rail." There have been a number of accidents, so take your time and drive defensively. There are no upgrades over about 14% going north or south, but underpowered three-speed vehicles, especially those with heavy loads or towing trailers, may encounter some tense moments. Set trip odometer.

Mile	Location
4.6	**Playa la Costilla** (Rib or Cutlet Beach). Boondocking, sand beach with stretches of gravel.
9.3	The dark hill to the east is Volcán Prieto (Dark Volcano). The shallows offshore are great for leopard grouper, and the small indentation in the shoreline just to the south has excellent corvina, pargo, and snapper.
11.2	Access to a sand-and-cobble beach with a natural breakwater. Beware of the 25% grade coming out.
16.6	Site of infamous grade in the "old" road; look up and to the south.
17.3	**El Huérfanito** (The Orphan). There are just a few homes here, opposite a tiny island. A rough concrete launch ramp (12%) leads to a pebble beach. Kids will have a ball with the hordes of small spotted bass.

■ Enchanted Islands

The Islas Encantadas are a group of 6 small islands stretching south along the coast for 18 miles, the most northerly lying offshore at this point. Their collective name stems from the facts that mirages are often seen in the area, currents on their eastern and western sides run in opposite directions, some of the beaches are black (lava sand), some rocks float (pumice), and others are made of glass (obsidian). The first four islands, El Huérfanito, El Muerto, Lobos, and Encantada, were formed by fault blocking of Miocene volcanic rock during the Pleistocene epoch.

The area east of Encantada is the focus of fishing in the area. About 700 yards to the east of the island is a tiny islet, covered with bird droppings and unworthy of a name, and even farther to the east is a large reef. Studded with pinnacles, it is loaded with gulf grouper, yellowtail, and cabrilla, as well as moderate numbers of white seabass. The eastern margin of the reef is marked by a wash rock that bares to three feet at low tide.

If you have a boat along, you should set aside a day to explore San Luis, the largest and most southern of the islands, and its companion Isla Pomo. Bufeo (to be described shortly) is a good place to launch. As you near San Luis, its western side gives few hints as to its violent volcanic birth during the Holocene epoch, but as you round the southern coast, layers of ash and pumice are encountered, and the east side proves to be far

more dramatic than the west. Even those without a graduate degree in geology will recognize that the semicircular bluff encountered there is the inside curve of a volcano, and that the 50-foot cone of dark, rough lava in the center is a vent plug, formed as volcanic activity ended. The eastern half of the volcano is missing, blasted into oblivion when it exploded. The coast on both sides of the volcano is a fantastic sculpture of volcanism and erosion.

There are numerous places on the island to land, including the long sand spit that sticks out from the southwestern side, and the volcano site, with its sloping beach of pumice and pebbles. The aid-to-navigation tower here, askew on its foundation, has been dubbed "The Leaning Tower of Pumice." A pebble beach on the east side, just south of the north tip of the island, provides another place to land. Rounding the north tip counterclockwise, you soon see a snug little harbor, but beware—the entrance may be awash at low tide, the rocks are sharp, and the place stinks to high heaven because of its popularity with sea birds. Just to the south, sun will be seen glinting off huge boulders of low-grade obsidian. Nearby is a "lunch cave," a small sea cave providing a cool, shaded place to take a break at low tides.

Isla Pomo, just to the northeast, is also of Holocene volcanic origin. Landings can be made in the cove on the east side, and there is a lunch cave on the south side. Above and adjacent to the cave is a mystery—are those white objects cactus covered by bird droppings, natural sculptures created by artistic birds using the same material, or stalagmites produced by an as-yet unknown geologic process?

Fishing is good around the islands, and trollers working yellowtail may have trouble keeping the numerous cabrilla off their hooks. Try the south and east sides of San Luis, the shallow channel across to Pomo, and several reefs a half mile or so north of both San Luis and Pomo. The islands are home to many sea birds, including ospreys, Heermann's gulls, frigates, and brown- and blue-footed boobies. Hundreds of pelicans often inhabit the sand spit on San Luis.

Mile	Location
🅿 24.4	Gas, water, food, sodas. The dominant plants in this area are *cardón*, *palo adán*, ocotillo, *garambullo*, elephant trees, acacias, and brittlebush, all described earlier. Freed from the "edge effect" seen along the Transpeninsular, brittlebushes in this area seem to be very neighborly; each plant allows its fellows a certain amount of living space, and the result is reminiscent of Foster City, California, with its orderly, row-after-row sameness.

36.3   La Encantada (signed). Sportfishing, food, drink, sand beach.

37.8   **Campo Bufeo** (signed). Restaurant, RV parking, cabins, gas, diesel. The long sand beach here is a good jumping-off place for visits to Islas San Luis and Pomo.

● ●

66 *Breakfast at Bufeo*

Many years ago, Reeve and I made our first trip to Baja, a foray in a Volkswagen camper along the shore of the Cortez south of San Felipe. After a number of battles with soft sand and the legendary "Terrible Three," the steepest and roughest grades in Baja, we finally parked on the sandy beach at Campo Bufeo. As night fell, we built a campfire and began to plan a long-awaited event, our first dive in the Cortez. There was excitement in the air; the visibility would be 200 feet, and the naive and unsuspecting fish would be fin-to-fin, of course. All we had to do was pick the one we wanted for supper and let him have it with a speargun! All fish are not created equal, at least in the frying pan, and the conversation turned towards speculation as to what species we might encounter. We knew that dolphinfish, grouper, and yellowtail were good eating, but we weren't sure they were to be found in the northern Cortez. To better plan the next day's menu, we got out a fish identification book, and the first page we looked at concerned the great white shark: "The star of 'Jaws'...reported to 36'...known to attack man or boats without provocation...uncommon but not rare in the Cortez." There was a lull in the conversation for several minutes as we digested these unhappy facts. I spoke first, recalling an old article by Baja explorer J. Ross Browne, something about manta rays hovering over pearl divers and then devouring them with formidable teeth and jaws. After another deep silence, Reeve told of someone he knew who had been bitten by a moray, and recounted a recent newspaper article about a similar event with a barracuda. As the embers turned to ashes, we lay down on our air mattresses, but there was to be little sleep that night as we silently mulled over every possible creature that could be waiting for us in the dark waters offshore. Could a giant grouper swallow a person whole? Does a marlin use its bill to impale things? Could a whale shark suck a diver into its huge mouth, by accident or design?

By dawn we were certain that every manta, moray, shark, and barracuda in the Cortez had migrated to the waters just off our beach in anticipation of a breakfast of human flesh, followed by a mob of piranhas, lampreys, wolf eels, and hungry hagfish arriving from other waters, hoping to clean up the leftovers. We reluctantly put on our fins, masks, and snorkels, cocked our spearguns, and warily backed into the water. When the water was chest deep I took a breath and stooped down for a first look. The visibility was poor, but the vague outline of a large fish could be seen not three feet away. As I pulled the trigger, the fish spooked, but there

was a pull on the line attached to the spear so heavy that the gun was almost jerked out of my hands, and I knew I had him. Standing up, I spat out the snorkel and let out a war whoop, and just at that instant, the fish leaped into the air behind me, landing in front of Reeve in a great spray of water. Hearing a scream and thinking we were under attack by sea creatures, just as we had expected, Reeve began beating a hasty retreat. I turned around and saw him heading for shore at top speed and started to follow him—perhaps he knew something I didn't. However, the fish had wrapped the line around my legs and I lost my balance and began to flounder around. With only a small amount of slack line left, the fish began thrashing the surface of the water in circles around me, and I yelled "Get this thing away from me!" Hearing the commotion, Reeve turned to see me under attack from all sides, drew his knife, and bravely swam back to save his only brother.

*Our adrenaline took several hours to return to normal levels, but as the corvina filets browned in the frying pan we laughed until our sides hurt; we had expected our first Cortez dive to be exciting, but not **this** exciting! We couldn't have been in the water two minutes! ——Walt* 99

● ●

Walt analyzes a mineral sample

Mile	Location
42.9	Campo el Faro; sportfishing.
43.2	**Papa Fernández'**, 1 mile east (signed), may have gas, oil, food, drink, and rental boats. Launch over a fairly hard sand-and-pebble beach. Fishing around Isla San Luis Gonzaga can be good from spring to fall for grouper, sierra, snapper, and spotted bass, and the area is frequently the northernmost range of significant numbers of migratory yellowtail. Hot spots in-

clude the waters off Punta Willard and along the shoreline just to the north. Commercial boats anchored in the bay may have fresh shrimp for sale.

45.8   Road east (signed) to Alfonsina's, two miles. This resort has rooms, restaurant, gas, water, limited supplies, rental boats, and possible mechanical repairs. Boats can be launched easily over the beach. There is a growing community of Americans.

50.9   Junction, take the right (210˚) fork. The other fork leads to Punta Final (Final Point).

64.5   **Las Arrastras**. Ranch, cold sodas, tire repair.

68.0   Intersection, go left (045˚) for Puerto Calamajué or right (164˚) for the Transpeninsular.

80.9   Arrive at the Transpeninsular Highway at KM 229+.

Mile 8.0 on the Punta Banda Road to Caleta Árbolitos, Kennedy's Cove, and Bahía Playon

Class 1-2, 2 miles; use the inset map on page 87. This area, on the southwest side of the Punta Banda peninsula, is very beautiful, and since it is usually quiet and empty, it serves as a good introduction to what Baja has to offer in its more remote areas. The road has been graded up to the crest, but the road down the southern slopes has loose rock and grades to 12%. In spite of the signs proclaiming the existence of an RV park, it would not be wise to attempt this road with a large mobile home or with any but the smallest of trailers.

Set trip odometer. Go left at Mile 0.5 for Árbolitos, right for Kennedy's Cove and Bahía Playon. If you head for Árbolitos and are towing a trailer, you might consider using the grove of trees giving the place its name (Small Trees) as a boondocking site, and continue on with your tow vehicle, dune buggy, ATV, or motorcycle; the road to this point is class 1, a marginal class 2 beyond.

If you wish to go to Kennedy's or El Playon, turn right at Mile 0.5, set trip odometer. At Mile 0.5 on the marginal class 2 road, you will encounter a fork at a concrete-block shed; turn left for Kennedy's, right for Playon. The coast in this area is rugged, and you will have to clamber down cliffs to get to the cobble beaches. A davit at Kennedy's can be used with a line to lower small boats to the beach.

The underwater life is typical Southern Californian, and kelp, lings, rock cod, lobsters, anemones, and sea urchins abound. Visibility averages 20 feet to 30 feet, but it can get as low as 8 feet and as high as 45 feet. An underwater arch can be found southeast of the two largest islets in Árbolitos, and friendly sea lions may accompany you while you swim through it. There are a number of sea caves, arches, and blowholes along the coast, and a cave near a prominent bird rock a mile east of Kennedy's has an open top that can be entered in calm weather.

66 Night dive

Reeve and I unloaded our camper at Kennedy's Cove and lowered our 12-foot aluminum boat, its engine, and our dive gear down the cliff with a rope to the rocky beach below. It was dark by the time we finished, and we quickly suited up for a night dive. After running several hundred yards through the choppy waters, we stopped the engine and dropped the anchor. After putting on our scubas, we tested the regulators, sat on the rail, and rolled over backwards into the water.

There were no shore lights, the sky was cloudy, and the water was pitch-black. We turned on our dive lights at the same time, and two brilliant shafts of light pierced the darkness, looking like the light sabers brandished by Luke Skywalker and Darth Vader. We headed for the bottom about 35 feet below and went our separate ways, looking at the fish, sea urchins, and abalone. As I followed a fish into a small cave, my light suddenly went out when I banged it into a rock. There was nothing I could do except to keep clicking the switch and banging on the case with a dive knife, but nothing helped. After several minutes I realized I could not see a thing; I was surrounded by utter darkness. This is a rare experience in the modern world, where there always seems to be light coming under a door, the glow of a clock dial, street lights shining through a window, or the loom of a distant city on the horizon. However, after a dozen good whacks, the light finally went on, its shaft aimed directly at a dozen lobsters in the back of the cave.

Now, the Mexican Fish and Game people take a dim view of foreigners taking lobsters, but there is a certain level of temptation beyond which mere mortals should not be tested. Raising a huge cloud of silt, I pursued the critters out the mouth of the cave and across sandy bottoms into stands of seaweed, until they attempted to hide in cracks and crevices. As I continued to stuff them one-by-one into a goody bag, I took a heavy pull on the scuba regulator, and was not greeted with the customary blast of cool air: my tank was virtually empty. I could still see one more lobster, but it was time to leave, and I began an ascent.

Switching to a snorkel at the surface, I took a few breaths and located the boat with my light, which went out again after several seconds. Arriving alongside, I pushed the bulging goody bag up into the boat and started to heave myself over the gunnel, when something struck a sharp blow to my forehead and tore off my mask. I groped around in the darkness and located the boat, which seemed to be upside down. Someone spoke, "The damn thing tipped over," and I realized Reeve was in the water next to me. As we collected our wits, it all became clear; Reeve had also given in to temptation, and on returning to the boat with his own bulg-

ing goody bag, he too had attempted to hoist himself into the boat, at the same time I did, each of us not realizing the other was there.

Hanging onto the upside-down boat, we exercised our full repertory of favorite Anglo-Saxon expletives. We were in no danger, but the outboard engine was underwater, a good deal of our gear had sunk to the bottom, including both dive lights and goody bags, and we were out of air. I put on my mask and could see a glow of light coming from the bottom—one of the dive lights had turned on—so I hyped up and kicked down to pick it up. It didn't take much effort to roll the boat over, but we could not bail it out because waves kept washing over the stern.

It took an hour to make a dozen free-dives to pick up the rest of our gear on the bottom and swim the sodden mess to shore. We finally got a bonfire going, and a pair of our ill-gotten gains were introduced to boiling water. Slathered with garlic butter and washed down with Chianti, the meal was great. The price extracted by the lobster god? Aching sinuses, sore muscles, a large black-and-blue mark across my forehead where the gunnel hit me, and an oar that had floated away. ——Walt 🙶

● ●

■■■■■■■■■■■■■■■■■■■■■■■■■■■■
Eréndira to Baja Malibu Sur RV Park

Class 2, 3.1 miles; use the map on pages 86–87. Turn southeast at the sign advertising the park as you enter town, set trip odometer. At Mile 0.2 cross the river (no problem in years of normal rainfall), at Mile 0.3 turn right (south), and at Mile 0.5 turn left (southeast). Encounter a group of metal agricultural buildings at Mile 1.2. Immediately south of these buildings, turn right (southwest) towards the ocean. The road soon swings south along the shore, passing hundreds of acres of tomato fields. Arrive at the park at Mile 3.1.

The park is still under construction, but it has full hookups, rest rooms, showers, laundry, and a sand beach. The road south from the park has many fine sand beaches and potentially excellent boondocking sites. However, a number of rough stream crossings, with grades up to 27%, make the road class 3, unsuitable for RVs. The road reaches San Vicente 18.8 miles from the park.

■■■■■■■■■■■■■■■■■■■■■■■■■■■■■■■
KM 44 on the road to Bahía de los Angeles to Misión San Borja

Class 3, 22.4 miles; use the map on pages 104–105. Set trip odometer. Take the right (245°) fork at Mile 2.1 and the left (180°) fork at Mile 4.0. The area is mineralized; note the quartz pavement at Mile 4.7 and the broad band of quartz on the hill at Mile 12.8. Deer, coyote, and many species of bird inhabit this area. Take the left (165°) fork at Mile 15.0

and arrive at the mission at Mile 22.4. Driven at safe speeds, this will take about three hours. The handsome stone church, built by the Dominicans in 1801 of stone quarried from the surrounding cliffs, and remaining in use until 1818, is the first well-preserved mission building south of the border. Treasure hunters have damaged its walls looking for hidden gold, and its two bells have been stolen (a cow bell now takes their place). A few people still live in the vicinity, so respect their privacy and avoid walking in the gardens. The church is still in use, and you may be asked for a small donation.

■■■■■■■■■■■■■■■■■■■■■■■■■■■
Bahía de los Angeles to Las Flores and on to Bahía San Francisquito

Class 1, 9.4 miles to Las Flores, then class 2, 72.6 more miles; use the map on page 184 and that on pages 104–105. The first part of this trip will take you to the location of a gold mine active in the late 1800s. The mine and the transportation system that was developed to serve it were one of the great engineering schemes in Baja at the time. The Bahía San Francisquito area offers fine fishing, as well as a taste of the "Old Baja" before the days of the Transpeninsular Highway.

Heading south on the "main drag" in Bahía de los Angeles, turn right (210°) at the white concrete-block fence marking the Casa Diaz complex, and then make the first left (135°) and set your trip odometer. At Mile 2.0 stop and note the large notches carved into the head of the ridge on the canyon's western side. These were cut to permit the operation of a cable-and-bucket conveyor for Mina Santa Marta. Ore was carried by the conveyor from the mine, passed over two large wheels sitting in these notches, crossed the canyon, and was dumped into narrow-gauge railroad cars, which carried it to an incline railway with two pairs of rails. The weight of the descending cart would pull an empty one up the incline. At the bottom, the ore was again dumped into rail cars and was then towed by a small steam locomotive to a stamping mill on the edge of the bay.

Continue on the road to Las Flores, arriving there at Mile 9.4. A smelter and boiler lie on the west side of the road. The buildings and machinery were salvaged long ago, but the stone vault used to store the silver still stands, its walls 3 feet thick. Old bricks that lined the smelter can be found, some having the inscription "Laclede, St. Louis" and the date "1826" cast in their sides. Small ceramic cups used as molds to form ingots also can be seen. Many artifacts from Las Flores are on display at the museum in Bahía de los Angeles.

Mina San Juan, located in the mountains about 11 miles south of Las Flores, was large and profitable, yielding $2 million in silver until production ended with the Mexican Revolution. Ore was carried from the mine by a narrow-gauge railroad to an overhead bucket-and-cable system, which led to another railroad, ending at a smelter at Las Flores. A tiny, almost toy-like locomotive used on the "San Juan-Las Flores Railroad" is on display in the park in Bahía de los Angeles.

The graded and improved gravel road from Las Flores continues 72.6 more miles to Bahía San Francisquito. Moderate RVs have made the trip, and trailer boats as large as 22 feet have been brought over this road and launched at Bahía San Francisquito across the gently sloping sand beach. However, the road is badly washboarded and is rapidly returning to the state intended by Mother Nature, and you will have to negotiate wash-outs, deep sand, and the like.

■■■■■■■■■■■■■■■■■■■■■■■■■■■■■■
KM 37 near Los Planes to El Sargento

7 miles, class 1; use the map on page 149. Turn right (north) at KM 37, enter the tiny village of La Ventana at KM 8. From this point, the road closely parallels the beach to the village of El Sargento at KM 11. There are beautiful sand beaches, great boardsailing conditions, and some of the world's finest fishing just offshore. There are no RV facilities, but there are numerous RV parking and boondocking sites, and several small stores. There is little doubt that the area's natural assets will bring development.

● ●

❝ *Coyote confrontation*

The exhaust of my Trail 90 was rapping loudly as I rode out of Bahía las Ánimas. Forty was too fast, but the sandy trail was smooth and I had to be back in Bahía de los Angeles by dark to have several new friends over for supper in my trailer. My mind was elsewhere, when two tawny shapes suddenly raced in front of me. Through the years I had encountered many coyotes, but none had let me get so close. A fraction of a second later my side vision caught something else; a third coyote had been following the pair and was on a collision course with the motorcycle, and I instinctively slammed on the brakes and swerved. I recall everything that happened from this point on in slow motion: after a long, slow fall to the left, I came to a stop in a gigantic cloud of dust. I felt no pain and knew I had been lucky that the fall had occurred on soft ground. As the dust settled, I began to extricate myself from under the motorcycle, when I was horrified to see the coyote crouched not 15 feet away, teeth bared and the black fur on his back standing on end.

I had heard conflicting accounts of coyotes; some said they are cowardly and vicious, others that they are brave and even gentle, at least to their own kind. This one was very young and weighed perhaps 25 pounds, but staring at him eye-to-eye with one leg pinned under the motorcycle, I had no wish to find out who was right. I thought about my belt knife and began fumbling to remove it from its sheath, but the corroded catch would not release. The dog-like creature just stood there, teeth bared, not emitting a sound nor moving a muscle. Slowly I began to work my leg out and was soon crouched next to the motorcycle. I remembered reading about an encounter with a rabid Baja coyote, a slobbering animal biting at the people behind a windshield; Erle Stanley Gardner, I thought. Should I run? Should I try to intimidate him by acting aggressive? Without arriving at a decision I found myself righting the motorcycle, on the side away from the coyote. There was still no sign of life except for those golden eyes. Moving with glacial speed, I mounted the motorcycle and placed my foot on the kick starter. Dozens of encounters with Mexican dogs had convinced me they have a genetic hatred of the sound of motorcycle exhausts, a fact learned at the cost of nothing more serious than several torn trouser legs and a set of tooth marks on a boot. Did this apply to coyotes? Again in slow motion, my boot followed the arc of the starter. The engine started instantly, but its noise had no effect on the creature. I shifted into first and slowly moved away, then into second, third, and fourth.

As I raced away I could see him in the mirror, dashing in the opposite direction, and I realized that he was probably as scared as I was. By the time I could stop and turn around for a final look, he had disappeared. ——Walt ❞

● ●

Appendix A

A Beginner's Course in Baja Fishing

When fishermen head south with a particular species in mind, it is likely to be wahoo, roosterfish, dolphinfish, yellowtail, or one of the four species of billfish, and the following sections describe the tackle, bait, and tactics used for each.

Billfish

Four species of billfish are found in Baja waters: black, blue, and striped marlin, and sailfish. Striped marlin are the most common, and there are probably more stripers hanging on the barbershop walls of America than any other species. All four feed on almost anything in the sea, including squid, albacore, mullet, mackerel, dolphinfish, flying fish, paper nautilus, and their own kind. Although most are caught on surface baits, they feed at any depth, even taking such bottom-dwellers as octopus. They are fearless when hungry, and have been known to use their bills to stab and stun. They have poor memories, and there are many records of individual fish being hooked over and over again. Most large bills are females.

Since they are pursued by legions of skilled sportfishermen, a great deal is known about baits and tactics. While there are differences among the four species, it all boils down to just two basic methods: drifting a live bait or trolling with a large whole bait like bonito, mackerel, or ballyhoo or an artificial lure specially designed for bills. Bills tend to be unevenly distributed, and asking around for recent information before you go out often pays off. They don't move far during the night, so if you find them one day, they should not be far away the next. Search for an area of clean, clear, warm water, determine its limits, and drift a live bait or troll in large circles or back and forth in straight lines. Troll an artificial just past the wake, at a speed high enough that it occasionally breaks the surface, probably about six knots.

Stripers, and to a lesser extent the other species, will "fin" or "sleep" on the surface with the top of their dorsal (back) and caudal (tail) fins exposed, especially in calm weather. Binoculars are thus a vital piece of equipment. In good years, it is not unusual to see 20 or 30 finning stripers in a day of fishing at the Bancos Gorda off San José del Cabo, often keeping company in groups of 2 or 3. Careful helmsmanship can place a bait in an irresistible position. When you see a fish, put on a live bait, let it out 60 or 70 yards, and troll slowly in a large circle, with no changes in throttle. Try to place it within sight of the fish, then stop and let the bait swim freely. Stripers are sometimes not too concerned about boats and they may let you troll within 20 or 30 yards without spooking. However, avoid putting a wake over a finning fish. If this scheme doesn't work and you have heavy casting gear aboard, stop the engine, drift down on the fish from upwind, and drop a bait or lure right in front of it. Sometimes "tailing" fish are seen, swimming with the swell, at about the same speed. This usually occurs in the late afternoon when the winds have come up. The most effective way to handle such fish is to get well ahead, start trolling a lure or bait and then slow down, letting the fish catch up.

You don't have to be an experienced fisherman to get a shot at a billfish, and it can be done with nothing more elaborate than a cartopper or an inflatable—see the simple and effective "recipe" on page 162.

Wahoo

It has been claimed that the name is derived from the shouts of people who catch them, for wahoo are among the swiftest fish in the sea, capable of reaching 50 miles an hour, and they can spool you (remove all the line on a reel) before you know what happened. Related to mackerel and tuna, they inhabit tropical and warmer temperate waters. Their bodies are slim and powerful, with a shape like barracuda, except that the first dorsal fin of a wahoo is much longer. They are pelagic and tend to swim alone or in small groups. Their migratory habits are hard to pin down. Wahoo generally like to winter at the Cape, returning in warmer months to more northerly locations off Bahía Magdalena and in the southern Cortez. Off Bahía Magdalena and at Banco Thetis they are found from June to December, off Cabo San Lucas all year, being most numerous from December to April, and from East Cape to north of La Paz from June to November. However, water temperatures can alter this pattern drastically, and during El Niño years, wahoo have been caught off the Islas los Coronados. Most are taken in water of at least 76°.

Gary Kramer

A wahoo is landed off San José del Cabo

Wahoo feed on almost anything they can catch, which is almost everything, but they prefer flying fish, mullet, ballyhoo, mackerel, and squid, and will take artificials, especially those that make surface noise. Trolling or casting vinyl-skirted and natural feather lures and jigs are the most popular methods, but on long-range trips from Southern California down the Pacific coast, between half and three-quarters of all wahoo are taken on live bait. They are not plentiful, but good numbers are taken in the Cape region, especially at Bancos San Jaime and Gorda, at the south tip of Isla Cerralvo, and off the east side of Isla Espíritu Santo. Wahoo are notorious morning-biters, and the best time of day is from first light until two hours after dawn. Since the hotel boats get going too late, plan to use your own.

Because they have bony mouths and they often shake their heads violently when they feel the hook, a relatively stiff rod and dacron line are best, and hooks must be needle-sharp. A wire leader is necessary, but, since the fish will often strike at them and cut the line, avoid bright-finish snaps and swivels. Make sure swivels do not ride at the surface, for wahoo will strike at the trail of bubbles. Because they are attracted by turbulence, place your lure at the end of the wake and be ready for close-in strikes. Wear shoes and use a billy at the first opportunity, for a wahoo will bite you if given the chance.

Roosterfish

Roosterfish have gray and silver bodies, with spectacular dorsal rays, which they erect when excited. Voracious predators of small fishes, they generally are found on shallow reefs and sandy bottoms from the surf line out to very moderate depths, usually no more than 15 feet, especially where shallow rocky bottoms come up to meet sandy beaches. Fishable populations extend from Bahía Magdalena to the Cape and occasionally as far north as Mulegé, the greatest concentrations being at East Cape. Baja is the best place in the world to fish for large roosters.

Fishing for these finicky, exciting fish is a real challenge. Often reputed to take only live bait, they will sometimes fall for artificials, especially in the surf or during a feeding frenzy. However, no single artificial produces consistently, and most fish are taken by slow trolling live bait, especially ladyfish, needlefish, halfbeaks, grunts, and mullet, the last being the bait of choice. Live baits tend to be too large for roosters to swallow in one gulp, so they drop them and hit again, especially if a feeding frenzy is not going on, making it difficult to know when to strike. Trollers often proceed at about one or two knots with the reel clutch out, the spool held with a thumb. When a strike is felt, the spool is released, allowing the fish to take the bait without resis-

Baja has the finest roosterfish grounds in the world

Gary Kramer

tance, and after 5 or 10 seconds, the clutch is engaged and the hook set. Once a school is located, usually involving less than a dozen fish, it pays to stop and drift a live bait. Roosters are powerful, long-range fighters, often greyhounding (leaping into the air repeatedly while moving rapidly forward) with their great dorsal fins raised, and some have been known to beach themselves in an effort to get away.

Favorite areas include the coast south from La Paz to Cabo Pulmo, especially Punta Arena de la Ventana and Punta Colorada, and the best months are generally May through October, primarily July and August, the very best usually being the last two weeks of July and the first two of August. The older fish disappear in the cold months and no one seems to know where they go. Opinion is divided as to their culinary value, but they are good eating if bled and quickly cooled.

Dolphinfish

Dolphinfish are the perfect gamefish: they take artificials readily, put on a fantastic aerial ballet of leaps, flips, twists, somersaults, and tailwalks when hooked, and if these efforts fail, they provide fine eating. Found throughout the world in tropical and warm temperate seas, they are

There are some big dolphinfish patrolling the waters off Cabo San Lucas; Tera Allegri and her world-record 82-pound, 2-ounce beauty, caught in 1993

Ethan Weitz

migratory and tend to be found in schools. Extremely beautiful, they have iridescent blue backs and compressed flanks. A freshly caught dolphinfish often turns the color and sheen of gold lamé, with waves of blue and green shimmering over its entire body.

Their favorite diet consists of squid, flying fish, and other small fish, and they can be taken in many ways, primarily by fast trolling dead or strip baits or artificials such as Rapalas or silver spoons 50 feet or 60 feet back of the boat, or by drifting live bait. Marlin fishermen often catch dolphinfish, but they are at their best on light tackle—a big meat stick (a heavy, stiff rod) takes the fun out of it. Individuals and small schools sometimes hang around floating objects like oil drums, forklift pallets, planks, logs, or seaweed, a habit of great usefulness to fisherman. They are not afraid of boats; it is often possible to look down and see schools milling about, and double and triple hookups are common. They can be chummed (ground or cut-up chunks of fish are dumped into the water to attract them), and chunk or strip baits work well once a school has been attracted. It often pays to let them have a free spool for a five-count before clutching in and setting the hook, but from that point on never give a dolphinfish an inch of slack line. When a fish is caught, his fellows will often escort him to the boat, and they can be taken by casting vinyl skirt or feather lures, especially those with a red and white color scheme.

Dolphinfish are found primarily from Bahía Magdalena to Mulegé in the hot months, although some stay off Cabo San Lucas and East Cape all year. Dolphinfish pileups (dense groups) have been reported in the Midriff, especially around Isla San Pedro Mártir. In years with unusually warm water, they are found as far north as Bahía de los Angeles, but occasionally things are so cool that few are taken in Baja waters. Superb eating (probably sold as mahi-mahi in your local fish market), dolphinfish do not keep well and should be consumed immediately.

Yellowtail

The California yellowtail is one of the most abundant and popular gamefish in Baja's Pacific and Cortez waters. Yellowtail are blue-gray to olive above and silver-white below, and have yellow-tinged fins and a yellow stripe down their sides. Large fish tend to be solitary, and often stay in one area, but smaller ones usually join schools and migrate in season.

"Psyching out" their migratory patterns is the key to productive fishing. March through December is often best on the Pacific coast south to Bahía Magdalena. In the Cortez, their habits are regular, but the dates are hard to predict. As the northern Cortez cools down in winter, yellows head south, leaving Bahía Gonzaga and showing up at Santa Rosalía, then Mulegé, and so on, and in summer the migration is reversed. From Bahía Gonzaga to the Midriff the warmer months are thus often the best, but from Mulegé to La Paz best is often winter and early spring. In the Cape region, large numbers are found from January to May. To complicate things, groups of year-around fish provide good fishing

Perry Studt

A trio of yellowtail and a large pinto cabrilla were the product of several hours of trolling. Since it was probably a very fertile female, the cabrilla was released unharmed

in many locations any time of year. Because of these migratory patterns, it does not pay to fish one area too long: if you are not getting bites, move on.

Yellows are structure-oriented, hanging around rocky points, headlands, and reefs, rather than flat, featureless underwater terrain, and are often found under kelp paddies. They feed in the morning and late afternoon on small fish, crabs, and other invertebrates, and will take live, strip, or chunk bait and cast, trolled or yoyoed (pulled up and down while near the bottom like the child's toy) jigs, and trolled or cast chrome spoons and swimmer-style lures like Rapalas. Live bait or slabs fished on the bottom in deep water with plenty of lead weight often take the largest fish.

Yellowtail can be strangely unpredictable: when crazed by the sight of squid, they will hit anything in the water, but sometimes they carefully ignore anything with even a suggestion of a protruding hook as they gobble up chum. When schools are "breezing" (swimming at the surface and creating a slight disturbance that looks like a wind ruffle) they may go into a frenzy of competition to see who will be first to the bait, may follow it without biting, or may spook and disappear. Yellows hit hard, make long sizzling runs, and provide excellent eating.

A mixed bag

Although the eight species just described are the most popular with small-boat fishermen, there are many others that deserve attention. In fact, many fishermen head for Baja without any specific type of fish in mind, seeking a mixed

bag of edible, sporty fish like sierra, grouper, or any of a hundred species. Some of these are of modest size and fighting ability, but others are large, first-rate gamefish. Some migrate seasonally, others are permanent residents; some inhabit rocky caves and reefs, others sandy bottoms, and still others are pelagic, roaming the seas. This diversity makes it highly likely that a fisherman who visits almost any location on Baja waters at any time of the year will find at least one species available and reasonably willing.

Fishing tackle

Because Baja is home to several hundred species of gamefish, ranging from delicate ladyfish to great black marlin, a one-rod fisherman will be handicapped. If fishing out of a boat, to take full advantage of what is available, you should have 4 rigs: a heavy-duty trolling rod with roller guides and a 6/0 revolving-spool reel loaded with 50- to 80-pound monofilament line; a medium-duty 6-foot trolling rod with aluminum oxide or hard alloy guides and a 4/0 reel loaded with 30-pound mono; a medium-duty 8-foot or 9-foot spinning outfit handling 20-pound mono; and a light spinning outfit with 8-pound mono. This array will handle almost any fish Baja has to offer and permit almost any technique except fly fishing and beach-casting. If your budget does not permit all four, the medium-duty trolling rig is the most versatile. Too light, you say? Not if you are careful and patient—a 315-pound blue marlin was caught on 8-pound-test line at East Cape in 1990, an astounding weight/test ratio of over 39:1.

If you wish to avoid problems, bring all the tackle you will need and a good supply of snaps, swivels, weights, leader, line, hooks, lures, and spare parts for reels. Although many supermarkets, hardware stores, hotels, and fleet reservations offices have a limited assortment of tackle, the only independent full-service tackle shops are Minerva's Baja Tackle and The Tackle Box in Cabo San Lucas.

■ Help from above and below

Fishermen have always sought divine intervention when things have been slow, but there is another source of help from above, the seabirds. Over millions of years of evolution, they have become skillful hunters, and fishermen can profit by observing their habits. Terns, gulls, boobies, shearwaters, and pelicans seldom indulge in recreational flying, and if you see these birds flying, you can be sure food is nearby. Gulls fly easily when scouting, with a steady motion of the wings, often gliding in level flight. When they see something edible, their demeanor changes and they become more purposeful, changing their wing motion, often hovering or circling to track the fish below before diving. The dramatic plunge of a pelican is a sure sign that small fish are below. When things are hot, pelicans do not waste time climbing to great heights, but will get up only a few yards before plunging in again.

One species deserves special attention, the frigate birds. Shaped like ancient pterodactyls (see page 127), they like to soar on thermals, using their keen eyes to spot food. They have learned that large game fish, especially marlin, will drive small fish to the surface, and they often hover or fly in circles above marlin, waiting for some action. Seeing a frigate acting in this way, the wise fisherman trolls his bait over the spot just below, not to compete for the little fish pursued by the frigates, but for the big fellows that drove them to the surface.

Help is also available from below. Two species of porpoise, the spotted and the spinner, are known to keep company with prized yellowfin tuna. In addition, yellowfin tuna and skipjack often keep company. Fishermen may thus encounter mixed schools of spotted porpoise, spinner porpoise, yellowfin, and skipjack. The spotted and spinner are very shy, and it is a related species, the gregarious bottlenose dolphin, that loves to escort boats, so if it's easy to get near them, they are probably the wrong species. Most tuna are caught when the porpoise are feeding, so keep an eye open for herds of porpoise going in different directions; if they are all going in the same direction they are traveling, not feeding. Approach slowly, avoid charging directly at them, and cast into the school. In these circumstances, the tuna are not particular as to what they eat, so just about anything in the tackle box ought to work.

Natural baits

Natural baits often take more fish than artificials. Live or fresh-dead baits can usually be purchased anywhere there are *panga* or cruiser fleets. If you can't buy bait, you can catch it yourself. Almost any kind of small fish makes good live bait, including herring, Pacific mackerel, sierra, ballyhoo, and goatfish. Mackerel-like fish often form dense schools which can be spotted with a fish-finder and taken with Lucky Joes, Handy-Dandys, mackerel snatchers, flies, or small chunks of bait. If they will not bite, cast a snag line with a half-dozen treble hooks and a three-ounce torpedo sinker through the school. Ladyfish, excellent light-tackle gamefish in their own right, and other small species can be caught with feathers, chrome spoons, or flies.

There are useful baits besides fish, including sand flea, crab, mussel, clam, lobster, limpet, sea worm, and abalone. Shrimpers are often seen at anchor along the western shores of the Cortez, and it is possible to buy whole shrimp or heads. A few cans of inexpensive shrimp or abalone bought locally are a useful backup. It would be well, of course, to bring a supply of natural baits from home. If your RV has a refrigerator/freezer, packages of frozen mackerel, anchovy, and squid will undoubtedly come in handy. Squid is so good a bait that Baja fishermen, especially shore-casters, have been known to bring 30-pound lots with them.

Artificial baits

The vast assortment of trinkets turned out by tackle manufacturers is proof that no artificial works all of the time everywhere, and specific advice as to make, model, and color has filled generations of fishing magazines. One manufacturer of lures offers them in 25 dazzling colors, including "electric strawberry," "June bug," and "chartreuse pepper." However, the basic guidelines are simple: you will need a variety of colors, types, and sizes of artificial baits, and those imitating natural foods, such as feathers, plastic shrimp, leadheads, chrome spoons, and candybars, continue to be sold year after year, while highly publicized gimmicks usually disappear in a year or two. Probably the most effective all-around lures are the jointed Rebel plug, the Rapala, and their look-alikes; one in our tackle box has worked so well that all the paint is gone and the underlying plastic is grooved by teeth marks, in some places so deeply that the eyes holding the hooks are in danger of pulling out. They come in a variety of sizes and three types: surface, medium depth, and deep-diving. Krocodile spoons and their clones also produce well. Although some species do not have sharp teeth, wire leader is recommended, for you can never tell what may accept your offering.

If you plan to go after billfish, the artificials just described do not work too well, and a lure specifically designed for the chore at hand will be needed. A billfish lure is generally about a foot long and has a clear plastic head with large eyes and prismatic strips of color embedded inside, and a brightly colored vinyl skirt. They are sold in many San Diego tackle stores, as well as the two in Cabo San Lucas mentioned earlier.

Cruisers and *pangas*

If you don't have a boat available, there are two basic types of boats available in Baja, *pangas* and fishing cruisers. *Pangas* are normally hired for sportfishing on a daily or hourly basis with a skipper-guide, and can comfortably fish three or four anglers. They are relatively inexpensive, and are fast and maneuverable, permitting access to rocky areas and shallow reefs. However, they have no accommodations beyond bench seats, no head, and no protection from the sun, although a few are starting to sport Bimini tops. The cost per day varies widely according to location, season, and the laws of supply and demand. In 1996, the average cost of a *panga* and its captain for a day of fishing was $116, and the lowest and highest rates typically encountered were $84 and $148. In San Felipe and Bahía de los Angeles, the winter price might get down to $60 or $70, while at the top of the season at Los Cabos, it might get up to $150 or even $160.

Cruisers come in a wide variety of sizes and types and are more expensive than *pangas*,. They usually feature live bait wells, fighting chairs, a cabin, and a head, and they can travel farther and faster than a *panga*, and can keep fishing in heavier weather. As with *pangas*, the cost per day varies widely according to location, season, and the laws of supply and demand. In 1996, the average cost for a day's fishing on a Baja cruiser was about $300. However, this number is skewed by a small number of very large and elaborate cruisers at Cabo San Lucas, and a more typical figure is $250 a day.

These figures are a bit deceptive, for different fleets place different limits on the number of fishermen allowed per boat, and some come equipped with lunch, drinks, tackle, and live bait, and others don't, and the number of hours at sea may be different. Since practices vary from place to place, make sure you clearly understand what will and will not be provided in the way of tackle, bait, food and drink, when to arrive in the morning, how long you will be out, and the price. The prices may seem high, but remember that with three or four fishermen sharing the cost of a *panga*, or five or six sharing a cruiser, it isn't all that bad. The prices are not necessarily fixed, so some haggling may be in order.

If you can't make up your mind whether you would rather troll or go beachcasting, there is a solution

There are many organizations scattered in strategic locations that can supply *pangas* and cruisers, including Tiburon's Pangas in San Quintín, Alfredo's Sports Fishing and Arturo's Sports Fishing Fleet in Loreto, and Dorado Velez Fleet and Bob Butler Baja Fishing in La Paz. There is a large and growing number of sportfishing fleets in the Cape region, including Victor's Aquatics, Finisterra Tortuga Sportfishing Fleet, Fleet Solmar, and Pisces Fleet. In addition, some hotels and resorts located between Mulegé and Cabo San Lucas have their own fleets. *Pangas* can also be located in the beach area of almost any town catering to sportfishermen and in commercial fishing settlements, although those in the latter locations are sometimes hard at work and unavailable. Raul Espinoza, and Deborah and Alberto Lucero offer *panga* fishing trips in the Bahía de los Angeles and Bahía San Francisquito areas, respectively. Appendix C provides information on the organizations and individuals specifically mentioned above, as well as many hotels, resorts, and fishing fleets.

Beach-casting

The beaches and rocky points along Baja's 1,980 miles of coastline are its least-known and most under-utilized fishery. These offer outstanding fishing for everyone from surf fishermen casting into crashing waves with highly specialized 12-foot poles and large spinning reels, to children with light spinning outfits dropping chunks of clam into rocky holes. A large number of species are available, including corbina, corvina, croaker, surfperch, ladyfish, flatfish, opaleye, cabezon, and ocean whitefish. The great sweep of Pacific beaches between El Rosario and Guerrero Negro, and between Bahía Tortugas and Bahía Magdalena, especially the outer beaches of the islands forming the latter bay, are usually deserted and frequently offer outstanding surf fishing. The beaches between Punta Santa Rosalillita and Guerrero Negro yield numerous large white seabass and even halibut. A few other Pacific locations in Baja Norte have

good roads and see fair numbers of fishermen, including Eréndira and San Quintín.

The coast between La Paz and San José del Cabo offers some of the most unusual and exciting beach-casting in the world, especially for roosterfish at Punta Pescadero and Punta Arena Sur. Ray Cannon's famous "Tuna Canyon" is located 4 miles south of Punta Pescadero, where a submarine canyon runs in close to the beach, providing a year-around population of yellowfin tuna that can occasionally be caught from shore.

An isolated population of white seabass lives in the upper Cortez, and they can be taken by casting from rocky points. Most yellowtail are caught from boats, and while they are not commonly thought of as an onshore species, they also feed in shallow water and even in the surf zone, although they don't stay any longer than necessary. It can be a real melee when they drive a school of bait into shallow water, and they will savagely attack anything offered. Don't expect to catch many yellowtail this way, for they fight hard and by the time you beach the first fish, the bite is usually over.

Fishing in a green jungle

Fishing in mangrove areas can be very profitable and exciting, but specialized techniques are required. The following information applies specifically to the Bahías Magdalena/las Almejas area, but can be utilized elsewhere, including Laguna Manuela, Estero la Bocana, and Laguna la Escondida.

A wide variety of fish can be caught in the mangrove areas fringing much of the eastern coastlines of both Bahía Magdalena and Bahía las Almejas, and the inland waterways to the north, including, but certainly not limited to, cabrilla, corvina, snook, mangrove snapper (red bass), yellowtail, and halibut. The variety of fish present is so large that usually something is biting. The best boat is a cartopper or an inflatable, since larger rigs will have trouble with extensive shoals. If you insist on using your big Whaler, make sure you have a length of line and a video camera so you will be able get some great shots of your crew doing Bogart/Hepburn *African Queen* routines when you stray from the channels.

The outside of a bend in a waterway will probably be deep and hold more fish, so anchor on the inside and cast across to the other side, giving you the advantage of playing the fish directly away from the cover. Trolling or casting parallel to the outside perimeter of the mangroves allows you to cover more territory, at the cost of allowing some fish to get into their roots when hooked. If you can't cast to an enticing location, use the current to drift a bait into place. Fish at high tide, for at low tide some of the big fish have left for deeper water. An incoming tide is usually better than the outgoing, because the previous low has concentrated fish in deeper spots and the water is clearer. If you are after snook, drift or anchor; they are spooked by even the smallest motors. Watch for large fish working mullet. Rays often can be seen "flapping" on the bottom to dislodge small organisms, and other species rush in to join the feast.

Fishing licenses and regulations

All persons, regardless of age, fishing in Mexico must have a fishing license. In addition, all persons aboard a boat must have a fishing license if any fishing tackle is aboard, even if it's just fish hooks and line in life rafts, whether fishing or not. Licenses are available for periods of one week, one month, and one year, and can be obtained from the Mexico Department of Fisheries at their office in San Diego and by mail. The current costs are as follows: one week $11.60; one month $17.45; and one year $22.70, but they change frequently. The Department has an automated telephone system providing current information on licenses. The Vagabundos del Mar, some travel clubs, a few sportfishing stores and insurance offices in San Diego, and all *Oficinas de Pesca* in Baja also sell licenses. The latter offices, called simply "Pesca offices" in the book, are found in numerous locations in Baja, many of which are identified in the text and on the town/city maps. Allow at least two weeks when obtaining licenses by mail. You must present your license to American officials at the border if you are bringing fish back.

Only one rod per person is allowed to be in use at any given time. Specific bag and possession limits are established. Pismo clams, oysters, abalone, lobster, and shrimp are reserved for the Mexican fishing cooperatives and may not be taken by sportfishermen, and no turtles or *totuava* may be taken by anyone, Mexican or American. If you purchase seafood, make sure you get a receipt. Cleaning and filleting fish for storage and transportation are permitted if the species can still be identified, but you cannot leave remnants of cleaning ashore. It is illegal to used artificial light to attract fish at night.

Underwater ecological reserves have been established at Scammon's Lagoon, Pulmo Reef, and the harbor at Cabo San Lucas. Mexican sportfishing regulations are enforced, and game wardens are afield. In addition, military personnel sometimes check licenses and the contents of coolers. Fishing regulations change frequently, so get a copy when you apply for a license and read it carefully.

Real-time information

The Tackle Box in Cabo San Lucas offers an up-to-date fishing report that can be received by telephone by calling them between 9 A.M. and 7 P.M. Information is also available from many of the *panga* and cruiser fleets, hotels, resorts, and RV parks listed in Appendix C. The objectivity of information from these sources may be suspect, of course.

Season and location

When is the best time of year for the mixed-bag fisherman? If you ask the question at a sportfishing office in Ensenada, you will get an inevitable answer, "Today! Today is best!" However, if the last boat has already left, the best time of year becomes "Tomorrow!" There is a certain logic to this, for any day is good to go fishing, but there are definite seasonal aspects to most locations and most species.

A great deal is known about when and where people have caught fish. The calendar on the next three pages was developed from a detailed review of over 250 books and magazine articles, some ranging as far back as the days of Zane Grey, a sportsman and popular writer of the early part of the century, as well as a review of the records maintained by the International Game Fish Association, and the scientific literature, all tempered with our own experience. It shows without question that the summer months are the most productive for most species, but that there is something biting almost everywhere throughout the year.

So, using the calendar, pick your location and species and the dates of your trip. Chapters 4 through 7 describe a number of hot-spots.

Fishing for the future

Mexico has aggressively expanded commercial fishing in Baja waters in recent years, permitting major increases in local gill-netting, and in purse-seining for species such as anchovy for reduction to fish meal, and even allowing Japanese long-liners to take massive numbers of billfish. (In 1991, Mexico announced that long-lining had been banned to protect the sportfishing industry.) Some Mexican fishing vessels casually discard the dead "bi-catch," fish with limited market value accidentally caught in their huge nets. The species often so wasted include large numbers of sailfish, marlin, skipjack, and manta ray. In addition, the completion of the Transpeninsular Highway and improved air transportation brought in new hordes of sportfishermen.

All this has placed stress on the fisheries, and there is no doubt that the fabulous fishing in Baja is declining and will continue to do so in coming years. Visiting fisherman can do little about laws that permit this decline, but they can help in a number of very direct and important ways.

	Jan.	Feb.	Mar.	Apr.	May	June	July	Aug.	Sept.	Oct.	Nov.	Dec.

Ensenada, Isla de Todos Santos

	Jan.	Feb.	Mar.	Apr.	May	June	July	Aug.	Sept.	Oct.	Nov.	Dec.
albacore						■	■	■	■	■		
barracuda				■	■	■	■	■	■	■	■	
bass, kelp				■	■	■	■	■	■	■	■	■
bonito				■	■	■	■	■	■	■	■	■
cod, rock	■	■				■	■	■	■	■	■	■
croaker				■	■	■	■	■	■	■	■	■
perch, barred	■	■				■	■	■	■	■	■	■
yellowtail						■	■	■	■	■		

Bahía San Quintín, Isla San Martín, Sacramento Reef

	Jan.	Feb.	Mar.	Apr.	May	June	July	Aug.	Sept.	Oct.	Nov.	Dec.
albacore						■	■	■	■	■		
barracuda				■	■	■	■	■	■	■	■	
bass, calico	■	■		■	■	■	■	■	■	■	■	■
bass, kelp				■	■	■	■	■	■	■	■	■
bonito				■	■	■	■	■	■	■	■	■
cod, rock	■	■	■	■	■	■	■	■	■	■	■	■
croaker				■	■	■	■	■	■	■	■	■
dolphinfish							■	■	■	■		
halibut			■	■	■	■	■					
perch, barred	■	■	■	■	■	■	■	■	■	■	■	■
tuna, yellowfin				■	■	■	■	■	■	■	■	
yellowtail			■	■	■	■	■	■	■	■	■	■

Bahía Tortugas

	Jan.	Feb.	Mar.	Apr.	May	June	July	Aug.	Sept.	Oct.	Nov.	Dec.
albacore						■	■	■	■	■		
bass, giant sea				■	■	■	■	■	■	■	■	
cabrilla				■	■	■	■	■	■	■	■	■
corvina	■	■								■	■	■
croaker			■	■	■	■	■	■	■			
dolphinfish							■	■	■	■	■	■
halibut			■	■	■	■	■					
tuna, yellowfin						■	■	■	■	■	■	■
yellowtail			■	■	■	■	■	■	■	■	■	■

Bahía Magdalena

	Jan.	Feb.	Mar.	Apr.	May	June	July	Aug.	Sept.	Oct.	Nov.	Dec.
bass, giant sea						■	■	■	■	■		
cabrilla						■	■	■	■	■		
corvina	■	■	■	■						■	■	■
dolphinfish						■	■	■	■	■		
halibut			■	■	■	■	■					
sailfish						■	■	■	■	■	■	■
snapper				■	■	■	■	■	■	■	■	
tuna, yellowfin						■	■	■	■	■	■	■

	Jan.	Feb.	Mar.	Apr.	May	June	July	Aug.	Sept.	Oct.	Nov.	Dec.
Bahía Magdalena (continued)												
wahoo					▓	▓	▓	▓	▓	▓	▓	▓
yellowtail			▓	▓	▓	▓	▓	▓	▓	▓	▓	▓
San José del Cabo, Cabo San Lucas												
cabrilla				▓	▓	▓	▓	▓	▓	▓		
dolphinfish	▓	▓	▓	▓	▓	▓	▓	▓	▓	▓	▓	▓
marlin, blue						▓	▓	▓	▓	▓	▓	▓
marlin, striped	▓	▓	▓	▓	▓	▓	▓	▓	▓	▓	▓	▓
roosterfish				▓	▓	▓	▓	▓	▓	▓		
sailfish	▓	▓	▓	▓	▓	▓	▓	▓	▓	▓	▓	▓
sierra	▓	▓	▓	▓							▓	▓
snapper						▓	▓	▓	▓			
swordfish					▓	▓	▓	▓	▓	▓		
tuna, yellowfin						▓	▓	▓	▓	▓	▓	▓
wahoo						▓	▓	▓	▓	▓	▓	▓
yellowtail	▓	▓	▓	▓	▓	▓						
Puertecitos, Bahía Gonzaga												
cabrilla					▓	▓	▓	▓	▓	▓		
corvina			▓	▓	▓	▓	▓	▓	▓	▓		
croaker	▓	▓	▓	▓	▓	▓	▓	▓	▓	▓	▓	▓
seabass, white					▓	▓	▓	▓	▓			
sierra					▓	▓	▓	▓	▓			
Bahía de los Angeles												
bass, giant sea			▓	▓	▓	▓	▓					
cabrilla				▓	▓	▓	▓	▓	▓	▓	▓	
corvina			▓	▓	▓	▓	▓	▓				
dolphinfish					▓	▓	▓	▓	▓			
grouper					▓	▓	▓	▓	▓	▓		
seabass, white					▓	▓						
sierra					▓	▓	▓	▓	▓			
yellowtail					▓	▓	▓	▓	▓	▓		
Mulegé												
cabrilla			▓	▓	▓	▓	▓	▓	▓	▓	▓	
corvina					▓	▓	▓	▓	▓	▓		
dolphinfish						▓	▓	▓	▓			
grouper					▓	▓	▓	▓	▓	▓		
marlin, striped						▓	▓	▓	▓			
sailfish					▓	▓	▓	▓				
sierra	▓	▓	▓									▓
tuna, yellowfin							▓	▓	▓			
yellowtail	▓	▓	▓								▓	▓

	Jan.	Feb.	Mar.	Apr.	May	June	July	Aug.	Sept.	Oct.	Nov.	Dec.
Loreto												
bonito	■	■	■	■						■	■	■
cabrilla			■	■	■	■	■	■	■	■	■	
corvina				■	■	■	■	■	■	■		
dolphinfish				■	■	■	■	■	■			
grouper				■	■	■	■	■	■	■	■	
marlin, striped					■	■	■	■	■	■	■	
roosterfish					■	■	■		■	■	■	
sailfish					■	■	■	■	■			
sierra	■	■	■							■	■	■
snapper				■	■	■	■	■	■	■	■	
tuna, yellowfin					■	■	■	■	■			
yellowtail	■	■	■							■	■	■
La Paz, Isla Espíritu Santo												
cabrilla				■	■	■	■	■	■	■	■	
crevalle, jack						■	■		■	■	■	
dolphinfish					■	■	■	■	■	■	■	■
grouper				■	■	■	■	■	■	■	■	■
marlin, black								■	■	■	■	
marlin, striped					■	■	■		■	■	■	
roosterfish					■	■	■	■	■	■	■	■
sailfish							■	■	■	■	■	■
sierra	■	■	■	■	■	■				■	■	■
snapper					■	■	■	■	■	■	■	■
tuna, yellowfin						■	■	■	■	■	■	■
wahoo						■	■	■	■	■	■	
yellowtail	■	■	■								■	■
East Cape, Punta Arena de la Ventana, Isla Cerralvo												
amberjack					■	■	■	■	■	■	■	■
cabrilla				■	■	■	■	■	■	■	■	■
crevalle, jack				■	■	■	■	■	■	■	■	
dolphinfish					■	■	■	■	■	■	■	■
grouper					■	■	■	■	■	■	■	■
marlin, black					■	■	■	■	■	■	■	
marlin, blue					■	■	■	■	■	■	■	
marlin, striped					■	■	■	■	■	■	■	■
roosterfish					■	■	■	■	■	■	■	■
sailfish					■	■	■	■	■	■	■	■
snapper				■	■	■	■	■	■	■	■	■
tuna, yellowfin				■	■	■	■	■	■		■	■
wahoo					■	■	■	■	■	■	■	
yellowtail	■	■	■	■								

Mexico places no restrictions on catch-and-release provided the fish are in good survival condition. If you are going to consume your catch, keep all fish of legal species caught, regardless of their small size; there are no current minimum size limits for any species in Baja waters. If you practice catch-and-release, you can't just jerk the fish off the hook, throw it back, and expect it to survive. Unless special precautions are taken, many caught fish succumb to shock, disorientation, suffocation, internal damage, or wounds. Fishermen go to great lengths to learn how to catch fish, but few know anything about how to let them go!

Blued, unplated long-shank iron hooks can be removed easily, and salt water and fish juices will eventually rust them away if the line breaks. Never use treble hooks, or hooks made from stainless steel. Consider using barbless hooks, or crimping down barbs with a pair of pliers. When a fish is alongside, keep it upright, and try to get the hook out while it is in the water and can breathe. A fish hung vertically can sustain internal injuries, so don't hoist it out of the water if you can avoid it. A fish's slimy coating protects it from bacteria, and fatal infections can occur if this is damaged, so try to get the hook out without touching the fish. If you must bring a fish aboard, use wet hands and grasp it by the lower lip or behind the gill plates, or ahead of the tail fin if it is toothy. Grasp a billfish in the obvious location. A net removes slime, and a gaff is almost always fatal. If the fish is deeply hooked, simply cut the line as close to the hook as possible. Bleeding fish are probably going to die, especially if their gills are involved, so keep such fish for food.

The largest individuals of most species tend to be females with high reproductive value, so let the big ones go. Large fish are probably going to be wasted anyway, since they cannot be consumed immediately and it is difficult or impossible to keep one under refrigeration until you get home. Besides, big fish don't taste any better than little ones. There is a lot of ego involved in dragging home a huge trophy, and letting one go may be about as popular as a rabid skunk, but it helps greatly.

Bottom fishermen often crank up from great depths fishes with their eyes bulging and stomachs protruding from their mouths. This is no place for catch-and-release, for the fish will almost certainly never make it back to the bottom. However, if you must release such fish, there is a right way to do it. The above ideas about hooks and release techniques apply, and in addition the fisherman should be prepared with a number 14 hypodermic needle, available from farm and ranch supply stores. Lay a pectoral fin (a "chest" fin, equivalent to a human arm) back against the fish's body, and with the point of the needle remove a scale from the body at the tip of the fin. Slowly insert the needle through the skin and abdominal wall. When the needle penetrates the gas bladder, air will rush out the end of the needle, telling you that it has penetrated far enough. Compress the sides of the fish

An ever-increasing number of fishing vessels like this ply the Cortez

until they appear normal or concave, pull out the needle and return the fish to the water. The fish will probably swim rapidly to the bottom, but if it doesn't, a few gentle prods from the blunt end of a net handle should send it on its way. This method works on almost any species of "bottom fish," regardless of size. No vital organs are harmed, and the chance of infection is slight if you keep the needle clean and store it in a vial of alcohol. Thus, for a dollar's worth of equipment and 30 seconds of effort, you can greatly reduce this unnecessary loss of fish—and who knows; perhaps the fish will eventually grow to monstrous proportions and fall for your bait a second time.

Fishermen occasionally catch seabirds, most often pelicans and boobies. If this happens do not cut the line, for the part still attached to the bird may become fouled in vegetation, rocks, or driftwood, and the bird will die of starvation. Slowly reel the bird in and get it under control by grasping the bill and one wing, near its base. A cloth put over the bird's head will help calm it down. A landing net can be used to help restrain the bird or bring it aboard a boat. Beware—a bird may defend itself by pecking, sometimes at eyes. Find the hook and push the barb through the skin, cut the barb off, and back the hook out, just as you would with a person who has been hooked. Good judgment is required if the hook is in a joint or near an eye or other vulnerable area, and it may be better to leave the hook alone and simply cut the line as close to the hook as possible. If the bird has swallowed the hook and it is not visible, cut the line at its bill. Inspect the bird carefully and remove all fishing line from it before letting it go. Look closely, for it is often hard to see monofilament line among the feathers.

If the line on your reels is getting brittle and frayed and must be changed while in Baja, burn it rather than simply discarding it. The same characteristics that make mono a good fishing line—durability, strength, and near-invisibility—make it deadly to wildlife. Birds often get caught in discarded mono, which soon becomes entangled in rocks or brush, causing them to starve to death. Hike down any Cortez beach and you will encounter the skeletons of birds fouled by mono.

● ●

❝ *Great, Dick, really great!*

Fishing for yellowtail had been excellent, and Reeve, our friend Dick Mandich and I were catching far more than we could eat. On the last day before heading home, Dick announced he was going to bring some fish along. Reeve and I pointed out that our ice was almost gone, and the fish would spoil by the time we could to get to a source of more. After a few minutes of deep thought, we could see by the look on Dick's face that he had come up with an idea. Working wordlessly, he began to collect cobbles from the beach and place them in a circle. Slowly the circle got taller, and began to lean inwards, assuming the shape of an igloo. We finally got the idea; Dick was going to smoke some yellow-tail!

Reeve and I went out in the boat and scoured nearby beaches for firewood, and soon collected a number of planks, four-by-fours, and fence posts. By the time we got back, the smokehouse was completed, and Dick started a fire, care-fully laid out the filets on the grill from the propane stove, put it into the smokehouse, and blocked the hole serving as an air vent so that the wood would smolder rather than ac-tively burn, producing the desired smoke.

After checking at 10-minute intervals for an hour or so, Dick reached in and removed the grill. The fish were a beautiful light-brown, with no trace of burning, and plump and properly moist. Dick was not too willing to allow us a sample, because we had been having some fun at his ex-pense as the project proceeded, but when he was off attend-ing to other chores, Reeve and I saw our chance and clipped several pieces that were cooling on the grill. With an appre-ciative grin, I propelled a sizable chunk into my mouth and took a robust bite. It is hard to describe the next five sec-onds, but I will try: there was an explosion of the most nau-seating taste I had ever experienced, my eyes teared shut, I began retching violently, my throat seized up, and I could hardly breathe. I managed to turn sideways and spit the hor-rid mess out, and as I turned back I could see that Reeve was in the same state of affairs. By Dick's return we had regained some of our composure, and he soon caught on and asked "Well, how was it?" "Great, Dick, really great!," was all we could stammer, adding a lack of candor to our misdemeanor.

After things calmed down, the source of the prob-lem became apparent: all the wood used in the igloo was from "civilized" sources, and some of it had been treated with creosote. No wonder the fish had such a beautiful light-brown hue! Except for the difficulty in swallowing, Reeve and I agreed that the fish would be an ideal remedy for tapeworm. That night when everyone else was asleep, I uncovered the fish in the hopes that the crabs, the gulls, and the sand fleas would find it appetizing, but the next morning it remained untouched. RVers intent on roasting weenies, smores, or marshmallows may profit from our experience. ——Walt ❞

● ●

Appendix B

Calendar of Holidays and Events

The following calendar provides the dates of a number of events. Make an effort to attend a day or two of Carnival or a similar civic event, for you may be pleasantly surprised. The sights and sounds are distinctively different that those of a carnival or county fair in the US, and you will be amazed at the riot of sights, sounds, and events that even such a small place as San José del Cabo can put on.

A few events, such as "spring break" and the Tecate SCORE Baja races, can be loud and rowdy. Others, like Easter, are popular dates for the citizens of Tijuana and Mexicali to go on vacation, filling up the hotels and RV parks at places like San Felipe, and Ensenada, and the campgrounds at Laguna Hanson and Cañon Guadalupe. If you value sanity, silence, and solitude, these locations should be avoided on the dates shown. Also, remember that many people north of the border head south during holidays in the US, often causing crowding, especially near border locations.

This calendar is by no means a comprehensive rendition of every holiday, festival, and event in Baja California. In addition, the dates of some vary from place to place and time to time. So, if you are interested in attending any of the festivities listed, or to learn of others, contact the appropriate tourism office listed in Appendix C well in advance.

January

January 1. New Year's Day. (Celebrations involving Christmas go on until January 6; see the December 16 entry.)

Last weekend in January. Arts and Crafts Show in Todos Santos.

February

February. Tecate SCORE Baja 250 race, variable dates.

February. Gray Whale Festival in Guerrero Negro and López Mateos.

February 5. Constitution Day.

February–March. Carnival, a pre-Lent festival similar to Mardi Gras. Ensenada and La Paz put on the largest and showiest events, but San Felipe and some of the smaller towns also participate. Ensenada's version is especially elaborate, and attracts over 300,000 people each year.

February 24. Flag Day.

March

March, odd years, during periods of full moon. Yacht race between Southern California and Cabo San Lucas. There is a great deal of merry-making and numerous festivities at the end of the race, and you need not be a yachtie to join in the fun. Why the full moon? So the sailors can enjoy night watches. Nice thinking!

March 16–21. San José del Cabo celebrates its "discovery" with a colorful and energetic parade, carnival rides, sideshows, fireworks, contests, and a series of dance and music events. The town's Saint's Day is on the 19th.

March 21. Birthday of Benito Juárez.

Late March, early April. Spring break is celebrated by *gringo* college students, primarily at Rosarito, Ensenada, San Felipe, San José del Cabo, and Cabo San Lucas.

Between March 22 and April 25; varies year to year. Easter. (The official Catholic definition is "the first Sunday after the first full moon after March 21.") Good Friday is observed the prior Friday.

April

Last full weekend in April. Rosarito-Ensenada Bicycle Ride, one of the largest bicycling events in the world, sponsored by Bicycling West.

Last full weekend in April. Newport-Ensenada Yacht Race. This is the largest international yacht race in the world, attracting between 400 and 800 yachts each year. You don't have to be a crewman to enjoy the festivities and partying that go on in Ensenada.

May

Early May. Food Festival in Rosarito.

May 1. International Labor Day.

May 3. La Paz celebrates its founding.

May 5. *Cinco de Mayo*, commemorating the 1862 defeat of the French army at the Battle of Puebla.

May 10. Mother's Day.

June

Early June. Tecate SCORE Baja 500 race.

June 1. Navy Day.

Late June. Seafood Festival in Rosarito.

July

July. Pitahaya Festival in El Triunfo and Miraflores.

July 22–25. Traditional festival in Santiago.

July 31. Saint's Day in San Ignacio. This also celebrates the annual date harvest, and features fiestas, musical events, and the crowning of the "Date Queen."

August

(None scheduled)

September

September 4. Saint's Day in Santa Rosalía, with music, festivities, and lots of food.

September 5–8. *Día de Nuestra Señora de Loreto*, celebrating the founding of the first mission in the Californias with a parade, masses, fiestas, music, and dancing.

September 16. *Diez y Seis*, Mexican Independence Day. Parades, music, dancing, fiestas, fireworks.

September 29. Saint's Day in San Miguel de Comondú, featuring fiestas, music, and dancing. (With continuing depopulation, this may soon become a thing of the past.)

Last Saturday in September. Another Rosarito-Ensenada bike race, sponsored by Bicycling West.

Last weekend in September. Seafood Fair in Ensenada.

October

October. Marlin fishing tournament in Cabo San Lucas, one of the most popular tournaments in the world.

October 2. Fiesta in Mulegé.

Second weekend in October. International Chili Cookoff in Ensenada, one of the town's most popular events.

October 12. Columbus Day. This would seem not too popular in Mexico, but it is known there as *Día de la Raza*, and celebrates the beginning of the Mexicans as a distinct people, commencing with Columbus's arrival. This is also Saint's Day at Todos Santos.

October 18. Saint's Day in Cabo San Lucas.

October 19–22. Santa Rosalía Fair and Festival.

October 19–25. Loreto celebrates its founding.

November

November 1–2. *Día de los Muertos* (Day of the Dead), a religious holiday similar to All Saint's Day.

Early November. San Felipe Shrimp Festival.

Mid-November. Tecate SCORE Baja 1000 race.

November 20. *Día de la Revolución*, commemorating the beginning of the Mexican Revolution in 1910. Many festivities, including parades in San Felipe and La Paz.

December

December 2 and 3. Saint's Day celebrations, San Javier.

December 12. *Día de Nuestra Señora de Guadalupe*, feast day of the Virgin of Guadalupe, Mexico's patron saint. The day is devoted to special masses, but the nearest Sunday to the 12th has fiestas, games, and music.

December 16–January 6. *Las Posadas*, which commemorate the Holy Family's search for lodging, the birth of Jesus, and Epiphany, in Mexico called the *Día de los Santos Reyes*, referring to the Three Wise Men. Religious candlelight processions are held nightly for the first nine days, and parties are frequent. Masses are held on December 25th, and on the last day, children open their Christmas gifts.

December 31. New Year's Eve.

Appendix C

Directory

Readers wanting addresses and phone numbers not provided below should contact the State Secretary of Tourism of the state involved. Telephone numbers in Baja California can also be obtained from US phones by dialing 00-0. The international operator of your long distance carrier will route your inquiry to a bilingual information operator. There is a fee for this service.

ABY Charters
% Giggling Marlin
Blvd. Marina y Matamoros
Cabo San Lucas, BCS, Mexico
011-52-114-3-0831
011-52-114-3-0874 fax

Activity Center
Playa Médano
Apdo. Postal 444
Cabo San Lucas, BCS, Mexico
011-52-114-3-3093

AeroCalifornia
800-237-6225

Agriculture Canada
Communications Branch
930 Carling Avenue
Ottawa, Ontario, Canada K1A 0C7

Air-Evac International, Inc.
8665 Gibbs Drive, Suite 202
San Diego, CA 92123
619-278-3822
800-854-2569

Airstream, Inc.
419 West Pike Street
Jackson Center, OH 45334-0825
513-596-6111
513-569-6092 fax

Alfredo's Sport Fishing
Avenidas Adolfo Mateos y Benito Juárez
Apdo. Postal 39
Loreto, BCS, Mexico
011-52-113-5-0165
011-52-113-5-0590 fax

Almar Dive Shop
Avenida Macheros Numero 149
Ensenada, BC, Mexico
011-52-617-8-3013

Amigos del Mar
Apdo. Postal 43
Cabo San Lucas, BCS, Mexico
011-52-114-3-0505
011-52-114-3-0887 fax
800-344-3349

Aqua Adventures Kayak School
7985 Dunbrook Road, Suite H
San Diego, CA 92126
619-695-1500
619-695-1659 fax

Aquamarina RV Park
Calle Nayarit Numero 10
Apdo. Postal 133
La Paz, BCS, Mexico
011-52-112-2-3761
011-52-112-5-6628 fax

Aqua Sports de Loreto
Loreto Inn Hotel
Blvd. Misíon Loreto
Apdo. Postal 35
Loreto, BCS, Mexico
011-52-113-3-0700
011-52-113-3-0377 fax

Arturo's Sports Fishing Fleet
Apdo. Postal 5
Loreto, BCS, Mexico
011-52-113-5-0409
011-52-113-5-0022 fax

Attorney General for the Protection of Tourists, State of Baja California [Norte]

Ensenada Office
Centro de Gobierno
Blvd. Lázaro Cardenas Numero 1477
Ensenada, BC, Mexico
011-52-617-2-3000
011-52-617-2-3081 fax

Mexicali Office
Plaza Baja California
Calzada Independencia y Calle Calafia
Local Numero 4
Mexicali, BC, Mexico
011-52-655-6-1712

Rosarito Office
Oficina de Secretaría de Turismo
Blvd. Benito Juárez Numero 100
Rosarito, BC, Mexico
011-52-661-2-0200

San Felipe Office
Avenida Mar de Cortez y Calle
  Manzanillo s/n
San Felipe, BC, Mexico
011-52-657-7-1155

Tecate Office
Oficina de Secretaría de Turismo
Callejon Libertad Numero 1350
Tecate, BC, Mexico
011-52-665-4-1095

Tijuana Office
Blvd. Diaz Ordaz y Avenida las Americas
Edificio Plaza Patria, 3er Nivel
Tijuana, BC, Mexico
011-52-668-1-9492
011-52-668-1-9579 fax

Attorney General for the Protection of Tourists, State of Baja California Sur
KM 5 1/2 Carretera Transpeninsular
  (FIDEPAZ)
Apdo. Postal 419
La Paz, BCS, Mexico
011-52-112-4-0100
011-52-112-4-0722 fax

16 de Septiembre y Alvaro Obregón
La Paz, BCS, Mexico
011-52-112-2-5939

Backroad Adventures
La Ventana de Mulegé
Apdo. Postal 47
Mulegé, BCS, Mexico
011-52-115-3-0245 phone and fax

Bahía de los Angeles
(Town satellite phone service)
011-52-665-0-3206 and 3207

Bahía los Frailes, Hotel
Apdo. Postal 230
San Jose del Cabo, BCS, Mexico
011-52-114-2-2246
800-762-2252

Baja Country Club
858 3rd Avenue, Suite 141
Chula Vista, CA 91911
011-52-617-3-0303
011-52-617-7-4013 fax

Baja Diving & Service
Avenida Obregón Numero 1665-2
Apdo. Postal 782
La Paz, BCS, Mexico
011-52-112-2-1826 shop
011-52-112-5-2575 home
011-52-112-2-8644 fax

Baja Life
P.O. Box 4917
Laguna Beach, CA 92652
714-376-2252
714-376-7575 fax

Bajamar Oceanfront Golf Resort
416 W. San Ysidro Blvd.
Box 1732
San Ysidro, CA 92173
011-52-615-5-0151
011-52-615-5-0150 fax
619-498-8234
800-225-2418

Baja Outback Tours
Plaza las Glorias, Local A-5
Cabo San Lucas, BCS, Mexico
011-52-114-3-2200

Baja Outdoor Activities
354 Madero, Centro
La Paz, BCS, Mexico
011-52-112-5-5636
011-52-112-5-3625 fax
    or
PO Box 265
Port Townsend, WA 98368
800-853-2252

Baja Ron's Motel
San Quintín, BC, Mexico
909-929-3883 8 A.M. to 3 P.M.
909-658-2333 5 P.M. to 8 P.M.
909-652-4041 fax

Baja Seasons
1177 Broadway, Suite Number 2
Chula Vista, CA 91911
619-422-2864
800-962-2252 from CA
800-356-2252 from rest of US
Call collect from Mexico

Baja Sun
Avenida Pedro Loyola Numero 295 y
    Avenida las Palmas
Fracc. Acapulco
Ensenada, BC, Mexico
011-52-617-7-7691
011-52-617-7-7693 fax
    or
Box 8530
Chula Vista, CA 91912-8530
800-946-2252

Baja Sur Internacional
Guerrero e/ Revolución y Serdan
La Paz, BCS, Mexico
011-52-112-2-7154

Bajarama Tours
Apdo. Postal 224
Ensenada, BC, Mexico
011-52-617-8-3512

Baja Travel
Baja Business Center
Madero y Guerrero
Apdo. Postal 535
Cabo San Lucas, BCS, Mexico
011-52-114-3-1934
011-52-114-3-1949 fax
800-777-2252

Baja Tropicales/Mulegé Kayaks
Apdo. Postal 60
Mulegé, BCS, Mexico
011-52-115-3-0190 fax
    or
3065 Claremont Drive, Suite C
San Diego, CA 92117
619-275-4225
619-275-1836 fax

Best Value Quality RV Tours
Box 889
Bonsall, CA 92003-0899
629-723-1912 fax and phone
800-823-1912

Bicycling West, Inc.
Box 15128
San Diego, CA 92175-5128
619-583-3001

Bob Butler's Fisherman's Fleet
Box 417
Palm Springs, CA 92263
011-52-112-2-1313
619-325-1379

Bodegas de Santo Tomás
Avenida Miramar Numero 666
Ensenada, BC, Mexico
011-52-617-8-2509

Brisa del Mar RV Resort
Apdo. Postal 45
Los Cabos, BCS, Mexico
011-52-114-2-2828 phone and fax

Bufadora Dive, La
Dale Erwin
Apdo. Postal 102
Maneadero, BC, Mexico
011-52-617-3-2092
714-776-1805

C & C Ground Services & Tours
Misión San Ignacio s/n
Apdo. Postal 7
Loreto, BCS, Mexico
011-52-113-3-0151 phone and fax

Cabo Acuadeportes
Apdo. Postal 136
Cabo San Lucas, BCS, Mexico
011-52-114-3-0117 phone and fax

Cabo Cielo RV Park
KM 3.8 Carretera Transpeninsular
Apdo. Postal 109
Cabo San Lucas, BCS, Mexico
011-52-114-3-0721
011-52-114-3-2527 fax

Cabo del Sol Golf Club
Blvd. de la Marina 39F, Suites 4-441
Cabo San Lucas, BCS, Mexico
011-52-114-3-3149
011-52-114-3-3340 fax
    or
4343 Von Karman Avenue
Newport Beach, CA 92660-2083
714-833-3033
800-637-2226

Cabo Diving Services
Blvd. Marina esq. Hidalgo
Apdo. Postal 195
Cabo San Lucas, BCS, Mexico
011-52-114-3-1109
011-52-114-3-1110 fax

Cabo Isla Marina
Apdo. Postal 371
Cabo San Lucas, BCS, Mexico
011-52-114-3-1251
011-52-114-3-1253 fax

Cabo Pulmo Divers
Rosaura Zapata e/ Morelos y Victoria
    Numero 955
Col. Loma Linda
La Paz, BCS, Mexico
011-52-112-2-1631

Cabo San Lucas Country Club
Blvd. Lázaro Cardenas s/n
Cabo San Lucas, BCS, Mexico
011-52-114-3-1922
011-52-114-3-1119 fax
800-854-2314

Campistre la Pila Trailer Park
Apdo. Postal 261
Ciudad Constitución, BCS, Mexico
011-52-113-2-0562

Campo de Golf de Loreto
Blvd. Misión de Loreto s/n
Loreto, BCS, Mexico
011-52-113-3-0788

Campo de Golf San José
Apdo. Postal 176
San José del Cabo, BCS, Mexico
011-52-114-2-0905
011-52-114-2-0882 fax

Cabo Real Golf Club
KM 19.5 Carretera Transpeninsular
Cabo San Lucas, BCS, Mexico
011-52-114-3-0040
011-52-114-3-0887 fax

Campo la Ventana *See Espinoza,*
Raul

Campo Playa RV Park
Apdo. Postal 789
Ensenada, BC, Mexico
011-52-617-6-2918
011-52-617-8-3767 fax

Canadian Consulate
German Gedovius Numero 5-201
Condominio del Parque
Tijuana, BC, Mexico
011-52-668-4-0461

**Canadian Department of External
Affairs**
Ottawa, Ontario, Canada K1A 0G2

Casa Blanca RV Park
KM 4 1/2 Carretera Transpeninsular
Apdo. Postal 681
La Paz, BCS, Mexico
011-52-112-2-5109

Casa Diaz
Bahía de los Angeles
Apdo. Postal 579
Ensenada, BC, Mexico

Castro's Fishing Place
Apdo. Postal 974
Ensenada, BC, Mexico
011-52-617-6-2895

Cavas Valmar
Calle Ambar Numero 810
Apdo. Postal 392
Ensenada, BC, Mexico
011-52-617-8-6405

Charters Mar de Cortez
Avenida Mar Caribe Numero 325
San Felipe, BC, Mexico
011-52-657-7-1278
011-52-657-7-1779 fax
or
355 W. 2nd. Street, Suite 310
Calexico, CA 92231

Chevrolet dealers

Motores de Ensenada
Blvd. Cardenas y Caracoles
Ensenada, BC, Mexico
011-52-617-0580

**Proveedora Agricola Automotriz
California**
Ciudad Constitución, BCS, Mexico
011-52-113-2-2180
011-52-113-2-0343 fax

**Proveedora Agricola Automotriz
California**
Bravo 1220
Apdo. Postal 242
La Paz, BCS, Mexico
011-52-112-2-2313

**Proveedora Agricola Automotriz
California**
Lázaro Cardenas, Camino al Médano
Cabo San Lucas, BCS, Mexico
011-52-114-3-2087
011-52-114-3-2088 fax

City View Beach RV Park
KM 15 Carretera al Norte
Apdo. Postal 680
La Paz, BCS, Mexico
011-52-112-4-6088

Club Cabo RV Park
Lista de Correos
Cabo San Lucas, BCS, Mexico
011-52-114-3-3348

Club de Pesca Trailer Park
Apdo. Postal 90
San Felipe, BC, Mexico
011-52-657-7-1180

Corona Beach RV Park
Apdo. Postal 1149
Ensenada, BC, Mexico

Critical Air Medicine
4141 Kearny Villa Road
San Diego, CA 92123
619-571-0482
619-571-0835 fax
800-247-8326

Cruise America
11 West Hampton Avenue
Mesa, AZ 85210
602-464-7310 fax
800-327-7799

Cruising Charts
Box 976
Patagonia, AZ 85624
520-394-2393

Dawson's Book Shop
535 North Larchmont Blvd.
Los Angeles, CA 90004
213-469-2186
213-469-9553 fax

Deportes Blazer
Paseo Hildalgo 23
Loreto, BCS, Mexico
011-52-113-5-0911

**DHL Worldwide Express offices in
Baja**

DHL International de Mexico
Avenida Abasolo Edificio Numero 78
Locales 4 y 5 Esq. Nayarit
Col. Pueblo Nuevo
La Paz, BCS, Mexico
011-52-112-5-6150

DHL International de Mexico
Calz. Cuauhtemoc (Antes Aviación)
Numero 10 Casi Esquina con Justo
Sierra Col. Cuauhtemoc Norte
Mexicali, BC, Mexico
011-52-656-8-1760

DHL International de Mexico
Paseo de los Heroes Numero 9105
Esq. Francisco Javier Mina
Zona del Río
Tijuana, BC, Mexico
011-52-668-4-8957

Dive Adventures
Plaza Bonita, Local 4-A
Apdo. Postal 146
Cabo San Lucas, BCS, Mexico
011-52-114-3-2630 phone and fax

Dive Palmilla *See* **Hotel Palmilla**

Dodge/Chrysler dealers

Autoproductos de Tijuana
Avenida Reforma y San Marcos
Ensenada, BC, Mexico
011-52-617-7-0204
011-52-617-6-5063 fax

Nueva Automotriz del Toro
Isabel la Católica Numero 1315
La Paz, BCS, Mexico
011-52-112-2-2557
011-52-112-2-1534 fax

Domecq Winery
KM 73 Carretera Tecate-El Sauzal
Apdo. Postal 987
Tijuana, BC, Mexico
011-52-662-3-2408
011-52-662-3-2414 fax

Dorado Velez Fleet
Apdo. Postal 402
La Paz, BCS, Mexico
011-52-112-2-2744, ext. 637

East Cape Divers *See Leonero, Rancho*

Ecoturismo Kuyima
Eduardo Sedano/José Varela
Domicilio Conocido
San Ignacio, BCS, Mexico
011-52-115-4-0026

El Arco Trailer Park
KM 5.5 Carretera a San José
Apdo. Postal 114
Cabo San Lucas, BCS, Mexico
011-52-114-3-1686 phone and fax

El Cardón Trailer Park
Apdo. Postal 104
La Paz, BCS, Mexico
011-52-112-4-0261

El Cardónal Resort
Los Barriles, BCS, Mexico
011-52-114-1-0040
514-767-6036
514-767-7180 fax

El Faro Beach RV Park
Apdo. Postal 1008
Ensenada, BC, Mexico
011-52-617-7-4620

El Faro Viejo Trailer Park
Apdo. Postal 64
Cabo San Lucas, BCS, Mexico
011-52-114-3-4211

El Monte RV Center
12061 E. Valley Blvd.
El Monte, CA 91732
818-443-6158
818-443-3549 fax
800-367-3687

El Moro RV Park
Rosendo Robles Numero 8
Loreto, BCS, Mexico
011-52-113-5-0542

El Palomar Trailer Park
Apdo. Postal 595
Ensenada, BC, Mexico
011-52-617-7-0650

Enchanted Island Excursions
Apdo. Postal 50
San Felipe, BC, Mexico
011-52-657-7-1431

or
233 Paulin, Number 8512
Calexico, CA 92231

Ensenada Sportfishing Center
2630 E. Beyer, Suite 676
San Ysidro, CA 92143
011-52-617-8-2185

Ernesto's Resort Motel *See Baja Ron's Motel*

Espinoza, Raul
12323 Carl Street
Pacoima, CA 91331
818-899-7876

Estero Beach Hotel
Apdo. Postal 86
Ensenada, BC, Mexico
011-52-617-6-6225
011-52-617-6-6925 fax

Finisterra, Hotel
Apdo. Postal 1
Cabo San Lucas, BCS, Mexico
011-52-114-3-3333

Ford dealers

Automotriz de Ensenada
Avenida Reforma y San Marcos
Ensenada, BC, Mexico
011-52-617-6-3668

Automotriz Baja California
Carretera Transpeninsular al Norte
Numero 3565
La Paz, BCS, Mexico
011-52-112-2-8870
011-52-112-2-8877 fax

Frances, Hotel
Col. Mesa Francia
Santa Rosalía, BCS, Mexico
011-52-115-2-2052

Good Sam Club
Box 6888
Englewood, CO 80155-6888
303-792-7306 fax
800-234-3450

Gordo's Sport Fishing
Apdo. Postal 35
Ensenada, BC, Mexico
011-52-617-8-3515
011-52-617-4-0481 fax

Hacienda Beach Resort, Hotel
Playa el Médano
Cabo San Lucas, BCS 23410
011-52-114-3-0122
011-52-114-3-0666 fax

Hacienda Santa Veronica
Avenida Revolucíon 1232 Desp. 507
Tijuana, BC, Mexico
011-52-66-85-9793

or
2272 Iris Avenue
San Diego, CA 92154
619-423-3830

Happy Campers Mobile RV Service & Repairs
Gigante Valle Dorado Local Numero 38
Ensenada, BC, Mexico
011-52-617-6-7580

Hyperbaric Technology, Inc.
200 W. Arbor Drive
San Diego, CA 92103
619-543-5222 (24 hours)

Instant Mexico Auto Insurance Services
223 Via de San Ysidro
San Ysidro, CA 92173
619-428-3583
619-690-6533 fax
800-345-47012

International Gateway Insurance Brokers
3450 Bonita Road, Suite 103
Chula Vista, CA 9190-3249
Box 609
Bonita, CA 91908-0609
619-422-3028
619-422-2671 fax
800-423-2646 from CA

Joker Hotel & RV Park
KM 12 1/2 Carretera Sur
Ensenada, BC, Mexico
011-52-617-6-7201

Juanita's Fleet
Plaza Karina Local Numero 1, Blvd. Marina
Apdo. Postal 29
Cabo San Lucas, BCS, Mexico
011-52-114-3-0522
800-421-8925

Juanito's Garden RV Park
Apdo. Postal 50
Los Barriles, BCS, Mexico
011-52-114-1-0024
011-52-114-1-0163 fax

Killer Hooks Surf Shop
Domicilio Conocido
San José del Cabo, BCS, Mexico
011-52-114-2-2430

La Jolla RV Park (San Felipe)
Box 978
El Centro, CA 92243
011-52-657-7-1222

La Paz Diving Service *See Aquamarina RV Park*

La Paz RV Park
Brecha California 120
Apdo. Postal 482
La Paz, BCS, Mexico
011-52-112-2-8787
011-52-112-2-9938 fax

Land's End Divers
Plaza las Glorias, Local A-5
Cabo San Lucas, BCS, Mexico
011-52-114-3-2200

Leonero, Rancho
8691 El Rancho
Fountain Valley, CA 92708
714-375-3720
800-334-2252

Loreto Inn Hotel
Blvd. Misíon Loreto
Apdo. Postal 35
Loreto, BCS, Mexico
011-52-113-3-0700
011-52-113-3-0377 fax

Loreto Shores Villas & RV Park
Apdo. Postal 219
Loreto, BCS, Mexico
619-223-8562
011-52-113-5-0629
011-52-113-5-0711 fax

Los Arcos Hotel
Avenida Obregón 498
Apdo. Postal 112
La Paz, BCS, Mexico
011-52-112-2-2744
011-52-112-5-4313 fax
800-347-2252

Los Cabos Fishing Center
Apdo. Postal 384
Cabo San Lucas, BCS, Mexico
011-52-114-3-3736

Los Dorados Fleet
Hotel Plaza las Glorias, Local 31630
Cabo San Lucas, BCS, Mexico
011-52-114-3-1630 phone and fax

Lucero, Deborah and Alberto
Apdo. Postal 7
San Ignacio, BCS, Mexico
and
7825 North Avenue
Lemon Grove, CA 91945

Mail Boxes Etc.
Marina Cabo Plaza, Local F
Blvd. Marina Numero 39
Cabo San Lucas, BCS, Mexico
011-52-114-3-3033
011-52-114-3-3031 fax

Malibu Beach Sur RV Park
Apdo. Postal 95
Maneadero, BC, Mexico
702-645-9155

Manfred's RV Trailer Park
KM 213 Transpeninsular
Apdo. Postal 120
Ciudad Constitución, BCS, Mexico
011-52-113-2-1103

Map Centre, Inc.
2611 University Avenue
San Diego, CA 92104-2894
619-291-3830
619-291-3840 fax

Marina de La Paz
Topete 3040 y Legaspi
Apdo. Postal 290
La Paz, BCS, Mexico
011-52-112-5-2112
011-52-112-5-5900 fax

Marina Palmira
KM 2.5 Carretera a Pichilingue
Apdo. Postal 34
La Paz, BCS, Mexico
011-52-112-5-3959
011-52-112-5-6242 fax

Mar del Sol RV Park
San Felipe, BC, Mexico
011-52-657-7-1280
800-336-5454

Mar-Co's RV Park
Avenida Golfo de California 788
San Felipe, BC, Mexico
011-52-655-7-2579

Marina, Hotel
KM 2.5 Carretera a Pichilingue
Apdo. Postal 34
La Paz, BCS, Mexico
011-52-112-2-6254
011-52-112-2-6277 fax

Martin Verdugo RV Resort
Apdo. Postal 17
Los Barriles, BCS, Mexico
011-52-114-1-0054 phone and fax

Mesón de Don Pepe RV Park
Apdo. Postal 7
Colonia Vicente Guerrero, BC, Mexico
011-52-616-6-2216
011-52-616-6-2268 fax

Mexican Consulate General
1549 India Street
San Diego, CA 92101
619-231-8414
619-231-4802 fax

Mexican Consulates and Consular Agencies in other cities

Albuquerque, NM	505-247-2139
Atlanta, GA	404-266-1913
Austin, TX	512-478-9031
Boston, MA	617-426-4942
Brownsville, TX	512-542-2051
Calexico, CA	619-357-3863
Chicago, IL	312-855-1380
Corpus Christi, TX	512-882-3375
Dallas, TX	214-630-7431
Del Rio, TX	512-775-9451
Denver, CO	303-830-6702
Detroit, MI	313-567-7709
Eagle Pass, TX	512-773-9255
El Paso, TX	915-533-3644
Fresno, CA	209-233-3065
Houston, TX	713-524-2300
Laredo, TX	210-723-6369
Los Angeles, CA	213-351-6800
McAllen, TX	210-686-0243
Miami, FL	305-441-8781
Midland, TX	915-687-2334
New Orleans, LA	505-522-3596
New York, NY	212-689-0456
Nogales, AZ	520-287-2521
Oxnard, CA	805-483-4684
Philadelphia, PA	215-922-4262
Phoenix, AZ	602-242-7398
Sacramento, CA	916-363-3885
Saint Louis, MO	314-436-3233
Salt Lake City, UT	801-521-8502
San Antonio, TX	210-227-9145
San Bernardino, CA	909-888-3155
San Francisco, CA	415-392-5554
San Jose, CA	408-294-3415
Santa Ana, CA	714-835-3069
Seattle, WA	206-448-6819
Tucson, AZ	602-882-5595
Washington, DC	202-736-1000

Mexican Ferry System (SEMATUR)

Guaymas Office
011-52-622-2-3390
011-52-622-2-3393 fax

La Paz Office
Guillermo Prieto and 5 de Mayo
011-52-112-5-3833
011-52-112-5-4666

La Paz, Pichilingue Terminal
011-52-112-2-9485
011-52-112-2-6588 fax

Mazatlán Office
011-52-698-1-7020
011-52-698-1-7023 fax

Santa Rosalía Office
011-52-115-2-0013
011-52-115-2-0014

Topolobampo Office
011-52-686-2-0141
011-52-686-2-0035 fax

Mexican Government Tourism Of-
fices

70 East Lake Street, Suite 1413
Chicago, IL 60601
312-606-9015
312-606-9012 fax

2707 North Loop W, Suite 450
Houston, TX 77008
713-880-1833
713-880-5153 fax

10100 Santa Monica Blvd., Suite 224
Los Angeles, CA 90067
310-203-8191
310-203-8316 fax

405 Park Avenue, Suite 1401
New York, NY 10022
212-755-7261
212-753-2874 fax

1911 Pennsylvania Avenue NW
Washington, DC 20006
202-728-1750
202-728-1758 fax

One Place Ville Marie, Suite 1526
Montreal, Quebec, Canada H3B 2B5
514-871-1052
514-871-3825 fax

2 Bloor Street West, Suite 1801
Toronto, Ontario, Canada M4W 3E2
416-925-0704
416-925-6061 fax

1610-999 West Hastings Street
Vancouver, BC, Canada V6C 2W2
604-669-2845
604-669-3498 fax

Mexico Department of Fisheries
2550 Fifth Avenue, Suite 101
San Diego, CA 92103-6622
619-233-6956
619-233-0344 fax

Minerva's Baja Tackle
Apdo. Postal 156
Cabo San Lucas, BCS, Mexico
011-52-114-3-1282
011-52-114-3-0440 fax

Molino Viejo Motel and RV Park
Apdo. Postal 90
Valle de San Quintín, BC, Mexico
800-479-7962

Mona Lisa RV Park
Apdo. Postal 607
Ensenada, BC, Mexico

Mulegé Divers
Gral. Martínez s/n
Mulegé, BCS, Mexico
011-52-115-3-0059 store
011-52-115-3-0134 home

Mulegé Kayaks *See Baja Tropicales/*
Mulegé Kayaks

Nissan dealers

Comercio Automotríz
KM 111 Carretera Transpeninsular
Ensenada, BCS, Mexico
011-52-617-6-6118

Grupo VAPSA Autocompactos
KM 212 Carretera Norte
Ciudad Constitución, BCS, Mexico
011-52-113-2-2222

Grupo VAPSA Autocompactos
5 de Febrero Numero 1050
La Paz, BCS, Mexico
011-52-112-2-2277
011-52-112-5-4100 fax

Grupo VAPSA Autocompactos
Blvd. San José Numero 2000
Zona FONATUR
San José del Cabo, BCS, Mexico
011-52-114-2-1666
011-52-114-2-1667 fax

NorthSouth de Mexico
310-337-7788
011-52-114-2-4144
800-010-1585 (from within Mexico)

Oasis Hotel
Apdo. Postal 17
Loreto, BCS, Mexico
011-52-113-5-0211
011-52-113-5-0795 fax

Oasis Hotel and RV Resort (north
of Ensenada)
Box 158
Imperial Beach, CA 91933
011-52-661-3-3255
011-52-661-3-3252 fax
800-426-7472

Oasis los Aripez Trailer Park
KM 15 Transpeninsular Norte
La Paz, BCS, Mexico
011-52-112-4-6090

Ojai, Rancho
PO Box 280
Tecate, CA 91980
011-52-665-4-4772

Old Mill Motel
223 Via de San Ysidro, Suite 7
San Ysidro, CA 92173
619-428-2779
619-428-6269 fax
800-479-7962

Orchard RV Park
Apdo. Postal 24
Mulegé, BCS, Mexico
011-52-115-3-0300

Pacific Coast Adventures
Plaza las Glorias
Cabo San Lucas, BCS, Mexico
011-52-114-3-1592
011-52-114-3-3922 fax
800-491-3483

Pacifico Tours
Blvd. Marina y Camino a la Plaza s/n
Cabo San Lucas, BCS, Mexico
011-52-112-6-8430

Palmas de Cortez, Hotel
Box 9016
Calabasas, CA 91372
818-222-7144

Palmilla Golf Club
Apdo. Postal 52
San José del Cabo, BCS, Mexico
011-52-114-2-0582, ext. 41

Palmilla, Hotel
Apdo. Postal 52
San José del Cabo, BCS, Mexico
011-52-114-2-0582
011-52-114-2-1706 fax
or
4343 Von Karman Avenue
Newport Beach, CA 92660-2083
714-833-3030
714-476-1648 fax
800-637-2226

Pepe's Dive Center
Cabo Pulmo via
La Rivera, BCS, Mexico
208-726-9233
208-726-5545 fax

Pisces Fleet
Blvd. Marina y Madero, Local 2
Apdo. Postal 137
Cabo San Lucas, BCS, Mexico
011-52-114-3-1288
011-52-114-3-0588 fax
800-950-4242

Pisces Water Sport Center
Club Cascadas de Baja
Cabo San Lucas, BCS, Mexico
011-52-114-3-1288

Playa Bonita RV Park
475 E. Badillo Street
Covina, CA 91723
909-595-4250

Playa de Laura RV Park
Avenida Mar de Cortez
San Felipe, BC, Mexico
011-52-657-7-1128

Playa del Sol, Hotel
Box 9016
Calabasas, CA 91372
818-591-9463

Playa de Oro RV Resort
3106 Capa Drive
Hacienda Heights, CA 91745
818-336-7494

Point South RV Tours, Inc.
11313 Edmonson Avenue
Moreno Valley, CA 92555
909-247-1222
909-924-3838 fax
800-421-1394

Posada Concepción
Apdo. Postal 14
Mulegé, BCS, Mexico
011-52-617-8-3329

Posada Don Diego
Apdo. Postal 126
Colonia Vicente Guerrero, BC, Mexico
011-52-616-6-2181

Posada Real los Cabos, Hotel
Zona Hotelera, Malecón s/n
Apdo. Postal 51
San José del Cabo, BCS, Mexico
011-52-114-2-0155
800-528-1234

Presidente Intercontinental Hotel
Blvd. Mijares s/n
Apdo. Postal 2
San José del Cabo, BCS, Mexico
011-52-114-2-0038
011-52-114-2-0232 fax
800-447-6147

Punta Chivato, Hotel
Apdo. Postal 18
Mulegé, BCS, Mexico
011-52-115-3-0188 phone and fax

Punta Colorada, Hotel
Box 9016
Calabasas, CA 91372
818-222-5066
800-368-4334

Real del Mar Golf Club
3171 Iris Avenue, Suite 84
San Diego, CA 92173
011-52-661-3-3401
011-52-661-3-3435 fax
800-803-6038

Recreation Industries Co.
Box 68386
Oak Grove, OR 97268
503-653-2833
503-654-0052 fax

Rob's Baja Tours
Box 4003
Balboa, CA 92661
714-673-2670

Ruben's Trailer Park
Golfo de California 703
San Felipe, BC, Mexico
011-52-657-7-1091

San Felipe Marina Resort and RV Park
San Felipe, BC, Mexico
011-52-657-7-1455
619-558-0295

San José, Rancho
219 Diamond Way Number 16
Vista, CA 92083-4452
619-758-2719

San Lucas Trailer Park
Apdo. Postal 131
Santa Rosalía, BCS, Mexico

San Perdito RV Park
KM 59 Carretera Todos Santos/ Cabo San Lucas
Todos Santos, BCS, Mexico
011-52-112-2-4520
011-52-112-2-2499 fax

SCORE International
12997 Las Vegas Blvd. South
Las Vegas, NV 89124
702-361-5404
702-361-5037 fax

Serenidad, Hotel
Apdo. Postal 9
Mulegé, BCS, Mexico
011-52-115-3-0111
011-52-115-3-0311 fax

Solmar, Hotel
Avenida Solmar Numero 1
Apdo. Postal 8
Cabo San Lucas, BCS, Mexico
011-52-114-3-3535
011-52-114-3-0410 fax

State Secretary of Tourism of Baja California [Norte]

Colonia Guerrero Office
011-52-616-6-2268

Ensenada Office
Centro de Gobierno
Blvd. Lázaro Cardenas Numero 1477
Ensenada, BC, Mexico
011-52-617-2-3000
011-52-617-2-3081 fax

Mexicali Office
Calzada Independencia y Calle Calafia
Centro Comercial Baja California
Local 4-C
Mexicali, BC, Mexico
011-52-655-6-1172
011-52-655-6-1282 fax

Rosarito Office
Blvd. Benito Juárez Numero 100
Rosarito, BC, Mexico
011-52-661-2-0200

San Felipe Office
Avenida Mar de Cortez y Calle Manzanillo s/n
San Felipe, BC, Mexico
011-52-657-7-1155

San Quintín Office
011-52-666-5-2376

San Vicente Office
011-52-616-5-6632

Tecate Office
Callejon Libertad Numero 1305
Tecate, BC, Mexico
011-52-665-4-1095

Tijuana Office
Blvd. Diaz Ordaz y Avenida las Americas
Edificio Plaza Patria 3er Nivel
Tijuana, BC, Mexico
011-52-668-1-9492
011-52-668-1-9579 fax

State Secretary of Tourism of Baja California Sur
KM 5 1/2 Carretera Transpeninsular (FIDEPAZ)
Apdo. Postal 419
La Paz, BCS, Mexico
011-52-112-4-0100
011-52-112-4-0722 fax

Tackle Box, The
Avenida Madero Numero 9
Apdo. Postal 503
Cabo San Lucas, BCS, Mexico
011-52-114-3-3736 fax and phone

Tiburon's Pangas Sportfishing
2011 Pacific Avenue
Long Beach, CA 90806
310-865-4490
310-599-0106 fax

Tío Watersports
Playa Médano
Cabo San Lucas, BCS, Mexico
011-52-114-3-444, ext. 778
011-52-114-3-1521 fax

Too Much Fun Promotions
Box 120089
Chula Vista, CA 91912
011-52-661-2-2525 phone and fax

Tracks to Adventure
2811 Jackson, Suite K
El Paso, TX 79930-9985
915-565-9627
800-351-6053

TRIPUI Resort RV Park
Apdo. Postal 100
Loreto, BCS, Mexico
011-52-113-3-0818
011-52-113-3-0828 fax

US Consular Agency
Blvd. Marina y Calle de Cerro
Cabo San Lucas, BCS, Mexico
011-52-114-3-3566 phone and fax

US Consulate General
Avenida Tapachula 96
Col. Hipódromo
Tijuana, BC, Mexico
011-52-668-1-7400
011-52-668-1-8016 fax
  or
Box 439039
San Ysidro, CA 92143
619-585-2000 24-hour answering service

US Customs Service
Box 7407
Washington, DC 20044
202-927-6724

US Fish and Wildlife Service
Department of the Interior
Washington, DC 20240
202-208-5634

US State Department
Citizen's Emergency Center
202-647-5225

University of Arizona
Printing & Publishing Support Services
Tucson, AZ 85721
602-621-2571
602-621-6478 fax

Ursula's Sport Fishing Charters
Hidalgo y Blvd. Marina
Cabo San Lucas, BCS, Mexico
011-52-114-3-1264 phone and fax

**Vagabundos del Mar Boat and
  Travel Club**
190 Main Street
Rio Vista, CA 94571
707-374-5511
707-374-6843 fax

Vagabundos del Mar Trailer Park
Apdo. Postal 197
Cabo San Lucas, BCS, Mexico
011-52-114-3-0290
011-52-114-3-0511 fax

Viajes Guayacura
Apdo. Postal 71
Ensenada, BC, Mexico
011-52-617-8-1641
011-52-617-8-1045 fax

Viajes Mar y Arena
Zona Porturia
Puerto San Carlos, BCS, Mexico
011-52-113-6-0076

Victor's Aquatics

  Hotel Posada Real Cabo
  Zona Hotelera, Malecón s/n
  San José del Cabo, BCS, Mexico
  011-52-114-2-1092
  800-528-1234
    or
  Jig Stop Tours
  3486 Coast Highway
  Dana Point, CA
  714-496-096
  714-496-1384 fax
  800-521-2281

Victor's el Cortez RV Park
San Felipe, BC, Mexico
011-52-657-7-1056
  or
Box 1227
Calexico, CA 92232

Villarino Camp
Apdo. Postal 1
Punta Banda, BC, Mexico
011-52-617-6-4246

Villa María Isabel RV & Trailer Park
KM 134 Carretera Transpeninsular
Mulegé, BCS, Mexico
011-52-115-3-0426
011-52-115-3-0246 fax

Villas de Loreto RV Park
Antonio Mijares y Playa
Colonia Zaragoza
Apdo. Postal 132
Loreto, BCS, Mexico
011-52-113-5-0586 phone and fax

Villa Serena RV Park
Apdo. Postal 111
Cabo San Lucas, BCS, Mexico
011-52-114-3-0509 phone and fax

Villa Vitta Hotel Resort
Box 462701
Escondido, CA 92046
011-52-665-0-3206
619-741-9583

Vista Sea Sport
Apdo. Postal 42
Buena Vista, BCS, Mexico
011-52-114-1-0031 phone and fax

Volkswagen dealers

  Concesionario Volkswagen
  Avenida Clark 41, Col. Moderna
  Ensenada, BC, Mexico
  011-52-617-4-4625

  Automotriz Transmar de Cortés
  KM 4 Carretera al Norte
  La Paz, BCS, Mexico
  011-52-112-2-2054
  011-52-112-5-0939 fax

  Automotriz Transmar de Cortés
  KM 38 Carretera Transpeninsular
  Santa Rosa, BCS, Mexico
  011-52-114-2-0854
  011-52-114-2-0880

Appendix D

Map Key, Distances, and Measurements

Town/City Map Key

Auto/truck parts	AP	Ice cream	IR	Post office	PO
Bakery	BK	Ice	IC	Rest rooms (public)	RR
Bank	BA	Immigration	IM	Restaurant/café	RE
Beer	BE	Laundry	LA	RV park/campsite	RV
Bus depot/stop	BD	Liquor	LI	Souvenirs/gifts/curios	SO
Car rental	CR	LPG	LP	Sporting goods	SG
Coffee/espresso	CO	Butcher shop	ME	Telegraph	TE
Customs	CU	Mechanic	MC	Telephone	TP
Dentist	DE	Money exchange	MY	Tire sales/repair	TS
Dive shop	DI	Motorcycle shop	MO	Tortilla factory	TF
Doctor	DO	Optical	OP	Tourist office	TO
Ferry	FE	Outboard parts/repairs	OB	Travel agency	TA
Fruit/vegetables	FR	*Pangas*, cruisers, guides	PA	Veterinarian	VE
Groceries	GR	PEMEX	PE	Video sales/rentals	VI
Hardware	HA	PESCA (fishing license) office	PS	Water	WA
Hospital/clinic	HO	Pharmacy	PH	Welding	WE
Hotel/motel	HT	Photography	PT		

Mileage Between Points—Transpeninsular Highway

	Tijuana	Ensenada	San Vicente	San Quintín	El Rosario	Cataviña	Parador Punta Prieta	Guerrero Negro	Vizcaíno	San Ignacio	Santa Rosalía	Mulegé	Loreto	Ciudad Constitución	La Paz	San José del Cabo
Tijuana																
Ensenada	69															
San Vicente	125	56														
San Quintín	186	117	61													
El Rosario	226	157	101	40												
Cataviña	299	230	174	113	73											
Parador Punta Prieta	365	296	240	179	139	66										
Guerrero Negro	447	378	322	261	221	148	82									
Vizcaíno	492	423	367	306	266	193	127	45								
San Ignacio	536	467	411	350	310	237	171	89	44							
Santa Rosalía	581	512	456	395	355	282	216	134	89	45						
Mulegé	619	550	494	433	393	320	254	172	127	83	38					
Loreto	703	634	578	517	477	404	338	256	211	167	122	84				
Ciudad Constitución	792	723	667	606	566	493	427	345	300	256	211	173	89			
La Paz	923	854	798	737	697	624	558	476	431	387	342	304	220	131		
San José del Cabo	1037	968	912	851	811	738	672	590	545	501	456	418	334	245	114	
Cabo San Lucas	1057	988	932	871	831	758	692	610	565	521	476	438	354	265	134	20

Measurements

1 pound	=	0.454 kilogram
1 kilogram	=	2.2046 pounds
1 gallon	=	3.784 liters
1 liter	=	0.264 gallon
1 liter	=	1.0567 liquid quarts
1 liquid quart	=	0.946 liter
1 meter	=	39.37 inches
1 meter	=	3.281 feet
1 foot	=	0.305 meter
1 inch	=	2.54 centimeters
1 centimeter	=	0.393 inch
1 kilometer	=	3,280.8 feet
1 kilometer	=	0.621 statute mile
1 kilometer	=	0.54 nautical mile
1 statute mile	=	1.61 kilometers
1 statute mile	=	5,280 feet
1 nautical mile	=	6,076.1 feet
1 nautical mile	=	1.15 statute miles
1 nautical mile	=	1.85 kilometers

Appendix E

Instant Spanish

Communicating with the locals in their own language is part of the fun, so this appendix provides a highly simplified approach to Spanish that will allow you to ask directions, interpret road signs, deal with menus, shop for food and supplies, obtain services, and generally understand and be understood.

Extra characters and pronunciation

Spanish has a few "peculiarities" that English-speakers often find a bit difficult to deal with. To start with, there are three "extra" alphabetical characters, *ch*, *ñ* (an ordinary "n" with a tilde over it), and *ll* (double l), each being separate and distinct from the "regular" *c*, *h*, *n* and *l*. Also, "*rr*" (two rs) is often encountered. Each *r* is separate, and the pair is not granted alphabetic character status as are *ch*, *ñ* and *ll*, but when "*rr*" is encountered, the pair is pronounced with a trill of the tongue. English-speaking people often find this sound difficult to master. To avoid many headaches, the English phonetic pronunciation of every Spanish word in the dictionary below is provided, as well as those in the model sentences at the end of this appendix.

Nouns and their articles

A noun is a word used to name a person, place, thing, quality or action. All Spanish nouns have gender, which can often be determined by the their endings; if a word ends with an -*o* it is usually masculine, and those ending with an -*a* are usually feminine, such as *amigo* and *amiga* (male friend and female friend).

Words called "articles" often precede nouns. Three English words can serve as articles: "a," "an," and "the." In Spanish, there are four singular articles, *un*, *una*, *el* and *la*, and their use is based on gender: the article must agree in gender with the noun it precedes. The Spanish articles *un* and *el* are masculine, *un* being the equivalent of **both** "a" and "an," and *el* meaning "the." The articles *una* and *la* are feminine, *una* being the equivalent of **both** "a" and "an," *la* meaning "the." The number of the article (singular or plural) must also agree with the noun, and there are thus four plural articles, each related to gender: the singular *un* becomes *unos*, *el* becomes *los*, and the feminine *una* and *la* become plural by just adding an -*s*, the words becoming *unas*

and *las*. Here is what it looks like in table form:

ARTICLES	SINGULAR		PLURAL	
English	a, an	the	a, an	the
Spanish, masculine	*un*	*el*	*unos*	*los*
Spanish, feminine	*una*	*la*	*unas*	*las*

To save you a lot grief, all nouns in the dictionary have been equipped with the appropriate singular articles. However, a few words are inherently plural, like "glasses," referring to eye glasses, and the correct plural articles are provided. This system provides a simple way of identifying nouns in the dictionary—if a word is associated with an article, it's a noun.

Adjectives

Adjectives are words used to limit or describe nouns and certain other classes of words, often denoting characteristics such as color, size, shape, quality, number, condition or status. Unlike English, Spanish adjectives usually **follow** the noun; "white house" is *casa blanca* ("house white"). However, one type of adjective is placed **before** the noun, and to keep things simple such adjectives are identified by a superscript [1] in the dictionary. Many Spanish adjectives in the dictionary end in -*o*, indicating they are masculine. Those which also have a feminine form are followed by -*a*, indicating that the -*o* can be exchanged with an -*a*, since adjective and noun must usually agree in gender. Some adjectives do not have a feminine form, and thus no -*a* is shown. (In several cases -*as* will also be encountered in the dictionary.) You might wish to spend a few minutes cruising the dictionary looking for Spanish words followed by -*a*. or -*as*. You will not spot all the adjectives this way, but it will refresh your memory as to their nature.

Verbs

Verbs are words that express existence, action, or occurrence. How do you recognize a verb in the dictionary? Simple—the English word will be followed by the word "to;" for instance "anchor, to." Most verbs in the dictionary are not conjugated. **There is no cause for panic**—you already

257

conjugate English verbs dozens of times every day, even though you may not know exactly what the term means—remember the old "I, you, he, we, you, they" stuff from English class? You need not fear—the model sentences are correctly conjugated, and it is thus perfectly possible to forget about the matter altogether.

The verbs in the dictionary are in the present tense. What, you say you don't know what tense means? Sure you do! The past tense refers to things that have already happened: "He caught a huge yellowtail yesterday;" present tense refers to things that are occurring now: "He is trolling too deep;" and future tense refers to things that will happen in the future: "You will catch a yellowtail if you do exactly what *Exploring Baja* says." You need not worry about tense—the model sentences often involve conjugated verbs, in the present, past, or future tense, as appropriate to the meaning of the sentence, and the correct usage is thus laid out in black and white.

Other parts of speech

Nouns, adjectives, and verbs are of great value to the Baja traveler, of course, but what about the other parts of speech: adverbs, pronouns, prepositions, and so forth? No, they have not been forgotten. A number of these parts of speech are included in the dictionary. However, in order to avoid submerging you in an unhappy quagmire of words and rules, the more important ones have also been made parts of the model sentences.

Numbers

The dictionary provides the translation for all numbers from zero to nineteen; from twenty to ninety by tens; from one hundred to nine hundred by hundreds; and the words for thousand and million. To form an intermediate number, simply "splice" numbers together as we do in English; twenty-six is *veinte seis*; three-hundred-fifty is *trescientos cincuenta*; two thousand is *dos mil*. If you can't understand this, there are several things you can do: write out the number (or ask the other person to do so), or simply speak out the number in digits—the year 1996 would thus be *uno nueve nueve seis*. The second approach may cause you to be regarded with a certain degree of sympathy, but at least you will be understood.

Advanced instant Spanish

Things have been kept exceedingly simple so far, but after some practice, you may want to spread your linguistic wings a bit. If you feel you can't handle this at the current state of your career as a Spanish linguist, simply skip the next four paragraphs.

You can pronounce Spanish words more skillfully than permitted by the English phonetic versions provided. The characters "b" and "v" have the same sounds in Spanish. Since the phonetic words are in English, we have opted for the "b" sound, but in fact the Spanish "b" and "v" are pronounced like the English "v," but are formed between the upper and lower lips, rather than between the lower lip and the upper teeth—call it half way between an English "b" and "v." The "*ll*" character in Spanish is pronounced like the "lli" in the English word "million," but the "l" and the "y" sounds are pronounced so closely that they become one sound. The "*ñ*" character is pronounced like the "ni" in the English word "onion." The "*rr*" sound can not be made part of the phonetic pronunciations provided in the dictionary and the model sentences, for the simple reason that no similar sound exists in English. When a pair of *r*s is encountered, you can sound a bit more authentic by trilling the sound with your tongue .

Almost all nouns in the dictionary are singular, but if you want to experiment with plurals, there is a useful (but not always correct) rule of thumb—add an -*s* at the end of Spanish words ending with *a, e, i, o* or *u* (vowels), and an -*es* at the end of all others. Virtually all adjectives in the dictionary are singular, but you can convert them to plural form by adding an -*s* at the end of words ending with a vowel, and an -*es* at the end of all others.

Some words have a formal and an informal form. The informal form is used when addressing relatives, friends, and children, the formal when addressing a stranger or a person to whom respect is due. Words in the dictionary having such forms are identified by a superscript [2]. If in doubt, use the formal form.

For those that would like to try getting rather fancy, the conjugations of three important Spanish verbs are provided in the dictionary. The verb "to be" and its conjugations (I am, you are, he is, we are, you are, they are) exists in two forms in Spanish, *estar* and *ser*. *Estar* is used to tell about or inquire about location, to tell or ask about health, or to describe a temporary, accidental, or readily changeable condition, an example being to be happy—I am happy, you are happy, we are happy, etc. *Ser* is used in situations not described in *estar*, an example being to be American—I am American, you are American, etc. *Estar* and the words in its conjugation are identified by a superscript [3] in the dictionary below, *ser* with a [4]. The third verb, *tener*, "to have" (I have, you have, he has, etc.) and the words in its conjugation are identified by a superscript [5].

Dictionary

The following Spanish/English dictionary contains a number of basic words and terms involving numbers, time, days of the week, colors, foods, directions, tools, natural history, geographic and meteorological terms, and "opposites" (left, right, hot, cold, up, down, rich, poor, etc.), as well are words of a more general nature. In addition, many boating, fishing, diving, driving, RVing, and health words and terms are provided. Many words in both languages often have more than one meaning, and scholarly Spanish/English dictionaries sometimes require several pages to explain the many shades of meaning of a single word. However, to avoid stranding you in a sea of confusion, we have limited most words to a single meaning, the most useful meaning in light of the purpose stated in the first paragraph of this appendix. We have also endeavored to choose those Spanish words bearing the closest resemblance to English in terms of their Latin roots, greatly simplifying the mental gymnastics required. If the meaning of the last three sentences is not clear, don't worry and just accept as a matter of faith that we have endeavored to keep things simple.

English and Spanish words and terms are provided in alphabetical order in separate columns, labeled ENGLISH and SPANISH. If you want to know the Spanish counterpart to an English word, locate the word in the ENGLISH column, and the SL column will provide the LINE number where the Spanish counterpart can be found. If you want to know the English counterpart of a Spanish word, locate the word in the SPANISH column and the EL column will provide the LINE number where the English counterpart can be found. The PRONUNCIATION column provides the English phonetic pronunciation of the Spanish word, with syllables that should be stressed shown in bold characters. Remember—this column is in English, even though it may not appear so. Don't make problems for yourself; if a phonetic word or syllable seems ambiguous, choose the simplest interpretation.

Try it out. If, for example, you want to know the Spanish word for "alternator" (the part attached to the engine in your RV that makes electricity to feed the battery), locate the word in the alphabetized ENGLISH column, which proves to be LINE 20, and the SL column says its Spanish counterpart can be found on LINE 49, and the word in the

SPANISH column on LINE 49 turns out to be *alternador*. Since the articles shown are *un* and *el*, you know that it is a singular masculine noun. Moving to the right along LINE 49, the PRONUNCIATION column shows that the word is pronounced "ahl-tehr-nah-**dohr**."

To find the English translation of a Spanish word, simply locate the word in the alphabetized SPANISH column, and the EL column will tell you the line of the English word. Try it out; you are driving and see a sign saying CURVA PELIGROSA. Locate the term in the alphabetized SPANISH column, which proves to be on LINE 299, and the EL column just to the right of the term says its English counterpart can be found on LINE 211, "dangerous curve." The PRONUNCIATION column on LINE 299 indicates it is pronounced "**cur**-bah peh-leeh-**groh**-sah."

This simple system is very compact compared to a conventional reverse, English/Spanish, Spanish/English dictionary, permitting a far more comprehensive dictionary in the space available. Specialized terms related to golf, tennis, kayaking, jet skiing, paragliding, hang gliding, sailboarding, water skiing, and surfing are not provided because the sports have become so thoroughly "Americanized" that no translations are necessary—the English terms are widely understood in Baja, at least in places frequented by *gringos*. Questions and statements concerning the availability of equipment, costs, schedules and so forth can be formed easily by adapting the sentences provided for boating, fishing, and diving.

LINE	ENGLISH	SL	SPANISH	EL	PRONUNCIATION
1	a (feminine plural article)	1098	*a*	999	ah
2	a (feminine singular article)	1095	*a la parrilla*	119	ah lah pahr-**reeh**-yah
3	a (masculine plural article)	1102	*a qué distancia*	449	ah keh dees-**tahn**-syah
4	a (masculine singular article)	1093	*abajo*	254	ah-**bah**-hoh
5	abalone (mollusk), an, the	8	*abierto, -a*	688	ah-**byehr**-toh
6	about (origin, composition, content, use)	303	*abril, un, el*	38	ah-**breel**
7	accident (mishap), an, the	10	*abrir*	689	ah-**breer**
8	adhesive tape, the	223	*abulón, una, la*	5	ah-buh-**lohn**
9	adjust, to	17	*acceso a playa*	74	ahk-**ces**-soh ah **plah**-yah
10	after	326	*accidente, un, el*	7	ahk-seeh-**dehn**-teh
11	afternoon, an, the	1017	*acedía, la*	420	ah-sayh-**deeh**-ah
12	against	397	*aceite para cocción, el*	675	ah-**seyh**-teh **pah**-ruh koh-**syohn**
13	air (atmosphere), the	27	*aceite para diferenciales, el*	228	ah-**seyh**-teh **pah**-ruh deeh-fehr-ehn-seeh-**ahl**-ehs
14	albacore (fish), an, the	33	*aceite para motores, el*	289	ah-**seyh**-teh **pah**-ruh moh-**tohr**-ehs
15	alcohol (beverage, medicine), the	36	*aceite, un, el*	676	ah-**seyh**-teh
16	alive (living)	1136	*acumulador, un, el*	69	ah-kooh-mooh-lah-**dohr**
17	all (every)	1061	*adaptar*	9	ah-**dahp**-tahr
18	all-terrain vehicle (ATV), an, the	288	*adelante*	343	ah-deh-**lahn**-teh
19	allergy (malady, an, the	37	*adiós*	379	ah-**dyohs**
20	alternator (vehicle part), an, the	49	*Aduana*	206	ah-**dwah**-nah

LINE	ENGLISH	SL	SPANISH	EL	PRONUNCIATION
21	amberjack (fish), an, the	812	*afuera de*	697	ah-**fweh**-rah deh
22	an (feminine plural article)	1099	*agosto, un, el*	47	ah-**gohs**-toh
23	an (feminine singular article)	1096	*agua, la*	1071	**ah**-gwah
24	an (masculine plural article)	1103	*águila, una, la*	267	**ah**-geeh-lah
25	an (masculine singular article)	1094	*aguja, una, la*	632	ah-**gooh**-hah
26	anchor, an, the	58	*ahora*	664	ah-**ohr**-ah
27	anchor, to	59	*aire, el*	13	**ahy**-reh
28	anchovy (fish), an, the	134	*ajo, el*	365	**ah**-hoh
29	and	1144	*al carbón*	156	ahl karh-**bohn**
30	angina (malady), the	61	*al horno*	59	ahl **ohr**-noh
31	ankle (body part), an, the	1059	*al vapor*	908	ahl bah-**pohr**
32	antacid (medicine), an, the	66	*alacrán, un, el*	824	ah-lah-**kranh**
33	antibiotic (medicine), an, the	67	*albacora, una, la*	14	ahl-bah-**corh**-ah
34	antiseptic (medicine), an, the	68	*alberca, una, la*	942	ahl-**behr**-kah
35	appendicitis, the	71	*alcantarilla, una, la*	266	ahl-kahn-tahr-**reeh**-ah
36	appendix (body part), an, the	70	*alcohol, el*	15	ahl-**koh**-holh
37	apple (food), an, the	641	*alergia, una, la*	19	ah-lehr-**geeh**-ah
38	April, an, the	6	*aleta de buzo, una, la*	314	ah-**layh**-tah deh **booh**-soh
39	arm (body part), an, the	139	*algo*	886	**ahl**-goh
40	arrive, to	616	*alicates, los*	727	ah-leeh-**kah**-teyhs
41	arthritis (malady), the	84	*alimento para gatos, el*	149	ah-leeh-**mahyn**-toh **pah**-rah gah-tohs
42	as	242	*alimento para niño, el*	52	ah-leeh-**mahyn**-toh **pah**-ruh neen-yoh
43	ask, to	859	*alimento para perros, el*	248	ah-**leeh**-mahyn-toh **pah**-rah **pehr**-rohs
44	aspirin (medicine), an, the	89	*alimento, un, el*	333	ah-leeh-**mahyn**-toh
45	asthma (malady), the	87	*almeja, una, la*	169	ahl-**mayh**-hah
46	at (position, time)	393	*almuerzo, un, el*	559	ahl-**mwehr**-soh
47	August, an, the	22	*alquilar*	434	ahl-keeh-**lahr**
48	automatic teller machine, an	155	*alquilar*	782	ahl-kweeh-**lahr**
49	available	350	*alternador, un, el*	20	ahl-tehr-nah-**dohr**
50	avenue (street), an, the	97	*alto*	915	**ahl**-toh
51	axle (vehicle part), an, the	376	*alto, -a*	431	**ahl**-toh
52	baby food, the	42	*alto-inspección*	480	al-toh eehn-spayk-**syohn**
53	back (body part), a, the	423	*amarillo, -a*	1130	ah-mah-**reeh**-yoh
54	backwards	507	*amiga, una, la*	353	ah-**meeh**-gah
55	bacon (food), the	1060	*amigo, un, el*	354	ah-**meeh**-goh
56	bad	632	*amortiguador, un, el*	853	ah-mohr-teeh-gwah-**dohr**
57	bait (cut, fishing), a, the	181	*añagaza, una, la*	561	ahn-nyah-**gah**-zah
58	bait (live, fishing), a, the	180	*ancla, una, la*	26	**ahn**-klah
59	baked (cooking method)	30	*anclar*	27	ahn-**klar**
60	bakery, a, the	771	*andar*	1066	ahn-**dahr**
61	banana (food), a, the	831	*angina, la*	30	ahn-**heeh**-nah
62	Band-Aid, a, the	298	*año, un, el*	1128	**ahn**-yoh
63	bandage, a, the	1117	*anoche*	518	ah-**noh**-chay
64	bank (fishing, money), a, the	107	*anteojos de sol, los*	931	ahn-teh-oh-**hohs** deh sohl
65	barbecue (cooking method)	110	*antes de*	83	**ahn**-tehs deh

LINE	ENGLISH	SL	SPANISH	EL	PRONUNCIATION
66	barracuda (fish), a, the	112	*antiácido, un, el*	32	ahn-teeh-**ah**-seeh-doh
67	bathe, to	106	*antibiótico, un, el*	33	ahn-teeh-beeh-**oh**-teeh-koh
68	bathroom, a, the	108	*antiséptico, un, el*	34	ahn-teeh-**sep**-teeh-koh
69	battery (electric), a, the	16	*aparato auditivo*	416	ah-pah-**rah**-toh auh-deeh-**teeh**-boh
70	bay (cove), a, the	102	*apéndice, un, el*	36	ah-**pen**-deeh-seh
71	be, to (... ... American)	965	*apendicitis, la*	35	ah-pen-deeh-**seeh**-teehs
72	be, to (... ... happy)	436	*aprender*	524	ah-prehn-**dehr**
73	beach (shore), a, the	834	*aquí*	429	ah-**keeh**
74	beach access (road sign)	9	*arandela, una, la*	1069	ah-rahn-**deh**-lah
75	beans (food, plural), the	475	*árbol de levas, un, el*	137	**ahr**-bol deh **leh**-bahs
76	bearing (vehicle part), a, the	235	*árbol de motor, un, el*	259	**ahr**-bohl deh moh-**tohr**
77	beautiful (handsome)	517	*arena, la*	815	ah-**reeh**-nah
78	because	853	*arpón, un, el*	362	ahr-**pohn**
79	because of	847	*arponear*	363	ahr-**pohn**-nyhr
80	beef (food), the	183	*arranque, un, el*	906	ahr-**rahn**-keh
81	beer (beverage), a, the	212	*arrecife, un, el*	775	ahr-reeh-**seeh**-feyh
82	beer distributor, a, the	211	*arriba*	1053	ahr-**reeh**-bah
83	before	65	*arroz, el*	793	ahr-**rohs**
84	begin (commence), to	238	*artritis, la*	41	ahr-**treeh**-teehs
85	beginning (start), a, the	241	*asado, -a*	803	ah-**sah**-doh
86	behind (in back of)	329	*asfalto fresco*	350	ahs-**fal**-toh **frays**-koh
87	believe, to	273	*asma, la*	45	**ahs**-mah
88	best (superior)	666	*asoleada, una, la*	937	ah-soh-leeh-**ah**-dah
89	between (intermediate location or time)	408	*aspirina, una, la*	44	ahs-peeh-**reeh**-nah
90	bird (large), a, the	96	*ataque al corazón, un, el*	418	ah-**tah**-kay ahl koh-rah-**sohn**
91	bird (small), a, the	764	*ataque, un, el*	927	ah-**tah**-kay
92	bite (insect or animal), a, the	817	*atascado*	928	ah-tahs-**kah**-doh
93	black (color)	711	*atún amarillo, un, el*	1131	ah-**toohn** ah-mah-**reeh**-yoh
94	black sea bass (fish), a, the	669	*atún, un, el*	1039	ah-**toohn**
95	bleed (malady), to	942	*autocasa, una, la*	606	auh-toh-**kah**-sah
96	blood (body part), the	943	*ave, una, la*	90	**ah**-beh
97	blue (color)	101	*avenida, una, la*	50	ah-bah-**neeh**-dah
98	boat, a, the	111	*ayer*	1134	ah-**yehr**
99	boiled (cooking method)	519	*ayudar*	425	ah-yooh-**dahr**
100	bolt (fastening, large), a, the	210	*azúcar, el*	929	ah-**sooh**-kahr
101	bolt (fastening, small), a, the	809	*azul*	97	ah-**soohl**
102	bone (body part), a, the	536	*bahía, una, la*	70	bah-**heeh**-ah
103	bonito (fish), a, the	133	*bajo, -a*	557	**bah**-hoh
104	booby (bird), a, the	789	*bajo, -a*	845	**bah**-hoh
105	book (printed work), a, the	600	*ballena, una, la*	1089	bah-**yeah**-nah
106	bottle (glass), a, the	138	*bañarse*	67	bahn-**yahr**-seh
107	bottom (lowest part), a, the	470	*banco, un, el*	64	**bahn**-koh
108	brain (body part), a, the	206	*baño, un, el*	68	**bahn**-yoh
109	brake (vehicle part), a, the	474	*barato, -a*	157	bah-**rah**-toh
110	brake fluid (vehicle part), the	466	*barbacoa*	65	bahr-bah-**koh**-ah
111	brake shoe (vehicle part), a, the	1148	*barco, un, el*	98	**bahr**-koh

LINE	ENGLISH	SL	SPANISH	EL	PRONUNCIATION
112	bread (food), the	770	*barracuda, una, la*	66	bar-rah-**kooh**-dah
113	breaded (cooking method)	391	*barrena, una, la*	255	bahr-**reeh**-nah
114	breakfast, a, the	322	*barrenar*	256	bahr-**reeh**-nahr
115	breast (body part), a, the	959	*barrilete, un, el*	874	barrh-eh-**leh**-teh
116	breathe, to	917	*bastante*	291	bahs-**tahn**-teh
117	bridge (for a road, dental) a, the	873	*basura, la*	364	bah-**sooh**-rah
118	bring, to	1075	*beber*	258	beh-**behr**
119	broiled (cooking method)	2	*bebida, una, la*	257	beh-**beeh**-dah
120	broken (fractured)	930	*berrendo, un, el*	744	behr-**rehn**-doh
121	brown (color)	780	*biblioteca, una, la*	534	beeb-leeh-oh-**teh**-kah
122	bruise (malady), a, the	258	*biela, una, la*	186	beeh-**ayh**-lah
123	building (structure), a, the	375	*bien*	1085	byehn
124	bump (in a road, speed bump), a, the	1065	*bien hecho, -a*	1086	byehn **eh**-choh
125	buoyancy compensator, a, the	245	*bifurcación, una, la*	341	beeh-fuhr-kah-**syohn**
126	burn (malady), a, the	887	*bistec, un, el*	907	beehs-**tehk**
127	but	801	*blanco, -a*	1100	**blahn**-koh
128	butcher shop, a, the	185	*blando, -a*	885	**blahn**-doh
129	butter (food), the	640	*blanquillo, un, el*	669	blahn-**keeh**-yoh
130	buy, to	246	*boca, una, la*	612	**boh**-kah
131	by (cause, mode)	848	*bomba, una, la*	749	**bohm**-bah
132	by accident	850	*bombear*	750	bohm-beeh-**ahr**
133	cabrilla (fish), a, the	152	*bonito, un, el*	103	boh-**neeh**-toh
134	call (telephone), a, the	607	*boquerón, un, el*	28	boh-kwer-**ohn**
135	calm (tranquil)	1077	*bordo de velas, un, el*	811	**bohr**-doh deh **beh**-lahs
136	camera, a, the	161	*borracho, -a*	263	bohr-**rah**-choh
137	camshaft (vehicle part), a, the	75	*borrego, un, el*	609	bohr-**reh**-goh
138	can (able to)	843	*botella, una, la*	106	boh-**teh**-yah
139	can (container), a, the	582	*brazo, un, el*	39	**brah**-soh
140	Canada	173	*brillante*	935	breeh-**yahn**-tayh
141	Canadian, a, the	174	*brújula, una, la*	184	**brooh**-hooh-lah
142	cancer (malady), a, the	175	*bucear*	238	booh-sayh-**ahr**
143	candy store, a, the	373	*bueno[1], -a*	378	**bweh**-noh
144	carburetor (vehicle part) a, the	179	*buitre, un, el*	1064	booh-**eeh**-treh
145	careful, to be	1034	*bujía, una, la*	895	booh-**heeh**-ah
146	carrot (food), a, the	1147	*buscar*	552	boohs-**kahr**
147	carry, to	619	*buzo, un, el*	239	**booh**-soh
148	cat (mammal), a, the	487	*caballo, un, el*	441	kah-**bah**-yoh
149	cat food, the	41	*cabeza, una, la*	411	kah-**beh**-sah
150	catch (... ... a fish), to	234	*cabra, una, la*	377	**kah**-brah
151	cattle (road sign)	482	*cabrilla pinta, una, la*	530	kah-**breeh**-yah **peehn**-tah
152	caution (road sign)	856	*cabrilla, una, la*	133	kah-**breeh**-yah
153	center (headquarters, middle), a, the	202	*cadera, una, la*	433	kah-**dehr**-ah
154	centimeter (measurement), a, the	200	*café, un, el*	179	kah-**feh**
155	change (alter), to	163	*cajero automático, un,*	48	kah-**hehr**-oh autoh-**mah**-teeh-koh
156	charcoal-grilled (cooking method)	29	*calamar, un, el*	903	kah-lah-**mahr**
157	cheap (inexpensive)	109	*calambres*	913	kah-**lahm**-breys
158	check (bank draft), a, the	215	*caliente*	444	kah-**lyehn**-teh

LINE	ENGLISH	SL	SPANISH	EL	PRONUNCIATION
159	check (bill in a restaurant), a, the	292	*calle, una, la*	926	**kah**-yeah
160	cheese (food), a, the	890	*calor, el*	421	kah-**lohr**
161	chest (body part), a, the	790	*cámara, una, la*	136	**kah**-mah-rah
162	chicken (food), a, the	845	*camarón, un, el*	864	kah-mah-**rohn**
163	child (female), a, the	714	*cambiar*	155	kahm-**byahr**
164	child (male), a, the	715	*camino cerrado*	799	kah-**meeh**-noh sehr-**rah**-doh
165	chocolate (food), the	216	*camino en reparación*	800	kah-**meeh**-noh ehn rayh-pah-rah-**syohn**
166	choose, to	417	*camino ondulado*	1073	kah-**meeh**-noh ohn-dooh-**lah**-doh
167	church, a, the	538	*camino sinuoso*	1106	kah-**meeh**-noh seeh-nooh-**oh**-soh
168	city, a, the	226	*camino, un, el*	801	kah-**meeh**-noh
169	clam (mollusk), a, the	45	*camión, un, el*	1035	kah-meeh-**yohn**
170	clean (not dirty)	605	*camisa, una, la*	852	kah-**meeh**-sah
171	clean, to	604	*caña de pescar, una, la*	805	**kahn**-nyah deh pehys-**kahr**
172	clinic (health), a, the	228	*caña, una, la*	729	**kahn**-yah
173	close to (near)	204	*Canadá*	140	can-nah-**dah**
174	closed (shut)	208	*canadiense, un, el*	141	kah-nah-**dyehn**-seh
175	clothes (garments), the	929	*cáncer, un, el*	142	**kahn**-sayhr
176	cloudy (overcast)	738	*cangrejo, un, el*	198	kahn-**greyh**-hoh
177	clutch (vehicle part), a, the	390	*cansado, -a*	998	kahn-**sah**-doh
178	coconut (food), a, the	231	*cara, una, la*	297	**kah**-rah
179	coffee (beverage), a, the	154	*carburador, un, el*	144	kah-booh-rah-**dohr**
180	cold (frigid)	476	*carnada viva, una, la*	58	khar-**nah**-dah **beeh**-bah
181	cold (malady), a, the	194	*carnada, una, la*	57	khar-**nah**-dah
182	color, a, the	237	*carne de cerdo, la*	733	**kahr**-nay deh **sher**-doh
183	come, to	1119	*carne de vaca, la*	80	**kahr**-neh deh **bah**-kah
184	compass, a, the	141	*carne, la*	584	**kahr**-nay
185	condom, a, the	249	*carnicería, una, la*	128	kahr-neeh-sayh-**reeh**-ah
186	connecting rod (vehicle part), a, the	122	*carrete, un, el*	776	kahr-**ray**-teh
187	constipation (malady), the	445	*carretera, una, la*	432	kahr-reh-**teh**-rah
188	contact lens, a, the	594	*carta, una, la*	532	**kahr**-tah
189	contraceptive, a, the	257	*casa de cambio*	601	**kah**-sah deh kahm-**beeh**-oh
190	cook, to	230	*casa de correos, una, la*	736	**kah**-sah deh kohr-**reah**-ohs
191	corbina (fish), a, the	260	*casa de telégrafo, una, la*	952	**kah**-sah deh teh-**layh**-grah-foh
192	corn (cooked ear), the	388	*casa, una, la*	439	**kah**-sah
193	corn (grain), the	630	*cascabel, una, la*	768	kahs-kah-**behl**
194	cough (malady), a, the	1071	*catarro, un, el*	181	kah-**tah**-roh
195	cough (malady), to	1072	*catorce*[1]	346	kah-**tohr**-seh
196	cough syrup (medicine), a, the	558	*cazo de aceite, un, el*	678	**cah**-soh deh ah-**seyh**-teh
197	coyote (mammal), a, the	272	*cebolla, una, la*	686	seh-**boh**-yah
198	crab (crustacean), a, the	176	*ceda el paso*	1135	**seeh**-dah ehl **pah**-soh
199	crankshaft (vehicle part), a, the	219	*cena, una, la*	938	**seh**-nah
200	cream (food), the	274	*centímetro, un, el*	154	sayhn-**teeh**-may-troh
201	credit card, a, the	1018	*centro de salud, un, el*	414	**sehn**-troh deh sah-**lood**
202	crown (dental), a, the	262	*centro, un, el*	153	**sehn**-troh
203	cruiser (boat), a, the	277	*cepillo de dientes*	1010	seh-**peeh**-yoh deh **dyehn**-tehs
204	cup (eating utensil), a, the	1021	*cerca de*	173	**cehr**-cah deh

LINE	ENGLISH	SL	SPANISH	EL	PRONUNCIATION
205	current (of water), a, the	266	*cerca de*	628	**cehr**-cah deh
206	Customs (Mexican govt. office)	20	*cerebro, un, el*	108	seh-**reh**-broh
207	cut (sever), to	267	*cero*[1]	1152	**say**-roh
208	cylinder (for LPG gas), a, the	220	*cerrado, -a*	174	sehr-**rah**-doh
209	danger (hazard), a, the	794	*cerradura, una, la*	547	sehr-rah-**dooh**-rah
210	dangerous (hazardous)	795	*cerrojo, un, el*	100	sehr-**oh**-hoh
211	dangerous curve (road sign)	299	*cervecería, una, la*	82	sehr-bey-seh-**reeh**-ah
212	date (of year), a, the	455	*cerveza, una, la*	81	sehr-**bey**-sah
213	daughter, a, the	522	*champiñónes, unos, los*	617	cham-peehn-**yoh**-nays
214	day, a, the	330	*cheque de viajeros, un, el*	1031	**cheh**-keh deh beeh-yah-**heh**-rohs
215	dead (expired)	697	*cheque, un, el*	158	**cheh**-keh
216	December, a, the	334	*chocolate, el*	165	choh-koh-**lah**-tahy
217	deep (in depth)	532	*chorizo, el*	819	chor-**reeh**-soh
218	deer (mammal), a, the	1116	*ciento*[1]	684	seeh-**yehn**-toh
219	delicatessen, a, the	1092	*cigüeñal, un, el*	199	seeh-goohn-**nahl**
220	dentist, a, the	317	*cilindro de gas, un, el*	208	seeh-**lyn**-droh deh gahs
221	dentures (false teeth, plural), the	316	*cinco*[1]	323	**seehn**-coh
222	dessert (food), a, the	855	*cincuenta*[1]	310	seehn-**kwehn**-tah
223	detour (road sign)	328	*cinta adhesiva, la*	8	**ceehn**-tah ahd-heeh-**seeh**-bah
224	diabetes (malady), the	331	*cinta de ventilador, una, la*	302	**ceehn**-tah deh bahyn-teeh-lah-**dohr**
225	diaper, a, the	772	*cinturón de buzo, un, el*	1082	seehn-tooh-**rohn** deh **booh**-soh
226	diarrhea (malady), the	333	*ciudad, una, la*	168	seeh-yooh-**dahd**
227	differential (vehicle part), a, the	341	*ciudad, una, la*	1024	seeh-yooh-**dahd**
228	differential oil (vehicle part), the	13	*clínica, una, la*	172	**kleehn**-eeh-cah
229	dim your brights (road sign)	251	*cocina, una, la*	923	koh-**seeh**-nah
230	dip (dip in road, road sign)	1109	*cocinar*	190	koh-seeh-**nahr**
231	direction (course towards), a, the	346	*coco, un, el*	178	**koh**-koh
232	dirty (unclean)	998	*codo, un, el*	281	**koh**-doh
233	discount, a, the	323	*codorniz, una, la*	755	koh-dohr-**neehs**
234	dislocation (malady), a, the	348	*coger*	150	koh-**her**
235	distance, a, the	351	*cojinete de bolas, un, el*	76	koh-heeh-**neh**-teh deh **boh**-lahs
236	distant (far, remote)	352	*colibrí, un, el*	453	koh-leeh-**breeh**
237	distributor (vehicle part), a, the	353	*color, un, el*	182	koh-**lohr**
238	dive (scuba dive, free dive), to	142	*comenzar*	84	koh-mehn-**sahr**
239	diver, a, the	147	*comer*	275	koh-**mehr**
240	dizzy (malady)	646	*comida, una, la*	583	koh-**meeh**-dah
241	do not enter (road sign)	719	*comienzo, un, el*	85	koh-meeh-**ehn**-soh
242	do not litter (road sign)	722	*como*	42	**koh**-moh
243	do not park (road sign)	718	*como*	537	**koh**-moh
244	do not pass (road sign)	721	*cómo*	447	**koh**-moh
245	do, (accomplish) to	504	*compensador de buzo, un, el*	125	kohm-pahyn-sah-**dohr** deh **booh**-soh
246	doctor (physician), a, the	664	*comprar*	130	kohm-**prahr**
247	dog (mammal), a, the	803	*comprender*	1050	kohm-prehn-**dehr**
248	dog food, the	43	*con*	1113	kohn
249	dollar, a, the	357	*condón, un, el*	185	cohn-**dohn**
250	dolphin (marine mammal), a, the	314	*conducir*	260	kohn-dooh-**seehr**
251	dolphinfish (fish), a, the	366	*coneceda cambio de luces*	229	koh-neh-**seeh**-dah kahm-**beeh**-oh deh **looh**-sehs

LINE	ENGLISH	SL	SPANISH	EL	PRONUNCIATION
252	door , a, the	874	*conejo, un, el*	758	kohn-**neh**-hoh
253	dove (bird), a, the	768	*conocer*	511	koh-noh-**sehr**
254	down	4	*conseguir*	370	kohn-seh-**geehr**
255	drill (tool), a, the	113	*conserve su derecha*	503	kohn-**sayhr**-bay sooh deh-**reh**-chah
256	drill, to	114	*conserve su izquierda*	502	kohn-**sayhr**-bay sooh eez-keeh-**ayhr**-dah
257	drink (beverage), a, the	119	*contraceptivo, un, el*	189	kohn-trah-sep-**teeh**-boh
258	drink (swallow), to	118	*contusión, una, la*	122	kohn-tooh-**syohn**
259	drive shaft (vehicle part), a, the	76	*corazón, un, el*	417	koh-rah-**sohn**
260	drive, to	250	*corbina, una, la*	191	kohr-**beeh**-nah
261	driver's license, a, the	601	*cordón, un, el*	1111	kohr-**dohn**
262	drug (medicine), a, the	370	*corona, una, la*	202	kohr-**oh**-nah
263	drunk (tipsy)	136	*correcamino, un, el*	802	cohreh-kah-**meeh**-noh
264	dry (not wet)	948	*correcto, -a*	795	kohr-**rayhc**-toh
265	dryer (laundry), a, the	947	*correo, el*	564	kohr-**reh**-oh
266	dump station (sewer), a, the	35	*corriente, una, la*	205	kohr-reeh-**ayhn**-teh
267	eagle (bird), a, the	24	*cortar*	207	kohr-**tahr**
268	ear (inner, body part), an, the	753	*corto, -a*	857	**kohr**-toh
269	ear (outer, body part), an, the	759	*corvina blanca, una, la*	1101	kohr-**beeh**-nah **blahn**-kah
270	ear/eye drops (medicine, plural), the	494	*costilla, una, la*	792	kohs-**teehl**-yah
271	earache (malady), an, the	361	*costoso, -a*	295	kohs-**toh**-soh
272	early (first, to get up...)	1031	*coyote, un, el*	197	coh-**yoh**-teh
273	east, the	439	*creer*	87	kreh-**ehr**
274	easy (not difficult)	447	*crema, la*	200	**kray**-mah
275	eat (consume), to	239	*cruce de peatónes*	709	**krooh**-sayh deh peh-ah-**tohn**-ehs
276	egg (food), an, the	537	*cruce, un, el*	498	**krooh**-sayh
277	eight	748	*crucero, un, el*	203	krooh-**seh**-roh
278	eight hundred	749	*cuál*	1097	kwahl
279	eighteen	337	*cuándo*	1094	**kwahn**-doh
280	eighty	747	*cuánto*	452	**kwahn**-toh
281	elbow (body part), an, the	232	*cuánto tiempo*	450	**kwahn**-toh **tyehm**-poh
282	electricity, the	383	*cuántos*	451	**kwahn**-tohs
283	eleven	757	*cuarenta*[1]	342	kwah-**rehn**-tah
284	empty	1108	*cuarto, -a*	756	**kwahr**-toh
285	end (finish), an, the	464	*cuarto, un, el*	806	**kwahr**-toh
286	end (terminate), to	1039	*cuatro*[1]	344	**kwah**-troh
287	end of pavement (road sign)	463	*cuatrocientos*[1]	345	kwah-troh-seeh-**yehn**-tohs
288	engine (vehicle part), an, the	692	*cuatromoto, un, el*	18	kwah-troh-**moh**-toh
289	engine oil (vehicle part), the	14	*cuchara, una, la*	898	kooh-**chah**-rah
290	English (language), the	545	*cuchillo, un, el*	509	kooh-**cheeh**-yoh
291	enough (sufficient)	116	*cuello, un, el*	630	**kweh**-yoh
292	entrance, an, the	407	*cuenta, una, la*	159	**kwehn**-tah
293	every (all of)	1062	*cuerda, una, la*	538	**kwher**-dah
294	exit, an, the	938	*cuerda, una, la*	808	kooh-**ayhr**-dah
295	expensive (costly)	271	*cuesta, una, la*	381	**kwehs**-tah
296	eye (body part), an, the	755	*cuidado con el ganado*	1070	kweeh-**dah**-doh kohn ehl gah-**nah**-doh

LINE	ENGLISH	SL	SPANISH	EL	PRONUNCIATION
297	face (body part), a, the	178	*cumbre, la*	1013	**koohm**-breh
298	faint (malady), to	324	*curita, una, la*	62	koohr-**ee**-tah
299	fall (season), the	760	*curva peligrosa*	211	**cur**-bah peh-leeh-**groh**-sah
300	false (not true)	448	*dar*	373	dahr
301	family, a, the	449	*dar una propina*	995	dahr **oohn**-ah proh-**peeh**-nah
302	fan belt (vehicle part), a, the	224	*darse prisa*	455	**dahr**-seh **preeh**-sah
303	far from	591	*de*	6	deh
304	fast (rapid)	899	*de*	357	deh
305	father, a, the	762	*de*	673	deh
306	February, a, the	454	*debajo de*	1049	deh-**bah**-hoh deh
307	fever (malady), a, the	460	*deber*	619	deh-**behr**
308	few (not many)	842	*débil*	1078	**deh**-beehl
309	fifteen	892	*decir*	820	deh-**seehr**
310	fifty	222	*dedo del pie, un, el*	1001	**deh**-doh dehl **peeh**-yeh
311	fill, to	617	*dedo, un, el*	315	**deh**-doh
312	film (for a camera), the	461	*del*	674	dehl
313	filter (gas, oil, water, air), a, the	462	*delante de*	472	deh-**lahn**-teh deh
314	fin (diving), a, the	38	*delfín, un, el*	250	dehl-**feehn**
315	finger (body part), a, the	311	*demasiado[1], -a*	1007	deh-mah-seeh-**yah**-doh
316	fire (blaze), a, the	480	*dentaduras postizas, las*	221	dehn-tah-**dooh**-rahs pohs-**teeh**-sahs
317	first	861	*dentista, un, el*	220	dehn-**teehs**-tah
318	fish (alive), a, the	816	*dentro de*	478	**dehn**-troh deh
319	fish (as food), a, the	805	*deporte, un, el*	899	deh-**pohr**-teh
320	fish, to	808	*derecho, -a*	796	deh-**reh**-choh
321	fisherman, a, the	806	*derecho, -a*	925	deh-**reh**-choh
322	fisherwoman, a, the	807	*desayuno, un, el*	114	deh-sah-**yooh**-noh
323	five	221	*descuento, un, el*	233	dehs-**kwen**-toh
324	five hundred	893	*desmayarse*	298	dehs-mah-**yarh**-seh
325	flat (level)	608	*despacio*	876	dehs-pah-**seeh**-oh
326	flat tire, a, the	826	*después de*	10	dehs-**pwehs** deh
327	floor (of a building), a, the	828	*destornillador, un, el*	827	dehs-tohr-neeh-yah-**dohr**
328	flour (food), the	512	*desviación*	223	dehs-byah-**syohn**
329	flower (plant), a, the	465	*detrás de*	86	deh-**trahs** deh
330	flying fish, a, the	1137	*día, un, el*	214	**deeh**-ah
331	follow, to	949	*diabetes, la*	224	deeh-ah-**bey**-tayhs
332	food stand or cart, a, the	622	*diario, un, el*	637	deeh-ah-**reeh**-oh
333	food, a, the	44	*diarrea, la*	226	deeh-ah-**reeh**-ah
334	foot (body part, measurement), a, the	818	*diciembre, un, el*	216	deeh-**syehm**-breh
335	for (in exchange)	849	*diente, un, el*	1009	**dyehn**-teh
336	for (purpose, destination)	777	*diez y nueve[1]*	643	deeh-**yhes** ee **nweh**-beh
337	for rent	945	*diez y ocho[1]*	279	deeh-**yhes** ee **oh**-choh
338	for sale	946	*diez y seis[1]*	871	deeh-**yhes** ee sayhs
339	forbidden	865	*diez y siete[1]*	843	deeh-**yhes** ee seeh-**ahy**-tahy
340	fork (eating utensil), a, the	1032	*diez[1]*	958	deeh-**yhes**
341	fork (in a road), a, the	125	*diferencial, una, la*	227	deeh-fehr-ehn-seeh-**ahl**
342	forty	283	*difícil*	401	deeh-**feeh**-seehl
343	forwards	18	*dinero, el*	600	deeh-**neh**-roh

LINE	ENGLISH	SL	SPANISH	EL	PRONUNCIATION
344	four	286	*dirección prohibida*	647	deeh-rehk-**syohn** proh-eeh-**beeh**-dah
345	four hundred	287	*dirección única*	685	deeh-rehk-**syohn ooh**-neeh-kah
346	fourteen	195	*dirección, una, la*	231	deeh-rehk-seeh-**yohn**
347	fox (mammal), a, the	1152	*director, un, el*	568	deeh-rehk-**tohr**
348	fracture (malady), a, the	473	*dislocación, una, la*	234	deehs-loh-kahs-**yohn**
349	French fries (food), the	774	*disminuya su velocidad*	878 seeh-**dad**	deehs-meen-**ooh**-yah sooh beh-loh-
350	fresh asphalt (road sign)	86	*disponible*	49	deehs-poh-**neeh**-bleh
351	Friday, a, the	1132	*distancia, una, la*	235	deehs-**tahn**-syah
352	fried (cooking method)	477	*distante*	236	deehs-**tahn**-teh
353	friend (female), a, the	54	*distribuidor, un, el*	237	dehs-treeh-bweeh-**dohr**
354	friend (male), a, the	55	*doblar*	1040	dohb-**lahr**
355	frigatebird, a, the	1053	*doble circulación*	1046	**dohb**-lay seehr-kooh-lah-**syohn**
356	frog (amphibian), a, the	897	*doce*[1]	1042	**doh**-say
357	from (origin, made ...)	304	*dólar, el, un*	249	**doh**-lahr
358	fruit (food), a, the	478	*dolor de cabeza, un, el*	412	doh-**lohr** deh kah-**beh**-sah
359	fruit store, a, the	479	*dolor de diente, un, el*	1012	doh-**lohr** deh **dyehn**-teh
360	full (brimming)	618	*dolor de garganta, un, el*	888	doh-**lohr** deh gar-**gahn**-tah
361	furniture, the	695	*dolor de oído, un, el*	271	doh-**lohr** deh oh-**eeh**-doh
362	gaff (fishing), a, the	78	*dolor, un, el*	701	doh-**lohr**
363	gaff (fishing), to	79	*domingo, un, el*	934	doh-**meehn**-goh
364	garbage (trash), the	117	*dónde*	1095	**dohn**-deh
365	garlic (seasoning), the	28	*dónde está*	1096	**dohn**-deh ehs-**tah**
366	gas station, a, the	431	*dorado, un, el*	251	dohr-**rah**-doh
367	gas tank (vehicle part), a, the	1012	*dormir*	875	dohr-**meehr**
368	gasoline, the	486	*dos*[1]	1044	dohs
369	gentleman, a, the	960	*doscientos*[1]	1045	dohs-seeh-**yehn**-tohs
370	get (obtain), to	254	*droga, una, la*	262	**droh**-gah
371	gift (present), a, the	907	*ducha, una, la*	863	**dooh**-chah
372	gin (beverage), the	491	*dulce*	940	**doolh**-seh
373	give, to	300	*dulcería, una, la*	143	doolh-seh-**reeh**-ah
374	glass (eating utensil), a, the	1112	*duro, -a*	402	**dooh**-roh
375	glasses (eye, plural), the	595	*edificio, un, el*	123	eh-deeh-**feeh**-syoh
376	go, to	552	*eje, un, el*	51	**eh**-heh
377	goat (mammal), a, the	150	*ejido, el*	747	ahy-**heeh**-doh
378	good (nice, kind, well)	143	*el*	966	ehl
379	good-by	19	*él*	407	ehl
380	gout (malady), the	493	*él es*[4]	409	ehl ehs
381	grade (slope of a road), a, the	295	*él está*[3]	410	ehl ehs-**tah**
382	grape, a, the	1106	*él tiene*[5]	408	ehl teeh-yehn-ayh
383	gray (color)	498	*electricidad, la*	282	eh-lehk-treeh-seeh-**dad**
384	grease (lubricate), to	405	*ella*	847	**eh**-yah
385	great white shark (fish), a, the	1044	*ella es*[4]	849	**eh**-yah ehs
386	green (color)	1125	*ella está*[3]	850	**eh**-yah ehs-**tah**
387	grocery store, a, the	1049	*ella tiene*[5]	848	**eh**-yah teeh-**yehn**-ayh
388	grouper (fish), a, the	671	*elote, el*	192	eh-**loh**-teh
389	guide (person), a, the	502	*embarazada*	740	ehm-bahr-ah-**sah**-dah

LINE	ENGLISH	SL	SPANISH	EL	PRONUNCIATION
390	gull (bird), a, the	490	*embrague, un, el*	177	ehm-**brah**-gheh
391	hacksaw (tool), a, the	974	*empanado, -a*	113	ehm-pah-**nah**-doh
392	half	665	*empujar*	753	aym-pooh-**hahr**
393	halibut (fish), a, the	510	*en*	46	ehn
394	ham (food), a, the	557	*en*	471	ehn
395	hamburger (food), a, the	511	*en*	486	ehn
396	hammer (tool), a, the	653	*en*	680	ehn
397	hammerhead shark (fish), a, the	814	*en contra de*	12	ehn **kohn**-trah deh
398	hand (body part), a, the	638	*en vez de*	481	ehn behs deh
399	happy (cheerful)	456	*encendido, el*	467	ehn-sehn-**deeh**-doh
400	harbor, a, the	875	*encima de*	681	ehn-**seeh**-mah deh
401	hard (difficult)	342	*enero, un, el*	492	eh-**neh**-roh
402	hard (opposite of soft)	374	*enfermedad del corazón, un, el*	419	ayn-fehr-meeh-**dad** dehl koh-rah-**sohn**
403	hat (cap), a, the	989	*enfermo, -a*	865	ehn-**fehr**-moh
404	have, to (to possess, ... a boat)	1037	*enganchar*	438	ehn-gahn-**char**
405	hawk (bird), a, the	509	*engrasar*	384	ehn-grah-**sahr**
406	hay fever (malady), the	459	*ensalada, una, la*	813	ehn-sah-**lah**-dah
407	he	379	*entrada, una, la*	292	ehn-**trah**-dah
408	he has (... ... a boat)	382	*entre*	89	**ehn**-treh
409	he is (... ... American)	380	*eres*[4]	1139	**eh**-rehs
410	he is (... ... happy)	381	*error, un, el*	598	ehr-**rohr**
411	head (body part), a, the	149	*erupción, una, la*	766	ayh-roohp-**syohn**
412	headache (malady), a, the	358	*es*	487	ehs
413	headlight (vehicle part), a, the	453	*esa*[1]	960	**eh**-sah
414	health center, a, the	201	*esas*[1]	984	**eh**-sahs
415	hear (listen), to	754	*escafando, un, el*	1088	ehs-cah-**fahn**-doh
416	hearing aid	69	*escafandra autónoma, una, la*	828	ehs-cah-**fahn**-drah auh-**toh**-noh-mah
417	heart (body part), a, the	259	*escoger*	166	ehs-koh-**hehr**
418	heart attack (malady), a, the	90	*escondido, -a*	430	ehs-kohn-**deeh**-doh
419	heart disease (malady), a, the	402	*escuchar*	541	ehs-kooh-**chahr**
420	heartburn (malady), the	11	*escuela, una, la*	821	ays-**kweh**-lah
421	heat, the	160	*ese*[1]	961	**eh**-seh
422	heatstroke (malady), the	546	*esos*[1]	985	**eh**-sohs
423	heavy (not light)	804	*espalda, una, la*	53	ehs-**pahl**-dah
424	hello	528	*español, el*	893	ehs-pahn-**nyohl**
425	help (aid), to	99	*espinazo, un, el*	897	ahy-speeh-**nah**-soh
426	hemorrhoids (malady), the	516	*esposa, una, la*	1104	ehs-**poh**-sah
427	her (formal, one person possessing more than one object, ... trucks)	1003	*esposo, un, el*	457	ehs-**poh**-soh
428	her (formal, one person possessing one object, ... truck)	993	*esta noche*	1006	**ehs**-tah **noh**-chay
429	here (this place)	73	*esta semana*	983	**ehs**-tah seh-**mah**-nah
430	hidden	418	*esta*[1]	981	**ehs**-tah
431	high (tall)	51	*estación de gasolina, una, la*	366	ehs-tah-**syohn** deh gah-soh-**leeh**-nah
432	highway, a, the	187	*estacionar*	704	ehs-tah-seeh-ohn-**ahr**
433	hip (body part), a, the	153	*Estados Unidos, los*	1051	ehs-**tah**-dohs ooh-**neeh**-dohs
434	hire, to	47	*estáis*[3]	1138	ehs-**tah**-eehs

LINE	ENGLISH	SL	SPANISH	EL	PRONUNCIATION
435	his (formal, one person possessing more than one object, ... trucks)	1004	*están*[3]	975	ehs-**tahn**
436	his (formal, one person possessing one object, ... truck)	994	*estar*[3]	72	ehs-**tahr**
437	history, a, the	526	*estas*[1]	973	**ehs**-tahs
438	hitch (... ... a trailer), to	404	*estás*[3]	1140	ehs-**tahs**
439	home (dwelling), a, the	192	*este, el*	273	**ehs**-teh
440	hook (fishing), a, the	483	*este*[1]	982	**ehs**-teh
441	horse (mammal), a, the	148	*estómago, un, el*	912	ehs-**tohm**-ah-goh
442	hose (garden), a, the	636	*estos*[1]	974	**ehs**-tohs
443	hospital, a, the	534	*estoy*[3]	462	ehs-**toy**
444	hot (very warm)	158	*estrella, una, la*	905	ehs-**treh**-yah
445	hot dog (food), a, the	802	*estreñimiento, el*	187	ehs-tray-neeh-**myehn**-toh
446	hour, an, the	533	*estufa, una, la*	924	ehs-**tooh**-fah
447	how (in what way)	244	*fácil*	274	**fah**-seehl
448	how (question, ... was the trip)	884	*falso, -a*	300	**fahl**-soh
449	how far (question)	3	*familia, una, la*	301	fah-**meehl**-yah
450	how long (question)	281	*fardela, una, la*	851	fahr-**deh**-lah
451	how many (question)	282	*farmacéutico, un, el*	716	far-mah-**sooh**-teeh-koh
452	how much (question)	280	*farmacia, una, la*	717	far-mah-**seeh**-ah
453	hummingbird, a, the	236	*faro, un, el*	413	**fah**-roh
454	hungry, to be	1035	*febrero, un, el*	306	feh-**breh**-roh
455	hurry (move quickly), to	302	*fecha, una, la*	212	**feh**-chah
456	hurt (malady), to	581	*feliz*	399	fey-**leehs**
457	husband, a, the	427	*feo, -a*	1047	**fah**-oh
458	hut (thatched shelter), a, the	767	*ferretería, una, la*	918	fehr-reh-teh-**reeh**-ah
459	hypertension (malady), the	525	*fiebre del heno, la*	406	**fyeh**-breh dehl **ayh**-noh
460	I (myself)	1146	*fiebre, una, la*	307	feeh-**yeh**-breh
461	I am (... ... American)	992	*filme, el*	312	**fehl**-meh
462	I am (... ... happy)	443	*filtro, un, el*	313	**feehl**-troh
463	I have (... ... a boat)	1038	*fin del pavimento*	287	feehn dehl pah-beeh-**mayn**-toh
464	ice cream (food), an, the	515	*fin, un, el*	285	feehn
465	ice, the	520	*flor, una, la*	329	flohr
466	if (... it rains)	971	*fluido para freno, el*	110	fluh-ee-doh **pah**-ruh **freh**-noh
467	ignition (vehicle part), the	399	*fluido para radiadores, el*	760	fluh-**ee**-doh **pah**-ruh rah-deeh-yah-**dorh**-ehs
468	Immigration (Mexican govt. office)	679	*fluido para transmisiones, el*	1029	fluh-**ee**-doh **pah**-ruh trahns-meeh-seeh-yohn-**ehs**
469	important	539	*foca, una, la*	834	**foh**-kah
470	impossible	540	*fondo, un, el*	107	**fohn**-doh
471	in (place, time, manner)	394	*fósforo, un, el*	579	**fohs**-foh-roh
472	in front of	313	*fotografía, una, la*	718	foh-toh-grah-**feeh**-ah
473	in order to	778	*fractura, una, la*	348	frahk-**tooh**-rah
474	inch (measurement), a, the	876	*freno, un, el*	109	**freh**-noh
475	infection (malady), an, the	543	*frijoles, los*	75	freeh-**hoh**-lehs
476	inflate, to	544	*frío, -a*	180	**freeh**-oh
477	influenza (malady), the	497	*frito, -a*	352	**freeh**-toh
478	inside of	318	*fruta, una, la*	358	**frooh**-tah

LINE	ENGLISH	SL	SPANISH	EL	PRONUNCIATION
479	insomnia (malady), the	547	*frutería, una, la*	359	frooh-tah-**reeh**-ah
480	inspection stop (road sign)	52	*fuego, un, el*	316	**fweh**-goh
481	instead of	398	*fuera de*	699	**fweh**-rah deh
482	insulin (medicine), the	548	*ganado*	151	gah-**nah**-doh
483	insurance, the	951	*gancho, un, el*	440	**gahn**-choh
484	interesting	549	*garganta, una, la*	989	gahr-**gahn**-tah
485	intestine (body part), an, the	550	*gas de cocinar*	540	gahs deh koh-seeh-**nahr**
486	into (enter ..., come in contact with)	395	*gasolina, la*	368	gah-soh-**leeh**-nah
487	is (he/she/it ...)	412	*gato, un, el*	148	**gah**-toh
488	island, an, the	554	*gato, un, el*	489	**gah**-toh
489	jack (vehicle part), a, the	488	*gavilán pescador, un, el*	693	gah-beeh-**lahn** peyhs-kah-**dohr**
490	jack crevalle (fish), a, the	1068	*gaviota, una, la*	390	gah-beeh-**oh**-tah
491	jack up, to	599	*ginebra, la*	372	heeh-**neh**-brah
492	January, a, the	401	*golondrina marina, una, la*	959	goh-lohn-**dreen**-nah mar-**een**-ah
493	jaw (body part), a, the	634	*gota, la*	380	**goh**-tah
494	joint, universal (vehicle part), a, the	568	*gotas para los oídos/ojos, las*	270	**goh**-tahs **pah**-rah lohs oh-**eeh**-dohs/ **oh**-hohs
495	journey, a, the	1128	*grande*	515	**grahn**-deh
496	juice (food), the	565	*grava suelta*	553	**grah**-bah sooh-**ayl**-tah
497	July, a, the	566	*gripe, la*	477	**greeh**-payh
498	junction (of roads), a, the	276	*gris*	383	greehs
499	June, a, the	567	*grúa remolque, una, la*	1019	**grooh**-ah reh-**mohl**-kay
500	junk (used parts for vehicles), the	562	*guardar*	501	gwahr-**dahr**
501	keep (retain), to	500	*guía de teléfono, un, el*	953	**gwee**-ah deh teh-**leh**-foh-noh
502	keep left (road sign)	256	*guía, un, el, una, la*	389	**gwee**-ah
503	keep right (road sign)	255	*hablar*	896	ahb-**lahr**
504	key (for a lock), a, the	614	*hacer*	245	ah-**sehr**
505	kidney (body part), a, the	924	*hacer*	565	ah-**sehr**
506	kilogram, a, the	570	*hacia*	1021	hah-**seh**-ah
507	kilometer, a, the	571	*hacia atrás*	54	hah-**seh**-ah ah-**trahs**
508	knee (body part), a, the	927	*Hacienda*	1032	hah-seeh-**ehn**-dah
509	knife (tool, eating utensil), a, the	290	*halcón, un, el*	405	ahl-**kohn**
510	know (a fact or how to), to	936	*halibut, un, el*	393	hahl-leh-**but**
511	know (a person or thing), to	253	*hamburguesa, una, la*	395	hahm-boorh-**ghay**-sah
512	lady (married) a, the	961	*harina, la*	328	ah-**reh**-nah
513	lady (unmarried), a, the	962	*hasta*	1052	**ahs**-tah
514	landslide area (road sign)	1151	*hay*	970	**ah**-eeh
515	large (big, great, grand)	495	*helado, un, el*	464	eh-**lah**-doh
516	larger	656	*hemorroides, las*	426	hayh-mohr-roh-**eeh**-dehs
517	last (final, ultimate)	1091	*hermoso, -a*	77	hehr-**moh**-soh
518	last night	63	*herramienta, una, la*	1008	heerah-meeh-**ehn**-tah
519	late (overdue, behind)	1016	*hervido, -a*	99	ehr-**beeh**-doh
520	launch ramp, a, the	583	*hielo, el*	465	**yeh**-loh
521	laundry machine, a, the	585	*hígado, un, el*	544	**eeh**-gah-doh
522	laxative (medicine), a, the	587	*hija, una, la*	213	**eeh**-hah
523	leader (fishing), a, the	991	*hijo, un, el*	887	**eeh**-hoh
524	learn, to	72	*hinchado, -a*	943	eehn-**chah**-doh

LINE	ENGLISH	SL	SPANISH	EL	PRONUNCIATION
525	leave (depart), to	939	*hipertensión, la*	459	heeh-payhr-tayhn-seeh-**ohn**
526	left (opposite of right)	555	*historia, una, la*	437	heehs-torh-**rheeh**-ah
527	left turn only (road sign)	985	*hoja de afeitar, una, la*	770	**oh**-hah deh ah-fey-**tahr**
528	leg (body part), a, the	821	*hola*	424	**oh**-lah
529	lemon (food), a, the	603	*hombre, un, el*	567	**ohm**-breh
530	leopard grouper (fish), a, the	151	*hombres trabajando*	588	**ohm**-breyhs trah-bah-**han**-doh
531	less than	667	*hombro, un, el*	861	**ohm**-broh
532	letter (mail), a, the	188	*hondo, -a*	217	**oohn**-doh
533	lettuce (food), the	589	*hora, una, la*	446	**ohr**-rah
534	library, a, the	121	*hospital, un, el*	443	ohs-peeh-**tahl**
535	license (permit), a, the	602	*hoy*	1000	ohy
536	life jacket, a, the	940	*hueso, un, el*	102	**weh**-soh
537	like	243	*huevo, un, el*	276	**hweh**-boh
538	line (fishing), a, the	293	*iglesia, una, la*	167	eeh-**gleh**-syah
539	lip (body part), a, the	573	*importante*	469	eehm-pohr-**tahn**-teh
540	liquefied petroleum gas (LPG)	485	*imposible*	470	eehm-poh-**seeh**-blayh
541	listen, to	419	*incorrecto, -a*	1126	eehn-kohr-**rayhc**-toh
542	liter (measurement), a, the	606	*indigestión, una, la*	1055	eehn-deeh-hes-**tyohn**
543	live, to	1135	*infección, una, la*	475	eehn-fek-seeh-**yohn**
544	liver (body part), a, the	521	*inflar*	476	eehn-**flahr**
545	lizard, a, the	574	*inglés, el*	290	eehn-**glehs**
546	lobster (crustacean), a, the	575	*insolación, la*	422	ehn-sol-lah-**syohn**
547	lock (on a door), a, the	209	*insomnio, el*	479	eehn-sohm-**neeh**-yoh
548	long (lengthy)	579	*insulina, la*	482	eehn-sooh-**leeh**-nah
549	long distance, a	577	*interesante*	484	eehn-teh-rehs-**sahn**-tahy
550	long time, a, the	578	*intestino, un, el*	485	eehn-tayhs-**teeh**-noh
551	look (appear), to	685	*invierno, el*	1110	eehn-**byehr**-noh
552	look for, to	146	*ir*	376	eehr
553	loose gravel (road sign)	496	*ir de compras*	856	eehr deh **kohm**-prahs
554	loosen (slacken), to	987	*isla, una, la*	488	**eehs**-lah
555	lose (suffer loss), to	799	*izquierdo, -a*	526	eehs-**kyehr**-doh
556	lost	800	*jabón, el*	884	hah-**bohn**
557	low (small, short)	103	*jamón, un, el*	394	hah-**mohn**
558	luck, the	1001	*jarabe para la tos, un, el*	196	hah-**rah**-bay **pah**-ruh lah tohs
559	lunch (midday meal), a, the	46	*jejéne, un, el*	659	hay-**hen**-ayh
560	lung (body part), a, the	878	*jeringa, una, la*	945	hehr-**reehn**-gah
561	lure (fishing), a, the	57	*jira, una, la*	719	**heeh**-rah
562	mackerel (fish), a, the	627	*jonke, el*	500	**yohn**-keh
563	magazine (to read), a, the	921	*joven*[1]	1143	**hoh**-behn
564	mail (letter), the	265	*jueves, un, el*	991	**hweh**-behs
565	make (construct), to	505	*jugo, el*	496	**hooh**-goh
566	mako shark (fish), a, the	1045	*julio, un, el*	497	**hoohl**-yoh
567	man, a, the	529	*junio, un, el*	499	**hooh**-nyoh
568	manager (director), a, the	347	*junta cardán, una, la*	494	**hoohn**-tah kahr-**dahn**
569	mango (food), a, the	635	*jurel, un, el*	1132	hooh-**rehl**
570	manta ray (fish), a, the	639	*kilogramo, un, el*	506	keeh-loh-**grah**-moh
571	mantle, gas (for LPG light), a, the	637	*kilómetro, un, el*	507	keeh-**loh**-meh-troh

LINE	ENGLISH	SL	SPANISH	EL	PRONUNCIATION
572	many (much, lots of)	694	*la*	964	lah
573	map (chart), a, the	642	*labio, un, el*	539	**lah**-byoh
574	March (month), a, the	654	*lagarto, un, el*	545	lah-**gahr**-toh
575	marlin, black (fish), a, the	649	*langosta, una, la*	546	lahn-**gohs**-tah
576	marlin, blue (fish), a, the	648	*lápiz, un, el*	712	**lah**-pees
577	marlin, striped (fish), a, the	650	*larga distancia, una*	549	**lahr**-gah dees-**tahn**-syah
578	mask (diving), a, the	657	*largo tiempo, un, el*	550	**lahr**-goh **tyehm**-poh
579	match (to light a fire), a, the	471	*largo, -a*	548	**lahr**-goh
580	May (month), a, the	658	*las*	963	lahs
581	mayonnaise (food), the	659	*lastimar*	456	lahs-teeh-**mahr**
582	me (myself)	660	*lata, una, la*	139	**lah**-tah
583	meal (lunch, etc.), a, the	240	*launcha rampa, una, la*	520	**lahn**-chah **rahm**-pah
584	meat (food), the	184	*lavabo, un, el*	787	lah-**bah**-boh
585	mechanic, a, the	661	*lavandería, una, la*	521	lah-bahn-deh-**reeh**-ah
586	medicine, a, the	663	*lavarse*	1068	yah-**bahr**-seh
587	medium (degree of cooking)	1040	*laxante, un, el*	522	lahk-**sahn**-teh
588	men working (road sign)	530	*leche, la*	594	**leh**-cheh
589	menu, a, the	668	*lechuga, la*	533	leh-**chooh**-gah
590	meter (measurement), a, the	674	*legumbres, las*	1059	leh-**gohm**-brehs
591	Mexican, a, the	675	*lejos de*	303	**leh**-hohs deh
592	microwave station, a, the	677	*leña, la*	1116	**layhn**-yah
593	mile, a, the	682	*lengua, una, la*	1005	**lehn**-gwah
594	milk (food), the	588	*lente de contacto, una, la*	188	**layn**-teh deh kohn-**tahc**-toh
595	millimeter (measurement), a, the	681	*lentes, los*	375	**lahn**-tayhs
596	million	683	*lento, -a*	877	**lehn**-toh
597	minute (time), a, the	684	*león de montaña, un, el*	608	leeh-**ohn** deh mohn-**tahn**-nah
598	mistake (error), a, the	410	*león marino, un, el*	830	layh-**ohn** ma-**reeh**-noh
599	Monday, a, the	626	*levantar con el gato*	491	leh-bahn-**tahr** kohn ehl **gah**-toh
600	money (cash), the	343	*libro, un, el*	105	**leeh**-broh
601	money exchange office	189	*licencia de manejar, una, la*	261	leeh-sen-**seeh**-ah deh mahn-**eeh**-harh
602	month, a, the	672	*licencia, una, la*	535	leeh-sen-**seeh**-ah
603	moon, the	625	*limón, un, el*	529	leeh-**mohn**
604	more (extra, added)	655	*limpiar*	171	leehm-**pyahr**
605	mother, a, the	629	*limpio, -a*	170	**leehm**-pyoh
606	motor home (vehicle), a, the	95	*litro, un, el*	542	**leeh**-troh
607	motorcycle (vehicle), a, the	689	*llamada telefónica, una, la*	134	yah-**mah**-dah teh-leh-**fohn**-neeh-cah
608	mountain lion (mammal), a, the	597	*llano, -a*	325	**yah**-noh
609	mountain sheep (mammal), a, the	137	*llano, -a*	880	**yah**-noh
610	mountain, a, the	687	*llanta, una, la*	996	**yahn**-tah
611	mouse (mammal), a, the	901	*llantera, una, la*	997	yahn-**tehr**-ah
612	mouth (body part, of a river), a, the	130	*llave de tubo, una, la*	1124	**yah**-beh deh **tooh**-boh
613	move (change location), to	693	*llave inglesa, una, la*	1123	**yah**-beh eehn-**gleh**-sah
614	movie (film), a, the	793	*llave, una, la*	504	**yah**-beh
615	mullet (fish), a, the	699	*llave, una, la*	1122	**yah**-beh
616	museum, a, the	701	*llegar*	40	yeh-**gahr**
617	mushrooms (food, plural), the	213	*llenar*	311	yeh-**nahr**
618	music, the	702	*lleno, -a*	360	**yeh**-noh

LINE	ENGLISH	SL	SPANISH	EL	PRONUNCIATION
619	must	307	*llevar*	147	yeh-**bahr**
620	mustard (food), the	688	*llover*	763	yoh-**behr**
621	my (one person possessing more than one object, ... trucks)	686	*lluvia, una, la*	762	yooh-**beeh**-ah
622	my (one person possessing one object, ... truck)	676	*lonchería, una, la*	332	lohn-chah-**reeh**-ah
623	name, a, the	727	*los*	965	lohs
624	napkin (eating utensil), a, the	967	*lubricar*	677	looh-breeh-**kahr**
625	napkin, sanitary, a, the	1057	*luna, la*	603	**looh**-nah
626	narrow bridge (road sign)	872	*lunes, un, el*	599	**looh**-nehs
627	nausea (malady), the	708	*macarela, una, la*	562	mah-cah-**reh**-lah
628	near to (close to, nearby)	205	*madera, la*	1117	mah-**deh**-rah
629	necessary (obligatory)	709	*madre, una, la*	605	**mah**-dreh
630	neck (body part), a, the	291	*maíz, el*	193	mah-**eehs**
631	need (require), to	710	*malecón, un, el*	831	mah-layh-**kohn**
632	needle (sewing, syringe), a, the	25	*malo[1], -a*	56	**mah**-loh
633	nerve (body part), a, the	712	*mañana*	1004	mahn-**yah**-nah
634	never	744	*mandíbula, una, la*	493	mahn-**deeh**-buh-lah
635	never mind	720	*mango, un, el*	569	**mahn**-goh
636	new	742	*manguera, una, la*	442	man-**gweh**-rah
637	newspaper, a, the	332	*manguito, un, el*	571	mahn-**gweeh**-toh
638	next	870	*mano, una, la*	398	**mah**-noh
639	next week	956	*manta raya, una, la*	570	**mahn**-tah **rayh**-yah
640	night, a, the	726	*mantequilla, la*	129	mahn-teh-**keeh**-yah
641	nine	741	*manzana, una, la*	37	mahn-**sah**-nah
642	nine hundred	735	*mapa, un, el*	573	**mah**-pah
643	nineteen	336	*maquinilla de afeitar, una, la*	769	mah-keeh-**neeh**-yah deh ah-fey-**tahr**
644	ninety	736	*mar, un, el, una, la*	832	mahr
645	no	716	*marea, una, la*	992	**mahr**-reah
646	no admittance (road sign)	862	*mareado, -a*	240	mah-reh-**yah**-doh
647	no entry (road sign)	344	*mariscos, los*	833	mah-**reehs**-kohs
648	no left turn (road sign)	724	*marlin azul, un, el*	576	**mahr**-leehn ah-**soohl**
649	no parking (road sign)	863	*marlin negro, un, el*	575	**mahr**-leehn **neh**-groh
650	no right turn (road sign)	723	*marlin, un, el*	577	**mahr**-leehn
651	no smoking	864	*marsopa, una, la*	734	mahr-**soh**-pah
652	no U-turn (road sign)	725	*martes, un, el*	1037	**mahr**-tehs
653	noise, a, the	933	*martillo, un, el*	396	mahr-**teeh**-yoh
654	noisy	934	*marzo, un, el*	574	**mahr**-soh
655	north, the	730	*más*	604	mahs
656	northeast, the	728	*más grande*	516	mahs **grahn**-deh
657	northwest, the	729	*máscara de buzo, una, la*	578	**mahs**-kah-rah deh **booh**-soh
658	nose (body part), a, the	707	*mayo, un, el*	580	**mah**-yoh
659	noseeum (biting insect), a, the	559	*mayonesa, la*	581	mah-yoh-**neeh**-sah
660	not	717	*me*	582	may
661	nothing	703	*mecánico, un, el*	585	meh-**kah**-neeh-koh
662	nothing else	704	*mecanismo de dirección, un, el*	909	meeh-kahn-**eehs**-moh deh deeh-rehk-**syohn**
663	November, a, the	737	*medicina, una, la*	586	meh-deeh-**seeh**-nah

LINE	ENGLISH	SL	SPANISH	EL	PRONUNCIATION
664	now	26	*médico, un, el*	246	**meh**-deeh-koh
665	number, a, the	743	*medio, -a*	392	**meh**-dyoh
666	nut (for a bolt), a, the	1086	*mejor*	88	meh-**hohr**
667	oar, an, the	911	*menos de*	531	**meh**-nohs deh
668	occupied	751	*menú, un, el*	589	meh-**nooh**
669	ocean whitefish (fish), an, the	129	*mero prieto, un, el*	94	**meh**-roh preeh-**ayh**-toh
670	ocean, an, the	746	*mero prieto, un, el*	829	**meh**-roh preeh-**ayh**-toh
671	October, an, the	750	*mero, un, el*	388	**meh**-roh
672	octopus (mollusk), an, the	880	*mes, un, el*	602	mayhs
673	of (belonging to)	305	*mesa, una, la*	946	**meh**-sah
674	of the	312	*metro, un, el*	590	**meh**-troh
675	oil (cooking), the	12	*mexicano, un, el*	591	meh-heeh-**kah**-noh
676	oil (lubricant), an, the	15	*mi[1]*	622	meeh
677	oil (lubricate), to	624	*microonda, una, la*	592	meeh-**kroohn**-dah
678	oil pan (vehicle part), a, the	196	*miércoles, un, el*	1080	meeh-**yehr**-koh-lehs
679	old	1130	*Migración*	468	meeh-grah-**syohn**
680	on (engaged, further ..., sit ...)	396	*mil[1]*	986	meehl
681	on top of	400	*milímetro, un, el*	595	meeh-**leeh**-mayh-troh
682	one (number)	1101	*milla, una, la*	593	**meeh**-yah
683	one hour parking (road sign)	1097	*millón[1]*	596	meehl-**yohn**
684	one hundred	218	*minuto, un, el*	597	meeh-**nooh**-toh
685	one way (road sign)	345	*mirar*	551	meeh-**rahr**
686	onion (food), an, the	197	*mis[1]*	621	meehs
687	only	986	*montaña, una, la*	610	mohn-**tahn**-nah
688	open (not closed)	5	*mostaza, la*	620	mohs-**tah**-sah
689	open, to	7	*motocicleta, una, la*	607	moh-toh-seeh-**klay**-tah
690	optician, an, the	758	*motor fuera de borda, un, el*	698	moh-**tohr fweh**-rah deh **boar**-dah
691	or	745	*motor popa, un, el*	911	moh-**tohr poh**-pah
692	orange (food), an, the	706	*motor, un, el*	288	moh-**tohr**
693	osprey (bird), an, the	489	*mover*	613	moh-**behr**
694	other	761	*muchos[1], -a*	572	**mooh**-chohs
695	our (formal, more than one person possessing more than one object, ... trucks)	740	*muebles, el*	361	moo-**eh**-blehs
696	our (formal, more than one person possessing one object, ... truck)	739	*muelle, un, el*	902	**mweh**-yeh
697	out	21	*muerto, -a*	215	**mwehr**-toh
698	outboard motor, a, the	690	*mujer, una, la*	1115	mooh-**hehr**
699	outside of	481	*mujol, un, el*	615	**mooh**-holh
700	owl (bird), a, the	1024	*muñeca, una, la*	1125	moohn-**yeh**-kah
701	pain (malady), a, the	362	*museo, un, el*	616	mooh-**seh**-oh
702	paper (for writing), the	776	*música, una*	618	**mooh**-seeh-kah
703	pargo (fish), a, the	782	*nada*	661	**nah**-dah
704	park (... ... a vehicle), to	432	*nada más*	662	**nah**-dah mahs
705	park (to play in), a, the	783	*nadar*	941	nah-**dahr**
706	past (former, earlier)	784	*naranja, una, la*	692	nah-**rahn**-hah
707	pastries (food, plural), the	786	*nariz, una, la*	658	nah-**reehs**
708	pay (compensate), to	763	*náusea, la*	627	**nauh**-sha

LINE	ENGLISH	SL	SPANISH	EL	PRONUNCIATION
709	pedestrian crossing (road sign)	275	*necesario, -a*	629	neh-seh-sah-**reeh**-oh
710	pelican (bird), a, the	792	*necesitar*	631	neh-seh-seeh-**tahr**
711	pen (for writing), a, the	836	*negro, -a*	93	**neh**-groh
712	pencil (for writing), a, the	576	*nervio, un, el*	633	**nehr**-byoh
713	pepper (food), a, the	824	*neumático de repuesto, un, el*	894	nooh-**mah**-teeh-koh deh reh-**pwehs**-toh
714	pepper (seasoning), the	823	*niña, una, la*	163	**neehn**-yah
715	perhaps	1008	*niño, un, el*	164	**neehn**-yoh
716	pharmacist, a, the	451	*no*	645	noh
717	pharmacy, a, the	452	*no*	660	noh
718	photograph, a, the	472	*no estacionar*	243	noh ahy-stah-seeh-ohn-**ahr**
719	picnic, a, the	561	*no hay paso*	241	noh ah-**eeh** pah-soh
720	pill (medicine), a, the	822	*no importa*	635	noh eehm-**pohr**-tah
721	pineapple (food), a, the	825	*no rebase*	244	noh reh-**bah**-sayh
722	piston (vehicle part), a, the	829	*no tire basura*	242	noh **teeh**-ray bah-**sooh**-rah
723	place (site), a, the	979	*no voltear a la derecha*	650	noh bohl-tayh-**ahr** ah lah deh-**reh**-chah
724	plant (shrub), a, the	830	*no voltear a la izquierda*	648	noh bohl-tayh-**ahr** ah lah eehs-**kyehr**-dah
725	plate (eating utensil), a, the	832	*no voltear en u*	652	noh bohl-tayh-**ahr** ayn ooh
726	please	851	*noche, una, la*	640	**noh**-chay
727	pliers (tool, plural), the	40	*nombre, un, el*	623	**nohm**-breh
728	pneumonia (malady), the	879	*noreste, el*	656	nohr-**ehs**-teh
729	pole (fishing), a, the	172	*noroeste, el*	657	noh-roh-**ehs**-teh
730	police (cop), the	844	*norte, el*	655	**nohr**-teh
731	pompano (fish), a, the	769	*nosotras somos*[4]	1075	noh-**soh**-trahs **soh**-mohs
732	poor (not well off, not done well)	837	*nosotros estamos*[3]	1074	noh-**soh**-trohs ehs-**tah**-mohs
733	pork (food), the	182	*nosotros somos*[4]	1076	noh-**soh**-trohs **soh**-mohs
734	porpoise (marine mammal), a, the	651	*nosotros tenemos*[5]	1077	noh-**soh**-trohs tehn-**neh**-mohs
735	possible	854	*novecientos*[1]	642	noh-beh-**syehn**-tohs
736	post office, a, the	190	*noventa*[1]	644	noh-**behn**-tah
737	postcard, a, the	1020	*noviembre, un, el*	663	noh-beeh-**ehm**-breh
738	potato (food), a, the	787	*nublado, -a*	176	nooh-**blah**-doh
739	prefer, to	858	*nuestro*[1], *-a*	696	**nwehs**-troh
740	pregnant	389	*nuestros*[1], *-as*	695	**nwehs**-trohs
741	prescription, a, the	902	*nueve*[1]	641	**nweh**-beh
742	price, a, the	857	*nuevo*[1], *-a*	636	**nweh**-boh
743	prohibit, to	866	*número, un, el*	665	**nooh**-meh-roh
744	pronghorn (mammal), a, the	120	*nunca*	634	**noohn**-kah
745	provide, to	869	*o*	691	oh
746	public beach, a, the	833	*océano, un, el*	670	oh-**sayh**-ah-noh
747	public land, the	377	*ochenta*[1]	280	oh-**chen**-tah
748	pull, to	1055	*ocho*[1]	277	**oh**-choh
749	pump (moves liquid or gas), a, the	131	*ochocientos*[1]	278	oh-choh-seeh-**yehn**-tohs
750	pump, to	132	*octubre, un, el*	671	ohk-**tooh**-breh
751	puncture (tire), a, the	827	*ocupado, -a*	668	oh-kooh-**pah**-doh
752	purified	881	*oeste, el*	1087	oh-**ehs**-teh
753	push, to	392	*oído, un, el*	268	oh-**eeh**-doh
754	put (place), to	846	*oír*	415	oh-**eehr**

LINE	ENGLISH	SL	SPANISH	EL	PRONUNCIATION
755	quail (bird), a, the	233	*ojo, un, el*	296	**oh**-hoh
756	quarter (a fourth of)	284	*ola, una, la*	1072	**oh**-lah
757	quick (fast)	867	*once*[1]	283	**ohn**-seh
758	rabbit (mammal), a, the	252	*óptico, un, el*	690	**ohp**-teeh-koh
759	radiator (vehicle part), a, the	894	*oreja, una, la*	269	oh-**reh**-hah
760	radiator fluid (vehicle part), the	467	*otoño, el*	299	oh-**tohn**-yoh
761	radio, a, the	895	*otro*[1]*, -a*	694	**oh**-troh
762	rain (precipitation), a, the	621	*padre, un, el*	305	**pah**-dreh
763	rain, to	620	*pagar*	708	pah-**gahr**
764	ranch, a, the	898	*pájaro, un, el*	91	**pah**-hah-roh
765	rare (degree of cooking)	839	*pala, una, la*	862	**pah**-lah
766	rash (malady), a, the	411	*palabra, una, la*	1118	pah-**lah**-brah
767	rat (mammal), a, the	900	*palapa, una, la*	458	pah-**lah**-pah
768	rattlesnake (reptile), a, the	193	*paloma, una, la*	253	pah-**loh**-mah
769	razor (to shave with), a, the	643	*pámpano, un, el*	731	**pahm**-pahn-noh
770	razor blade, a, the	527	*pan, el*	112	pahn
771	receipt, a, the	903	*panadería, una, la*	60	pah-nah-deh-**reeh**-ah
772	recreational vehicle, a, the	1113	*pañal, un, el*	225	pah-**nyahl**
773	rectum (body part), the	904	*pantalones, los*	1034	pahn-tah-**loh**-nahys
774	red (color)	928	*papas fritas, las*	349	**pah**-pahs **freeh**-tas
775	reef (shallow spot), a, the	81	*papel higiénico, el*	1002	pah-**pehl** heeh-geeh-**ehn**-eeh-koh
776	reel (fishing), a, the	186	*papel, el*	702	pah-**pehl**
777	refrigerator, a, the	906	*para*	336	**pah**-rah
778	registration (vehicle, etc.), the	1056	*para*	473	**pah**-rah
779	regulator (diving), a, the	909	*parar*	916	pah-**rarh**
780	regulator (gas), a, the	910	*pardo, -a*	121	**pahr**-doh
781	release, to	988	*pargo amarillo, un, el*	882	**pahr**-goh ah-mah-**reeh**-yoh
782	rent, to	48	*pargo, un, el*	703	**pahr**-goh
783	repair, to	914	*parque, un, el*	705	**pahr**-keh
784	repeat, to	915	*pasado, -a*	706	pah-**sah**-doh
785	request, to	791	*pasta dentífrica, la*	1011	**pahs**-tah dayhn-**teeh**-freeh-kah
786	reservation (place in line), a, the	916	*pasteles, los*	707	pahs-**teh**-lehs
787	rest room, a, the	584	*patata, una, la*	738	pah-**tah**-tah
788	restaurant, a, the	918	*patín de mar, el, un*	939	pah-**teehn** deh mahr
789	return (go back), to	1139	*pato bobo, un, el*	104	**pah**-toh **boh**-boh
790	return, a, the	919	*pecho, un, el*	161	**peh**-choh
791	rheumatism (malady), the	920	*pedir*	785	payh-**deehr**
792	rib (body part), a, the	270	*pelícano, un, el*	710	pehl-**leeh**-kah-noh
793	rice (food), the	83	*película, una, la*	614	peh-**leeh**-kooh-lah
794	rich (wealthy, ... in virtues)	923	*peligro, un, el*	209	peh-**leeh**-groh
795	right (correct, proper)	264	*peligroso, -a*	210	peh-leeh-**groh**-soh
796	right (opposite of left)	320	*pensar*	977	pahyn-**sahr**
797	right turn only (road sign)	984	*peor*	1121	pay-**ohr**
798	river, a, the	925	*pequeño*[1]*, -a*	879	peh-**kehn**-yoh
799	road closed (road sign)	164	*perder*	555	pehr-**dehr**
800	road under repair (road sign)	165	*perdido, -a*	556	pehr-**deeh**-doh
801	road, a, the	168	*pero*	127	**peh**-roh

LINE	ENGLISH	SL	SPANISH	EL	PRONUNCIATION
802	roadrunner (bird), a, the	263	*perro caliente, un, el*	445	**pehr**-roh kah-**lyehn**-teh
803	roasted (cooking method)	85	*perro, un, el*	247	**pehr**-roh
804	rock (stone), a, the	926	*pesado, -a*	423	peh-**sah**-doh
805	rod (fishing), a, the	171	*pescado, un, el*	319	peyhs-**kah**-doh
806	room, a, the	285	*pescador, un, el*	321	peyhs-kah-**dohr**
807	roosterfish (fish), a, the	813	*pescadora, una, la*	322	peyhs-kah-**dohr**-ah
808	rope, a, the	294	*pescar*	320	peyhs-**kahr**
809	rough (bumpy, coarse)	931	*pestillo, un, el*	101	pehs-**teeh**-yoh
810	ruler (to measure with), a, the	908	*pez ballesta, un, el*	1033	peyhs bahl-**lesth**-trah
811	sailboard, a, the	135	*pez espada, un, el*	944	peyhs ehs-**pah**-dah
812	sailfish (fish), a, the	815	*pez fuerte, una, la*	21	peyhs **fuerh**-teh
813	salad (food), a, the	406	*pez gallo, un, el*	807	peyhs **gah**-yoh
814	salt (... water, seasoning), the	937	*pez martillo, un, el*	397	peyhs mahr-**teeh**-yoh
815	sand (on the beach), the	77	*pez vela, un, el*	812	peyhs **beh**-lah
816	sandwich (food), a, the	941	*pez, un, el*	318	peyhs
817	sargo (fish), a, the	944	*picadura, una, la*	92	peeh-kah-**dooh**-rah
818	Saturday, a, the	935	*pie, un, el*	334	**peeh**-ahy
819	sausage (food, spicy Mexican), the	217	*piedra, una, la*	914	peeh-**ahy**-drah
820	say, to	309	*piel, la*	873	peeh-**yehl**
821	school (place for students), a, the	420	*pierna, una, la*	528	peeh-**yehr**-nah
822	scissors (tool, plural), the	1054	*píldora, una, la*	720	**peel**-dorh-ah
823	score (of a game or sport), a, the	1013	*pimienta, la*	714	peeh-meeh-**ehn**-tah
824	scorpion (arachnid), a, the	32	*pimiento, un, el*	713	peeh-**myehn**-toh
825	scrambled (cooking method)	922	*piña, una, la*	721	**peehn**-yah
826	screw (fastening), a, the	1067	*pinchazo, un, el*	326	peehn-**chah**-soh
827	screwdriver (tool), a, the	327	*pinchazo, un, el*	751	peehn-**chah**-soh
828	scuba (diving apparatus), a, the	416	*piso, un, el*	327	**peeh**-soh
829	sea bass, giant (fish), a, the	670	*pistón, un, el*	722	peehs-**tohn**
830	sea lion (marine mammal), a, the	598	*planta, una, la*	724	**plahn**-tah
831	sea wall, a, the	631	*plátano, un, el*	61	**plah**-tah-noh
832	sea, a, the	644	*plato, un, el*	725	**plah**-toh
833	seafoods (plural), the	647	*playa pública, una, la*	746	**plah**-yah **pooh**-bleeh-kah
834	seal (marine mammal), a, the	469	*playa, una, la*	73	**plah**-yah
835	seal (mechanical part), a, the	954	*plomo, un, el*	867	**ploh**-moh
836	second (of time), a, the	950	*pluma, una, la*	711	**ploo**-mah
837	secondary side road, a, the	896	*pobre*	732	**poh**-breh
838	see, to	1122	*poca distancia, una*	859	**poh**-kah dees-**tahn**-syah
839	sell, to	1118	*poco hecho*	765	**poh**-koh **eh**-choh
840	September, a, the	964	*poco tiempo, un, el*	860	**poh**-koh **tyehm**-poh
841	seven	976	*poco, -a*	858	**poh**-koh
842	seven hundred	969	*poco[1], -a*	308	**poh**-koh
843	seventeen	339	*poder*	138	poh-**dehr**
844	seventy	970	*policía, la*	730	poh-leeh-**seeh**-ah
845	shallow (not deep, shoal)	104	*pollo, un, el*	162	**poh**-yoh
846	shark (fish), a, the	1046	*poner*	754	poh-**nehr**
847	she	384	*por*	79	pohr
848	she has (... ... a shirt)	387	*por*	131	pohr

LINE	ENGLISH	SL	SPANISH	EL	PRONUNCIATION
849	she is (... ... American)	385	*por*	335	pohr
850	she is (... ... happy)	386	*por casualidad*	132	pohr kah-sooh-**leeh**-dad
851	shearwater (bird), a, the	450	*por favor*	726	pohr fah-**bohr**
852	shirt, a, the	170	*por qué*	1103	pohr keh
853	shock absorber (vehicle part), a, the	56	*porque*	78	**pohr**-keh
854	shoe, a, the	1150	*posible*	735	poh-**seeh**-blayh
855	shop, auto electrical, an, the	1009	*postre, un, el*	222	pohs-**treh**
856	shopping, to go	553	*precaución*	152	preh-kaw-seeh-**yohn**
857	short (in length)	268	*precio, un, el*	742	**preh**-syoh
858	short (little)	841	*preferir*	739	preh-feh-**reehr**
859	short distance, a	838	*preguntar*	43	preh-goohn-**tahr**
860	short time, a, the	840	*primavera, la*	901	preeh-mah-**beh**-rah
861	shoulder (body part), a, the	531	*primero, -a*	317	preeh-**meh**-roh
862	shovel (tool), a, the	765	*prohibida la entrada*	646	proh-eeh-**beeh**-dah lah ayhn-**trah**-dah
863	shower (bath), a, the	371	*prohibido estacionarse*	649	proh-eeh-**beeh**-doh ehs-tah-seeh-oh-**nahr**-seh
864	shrimp (crustacean), a, the	162	*prohibido fumar*	651	proh-eeh-**beeh**-doh fooh-**mar**
865	sick (malady)	403	*prohibido, -a*	339	proh-eeh-**beeh**-doh
866	sierra (fish), a, the	975	*prohibir*	743	pro-heeh-**beehr**
867	sinker (fishing), a, the	835	*pronto, -a*	757	**prohn**-toh
868	sit, to	963	*propina, una, la*	994	proh-**peeh**-nah
869	six	952	*proveer*	745	proh-**behr**
870	six hundred	953	*próximo, -a*	638	**prohk**-seeh-moh
871	sixteen	338	*pueblo, un, el*	1023	**pweh**-bloh
872	sixty	968	*puente angosto*	626	**pwehn**-teh ahn-**gohs**-toh
873	skin (body part), the	820	*puente, un, el*	117	**pwehn**-teh
874	skipjack (fish), a, the	115	*puerta, una, la*	252	**pwehr**-tah
875	sleep, to	367	*puerto, un, el*	400	**pwehr**-toh
876	slow (road sign)	325	*pulgada, una, la*	474	poohl-**gah**-dah
877	slow (unhurried)	596	*pulgar, un, el*	990	poohl-**gahr**
878	slow down (road sign)	349	*pulmón, un, el*	560	poolh-**mohn**
879	small (little)	798	*pulmonía, la*	728	poohl-mohn-**eeh**-ah
880	smooth (flat, level, even)	609	*pulpo, un, el*	672	**poolh**-poh
881	snake (reptile), a, the	966	*purificada*	752	purh-eeh-fah-**cah**-dah
882	snapper (fish), a, the	781	*que*	962	keh
883	snorkel (diving), a, the	1085	*que*	1098	keh
884	soap, the	556	*qué*	448	keh
885	soft (not hard, tender)	128	*qué*	1091	keh
886	something (... else, ... more)	39	*quemadura de sol, una, la*	933	keh-mah-**dooh**-rah deh sohl
887	son, a, the	523	*quemadura, una, la*	126	keh-mah-**dooh**-rah
888	sore throat (malady), a, the	360	*querer*	1067	keh-**rehr**
889	soup (food), the	990	*querer*	1112	keh-**rehr**
890	south, the	1002	*queso, un, el*	160	**keh**-soh
891	southeast, the	999	*quién*	1102	keh-**ehn**
892	southwest, the	1000	*quince*[1]	309	**keehn**-seh
893	Spanish (language), the	424	*quinientos*[1]	324	keeh-nyeh-**ehn**-tohs
894	spare tire (vehicle part), a, the	713	*radiador, un, el*	759	rah-deeh-yah-**dohr**

LINE	ENGLISH	SL	SPANISH	EL	PRONUNCIATION
895	spark plug (vehicle part), a, the	145	*radio, una, la*	761	**rah**-dyoh
896	speak, to	503	*ramal, un, el*	837	rah-**mahl**
897	spine (body part), a, the	425	*rana, una, la*	356	**rah**-nah
898	spoon (eating utensil), a, the	289	*rancho, un, el*	764	**rahn**-choh
899	sport, a, the	319	*rápido, -a*	304	**rah**-peeh-doh
900	sprain (malady), a, the	1066	*rata, una, la*	767	**rah**-tah
901	spring (season), the	860	*ratón, un, el*	611	rah-**tohn**
902	spring (vehicle part), a, the	696	*receta, una, la*	741	reh-**say**-tah
903	squid (invertebrate), a, the	156	*recibo, un, el*	771	reh-**seeh**-boh
904	stamp (postage), a, the	955	*recto, el*	773	**rech**-toh
905	star (in sky, movie), a, the	444	*refaccionaria, una, la*	920	rayh-fahk-seeh-oh-nayh-**reeh**-ah
906	starter (vehicle part), a, the	80	*refrigerador, un, el*	777	ray-free-geeh-rah-**dohr**
907	steak (food), a, the	126	*regalo, un, el*	371	reh-**gah**-loh
908	steamed (cooking method)	31	*regla, una, la*	810	**rehg**-lah
909	steering gear (vehicle part), a, the	662	*regulador de buzo, un, el*	779	rayh-gooh-lah-**dohr** deh **booh**-soh
910	steering wheel (vehicle part), a, the	1138	*regulador de gas, un, el*	780	rayh-gooh-lah-**dohr** deh gahs
911	stern drive motor, a, the	691	*remo, un, el*	667	**rayh**-moh
912	stomach (body part), a, the	441	*remolcar*	1020	reh-mohl-**kahr**
913	stomach cramps (malady)	157	*remolque, una, la*	1026	reh-**mohl**-kay
914	stone (rock), a, the	819	*reparar*	783	reh-pah-**rahr**
915	stop (road sign)	50	*repetir*	784	reh-peh-**teehr**
916	stop, to	779	*reservación, una, la*	786	ray-sehr-bah-**syohn**
917	store (general term), a, the	1050	*respirar*	116	rehs-peeh-**rahr**
918	store (hardware), a, the	458	*restaurante, un, el*	788	rehs-tauh-**rahn**-teh
919	store (shoe), a, the	1149	*retorno, un, el*	790	rayh-**tohr**-noh
920	store, auto parts, an, the	905	*reumatismo, el*	791	rayh-oohm-ah-**teehs**-moh
921	storm (tempest), a, the	1029	*revista, una, la*	563	reh-**beehs**-tah
922	stormy (turbulent)	1030	*revueltos*	825	reh-**bwehl**-tohs
923	stove (for cooking), a, the	229	*rico, -a*	794	**reeh**-koh
924	stove (for heating), a, the	446	*riñón, un, el*	505	reehn-**yohn**
925	straight (not bent)	321	*río, un, el*	798	**reeh**-oh
926	street, a, the	159	*roca, un, el*	804	**roh**-kah
927	stroke (malady), a, the	91	*rodilla, una, la*	508	roh-**deeh**-yah
928	stuck (unable to move), to be	92	*rojo, -a*	774	**roh**-hoh
929	sugar (food), the	100	*ropas, las*	175	**roh**-pahs
930	summer, the	1123	*roto, -a*	120	**roh**-toh
931	sun glasses (plural), the	64	*rudo, -a*	809	**ruh**-doh
932	sun, the	981	*rueda, una, la*	1093	ruh-**ayh**-dah
933	sunburn (malady), a, the	886	*ruido, un, el*	653	ruh-**eeh**-doh
934	Sunday, a, the	363	*ruidoso, -a*	654	ruh-eeh-**doh**-soh
935	sunny (bright, brilliant)	140	*sábado, un, el*	818	**sah**-bah-doh
936	sunscreen (medicine), a, the	1100	*saber*	510	sah-**behr**
937	sunstroke (malady), a, the	88	*sal, la*	814	sahl
938	supper, a, the	199	*salida, una, la*	294	sah-**leeh**-dah
939	surfboard, a, the	788	*salir*	525	sah-**leehr**
940	sweet	372	*salvavidas, unos, los*	536	sahl-bah-**beeh**-dahs
941	swim, to	705	*sándwich, un, el*	816	**sahnd**-weech

LINE	ENGLISH	SL	SPANISH	EL	PRONUNCIATION
942	swimming pool, a, the	34	*sangrar*	95	sahn-**ghrar**
943	swollen (distended, malady)	524	*sangre, la*	96	**sahn**-greh
944	swordfish (fish), a, the	811	*sargo, un, el*	817	**sahr**-goh
945	syringe, a, the	560	*se renta*	337	seyh **rayhn**-tah
946	table (counter), a, the	673	*se vende*	338	seyh **bahyn**-dayh
947	taco shop, a, the	1015	*secadora, una, la*	265	seeh-kah-**dohr**-ah
948	take, to	1063	*seco, -a*	264	**seh**-koh
949	tampon, a, the	1014	*seguir*	331	seh-**geehr**
950	tank (scuba), a, the	1011	*segundo, un, el*	836	sayh-**goohn**-doh
951	tea (beverage), the	1022	*seguro, el*	483	seh-**gooh**-roh
952	telegraph office, a, the	191	*seis*[1]	869	sayhs
953	telephone book, a, the	501	*seiscientos*[1]	870	sayhs-seeh-**yehn**-tohs
954	telephone, a, the	1026	*sello de metal, un, el*	835	**sayh**-yoh deh meh-**tahl**
955	telephone, to	1025	*sello, un, el*	904	**seh**-yoh
956	television, a, the	1027	*semana próxima*	639	seh-**mah**-nah **prohk**-seeh-mah
957	temperature, a, the	1028	*semana, una, la*	1081	seh-**mah**-nah
958	ten	340	*sendero, un, el*	1025	sayhn-**deyh**-roh
959	tern (bird), a, the	492	*seno, un, el*	115	**sah**-noh
960	that (referring to one feminine person or object, ... woman, ... flower)	413	*señor, un, el*	369	sehn-**yohr**
961	that (referring to one masculine person or object, ... man, ... reel)	421	*señora, una, la*	512	sehn-**yohr**-ah
962	that (the reel ... I am using)	882	*señorita, una, la*	513	sehn-yohr-**eeh**-tah
963	the (feminine plural article)	580	*sentarse*	868	sehn-**thar**-seh
964	the (feminine singular article)	572	*septiembre, un, el*	840	sehp-**tyehm**-breh
965	the (masculine plural article)	623	*ser*[4]	71	sehr
966	the (masculine singular article)	378	*serpiente, una, la*	881	sayhr-peeh-**yahn**-teh
967	theater , a, the	1023	*servilleta, una, la*	624	sehr-beeh-**yeh**-tah
968	their (formal, more than one person possessing more than one object)	1005	*sesenta*[1]	872	sayh-**sen**-tah
969	their (formal, more than one person possessing one object, ... truck)	995	*setecientos*[1]	842	seh-teh-**syehn**-tohs
970	there is, there are	514	*setenta*[1]	844	say-**ten**-tah
971	thermometer, a, the	1041	*si*	466	seeh
972	thermostat (vehicle part), a, the	1042	*sí*	1133	seeh
973	these (referring to more than one feminine person or object, ... women, ... flowers)	437	*sierra golfina, una, la*	1065	see-**ahr**-rah gohl-**feehn**-ah
974	these (referring to more than one masculine person or object, ... men, ... reels)	442	*sierra para metales, una, la*	391	seeh-**arh**-hah **pah**-ruh meh-**tah**-lehs
975	they are (... ... happy)	435	*sierra, una, la*	866	see-**arh**-ah
976	they have (... ... a boat)	1051	*siete*[1]	841	seeh-**ahy**-tahy
977	think, to	796	*sin*	1114	seehn
978	thirsty, to be	1036	*sirga una, la*	1018	**seer**-gah
979	thirteen	1079	*sitio, un, el*	723	**seeh**-tyoh
980	thirty	1080	*sobre*	1054	**soh**-breh
981	this (referring to one feminine person or object, ... woman, ... flower)	430	*sol, el*	932	sohl
982	this (referring to one masculine person or object, ... man, ... reel)	440	*soldador, un, el*	1084	sol-dah-**dohr**

LINE	ENGLISH	SL	SPANISH	EL	PRONUNCIATION
983	this week	429	*soldar*	1083	sol-**dahr**
984	those (referring to more than one feminine person or object, ... women, ... flowers)	414	*sólo derecha*	797	**soh**-loh deh-**reh**-chah
985	those (referring to more than one masculine person or object, ... men, ... reels)	422	*sólo izquierdo*	527	**soh**-loh eehs-**kyehr**-dah
986	thousand	680	*sólo, -a*	687	**soh**-loh
987	three	1081	*soltar*	554	sohl-**tahr**
988	three hundred	1082	*soltar*	781	sohl-**tahr**
989	throat (body part), a, the	484	*sombrero, un, el*	403	sohm-**breh**-roh
990	thumb (body part), a, the	877	*sopa, la*	889	**soh**-pah
991	Thursday, a, the	564	*sotileza, una, la*	523	soh-teh-**leh**-sah
992	tide, a, the	645	*soy*[4]	461	sohy
993	time, a, the	1048	*su*[1,2]	428	sooh
994	tip (gratuity), a, the	868	*su*[1,2]	436	sooh
995	tip (pay a gratuity), to	301	*su*[1,2]	969	sooh
996	tire (vehicle part), a, the	610	*su*[1,2]	1147	sooh
997	tire repair shop, a, the	611	*su*[1,2]	1145	sooh
998	tired (weary), to be	177	*sucio, -a*	232	**sooh**-syoh
999	to (direction)	1	*sudeste, el*	891	soohd-**ehs**-teh
1000	today (now)	535	*sudoeste, el*	892	soohd-oh-**ehs**-teh
1001	toe (body part) a, the	310	*suerte, la*	558	**swehr**-teh
1002	toilet paper, the	775	*sur, el*	890	soorh
1003	tomato (food), a, the	1064	*sus*[1,2]	427	soohs
1004	tomorrow	633	*sus*[1,2]	435	soohs
1005	tongue (body part), a, the	593	*sus*[1,2]	968	soohs
1006	tonight	428	*sus*[1,2]	1144	soohs
1007	too much	315	*sus*[1,2]	1146	sooh
1008	tool, a, the	518	*tal vez*	715	tahl behs
1009	tooth (body part), a, the	335	*taller auto-eléctrico, un, el*	855	**tahl**-yehr **auh**-toh eh-**lehk**-treeh-koh
1010	tooth brush, a, the	203	*taller, un, el*	1120	**tahl**-yehr
1011	tooth paste, the	785	*tanque de escafandra, un, el*	950	**tahn**-kay deh ehs-cah-**fahn**-drah
1012	toothache (malady), a, the	359	*tanque de gasolina, un, el*	367	**tahn**-kay deh gah-soh-**leeh**-nah
1013	top (summit), the	297	*tanteo, un, el*	823	tahn-**teh**-oh
1014	tortilla factory, a, the	1069	*tapón, un, el*	949	tah-**pohn**
1015	totuava (fish), a, the	1073	*taquería, una, la*	947	tah-kay-**reeh**-ah
1016	Tourism (Mexican govt. office)	1088	*tarde*	519	**tahr**-deh
1017	tourist card, a, the	1019	*tarde, una, la*	11	**tahr**-deh
1018	tow rope, a, the	978	*tarjeta de crédito, una, la*	201	tahr-**heh**-tah deh **kred**-eeh-toh
1019	tow truck (vehicle), a, the	499	*tarjeta de turista, una, la*	1017	tarh-**hay**-tah deh tooh-**reehs**-tah
1020	tow, to	912	*tarjeta postal, una, la*	737	tahr-**heh**-tah pohs-**tahl**
1021	toward (in the direction of)	506	*taza, una, la*	204	**tah**-sah
1022	towel, a, the	1058	*té, el*	951	tahy
1023	town (small), a, the	871	*teatro, un, el*	967	teh-**at**-roh
1024	town, a, the	227	*tecolote, un, el*	700	teh-coh-**loh**-teh
1025	trail (path), a, the	958	*telefonear*	955	teh-leh-foh-neh-**ahr**
1026	trailer (vehicle), a, the	913	*teléfono, un, el*	954	teh-**leh**-foh-noh
1027	tranquilizer (medicine), a, the	1076	*televisión, una, la*	956	teh-lay-beeh-**showhn**

LINE	ENGLISH	SL	SPANISH	EL	PRONUNCIATION
1028	transmission (vehicle part), a, the	1078	*temperatura, una, la*	957	tayhm-pay-rah-**tooh**-rah
1029	transmission fluid (vehicle part), the	468	*tempestad, una, la*	921	tayhm-payh-**stad**
1030	travel, to	1127	*tempestuoso, -a*	922	tayhm-payhs-tooh-**oh**-soh
1031	traveler's check, a, the	214	*temprano, -a*	272	tehm-**prah**-noh
1032	Treasury (Mexican govt. office)	508	*tenedor, un, el*	340	teh-neh-**dohr**
1033	triggerfish (fish), a, the	810	*tenéis⁵*	1141	teh-**neh**-eehs
1034	trousers (plural), the	773	*tener cuidado*	145	teh-**nehr** kweeh-**dah**-doh
1035	truck (vehicle), a, the	169	*tener hambre*	454	teh-**nehr ahm**-breh
1036	true (not false)	1124	*tener sed*	978	teh-**nehr** sedh
1037	Tuesday, a, the	652	*tener⁵*	404	teh-**nehr**
1038	tumor (malady), a, the	1087	*tengo⁵*	463	**ten**-goh
1039	tuna (fish), a, the	94	*terminar*	286	tehr-meeh-**nahr**
1040	turn (... ... a corner, ... over), to	354	*término medio*	587	**tehr**-meeh-noh **mehd**-yoh
1041	turtle (reptile), a, the	1070	*termómetro, un, el*	971	tehr-**moh**-met-troh
1042	twelve	356	*termostato, un, el*	972	tehr-moh-**stah**-toh
1043	twenty	1115	*tiburón ballena, un, el*	1090	teeh-buhr-**ohn** bah-**yeah**-nah
1044	two	368	*tiburón blanco, un, el*	385	teeh-buhr-**ohn blahn**-koh
1045	two hundred	369	*tiburón bonito, un, el*	566	teeh-buhr-**ohn** boh-**neeh**-toh
1046	two way (road sign)	355	*tiburón, un, el*	846	teeh-buhr-**ohn**
1047	ugly (not handsome)	457	*tiempo, el*	1079	**tyehm**-poh
1048	ulcer (malady), an, the	1090	*tiempo, un, el*	993	**tyehm**-poh
1049	under	306	*tienda de abarrotes, una, la*	387	**tyehn**-dah deh ah-bahr-**roh**-tayhs
1050	understand, to	247	*tienda, una, la*	917	**tyehn**-dah
1051	United States, the	433	*tienen⁵*	976	teh-**ehn**-en
1052	until	513	*tienes⁵*	1142	teh-**ehn**-ehs
1053	up	82	*tijera, una, la*	355	teeh-**heh**-rah
1054	upon	980	*tijeras, las*	822	teeh-**heh**-rahs
1055	upset stomach (malady), an, the	542	*tirar de*	748	teeh-**rahr** deh
1056	vacancy, a, the	1107	*título de propiedad, el*	778	**teeh**-tooh-yoh deh proh-**peeh**-dahd
1057	valley, a, the	1110	*toalla sanitaria, una, la*	625	toh-**ah**-yah sah-nah-tah-**reeh**-ah
1058	valve (vehicle part, engine, tire), a, the	1111	*toalla, una, la*	1022	toh-**ah**-yah
1059	vegetables (food, plural), the	590	*tobillo, un, el*	31	toh-**beeh**-yoh
1060	vehicle, a, the	1114	*tocino, el*	55	toh-**seeh**-noh
1061	veterinarian, a, the	1126	*todo¹, -a*	17	**toh**-doh
1062	view (vista), a, the	1134	*todo¹, -a*	293	**toh**-doh
1063	vomit (malady), to	1140	*tomar*	948	toh-**mahr**
1064	vulture (bird), a, the	144	*tomate, un, el*	1003	toh-**mah**-teh
1065	wahoo (fish), a, the	973	*tope, un, el*	124	**toh**-peh
1066	walk, to	60	*torcedura, una, la*	900	toohr-sayh-**dooh**-rah
1067	want, to	888	*tornillo, un, el*	826	tohr-**neeh**-yoh
1068	wash, to	586	*toro, un, el*	490	**toh**-roh
1069	washer (for a bolt), a, the	74	*tortillera, una, la*	1014	tohr-teeh-**yhea**-rah
1070	watch out for cattle (road sign)	296	*tortuga, una, la*	1041	tohr-**tooh**-gah
1071	water (liquid), the	23	*tos, una, la*	194	tohs
1072	wave (swell), a, the	756	*toser*	195	toh-**sehr**
1073	wavy or irregular road (road sign)	166	*totuava, una, la*	1015	toh-**twa**-bah
1074	we are (... ... happy)	732	*trabajar*	1119	trah-bah-**hahr**

LINE	ENGLISH	SL	SPANISH	EL	PRONUNCIATION
1075	we are (feminine, ... American)	731	*traer*	118	trah-**ehr**
1076	we are (masculine, ... American)	733	*tranquilizante, un, el*	1027	trahn-kweeh-leeh-**sahn**-teh
1077	we have (... ... a boat)	734	*tranquilo, -a*	135	trahn-**kweeh**-loh
1078	weak (feeble, not strong)	308	*transmisión, una, la*	1028	trahns-meeh-seeh-**yohn**
1079	weather, the	1047	*trece*[1]	979	**treh**-seh
1080	Wednesday, a, the	678	*treinta*[1]	980	**treyn**-tah
1081	week, a, the	957	*tres*[1]	987	trehs
1082	weight belt (diving), a, the	225	*trescientos*[1]	988	trehs-seeh-**yehn**-tohs
1083	weld, to	983	*trigo, el*	1092	**treeh**-goh
1084	welder (person who welds), a, the	982	*tu*[1,2]	1151	tooh
1085	well (good, pleasant)	123	*tubo de respiración, una, la*	883	**tooh**-boh deh rayh-speeh-rah-**syohn**
1086	well-done (degree of cooking)	124	*tuerca, una, la*	666	**twehr**-kah
1087	west, the	752	*tumor, un, el*	1038	tooh-**mohr**
1088	wet suit (diving), a, the	415	*Turismo*	1016	tooh-**reehs**-moh
1089	whale (marine mammal), a, the	105	*tus*[1,2]	1150	toohs
1090	whale shark (fish), a, the	1043	*úlcera, una, la*	1048	**oohl**-sahy-rah
1091	what (question, ... time is it)	885	*último*[1]*, -a*	517	**oohl**-teh-moh
1092	wheat (food), the	1083	*ultramarino, una, la*	219	oohl-trah-mah-**reeh**-noh
1093	wheel (vehicle part), a, the	932	*un*	4	oohn
1094	when (question)	279	*un*	25	oohn
1095	where (question)	364	*una*	2	**oohn**-ah
1096	where is (question)	365	*una*	23	**oohn**-ah
1097	which (question)	278	*una hora*	683	**ooh**-nah **ohr**-rah
1098	which (question)	883	*unas*	1	**oohn**-ahs
1099	whiskey, the	1143	*unas*	22	**oohn**-ahs
1100	white (color)	127	*ungüento de sol, un, el*	936	oohn-**gwehn**-toh deh sohl
1101	white seabass (fish), a, the	269	*uno*[1]	682	**ooh**-noh
1102	who (question)	891	*unos*	3	**oohn**-nohs
1103	why (question)	852	*unos*	24	**oohn**-nohs
1104	wife, a, the	426	*usted*[2]	1137	ooh-**stehd**
1105	wind (breeze), a, the	1131	*ustedes*[2]	1136	ooh-**steh**-dehs
1106	winding road (road sign)	167	*uva, una, la*	382	**ooh**-bah
1107	window, a, the	1120	*vacante, una, la*	1056	bayh-**kahn**-teh
1108	windy	1121	*vacío, -a*	284	bah-**seeh**-oh
1109	wine (beverage), the	1133	*vado*	230	**bah**-doh
1110	winter, the	551	*valle, un, el*	1057	**bah**-yeah
1111	wire (electrical), a, the	261	*válvula, una, la*	1058	**bal**-booh-lah
1112	wish, to	889	*vaso, un, el*	374	**bah**-soh
1113	with	248	*vehículo recreativo, un, el*	772	bay-**heeh**-koh-loh rech-reh-**teh**-boh
1114	without	977	*vehículo, un, el*	1060	bay-**heeh**-koh-loh
1115	woman, a, the	698	*veinte*[1]	1043	**beyn**-teh
1116	wood (for a fire), the	592	*venado, un, el*	218	bahy-**nah**-doh
1117	wood (lumber), the	628	*venda, una, la*	63	**behn**-dah
1118	word (expression), a, the	766	*vender*	839	behn-**dehr**
1119	work, to	1074	*venir*	183	beh-**neehr**
1120	workshop, a, the	1010	*ventana, una, la*	1107	behn-**tah**-nah
1121	worse	797	*ventoso, -a*	1108	behn-**toh**-soh

LINE	ENGLISH	SL	SPANISH	EL	PRONUNCIATION
1122	wrench (tool), a, the	615	*ver*	838	behr
1123	wrench, adjustable (tool), an, the	613	*verano, el*	930	beh-**rah**-noh
1124	wrench, socket (tool), a, the	612	*verdadero, -a*	1036	behr-dadh-**deh**-roh
1125	wrist, a, the	700	*verde*	386	**behr**-deh
1126	wrong (incorrect)	541	*veterinario, un, el*	1061	beh-teh-reeh-nah-**reeh**-yoh
1127	yard (measurement), a, the	1145	*viajar*	1030	beeh-yah-**har**
1128	year, a, the	62	*viaje, un, el*	495	**byah**-heh
1130	yellow (color)	53	*viejo[1], -a*	679	**byeh**-hoh
1131	yellowfin tuna (fish), a, the	93	*viento, un, el*	1105	**byehn**-toh
1132	yellowtail (fish), a, the	569	*viernes, un, el*	351	**byehr**-nehs
1133	yes	972	*vino, el*	1109	**beeh**-noh
1134	yesterday	98	*vista, una, la*	1062	**beehs**-tah
1135	yield right of way (road sign)	198	*vivir*	543	beeh-**beehr**
1136	you (formal and informal, referring to more than one person, ... fishermen)	1105	*vivo, -a*	16	**beeh**-boh
1137	you (formal, referring to one person, ... should rest)	1104	*volador, un, el*	330	boh-lah-**dohr**
1138	you are (referring to more than one person, ... happy)	434	*volante, un, el*	910	boh-**lahn**-teh
1139	you are (referring to one person, ... American)	409	*volver*	789	bol-**behr**
1140	you are (referring to one person, ... happy)	438	*vomitar*	1063	boh-meeh-**tahr**
1141	you have (referring to more than one person, ... a truck)	1033	*vuestro[1, 2,] -a*	1149	booh-**ehs**-troh
1142	you have (referring to one person, ... a truck)	1052	*vuestros[1, 2,] -as*	1148	booh-**ehs**-trohs
1143	young, to be	563	*whisky, el*	1099	**weehs**-keeh
1144	your (formal, more than one person possessing more than one object, ... trucks)	1006	*y*	29	ee
1145	your (formal, more than one person possessing one object, ... truck)	997	*yarda, una, la*	1127	**yahr**-dah
1146	your (formal, one person possessing more than one object, ... trucks)	1007	*yo*	460	yoh
1147	your (formal, one person possessing one object, ... truck)	996	*zanahoria, una, la*	146	sah-nah-**hor**-eeah
1148	your (informal, more than one person possessing more than one object, ... trucks)	1142	*zapata del freno, una, la*	111	sah-**pah**-tah dehl **freh**-noh
1149	your (informal, more than one person possessing one object, ... truck)	1141	*zapatería, una, la*	919	sah-pah-teh-**reeh**-ah
1150	your (informal, one person possessing more than one object, ... trucks)	1089	*zapato, un, el*	854	sah-**pah**-toh
1151	your (informal, one person possessing one object, ... truck)	1084	*zona de derrumbes*	514	**sohn**-ah deh deh-**rohm**-behs
1152	zero	207	*zorra, una, la*	347	**sorah**-ah

Footnotes:

1. Placed before the noun when used as an adjective.
2. The informal form is used when addressing relatives, friends, and children, the formal when addressing a stranger or a person to whom respect is due.
3. The Spanish verb *estar*, "to be," and the words in its conjugation are used to tell about or inquire about location, to tell or ask about health, or to describe a temporary, accidental, or readily changeable condition.
4. The Spanish verb *ser*, "to be," and the words in its conjugation are used in situations not described in [3] above.
5. The Spanish verb *tener*, "to have," and the words in its conjugation.

Speaking sentences

A number of useful sentences will be found below. They are very simple and have been designed to convey your meaning as simply as possible while fracturing Spanish as little as feasible. For instance: you need not worry about tense, for they are phrased in the present, past, or future tense, as appropriate; all verbs are correctly conjugated; the necessary adverbs, pronouns, and prepositions are included; and the phonetic pronunciation of all Spanish words is provided. Except for adjectives, you need not worry about syntax (the order in which words appear in a sentence) because it is all laid out in black and white.

Some sentences are complete in themselves, but others have missing words or terms. In many cases, these are nouns denoting the name of a town, restaurant, beach, etc., such as "La Paz," "Restaurant Bismark," or "Playa Tecolote," or products such as "fish hooks," "LPG, "or "steak," or an article and noun, such as "the beach," "a telephone," "an outboard motor," "a marlin," "a mechanic," etc. In some cases, the missing word is a verb, such as "to fish" and "to anchor." If a specific characteristic, such as color, size, shape, quality, number, condition, or status is required, simply add an adjective.

As an example, assume you got sunburned during a day of fishing, and want to know where a hat can be purchased. First, locate the sentence "Where can I buy (article and noun)?", which turns out to be *¿Dónde puedo comprar ___?*, then look up the Spanish article and noun for "a hat," which prove to be *un sombrero* (note that the gender and number of noun and article are the same, masculine singular). With the article and noun added, the sentence is thus *¿Dónde puedo comprar un sombrero?*, "Where can I buy a hat?" However, not just any hat will do, for this one must have a specific characteristic—it must be large. You must therefore introduce the adjective *grande* , which, since it does not have a superscript [1] in the dictionary, is placed after the noun. The sentence it thus *¿Dónde puedo comprar un sombrero grande?* "Where can I buy a large hat?" What could be more simple?

You have probably noted what appear to be typographical errors in the dictionary, including uncapitalized Spanish words for the months and the days of the week and for "Canadian," "Spanish," "English," and "Mexican," and in the sentences that follow there will be "upside-down" question marks and exclamation points before some sentences. These are not errors; that's the way things are done in Spanish. Most sentences are provided in blunt, Yankee-style terms, but to avoid appearing rude and aggressive, it is necessary to include appropriate Preliminaries and a few Magic Words, which are provided. A "*por favor*" (please) included in a request or question never hurts: *Tráigame usted más cerveza, por favor!* (Bring me more beer, please!)

Preliminaries

Do you speak English? *¿Habla usted inglés?* **Ah**-blah ooh-**stehd** eehn-**glehs**?

Good afternoon/evening. *Buenas tardes/noches.* **Bweh**-nahs **tahr**-dehs/**noh**-chays.

Good morning. *Buenos días.* **Bweh**-nohs **deeh**-ahs.

Hello! *¡Hola!* **Oh**-lah!

How are you? *¿Cómo está usted?* **Koh**-moh ehs-**tah** ooh-**stehd**?

I am fine. And you? *Estoy bien. ¿Y usted?* Ehs-**toy** byehn. Ee ooh-**stehd**?

I am from (city, state, region, country). *Soy de ___.* Sohy deh ___.

My name is (___). *Mí nombre es ___.* Meeh **nohm**-breh ___.

What is your name? *¿Cómo se llama usted?* **Koh**-moh seh **yah**-mah ooh-**stehd**?

Where are you from? *¿De dónde es usted?* Deh **dohn**-deh ehs ooh-**stehd**?

Magic words

I'm sorry. *Lo siento.* Loh see-**ehn**-toh.

Please. *Por favor.* Pohr fah-**bohr**.

Thank you very much. *Muchas gracias.* **Mooh**-chahs **grah**-see-ahs.

You're welcome. *De nada.* (Literally, "it's nothing.") Deh **nah**-dah.

Frequently used expressions

As soon as possible. *Lo más pronto posible.* Loh mahs **prohn**-toh poh-**seeh**-blayh.

Can you help me? *¿Me podría ayudar?* May poh-**dree**-ah ah-yooh-**dahr**?

Do you understand? *¿Comprende usted?* Kohm-prehn-**deh** ooh-**stehd**?

How do you say (English word) in Spanish? *¿Cómo se dice ___ en español?* **Koh**-moh say **deeh**-sayh ___ ehn ehs-pahn-**nyohl**?

How long (in time)? *¿Cuánto tiempo?* **Kwahn**-toh **tyehm**-poh?

How much does it cost per (hour, day, week, month, year)? *¿Cuánto cuesta por ___?* **Kwahn**-toh **kwehs**-tah pohr ___?

I (don't) like it. *(No) Me gusta.* (Noh) May **goohs**-tah.

I am looking for (noun, or article and noun, and an adjective as necessary, such as "the beach," "a large hat," "a good restaurant"). *Busco ___.* **Boos**-koh ___.

I don't know. *No sé.* Noh seh.

I don't understand. *No comprendo.* Noh kohm-**prehn**-doh.

I need (noun, article and noun, or verb, and an adjective as necessary, such as "a wrench," "five steaks," "to sleep"). *Necesito ___.* Neh-seh-**see**-toh ___.

I need it by (today, tomorrow, Saturday, October, etc.). *Lo necesito para ___.* Loh neh-seh-**see**-toh **pah**-ruh ___.

I think it is (adjective, such "beautiful," "cold," "expensive," etc.). *Creo que es ___.* **Kreh**-oh kay ehs ___.

I understand. *Yo comprendo.* Yoh kohm-**prehn**-doh.

I want (noun, article and noun, or verb, and an adjective as necessary. such as "to fish," "a large reel," "ten tomatoes"). *Quiero ___.* Keeh-**yehr**-oh ___.

I will be back by (hour, today, tonight, tomorrow, day of the week, month, etc.). *Regresaré para ___.* Reh-greh-sah-**reh pah**-rah ___.

It doesn't matter. *No importa.* Noh eehm-**pohr**-tah.

Just a second. *Un momento.* Oohn moh-**men**-toh.

Please repeat. *Repita, por favor.* Ray-**pee**-tah pohr fah-**bohr**.

Please speak slowly. *Hable despacio, por favor.* **Ah**-blayh dehs-pah-**seeh**-oh, pohr fah-**bohr**.

See you later. *Hasta la vista.* **Ah**-stah lah **beeh**-stah.

What do you call this/that in Spanish? *¿Cómo se llama esto/eso en español?* **Koh**-moh say **yah**-mah **ehs**-toh/**eh**-soh ehn ehs-pahn-**nyohl**?

What is this/that? *¿Qué es esto/eso?* Keh ehs **ehs**-toh/**eh-soh**?

What time in the morning will we leave? *¿A qué hora por la mañana salimos?* Ah keh **oh**-rah pohr lah mahn-**yah**-nah sah-**leeh**-mohs?

What time will we return? *¿A qué hora regresamos?* Ah keh **oh**-rah reh-greh-**sah**-mohs?

What?, or What did you say? *¿Cómo?* **Koh**-moh?

Where do they leave from? *¿De dónde salen?* Deh **dohn**-deh **sahl**-ehn?

Obtaining directions

Can you show it to me on the map? *¿Puede indicármelo en el mapa?* **Pweh**-deh een-deeh-**kahr**-may-loh ehn ehl **mah**-pah?

How far away is (noun, or article and noun, such as "Loreto," "the beach")? *¿A qué distancia está ___?* Ah keh dees-**tahn**-syah ehs-**tah** ___?

I am lost. *Me he perdido.* May hay pehr-**deeh**-doh.

I want to go to (noun, or article and noun, such as "La Paz," "the mountains"). *Quiero ir a ___.* Keeh-**yehr**-oh eer ah ___.

Is it a good/bad road? *¿Es bueno/malo el camino?* Ehs **bweh**-noh/**mah**-loh ehl kah-**meeh**-noh?

Where is (noun, or article and noun, such as "Comondú," "the reef," "the fuel pump")? *¿Dónde está ___?* **Dohn**-deh ehs-**tah** ___?

Which direction is (noun, article and noun, and an adjective as necessary, such as "San Carlos," "the gas station," "the best beach")? *¿En qué dirección es ___?* Ehn keh deeh-rehk-**syohn** ehs ___?

Restaurants, shopping, and tours

Are there any sightseeing tours? *¿Hay excursiones turísticas?* **Ah**-eeh ehs-koohr-**seeh**-ohnes too-**reehs**-teeh-kahs?

At what time do they open/close? *¿A qué hora abren/cierran?* Ah keh **or**-rah **ah**-brehn/see-**ehr**-ahn?

Bring me (noun, or article and noun, such as "a menu," "coffee," "a steak," stating cooking method and cooking degree as necessary). *Tráigame ___.* **Traih**-gah-meh ___.

Do you have it in (adjective, such as "red," "large")? *¿Tiene algo en ___?* Teeh-**yehn**-ayh **ahl**-goh ehn ___?

Do you know a good restaurant? *¿Conoce usted un buen restaurante?* Koh-**noh**-say ooh-**stehd** oohn bwehn rehs-tauh-**rahn**-teh?

Do you take credit cards/traveler's checks/personal checks? *¿Se aceptan tarjetas de crédito/cheques de viajeros/cheques personales?* Seh ah-**sep**-tahn tahr-**heh**-tahs deh **kred**-eeh-tohs/**cheh**-kehs deh byah-**heh**-rohs/**cheh**-kehs perh-sohn-**ahl**-ehs?

How much is it? *¿Cuánto es?* **Kwahn**-toh ehs?

I like the meat (cooking method and degree of cooking). *Me gusta la carne ___.* May **goohs**-tah lah **kahr**-nay ___.

I want to buy (noun or article and noun, and an adjective as necessary, such as "hamburger," "hooks," "a long rope"). *Quiero comprar ___.* Keeh-**yehr**-oh kohm-**prahr** ___.

I'd like (noun, article and noun, or verb, and an adjective as necessary, such as "dessert," "the yellow shirt," "to fish"). *Quisiera ___.* Keeh-seeh-**yehr**-ah ___.

I'm thirsty/hungry. *Tengo sed/hambre.* **Ten**-goh sedh/**ahm**-breh.

It is too much. *Eso es demasiado.* **Eh**-soh ehs deh-mah-seeh-**ah**-doh.

The check, please. *La cuenta, por favor.* Lah **kwehn**-tah, pohr fah-**bohr**.

Waiter, we need (noun, or article and noun, such as "water," "a spoon," "a napkin"). *Camarero, necesitamos ___.* Kah-mah-**rehr**-oh, neh-seh-see-**tah**-mohs ___.

What's the exchange rate today for American/Canadian dollars? *¿A qué está el cambio hoy por dólares de Estados Unidos/Canadá?* Ah keh ehs-**tah** ehl kahm-**beeh**-oh ohy pohr doh-**lahr**-ehs deh Ehs-**tah**-dohs Ooh-**nee**-dohs/Can-nah-**dah**?

Where can I buy (noun, or article and noun, and an adjective as necessary, such as "pizza," "film," "good clothes")? *¿Dónde puedo comprar ___?* **Dohn**-deh **pweh**-doh kohm-**prahr** ___?

Where can I change some money? *¿Dónde puedo cambiar dinero?* **Dohn**-deh **pweh**-doh kahm-**byahr** deeh-**neh**-roh?

Vehicle matters

Can you fix (article and noun, such as "the transmission," "the tire")? *¿Puede usted reparar ___?* **Pweh**-deh ooh-**stehd** ray-pah-**rahr** ___?

Can you lend me (article and noun, such as "a wrench," "a hammer") *¿Puede usted prestarme ___?* **Pweh**-deh ooh-**stehd** prehs-**tahr**-may ___?

Can you tow my (noun, such as "truck," "motor home," "boat")? *¿Puede usted remolcar mi ___?* **Pweh**-deh ooh-**stehd** reh-mohl-**kahr** meeh ___?

Do you have the part? *¿Tiene la pieza?* Teeh-**yehn**-ayh lah **pyeh**-sah?

Fill it up with ("Magnasin," "Nova," "water," etc.). *Llénelo con ___.* **Yeh**-nayh-loh kohn ___.

I have a flat tire. *Tengo un pinchazo.* **Ten**-goh oohn peehn-**chah**-soh.

I need (noun or article and noun, and an adjective as necessary, such as "gasoline," "engine oil," "a mechanic," "a tow truck," "a new transmission"). *Necesito ___.* Neh-seh-**see**-toh ___.

I think there is something wrong with (article and noun, such as "the alternator," "the brakes"). *Creo que pasa algo con ___.* **Kray**-oh kay **pah**-sah **ahl**-goh kohn ___.

It won't start. *No arranca.* Noh ah-**rahn**-kah.

My (noun such as "truck," "motor home") is stuck. *Mi ___ se atascó.* Meeh ___ seh ah-tahs-**coh**.

The (noun, such as "radiator," "gas tank," "oil pan") is leaking. *El/La ___ tiene un agujero.* Ehl/Lah ___ teeh-**yehn**-ayh oohn ah-goo-**hehr**-oh.

The (noun, such as "radiator," "bearing") overheats. *El/La ___ se calienta demasiado.* Ehl/Lah ___ seh kah-**lyehn**-tah deh-mah-seeh-**yah**-doh.

The battery is dead. *El acumulador está muerto.* Ehl ah-kooh-mooh-lah-**dohr** ehs-**tah** mwehr-toh.

The keys are lost/inside. *Las llaves están perdidas/adentro.* Lahs **yah**-behs ehs-**tahn** pehr-**deeh**-dahs/ah-**dehn**-troh.

Boating, fishing, and diving

Boat the fish. *Engánchalo.* Ehn-**gahn**-chah-loh.

Bring in the line. *Enrolla la cuerda.* Ehn-**rohl**-yah lah kooh-**ayhr**-dah.

Change the bait. *Cambia la carnada.* Kahm-**beeh**-yah lah khar-**nah**-dah.

Do you have (noun, or article and noun, such as "fins," "reels," "a compressor")? *¿Tiene ___?* Teeh-**yehn**-ayh ___?

Fill the scuba tank. *Llene el tanque de escafandra.* **Yeh**-neh ehl **tahn**-kay deh ehs-cah-**fahn**-drah.

How deep is it here? *¿Qué tan hondo está aquí?* Kay tahn **hon**-doh ehs-**tah** ah-**keeh**?

How many hours will we be out in the boat? *¿Cuántas horas estaremos en el barco?* **Kwahn**-tahs **or**-rahs ehs-tah-**reh**-mohs ehn ehl **bahr**-koh?

I need/have a fishing license. *Necesito/Tengo una licencia de pescar.* Neh-seh-**seeh**-toh/**Ten**-goh una leeh-sen-**seeh**-ah deh pehys-**kahr**.

I want to fish ("shallow," "deep," "near the beach"). *Quiero pescar ___.* Keeh-**yehr**-oh peyhs-**kahr** ___.

I want to fish for (noun, such as "marlin," "roosterfish"). *Quiero pescar por ___.* Keeh-**yehr**-oh peyhs-**kahr** pohr ___.

I want to fish/dive at (noun, or article and noun, such as "Guardian Angel," "the reef"). *Quiero pescar/bucear en ___.* Keeh-**yehr**-oh ehn peyhs-**kahr**/booh-**sayh**-ahr ehn ___.

I want to release the fish unharmed. *Quiero soltar el pez ileso.* Keeh-**yehr**-oh sohl-**tahr** ehl peyhs eehl-**eh**-soh.

Is the boat equipped with (noun, or article and noun, such as "life jackets," "an anchor")? *¿Está equipado el barco con ___?* Ehs-**tah** eh-kweeh-**pah**-doh ehl **bahr**-koh kohn ___?

Let's anchor. *Tiremos la ancla.* Teeh-**reh**-mos lah **ahn**-klah.

Let's go to the same spot. *Vamos al mismo lugar.* **Bah**-mohs ahl **meehs**-moh looh-**gahr**.

What is the price of a day of fishing/diving? *¿Qué es el precio de un día de pesca/buceo?* Keh ehs ehl **preh**-syoh de oohn **deeh**-ah deh peyhs-**kahr**/booh-**seeh**-oh?

What kind of fish are here? *¿Qué clase de pez hay aquí?* Keh **klah**-seh deh peyhs **ah**-eeh ah-**keeh**?

What kind of fish is this? *¿Qué clase de pez es?* Keh **klah**-seh deh peyhs ehs?

What time is high/low tide? *¿A qué hora está alta/baja la marea?* Ah keh **oh**-rah ehs-**tah ahl**-tah/**bah**-hah lah **mahr**-reah?

Where can I buy/rent fishing/diving gear? *¿Dónde puedo comprar/alquilar aparejo de pesca/buceo?* **Dohn**-deh **pweh**-doh kohm-**prahr**/ahl-keeh-**lahr** ah-pah-**reh**-hoh deh peyhs-**kah**/booh-**seeh**-oh?

Where is the best place (verb, such as "to fish," "to dive")? *¿Dónde está el mejor sitio ___?* **Dohn**-deh ehs-**tah** ehl meh-**hohr** seeh-tyoh ___?

Where is the fishing tackle/dive shop? *¿Dónde está la tienda de aparejo de pesca/buceo?* **Dohn**-deh ehs-**tah** lah **tyehn**-dah deh ah-pah-**reh**-hoh de **peyhs**-kah/booh-**seeh**-oh?

Will live bait be available? *¿Tendrán carnada viva?* Tehn-**drahn** khar-**nah**-dah **beeh**-bah?

Will you supply lunch and drinks? *¿Nos proveerás almuerzo y bebidas?* Nohs proh-beeh-**rahs** ahl-**mwehr**-soh ee beh-**beeh**-dahs?

Medical, dental, pharmacy, and optical

Can you fix this (noun, such as "dental bridge")? *¿Puede usted reparar ___?* **Pweh**-deh ooh-**stehd** reh-pah-**rahr** ___?

Do you have medicine for (malady, such as "hypertension," "an infection")? *¿Tiene medicina para ___?* Teeh-**yehn**-ayh meh-deeh-**seeh**-nah **pah**-ruh ___?

Do you know a ("doctor," "dentist," "pharmacist," "optician") who speaks English? *¿Conoce a un ___ que hable inglés?* Koh-**noh**-say ah oohn ___ kay **ah**-blayh eehn-**glehs**?

How many times a day must I take this medicine? *¿Cuántas veces al día tengo que tomar esta medicina?*

Kwahn-tahs **beh**-says ahl **deeh**-ah **ten**-goh kay toh-**mahr** ehs-tah meh-deeh-**seeh**-nah?

I don't feel well. *No me siento bien.* Noh may seeh-**yen**-toh byehn.

I feel better/worse. *Me siento mejor/peor.* May seeh-**yen**-toh may-**hohr**/pay-**ohr**.

I had (malady, such as "hemorrhoids") (number, such as "two," and "years," "months," or "days") ago. *Tuve ___ hace ___.* **Tooh**-bay ___ ah-seh ___.

I have (malady, such as "influenza," "appendicitis"). *Tengo ___.* **Ten**-goh ___.

I have a pain in my (body part, such as "arm," "stomach"). *Tengo dolor de mi ___.* **Ten**-goh doh-**lohr** deh meeh ___.

I need a ("doctor," "dentist," "pharmacist," "optician"). *Necesito a un ___.* Neh-seh-**seeh**-toh ah oohn ___.

I'm (not) allergic to (substance, food, medicine). *(No) Soy alérgico (-a) a ___.* (Noh) Sohy ah-**lehr**-geeh-koh (-a) ah ___.

I'm pregnant. *Estoy embarazada.* Ehs-**toy** ehm-bahr-ah-**sah**-dah.

I'm taking (medicine). *Tomo ___.* **Toh**-moh ___.

It hurts me here (pointing to spot). *Me duele aquí.* May **dweh**-ley ah-**keeh**.

There is (no) history of (malady) in my family. *(No) Hay historia de ___ en mi familia.* (Noh) **Ah**-eeh heehs-torh-**rheeh**-ah deh ___ ehn meeh fah-**meehl**-yah.

RV parks

Do you have a vacancy? *¿Tiene vacante?* Teeh-**yehn**-ahy bayh-**kahn**-teh?

Do you offer discounts? *¿Ofrece usted descuentos?* Ohf-**reh**-seh ooh-**stehd** dehs-**kwen**-tohs?

How much is the site per ("night," "week," "month," "year")? *¿Cuánto cuesta el sitio por ___?* **Kwahn**-toh **kwehs**-tah ehl seeh-**tyoh** pohr ___?

I am a member of (Good Sam, Vagabundos del Mar, etc.). *Soy un miembro de ___.* Sohy oohn meeh-**ehm**-broh deh ___.

I would like to make a reservation. *Quisiera hacer una reservación.* Keeh-see-**ehr**-ah ah-**sehr oohn**-ah ray-sehr-bah-**syohn**.

Is (article and noun, such as "a shower," "a laundry machine," "a launch ramp") available? *¿Hay ___ disponible?* **Ah**-eeh ___ deehs-poh-**neeh**-bleh?

Is ("water," "electricity," "a sewer," "a *palapa*") available at the site? *¿Hay ___ disponible en el sitio?* **Ah**-eeh ___ deehs-poh-**neeh**-bleh ehn ehl seeh-**tyoh**?

We are leaving ("tomorrow," "next week," "next month"). *Salimos ___.* Sah-**leeh**-mohs ___.

We will be staying (number, such as "ten") ("days," "weeks," "months"). *Nos quedaremos ___ ___.* Nohs kay-dahr-**eh**-mohs ___ ___.

Appendix F

Learning More

Your next Baja book should be...

So you have made your first trip to Baja and were fascinated and want to read more? Do you agree that Baja is not "a land accursed by God?" If so, the first book to consider is Walt's highly praised book on travel, outdoor adventure, and natural history, available from your bookseller or directly from Wilderness Press:

> Peterson, Walt, *The Baja Adventure Book*. 2nd. ed. Berkeley: Wilderness Press, 1995.

Baja's human history

The following books will round out your knowledge of the human history of Baja California:

> Browne, John Ross, *Explorations in Lower California*. Studio City (CA): Vaquero Books, 1966. Browne was a well-known writer and journalist, as well as an undercover agent for the US Treasury Department. In 1866, representing the Lower California Company, Ross explored much of the southern half of the peninsula.

> Clavigero, Don Francisco Javier, *The History of Lower California*. Translated by Sara E. Lake. Edited by A. A. Gray. Sparks (NV): Ransom Distributing Co., 1971. Although no match for the humor and insight of Father Baegert's letters (Nunis 1982), this book contains interesting and useful information about the natural history of the peninsula and the people who lived there.

> Crosby, Harry W., *Antigua California*. Albuquerque: University of New Mexico Press, 1994. Covering the years 1697 through 1768, this fine new book describes the motives, politics, and methods of the Jesuits, and the family and social life of the Indian and Hispanic peoples under their sway. See below for other books by Crosby.

> Dunne, Peter Masten, *Black Robes in Lower California*. Berkeley: University of California Press, 1968. A Jesuit writing about Jesuits, Dunne has been criticized for an excessively rosy outlook. True to its title, the book is about the Jesuits and their activities, not their religious charges; only 25 pages describe the penin-

sula and the culture of its native inhabitants, almost always cast in negative terms. Read with these aspects in mind, the book is a valuable and scholarly resource.

> Henderson, David A., *Men and Whales at Scammon's Lagoon*. Los Angeles: Dawson's Book Shop, 1972. A detailed history of Captain Scammon's rediscovery of the lagoon that bears his name, as well as the ensuing slaughter.

> Huycke, Harold D., *To Santa Rosalía: Further and Back*. Newport News (VA): Mariners Museum, 1970. An interesting history of the copper mines in Santa Rosalía, the great square-riggers that visited the port, and the men that sailed them.

> Nunis, Doyce B., ed., *Journey of James H. Bull, Baja California, October 1843 to January 1844*. Los Angeles: Dawson's Book Shop, 1965. Describes Bull's muleback travels from Mulegé to San Diego along El Camino Real. Bull was the first American to travel extensively in Baja.

> _____, *The Letters of Jacob Baegert, 1749-1761, Jesuit Missionary in Baja California*. Los Angeles: Dawson's Book Shop, 1982. Jesuit Father Baegert's letters are interesting, very human, and often very funny, although presumably not intended as such.

Although outdated by recent events, the following book provides a good analysis of the complicated historical, social, political, and economic relationships between Mexico and the US:

> Riding, Alan, *Distant Neighbors*. New York: Vintage Books, 1986.

Baja's natural history

If you have an interest in natural history, the following books are recommended:

> Behrens, David W., *Pacific Coast Nudibranchs, A Guide to the Opisthobranchs, Alaska to Baja California*. Monterey (CA): Sea Challengers, 1991. Some of the most colorful and spectacular living organisms on earth come in the unlikely forms of the gelatinous, slug-like nudibranchs. Don't miss this book if you are a diver with a taste for the small, the flamboy-

ant, and the beautiful.

Brusca, Richard C., *Common Intertidal Invertebrates of the Gulf of California*. Tucson: University of Arizona Press, 1980. A scholarly handbook, with numerous photos and sketches, and an extensive bibliography.

Case, Ted J., and Martin L. Cody, eds., *Island Biogeography in the Sea of Cortez*. Berkeley: University of California Press, 1983. Contains scientific papers on the biology and geology of the islands in the Cortez, with useful bibliographies. Too technical for casual reading, but very useful if you are willing to do the digging.

Gordon, David, and Alan Baldridge, *Gray Whales*. Monterey (CA): Monterey Bay Aquarium, 1991. With many color and black-and-white photos, this book is one of the best on the subject.

Gotshall, Daniel W., *Marine Animals of Baja California/A Guide to the Common Fishes and Invertebrates*. Los Osos (CA): Sea Challengers, 1987. Detailed descriptions and 213 color photos of fish and invertebrates from Isla Cedros to the Cape and north to Bahía de los Angeles.

_____, *Pacific Coast Inshore Fishes*. Los Osos (CA): Sea Challengers, 1989. If you have not been able to get your spouse into mask and fins, the color photos of garibaldi, butterfly fish, and bluebanded goby should do the trick. Excellent descriptions and photos of 126 species, covering Alaska south.

_____, *Guide to Marine Invertebrates-Alaska to Baja California*. Los Osos (CA): Sea Challengers, 1994. Descriptions and 253 color photos of the most common shallow-water invertebrates found from Alaska to Baja.

Keen, A. Myra, and James A. Mclean, *Sea Shells of Tropical West America*. Stanford (CA): Stanford University Press, 1958. A monumental reference book covering sea shells from the Cortez to Colombia, with descriptions of 1,650 species and about 1,500 illustrations.

Kerstitch, Alex, *Sea of Cortez Marine Invertebrates: A Guide to the Pacific Coast, Mexico to Ecuador*. Monterey (CA): Sea Challengers, 1989. This excellent book contains information and color pictures of the sponges, hydroids, corals, gorgonians, worms, sea stars, brittle stars, nudibranchs, and other critters many have heard about and even seen but seldom recognize.

Leatherwood, Stephen, and Randall R. Reeves, *The Sierra Club Handbook of Whales and Dolphins*. San Francisco: Sierra Club Books, 1983. A fine general guide to whales and dolphins, with 200 paintings and photographs, and detailed information on identification, natural history, and distribution.

Minch, John, and Thomas Leslie, *The Baja Highway*. San Juan Capistrano (CA): John Minch and Associates, Inc., 1991. Although in need of an index and the lash and blue pencil of a professional editor, this book is valuable to those who have an interest in the geology and biology of the peninsula. Presented in a road-log style keyed to the KM markers, the information is very accessible to laymen without scientific training.

Morris, Percy A., *A Field Guide to Pacific Coast Shells*. Boston: Houghton Mifflin Co., 1966. A useful handbook, with a major section on Cortez gastropods and pelecypods, and many illustrations.

Nelson, Edward W., *Lower California and Its Natural Resources*. Riverside (CA): Manessier Publishing Co., 1966. Sober, scientific, and scholarly, but fact-filled and interesting, this book describes the peninsula as it was in the early part of the century, and provides information available from no other source.

Ricketts, Edward F., and Jack Calvin, revised by David W. Phillips. *Between Pacific Tides*. Stanford (CA): Stanford University Press, 1985. Not specifically about Baja waters, but very useful to those interested in intertidal organisms.

Roberts, Norman C., *Baja California Plant Field Guide*. La Jolla (CA): Natural History Publishing Co., 1989. A useful and highly recommended popular-level book with many color photographs.

Thomson, Donald A., Lloyd T. Findley and Alex N. Kerstitch, *Reef Fishes of the Sea of Cortez*. New York: John Wiley & Sons, 1979. The best guide available to the many reef fishes seen by scuba divers and snorkelers in the Cortez.

Violette, Paul E., *Shelling in the Sea of Cortez*. Tucson (AZ): Dale Stuart King, Publisher, 1964. Concerns the eastern portions of the Cortez.

Wiggins, Ira L., *Flora of Baja California*. Stanford (CA): Stanford University Press, 1980. Comprehensive, technical, and scholarly.

Wilbur, Sanford R., *Birds of Baja California*. Berkeley: University of California Press, 1987. The most complete technical reference on the subject available, this book includes an annotated checklist of all birds known to occur in Baja, with detailed seasonal and distributional information, and a record of sightings.

Zwinger, Ann, *A Desert Country Near the Sea*. New York: Harper & Row Publishers, 1983. This well-written book describes the Cape region, and contains descriptions of many birds.

Mineral collecting

If you are a mineral collector, you may be interested in the following books:

Shedenhelm, W. R., *Rockhounding in Baja*. Glendale: La Siesta Press, 1980.

Sinkankas, John, *Gemstones of North America, Vol. I*. New York: Van Nostrand Reinhold Co., 1959.

_____, *Gemstones of North America, Vol. II*. New York: Van Nostrand Reinhold Co., 1976.

Shedenhelm 1980 is the only book devoted completely to Baja mineral collecting, but it is useful primarily as a summary of the literature. Sinkankas' books have many references to Baja gems and minerals, but most of the sites discussed are from second- and third-hand sources, and are so dependent on ever-changing local place names as to be of limited use in relocating sites. Still, every little bit helps, and there is little else available.

Adventuring

If you crave adventure, the following are recommended.

Harry Crosby is a modern-day Baja adventurer, and three of his books provide interesting reading and an insight into aspects of Baja California not available from any other source.

> Crosby, Harry W., *The King's Highway*. Salt Lake City: Copley Books, 1974. In 1967, Crosby made a mule trip retracing the route of El Camino Real from Loreto to Misión San Fernando. His book about the adventure is very readable and contains the most extensive information available on the subject.
>
> _____, *Last of the Californios*. Salt Lake City: Copley Books, 1981. The story of the descendants of the Hispanic people who settled Baja California, now living in remote regions of the peninsula in the manner of their ancestors two centuries ago.
>
> _____, *The Cave Paintings of Baja California*. Salt Lake City: Copley Books, 1984. The best available book on the Indian art gracing the peninsula.

Erle Stanley Gardner, of *Perry Mason* fame, made a number of adventurous trips to Baja, which he recorded in six books, now out of print. Although outdated and subject to factual errors, they make good reading.

> Gardner, Erle Stanley, *The Land of Shorter Shadows*. New York: William Morrow and Company, 1948. Describes a trip by vehicle to Cabo San Lucas.
>
> _____, *Hunting the Desert Whale*. New York: William Morrow and Company, 1960. Covers several trips to the Scammon's Lagoon area to see the whales and to beachcomb.
>
> _____, *Hovering Over Baja*. New York: William Morrow and Company, 1961. Describes two trips to Baja to explore Cañons Asamblea and Sal Si Puede, north of Bahía de los Angeles, one by trail scooter, the other by helicopter.
>
> _____, *The Hidden Heart of Baja*. New York: William Morrow and Company, 1962. Recounts the expedition which brought the rock art to public attention, although it contains little about the art itself.
>
> _____, *Off the Beaten Track in Baja*. New York: William Morrow and Company, 1967. More Baja adventures, including trips by jet helicopter.
>
> _____, *Mexico's Magic Square*. New York: William Morrow and Company, 1968. Tells of travels in northern Baja, including a trip to Tijuana and Ensenada aboard the Goodyear blimp.

> Hale, Howard, *Long Walk to Mulegé*. Santee (CA): Pinkerton Publishing Co., 1980. Concerns an adventurous 450-mile hike down the desolate peninsula made by two University of California students in 1921.
>
> Hancock, Ralph, *Baja California*. Los Angeles: Academy Publishers, 1953. Tells of the travels during the 1950s by a group of sportsmen, including a trip from Los Angles to Cape San Lucas aboard their Jeep truck. Contains an interesting section about El Mármol in the days of the Browns, with photos of the village and the people.
>
> Lamb, Dana, *Enchanted Vagabonds*. New York: Harper and Brothers, Publishers, 1938. Lamb tells of the kayak trip he and his wife made from San Diego to the Panama Canal, with many adventures in Baja *en route*.
>
> Murray, Spencer, *Cruising the Sea of Cortez*. Palm Desert (CA): Desert-Southwest, Inc., 1963. Although much of the factual information is outdated, this book makes good reading and stands as the classic of Baja trailer boating.
>
> North, Arthur W., *Camp and Camino in Lower California*. Glorieta (NM): Rio Grande Press, 1977. Tells of the author's many adventures while exploring the peninsula with burro and mule in the early part of the century. North has been described as Baja's first tourist.

Self-propelled in Baja

If you like healthy outdoor exercise, the following may prove useful:

> Robinson, John W., *Camping and Climbing in Baja*. Glendale (CA): La Siesta Press, 1983. Many hikes and climbs in Baja Norte.
>
> Romano-Lax, Andromeda, *Sea Kayaking in Baja*. Berkeley (CA): Wilderness Press, 1993. The only book devoted completely to kayaking in Baja waters.
>
> Wong, Bonnie, *Bicycling Baja*. San Diego: Sunbelt Publications, 1988. Completely devoted to conquering the Transpeninsular the hard way.

Fishing

Like to fish? Try these:

> Cannon, Ray, *How to Fish the Pacific Coast*. Menlo Park (CA): Lane Books, 1967. Not specifically about Baja, but contains useful basic information for novice fishermen planning a trip.
>
> Curcione, Nick, *Hot Rail*. Oakland (CA): Angler Publications, 1985. Aimed primarily at fishermen aboard the long-range boats out of San Diego fishing Baja's Pacific coast, but also helpful to those bringing their own boats.
>
> Kelly, Neil, and Gene Kira, *The Baja Catch*. Valley Center (CA): Apples and Oranges, Inc., 1988. A helpful book covering the inshore fisheries.

Special works...

The following book defies precise categorization, but no Baja library is complete without it:

> Steinbeck, John, and Edward R. Ricketts, *The Log From the Sea of Cortez*. New York: Viking Press, 1941.

Although outdated by the construction of the Transpeninsular Highway, the next book provides rousing stories of fishing action and good times, and is considered one of the classics of Baja literature:

> Cannon, Ray, *The Sea of Cortez*. Menlo Park (CA): Lane Books, 1966.

Baja-related fiction

Magazine articles written by fishermen are not the only fictional works about Baja:

> Benchley, Peter A., *The Girl of the Sea of Cortez*. New York: Doubleday & Co., Inc., 1982. An enjoyable book based on the author's experiences with the manta rays at Marisla Seamount.
>
> Nordhoff, Charles (Antonio de Fierro Blanco), *The Journey of the Flame*. Boston: Houghton Mifflin Co., 1941. Written by one of the authors of the *Bounty* trilogy, this book is so detailed that many people have been fooled into believing that it depicts historical events.

The following novels are adventure stories aimed at young readers:

> Dusoe, Robert C., *Only the Strong*. New York: Longmans, Green, and Company, 1955. Increasing drought slowly brings hard times to a Cochimí family named Webb, the odd name due to the introduction of a New England ship captain into the gene pool many generations ago. Greedy capitalists attempt to take over the family ranch, and rising water in their gold mine portends economic disaster. However, three kegs of blasting power bring about a happy ending.

> _____, *Three Without Fear*. New York: David McKay Company, 1947. A boy leads an adventurous life when he is shipwrecked along the coast of Baja.
>
> O'Dell, Scott, *The Black Pearl*. Boston: Houghton Mifflin, 1967. A 16-year-old boy dreams of diving for a giant pearl, an enemy in the form of a manta "as big as the largest ship in the harbor [La Paz]...the most dangerous creature in [the Vermilion Sea]...guarding a secret cave," and an ending reminiscent of *Moby Dick*. What more could a young reader ask for?
>
> Steinbeck, John, *The Pearl*. New York: Viking Press, 1961. John takes us a-pearling. Feeling "the creeping of fate, the circling of wolves, the hover of vultures," the young hero encounters misfortune when the pearl he has found is judged to be too large to sell and thus of interest only to a museum or as a curiosity.

Where to get Baja books

The Map Centre, Inc. in San Diego carries a wide variety of books about Baja, as well as maps and nautical and aeronautical charts. Dawson's Book Shop offers out-of-print books on Baja, as well as the 50-volume Baja California Travels Series, covering such disparate Baja subjects as history, ethnology, linguistics, Indian art, whales, pirates, the Gold Rush, railroads, and cattle drives and brands. Both will send lists of their offerings upon request.

Where to get Baja news

A monthly English-language newspaper is published about Baja, the *Baja Sun*. Lively and interesting, it provides articles on a wide variety of subjects. In addition, there is a fine new magazine, *Baja Life*. Filled with articles on such subjects as golf, whales, Bahía Magdalena, the desert's seasonal show of colorful plant blooms, volleyball, a whale shark encounter, La Paz, and Misión San Javier, complemented by excellent color photographs. It also contains departments on yachting, retirement and living in Baja, ecological matters, fishing, and other subjects.

Index

References to specific bakeries, butcher shops, dentists, doctors, grocery stores, hospitals, liquor and beer stores, opticians, pharmacies, post offices, seafood and fruit markets, shopping malls, supermarkets, telephones, and tire shops are not included in the index and can be found on the town/city maps and in the narratives and road logs. In addition, the system of icons described on page 5 can be used to quickly locate basic facilities of interest to RVers.